Selected works of Chaucer

Selected works of Chaucer

CHANCELLOR
PRESS

First published in 1912 by the Macmillan Company under the title
The Complete Poetical Works of Geoffrey Chaucer

This edition first published in 1994 by Chancellor Press
an imprint of Reed Consumer Books Limited
Michelin House, 81 Fulham Road, London SW3 6RB
and Auckland, Melbourne, Singapore and Toronto

ISBN 1 85152 585 8

A CIP catalogue record for this book is available from the British Library

Printed in Great Britain by The Bath Press

Contents

Contents

Preface

This volume is complete for Chaucer's poetry. The only poems in recent editions here omitted are one or two short poems which there seems no reliable reason for ascribing to him, and the translation of *Le Roman de la Rose*, in no sense an original poem, and in part certainly, and elsewhere possibly, not by him at all. The prose works wholly omitted are the translation of Boethius' *De Consolatione Philosophiæ* and the *Treatise on the Astrolabe* (also largely a translation); his other two prose works, the *Tale of Melibeus* and the *Parson's Tale* (both largely or wholly unoriginal and hardly appealing to modern tastes), being inherent parts of the *Canterbury Tales*, are represented by specimens. The text followed throughout (not without occasional reference to the manuscripts) is Professor Skeat's, except for the *Troilus and Criseyde*, in which Professor McCormick's (in the *Globe Chaucer*) is followed.

The combined glossary and notes (alphabetically arranged by obvious catch-words) contain only such explanations as seem really essential, or are not easily accessible elsewhere, as in a good English dictionary, or classical dictionary, or the like. For fuller ones the reader must be referred to the commentary in Skeat's *Oxford Chaucer*. Immediately before the glossary is given a slight sketch of Chaucer's life, and also remarks as to the source or circumstances which gave rise to a poem, when such seemed necessary to the full appreciation of it.

P. M-K.
CORNISH, NEW HAMPSHIRE

J. S. P. T.
UNIVERSITY OF MICHIGAN
1911

The Canterbury Tales

The Prologue

When the sweet showers of April have pierced to the root the dryness of March, and bathed every vein in moisture whose quickening brings forth the flowers; when Zephyr also with his sweet breath has quickened the tender new shoots in holt and moor, and the young sun has run his half-course in the Ram, and little birds make melody and sleep all night with eyes open, so nature pricks them in their hearts: then folk long to go on pilgrimage to renowned shrines in sundry distant lands, and palmers to seek strange shores. And especially from every shire's end in England they go their way to Canterbury, to seek the holy blessed martyr who helped them when they were sick.

On a day in that season, as I was biding at the Tabard Inn at Southwark, about to make my pilgrimage with devout heart to Canterbury, it befell that there came at night to that hostelry a company of full nine-and-twenty sundry folk, who by chance had fallen into fellowship. All were pilgrims, riding to Canterbury. The chambers and the stables were wide, and we were right well lodged. But in brief, when the sun had gone to rest, I had spoken with every one of them and was soon of their company, and agreed to rise early to take our way whither I have told you. Nevertheless, whilst I have time and space, before this tale goes farther, I think it is reason to tell you all the quality of each of them, as they appeared to me, what sort of folk they were, of what station and how they were accoutred. With a knight I will begin.

There was a Knight and that a worthy, who, from the time when he first rode abroad, loved knighthood, faithfulness and honour, liberality and courtesy. He was full valiant in his lord's war and had campaigned, no man farther, both in Christendom and in heathen lands, ever honoured for his worth. He was at Alexandria when it was won; many a time in Prussia he had headed the board, before all the foreign knights; he had fought in Lithuania and in Russia, no Christian man of his degree oftener; he had been in Granada at the seige of Algeciras and in Belmaria; he was at Lyeys and in Attalia when they were won, and had landed with many a noble army in the Levant. He had been in fifteen mortal battles, and had thrice fought for our faith in the lists at Tremessen and ever slain his foe; he had been also, long before, with the lord of Palathia against another heathen host in Turkey; and ever he had exceeding renown. And though he was valorous he was prudent, and as meek as a maid of his bearing. In all his life he never yet spoke discourtesy to any living creature, but was truly a perfect gentle knight. To tell you of his equipment, his horses were good but he was not gaily clad. He wore a jerkin of fustian all begrimed by his coat of mail, for he had just returned from his travels and went to do his pilgrimage.

His son was with him, a young Squire, a lover and a lusty young soldier. His locks were curled as if laid in a press. He may have been twenty years of age, middling in height, wondrous nimble and great of strength. He had been, upon a time, in a campaign in Flanders, Artois, and Picardy, and had borne him well, in so little time, in hope to stand in his lady's grace. His clothes were embroidered, red and white, as it were a meadow full of fresh flowers. All the day long he was singing or playing upon the flute; he was a fresh as the month of May. His coat was short, with long, wide sleeves. Well could he sit a horse and ride, make songs, joust and dance, draw and write. He loved so ardently that at night-time he slept no more than a nightingale. He was courteous, modest and helpful, and carved before his father at table.

They had a Yeoman with them; on that journey they would have none other servants. He was clad in coat and hood of green, and in his hand bore a mighty bow and under his belt a neat sheaf of arrows, bright and sharp, with peacock feathers. He knew how to handle his gear like a good yeoman; his arrows flew not aslant with feathers trailing. His head was cropped and his visage brown. He understood well all the practice of wood-craft. He wore a gay arm-guard of leather and at one side a sword and buckler; at the other a fine dagger, well accoutred and as sharp as a spear-point; on his breast a St. Christopher in bright silver, and over his shoulder a horn on a green baldric. He was a woodman indeed, I believe.

There was also a nun, a Prioress, full quiet and simple in her smiling; her greatest oath was but by Saint Loy. She was named Madame Eglantine. Well she sang divine service, intoned full seemly in her nose, and spoke French elegantly, after the manner of Stratford-le-Bow, for Parisian French she knew naught of. She had been well taught the art of eating, and let no morsel fall from her lips, and wet but her finger-tips in the sauce. She knew how to lift and how to hold a bit so that not a drop fell upon her breast. Her pleasure was all in courtesy. She wiped her upper lip so well that no film of grease was to be seen in her cup after she had drunk; and very dainty she was in reaching for her food. In truth she was full diverting, pleasant and amiable of bearing. She took pains to imitate court manners, to be stately in her demeanour and to be held worthy of reverence. But to tell you of her character, she was so charitable and so tender-hearted she would weep if she saw a mouse caught in a trap if it were dead or bleeding. She had certain small dogs, which she fed upon roasted meat or milk and finest wheaten bread. She would weep sore if one of them died or was struck at sharply with a stick. She was all warm feeling and tender heart. Her wimple was plaited neatly. Her nose was slender, her eyes as gray as glass, her mouth small and soft and red withal. Certainly she had a fine forehead, almost a span high, — verily she was not undersized. Her cloak was neatly made, I was ware. About her arm was a coral rosary, the larger beads of green, upon which hung a brooch of shining gold; on it was engraved first an *A* with a crown, and after that *Amor vincit omnia.*

Another Nun, her chaplain, was with her, and three Priests.

There was a Monk, exceeding fine and imposing, a great rider about the country-side and a lover of hunting, a manly man withal, fit to be an abbot. He had many a blooded horse in his stable, and when he rode, men could hear his bridle jingling in a whistling wind as clear and loud as the chapel-bell where this lord was prior. Because the rule of St. Maur or of St. Bennet was old and something austere, this same monk let such old things pass and followed the ways of the newer world. He gave not a plucked hen for the text that hunters are not holy, or that a careless monk (that is to say, one out of his cloister) is like a fish out of water; for that text he would not give a herring. And I said his opinion was right; why should he study and lose his wits ever poring over a book in the cloister, or toil with his hands and labour as St. Austin bids? How shall the world be served? Let St. Austin have his work to himself. Therefore he rode hard, followed greyhounds as swift as birds on the wing. All his pleasure was in riding and hunting the hare, and he spared no cost thereon. I saw his sleeves edged at the wrist with fine dark fur, the finest in the country, and to fasten his hood under his chin he had a fine-wrought brooch of gold; in the larger end was a love-knot. His bald head shone like glass; so did his face, as if it had been anointed. He was a sleek, fat lord. His bright eyes rolled in his head, glowing like the fire under a cauldron. His boots were of rich soft leather, his horse in fine fettle. Now certainly he was a fair prelate. He was not pale, like a wasted ghost; best of any viand he loved a fat roasted swan. His palfrey was as brown as a berry.

There was a begging Friar, wanton and jolly, a very self-important fellow. In all the four orders is not one so skilled in gay and flattering talk. He had, at his own expense, married off many a young woman; he was a noble pillar of his order! He was well beloved and familiar amongst franklins everywhere in his country-side, and likewise with worthy town women, for he had, as he said himself, more virtue as confessor than a parson, for he held a papal licence. Full sweetly he heard confession, and his absolution was pleasant; he was an easy man to give penance, when he looked to have a good dinner. Gifts to a poor order are a sign that a man has been well shriven, he maintained; if a man gave, he knew he was contrite. For many a man is so stern of heart that he cannot weep though he suffer sore; therefore, instead of weeping and praying, men may give silver to the poor friars. His tippet was stuffed full of knives and pins as presents to comely women. And certainly he had a pleasant voice in singing, and well could play the fiddle; in singing ballads he bore off the prize. His neck was as white as the flower-de-luce, and he was as strong as a champion. He knew all the town taverns, and every inn-keeper and bar-maid, better than the lepers and beggar-women. For it accorded not with a man of his importance to have acquaintance with sick lepers; it was not seemly, it profited not, to deal with any such poor trash, but all with rich folk and sellers of victual. But everywhere that advantage might follow he was courteous, lowly and serviceable. Nowhere was any so capable; he was the best beggar in his convent, and gave a certain yearly payment that none of his brethren might trespass on his routes. Though a widow might not have an old shoe to give, so pleasant was his 'In principio,' he would have his farthing ere he went. He gained more from his begging than from his poverty, I believe! He would romp about like a puppy-dog. In love-days he was right efficacious, for he was not like a cloister-monk or a poor scholar with a threadbare cope, but like a Master of Arts or a cardinal. His half-cope was of double worsted and came from the clothes-press rounding out like a bell. He pleased his whim by lisping a little, to make his English sound sweet upon his tongue, and in his harping and singing his eyes twinkled in his head as the stars on a frosty night. This worthy friar was named Hubert.

There was a Merchant with a forked beard, in parti-coloured garb. High he sat upon his horse, a Flanders beaver-hat on his head, and boots fastened neatly with rich clasps. He uttered his opinions pompously, ever tending to the increase of his own profit; at any cost he would the sea were safeguarded betwixt Middleburg and Orwell. In selling crown-pieces he knew how to profit by the exchange. This worthy man employed his wit full cunningly; no body could tell that he was in debt, so stately he was of demeanour in bargaining and borrowing. He was a worthy man withal, but, to say the truth, I know not his name.

There was also an Oxford Clerk who had long gone to lectures on logic. His horse was as lean as a rake, and he was not right fat, I believe, but looked hollow-cheeked, and grave likewise. His little outer cloak was threadbare, for he had no worldly craft to beg office, and as yet had got him no benefice. He would rather have had at his bed's head twenty volumes of Aristotle and his philosophy, bound in red or black, than rich robes or a fiddle or gay psaltery. Albeit he was a philosopher, he had but little gold in his money-box! But all that he could get from his friends he spent on books and learning, and would pray diligently for the souls of them that gave him wherewith to stay at the schools. Of study he took most heed and care. Not a word spoke he more than was needful, and that little was formal and modest, in utterance short and quick, and full of high matter. All that he said tended toward moral virtue. Above all things he loved to learn and to teach.

There was also a Sergeant of the Law, an excellent man, wary and wise, a frequenter of the porch of Paul's Church. He was discreet and of great distinction; or seemed such, his words were so sage. He had been judge at assizes, by patent and full commission; with his learning and great repute he had earned many a fee and robe. Such a man as he for acquiring goods there never was; aught that he desired could be shown to be held in fee-simple, and none could find a flaw in his deeds. Nowhere was there so busy a man, and yet he seemed busier than he was. He knew in precise terms every case and judgment since King William the Conqueror, and every statute fully, word for word, and none could chide at his writing. He rode in homely style in a coat of mixed stuff and a girdle of silk with small cross-bars. Of his appearance I will not make a longer story.

A Franklin was travelling with him, bearded white as a daisy, ruddy of face and sanguine of temper. Well he loved a sop in wine of a morning. He was ever wont to live in pleasure, for he was a very son of Epicurus, who held the opinion that perfect felicity stands in pleasure alone. He ever kept open house, as a very St. Julian in his own country-side. His bread and his wine were ever alike of the best; never were a man's wine-vaults better stored. His house was never without a huge pasty of fish or flesh-meat; in his house it snowed meat and drink, and every dainty that a man could dream of. According to the season of the year he varied his meats and his suppers. Many a fat partridge was in his mew and many a bream and pike in his fish-pond. Woe to his cook unless his sauces were pungent and sharp, and his gear ever in order! All the long day stood a great table in his hall ready laid. When the justices met at sessions, there he lorded it full grandly, and many a time he sat as knight of the shire in parliament. A dagger hung at his girdle, and a pouch of taffeta, white as morning's milk. He had been sheriff and auditor; nowhere was so worthy a vassal.

A Haberdasher, a Carpenter, a Weaver, A Dyer and an Upholsterer were with us as well, all in the same livery of a great and splendid guild. All fresh and new was their gear. Their knives were not tipped with brass but all with fine-wrought silver, like their girdles and their pouches. Each of them seemed a fair burgess to sit in a guildhall on a dais. Each for his discretion was fit to be alderman of his guild, and had goods and income sufficient therefor. Their wives would have consented, I trust! And else were they to blame; it is a full fair thing to be called *madame*, and to walk ahead of other folks to vigils, and to have a mantle carried royally before them.

They had a Cook with them for that journey, to boil chickens with the marrow-bones and tart powder-merchant and cyperus-root. Well he knew a draught of London ale! He could roast and fry and boil and stew, make dainty pottage and bake pies well. It was a great pity, methought, that he had a great sore on his shin, for he made capon-in-cream with the best of them.

There was a Shipman, from far in the West; for aught I know, he was from Dartmouth. He rode a nag, as well as he knew how, in a gown of frieze to the knee. He had a dagger hanging on a lace around his neck and under his arm. The hot summer had made his hue brown. Of a truth he was a good fellow: many a draught of wine had he drawn at Bordeaux whilst the merchant slept. He paid no heed to nice conscience; on the high seas, if he fought and had the upper hand, he made his victims walk the plank. But in skill to reckon his moon, his tides, his currents and dangers at hand, his harbours and steersmanship, there was none such from Hull to Carthage. In an emprise he was bold and shrewd. His beard had been shaken by many a tempest. He knew the harbours well from Gothland to Cape Finisterre, and every creek in Spain and in Brittany. His ship was called the *Maudelayne*.

With us was a Doctor of Physic; for skill in medicine and in surgery was not his peer in all this world. He watched sharply for favourable hours and an auspicious ascendent for his patients' treatment, for he was full well grounded in astrology. He knew the cause of each malady, were it from a humour hot, cold, dry or moist, whence it had sprung and of what humour. He was a thorough and a perfect practitioner. Having found the cause and source of his trouble, anon he had ready the sick man's physic. He had his apothecaries all prepared to send him electuaries and drugs, for each helped the other's gain; their friendship was not formed of late! He knew well the old Æsculapius, Dioscorides and Rufus, Hippocrates, Haly and Galen, Serapion, Rhasis and Avicenna, Averroes, Damascene and Constantine, Bernard, Gatisden and Gilbertine. His own diet was moderate, with no superfluity, but nourishing and simple to digest. His study was but little on Scripture. He was clad in sanguine and light blue, lined with taffeta and sarcenet. Yet he was but moderate in spending, and kept what he won during the pestilence. Gold is a cordial in physic; doubtless that was why he loved gold above all else.

There was a Goodwife from near Bath, but she was somewhat deaf and that was pity. She was so skilled in making cloth that she passed them of Ypres and Ghent. In all the parish was no wife who should march up to make an offering before her, and if any did, of a truth so wroth she was that she was out of all charity. Her kerchiefs were full fine of texture; and I durst swear they weighed ten pound that were on her head of a Sunday. Her hose were of a fine scarlet and tightly fastened, and her shoes full soft and new. Her face was bold and fair and red. All her life she was a worthy woman; she had had five husbands at church-door, besides other company in her youth, but thereof it needs not speak now. She had thrice been at Jerusalem; many a distant stream had she crossed; she had been on pilgrimages to Boulogne and to Rome, to Santiago in Galicia and to Cologne. This wandering by the way had taught her sundry things. Sooth to say, she was gap-toothed; she sat full easily on an ambling horse, wearing a fair wimple and on her head a hat as broad as a buckler or target. About her broad hips was a short riding skirt and on her feet a pair of sharp spurs. Well could she laugh and prate in company. Love and its remedies she knew all about, I dare be bound, for she had been through the old game.

There was a good man of religion, a poor Parson, but rich in holy thought and deed. He was also a learned man, a clerk, and would faithfully preach Christ's gospel and devoutly instruct his parishioners. Benign, wondrous diligent, and patient in adversity, such he was oftentimes proved. Right loath he was to excommunicate for unpaid tithes, but rather would give to his poor parishioners out of the church alms and also of his own substance; in little he found sufficiency. His parish was wide and the houses far apart, but for thunder or rain he neglected not to visit the farthest, great or small, in sickness or misfortune, going a-foot, a staff in his hand. This noble example he gave to his sheep, that first he wrought and afterward taught; these words he took out of the gospel, and this similitude he added as well, that if gold rust, what shall iron do? For if a priest upon whom we trust be foul, no wonder though an ignorant layman be corrupt; and it is shame (if a priest will but heed it) that a shepherd should be defiled and the sheep clean. A priest should give good ensample by his cleanness how his sheep should live. He would not farm out his benefice, nor leave his sheep stuck fast in the mire, whilst he ran to London to St. Paul's, to get an easy office of chantry-priest, or to be retained by some guild, but dwelt at home and guarded his fold full well, so that the wolf made it not miscarry. He was no hireling, but a shepherd. And though he were holy and virtuous, he was not pitiless to sinful men, nor cold or haughty of speech, but both discreet and benign in his teaching; to draw folk up to heaven by his fair life and good ensample, this was his care. But when a man were stubborn, whether of high or low estate, he would chide him sharply. There was nowhere a better priest than he. He looked for no pomp and reverence, nor yet was his conscience over-nice; but the teaching of Christ and his apostles he taught, and first he followed it himself.

With him was his brother, a Ploughman, who had drawn many a cartload of dung. He was a faithful and good toiler, living in peace and perfect charity. He loved God best at all times with all his whole heart, in good and ill fortune, and then his neighbour even as himself. He would thresh and ditch and delve for every poor person without pay, but for Christ's sake, if it lay in his might. He paid his tithes fairly and well on both his produce and his goods. He wore a ploughman's frock and rode upon a mare.

There was a Reeve also and a Miller, a Sumner and a Pardoner, a Manciple and myself. There were no more.

The Miller was a stout fellow, full big of bones and brawn; and well he showed them, for everywhere he came to a wrestling match he would ever carry off the prize ram. He was short-shouldered and broad, a thick, knotty fellow. There was no door that he could not heave off its hinges, or break with his head at a running. His beard was as red as any sow or fox, and also broad like a spade. Upon the very tip of his nose he had a wart, and on it stood a tuft of red hair like the bristles on a sow's ears, and his nostrils were black and wide. At his thigh hung a sword and buckler. His mouth was as great as a great furnace. He was a loud prater and a ribald jester, and it was mostly of sin and scurrility. He knew well how to steal corn and take his toll of meal three times over; and yet he had a golden thumb, perdy! He wore a white coat and a blue hood. He could blow and play the bagpipe well, and with its noise he brought us out of town.

There was a gentle Manciple of an Inn of Court, of whom other stewards might take ensample for craftiness in buying victual. Whether he paid in cash or took on credit, he was so watchful in his buying that he was ever before others and in good case. Now is it not a full fair gift of God that the wit of such an unlettered man shall pass the wisdom of a great body of learned men? He had more than a score of masters, expert and diligent in law, of whom in that house there were a dozen worthy to be stewards of lands and revenues of any lord in England, to let him live upon his income, honorably, free from debt, unless he were mad, or live as plainly as he would; or able to help a whole shire in any case which might befall. And yet this Manciple hoodwinked all of them.

The Reeve was a slender, bilious man. His beard was shaven as close as could be, his hair was cut short around his ears and docked in front like a priest's. His legs were full long and lean like a stick; I could see no calf. He could well keep a bin and a garner and no inspector could get the best of him. In the drought or in the wet he could foretell the yield of his grain and seed. His lord's sheep, poultry and cattle, his dairy and swine and horses and all his stock, this Reeve had wholly under his governance, and submitted his accounts thereon ever since his lord was twenty years of age; and none could ever find him out in arrears. There was no bailiff nor herdsman nor other churl whose tricks and craftiness he knew not. They were as afraid of him as of the plague. His dwelling-place was a pleasant one on a heath, all shaded with green trees. Better than his lord he knew how to pick up wealth, and had a rich privy hoard; he knew how to please his master cunningly by giving and lending him out of what was his master's by right, and to win thanks therefor, and a cast coat and hood withal. In his youth he had learned a good trade and was a full good carpenter and wright. This Reeve sat upon a fine dapple gray cob named Scot. He wore a long surcoat of blue and at his side a rusty blade. He was from Norfolk, near a town they call Baldeswell. His coat was tucked up around him like a friar's, and he ever rode last of us all.

A Sumner was with us there, a fire-red cherubin-faced fellow, salt-phlegmed and pimply, with slits for eyes, scabby black eyebrows and thin ragged beard, and as hot and lecherous as a sparrow. Children were terrified at his visage. No quick-silver, white-lead, brimstone, borax nor ceruse, no cream of tartar nor any ointment that would clean and burn, could help his white blotches or the knobs on his chaps. He loved garlic, onions and leeks too well, and to drink strong wine as red as blood, and then he would talk and cry out like mad. And after drinking deep of wine he would speak no word but Latin, in which he had a few terms, two or three, learned out of some canon. No wonder was that, for he heard it all day long, and you know well how a jay can call 'Wat,' after long hearing it, as well as the pope could. But if he were tested in any other point, his learning was found to be all spent. *Questio quid juris*, he was ever crying. He was a kind rogue and a gentle, a better fellow I never knew; for a quart of wine he would suffer a good fellow to have his paramour a twelvemonth and utterly wink at it, and privily he practised the same himself! And if anywhere he found a good fellow, he would teach him in such case to have no fear of the archdeacon's excommunication, unless a man's soul is in his purse, for it was in his purse he should be punished. 'The Archdeacon's hell is your purse,' he said. But well I wot he lied in his teeth; every guilty man should fear the church's curse, for it will slay even as absolution saves, — and also let him beware of a *significavit*. Within his jurisdiction on his own terms he held all the young folk of the diocese, and knew their guilty secrets and was their chief adviser. He had a garland on his head large enough for an ale-house sign, and carried a round loaf of bread as big as a buckler.

With him rode a gentle Pardoner, of Roncesvalles, his friend and crony, come straight from the Court of Rome. He sang full loudly,

'Come hither, love, to me,'

whilst the Sumner bore him a stiff bass; never was trumpet of half such a sound. This Pardoner had waxy-yellow hair, hanging smooth, like a hank of flax, spread over his shoulders in thin strands. For sport he wore no hood, which was trussed up in his wallet; riding with his hair dishevelled, bare-headed save for his cap, he thought he was all in the newest fashion. His eyes were glaring like a hare's. He had a vernicle sewed on his cap, and his wallet, brimful of pardons hot from Rome, lay before him on his saddle. His voice was as small as a goat's. He had no beard nor ever would have, his face was as smooth as if lately shaven; I believe he was a mare or a gelding. But as for his trade, from Berwick to Dover there was not such another pardoner. In his bag he had a pillow-case which he said was our Lady's kerchief, and a small piece of the sail which he said St. Peter had when he walked upon the sea and Jesu Christ caught him. He had a cross of latten, set full of false gems, and pigs' bones in a glass. But with these relics, when he found a poor parson dwelling in the country, in one day he gat him more money than the parson gat in two months. And thus, with flattering deceit and tricks, he made the parson and the people his dupes. But to give him his due, after all he was a noble ecclesiastic in church; he could read well a lesson or legend and best of all sing an offertory. For he knew well that when that was done he must preach and file his tongue smooth, to win silver as he well knew how. Therefore he sang merrily and loud.

Now I have told you in few words the station, the array, the number of this company and also why they were assembled in Southwark, at this noble hostelry the Tabard, hard by the Bell. But now it is time to say how we bore us that same even, when we had alighted at that hostelry; and afterward I will tell you of our journey and the remnant of our pilgrimage. But first I pray that of our courtesy ye ascribe it not to mine ill manners if I speak plainly in this matter, telling you their words and cheer, and if I speak their very words as they were. For this ye know as well as I, that whoso tells a tale that another has told, he must repeat every word, as near as he can, although he speak never so rudely and broad. Else he must tell his tale falsely, or feign, or find new words. He may not spare any, were it his own brother; he is bound to say one word as well as the next. Christ himself spoke full plainly in Holy Writ and ye know well that it is no baseness. And Plato says, whoever can read him, that the word must be cousin to the act. I also pray you to forgive me though I have not set folk here in this tale according to their station, as they should be. My wit is short, ye can well understand.

Our host made us all great cheer, and anon brought us to supper and served us with the best of victual. The wine was strong and right glad we were to drink. Our Host was a seemly man, fit to be marshal in a banquet-hall, a large man with bright eyes, bold in speech, wise and discreet, lacking naught of manhood: there is not a fairer burgess in Cheapside. He was withal a right merry fellow, and after supper, when we had paid our scores, he began to jest and speak of mirth amongst other things. 'Now lordings,' he said, 'verily you are right heartily welcome to me, for by my troth, if I shall say sooth, I have not seen this year so merry a company at this inn at once. I would fain make mirth if I but knew how. And I have even now bethought me of a mirthful thing to give you pleasure, which shall cost nothing. You go to Canterbury, — God speed you, and the blessed martyr duly reward you! I know full well, along the way you mean to tell tales and make sport, for in truth it is no comfort nor mirth to ride by the way dumb as a stone. And therefore, as I said, I will make you sport. If it please you all by common consent to stand by my words and to do as I shall tell you, now by my father's soul (and he is in heaven) to-morrow as you ride along, if you be not merry, I will give you my head. Hold up your hands, without more words!'

Our mind was not long to seek. We thought it not worth debating, and agreed with him without more thought, and bade him to say his verdict as he would.

'Lordings,' quoth he, 'pray hearken now, but take it not, I pray you, disdainfully. To speak briefly and plainly, this is the point, that each of you for pastime shall tell two tales in this journey to Canterbury, and two others on the way home, of chances that have once befallen you. And whichever of you bears him best, that is to say, that tells now tales most instructive and diverting, shall have a supper at the expense of us all, sitting here in this place, beside this post, when we come back from Canterbury. And to add to your sport, I will gladly go with you at mine own cost, and be your guide. And whoever opposes my judgment shall pay all that we spend on the way. If you agree that this be so, tell me now, without more words, and straightway I will plan therefor.'

We agreed to this thing and pledged our word with glad hearts, and prayed him to do so, and to be our ruler and to remember and judge our tales, and to appoint a supper at a certain price. We would be ruled at his will in great and small, and thus with one voice we agreed to his judgment. Thereupon the wine was fetched, and we drank and then each went to rest without longer stay.

On the morrow, when the day began to spring, our host arose and played Chanticleer to us all, and gathered us in a flock. Forth we rode, a little faster than a walk, to St. Thomas-a-Waterings. There our Host drew up his horse and said, 'Hearken, lordings, if you will. You know your agreement; I remind you of it. If evensong and matins accord, let see who shall tell the first tale. So may I ever drink beer or wine, whoso rebels against my judgment shall pay all that is spent on the journey. Now draw cuts, ere we separate further; he who has the shortest shall begin the tales. Sir Knight, my master and my lord,' quoth he, 'now draw your lot, for this is my will. Come nearer, my lady Prioress, and you, sir Clerk, be not shamefast, study not; lay hand to, every man of you.'

Anon every one began to draw, and in short, were it by chance or not, the truth is, the lot fell to the Knight, at which every one was full blithe and glad; he must tell his tale, as was reason, according to the agreement which ye have heard, — what need of more words? When this good man saw it was so, as one discreet and obedient to his free promise he said, 'Since I begin the sport, what! in God's name, welcome be the cut! Now let us ride on, and hearken to what I say.'

And at that word we rode forth on our journey. And he began his tale anon with right glad cheer, and spoke in this wise.

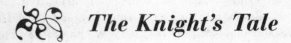

The Knight's Tale

Once, as old histories tell us, there was a duke called Theseus, lord and ruler of Athens, and in his time such a conqueror that there was none greater under the sun. He had subdued many a rich country, and what with his wisdom and his knighthood had conquered all the kingdom of the Amazons, which whilom was called Scythia. He wedded the Queen Hippolyta and brought her home with him to his country in great glory and pomp, and her young sister Emily with her. And thus with victory and melody I leave this noble duke riding on to Athens, with all his host in arms behind him.

And were it not too long to hear, certes I would have told you fully how the kingdom of the Amazons was won by Theseus and his knightly valour; and, whilst I was about it, of the great battle betwixt the Athenians and the Amazons; how Hippolyta was besieged, the fair, hardy queen of the Scythians; of her wedding-feast, and of the tempest at her home-coming. But all that I must forbear now; God wot, I have a large field to plough, and mine oxen are but weak. The remainder of my tale is long enough, and also I would not hinder any of this company; let every comrade in turn tell his tale, and let see who shall win the supper. And where I left off I will begin again.

When this duke was come well-nigh to the town in all his triumph and highest pomp, he cast his eye at one side and was ware of a company of ladies, clad in black, kneeling in the highway, two by two. But such a cry and woe they made that no living creature in this world heard ever such another; nor would they stint this crying till they had caught the reins of his bridle.

'What folk are you that disturb the festival of my home-coming thus with lamentations?' quoth Theseus. 'Have you so great ill-will toward my honours that you so complain and cry? Or who has done you ill? Tell me if it may be amended, and why you are thus clothed in black.'

The eldest lady of them all spoke (but first she swooned with such a deathly look that it was pitiful to see): 'Lord, to whom Fortune has granted victory and to live as a conqueror, your glory and honour grieve us not. We beg for succour and for mercy upon our woe and distress. Of your nobility let fall some drop of pity upon us wretched women; for certes, there is none of us all, lord, but has been a queen or a duchess. Now are we poor caitiffs, as men may see, thanks to Fortune and her false wheel, that ensures not prosperity to any estate. And certes, lord, here in the temple of the goddess Clemency we have been all this fortnight awaiting your coming. Now help us, lord, since it is within your power! I, wretch that I am, thus weeping, and wailing, was once wife to King Capaneus, who perished at Thebes, cursed be the day! And we who are in this plight and make this lament all lost our husbands whilst the siege lay about that town. And now, alack! old Creon who is now lord of Thebes, full of ire and iniquity, of his tyrannical malice has drawn the dead bodies of our slain lords upon an heap, to do them indignity, and will suffer them by no means to be either buried or burned, but in scorn gives them to hounds to eat.' And with that word, without more ado, they all fell on their faces and cried piteously, 'Have some mercy upon us wretched women, and let our woe sink into your bosom!'

The noble duke sprang from his charger with pitying heart, when he heard them speak; his heart wellnigh broke when he saw them who had once been of high degree so piteous and cast down. And he raised them all up in his arms and comforted them full kindly, and swore an oath that, as he was a true knight, he would strive to take such vengeance upon the tyrant Creon that all the people of Greece should tell how he was served by Theseus, as a man that had well merited his death. And right anon, without more delay, he unfurled his banner and rode forth to Thebes with all his host. No nearer to Athens would he travel, nor take his ease half a day, but lodged that night far on toward Thebes, and anon sent Hippolyta the queen and Emily her fair young sister to abide in the town of Athens; and then onward he rode. There is no more to be told.

The red image of Mars with spear and targe so shone upon his broad white banner that all the fields glittered round about. And by his banner was borne his pennant of gold full rich, whereon was hammered out the Minotaur, which he had slain in Crete. Thus rode this duke, this conqueror, and in his host all the flower of chivalry, till he came to Thebes and dismounted in a fair open field where he thought to fight. To tell shortly of this matter, he fought with Creon, King of Thebes, like a worthy knight, and slew him in manly wise in open battle, and put his folk to rout; and then by assault he won the city and rent down wall and beam and rafter. He restored to the ladies the bones of their husbands, to perform their obsequies which were then in use. But it were all too long to tell the clamour and lament of the ladies at the burning of the bodies, and the great honour done them by the noble conqueror Theseus, when they departed from him. To be brief is all my wish. When this worthy duke had slain Creon and thus won Thebes, he took his rest in the field all that night and then dealt with all that country as he would.

After the battle and defeat, the pillagers were busy to search through the heaps of dead, to strip them of harness and garments; and so befell that in the heap they came upon two young knights, lying hard by each other, pierced through and through by many a grievous, bloody wound, both bearing arms of one style, richly wrought; of which two, the one was called Arcite and the other knight Palamon. They were not fully alive nor fully dead, but by their escutcheons and their accoutrements the heralds knew them amongst the rest to be of the royal blood of Thebes and born of two sisters. Out of the heap the pillagers dragged them, and bore them softly to Theseus' tent. And he despatched them full soon to Athens to dwell in prison perpetually; no ransom would he take. And when this worthy duke had done this, anon he rode homeward with all his host, crowned with laurel like a conqueror, and there in joy and honour he lived to the end of his life; what need of more words? And Palamon and Arcite in a tower dwelt in anguish and woe; no gold should free them.

This passed on by day and by year till it befell, once upon a May morning ere daybreak, that Emily, who was fairer to see than the lily upon its green stalk, and fresher than the May with its new flowers (for her cheeks strove with the rose, I know not which was the fairer), Emily, I say, as was her wont, had arisen and was all ready clad, for May will have no slug-a-beds. The season pricks every gentle heart and arouses it out of sleep and says, 'Arise, pay thy service.' Thus Emily bethought her to rise and do honour to May. She was full freshly clothed and her yellow hair was braided in a tress behind her back, a yard long, I believe; and in the garden at sunrise she walked up and down gathering the red and white flowers at will, to make a delicate garland for her head; and she sang heavenly, like an angel.

This great tower so thick and strong, where the knights were imprisoned, was the chief donjon of the castle and joined with the wall of the garden where Emily was diverting her. Clear was the morning and bright the sun, and Palamon, the woful prisoner, was risen and by his jailer's leave, as was his wont, was pacing in a chamber on high, whence he saw all the noble city, and also the garden, full of its green branches, where this fresh Emily was walking and rambling up and down. Palamon, the sorrowful prisoner, went about pacing to and fro in the chamber, complaining to himself in his misery. Full often he cried, Alas that he was born! And so befell, by chance or hap, that through a window set thick with many an iron bar, great and square as any beam, he cast his eye upon Emily, and therewith he started and cried 'Ah!,' as though he were stricken through the heart. And at that cry Arcite anon started up and said, 'Cousin mine, what ails you that you are so pale and deathlike to look upon? Why cried you out? Who has done you hurt? For the love of God, take our prison all in patience, for it may be none otherwise. This adversity was given us by Fortune. Some evil aspect or disposition of Saturn by some constellation has given us this, though we had vowed it should not be. So stood the heavens when we were born, and we must endure it; this is all.'

This Palamon answered anon, 'Cousin, in sooth this thought of yours is vainly imagined. This prison caused not my groan. I have got but now a wound through mine eye into my heart, that will be my death. The fairness of that lady whom I see yonder in the garden, roaming to and fro, is cause of all

15

my crying and pains. I know not whether she be woman or goddess; but in very sooth I swear it is Venus.' Therewithal he fell upon his knees and said, 'Venus, if it be thy will to transfigure thee here in this garden thus before me, a sorrowful wretched creature, help us to escape out of this prison. But if my destiny be decreed by eternal word that I die in prison, have some compassion upon our lineage that is brought so low by tyranny.'

And upon that, Arcite began to espy where this lady roamed about, and the sight of her beauty so hurt him that if Palamon was sore wounded Arcite was hurt as much or worse; and he said piteously with a sigh, 'The fair beauty of her who roams in yonder spot suddenly slays me, and if I have not her pity and her grace, at least to see her, I am but dead; and there an end.'

When Palamon heard these words, he looked at him furiously and answered, 'Say you this in earnest or sport?'

'Nay, in earnest, by my faith,' quoth Arcite. 'So God help me, I have full little stomach for sport!'

This Palamon began to knit his brows. 'It were no great honour to you,' quoth he, 'to be false or a traitor to me your cousin and sworn full deep to be your brother; as each of us is pledged that never, till death part us two, though we die by torture, shall either of us hinder the other in love or in any case, dear brother; but that you should faithfully further me in every case and I shall further you. This was your oath, and, of a surety, mine also; I know right well you dare not gainsay it. Thus you are pledged to be my trusty friend, and now you would falsely be about loving my lady, whom I love and serve and ever shall till my heart die. Now, certes, false Arcite, you shall not so. I loved her first and told you my pain, as to my trusty friend and my brother pledged to help me as I said. Wherefore you are bound as a knight to help me if you can, else are you false, I hold.'

Arcite spoke again full proudly: 'You will be seen to be false ere I am; and you are false, I tell you flatly. For with earthly love I loved her ere you did. What will you say? You knew not but now whether she were goddess or woman. Yours is a holy sentiment, and mine is love as toward a creature; wherefore I told you my case as to my cousin and sworn brother. Put case you loved her first. Know you not well the old clerk's saying,

'Who on a lover sets a law?'

By my pate, love is a greater law than can be given to any man on the earth. And therefore all human law and decrees and such-like are broken every day for love by folk in every station. A man must needs love in spite of his teeth! He cannot flee it though he die, be she maid, married, or widow. And also you are not likely, all your life, to stand in her grace, and no more shall I; for you know full well that you and I are doomed to prison perpetually, no ransom shall help us. We strive like the hounds for the bone, that fought all day and won naught; amidst all their rage came a kite and bore away the bone from betwixt them. Therefore at the king's court each man for himself is the only rule, my brother. Love if you will, for I love and ever shall, dear brother, and truly this is all. We must remain here in this prison and each of us take his lot!'

Great and long was the strife betwixt them, if I had but leisure to tell it; but to the point. It happened on a day (to tell it you shortly) that a worthy duke named Pirothous, comrade unto duke Theseus since they were little children, was come to Athens to visit his fellow, as he was wont, and to divert himself. For he so loved none other man in this world, and Theseus loved him as tenderly; so well they loved that when the one was dead, in very sooth his friend went and sought him down in hell, as the old books say. But that story I list not write. Duke Pirothous loved Arcite well, and had known him at Thebes many a year. Finally, at the prayer of Pirothous, Duke Theseus released him from prison without ransom, to go freely where he would on such terms as I shall tell you. This in short was the agreement of Arcite, that if ever in his life he were found by day or night in any realm of Theseus and were caught, he should lose his head by the sword. There were no better terms, but he took his leave and sped homeward. Let him beware, his neck is in pledge!

How great is Arcite's sorrow now! He feels death stab him through his heart. He weeps, wails, piteously cries, and watches a time to slay himself privily. He said, 'Alas the day that I was born! Now is my prison worse than ever; now I am doomed forever not to purgatory but to hell. Alas that ever I knew Pirothous; else I had dwelt with Theseus evermore fettered in his prison. Then had I been in bliss, not woe. Though I never win the grace of her whom I serve, only the sight of her would have sufficed me right well. O dear cousin Palamon, thine is the victory in this thing. Full blissfully mayst thou dwell in prison, — in prison? — nay, in paradise, certes. Well has Fortune cast the die for thee, who has the sight of her, as I only the absence! For it is possible, since thou art near her and art a knight, a worthy and an able, by some chance of changeful Fortune thou mayst sometime attain thy desire. But I that am exile and so barren of all grace and hope that neither earth, water, fire nor air, nor any creature made of them, can help or give me comfort, well may I die in distress and despair! Farewell, my life, my joy and gladness! Alas, why complain folk so generally of God's providence or of Fortune, that full often gives them in manifold wise better hap than they could choose for themselves? One man desires riches, which become cause of his murder or great sickness.

Another would fain be out of prison; and at home he is slain by his household. Herein is infinite peril; we wot not here what thing thing we pray for. We fare as a man drunk as a rat; a drunken man knows well that he has an house, but not the right way thither, and for him slippery is the path thereto! Certes, so fare we in this world. We seek diligently after felicity, but in sooth go wrong full often. Thus may we all say, and chiefly I, that supposed and had a great notion that if I could escape from prison I were in weal and perfect joy, where now I am exiled from my weal. Since I cannot see thee, Emily, I am but dead; naught can cure me.'

On the other hand, Palamon, when he knew Arcite was gone made such sorrow that the great tower resounded with his clamour and lament, and the very fetters about his great shins were wet with his bitter, salt tears. 'Alas!' quoth he, 'my cousin Arcite, the profit of all our strife is thine, God wot. Thou walkest now at large in Thebes, and givest little thought to my woe. With thy wisdom and manhood thou mayst assemble all the folk of our kindred and make so sharp war upon this city that by some chance or treaty thou mayst have her to wife and lady for whom I must die. For by way of possibilities, great is thine advantage, since thou art a lord, and at large and free from prison, above mine, that die here in a cage. Whilst I live I must weep and wail with all the woe of a prisoner, and also with the pain that love gives me, which doubles all my torment.' Therewith the fire of jealousy blazed up within his breast and seized him so madly by the heart that he was livid as a box-tree to look upon, or as the dead and cold ashes.

Then he said, 'O cruel gods, that govern this world with the bond of your eternal word, and write your laws and eternal decrees upon tables of adamant, how is mankind more bounden unto you than the sheep that cowers in the fold? Man is slain like any beast, and dwells also in prison and constraint, and is sick and in adversity, and ofttimes guiltless, in faith. What just governance is in this Providence that so torments the innocent? And yet this increases all my pain, that man is bound to his duty, for God's sake to refrain from his desires, where a beast may fulfill all its pleasure. And when a beast is dead, its trouble is past, but after death a man must weep and lament though he have had care and woe in this world. Without doubt it may be thus; the answer to all this I leave to divines, but well I wot that on this earth is great sorrow! Alas! I see a serpent or a thief, that has done mischief to many a faithful man, go at large and where he list. But I must be in prison through Saturn and the jealous rage of Juno, who has destroyed wellnigh all the blood of Thebes and laid waste its wide walls. And on the other hand, Venus slays me for jealousy and fear of Arcite.'

Now for a season will I leave Palamon ever lying in prison, and will tell you forth of Arcite.

The summer passed, and the long nights doubled both the bitter pain of the lover and of the prisoner. I wot not which has the wofuller occupation! For, to tell shortly, Palamon is perpetually doomed to prison, to die in chains and fetters; and Arcite is exiled on pain of death from that country for evermore, and nevermore shall he see his lady. Ye lovers, I ask now the question, which is in the worse case, Palamon or Arcite? The one may see his lady daily, but must dwell ever in prison. The other may ride or walk where he list, but shall never see his lady more. Now ye that know how, deem as ye list, for I will tell forth as I began.

II

When Arcite was come to Thebes, many a day he languished and said 'Alas!', for never again should he see his lady. And shortly to conclude of his woe, so much sorrow had never creature that is or shall be whilst the world shall last. He was bereft of sleep, meat and drink, and waxed lean and dry as a stick; his eyes hollow, grisly to see, his hue sallow, pale as cold ashes. He was ever solitary, wailing all night and making his moan. If he heard songs or instruments of music, then would he weep and could not be consoled: So feeble and low and changed were his spirits, that none could recognize his speech nor his voice though they heard them. And in his transports he fared not only as if he had the lover's malady of Eros, but rather like madness engendered of melancholy in the cell of imagination in his brain. In short, both disposition and habits of this woful lover, lord Arcite, were turned all upside-down.

Why should I endite all day of his woe? When he had endured a year or two of this cruel torment in Thebes his country, on a night as he lay in his sleep the winged god Mercury seemed to stand before him, and bade him be of good cheer. In his hand upright he bore his wand of sleep, and upon his bright hair he wore a hat; in such guise he came, Arcite took heed, as when he put Argus to sleep. And thus he spoke to him: 'Thou shalt to Athens; there an end of thy woe is prepared.'

And at that word Arcite started up. 'Now truly,' quoth he, 'howsoever I pay for it, I will fare straightway to Athens. Not for the dread of death will I fail to see my lady whom I love and serve. I reck not though I die, if I behold her once!' And with that word he caught up a great mirror and saw that all his hue was changed, and his visage all of another fashion; and it ran into his mind anon that since his face was so disfigured with his malady, he might well, if he bore him humbly, live in Athens unknown evermore and see his lady wellnigh daily. And anon he changed his garb to that of a poor labourer, and all alone save for a squire, who was disguised poorly as he was and knew all his secret, he took the nearest way to Athens; and on a day he went to the court, and at the gate proffered his service to drudge and draw whatsoever men should bid him. And shortly to end this matter, he fell into office with Emily's chamberlain, who was wise and could well espy a good servant. Well could Arcite hew wood and carry water, for he was young and mighty therein, and strong and big of bones to do whatever he was bid. A year or two he was in this service, page of the chamber to Emily the bright, and he called his name Philostrate. But never in the court was half so well beloved a man of his station; for he seemed so noble a person that his renown spread throughout the court. They said that it were a charity for Theseus to raise his station, and put him in worshipful service, where he might employ all his powers. Thus within a while the report of his deeds and fair tongue was so spread abroad that Theseus took him unto himself as squire of his chamber, with gold enough to maintain his station. And also from year to year men brought him full privily his revenue from his own country; but this he spent in so seemly and cunning wise that no man wondered whence he had it. And three years he led his life in this wise, and bore him so in war and in peace that Theseus held no man dearer. And in this bliss I now leave Arcite, and will speak a little of Palamon.

Seven years in darkness and in horrible and strong prison has Palamon sat, worn away with woe and hardship. Who feels now a double wound and heaviness but Palamon, whom love so distrains that he goes out of his wit for woe! And also he is a prisoner, not only for a year but perpetually. Who could properly in English rhyme his martyrdom? Not I, in sooth. Therefore I pass it over as lightly as I can.

Now in the seventh year, on the third night of May, as the old books tell which relate this history more fully, were it by chance or by destiny (as thus, that when a thing is decreed, it shall be), it befell that Palamon, soon after midnight, by the helping of a friend broke his prison and fled the city as fast as he could go. For he had given his jailer to drink of a cordial, made of a certain wine with narcotics and fine opium of Thebes, so that all that night, though men should smite him, he could not awake, but slept ever. And thus Palamon fled away as fast as ever he could. The night was short and dawn at hand; he needs must hide, and to a grove hard by he crept with fearful foot. For in short this was his intent, to hide him in that grove all day and at night to take the road toward Thebes, and pray his friends to help him war upon

Theseus; and in brief, either he should lose his life or win Emily in marriage. This is the sum of it, and his full intent.

Now will I return again to Arcite, who little wist how nigh was his trouble till Fortine had brought him in the snare. The busy lark, messenger of day, saluted with her song the grey morn; and Phœbus rose up so fiery that all the orient laughed with light; and with his beams he dried in the thickets the silver drops hanging on the leaves. And Arcite, dwelling in the royal court with Theseus, a chief squire, was risen and looked out upon the merry morn. To do observance to May, and thinking ever upon his desire, he rode out of the court upon a charger that leapt like the flame, into the fields a mile or more to divert him. And into that grove of which I have told you he began by chance to take his way, to make him a garland of sprays, were it woodbine or hawthorn leaves. And loud he sang in the bright sun,

> 'May, with thy flowers and thy green,
> Right welcome be thou, fair fresh May,
> I hope to get some green this day.'

With lusty heart he sprang from his charger into the grove, and wandered up and down along a path, where by hap was Palamon behind a bush, that none might see him, for sore afraid of his death was he. He knew not at all that it was Arcite, — God wot he would have believed it full little. But the sooth is said, many years agone,

> 'The field hath eyes, the wood hath ears.'

A man does right well to hear a steady spirit, for ever betide unlooked-for meetings. Little wist Arcite of his old comrade, who was so nigh to hear all that he said, for Palamon sat full quietly in the bush.

When Arcite had roamed his fill, and sung his roundel lustily, forthwith he fell into a study, as do these lovers in their odd, changeful way, now in the tree-tops, now down amongst briers, now up, now down, like a bucket in a well. Even as on the Friday now it shines and now it rains hard, so can fickle Venus overcast the hearts of her folk; even as her day is changeful, so changes she her aspect; seldom is the Friday like all the rest of the week. When Arcite had sung he began to sigh, and without more ado sat him down. 'Alas,' quoth he, 'alas the day that I was born! How long through thy cruelty wilt thou war upon Thebes, O Juno? Alas! all the royal blood of Cadmus and Amphion is brought to confusion. Of the lineage of Cadmus am I, the first man that built Thebes and founded the city, and was crowned first king thereof; I am off-spring of his true line, and of the royal stock. And now I am such a caitiff and thrall that I serve him as his poor squire who is my mortal enemy. And yet Juno does me this indignity, also — that I dare not acknowledge my own name. Where I was wont to be called Arcite, now am I Philostrate, not worth a farthing! Alas fell Mars! alas Juno! thus hath your ire undone all our kindred, save me only, and wretched Palamon whom Theseus martyrs in his dungeon. And over all this, Love has shot his fiery dart through my true, anxious breast so burningly, to make a final end of me, that my death was shapen for me before my shirt! Thou slayest me with thine eyes, Emily; thou art the cause of my dying. I set not the value of a peascod upon all the remnant of my care, so I could do aught to thy pleasure!' And with that word he fell down in a trance for a long time.

Palamon, who thought he felt a cold sword glide suddenly through his heart, quaked for ire and could tarry no longer; but when he heard Arcite's words, started as a madman up out of the thick bushes with a pale, deathlike face, and 'Arcite' he said, 'false wicked traitor, now are you caught, who love my lady for whom I have all this pain and woe! You are my own blood and sworn to my confidence, as I have told you full oft before; and have cozened Duke Theseus and falsely changed your name. Either you or I shall die. You shall not love my lady; I alone will love her and none other. For I am your mortal enemy Palamon, and though I have no weapon here, but have escaped by grace of Fortune from prison, I doubt not that either I shall slay you or you shall not love Emily. Choose whichever you will, for you shall not escape me.'

When Arcite knew him and had heard his tale, with full savage heart he pulled out a sword and as fierce as a lion he spoke: 'By the God Who sits in heaven, were it not that you are sick and made for love and have no weapon here, you should never pass out of this grove but you should die by mine hand. For I defy the pledge and bond which you say I have made you. What, very fool! know that love is free, and that I will love her in spite of all your power. But have here my troth, forasmuch as you are a worthy knight and would fain contend for her by battle, I will not fail, but without the knowledge of any I will be here to-morrow, by my knightly honour, and bring armour sufficient for you, and you shall choose the best and leave the worst for me. And this night I will bring you meat and drink enough, and clothes for your bedding. And if so be you win my lady and slay me in this wood, you may well have your lady, for all me.'

Palamon answered, 'I assent.' And thus each of them pledged his faith and parted from the other till the morrow.

Ah, Cupid, who hast no charity! Ah, kingdom that wilt have no fellow! Full truly is it said that neither love nor lordship will have a partner; and that indeed Arcite and Palamon found.

Arcite rode anon to the town; and on the morrow ere daylight he privily prepared two suits of armour, each sufficient and meet for the battle in the field betwixt them. And this armour, along as he was born, he carried before him on his horse, and in the grove, at time and place appointed, this Arcite and Palamon met. Then began the colour in their visages to change. Even as the hunter in the realm of Thrace stands at a gap in the forest with a spear, when bear or lion is hunted, and hears him come rushing through the branches, breaking boughs and leaves, and thinks, 'Here comes my mortal foe; without fail, he must die or I, for I must slay him at this gap, or he me, if ill befall me; so were they, and so their hue altered, as far off as each could know the other. There was no 'Good-day', no salutation, but straightway, without word or rehearsing, each helped the other to arm, as courteously as if he were his dear friend; and after that they thrust at each other wondrous long time with spears sharp and stout. Ye might deem that Palamon in his fighting were a mad lion and Arcite a cruel tiger. They smote together like wild boars that forth white as foam in mad anger; up to the ankles they fought in blood. And in this wise I leave them fighting, and will tell you forth of Theseus.

The Destiny, God's general vicar, which executes over all the world the providence which He has foreordained, so strong it is that though the world wore the contrary of a thing, yea or nay, yet on a time that shall befall which befalls not again in a thousand years. For certainly our lusts here, be they of war, or peace, of love or hate, are all ruled by the eye above us. I am put now in mind of this by the mighty Theseus, that is so zealous on the hunt, and chiefly in May for the great hart, that no day dawns upon him in bed, that he is not clad and ready to ride with huntsman and horn, and hounds before him. For in hunting he has such delight that all his joy and passion is to be himself the great harts' destroyer, for after Mars now he serves Dian.

Clear was the day, as I have told, and Theseus in all joy and mirth rode a-hunting royally, with his fair Hippolyta and Emily clothed all in green; and to the grove, not far away, in which men told him was an hart, he held the straight course, and over a brook and so forth on his way toward the glade whither the hart was wont to have his flight. The duke would have a course or two at him with hounds such as he list to order. When he had come to the opening he shaded his eyes from the sun and looked about, and anon was ware of Palamon and Arcite that fought furiously, as it were two boards. The bright swords went to and fro so hideously that with the least blow it seemed they would fell an oak; but what they were he wist not at all. The duke smote his charger with his spurs and at a bound was betwixt the two, and pulled out a sword and cried, 'Ho' no more upon pain of losing your heads! By mighty Mars, he shall die forthwith that I see smite a stroke! But tell me what sort of men are you that are so bold as to fight here without a judge or other officer, as it were in royal lists?'

This Palamon answered forthwith, 'Sire, what need of more words? Both of is have deserved the death. Two woful wretches we are, two caitiffs, weary of our own lives, and as you are a just lord and judge, grant us no mercy nor escape, but slay me first, for the love of holy charity; but slay my fellow also as well. Or slay him first, for though you little know it, this is your mortal foe, this is Arcite, that is banished from your land on pain of death, for which he deserves to die; this is he who came to your doors and called himself Philostrate. Thus he has cozened you many a year. And you have made him your chief squire, and this is he that loves Emily. For since the day of my death is come, I fully confess that I am that woful Palamon that broke your prison wickedly. I am your mortal foe, and it is I who bear so hot a love to Emily the bright that I will die here before her eyes. Therefore I ask my death and my doom. But slay my companion in the same wise, for we both have deserved to die.'

The worthy duke answered anon, 'This is a speedy judgment. Your own mouth by your confession has condemned you, and I bear witness to it. It needs not torture you on the rack. You shall die, by mighty Mars the red!'

The queen for her very womanhood began to weep, and so did Emily and all the ladies in the troop. It was great pity, as they all deemed, that ever such a mischance should befall, for they were gentle youths, of great station, and only for love was this combat. They beheld their bloody wounds wide and sore, and one and all they cried, 'Have mercy upon us women, lord!' and upon their bare knees down they fell, and would have kissed his feet where he was, until at the last his mood was softened, for pity runs soon into a noble heart. And though at first he quaked for ire, yet he considered in brief the trespass of them both and the cause thereof; and although his ire arraigned them of guilt, yet his reason held them excused; as thus — he considered that every man will help himself in love, if he is able, and also deliver himself from prison. And likewise his heart had pity upon the women, who wept ever, and anon he thought in his noble heart, and said softly to himself, 'Fie upon a lord that will have no mercy, but be a lion in word and deed to them that repent and tremble, as well as to a proud, scornful man who ever upholds what he has done. That lord has little of discernment who knows no difference in such a case, but measures pride and humility alike.' And, in brief, when his ire was thus departed, he began to look up with shining eyes and spoke these words aloud: 'Ah, the God of Love! *Benedicite*, how mighty and great a lord he is! Against his might no impediments avail; well may he be called a god by reason of his miracles, for of every heart he can make what he will. Lo here are this Palamon and this Arcite, that were all quit of my prison, and might have lived royally in Thebes, and know that I am their mortal foe and that their death lies in my power; yet love, maugre their two eyes, has brought them hither both to die! Look now, is not that an high folly? Who is a fool but a lover? Behold how they bleed, for God's sake in heaven! Are they not in a noble plight? Thus has their lord, the god of love, paid their wages and their guerdon for serving him! And yet they that serve love deem themselves full wise, for aught that may betide! But this is the best sport of all, that she for whom they have this mirth thanks them therefore no more than me; for she knows no more of this hot to-do then a cuckoo or an hare! But all things must be assayed, both good and bad; young or old, a man must sometime be a fool. I wot it by myself, for in my time, years agone, I was a servant of love. And therefore, since I know of love's pain, as one oft caught in his snare, and how sore it can clutch a man, I forgive you this trespass all wholly, at the request of the queen kneeling here and also of Emily, my sweet sister; and you shall both anon swear to me never again to hurt my country nor war upon me by day or night, but be my friends in all that you can. I forgive you this trespass, every whit!'

Fairly and well they swore to him as he asked, and prayed him for mercy and to be their good lord; and he granted them his grace and said thus: 'To speak of royal lineage and riches, each of you is worthy, doubtless, to wed in due season, though she were a queen or a princess; but nevertheless, to speak of my sister for whom you have all this strife and jealousy, you know yourselves she may not wed two at once, though you fight forevermore. One of you, willy-nilly, must go whistle in an ivy-leaf; this is to say, she may not have both of you, be you never so jealous. And therefore I give you these terms, that each of you shall have his destiny as it is ordained for him, and hearken in what manner. Lo here I set your terms! My will is this, for flat conclusion, not to be replied to, and take it for the best, if it like you; that each of you go where he list, freely, without ransom or control, and this day fifty weeks, neither more nor less, each of you shall bring an hundred knights, armed in all perfection for the lists, ready to contender for her in battle. And this I promise you, without fail and upon my troth as a knight, that whichever of you both that has the strength, — that is to say, whether he or you with your hundred that I spoke of can slay your adversary or drive out of the lists, to him shall I give Emily, to that one whom Fortune grants so fair a grace. The lists I shall make here, and God so surely have mercy upon my soul as I shall be an even and faithful judge! None other terms shall you make with me, but that one of you shall be either dead or prisoner. And if this seem to you well said, speak your mind, and hold you content. This end and conclusion I set you!'

Whose look is light now but Arcite's? Who springs up for joy but Palamon? Who could tell or write of the joy there when Theseus granted so fair a grace? But down on their knees went every person and thanked him with heart and soul, and chiefest the Thebans many times over. And thus with good hope and blithe hearts they took their leave, and rode homeward to Thebes, with its broad old walls.

III

I believe men would deem me negligent if I forgot to tell of Theseus' outlay, who went busily to work to build up royal lists; such a noble theatre I dare to say was nowhere in this world. The circuit was a mile around, with a wall of stone and a ditch without. Round was the shape, in a circle, full of steps to the height of sixty paces, so that when a man was set on one step he hindered not his neighbour behind from seeing. Eastward stood a gate of white marble, and even such another opposite westward; and, to conclude briefly, within a like space was no such fabric on the earth. For there was no crafty man in the land that knew geometry or arithmetic, nor any cunning portrayer nor carver of images, that Theseus gave him not meat and hire to plan and build the theatre. And to do his rites and sacrifice, he built an oratory and an altar eastward above the gate, in honour of Venus, goddess of love; and westward, in commemoration of Mars, he built even such another, that cost an huge load of gold. And northward, in a turret on the wall, Theseus had wrought in noble wise an oratory rich to behold, of white alabaster and coral red, in honour of Dian the chaste.

And I have yet forgotten to describe the noble carving, the portrayings, the devices, the emblazonings and the figures in these three oratories. First, in the temple of Venus ye might have seen wrought upon the wall, in imagery piteous to behold, the broken sleeps and cold sighs, the sacred tears and lamentings, the fiery pangs of desire that love's servants endure in this life; the oaths which secure their covenants; pleasance and hope, desire and foolhardiness, beauty and youth, mirth, riches, love-charms and violence, deceits, flattery, extravagance, anxiety and jealousy (that wore a garland of yellow marigolds, with a cuckoo sitting on her hand); feasts, instruments of music, singing with dancing, pleasures and gay garments, with all the circumstance of love which I have reckoned and shall reckon, were painted by order upon the wall, and more than I can make mention of. In sooth all the mount of Cithæron, where Venus has her principal dwelling, was drawn upon the wall, with all the garden and the lustiness thereof. Idleness, the porter, was not forgotten, nor Narcissus the fair of long ago, nor the folly of King Solomon, nor yet the great strength of Hercules; the enchantments of Medea and Circe, nor the hardy fierce heart of Turnus, nor the rich Crœsus, captive and in servitude. Thus may ye see that neither wisdom nor riches, beauty nor cunning, strength nor hardihood can hold rivalry with Venus, for she can guide all the world as she list. Lo, all these folk were so caught in her snare till for woe they cried oft 'Alas!' One or two ensamples shall suffice here, though I could reckon a thousand more. The naked statue of Venus, glorious to look upon, was floating in a great sea, and from the navel down all was covered with green waves, bright as any glass. She had a lyre in her right hand, and on her head a rose-garland, fresh and well-smelling, and seemly to see. Above her head fluttered her doves, and before her stood her son Cupid, blind, as he is often shown, with two wings upon his shoulders. He carried a bow and bright, keen arrows.

Why should I not tell you as well the portrayings on the wall in the temple of mighty Mars the red? The walls were painted, in length and breadth, like to the inner parts of the grisly, great temple of Mars in Thrace, in that cold, frosty region where Mars has his supreme habitation. On the wall was painted first a forest, in which dwelt neither beast nor man, with barren old trees, knotty and gnarled, with sharp and hideous stumps. Through it ran a rumbling and a rushing noise, as though every bough should break in the tempest. Beneath a hill, under the slope, stood the temple of armipotent Mars, wrought all of burnished steel, the portal deep and narrow, ghastly to see; and thereout came such a raging blast as made all the gates to shake. The chill light from the north shone in at the door, for window in the wall was there none through which men could discern any light. The doors were all of everlasting adamant, clamped overthwart and endlong with tough iron, and every pillar that strongly held the temple almost was of the bigness of a tun and of bright and shining iron.

There I saw first the dark contriving of felony and all the compassing thereof; cruel ire, red as a coal; the pick-purse and also pale dread; the smiler with a knife under the mantle; the stable burning in its black smoke; the treacherous murder in the bed, and open war with wounds all bleeding, and strife with bloody knife and sharp menace. That sorry spot was all full of shrieks. Further on I saw there the slayer of himself with his hair bathed in his heart's blood; the nail driven in the temples by night; cold death upon his back, with mouth gaping. In the midst of the fane sat misfortune, with dejection and sorry visage. Farther yet I saw madness laughing in his frenzy, armed complaint, outcry and fierce fury; the corpse in the bushes with throat cut; a thousand slain, but not by pestilence; the tyrant with his prey ravined by force, and the town utterly left in ruins. Yet again I saw the dancing ships burned, the hunter strangled by the wild bears, the sow devouring the child in the very cradle, the cook scalded, for all his long spoon. Naught was forgotten that comes by the evil aspects of Mars. The carter run over by his cart lay full low under the wheel. There were also, of Mars' clan, the barber, the butcher, and the smith forging sharp swords upon his anvil. And above, in a tower, was depicted conquest sitting in great state, with the sharp sword hanging above him by a subtle thread of twine. The slaughter of Julius Cæsar was painted there, and of great Nero and Antony. Albeit they were unborn at that time, yet so long before were their deaths through the menacing of Mars depicted in clear blazonry. So was it shown in these portrayals even as it is drawn at large in the stars of heaven, who shall be slain and who die for love. One or two ensamples from old histories shall suffice; I cannot reckon them all even though I would.

The statue of Mars stood armed upon a chariot, grim as a madman, and over his head shone two figures of stars called in clerks' writings Puella and Rubeus; in this guise was the god of arms shown. A wolf stood before him at his feet, red-eyed and devouring a man. With subtle pencil were these figures depicted, to the glory of redoubtable Mars.

Now to the temple of Dian the chaste I will get me as fast as I can, to tell you all the description thereof. The walls up and down were painted with ensamples of hunting and of shamefast chastity. There I saw how woful Callisto, when Dian was angered with her, was turned from a woman to a bear (and she was made the lode-star afterwards). Thus was it painted, I can tell you no more; her son is a star as well, as men may behold. There I saw Dane, turned into a tree; I mean not the goddess Dian, but the daughter of Peneus, that was named Dane. There I saw Actæon made an hart, for vengeance because he saw Dian all naked; I saw also how his hounds caught and devoured him because they knew him not. There was painted how Atalanta also hunted the wild boar, with Meleager and many another, for which Dian wrought him woe. There I saw many another wondrous history, which I list not call to mind. This goddess sat full high on an hart, with small hounds about her feet, and underneath her feet she had a waxing moon that would soon wane. Her statue was clothed in green, bow in hand and arrows in a quiver. Her eyes she cast adown full low, where Pluto holds his dark region. Before her was a woman in travail, and because her child was so long unborn she called full piteously upon Lucina, 'Help, for thou canst better than any.' Fair and lifelike could he make his likeness that wrought her, and many a florin he paid for his colours.

Now were these lists all made, and Theseus, who at his own great cost had thus every whit appointed the temples and the theatre, was wondrous well pleased. But I will pass on a little from Theseus, and speak of Arcite and Palamon.

The day of their returning approached, when each should bring an hundred knights to contest in battle as I told you; and to Athens each of them came to keep his covenant, with an hundred knights all well and duly armed for the combat. And verily many a man said that never since the world was, as far as God has made sea or land, was so noble a fellowship, of a few men, in the knightly exploits of their hands. For every person that loved chivalry and would fain have an exalted name had prayed to be in those jousts. Joyful was he that was chosen! For ye know well that, if such a case befell to-morrow, every lusty knight that had his strength and was acquainted with love would be eager to be there. To fight for a lady — *benedicite*, it were a lusty sight to see! And so it was with many a knight that came with Palamon. One would be armed in a hauberk, a breastplate and a light upon; some would wear a pair of broad plates on front and back; some would have a Prussian shield or target; some would be armed well on their legs, and have an ax or a steel mace. There is no new guise that is not old. Armed they were, even as I have said, each after his own conceit.

There you might have seen, coming with Palamon, the great king of Thrace, Lycurgus himself. Black was his beard and manly his visage. His eyes glowed of a hue betwixt yellow and red, and like a griffin he looked about, with shaggy hairs in his dogged brows, his limbs great, his brawn hard, his shoulders broad, his arms round and long. And as the manner was in his country, full high he stood upon a chariot of gold, with four white bulls in the traces. Instead of an armorial tunic over his harness, he had an ancient bearskin, coal-black, with yellow nails bright as any gold. His long hair was combed down behind, and shone black as any raven's feather; on his head was a diadem of gold as great as an arm, of huge weight, set full of bright stones, of fine rubies and diamonds. About his chariot marched white mastiffs, twenty and more, as great as any steer, to hunt at the lion or hart; and followed him with collars of gold and holes filed therein, and muzzles fast bound. An hundred lords armed full well he had in his troop, with hearts stern and stout.

With Arcite, as men read in the histories, came riding, like Mars, the god of arms, the great Emetreus, king of Ind, upon a bay steed trapped in steel and covered with a diapered cloth of gold. His tunic, blazoned with his arms, was of cloth of Tartary, laid with pearls, white, round, and great. His saddle was of burnished gold, fresh forged. A short mantle hung upon his shoulders, stiff with red rubies sparkling as fire. His crisp hair ran in rings, yellow, glittering as the sun. His nose was high, his lips full, his eyes bright citron, and his colour sanguine, with a few freckles betwixt yellow and black sprinkled in his face; and as a lion he cast his looking about. His age I reckon at five-and-twenty; his beard was well begun to spring, and his voice as a thunderous trump. Upon his head he wore a garland of green laurel, fresh and lusty to see; and upon his hand he bore for his pleasure a tame eagle, white as any lily. He had with him an hundred lords, all armed full richly in all their gear, save for their heads. For dukes and earls and kings were gathered in this noble company, trust me well, for the advancement of knighthood and for love's sake. On every side about this king ran full many a tame lion and leopard.

And in this wise on the Sunday about prime these lords one and all were come to the city and alighted. This worthy Duke Theseus, when he had brought them into his city and lodged them, each after his rank, took such pains to feast and entertain them and do them all honour that even yet men deem that no man's wit could amend it. The service at the banquet, the minstrelsy, the great gifts to high and low, the rich array of Theseus' palace, what ladies were fairest and best on the dance, or which could best dance and sing, or who spoke of love most tenderly, who sat first or last on the dais, what hawks were perched above, what hounds lay on the floor — of all this I make no mention now; but all the pith of it, that methinks is best to tell. Now comes the point; hearken if you will.

The Sunday night ere daybreak, when Palamon heard the lark sing (though it were not day by two hours, yet sang the lark, and Palamon also), he arose with holy heart and high spirit to wend on his pilgrimage to the blessed benign Cytherea, I mean Venus, worthy of all reverence; and in her hour he walked forth a-foot to the lists, and into her temple. And down he kneeled, and with humble cheer and aching heart he said as I shall tell you.

Fairest of fair, daughter to Jove and spouse to Vulcan, O Venus my lady, thou that gladdenest the mount of Cithæron, have pity on my bitter burning tears and receive mine humble prayer at thine heart, by that love thou borest to Adon. Alas, I have no language to express the torments of this hell! My heart cannot reveal my woes, I am so bewildered that I can say naught. But mercy, lady bright, that well knowest my thought and seest my pain; consider all this and have pity, and so surely shall I evermore be thy true servant with all my might, and hold warface ever with chastity. That vow I make, so thou wilt help me. I care not to boast of arms, nor ask tomorrow to have victory, nor renown in this combat nor vain praise for mine exploits trumpeted up and down. But I would fully have possession of Emily, and die in thy service. Find thou the manner how; I reck not whether it be better to have victory of them, or they of me, so I have my lady in mine arms. For though Mars be god of battle, thy virtue is so great in heaven that if thou wilt I shall have my love. Thy temple evermore will I honour, wherever I go, and on thine altar I will maintain a fire and do sacrifice. And if thou deny me, my sweet lady, then I pray that to-morrow with a spear Arcite may bear me through the heart. Then, when I am dead, I reck not though Arcite win her to wife. This is the sum and end of my prayer — grant me my love, thou blessed lady.'

When his orison was done, Palamon did his sacrifice anon full devoutly, with all ceremony, though I tell not his rites now. But at last the statue of Venus shook, and made a sign whereby he understood that his prayer that day was accepted. For though the sign showed delay, yet he knew well that his boon was granted, and went home with glad heart.

About the third hour after Palamon set forth for Venus' temple, up rose the sun, and up rose Emily, and hastened forth to the temple of Dian. Her maidens that she led with her had with them, all prepared, the fire, the incense, the vestures, horns full of mead, as was the manner, and all the remnant that appertained to the sacrifice; naught was lacking. Whilst the temple, full of fair hangings, smoked with sweet odours, this Emily with mild heart washed her body with water of a spring. But how she did her rite, unless it be something in general, I dare not tell. (Yet it were a pleasure to hear more. For a man of blameless mind it were no harm; it is good that a man be free of his speech). Her bright hair was combed and all untressed, and on her head was set a crown of green oak, fair and meet. She kindled two fires on the altar, and did her rites as men may read in Theban Statius and these old books. When the fire was kindled she spoke thus to Dian with pious cheer.

'Chaste goddess of the green woods, to whom heaven and earth and sea are visible, queen of the low dark realm of Pluto, goddess of maidens, that many a year hast known my heart and what I desire, keep me now from thy wrath and vengeance, which Actæon cruelly bore. Chaste goddess, thou well knowest that I desire to be a maid till I die, never would I be love nor wife. I am a maiden, thou knowest, yet of thy band, and love hunting and the chase and to walk in the savage woods, and not to be a wife and to be with child. I would not know man's society. Now lady, I adjure thee by thine own three forms, help me, since thou canst, and grant me this one grace — send love and peace betwixt Arcite and Palamon, that love me so sore; and so turn away their hearts from me that all their hot desire and love and busy torment and flames be quenched or turned elsewhere. And if thou wilt not favour me, or my destiny be ordered that I needs must have one of the two, send me him that desires me most. Goddess of clean chastity, behold the bitter tears that drop on my cheeks. Since thou, a maiden thyself, art warder of us all, keep and defend my maidenhead, and whilst I live I will serve thee as a maiden.'

The fires burned steady upon the altar whilst Emily was thus praying, but suddenly she saw a marvellous sight. For right anon one of the fires was quenched and quickened again, and anon after that the other fire was quenched and quite extinct. And as it was extinguished it made a whistling as these wet brands do when they burn, and at the end of the brand out ran as it were many bloody drops. At which Emily was so sore aghast that she began to cry aloud and was wellnigh mad; for she knew not what it signified, but only called out for fear and so wept that it was piteous to listen. And thereupon Dian appeared, in the guise of an huntress with bow in hand, and said, 'Daughter, cease thy heaviness. It is decreed amongst the high gods, and written and confirmed in eternal words, that thou shalt be wedded unto one of them that have had so much care and woe for thee; but unto which I may not tell. Farewell, I may remain no longer. The fires burning on mine altar, ere thou go hence, shall declare to thee thy lot in this love matter.'

And with that word the arrows in the goddess' quiver clattered and rung aloud, and forth she went and vanished. At which Emily was astonied, and said, 'Alas! what signifies this? I put me in thy protection, Dian, and in thy control.' And home she went straight. This is the sum of it, there is no more to say.

In the next hour of Mars after this Arcite went forth on foot to the temple of fierce Mars, to do his sacrifice with all the rites of his pagan faith. With devout heart and high reverence he said his orison to Mars right thus.

'O strong god, that in the cold realms of Thrace art honoured and held as lord, and in every country and every realm hast in thine hand all the bridle of war, and disposest fortune therein as thou wilt, accept from me my devout sacrifice. If so be my youth have such merit, and my might be worthy to serve thy godhead, and I may be one of thine, then pity my pains, I pray. For that pain and those hot flames in which thou burnedst for desire once when thou hadst at will all the beauty of fair, young, fresh Venus (although once on a time it went amiss with thee, when Vulcan caught thee in his cords, alas!), for that sorrow that was in thine heart then, pity my bitter pains as well. Thou knowest I am young and uncunning, and hurt more with love, I believe, than ever was any living creature. For she who gives me all this woe recks never if I sink or float. And well I wot I must win her with force of arms upon the field, ere she will promise me mercy; and well I wot without help or grace from thee my strength cannot avail. Then help me to-morrow in my fight, and bethink thee of that fire that once burned thee, lord, as this fire now burns me; and grant that to-morrow I may conquer. Mine be the travail, thine be the glory! Thy supreme temple will I most revere of any place, and ever most toil in thy strong calling and to do thy pleasure; and in thy temple I will hang up my banner and all the arms of my fellows, and evermore till the day I die I will maintain an eternal fire before thee. And I will bind me to this vow also; my beard and my hair I will give thee, that now hang adown long and never yet felt offence of razor or shears, and I will be thy true servant whilst I live. Now, lord, have pity on my bitter sorrows, and give me victory; I ask of thee no more.'

The prayer of Arcite the strong being done, the temple-doors and also the rings that hung thereon clattered full loud, at which Arcite was somewhat aghast. The fires burned brightly upon the altar and illumined all the temple, and anon the ground gave out a sweet smell. And Arcite lifted his hand and cast more incense into the fire, and did other rites. And at last the statue of Mars began to ring his hauberk. And with that sound Arcite heard a murmur full low and dim which said 'Victory!' wherefore he gave laud and honour to Mars. Thus with joy and high hope of fairing well, Arcite went anon to his lodging, as fain as a bird at the bright sun.

Forthwith such strife for that grant began in heaven betwixt Venus, goddess of love, and Mars, the stern god armipotent, that Jupiter had much ado to calm it; till Saturn the pale and cold, who knew so many things that had chanced aforetime, in his old experience found a manner to content either side full soon. Sooth is the saying, age has great advantage; in age is both wisdom and experience. Men can outrun the old, but not outwit him. Anon, to appease strife and dread, albeit that is against his nature, Saturn began to find remedy.

'My dear daughter Venus.' quoth he, 'my course which circles so widely hath more power than any man comprehends. Mine is the drowning in the wan sea, mine the imprisoning in the dark cottage, mine the strangling and the hanging by the throat; the murmurs, the groaning, the churls' rebellion, the privy poisoning. I do vengeance and full chastisement when I dwell in the sign of the Lion. Mine is the ruin of high mansions, the falling of towers and walls on the sapper and the carpenter. When Samson shook the pillar, it was I slew him. And mine be the cold maladies, the dark treasons and ancient plots; mine aspect begets the plague. Weep no more now, I will do my diligence that thine own knight Palamon shall have his lady as thou hast promised him. Though Mars may help his knight, nevertheless at last there must be peace betwixt you; albeit ye are not of one nature, which causes ever such division. Weep thou no more; I am thy grandfather, ready at thy command, and I will fulfil thy pleasure.'

Now will I leave the gods of heaven, Venus, goddess of love, and Mars; and tell you as plainly as may be the main substance, for which I began.

IV

Great was the festival in Athens, and also for that lusty season of May every person was in such mirth that they jousted and danced all the Monday, and spent it in Venus' high service. But because all should be up early to see the great tourney, they went to rest betimes that night.

When day began to spring on the morrow, there was clattering and noise of horses and mail in hostelries all about, and to the palace rode many a troop of lords upon steeds and palfreys. There could you have seen armour devised full rare and richly, and wrought well in steel-work and goldsmithry and embroidery; bright shields, horses' trappings, steel caps, gold-beaten helmets, hauberks, armorial tunics; lords on their chargers in splendid vesture above their armour; knights-retainers, and squires nailing on spear-heads, buckling helms, strapping shields and lacing with thongs. Where need was, all were busy. Foamy steeds were gnawing on golden bridles, armourers were spurring to and fro in haste with file and hammer; there were yeomen on foot, and many a burgess, with short staves in hand, as thick as they could crowd, pipes, trumpets, drums, clarions, that in battle sound bloody blasts; the palace up and down full of people holding talk, here three, there ten, surmising as to these two Theban knights. Some said it shall be so, some said thus, some held with him of the black beard, some with the thick-haired, some with the bald; some said that one looked grim and would fight indeed, and that one had a battle-ax that weighed twenty pound. Thus for long the hall was full of conjecture from the time the sun began to spring.

The great Theseus, awaked from his sleep with the minstrelsy and noise, held yet his chamber in his rich palace till the Theban knights with equal honour were fetched thither. Duke Theseus was set at a window, arrayed right as if he were a god on his throne. The people pressed thitherward to see him and do him high reverence, and also to hearken to his pronouncement and behest. An herald on a scaffold proclaimed silence till all the people's noise was hushed, and then he declared the mighty duke's will.

'The lord duke, of his high prudence, hath considered that it were mere destruction to noble blood, if men should now in this emprise fight in the fashion of mortal battle. Wherefore, to ordain that they shall not perish, he will modify his first purpose. On pain of death, therefore, no man shall send or bring into the lists any manner of missile, or pole-ax, or short knife; no man shall draw or bear by his side any short sword with sharp point for stabbing; no man shall ride against his adversary with a sharp-ground spear more than one course, but on foot he may thrust, if he will, to defend himself. He that is worsted shall be captured, not slain, but brought to the stake that shall be ordained on either side; thither he must perforce and remain there. And if so befall that the chieftain on either side be taken, or else be slain, the tourneying shall last no longer. God speed you! Go forth, lay on hard! With maces and long swords fight your fill. This is the lord duke's decree, and now go your ways.'

The voice of the people reached the sky, so loud they cried with joyful voice: 'God say so good a lord, he will have no bloody destruction!' Up go trump and melody, and the bands of knights ride to the lists in order through the broad city, which was all hung with no serge but with cloth of gold. Like a lord indeed rode this noble duke, the two Thebans on either side; next rode Emily and the queen, and then another company ordered according to their station. Thus they passed through the city and came early to the lists. It was not yet full prime of day when Theseus was set down in high state, and Hippolyta the queen, and Emily, and the other ladies in tiers about. All the crowd pressed to their seats. And then through the western gates, under the shrine of Mars, Arcite and his hundred entered anon with red banner: and at the same moment Palamon and his men entered from the east under the shrine of Venus, with white banner and hardy cheer and face. In all the world, if men should seek up and down, were no two such companies, so even, without inequality. None was so discerning who could say that either had advantage of other in valour, rank or age. And they dressed them in two fair ranks. When all their names had been read, that there might be no guile as to their number, then were the gates shut and a herald cried on high, 'Do now your devoir, proud young knights!'

The heralds left their spurring about, trumpets and clarions rang aloud; there is no more to say but that in either line the spears were put full firmly in rest, in went sharp spurs into flanks, and men saw who could ride and who could joust. Shafts were shivering upon thick shields, one man felt the stab through the breast-bone, up sprung spears twenty foot on high, out came swords bright as silver, and hewed and split helms, out burst the blood with stern red streams, with mighty maces they crushed bones; one thrust through the thickest of the throng, there stumbled mighty steeds and down went knight and all, one on foot thrust with his spear-stump, one was hurtled down with his horse, and rolled like a ball under foot. One was hurt through the body, and then seized and, maugre his head, brought to the stake, and there he must abide by agreement; and thither one was brought from the other party. At times Theseus made them to rest and refresh them, and drink if they would. Full often in that day those two Thebans met together and wrought woe each to his adversary; each unhorsed the other twice. There is no tiger in the vale of Gargaphil, when her little whelp is stolen, so cruel on the hunt as Arcite's jealous heart was against this Palamon. Nor is a lion in Belmary so fell after the blood of his prey, when he is hunted or mad with hunger, as Palamon to slay Arcite his foe. The jealous strokes bit on their helms, out ran the red blood on both their flanks.

Some time there must be an end of every deed. For ere the sun went to rest, the strong king Emetreus made shift to seize upon Palamon as he fought, and made his sword to bite deep into his flesh; and by the arms of twenty he was drawn, ever resisting, unto the stake. Striving to rescue him, the strong king Lycurgus was borne down, and for all his valour king Emetreus was borne a sword's length out of his saddle, so Palamon hit him ere he was overpowered. But all for naught, he was dragged to the stake. His hardy heart could not help him; when he was caught he must abide, perforce and also by agreement. Who but woful Palamon sorrows now, that may now no more go to the fight?

And when Theseus had seen it, he cried to the folk, who fought ever, 'Ho! no more, it is done! I shall be a faithful judge and not a partial. Arcite of Thebes shall have Emily, whose good fortune has granted him to win her nobly. And straightway for joy of this began such an uproar amongst the people, so loud and high, it seemed the lists would fall.

What now can fair Venus in heaven do? What says she, what does this queen of love? She wept so, for lack of her desire, that her tears fell into the lists. 'I am ever disgraced, without doubt.' she said.

'Hold thy peace, daughter,' Saturn replied. 'Mars hath his will, and his knight all that he prayed for, and thou shalt be eased ere long, by mine head!'

The trumpets, the heralds that called and cried on high, and all the loud minstrelsy, made high festival for joy of Lord Arcite. But hold your peace a little now, and hearken what miracle befell straightway.

This fierce Arcite had doffed his helm to show his face, and on a charger spurred down the long field, looking upward on Emily. And she cast a friendly eye on him in return, for women, to speak generally, follow ever the favour of fortune. And in his heart she made all his cheer. Out of the ground burst an infernal Fury, sent from Pluto at request of Saturn, for fear of which his horse suddenly turned and leapt aside and, as he leapt, foundered; and, ere Arcite could take heed, pitched him on the crown of his head. He lay on the ground as lifeless, his breast all crushed by his saddle-bows; as black was his face as any raven or coal, so was the blood run therein Anon he was borne thence with mourning unto Theseus' castle. Then was he carved out of his harness, and brought fairly and soon into a bed, for he was yet alive and conscious, crying alway for Emily.

Duke Theseus with all his suite and guests were come home to Athens his city with all pomp and great festivity. Albeit this misadventure was befallen, he would not dishearten them all. Men said also that Arcite should not die, he should be healed of his hurt. And they were as fain of another thing, that of them all none was killed, though they were sore wounded, and especially one whose breast-bone was pierced by a spear. For other wounds and for broken bones some had charms and some had salves; they drunk sage and physic of herbs to preserve their limbs. Wherefore this noble duke cheered and honoured every man, as he well could; and made revelry all the long night, as was due, for the foreign lords. Nor was there held to have been any discomfiture, but only as in a joust or a tourney; there was no discomfiture, in sooth, for it is but a misadventure to fall, or to be held by twenty knights and carried unyielding and by force unto the stake, one man alone without a defender, dragged forth by arm, foot and toe, and his steed also driven forth with staves by yeoman and pages on foot. It could not mark him with ignominy, none could call it cowardice. Wherefore, to stop all rancour and malice, Duke Theseus anon bade proclaim the eminence of either side to be alike, as of brethren, and gave gifts to all after their station, and held high festival three days; and honourably escorted the kings out of his town a full day's journey. And home went every man straight; there was no more but, 'Farewell, have good day!' Of this battle I will speak no more, but tell of Arcite and Palamon.

Swelled the breast of Arcite, and the malady about his heart increased more and more. The clotted blood corrupted, in spite of any leech-craft, and remained so in his trunk that neither breathing a vein nor cupping nor drink of herbs could help him. The animal or expulsive virtue, which derives from that force called natural, availed not to void the venom. The pipes of his lungs began to swell, and every muscle in his breast and downward was sore harmed with venom and corruption. Neither vomit upward nor other physic availed him, to save his life. Crushed was all that region, Nature no longer had dominion. And certainly wherever Nature will not act, farewell physic; go bear the man to church! This is the sum of it — Arcite must die; wherefore he sent after Palamon, his dear cousin, and after Emily, and then said as ye shall hear.

'The woful spirit in mine heart cannot declare one point of all my bitter sorrows to you my lady, that I love most; but since my life can last no longer, to you above every creature I bequeath the devotion of my soul. Alas for the woe! alas for the strong pains that I have suffered for you, and through so long time! Alas the death! alas Emily mine! alas for our parting! alas my heart's queen! alas my bride, my heart's lady, ender of my life! What is this world, what looks a man for? Now with his love, now in his cold grave alone, without any company! Farewell, mine Emily, my sweet foe, and for the love of God take me softly in your two arms and hearken to my words.

'Many a day I have had strife and rancour here with my cousin Palamon, for the love of you and for jealousy. And may Jupiter so surely have mercy on my soul, to speak becomingly of a lover and faithfully in all points, that is to say, of fidelity, honour and knighthood, prudence, humility, station and high kindred, liberality and all such virtues, — so may Jupiter have part and lot in my soul as I know of none now in this world so worthy of love as Palamon, who serves you and will all his life. And if you shall ever wed, forget not the noble Palamon.

With that word his speech began to fail, for from his feet up to his breast had crept the cold of death that had vanquished him; and in his arms likewise the vital strength was lost and all gone. The intellect that dwelt in his sick and sore heart began to wane only when the heart felt death. Dusk grew before his two eyes, and breathing failed, but yet he cast his eye on his lady. His last word was 'Your favour, Emily!' His spirit changed house and went to a place where I never was, I cannot tell where. Therefore I leave off, I am no diviner; I find naught about souls in this volume that I follow, nor care I to repeat the opinions of them that write where spirits dwell. Arcite is cold and may Mars have care of his soul; now I will tell on of Emily.

Emily shrieked and Palamon roared, and Theseus took his swooning sister and bore her away from the corse. What boots it to take all day to tell how she wept both morn and night? At such times women have such sorrow, when their husbands have departed from them, for the more part they so grieve, or else fall into such sickness, that certainly they die, at last.

Infinite were the sorrow and tears of folk both old and of tender age throughout the town for the death of this knight; for him wept man and child.

No such weeping was there, sure, when Hector was brought, fresh slain, to Troy. Alas for the piteous sight, — scratching of cheeks, rending of hair! 'Why wouldst be dead?' these women sobbed. 'And hadst gold enough, and Emily!'

No man could cheer Theseus save Ægeus, his old father, that knew this world's transmutation as he had seen it change back and forth, joy after woe, woe after gladness; and he showed them ensamples and similitudes. 'Even as never a man died, that had not lived on earth in some station, even so never a man lived in all this world,' said he, 'that some time he died not. This world is but a thoroughfare full of misery, and we be pilgrims that pass to and fro; death is an end to every pain and grief in this world.' Above this he said much more to the same effect, wisely exhorting the people to be consoled.

Duke Theseus deliberated with all anxious care where the sepulchre of good Arcite might best be made and most honourably to his rank. And at last his conclusion was that where first Palamon and Arcite had the battle betwixt them for love, in that same green and sweet grove where Arcite made his complaint and bore his amorous desires and the hot flames of love, there he should make a fire in which the funeral office should be performed. Anon he gave orders to hew and hack the aged oaks, and lay them on rows in pieces well disposed for burning. With swift feet his officers ran and rode anon at his command. And then Theseus sent after a bier and overspread it all with cloth of gold, the richest that he had, and in the same he clad Arcite, with white gloves on his hands, a crown of green laurel on his head, and in his hand a bright sharp sword. He laid him on the bier with uncovered visage, weeping so the while that it was pity to behold. And that all the people might see the corse, when it was day it was brought into the hall, that resounded with the sound of lament.

Then came this woful Palamon, with torn beard and rough hair all ash-besprent, and then Emily, passing others in weeping, the ruefullest in all the procession. That the service might be the richer and more noble, Duke Theseus bade lead forth three steeds, trapped in steel all glittering and bearing the armours of Lord Arcite. Upon these tall white steeds sat folk of whom one bore his shield, another held his spear upright in his hands, and the third bore his Turkish bow, with quiver and trappings of burnished gold; and all rode forth at a walk with sorrowful cheer toward the grove. The noblest of the Greeks there present carried the bier upon their shoulders, with slow pace and eyes wet and red, through all the city by the chief street, which was spread all with black, and hung wondrous high with the same. On the right hand went Ægeus the old, and on the left Duke Theseus, with vessels of pure gold in their hands full of honey, milk, wine and blood. Then came Palamon, with a great troop, and then woeful Emily, with fire in her hand, to do her office at the obsequies, as was then the usage.

High labour and full great ordinance was at the service and the making of the pyre, which reached heaven with its green top and stretched its arms twenty fathom in breadth; that is to say, the boughs reached so far. There was first laid many a load of straw. But how the pyre was built up on high, and also the kinds of the trees (as oak, fir, birch, aspen, alder, holm, poplar, willow, elm, plane, ash, box, chestnut, linden, laurel, maple thorn, beech, hazel, yew, cornel), how they were felled shall not be told for all me! And how the gods ran up and down, disinherited of their habitation, in which they had long time dwelt in peace and rest, nymphs, fauns and hamadryads; and how all the beasts and birds fled for fear when the wood was felled; and how the ground was aghast of the light, that was not wont to see the bright sun; and how the fire was laid first with a bed of straw, and then with dry sticks cloven in three, and green wood, and then with spicery and cloth of gold and gems, and garlands hanging with many a flower, and myrrh and incense and sweet odours; and how Arcite lay amongst all this and amidst what treasures; and how Emily, as was the usage, applied the funeral torch, how she swooned when men made the fire and what she spoke and what she thought; what jewels men cast into the fire when it was burning high; how come cast shields and some spears and certain of their vestures, and cups full of wine, milk and blood into the furious fire; and how the Greeks in a huge company rode thrice about the fire toward the left with loud shouts, clattering their spears thrice; how the ladies cried aloud thrice, and Emily was led homeward; how Arcite was burned to cold ashes; and how the corpse-wake was held all that night, and how the Greeks played in the wake-games: — all this I care not to say. Nor who wrestled best, naked and anoint with oil, nor who bore him best in a hard pinch; nor will I tell how they went home to Athens when the games were done. But I will go shortly to the point and make an end of my long tale.

In process of certain years all the lament and mourning of the Greeks was ended by one general accord. Then I learn a parliament was held in Athens upon certain matters and cases, amongst which points there was consultation concerning an alliance with certain countries, and how to have full submission of the Thebans. Thereupon this noble Theseus sent after gentle Palamon, who little wist what was the cause; but in his black clothes and with his sorrow he came hastening at the command. Then sent Theseus for Emily. When they were sat down and all the place hushed, and Theseus had tarried a season, ere a word came from his wise bosom he fixed his eyes where he would, and sighed softly with a grave visage, and then spoke his will thus.

'When the high First Cause and Mover created the fair chain of love, great was the deed and high His intent; well He knew why, and what He designed therein. For with that fair chain of love He bound, to certain limits that they could not flee, the water and the earth, the fire and the air. That same Prince and Mover in this wretched world below has established a certain duration of days for all that is engendered here, beyond which days they may not pass, albeit indeed they may shorten those days. It needs allege non authority, for it is proved by experience; only I would declare that which is in my mind. Then may men well perceive by this order of things that this same Mover is stable and eternal. Well may a man know, unless he be a simpleton, that every part derives from its whole. Therefore Nature took not her origin from any fragment or part of a thing, but from a being stable and perfect, descending thence so far till she become corruptible. Therefore of His wise providence He has so well ordered His works that species and courses of things shall endure only by succession and not eternally. That this is true you may well understand and plainly see. Lo the oak, which has so long a time of youth after it first begins to spring, and, as we may see, has so long a life, yet at last wastes it away. Consider also how that the hard stone under out feet, on which we walk and tread, yet wears down as it lies by the way. The broad river at last waxes dry; the great towns we see wane and pass. Then you may see that all these earthly things come to an end. Of man and woman we see well also that at one time or the other, in youth or else age, they must die, king and serving-boy alike; one in the deep sea, one in the broad plain, one in his bed. Naught avails, all go that same way, and I may well say then that all things must die. Who has ordained things thus but Jupiter the king, prince and cause of all creatures, converting all things again to their proper source whence they were derived? And to strive against this avails no creature on earth of any degree. Then methinks it is wisdom to make a virtue of necessity, and to take well what we cannot eschew, and chiefest that which is decreed for us all. And whoso murmurs does folly, and is rebel against the governor of all things.

'And certainly it is most honour to a man to die in the flower of his excellence, when he is secure of his fair repute and has brought no shame to himself or his friend. And when he has breathed his last in honour, his friend ought to be gladder of his death than if his name were grown pale with age and his valour all forgot. For a man's glory, then, is it best to die when he is highest in fame. To think the contrary of all this is wilfulness. Why go we heavily? why murmur we that good Arcite, flower of chivalry, is departed in the course of duty and in honour out of this life, this foul prison? why murmur here his bride and cousin at the welfare of him that loved them so well? Will he thank them for it? Nay, God wot, never a bit! They hurt both his soul and also themselves, and profit themselves not at all. How shall I conclude after this long discourse, but that after woe I counsel that we be merry and thank Jupiter for his grace? And, ere we depart hence, I counsel that of two sorrows we make one perfect joy that shall last evermore; and look now where most sorrow is, for there will we first begin and make amends.

'Sister,' quoth he, 'with the full accord of my parliament, this is my decree, that of your grace you shall have pity on noble Palamon, your own knight, who serves you with will, heart and strength, and ever has since first you knew him, and that you shall take him for lord and husband. Reach me your hand, for this is our mandate. Show now your womanly pity. In faith, he is a king's brother's son; and though he were a poor squire, he has served you so many years in so great adversity, believe me this ought to be considered. For gentle mercy ought to go beyond mere justice.'

Then said he forthwith to Palamon, 'I trust there needs little sermoning to make you assent to this. Draw nigh, take your lady's hand!'

Anon there was made betwixt them the bond of marriage or matrimony by all the council and all the baronage. And thus with all bliss and music has Palamon wedded Emily, and may God That wrought all this wide world send him the joy of love that has paid for it so dear. Now is Palamon living in all weal, in bliss, in health and wealth. And he served Emily ever with such noble kindness, and she loved him so tenderly, that never was a word betwixt them of jealousy or any other vexation. Thus end Emily and Palamon. And God save all this fair fellowship! Amen.

Prologue to the Miller's Tale

When the Knight had thus ended his tale, in all the crowd was there none, young nor old, but said it was a noble history and worthy to be called to mind; and especially each of the gentlefolk. Our Host laughed and swore, 'So may I thrive, this goes well! The bag is unbuckled, let see now who shall tell another tale, for truly the sport is well begun. Now you, Sir Monk, if you can, tell somewhat to cap the Knight's story with.'

The Miller, who had drunk himself all pale, so that he could scarce sit his horse, would doff hood or hat or wait and mind his manners for no one, but began to cry aloud in Pilate's voice, and swore by arms and blood and head, 'I know a noble tale for the nonce, to cap the Knight's story with.'

Our Host saw that he was all drunken with ale, and said, 'Abide, Robin, dear brother, some better men shall speak first; abide, and let us go on in a seemly fashion.'

'God's soul!' quoth he, 'that will I not! I will speak, or else go my way!'

'Tell on, in the Devil's name!' answered our Host. 'You are a fool, your wits are afloat.'

'Now hearken, one and all! But first,' quoth the Miller, 'I make a protestation that I am drunk; I know it by my voice. And therefore if I speak as I should not, blame it upon the ale of Southwark, I pray you; for I will tell a life and a legend of a carpenter and his wife, and how a clerk bamboozled him.'

'No more of your prating!' the Reeve answered and said, 'Let be your rude drunken ribaldry. It is great folly and sin to injure or defame any man, and to bring women into such ill repute. You can tell enough of other matters.'

This drunken Miller answered back anon and said, 'Oswald, dear brother, he is no cuckold who has no wife. But I say not therefore that you are one. There is many a full good wife, and ever a thousand good to one bad, and that you know well yourself, if you have not lost your senses. Why are you angry now with my tale? I have a wife as well as you, perdy, yet for all the oxen in my plough I would not be over-curious and suspicious, as to deem of myself that I am a cuckold; I will believe well I am none. A husband shall not pry too curiously into God's mysteries or into his wife's. So he find God's plenty for himself, he need not enquire as to the remnant.'

What more can I say, but this Miller would forbear his word for no man, and told his churl's tale in his own fashion, and methinks, I shall rehearse it here. And therefore I pray every gentle creature, for the love of God, deem not that I tell it thus out of evil intent, but only because I must truly repeat all their tales, be they better or worse, or else tell some of my matter falsely. And therefore whoso will not hear it, let him turn the leaf over and choose another tale; for he shall find historical things enough, great and small, touching on noble deeds, and also on morality and holiness. Blame not me if you choose amiss. The Miller is a churl, you know well, and so was the Reeve and many another, and ribaldry they told, the two of them. Bethink you, and have me excused, and likewise men must not make earnest of sport.

The Miller's Tale

Once there dwelt at Oxford a rich churl, of his craft a carpenter, who took guests to board. With him dwelt a poor scholar, who had studied the liberal arts, but all his delight was turned to learning astrology. He knew how to work out certain problems; for instance, if men asked him at certain celestial hours when there should be drought or rain, or what should befall in any matter; I cannot reckon every one.

This gentle clerk was named Nicholas. He was well skilled in secret love and pleasure, and also full sly and cautious, and as meek as a maiden to look upon. He had a chamber to himself in that lodging-house, without any company, and full trimly decked with sweet herbs; and he himself was as sweet as the root of licorice. His *Almagest*, and other books great and small, his astrolabe that he used in his art, and his counters for calculating, all lay fairly by themselves on shelves at his bed's head. His clothes-press stood covered with scarlet frieze, and above it lay a gay psaltery, on which he made melody at night so sweetly that all the chamber was full of it. He would sing the hymn *Angelus ad Virginem*, and after that the King's Note; full oft was his merry throat exultant. And so this sweet clerk passed his time by help of what income he had and his friends provided.

This carpenter had newly wedded a wife, eighteen years of age, whom he loved more than his own soul. He was jealous, and held her closely mewed up, for she was wild and young, and he was on in years and deemed himself like to be made a cuckold. His wit was rude, and he knew not Cato's sentence that bade man should wed his like. Men should wed after their own kind, for youth and age are oft at odds. But since he was fallen in the snare, he must endure his pain, like other folk. Fair was this young wench, and her body withal graceful and slim as any weasel. She wore a striped silken girdle, and over her loins an apron white as morning's milk, all flounced out. Her smock was white, and embroidered about on the collar, within and without, before and behind, with coal-black silk; and of the same black silk were the strings of her white hood, and she wore a broad fillet of silk, wrapped high about her hair.

And in sooth she had a wanton eye; her eyebrows were arched and black as a sloe, and partly plucked out to make them narrow. She was more delicious to look on than the young pear-tree in bloom, and softer than a lamb's wool. From her girdle hung a leathern purse, tasselled with silk and with beads of latten. In all this world is no man so wise who could think of such a wench, or so gay a darling. Her hue shone more brightly than the florin newly forged in the Tower, and for her singing, it was as loud and lively as a swallow's sitting on a barn, and she could skip and make merry withal as any kid or calf following its dam. She was skittish as a jolly colt, long as a mast and straight as a wand. Her mouth was as sweet as honey or mead or a hoard of apples laid up in hay or heather. She wore a brooch on her low collar as broad as the boss on a shield, and her shoes were laced high on her legs. She was a primrose, a dear little pig's-eye, to be any lord's sweetheart, or yet for a good yeoman to wed.

Now sir, and again sir, it so chanced that this gentle Nicholas fell to romping with this young wife, on a day when her husband was at Oseney (as clerks are full subtle and sly), and suddenly he caught hold of her and said: 'Unless you will love me, sweetheart, truly I shall die for hidden love of you. Deary, love me now, or I will die, so God save me!' And he held her hard about the waist.

She sprang back like a colt in the halter, and wriggled away with her head. 'I will not kiss you, in faith,' quoth she. 'Why! let be, let be, Nicholas, or I will cry out "Alas! Help!." Take away your hands, of your courtesy!'

But this Nicholas began to beg for her grace, and spoke so fair and made such offers that at last she granted him her love, and swore by St. Thomas of Kent that she would do his will when she should see her chance. 'My husband is so jealous that unless you are privy and watch your time, I know right well I am no better than dead. You must be full sly in this thing.'

'Nay, have no fear therefor,' quoth Nicholas. 'A clerk had ill spent his time unless he could beguile a carpenter!'

And thus they were accorded and pledged to watch for a time, as I have told. When Nicholas had done thus, petted her well and kissed her sweetly, he took his psaltery, and made melody and played long and loud.

Then it befell on an holy day that his good wife betook her to the parish-church to work Christ's own works. Her forehead shone as bright as day, so had she scrubbed it when she had finished her tasks. Now at that church there was a parish-clerk named Absalom. Curly was his hair, and shone like gold, and spread out like a large broad fan; its neat parting ran straight and even, his cheeks were rosy and his eyes as gray as goose-quills. His leathern shoes were of openwork, like a window in Paul's Church. He went clad full trimly and neatly all in red hosen and a kirtle of a light watchet-blue; full fair and thick were the laces set in, and over it he had a gay surplice, as white as blossom on twig. God bless me, but he was a sweet lad! Well he knew how to clip and shave and let blood, and make a quittance or a charter for land. He could trip and dance in twenty ways after the manner of Oxford in that day, and cast with his legs to and fro, and play songs on a small fiddle. He could play on his gittern as well, and sometimes sang in a loud treble. In all the town was no brewhouse or tavern that he visited not in his merrymaking. But sooth to say he was somewhat dainty, and bashful of his speech.

This Absalom, so pretty and fine, went on this holy day with a censer, diligently incensing the goodwives of the parish, and many a killing look he cast on them. And chiefest on this carpenter's wife; to look at her seemed to him a sweet employment, she was so neat and sweet and bewitching. I dare be bound, if she had been a mouse and he a cat, he would have caught her straightway. And this sweet parish-clerk had such a love-longing in his heart that at the offertory he would take naught from any wife; for courtesy, he said, he could take none.

That night the moon shone full fair, and Absalom thought to wake all night for love's sake; he took his gittern and went forth, amorous and gay, till he came to the carpenter's house a little after the cocks had crowed, and drew him up by a casement window.

> 'Dear lady, if your will so be,
> I pray, you that you pity me!'

he sang in his sweet small voice, in nice harmony with his gitterning.

This carpenter woke, heard his song and said anon to his wife, 'What, Alison! Hear you not Absalom chanting thus under our own bower-wall?'

'Yes, God wot, John,' she answered him, 'I hear it every bit.'

Thus it went on; what would you have better than well-enough? From day to day this sportive Absalom wooed her till he was all woe-begone. He woke all night and all day, he combed his spreading locks and made him fine, he woed her by go-betweens and agents, and swore he would be her own page; he sang quavering like a nightingale; he sent her mead, and wines sweetened and spiced, and wafers piping hot from the coals, and because she was a town-wench he proffered her money. For some folk will be won by rich gifts, and some by blows, and some by courtesy. One time he played Herod on a high scaffold, to show his nimbleness and skill. But in such a case what could avail him? She so loved gentle Nicholas that Absalom may go blow the buck's-horn. For all his labour he had but a flout, and thus she made Absalom her ape and turned all his earnest to a jest. Men say this proverb, which is full sooth, 'Ever the nigh sly one maketh the far lief one to be a loathed one.' For though Absalom go mad for it, because he was far from her eye this nigh Nicholas stood in his light. Now bear you well, gentle Nicholas, for Absalom is fain to wail and sing 'Alack!'

And so befell one Saturday that the carpenter was gone to Oseney, and gentle Nicholas and Alison were agreed upon this, that Nicholas shall find a fetch to beguile this poor jealous husband; and if so be the game went aright, she should be his, for this was his desire and hers also. And anon, without more words, Nicholas would delay no longer, but had meat and drink for a day or two carried softly into his chamber, and bade her say to her husband, if he asked after him, that she knew not where he was; that she had not set eyes upon him all that day, she believed he was in some malady, for not by any crying out could her maid rouse him; he would not answer at all, for nothing.

Thus passed forth all that Saturday; Nicholas lay still in his chamber, and ate and slept or did what he would, till Sunday, toward sundown. This simple carpenter had great marvel about Nicholas, what could ail him. 'By Saint Thomas,' he said, 'I am afeared it stands not aright with Nicholas. God forbid that he has died suddenly! This world nowadays is full ticklish, of a truth; to-day I saw a corse borne to church that I saw at work last Monday. Go up, call at his door,' he said to his boy, 'or knock with a stone; look how it is, and tell me straight.'

This boy went up full sturdily, stood at the chamber-door and cried and knocked like mad: 'What! how! what do you, master Nick? How can you sleep all day long?'

But all was for naught, he heard not a word. Then he found a hole, low down in the wall, where the cat was wont to creep in; and through that he looked in far and at last caught sight of him. This Nicholas sat ever gaping upward as if he were peering at the new moon. Down went the boy, and told his master in what plight he saw this man.

This carpenter began to cross himself and said, 'Help us, Saint Frideswide! A man knows little what shall befall him! This man with his astronomy is fallen into some madness or some fit; I thought how it should end this way. Men were not intended to know God's secrets. Yea, happy is a man that never had schooling, that knows naught but only his *I believe!* So fared another clerk with his astronomy; he walked in the fields to peer upon the stars, to see what was to happen, till he fell into a marl-pit that he saw not! But yet, by Saint Thomas, I am right sorry about gentle Nicholas. By Jesu, King of heaven, he shall be chidden for his studying if I live. Get me a staff, Robin, that I may pry under the door whilst you heave it up. I believe we shall rouse him from his studying!'

And so he betook him to the chamber-door. His boy was a strong lad, and anon heaved the door up by the hasp, and in upon the floor it fell straightway. This Nicholas sat ever as still as a stone, ever gaping into the air. This carpenter weened he were fallen into a desperation, and seized him mightily by the shoulders and shook him hard and cried wildly, 'What, Nick! what, how! what, look down! Awake, think on Christ's passion; I cross thee from elves and spooks!' And thereupon he said the night-spell, toward the four corners of the house and without on the threshold of the door: —

> 'Jesu Christ and sweet Saint Benedight
> Bless this house from every wicked sprite.
> For the night-hag, the white *pater noster*;
> Where wentest thou, Saint Peter's sister?'

At last this gentle Nicholas began to sigh sore, and said, 'Alack! shall all the world be destroyed again now?'

'What say?' quoth the carpenter. 'What now! Think on God, as we do, men that work.'

'Fetch me drink,' quoth Nicholas, 'and after I will speak privily of a certain thing which touches you and me both. I will tell it to no other man, be sure.'

This carpenter went down and came again bringing a large quart of mighty ale; and when each of them had drunk his share, Nicholas shut his door fast and set the carpenter down beside him.

'John, my dear host,' he said, 'you shall swear me here on your troth that you will reveal this secret to no one; for it is Christ's own secret that I show you, and if you tell it to any you are a lost man. For this vengeance you will receive therefor if you betray me, that you shall run mad!'

'Nay, Christ and His holy blood forbid!' quoth this simple man. 'I am no blabber, and though I say it myself, I am not wont to prate. Say what you will, I shall never utter it to man, woman or child, by Him That harrowed hell!'

'Now, John, I will not deceive you,' quoth Nicholas; 'I have found by mine astrology, as I have been looking in the shining moon, that now a' Monday next, about a quarter through the night, there shall fall a rain so wild and mad that never was Noah's flood half so great. This world shall all be drowned in less than an hour, so hideous shall be the downpour. Thus shall all mankind perish in the flood.'

'Alas, my wife! And shall she drown?' this carpenter answered, and wellnigh fell over for sorrow. 'Alas mine Alison! Is there no remedy?'

'Why yes, 'fore God, if you will work after wise counsel,' quoth gentle Nicholas; 'but you may not work out of your own head. For thus says Solomon, and he was right trustworthy, "Work all by counsel, and thou shalt never repent." And if you will work after good advice, I undertake without mast or sail to save both her and you and me. Have you not heard how Noah was saved, when our Lord had warned him that all the world should be destroyed with water?'

'Yes,' quoth the carpenter, 'I heard it long, long ago.'

'Have you not heard also,' quoth Nicholas, 'the woe that Noah and his sons had ere he could get his wife aboard? He had rather than all his black rams then, I dare be bound, that she had had a ship all to herself! Know you then what is best to do? This thing calls for haste, and on an urgent matter men may not preach or delay. Go anon and get us forthwith into this house a kneading-trough or else a brewing-tub for each of us (but look that they be big), in which we may swim as in a barge and have therein victual enough for a day, — there needs no more. The water shall slacken and run off about prime on the next day. But Robin your boy must not know of this, nor I cannot save your maid Jill; ask not why, for though you ask me I will not tell God's secret. It ought to suffice you, if your wits not be turning, to have as great grace as Noah had. Your wife I shall save, I promise you. Go your way now, and make haste. But when you have got these kneading-tubs for us three, then you shall hang them from the rafters high in the roof, that no man spy upon our device. And when you have done thus, and laid our victual in them full fairly, and also an axe to smite the cord in two when the water comes, and when you have broken a hole on high in the gable toward the garden over the barn, that we may freely go on our way when the great shower is past, — then you will float as merrily, I will be bound, as the white duck after her drake. Then will I call out, "How, Alison! How, John! Be merry; the flood will soon pass." And you will answer, "Hail, Master Nick! Good morrow, I see you well, it is daylight now!" And then we shall be lords over all the world till we die, even as Noah and his wife!

'But one thing I warn you of strictly. Be well advised on that night when we be entered aboard ship that none of us speaks a word, nor calls nor cries, but we must be in our prayers. For that is God's own precious command. And your wife and you must hang far apart, that there be no folly betwixt you, any more in looking than in act. Now all this device is told you; go, and God speed you! To-morrow at night, when folks are all abed, we will creep into our kneading-tubs and sit there, awaiting God's grace. Go your way now, I have no time to make longer sermoning of this. Men say thus: "Send the wise and say nothing." You are so wise it needs not teach you. Go, save our lives, I entreat.'

This simple carpenter went his way with full many an 'alack!' and 'alas!', and told the secret to his wife. And she was wary, and knew better than he what all this quaint device was about. But nevertheless she fared as if she should die, and said, 'Alas! go your way at once and help us to escape, else we are all lost; I am your true, faithful wedded wife. Go, dear spouse, and help to save us!'

Lo, how great a thing is feeling! Men may die of imagination, so deep may the impression be. This simple fellow began to quake; he thought verily he could hear Noah's flood come wallowing like the sea to drown Alison his honey sweeting; he wept, wailed and made sorry cheer, and sighed with many a sorry gust. He went and got him a kneading-trough, and after that a tub and a cask, sent them privily to his house and hung them in the roof. With his own hand he made three ladders, to climb by the rungs and uprights into the tubs hanging amongst the beams; and victualed tub and trough and cask with bread and cheese, and good ale in a great vessel, right sufficient for a day. But ere he had made all this gear, he sent his boy and also his wench to London about his business. And as it drew toward night on the Monday, he lit no candle, but shut the door and ordered all things as they should be; and, in brief, up they all three climbed, and sat still whilst a man could walk a furlong.

'Now mum, and say a *pater noster!*' said Nick; and 'Mum!' quoth John, and 'Mum!' Alison. This carpenter sat still and said his prayers, ever listening for the rain, if he could hear it.

The dead sleep, for very weariness and apprehension, fell on this carpenter even about curfew-time or a little later, as I suppose; he groaned sorely in the travail of his spirit, and also snored, for his head lay uneasily. Down the ladder stalked Nicholas, and Alison sped down full softly; and they were in mirth and glee, till the bells began to sound for lauds, and friars in the chapel began to sing.

This parish-clerk, amorous Absalom, always so woe-begone for love, was at Oseney upon that Monday to divert him and make merry, with a party; and by chance he privily asked a cloister-monk after John the carpenter. The monk drew him aside out of the church. 'I wot not,' he said; 'I have not seen him work here since Saturday; I believe he be gone where our abbot has sent him for timber. For he is wont to go for timber and remain at the grange a day or two. Or else he is at home, certainly. In sooth I cannot say where he is.'

This Absalom waxed fully merry of heart, and thought, 'Now is the time to wake all night, for certainly since daybreak I have not seen him stirring about his door. On my soul, at cockcrow I shall knock fully privily at his casement which stands low upon his chamber-wall. To Alison now will I tell the whole of my love-longing, and now I shall not fail at the least to have a kiss from her. I shall have some sort of comfort, in faith. My mouth has itched all day long; that is a sign of kissing at least. All night also I dreamed I was at a festival. Therefore I will go sleep an hour or two, and then I will wake all night in mirth.'

When the first cock had crowed, up rose this frisky lover, and arrayed him in his gayest with all nicety. But first he chewed cardamoms and licorice to smell sweetly, ere he had combed his hair, and put a true-love charm under his tongue, for thereby he hoped to find favour. He rambled to the carpenter's house, and stood still under the casement, which was so low it reached to his breast. He gave a soft half-cough, — 'What do you, sweet Alison, honeycomb? My fair bird, my darling! Awake, sweet cinnamon, and speak to me. You think right little upon my sorrow, who sweat for your love wherever I go! No wonder though I languish and sweat! I mourn like a lamb after the dug. In faith, darling, I have such love-longing that I mourn like the true turtle-dove. I cannot eat, no more than a maiden.'

'Go from my window, Jack-fool,' quoth she. 'On my soul, there will be no singing.'

'Come buss me now.'

I love another better than you, by heaven, Absalom, and else I were at fault. Go your ways, or I will cast a stone at you, and let me sleep, in the Devil's name!'

'Alas!' quoth he. 'Alackaday that true love was ever so ill bestowed!'

This Absalom walked slowly across the street to a smith men called Master Gervase, who smithied plough-instruments at his forge. He was busily sharpening coulter and share when Absalom knocked full gently and said, 'Undo, Gervase, and that anon.'

'What! Who are you?'

'It is me, Absalom.'

'What, Absalom! By the rood, why rise ye so early? — Eh, *benedicte!* What ails you? Some gay girl, God wot, has brought you so early astir. By Saint Neot, you wot well what I mean!'

This Absalom recked not a peascod for all his mocking, and returned not a word in kind. He had more tow on his distaff than Gervase knew, and said,

'Dear friend, that hot coulter in the chimney — lend it me, I have somewhat to do with it; and I will bring it you straightway again.'

'Certes,' answered Gervase, 'were it gold or nobles in a poke all uncounted, you should have it, as I am a faithful smith! Eh, the Devil, what will ye do with it?'

'That is as it may be,' quoth Absalom. 'I shall tell you to-morrow-day;' and he caught the coulter by the cool handle.

Full softly he stole out at the door and went to the wall of the carpenter's house. He coughed first, and knocked withal upon the window, as he did before.

'Who is there that knocks so?' Alison answered. 'I warrant it a thief!'

'Why nay,' quoth he, 'God wot, my sweeting, I am your Absalom, my sweetheart. I have brought you a ring of gold; my mother gave it me, on my life! It is full fine and well graven withal. This I will give you if you kiss me!'

This Nicholas thought he would amend all the sport; he should kiss him ere he escaped! Back he put the window in haste, and out he put himself. Thereupon spoke this clerk Absalom, 'Speak, sweet bird, I wot not where thou art;' and then he was ready with his hot iron and smote Nicholas therewith.

Off went the skin a hand-breadth about, the hot coulter so burned him, and for the pain he thought he should die. 'Help! Water, water! Help, help for God's sake!' he cried like one mad.

The carpenter started out of his slumber; he heard one cry wildly 'Water!', and thought, 'Alas! now comes Nowell's flood!' He sat up without a word, and with his axe smote the cord a-two, and down went the tub and all; they stopped for nothing till they came to the floor, and there he lay in a swoon.

Up started Alison and Nick, and cried 'Help!' and 'Alack!' in the street. The neighbours young and old ran to stare upon him as he lay yet in a swoon, for with the fall he had broken his arm. But he must even digest his own trouble, for when he spoke he was overborne by Alison and gentle Nicholas. They told every man he was mad, he was aghast so of 'Nowell's flood' in his fantasy, that of his folly he had brought him three kneading-tubs and had hung them above in the roof; and had prayed them for God's sake to sit with him in the roof, *par compagnie*. Folks laughed at his odd quirk; into the roof they peered and gaped, and turned all his trouble into mirth. For whatsoever the carpenter answered, it was all for naught; no man heard his speeches, he was so sworn down by the great oaths of the others that in all the city he was held as mad. Every clerk anon held with every other clerk: 'the man is mad, my dear brother!' And every person laughed over his contention.

Thus the carpenter lost his wife, for all his watching and jealousy; and Nicholas was sore burned. This tale is done, and God save all the company!

Prologue to the Reeve's Tale

When folks had laughed at this plight of Absalom and of gentle Nicholas, sundry folk said sundry things, bit for the more part they laughed and made merry over the tale, nor saw I any man take it ill except only Oswald the Reeve. Because he was of his trade a carpenter, a little ire was yet lingering in his heart, and he began to grumble and to censure it a little.

'By my soul, I could pay 'ee back full well,' quoth he, 'with a tale about the hoodwinking of a bold miller, if I would speak of ribaldry. But I be old, I list not make sport; grass-time is over, all my fodder now is hay; this white pate writes me down an old man, and my heart is as dried up as my hair, — if I be not like a medlar, that ever grows softer and worse till it lie rotten amongst muck or straw. We old men, I doubt, we fare even so, we cannot ripen till we be rotten. We hop ever whilst the world will pipe to us, for ever it sticks in our desire to have a hoar head and a green tail, as has a leek. Though our might be gone, ever alike our will hankers after folly, for when we cannot do it yet will we talk of it. Still is the fire there, raked over in our old ashes. We have four burning coals — boasting, lying, anger and covetousness; these four sparks belong to age. In very deed, for all that our old limbs may be feeble, our desire fails us not. Ever I have kept my colt's-tooth, many a year as is passed since my tap of life began to run. Verily, when I was born, Death drew out the tap of life and let it run, and ever since has it so run till now the cask is wellnigh empty. The stream of life now trickles in upon the rim. The poor old tongue may well chime and ring of wretchedness long past; with old folk naught is left save dotage.'

When our Host had heard this homily, he began to speak as lordly as a king. 'Why all this wisdom?' he said. 'Are we to talk all day of Holy Writ? Dally not with the time; the Devil made a shipman or a doctor out of a cobbler, and the Devil made a reeve to preach. Tell forth your tale. Lo Deptford, and it is half-way prime; lo Greenwich, where is many a rascal! It were fully time to begin your tale.'

'Now, sirs, I pray you all not to take it ill,' quoth this Oswald the Reeve, 'though I answer this Miller with a gibe or flout. For it is lawful for a man to shove off force with force. This drunken Miller has told us here how a carpenter was beguiled, peradventure in mockery, because I am one. And by your leave I shall forthwith requite him, even in his own churl's language. I pray God, may his neck break! He can well see a stick in mine eye, but cannot see a beam in his own.'

The Reeve's Tale

At Trumpington, not far from Cambridge, there goes a brook over which stand a bridge and a mill; and this is very truth that I tell you. Long time there dwelt a miller, as proud and gay as any peacock. He could fish and mend nets and turn cups on a lathe, pipe and wrestle well and shoot; he wore by his belt a full sharp-bladed sword, and a long cutlass, and in his pouch he carried a jolly dagger. There was no man durst touch him for the peril! And also in his hose he carried a Sheffield knife. His skull was as bald as an ape's, round was his face and his nose a pug. He was a notable swaggerer at markets; there durst no person lay hand on him but he swore he should pay dear for it. He was a thief of corn and meal, and that a sly and unwearying, in very sooth. His name was called Bully Simkin. He had a wife, of gentle blood; the parson of the town was her father, who gave as her dowry many a brazen pan, the Simkin might marry into his kin. She had been brought up in a nunnery; Simkin would have no wife, he affirmed, but she were well nurtured and a maiden, for the sake of his honour as a yeoman. And she was proud and pert as a magpie. A full fair sight were the two together on holy days; he would walk before her with the tail of his hood wound about his head, and she came after in a scarlet petticoat, and Simkin wore hose of the like. No person durst call her aught but 'dame'; no man so bold walked by the way that durst once trifle or dally with her, unless he would be slain by Simkin with cutlass or knife or dagger. For jealous folk are evermore perilous; leastways they would have their wives believe so. And also, because she was somewhat smirched in her name, she was as repellent as water in a ditch, and full of disdain and of insolence. She thought ladies should treat her with respect, what with her gentle kin and her elegance that she had learned in the nunnery.

They had betwixt them a daughter twenty years old, and no other children save one of six months; it lay in a cradle, and was a proper lad. This wench was stout and well-grown, with broad hips and round high breast, and a pug-nose and eyes grey as glass. Right pretty was her hair, I will not deny it. Because she was comely, the parson of the town purposed to make her his heir, both of his movable property and his house, and full nice and captious he was about her marriage; his purpose was to bestow her well, into some family of exalted lineage and blood. For Holy Church's goods must be spent on the blood that is descended from Holy Church; therefore he meant to dignify his holy blood, though to do so he should devour Holy Church.

A great toll, of a surety, did this miller collect on the wheat and malt from all the land round about. And chiefest there was a great college that men call King's Hall at Cambridge, all the wheat and malt for which were ground by him. It happened on a day that the manciple of the college fell sick of some malady; men deemed that surely he could never recover. Wherefore this miller stole of the meal and corn a hundred times more than aforetime; of old he stole but courteously, but now he was an outrageous plunderer. Threat the warden chid and made much ado, but the miller recked not a straw, and blustered and said it was not so.

Now there dwelt in this Hall that I tell of two young poor clerks; bold and headstrong there were, and lusty in sport, and only for the frolic of it they begged eagerly of the warden to grant them a leave for but a little while to go to the mill and see their corn ground; and verily they would wager their heads the miller should not steal half a peck of corn from them by cunning, nor plunder from them by force. And at last the warden gave them leave. John one of them was named, and the second Alan. They were born in the same town, that was called Strother, far in the north, I cannot tell where.

This Alan, the clerk, made ready all that he must take, cast the sack of corn over a horse, and forth he went with John, and good swords and bucklers by their thighs. John knew the way, they needed no guide, and at the mill door he laid down the sack. Alan spoke first: 'All hail, Simon, in faith! How fares your wife, and your fair daughter?'

'Alan, welcome, by my head!' quoth Simkin. 'And John too! How now, what do you at Trumpington?'

'Simon,' replied John, 'by God, need has na peer. It behooves him serve himself that has na swain, as clerks say, or else he is a fool. I believe our manciple will die anon, so the jaws waggle in his head. And therefore I is come with Alan to grind our corn and carry it home. I pray you speed us hence as fast as you may.'

'In faith it shall be done,' quoth Simkin. 'What will you do whilst it is in hand?'

'By God, I will be here right by the hopper,' quoth John, 'and see how that the corn gaes in. By my father's soul, I never yet saw how that the hopper wags till and fra.'

'And will you swa?' answered Alan. 'Then by my pate I will be beneath, and see how that the meal falls down into the trough; that sall be my disport. In faith, John, I must be of your class, I is as ill a miller as you.'

This miller smiled at their simplicity. 'All this is but done for a fetch,' he thought; 'they deem no man can beguile them. But I vow by my trade, for all the craft in their philosophy, I shall blear their eyes yet. The more cunning wiles they put on, the more I will take when I steal. I shall give them bran yet in the place of flour.

> "The greatest clerks be not the wisest men,"

as the mare once said to the wolf. I care not a peascod for their art!'

Out at the door he privily went when he saw his time. He looked up and down till he found the clerks' horse where he stood tied under an arbor behind the mill; and went softly to the horse and anon stripped off the bridle. And when the horse was loose, forth he started with a 'Wehee!' through thick and thin toward the fen, where wild mares were running.

This miller went back; not a word he said, but did his business and chaffed with the clerks till their corn was ground all fair and well. And when the meal was sacked and fastened, this John went out and found his horse gone, and began to cry, 'Help! Alackaday, our horse is lost! Alan, for God's sake, man, step on your feet, come out at once! Alas, our warden has lost his palfrey!'

This Alan forgot all his thrifty mood; clean out of his mind went meal and corn and all, and he began to cry, 'What! whilk way is he gane?'

The goodwife came leaping in with a run. 'Alas!' she said, 'your horse is going to the fen with the wild mares, as fast as he can gallop. Bad luck on his hand that bound him so ill, and should have knit the rein better.'

'Alas!' quoth John. 'By the rood, Alan, lay down your sword, and I will mind alswa. I is full nimble, God wot, as a deer. By God! he sall not escape us baith. Why had you not pit the nag in the barn? Ill luck to thee, Alan, thou is a fool.'

These poor clerks ran full hard toward the fen, both Alan and John. And when the miller saw they were off, he took half a bushel of their flour, and bade his wife go and knead it in a loaf. 'I believe the clerks were afeared what I might do. Yet can a miller,' he said, 'trim a clerk's beard for all his art; now let them go where they will. Lo where they go! By my pate, they get him not so lightly. Yea, let the children play!'

These poor clerks ran up and down, with 'Whoa, whoa! Gee! Stop, stop! Ha! Look out behind! Gae whistle you whilst I head him off here!' But in brief, till it was dark night, with all their power they could not catch their nag, he ran alway so fast, till at length they caught him in a ditch.

Wet and weary, like a beast in the rain, came poor John and Alan with him. 'Alack the day I was born!' quoth John. 'Now we are brought till mockery and derision. Our corn is stolen; men will call us fools, baith the warden and all our friends, and chiefest the miller. Alack the day!' Thus John lamented as he walked along the road toward the mill, leading Bayard by the bridle. He found the miller sitting by the fire, for it was night. They could go no further then, but besought him for the love of God to give them lodging and entertainment, for their pence.

'If there be any', the miller replied, 'such as it is, you shall have your part in it. My house is strait; but you have studied book-learning, you know how to make twenty foot of space a mile broad by arguments. Let see now if this house may suffice, or make it bigger by talking, as you clerks do.'

'Now, Simon,' said John, 'thou is ever merry, by Saint Cuthbert, and that was fairly answered. I have heard say a man sall take ane of the twa, such-like as he finds or such-like as he brings. But specially I pray thee, dear host, get us some meat and drink and make us some cheer, and we will pay faithfully and fully. Men lure no hawks with empty hand; lo here our silver all ready to spend!'

This miller despatched his daughter into town for ale and bread, and roasted a goose for them, and secured their horse so that it should go astray no more. He made them a bed in his own chamber, fairly dight with sheets and blankets, only eight foot or ten from his own bed. His daughter had a bed to herself right in the same chamber and full near; it could be no other, and reason why, because there was no more room in the place. They supped and talked and disported them, and drank ever deeper of the strong ale, and about midnight went to rest.

Well had this miller varnished his head with the beer, and had drunk himself all pale when he went to bed. He hiccoughed and spoke through his nose as if he had a rheum or a hoarseness. To bed went his wife also, as light and frisky as any jay, so well had she wet her jolly whistle. The cradle was put at her bed's foot, that she might rock it and nurse the child. And when all that was in the crock had been drunk, anon the daughter went to bed; and to bed went Alan and John. None of them took aught else, they needed no opiate! Verily, so had the miller bibbed his ale that he snorted in his sleep as a horse. His wife bore him the bass, a full strong one; men might have heard their snoring two furlongs away. The wench snored, also *par compagnie.*

Alan the clerk, hearing all this tunefulness, poked John and said, 'Sleeps thou? Heard thou ever such-like a sange ere this? Lo, whilk a compline they are singing amongst them, Saint Antony's fire fall on their bodies! Wha hearkened ever to such-like a marvellous thing? Yea, may they come to the worst of bad ends! This lang night I sall get na sleep; but yet na matter, all sall be for the best. For, John, swa may I ever thrive, some easement the law allows us. For, John, there is a law says that gif a man be harmed in ane point, he sall be relieved in another. Our corn is stolen, without a doubt, and all day we have had an ill fit; and since all that cannot be remedied, I sall have some easement to countervail my loss. By my sawl, it sall be nane otherwise!'

'Have a care, Alan,' John answered. 'The miller is a parlous man, and gif he started out of his sleep he might do us baith a shrewd turn.'

'I count him not a fly,' Alan replied, and up he rose.

John lay still whilst a man might walk, a furlong or two; then he arose and went softly unto the cradle, took it in his hands and bore it quietly unto his bed's foot.

About dawn, when the third cock began to sing, the miller's daughter said to Alan, 'One thing I will tell you. When you pass the mill going homeward, even at the entrance behind the door you will find a loaf that was made of half a bushel of your own meal, which I helped my father to take. And now, good friend, God save and keep you!' And with that word she wellnigh wept.

Alan thought, 'Ere it be day I will go creep in by my fellow;' and anon his hand touched the cradle. 'By God,' he thought, 'I have misgone all wrangly; my head is all giddy to-night, and therefore I walk not straight. I wot well by the cradle, here lie the miller and his wife, and I have misgone.'

And with the Devil's own luck, forth he went to the bed where the miller lay He thought to have crept in by his fellow John, and he crept in by the miller and caught him by the neck, and said softly, 'Thou John, thou swine's-head, awake, and hear a noble sport, for thy father's soul!'

'Yea, false knave!' quoth the miller. 'Ah, false traitor, false clerk! You shall die, by God's dignity!' And he caught Alan by the throat. Alan caught him in turn furiously, and smote him on the nose with his fist. Down ran the bloody stream on the miller's breast, and on the floor they wallowed like two pigs in a poke, with nose and mouth crushed and bleeding. Up they got, and down again, till the miller stumbled against a stone and fell down backward upon his wife, who knew naught of this ridiculous fight. With the shock she started up, and cried, 'Help, holy cross of Bromholm! Lord, I call to thee! *In manus tuas!* Awake, Simon, the fiend has dropped on us. My heart is crushed; help, I am killed! Some one lies on my head and body; help, Simon! The false clerks fight!'

John started up as fast as ever he could, and groped to and fro by the wall to find a staff. She started up also, and knew the room better than did John, and forthwith found a staff by the wall. She saw a little shimmer of light where the moon shone in by a hole, and by it she saw the two on the floor, but in truth knew not which was which. When she caught sight of a white thing, she weened one of the clerks had worn a night-cap, and drew nearer with the staff and thought to smite this Alan a shrewd rap, but smote the miller on the bald pate. Down he went, crying, 'Help, I am killed!' These clerks beat him well, and let him lie, and clad them, and anon took their horse and also their meal and went their way. And at the mill they took their loaf also, full well baked, of half a bushel of flour.

Thus is the proud miller well beaten, and has lost his toll for grinding their corn, and paid every penny for the supper of Alan and John who beat him. Lo, such a thing it is for a miller to be false! And therefore this proverb is full sooth,

> 'Look not for good and do iniquity,
> the guileful shall himself beguiled be.'

And God That sits on high in glory save all this company, high and low. Thus have I requited the Miller in my tale.

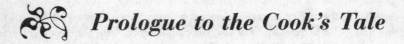# *Prologue to the Cook's Tale*

Whilst the Reeve was speaking, the Cook from London clawed him on the back for joy. 'Ha, ha!' quoth he. 'By the rood, this miller had a sharp experience in the matter of lodging for the night. Well said Solomon, "Bring not every man into thine house;" lodging by night is perilous. A man ought to advise well with himself whom he brings into his privacy. May I come to a bad end if ever I heard of a miller better set a-work, since I was called Hodge of Ware; he had a shrewd turn in the dark. But God forbid that we stop here! And therefore, if you vouchsafe to listen to tale from me, that am a poor man, I will tell you as well as I am able a little jest that befell in our town.'

Our Host answered and said, 'I agree; now tell on, Roger, look it be good. Many a meat-pie have you served out that has been twice hot and twice cold, and many a pasty have you let blood. From many a pilgrim have you had Christ's malison, for of your parsley that they have eaten with your fatted goose they fare the worse yet; for many a fly is at large in your shop. Now tell on, gentle Roger. But yet I prithee be not wroth for a privy nip; a man many say full sooth in jest.'

'You say full sooth, by my faith,' answered Roger. 'But "sooth jest, ill jest," as the Flemings say. And therefore, Harry Bailey, be not you wroth, by your faith, if my tale be of an inn-keeper ere we part. Nevertheless, I will not tell it yet, but ere we part you shall be paid back, of a surety.' Thereat he laughed and made merry cheer, and began his tale thus.

The Cook's Tale

A prentice dwelt once in our city, of a guild of victuallers. He was as blithe as a goldfinch in the shaw, a short comely fellow, as brown as a berry, with black locks full neatly combed. He could dance so merrily and well that he was called Perkin the Reveller. He was full of amorous gallantry as the hive of sweet honey; well was the wench that met with him. At every bridal he would sing and caper; he loved the tavern more than the shop. For when there was any procession in Cheapside he would spring thither; till he had seen all the sight and danced well, he would not come to the shop again. And he would gather to him a crew of the likes of him to hop and sing and make such disport, and they would set an hour to meet in such a lane to play at dice. For there was no prentice in the town could cast a pair of dice more prettily than Perkin could, and he was free withal of his coin in his privy resorts. That his master found full often in his accounts; often-times he found the till bare. Verily, with a revelling prentice that haunts wenches and dice and riotous living, his master shall suffer for it in his shop, though he have no part in the merry-making. For revelry and theft turn into one another, however well the prentice play on gittern or fiddle. Revel and fidelity, amongst folk of low degree, are ever at odds, as a man may well behold.

This jolly prentice abode with his master till he had nigh served out his prenticeship, though he was chidden morn and night, and sometimes escorted to Newgate gaol with a band of minstrels ahead. But upon a day, when his master looked over his indentures, he bethought him of a proverb which says thus,

> 'Better is rotten apple out of hoard
> Than that it rot the remnant on the board.'

So it is with a riotous servant; it is far less harm to let him go than that he corrupt all the servants in the place. Therefore his master gave him letters of discharge and bade him go, and bad luck with him! And thus the jolly prentice was given his leave; now let him riot all the night if he will!

And as there is no thief but has a confederate that helps him to suck in and squander all that he can borrow or filch, anon he sent his bed and his clothes to a compeer of his own kind that loved dice and disport and revelry; and had a wife that kept a shop for show, and made her living another wise.

The Words of the Host to the Company

Our Host saw well that the bright sun had sped over a fourth part of the arc of the artificial day, and half an hour and more besides; and though he was not deeply expert in learning, he knew it was the eighteenth morn of April, which is harbinger of May. He saw also that the shadow of every tree was the same in length as the erect body that formed it; and therefore by the shadow his wit told him that Phœbus, shining so clear and bright, had climbed five-and-forty degrees on high, and for that day, in that latitude, that it must be ten of the clock. Speedily he pulled his horse about.

'Lordings,' quoth he, 'I warn you, all this company, the fourth part of the day is spent. For the love of God and St. John, now lose no more time than may be. Sirs, time wastes away from us day and night; what with privy sleeping and negligence whilst we wake, it steels away from us as a stream that descends from the mountain to the plain and never turns back. Well may Seneca and many a philosopher bewail time lost more than gold gone from chest, for "loss of goods may be repaired, but loss of time confounds us," he said. Of a surety, it comes back no more than Malkin's maidenhead, which she has lost in wantonness. Let us not grow mouldy thus in sloth. — Sir Man of Law!' quoth he, 'as ever you hope for bliss, tell us a tale, according to agreement. You submitted freely to stand by my judgment in this thing; hold to your promise now and discharge it. Then at the worst you will have done your duty.'

'Host,' quoth he, 'I agree in God's name; my intent in no wise is to break agreement. A promise is a debt, and I will gladly perform all mine; I can say no better than this. For what laws a man imposes on another he should himself in justice observe; such is the old saw. But natheless, certain it is that at this time I know not how to tell a profitable tale. But Chaucer, as many a man knows, though he be little skilled in metres and crafty rhymings, has told such tales, now of long time, in the best English he has. And if he has not told them in one book, dear friend, he has in another. He has told of more lovers than Ovid made mention of in his old Epistles. Why should I tell of them again? In youth he wrote verses of Ceyx and Alcyone, and since then he has spoken of every one of these noble wives and true lovers likewise. Whoso will look in his large volume called *The Legend of Cupid's Saints* may see there the large open wounds of Lucrece and of Thisbe of Babylon, Dido's sword-stroke for the false Æneas, Phyllis hanging on the tree for love of her Demophon; the lament of Dejanira, Hermione, and Hypsipyle, and of Ariadne upon the barren island standing in the sea; Leander drowned for Hero; the tears of Helen, the woe of Briseis and of thee, Laodamia; thy cruelty, Queen Medea, thy little children hanging by the neck because thy Jason was false to love; Hypermnestra, Penelope, Alcestis, your wifehood he commends full well!

'But certainly he writes no word of that wicked tale of Canacè and her sinful love — I say *fie!* to such cursed stories; or of the story of Apollonius of Tyre, how the cursed king Antiochus ill-used his daughter, so horrible a story, where he threw her upon the pavement. And therefore, of full purpose, Chaucer never writes in any of his discourses of such abominations, nor will I rehearse such.

'But now for my tale, what shall I do this day? I were loath to be likened to the Muses called Pierides (the book of Metamorphoses knows what I mean). But natheless, though I come after him with naught but baked haws, I reck not a bean. I speak in prose and leave him to make the rhymes.' And at that, with a sober countenance, he began his tale as you shall now hear.

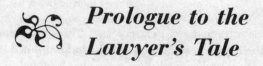# *Prologue to the Lawyer's Tale*

Oh hateful ill! Oh Poverty so confounded with thirst, with cold, with hunger! Thou art ashamed in thy heart to ask help; yet if thou ask not, then art thou so pierced with want that very destitution uncovers all thy hidden wound. In spite of thyself, thou must either steal or beg or borrow thy livelihood. Thou blamest Christ, and sayest bitterly that he divides temporal riches amiss. Thou sinfully blamest thy neighbour and sayest thou has too little and he all.

'I' faith,' sayest thou, 'sometime he shall pay for it, when his carcass burns in the coals, because he helped not the needy in their want.' Hearken to the judgment of the wise man.

> 'Better to die than live in penury.'
> 'If thou be poor, farewell thy dignity!'
> 'Thy very neighbour will despise thee.'

Hear again the saw of the wise man.

> 'All the days of the poor are evil.'

Have a care then, lest thou come to that point.

> 'If thou be poor, thy brother hateth thee;
> Much more, alas! thy friends afar do flee.'

But ah rich merchants, full of weal; ah noble, prudent folk! Your bags are full, at dice you throw not double aces but six and five, and merry may you dance at Christmas! Ye search through land and sea for your profits; like wise folk, ye know the whole estate of kingdoms; ye are fathers of tales and tidings both of peace and strife. And now I should be destitute of tales were it not that a merchant, many a year ago, taught me one which I shall now tell.

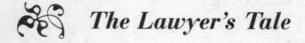

The Lawyer's Tale

Once there dwelt in Syria a company of rich merchants, grave and upright, that sent far and wide their spicery, their cloth of gold and rich-hued satins. Their wares were so excellent and so fresh that every one delighted to trade with them, and also to sell to them. Now it befell that the chief men of this craft prepared to go to Rome, whether for trade or pleasure, they would send no other messenger, but, in a word, went themselves to Rome, and took their lodging in such place as suited their purpose.

When these merchants had sojourned in that city a certain time, as suited their pleasure, it befell that from day to day the excellent renown of the emperor's daughter, dame Constance, was reported to them with every particular, even as I shall tell you. The common talk of every man was, 'Our Emperor of Rome, God protect him! has such a daughter that for goodness and beauty there was never such another since the world began. I pray God to uphold her in honour. Would she were queen of all Europe! In her is high beauty without vanity, youth without folly or crudeness; virtue is her guide in all her works, humility has slain all arrogance in her, she is mirror of courtesy. Her heart is a very shrine of holiness; her hand, a liberal minister of alms-giving.' And all this report was true, even as God is. But now to the merchants. They had their ships laden once more, and when they had seen this blessed maiden, they went merrily home to Syria and did their affairs as of yore and lived in weal. I can say naught else of them.

Now it chanced that these merchants stood in the favour of him that was soldan of Syria, and when they came from a foreign place he would make them good cheer with benign courtesy, and diligently inquire for tidings of sundry realms, to learn of the wonders which they might have seen or heard. Amongst other things, these merchants gave him especially so noble and full a report of dame Constance that the soldan conceived great delight to have her in mind, and all his pleasure and care was to love her his life long.

Peradventure in that broad book which men call the heavens it was writ with stars, at his birth, that he should die for love, alack! For in the stars is written, clearer than glass, could men but read it, the death of every man. In the stars was written the death of Hector, Achilles, Pompey, Julius, many a year before they were born; the strife of Thebes, the death of Hercules, of Samson, Turnus and Socrates. But men's wits are so dull that none can wholly read it.

This soldan sent for his privy council, and, in short, showed them all his mind and told them verily that unless he might have grace to win Constance within a short time, he was no better than dead, and charged them speedily to devise some means to save him. Different men said different things. They argued, debated back and forth, brought forth many a subtle opinion, talked of magic and deceit, but finally could see no help in that nor in aught else save marriage. And in this their reason showed them great difficulty, because of the difference in creed. They said they thought 'no Christian prince would fain wed his child under our sweet faith that was taught us by Mahomet our prophet.'

'Rather than lose Constance,' he answered, 'I will be christened without grudging. I must be hers, I can choose none other. I pray you hold your peace with your arguments. Save my life and neglect not to get her who has my life in her power, for I cannot longer endure this woe.'

What need of greater diffuseness? I say that by treaty and embassies, and by mediation of the Pope and all the Church and knighthood, for the destruction of Mahomet's religion and the profit of Christ's dear faith, such an agreement was made as you shall hear. The soldan and his barons and all his subjects should be christened and he should have Constance in marriage and a certain amount of gold, I know not what. This agreement was sworn to me by either side, with sufficient pledges. Now, fair Constance, may God almighty guide thee!

Some people, I believe, will now look for me to describe all the provision that the emperor, in his great splendour, prepared for his daughter, dame Constance. But all men will see that none could tell in a few words of all that was ordained for so high a matter. Bishops were appointed to go with her, lords, ladies, famous knights and sufficient other folk. Throughout the town it was proclaimed that every one should devoutly pray Christ to bless this marriage and speed this journey.

The day of her departing was come, the woful, fatal day. No more tarrying now; one and all they prepared to go forth and away. Constance arose all pale and overcome with sorrow, and made ready to wend her way, for she saw well there was no help. Alas! what wonder if she wept, that was to be sent to a strange nation, away from the friends who had protected her so tenderly, and to be bound in subjection to one whose manners she knew not? Husbands are all good and always were; this wives know, — but enough of this!

'Father,' she said, 'and you, my mother, my sovereign pleasure above all save Christ on high, Constance, your wretched child, your young daughter, commends her earnestly to your grace, for I go to Syria, nor shall I ever see you more with mine eyes. Alas! I must anon to the nation of Barbary, since it is your will. May Christ, that died to redeem us, give me grace to fulfill his commands, no matter though I, wretched woman, perish. Women are born to thralldom and pain, and to be under man's governing.'

Not at Troy, when Pyrrhus broke down the wall before Ilium was burnt, nor at the city of Thebes, nor at Rome when Hannibal had thrice vanquished the Romans, was heard such tender piteous weeping as in the chamber at her departure. But sing she, weep she, forth she must go.

Oh cruel firmament, the first-moved, that with thy diurnul swing ever pushest and hurlest everything from east to west, which in natural motion would hold the other course, thy pushing set the heaven in such array at the beginning of this disastrous journey that cruel Mars blasted this marriage. Inauspicious tortuous ascendant, the lord of which alas! is fallen helpless out of his angle into the darkest house! Ah, malevolent planet Mars! Ah, feeble moon, luckless are thy steps! Thou art in conjunction where thou art not well received; where thou wert auspicious, thence art thou departed. Alas, imprudent emperor! Was there no astrologer in thy whole town? Is no time more propitious than another for such a wedding? Is there no choice of time for a journey, especially to folk of high station, even when a person's horoscope is known? Alas, we are too ignorant or too slothful!

This fair and woful maid is come to ship with pomp and circumstance. 'Jesu Christ be with you all now!' she said, and that was all except 'Farewell, fair Constance!' She strove to show a cheerful look, and forth I leave her sailing thus and will return to the Syrians.

The mother of the soldan, a well-spring of all sin, espied her son's full intent to forsake his old sacrifices. At once she summoned her council; and when they were assembled to learn her will, she sat her down and spoke as you shall now hear. 'Lords,' quoth she, 'every one of you knows that my son is in point to abandon the holy laws of our Alcoran given by God's messenger Mahomet. But one vow I make to the great God — the life shall sooner vanish out of my body than Mahomet's law out of mine heart. What should this new faith bring us but thralldom and penance to our bodies, and afterward to be dragged to hell because we denied Mahomet, the founder of our faith? But sirs, will you give me your pledges, assenting to my plan which I shall tell you, that may secure us evermore?'

They swore and agreed, everyman of them, to stand by her in life and death, and each as best he could to draw all his friends to strengthen her cause. Thereupon she undertook the emprise of which you shall hear, and spoke to them thus: 'First we shall feign to accept the Christian faith, — cold water will not grieve us except a little! Then I will make such a feast and revel that I shall requite the soldan for his deeds, I trust. Be his wife christened never so white, she will need to wash away the red though she brought with her a font-full of water.' Ah soldaness, thou virago, root of iniquity, thou second Semiramis! Ah serpent under the form of woman, like to that serpent that is bound deep in hell! Ah treacherous woman, all that can destroy virtue and innocence through thy malice is bred in thee, nest of every sin! Oh Satan, envious since that day thou wert chased from our heritage, thou knowest well the old path to women! Thou madest Eve bring us into servitude; and wilt ruin this Christian marriage. Alas, alas! thou makest of women thine instrument, when thou wilt beguile.

This soldaness, whom I blame thus and curse, privily dismissed her council. Why delay the tale longer? On a day she rode to the soldan and told him that she would renounce her faith and receive baptism from priests' hands, repenting that she had been an heathen so long; and besought him to grant her the honour to have the Christian folk to a feast, — 'and I will do my diligence to please them.'

The soldan replied, 'I will do your will,' and kneeling thanked her for that request, so glad he knew not what to say. Then she kissed her son and went homeward.

II

These Christian folk arrived in Syria with a large and stately following. Straightway the soldan sent his messenger, first to his mother and then to all the realm about, to say his wife had truly come. He prayed his mother to ride to meet the queen for the honour of his realm. Great was the press and rich the spectacle when the Syrians and Romans met together. The soldan's mother, rich and gay of garb, received Constance with as glad a countenance as any mother could show to her dear daughter, and then with slow and stately gait they rode to the nearest city hard by. Not the triumph of Julius of which Lucan boasts was more royal or more sumptuous than this joyous assembly. But under it all this scorpion, this wicked spirit, the soldaness, for all her flattery, was planning to give a mortal sting. The soldan himself came soon after in royal wise wondrous to tell of, and welcomed her with all joy and bliss. Thus in mirth and joy I leave them, for the fruit of it all is what I tell. In due time men thought it wise that the revelry should cease, and all went to rest.

The time came for the feast which this old soldaness had ordained, and to it all the Christian folk betook them, both young and old. Here could men see a royal feast, and more dainties than I can describe to you. But all too dear they had bought it, before they rose. Oh sudden woe, ever successor to bliss of this world, which is ever sprinkled with bitterness, the end of the joy of our earthly labours! Woe is the end of our gladness. Hearken to this counsel for thy security: on the day of joy forget not the unknown woe or harm that comes behind. For to tell shortly, in a word, the soldan and every Christian save dame Constance only were stabbed and hewn in pieces at the table. This old soldaness, cursed crone, had through her friends done this cursed deed, because she wished to govern all the country. Nor was there a Syrian that was converted and knew the counsel of the soldan, who was not all hewn asunder ere he could escape. Constance they took without pause and set her on a ship, without a rudder, God wot!, and bade her learn navigation out of Syria back again to Italy. A certain treasure that she had brought they put with her and, sooth to say, great store of victual and also clothes, and then she sailed forth on the salt sea. Ah my Constance, full of kindness, ah beloved young daughter of an emperor, may He that is lord of fortune be thy rudder!

She crossed herself and in a full piteous voice cried unto the cross of Christ: 'Oh bright blessed altar, holy cross, red with the piteous blood of the Lamb that washed the world clean of the old iniquity, guard me from the fiend and from his claws on that day when I shall be drowned in the deep. Victorious tree, protection of the faithful, which alone wast worthy to bear the king of heaven with His fresh wounds, the white Lamb That was hurt with the spear — thou expeller of fiends out of man and woman, over whom thy sheltering arms reach out, preserve me and give me might to amend my life.'

For days and years this hapless creature sailed through the sea of Greece to the straits of Morocco, as Fortune would. On many a sorry meal she fed and often she looked for her death, before the wild waves drove her to a resting-place. Men may ask why she was not slain; who saved her body at the feast? Who saved Daniel, I answer, in the horrible cave where every one, master and man, save he, was devoured by the lion ere he could escape? None but God, whom he bore in his heart. On her God would show His wondrous miracle, that we might see His mighty acts. Christ, who is every harm's sovereign remedy, does a thing often, as clerks know, by certain means for certain ends, full dark to man's wit; we are too ignorant to understand His wise providence. But now, since she was not slain at the feast, who saved her from drowning in the sea? Who kept Jonas in the maw of the fish till he was pouted up at Nineveh? Well may men know it was none but He who saved the Hebrew people from drowning, and led them with dry feet through the sea. Who bade the four spirits of the tempest, powerful to vex the whole earth, 'Both north and south and east and west, trouble not sea nor land nor tree'? Truly, He who gave that command preserved this woman, sleeping and waking, from the tempest. Whence could this woman have meat and drink, how lasted her victual three years and more? Who fed St. Mary the Egyptian in the cavern or in the desert? None but Christ, indeed; it was as great a marvel to feed five thousand folk with five loaves and two fishes. God sent His abundance in her great need.

She drove forth into our wild ocean and through it until at length the waves cast her up under a stronghold whose name I know not, far in Northumberland. Her ship stuck so fast in the sand that for long it could not stir thence; Christ's will was that she should abide there. The constable of the castle came down to see the wreck, and searched the whole ship and found this weary careworn woman, and also her treasure. In her own language she prayed him for grace, and to take the life from her body, to deliver her from her woe; her speech was a manner of corrupt Latin, but nevertheless he understood her. When the constable had seen enough, he took this woful woman to land, who kneeled down and thanked God's dispensation, but what she was she would tell no man for weal or woe, though she died for it; she said that, by her troth, she was so bewildered in the sea that she had lost her memory. The constable, and his wife also, felt such pity for her that they wept in compassion. She was so diligent and eager to serve and please every one in that castle that all loved her who looked on her face.

This constable and his wife, dame Hermengild, and all that country were pagans, but Hermengild loved her as her own soul, and Constance sojourned so long with many a bitter tear and fervent orison that Jesu of His grace converted dame Hermengild, the constabless. No Christians in all that land durst assemble; the Christian folk had fled thence in fear of the pagans, who had conquered all the regions of the north, by sea and land. The old Christian Britons that dwelt in this isle had fled to Wales, which was their refuge for the time. Yet the Briton Christians were not so banished that there were not some who privily honoured Christ and beguiled the heathen folk, and near the castle dwelt three such, one of them blind, who could see only with the eyes of the soul, with which men see when they are blind. Bright was the sun on that summer's day when the constable and his wife and Constance took the road toward the sea for a little season, to divert them and to roam about.

'In the name of Christ,' cried this blind Briton, 'give me back my sight, dame Hermengild.'

This lady waxed fearful at the words, lest her husband would slay her for her love to Jesu Christ. But Constance emboldened her and bade her do the will of Christ, as a daughter of His church.

The constable was abashed at this. 'What means this gear?' he said.

'Sir, it is the power of Christ,' Constance answered, 'that saves folk from the snare of the fiend.' And so far she set forth our faith that, ere evening came, she had converted the constable and made him believe on Christ.

This constable was not lord of this place of which I speak, where he had found Constance, but had held it strongly, many years long, under Ælla, king of Northumberland; who was wise and valiant of his deeds against the Scots, as men read in books. But now I return to my story.

Satan, who watches ever to beguile us, saw all Constance's perfection and plotted how he might pay her back. He caused a young knight of that town to love her so hot, of foul love, that he verily thought he should perish unless he could have his will. He wooed her, but it availed not, she would do no sin. Then, for cruel hate, he compassed a way to make her die a shameful death.

He watched for a time when the constable was away and one night crept privily into Hermengild's chamber. Weary with vigils and prayers, Constance and Hermengild were sleeping. Tempted by Satan, this knight went all softly to the bed, and cut Hermengild's throat in twain, and laid the bloody knife beside dame Constance; then went his way, ill luck to him!

Soon after the constable came home with Ælla, king of that country, and saw his wife cruelly slain, and wept and wrung his hands full often; and beside Constance in the bed he found the bloody knife. Alas! what could she say? For very grief her wit had left her. To King Ælla all this calamity was told, as well as the time, the place, and in what wise dame Constance was found in a ship, as ye have heard it told before. The king's heart began to tremble with pity when he saw so gentle a creature fallen into grief and misfortune. For like a lamb led to his death this innocent stood before the king, whilst the false knight who had wrought the treason accused her of the crime. Nevertheless there was great mourning amongst the people, who said they could not deem that she had done such wickedness. For they had seen her ever virtuous and loving Hermengild as her own soul; and to this every one in that household bore witness save he who had slain Hermengild with his knife. And now the noble king caught a clue to this witness, and thought he would inquire deeper into these things to learn a truth.

Alas Constance! thou hast no champion at arms nor canst thou fight for thyself, alack! But may He that died to redeem us and bound Satan there where he still lies, be thy strong champion this day! For unless Christ show an open miracle, thou shalt straightway be slain, though guiltless. — She dropped upon her knees and said, 'Immortal God, Who didst save Susanna from false blame, and thou, merciful maiden, Mary, before whose Child angels sing "Alleluia," if I be guiltless of this crime, save me; else I die!'

Have ye not sometimes seen in a crowd the pale face of one who is led to instant death? By its hue men might know his face that was in peril amongst all the faces in that crowd. So stood Constance and looked about her. Ah ye queens, living in prosperity, duchesses and ladies all, have some pity on her plight. It is an emperor's daughter that stands alone, with none to whom she may lament. Ah, seed of kings thus in peril, far away are thy friends in thy necessity.

King Ælla had such compassion (as a gentle heart is ever full of pity) that from his eyes the tears ran down. 'Now straightway fetch a book,' quoth he, 'and if this knight will swear she slew this woman, then we will consider whom we will have for judge.' A book of the Gospels in British was fetched and upon it the knight swore that she was guilty. Thereupon a hand smote him on the neck so that he straightway fell down like a stone, and in the sight of all both his eyes burst from his face. A voice came in the hearing of all, 'Thou hast slandered guiltless the daughter of holy Church. In royal presence thou has done this and yet hold I my peace.'

At this marvel all the crowd was aghast, save Constance alone, and stood all in a maze in dread of vengeance. Great was the dread and repentance of them that had wrongly suspected this innocent Constance. And by this miracle and by Constance's mediation, in the end the king and many another there were converted, thanks to Christ's grace! This false knight was speedily slain for his treachery by Ælla's judgment; yet Constance had great pity for his death. And after this, in His mercy, Jesu made Ælla wed with all honour this holy maid, so bright and fair. Thus Christ made Constance a queen.

But who, in very sooth, was woful for their marriage but Donegild, the mother of the king, full of arrogance? It seemed her cursed heart would burst at her son's deed; it seemed a dishonour that he should take for his mate so alien a creature.

I would not take such account of the chaff and straw as of the corn; why should I speak of the royal array at the marriage, what course went first at the banquet, who blows a horn or trumpet? Only the cream of every tale is to be set forth; there was eating and drinking, and folk danced and sang and made merry. Constance went apart with her husband, as was but reason; for though wives be full holy creatures, they must needs take in patience the will of folk that have wedded them with rings, and lay a little their holiness aside for a season, — they can do no less. In due time Ælla begat on her a boy-child, and when he went toward Scotland to encounter his foes, he committed her to a bishop and his constable. And soon fair Constance, the humble and meek, was so far gone with child that she kept her chamber quietly, awaiting Christ's pleasure, until her time came and she brought forth a boy; Maurice they called him at the font-stone.

The constable called a messenger and wrote to his king Ælla the happy tidings, and other tidings profitable to be told. He took the letter and went his way, but seeking his own advantage rode first to the king's mother and saluted her fairly: 'Madame, you may be glad and blithe and thank God an hundred thousand times. My lady queen truly has a child, to the joy and bliss of all this realm. Lo, here are the sealed letters concerning it, which I must carry out with all haste. If you would say aught to your son the king, I am your servant, day and night.'

'Naught as at this time,' Donegild replied; 'but I will that you rest here all night and to-morrow I will tell you what I wish.'

The messenger drank heavily of wine and ale and whilst he slept like a swine his letters were privily stolen from his box; and another letter concerning this thing was subtly counterfeited and full sinfully wrought, addressed to the king as from the constable. The letter said, 'The queen was delivered of so horrible and fiendly a creature that none was so bold as to remain in the castle. The mother was an elf, come there by chance or charm or magic, and every person hates her company.'

Woful was the king at this letter, but he told his sore distress to none and wrote back with his own hand, 'Evermore welcome by the will of Christ to me who am now versed in His doctrine. Lord, welcome be Thy will and pleasure; all my desires I place under Thy governance. My folk shall keep my wife and this child, be it foul or fair, till my home-coming. When it so pleases Him, Christ may send me a son more to my mind.' Privily weeping he sealed the letter and delivered it to the messenger, who went forth and away.

Oh messenger, full of drunkenness, thy breath is strong, thy face is distorted and thy limbs falter ever. Thou revealest all secrets, thy mind is gone, thou pratest as a jay. Where drunkenness abounds no secret is hid. Oh Donegild, I have no English fit for thy tyrannous malice! Therefore I commit thee to the fiend — let him tell of thy treachery! Fie brutish, nay, by heaven I lie, fie fiendish spirit! for I dare to say thy spirit is in hell, though thou walk here.

The messenger returned and again alighted at the court of the king's mother, to her great joy, who pleased him in all that she could. He drank and well stuffed out his girdle, and slept and snored in his swinish way all night. Again his letters were stolen, every one, and counterfeited letters made thus, 'The king commands his constable straightway, on pain of condign judgment and hanging, by no means to suffer Constance to remain in his kingdom so much as an hour beyond three days; but he shall put her, her young son, and all her gear in the same ship in which he found her, and push her out from the shore and charge her never more to return.' Ah my Constance, well may thy spirit shudder and thy dreams be of pain, when Donegild devised this order!

On the morrow, when he woke, the messenger took the straight course to the castle and delivered to the constable his letter. Who, when he saw its pitiful meaning, said many a time, 'alack!' and 'alas!' 'Lord Christ, how can this world endure,' quoth he, 'so full of sin is many a man? O mighty God, since Thou art a just judge, how is it, so I offend Thee not, that Thou wilt suffer the innocent to perish and the wicked to reign in prosperity? Ah good Constance, alas! Woe is me that I must be thine executioner, or die a death of shame. Yet is there no escape!'

Both young and old in all that castle wept when the king sent this accursed letter. On the fourth day, Constance with a deadly pale face went her way towards the ship; full meekly she bore Christ's pleasure and kneeling on the shore said, 'Lord, ever welcome be Thy will! He that kept me from the false accusation whilst I dwelt amongst you on land, will keep me safe from harm and shame on the salt sea, though I know not how. He is yet as strong as ever He was. In Him I trust and in His dear Mother, who is my sail and helm.' Her little child lay weeping upon her arm, and kneeling she said pityingly to him, 'Peace, little son, I will not harm thee,' and then she drew her kerchief from her head and laid it over his little eyes and lulled him in her arms. Then she cast her eyes to heaven; 'Mother,' she said, 'Mary, bright maid, true it is that through woman's tempting, mankind was lost and ever doomed to death; wherefore thy Child was all torn upon the cross. Thy blessed eyes beheld all His torment; then is there no comparison betwixt thy woe and any that man may endure. Thou sawest thy Child slain before thine eyes; yet my little child still lives. Now lady bright, to whom all sufferers cry for aid, glory of womanhood, fair maiden, haven of refuge, bright star of day, pity my child, who of thy nobility pitiest every piteous distressed person! Alas, little child! What is thy guilt who has never yet sinned? Why would thy harsh father destroy thee? Oh help me, dear constable! Let my little child dwell here with thee. But if thou darest not save him, kiss him once in his father's name.' Then looking back toward the land she said, 'Farewell ruthless husband!'; and rose and walked down the shore to the ship. All the people followed her; and ever she soothed her weeping child, and she took her leave, crossed herself with a holy heart and entered into the ship.

The ship was provisioned, to say the sooth, abundantly for her needs for many a day; and enough she had of other necessaries, praised be God's grace. May God almighty control the wind and weather and bring her home! I can say no more but that she drove on over the sea.

III

Soon after this Ælla the king came home to his castle, and asked after his wife and child. The constable turned chill about his heart, but told him fully all the deeds that ye have heard, — I can tell it no better again; and showed the king his hand and seal. 'Lord, as you commanded me on pain of death, so have I verily done.' The messenger was tortured till he must confess, flat and plain, where he had lodged from night to night; and thus by wit and subtle inquiry they imagined whence this evil sprang. The hand that had written the letter was discovered, and all this venomous cursed deed; but in what wise I know not. The end was, as men may find in books, that Ælla slew his mother because she was a traitor to her allegiance, and thus ends old Donegild, a plague on her! But the sorrow of Ælla for his wife and child, night and day, no tongue can tell. Now I will return to Constance.

In pain and woe she floated on the seas five years and more as pleased Christ's providence, ere her ship approached land. Under a heathen castle at last, of which I find not the name in my text, the sea threw her and her child. Almighty God, Who savest mankind, forget not Constance and her child, that are fallen again on an heathen land, in point to perish, as ye shall all soon see. Down from the castle came many a person to gape at Constance and the ship. Briefly, one night the lord's steward, God send him evil! a thief who had denied our faith, came down from the castle into the ship alone; and said he would be her lover, whether she would or no. Woebegone indeed was this wretched woman then; her child and she cried lamentably. But blessed Mary helped her anon, for with her violent struggling the thief speedily fell overboard, and was drowned in the sea for punishment. Thus Christ kept Constance spotless.

Author. O foul sin of lust, behold thine end! Not only dost thou enfeeble the mind of man, but wilt ruin his body too. The end of thy deed and of thy blind desires is lamentation. How many there be who are either slain or shamed, not only for the deed but only for the intent to do the sin! But how should this weak woman have the strength to defend her against this renegade? O Goliath, immeasurable and huge, how could David overthrow thee, he so young and bare of armour? How durst he look on thy dread face? Man may see it was through God's favour. Who gave Judith the hardihood to kill Holofernes in his tent and deliver God's people from wretchedness? I ask it for this reason, that just as God sent to her the spirit of vigour to save her from disaster, so he sent might and vigour to Constance.

Out through the narrow mouth betwixt Gibraltar and Ceuta went her ship driving ever, sometimes west, sometimes south and north and east, for many a weary day. At length Christ's mother (be she ever blessed!) of her love wrought an end for her heaviness.

Now let us leave Constance for a little and speak of the Roman emperor. Through letters out of Syria he had learned the slaughter of Christian folk and the shame done to his daughter by a false traitor, I mean the cursed wicked Soldaness, and how at the feast she had caused the murder of great and small. Wherefore, to take high vengeance on the Syrians, he had sent, under royal ordinance, his senator and many other lords, God wot. For many a day they burned and slew and laid waste; but at the last they were repairing victoriously to Rome. As the senator was royally sailing, the book tells, he met the ship driving on in which Constance sat full piteously. He knew not at all what she was nor why she was in such a plight; nor would she tell of her estate, even to save her life. He brought her to Rome and delivered her and her young son to his wife; and there she lived a season. Thus could our Lady bring poor Constance out of woe; and many another since. Long time God granted her to dwell in that place in holy works. The senator's wife was her aunt, yet knew her never the more for that. But I will tarry no longer here; I will return to King Ælla, whom I left weeping and sore sighing for his wife, and I will now leave Constance in the senator's care.

King Ælla having slain his mother, on a day fell into such remorse that at last he came to Rome to receive penance. He submitted him to the pope's behest in things great and small, and besought Jesu Christ to forgive the wicked works he had done. The news spread throughout Rome-town, by couriers that went before him, how Ælla the king was coming on pilgrimage. Wherefore the senator and many of his lineage rode to meet him, according to the custom, as well to display his own splendid courtesy as to do reverence to a king. This noble senator and King Ælla did great cheer one to the other; great honour and friendship the noble senator showed to Ælla, and he to the senator also. Within a day or two, it befell the senator feasted with King Ælla and, in a word, if I err not, Constance's son went with him. Some men say that it was at Constance's request that he led this child to the feast. I cannot tell every point. Be as be may, there he was; and true it is that at his mother's bidding, during meat, the child stood looking in the king's face. Ælla had great marvel at the child and asked the senator anon, 'Whose is the fair child standing yonder?'

'By God and St. John,' he answered, 'I know not! He has a mother, but father has he none that I know of;' and briefly he told Ælla how the child was found. 'But God wot,' said the senator also, 'one of so virtuous life as his mother I never saw nor heard of amongst all women of this world, maids or wives. I dare well say she would rather have a blade through her breast than be a sinful woman; no man could bring her to that deed.'

Now this child was as like to Constance as a creature could be. Ælla had her face in his heart, and mused thereon if the child's mother could perchance be she that had been his wife. Privily he sighed, and made such speed from the table as he could. 'My faith!' he thought, 'there is a phantom in my head. Of reasonable judgment I ought to deem that my wife is drowned in the salt sea.' Yet again he reasoned, 'How know I but Christ has sent her hither by sea even as he sent her to my country from another?'

After noon, home went Ælla with the senator to prove this wondrous thing. The senator did him great honour and straightway sent for Constance. Trust me, she cared not to dance when she understood the message; scarce could she stand upon her feet. When Ælla saw his wife he gave her fair greeting and so wept that it was pity to behold. At the first look he cast upon her he knew her full well to be his wife. But she, for sorrow, stood dumb as a tree; so was her heart shut up in pain when she remembered his unkindness, and twice she swooned before his eyes. He wept and piteously made his defence: 'Now may God and all His bright saints so surely have mercy on my soul as I am as guiltless of your woe as Maurice my son, who is so like you. Else may the fiend fetch me from this place!'

It was long before the sobbing and the bitter pangs could ease their hearts; it was piteous to hear their weeping, which seemed to increase their woe. I pray you release me from my labours; I cannot tell of their woe all the long day, I am aweary of sorrow. But finally, when the truth was known, that Ælla was guiltless of her pain, they kissed a hundred times, I believe. There was such bliss betwixt them that, except the joy everlasting, no creature has ever seen the like nor shall see, whilst the world endures.

Then she prayed meekly that her husband in relief of her long, pitiful pains would pray her father especially that of his majesty he might vouchsafe to dine with him some day. She begged also that he should by no means say a word to him of her. Some men say that the child Maurice took this message to the emperor. But I believe Ælla was not so foolish as to send any child to one of such sovereign dignity, the flower of Christendom; it is better to suppose he went himself. This emperor courteously agreed to dine as he was asked, and I find it in the books that he looked earnestly upon the child and thought on his daughter. Ælla went to his lodging, and, as became him, furnished out the feast in every way so far as his cunning could reach. The morrow came and Ælla and his wife prepared to escort the emperor, and forth they rode in joy and gladness. When she saw her father she alighted down from her horse and fell on her knees. 'Father,' she said, 'your young child Constance is now clean gone from your mind. But I am your daughter Constance whom you once sent to Syria. It is I, father, who was put alone upon the salt sea and doomed to die. Now, good father, I cry you mercy. Send me no more to heathen lands, but thank my lord here for his kindness.'

Who can describe the pathetic joy of those three, thus united? But I must make an end of my tale; the day goes fast and I must tarry no more. These happy folk sat them down to dine, and I will leave them in a thousand-fold more joy and bliss than I can tell.

This child Maurice was afterwards made emperor by the pope, and lived as a good Christian and did great honour to Christ's church. But all his story I will pass by, for my tale is most of Constance. In old Roman chronicles men may read Maurice's life; I bear it not in mind. When he saw his time, King Ælla came back to England straight, with Constance his sweet and holy wife, and there they lived in joy and quiet.

But little while the joy of this world lasts, I promise you; time will not abide, from day to night it changes. Who lived ever one day in such delight that neither conscience moved him, ire, appetite nor some kind of terror, envy, pride, passion nor some injury? I set down this truth only for this reason, that Ælla's bliss with Constance endured but a little while in joy and in delight. For death, that takes his tax from high and low, caught away King Ælla out of this world when a year was passed; let us pray God's mercy on his soul! For him dame Constance had full great heaviness, but at last went her way back to the town of Rome. There the holy creature found her friends all safe and sound; and thus had she escaped out of all her misadventures. When she met her father she fell upon her knees to the earth, and weeping for the pathetic joy of her heart, she praised God a hundred thousand times. In virtue and holy almsdeeds they lived together, and never went asunder till death parted them.

And now farewell, my tale is done. And may Jesu Christ, Who is mighty to send joy after woe, govern us in His grace and guard us all that are here. Amen.

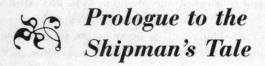 *Prologue to the Shipman's Tale*

Our Host stood up in his stirrups and said, 'Good men, hearken, all of you. This was a profitable tale and a timely. Sir parish priest, by God's bones, tell us a tale as you agreed. By God's dignity, I see that you men learned in lore know many a good thing.'

The Parson answered, 'Bless me! What ails the man, to swear so sinfully?'

Our Host answered, 'Ho, Johnnykin, ye are there, are ye? I smell a Lollard in the wind. How now, good men, listen and stay a bit, for by God's worthy pains we shall have a predication. This Lollard here will preach us somewhat!'

'Nay, that shall he not, by my father's soul,' quoth the Shipman. 'He shall not preach here, nor interpret any gospel text. We all believe in the one great God; he would spring some difficulty, or sow tares in our clean corn. Therefore, Host, I warn you in advance, my jolly body shall give you a story, and I shall clink you so merry a bell that I shall wake you all! But it shall not be of philosophy, nor physic, nor curious law-phrases. I have but small Latin in my belly!'

The Shipman's Tale

At St. Denis once there dwelt a merchant, who was rich and therefore men deemed him wise. His wife was of excellent fairness, and loved company and revelry; a thing which causes more expense than all the noble cheer and respect are worth that men do such dames at feasts and dances. Such salutations and fair looks pass away like a shadow upon the wall. But woe to him who must always pay! For his own honour's sake, the hapless husband must clothe us and deck us out in the rich array wherein we merrily dance. If peradventure he cannot, or else will not suffer such expenditure, but deem it but loss and waste, then must some other man pay our cost or lend us gold; and that is perilous.

This worthy merchant kept noble house, to which there was ever wondrous great resort, for his liberality and his fair wife. But hearken to my tale. Amongst his other guests great and small was a monk, a bold man and a fair, thirty years of age, I believe, who ever resorted thither. This young comely monk had been so well acquainted with the goodman of the house since they had known each other, that he was as familiar in his house as any friend could be. Inasmuch as they had both been born in one village, the monk claimed cousinship with the goodman; and he again said him not nay, but was as glad of it as a bird is of the dawn. Thus they were knit in eternal alliance and each assured the other of brotherhood for life. Free and liberal was Brother John, and chiefest with his money in that house, and diligent to give pleasure; he forgot not to tip the smallest page in all that house, and when he came would give some manner of fit and handsome thing to the lord and after that to all his household after their station. Wherefore they were as glad of his coming as fowl is fain of sunrise. But no more of this now, for this suffices.

It so befell on a day that this merchant made ready to go to the town of Bruges to buy there certain goods. Therefore he sent anon a messenger to Paris, praying Brother John to come to St. Denis to divert himself with him and his wife for a day or two before he went to Bruges. This noble monk had license from his abbot to go when he would, because he was a man of great discretion, and also bailiff of the convent, and rode about to inspect their granges and wide barns; and he came anon to St. Denis. Who was so welcome as my lord Brother John, our dear cousin, full of courtesy? He brought with him a great jug of Malmsey and another full of fine Vernage, and certain wild fowl, as he was wont. Thus I leave them eating and drinking and diverting them for a day or two.

The third day the merchant rose up and gravely considered his business. Up he went into his counting-house to reckon with himself how things this year stood with him and how he had expended his money, and whether he had gained or no. Many a ledger and bag he laid before him on his counting-board. Full rich were his treasure and his money-bags, and therefore he shut fast the counting-house door; and also he would not that any should break in upon his figuring; and thus he sat till past prime. Brother John was also risen on this morrow and walked to and fro in the garden, saying his office like a gentleman. The goodwife came walking privily into the garden where he was pacing softly, and saluted him as she had often done before. A maid-child came in her company, whom she ruled and guided as she would, for the maid was yet under the rod. 'Oh my dear cousin, Brother John,' quoth she, 'what ails you to rise so early?'

'Niece,' said he, 'it ought to suffice to sleep five hours, unless one is an old enfeebled creature, like these married men who lie and cower, as a tired hare distracted by the hounds sits in her form. But, dear niece, why are you so pale? I believe you have need to rest you soon.' And with that word he laughed merrily, and waxed all red at his own thought.

This fair wife began to shake her head. 'Yea, God wot all,' quoth she; 'well may I sing Alack! and Alas that I was born! But to no person dare I tell how it stands with me. Wherefore I think either to go my way out of this land or else to make an end of myself; I am so full of trouble and dread.'

The monk began to stare upon this wife. 'Alack, my niece,' said he, 'God forbid that for any sorrow or fear you should destroy yourself! But tell me your trouble; perchance I may counsel or help you in your mischief, and therefore tell me all, for it shall be secret. For on my breviary here I take my oath never to betray your counsel for fair or foul.'

'I say the same to you again,' quoth she. 'By God and this breviary I swear, though I be torn to pieces or though I go to hell for it, never to betray a word of what you tell me. This I say not for our kinship but truly for friendship and good trust.' Thus they swore and kissed upon it, and each said to the other what they would.

'Cousin,' she said, 'if I had a fit time, — as I have not, most of all in this place, — I would tell you the legend of my life, what I have suffered from my husband since I wedded him, kin though he be to you.'

'Nay,' quoth the monk, 'by God and St. Martin, he is no more my kin than is the leaf hanging on the tree! By St. Denis of France, I call him so to have the more ground for acquaintance with you, whom of a truth I have loved especially above all women; this I swear on my order. Tell your grief and hasten you, and anon go your way, lest he come down.'

'My dear love, oh my Brother John!' quoth she. 'Would I could keep this secret, but out it must, I can wait no longer. My husband is the worst man to me, that ever was since the world was made. But since I am a wife, it befits me not to tell any person of our private matters, either a-bed or elsewhere. God of His grace forbid that I tell them. A wife should say naught but honour of her husband, I know full well, save that to you thus much I may say — so may God help me, as he is not worth in any degree at all the value of a fly! Yet most of all his stinginess grieves me. You well know that all women by nature desire six things as well as I do; they would have their husbands bold and wise and rich, and generous too, and submissive to their wives, and lusty. But by the rood, for array that I have bought, only to do him credit, a' Sunday next I must pay an hundred francs, or else I am lost. Rather would I never have been born than there should be scandal or dishonour for it; yet if my husband should espy it, I am as good as lost; therefore, I pray you, lend me this sum or I must die. Brother John, I say, lend me these hundred francs, and by my faith, I will not fail in gratitude if you grant to do what I ask. At a certain day I will repay you and do you whatever pleasure and service I can, even as you will appoint. If I do not, may God take vengeance upon me as foul as ever had Ganelon for his treason to France!'

This noble monk answered thus, — 'Now truly, mine own dear lady, I have such pity for you that I swear to you and plight my troth that when you husband has gone to Flanders I will deliver you out of this care. I will bring you an hundred francs.' And at that he caught and kissed her many times.

'Now go,' he said, 'all swiftly, and let us dine as soon as may be, for it is prime of day by the sun-dial. Go now, and be as trusty as I shall be.'

'God forbid it be otherwise, Sir,' she said, and went forth as merry as a magpie, and bade the cooks make haste that they all might dine anon. Then up to her husband she went, and knocked at his counting-house door full boldly. '*Qui là?*' he said.

'By Peter, it is I,' said she; 'What, sir, how long would you fast? How long will you reckon and figure your sums and your books and things? The Devil have a share in all such sums! You have enough of God's sending, perdy! Come down to-day and let your bags be; are you not ashamed that Brother John should fast wretchedly all this long day? What! Let us hear a mass and then to dinner!'

Quoth this man, 'Wife, little can you fancy this intricate and anxious business of ours. For so may God help me and my lord St. Ive, amongst twelve of us merchants scarce two shall prosper continually until old age. We are fain to make good cheer and put as good face on it as may be, and let the world wag as it will and keep our affairs privy, till we be dead or else feign a pilgrimage or take ourselves off somewhere. Therefore is it full needful for me to plan my course in this queer world, for evermore in trade we must stand in dread of hap and fortune. To-morrow at sunrise I will to Flanders, and return as soon as ever I can. Wherefore I beseech you, dear wife, be gentle and meek toward every creature and careful to watch over our goods and govern our house decently and well. You have enough, in every wise, for a provident household. You want for neither array nor victual, and you shall lack no silver in your purse.'

With that he shut his counting-house door and straightway went down. Without delay a mass was said and quickly the tables were set and they sped them to dinner; and right richly this merchant fed the monk.

After dinner Brother John gravely took the merchant aside and said to him privily, 'Cousin, I see it stands so that you will to Bruges. God and St. Austin speed and guide you! I pray you, cousin, be careful in your journey; govern your diet temperately also; most chiefly in this heat. And so farewell, cousin; there needs no more ceremony betwixt us; God shield you from trouble! Day or night, if there be aught in my power that you will command me in any wise, it shall be done, even as you will have it. — One thing ere you go, I would pray you, if it may be; to lend me an hundred francs, a week or two, for certain beasts that I must buy to stock a place with that is ours. God so help me, I would it were yours! I will surely not fail my day, by an hour, not for a thousand francs. But let this thing be secret, I beg, for I must buy these beasts to-night. And now farewell, mine own dear cousin; gramercy for your generosity and good cheer.'

This noble merchant anon answered courteously, 'Brother John, cousin mine, truly this is a small request. My gold is yours whenever you will have it, and not only my gold but my merchandise. Take what you will, God forbid you should spare. But there is one thing with us merchants, — you know it full well — that our money is our plough. We may borrow whilst we have credit, but it is no jest to be goldless. Pay it again at your ease. I am full fain to serve you as I can.' He fetched these hundred francs anon and delivered them privily to the monk, and no one in all the world knew of this loan saving these two. They drank and talked and rambled about a while and diverted them till Brother John rode away to his abbey.

The morrow came and the merchant rode toward Flanders; his apprentice guided him till he came merrily into Bruges. There he went diligently about his needs, buying and borrowing; he neither played at dice nor danced, but only minded his merchandise; and thus I leave him.

The Sunday next after this merchant had gone, Brother John arrived at St. Denis, his crown and head all freshly shaven. In all that house was no page so small or anyone else but was full fain that my lord Brother John was returned. But to go shortly to the point, this fair wife agreed with Brother John that she would grant him her love for these hundred francs.

And on the morrow Brother John went his way, bidding the household 'farewell, adieu!' None of them and no one in the town had suspicion of my lord John. And he rode back to his abbey, or whither he would; I say no more of him.

When the market was over, the merchants repaired to St. Denis, where he made good cheer to his wife. He told her that merchandise was so dear that me must needs borrow money, for he was bound in a recognizance to pay forthwith twenty thousand crowns, wherefore he went to Paris to borrow a sum of francs from certain of his friends, and took certain moneys with him. When he came to the town, of his great fondness he went first to Brother John for a friendly visit; not to ask or borrow money of him, but to learn of his welfare and to tell him of his business, as friends do when they are met. Brother John made him merry cheer, and the merchant in turn told how propitiously he had bought his goods, God be thanked; save that he must without fail secure a loan; and then he should be in joy and rest. 'Certes,' Brother John answered, 'I am full fain that you are come back safe and sound. If I were rich, as I hope for bliss, you should not want for twenty thousand crowns, because you so kindly lent me gold the other day; and as I best can, I thank you, by heaven and by St. Peter! But nevertheless I paid down that money upon your bench to our dame, you wife at home. She knows it well, in faith, by certain tokens that I cannot tell her. Now, by your leave, I cannot tarry longer; our abbot will out of this town anon and I must go in his company. Greet well our dame, mine own dear niece, and farewell, dear cousin, till we meet again.'

This merchant wary and wise made his borrowings and paid down the money in Paris to certain Lombards, into their hands, and got his bond back from them. Then he went home as merry as a popinjay, for he well knew the affair so stood that he must needs win on that journey a thousand francs above all his expense.

His wife met him at the gate as she was wont to do. That night they made merry, for he was rich and entirely out of debt. At length this merchant said, 'In faith I am a little wroth with you, my wife, much though it grieve me. And know you why? I deem you have made a manner of strangeness twixt me and my cousin, Brother John. You should have warned me ere I went that he had paid you an hundred francs and had a token of it. He was ill pleased – he seemed so by his face, when I spoke to him of my borrowing. Yet by our heavenly King, I thought not to ask aught of him. I pray you, wife, do so no more. Tell me ever, ere I leave you, if any debtor have paid you in my absence, lest by your negligence I might ask him for a thing which he has paid.'

His wife was never a bit affrighted, but said boldly, and that at once, 'Marry, I defy this false monk, Brother John! I care not a whit for his tokens. He gave me certain money, that I know well. What! ill luck to his monk's snout! God wot, I thought he had given it me for your sake, to spend for mine own credit and profit, in a-cousinly way and by reason of the good cheer he has ofttimes had in this house. But since I see I am in this pickle, I will answer you to the point. You have slacker debtors than I. For I will pay you readily from day to day; and if so be I fail, I am your wife — score it upon my account and I will pay it as soon as ever I can. By my troth, I have bestowed every whit of it upon my array, and not on waste! And because I have bestowed it so well and to your credit, for heaven's love, I say, be not worth, but let us laugh and sport. You shall have my merry face for pledge; forgive it me, mine own dear spouse. Turn to me again and make better cheer.'

This merchant saw there was no help, and that it were but folly to chide, since the thing could not be amended. 'Now, wife,' he said, 'I forgive you, but on your soul be not so lavish again. Take better care of our means, I charge you.'

Thus ends my tale now, and may God send us tales enough to the end of our lives. Amen.

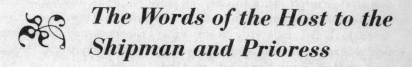

The Words of the Host to the Shipman and Prioress

'Well said,' quoth our Host, 'by *Corpus Dominus!* Long may you sail by the shore, sir gentle master, gentle mariner! May God give this monk a thousand cartloads of bad years! Aha, comrades, beware such a trick! The monk put a dupe in the man's hood and in his wife's too, by St. Austin! Nevermore bring monks to your house!

'But let that pass and now let us seek about; who shall tell another tale of all this company?' And with that word he spoke as courteously as a maid: 'My lady Prioress, by your leave, so I knew I should not vex you, I would deem that you should tell a tale next, if so be you would. Now will you vouchsafe, my lady dear?'

'Gladly,' said she, and spoke as I will now tell you.

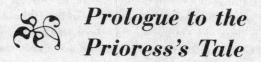

Prologue to the Prioress's Tale

O Lord, our Lord, how marvellously is Thy name spread through this great world! For not only is Thy worthy praise performed by men of dignity, but by the mouth of children Thy goodness is celebrated, for sometimes when sucking at the breast they show Thy praise. Wherefore, as I best can, I will do my diligence to tell a story in praise of Thee and of the white lily-flower which bore Thee, who is maid forever. Not that I can increase her honour, for she herself is honour and, next after her Son, the root of bounty and the medicine of souls.

O mother-maid! O noble maid-mother! O bush unburnt, though burning in the sight of Moses, that through thy humility didst drawn down from the

Deity the Spirit that alighted in thee; of whose virtue, when He had illumined thy heart, was conceived the Father's Wisdom! Help me to tell my tale in thine honour. Lady, thy kindness, thy nobility, thy might and thy great humility, no wit and no tongue can express. For sometimes, lady, of thy benignity, thou dost even go before men's prayers, and procurest for us, through thine intercession, the light to guide us unto thy dear Son. My skill is so weak, O blessed queen, to declare thy worthy greatness that I cannot sustain the burden; but fare as a twelve-months' child that can scarce utter any word. Therefore I pray, guide my song which I shall say of thee.

The Prioress's Tale

In a great city in Asia amongst the Christian folk was a Jewish quarter, maintained by a lord of that country for foul usury and vile gain, hateful to Christ and His followers. And men could ride or walk all through the streets of it, for it was open at either end. Down beyond the farther part stood a little school of Christian folk, in which were many children of Christian blood. Year by year they studied such things as were in use in that country, that is to say, singing and reading, as small children do. Amongst these little school-boys was a widow's son, seven years old. On his way to school, day by day, wherever he saw the image of Christ's mother he would kneel down and say his *Ave Maria*. Thus had the widow taught her little son to honour our Lady, Christ's dear mother, and he forgot it not, for a good child will learn quickly. But ever, when I think of this thing, St. Nicholas stands in my memory, because he did reverence to Christ so young.

As this little child sat in school, studying his little book of prayers, he heard *Alma redemptoris* sung, as the children learned their book of antiphons, and he drew nearer and nearer as he durst, ever hearkening to the words and the melody until he knew the first verse all by heart. He knew nothing of what the Latin meant, he was too young and tender of age, but on a day he begged his fellow to expound this song to him in his own speech or tell him why it was in use. Many a time upon his bare knees he prayed him to construe and explain it to him. His fellow, who was older than he, answered, 'I have heard tell that this song was made to salute our blessed Lady and pray her to be our help and succour when we die. I cannot expound more of it. I learn singing, I know but small grammar.'

'And is this song made in honour of Christ's mother?' said this innocent. 'Now I will do my diligence, certes, to learn it all ere Christmas is past. Though I be chidden for mine own book, and beaten thrice in an hour, I will learn it in honour of our Lady.'

On the way home from day to day his fellow taught him privily till he knew it by heart, and then he sang it boldly and well from word to word after the true melody. Twice a day it passed through his throat, as he went to school and home again through the Jewry, evermore sweetly singing and crying *O alma redemptoris*. His mind was set ever upon our Lady; the sweetness of Christ's mother had so pierced his heart that to invoke her he could not cease his singing on the way.

Our first foe, the serpent Satan, who has his wasp's nest in the Jewish heart, swelled up and said, 'Ye Hebrew people, alas! is this honourable to you that such a boy shall walk at will in your despite and sing of such matter as is against the reverence due your faith?' Thenceforth the Jews conspired to drive this innocent out of the world. Thereto they suborned a murderer who had a privy place in an alley, and as the child went by, this cursed Jew seized and held him, then cut his throat and cast him into a foul pit.

O cursed folk of modern Herods, what avails your evil intent? Murder will out, verily it will not fail, and chiefly where it touches the honour of God. Blood cries out on your cursed deed. O martyr made fast in virginity (the Prioress cried), now mayst thou sing, following ever the white celestial Lamb. Of thee wrote St. John, the great evangelist, in Patmos, and said that they go before the Lamb and sing an ever-new song, who never knew women fleshly.

This widow waited all that night for her little child, but he came not. Wherefore, as soon as it was day, with pale face and anxious dread she sought him at school and elsewhere, till finally she learned so much, that he was last seen in the Jewry. With mother's pity in her breast, as if half out of her mind she went to every place where she fancied a likelihood to find her little child, and ever she cried on Christ's mother the meek and tender; and at length she sought him amongst the cursed Jews. She questioned every Jew that dwelt there and prayed them piteously to tell her if her child had passed by. They said, 'Nay.' But Jesu of His grace presently put it into her mind that she cried out to her son, where he was cast in the pit beside the way.

O great God that performest thy laud by the mouth of innocents, behold here thy power! This gem of chastity, this emerald, and this bright ruby of martyrdom, where he lay with throat all cut, he began to sing *alma redemptoris* so loudly that the place all rung. The Christian folk passing through the street came to marvel upon the deed and in haste sent after the provost. He came thither, he tarried not, and praised Christ, the King of heaven, and also His mother, the glory of mankind. And then he bade the Jews should be bound. With piteous lamentations the child was taken up, ever singing his song, and carried to the nearest abbey with a great and noble procession. His mother lay by the bier swooning; scarce could the people draw away this second Rachel from the bier. Each one of the Jews who knew of this murder the provost caused to die in torment and by a shameful death, and that straightway. No such cursedness would he tolerate. Evil he shall have who evil deserves. Therefore he had them drawn with wild horses and after that hung them, according to law.

Upon his bier before the chief altar this innocent lay ever whilst the mass went on, and then the abbot and his convent spend them to bury him. But when they sprinkled holy water on him, the child spoke again, and sang, *O alma redemptoris mater!* This abbot, a holy man, as monks be (or else ought to be), began to conjure this young child. 'O dear child, I beseech thee, in the name of the holy Trinity, tell me why thou singest, since to mine eyes thy throat is cut.'

'My throat is cut to my neck-bone,' said the child, 'and in the course of nature I should have died, yea, long since. But as ye will find in books, Jesu Christ will have His glory abide and be remembered. Therefore in honour of His dear mother, I still may sing loud and clear *O alma*. After my little wit, I ever loved Christ's sweet mother, this well of mercy, and when I was in point to die, she came to me and bade me sing this anthem in my death, as ye have heard, and as I sang methought she laid a grain on my tongue. Wherefore I sing and sing I must needs in honour of that blessed noble maiden till the grain is taken from my tongue. And afterward she said to me, "My little child, now will I fetch thee when the grain is taken away. Be not afraid, I will not forsake thee!"'

This holy monk, the abbot I mean, drew out the child's tongue and took off the grain, and he softly yielded up the ghost. When the abbot saw this marvel, his salt tears trickled down like a shower, and he fell flat upon the pavement and lay still as if bound and all the monks also lay weeping upon the floor, blessing Christ's dear mother. At length they rose and went forth and took this martyr from his bier, and enclosed his little sweet body in a tomb of pure marble-stones. Where he now is, God grant we may all see him!

O young Hugh of Lincoln, slain also by cursed Jews, as all men know (for it is but a little while since), pray thou also for us, sinful unstable folk, that God in His Mercy multiply His grace upon us in reverence of His Mother Mary. Amen.

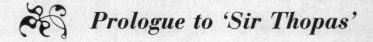

Prologue to 'Sir Thopas'

When all this miracle had been told, every man was wondrous sober; until our Host began to jest, and then for the first time he looked on me and said, 'What man are you? Are you watching to see an hare? Ever I see you staring upon the ground. Come nearer and look up merrily. Now make way, sirs, — give this man room! He is full shapely in the waist like myself, small and fair of visage; he were a dolly for any woman to embrace in her arms! He seems elf-like by his countenance, for he chats with no man. Now tell us somewhat, as other folk have done. Tell us anon a tale of mirth.'

'Host,' said I, 'be not displeased, for certes I know none other tale but a rhyme that I learned long ago.'

'Yea, that is good,' said he. 'Now methinks by his face we shall hear some rare thing.'

The Tale of Sir Thopas

Listen, lords, with good will, and verily I will tell you of mirth and joy; all of a knight, fair and noble in battle and tournament, Sir Thopas was his name. Born as he was in a far country, beyond the sea, in Flanders, at Poppering in the manorhouse. His father stood in full high degree, by God's grace lord of that county. Sir Thopas waxed into a doughty swain, with a face as white as wheaten bread and lips as red as a rosebud. His hue was like fast scarlet dyes, and I tell you of a truth he had a seemly nose. Like saffron was his hair and also his beard, which reached unto his girdle. His shoes were of Cardovan leather and his brown hose from Bruges. His robe was a rich brocade which cost many a half-penny. He could hunt wild deer and ride along the river hawking, with a gray goshawk on hand. He was a good archer to boot and at wrestling he had no peer, wherever a ram was staked. Many a maid, bright in her bower, mourned for love of him when she had better have slept; but he was chaste, and no lecher, and sweet as flower of the thorn that bears the red hip.

On a morrow it so befell that Sir Thopas would ride forth, and he got upon his grey steed, in his hand a lance, and a long sword by his thigh. Through a fair forest he spurred, where were many wild beasts, yea, both bucks and hares; but as he rode south and rode north, I tell you a sorry hap had wellnigh betided him. There sprung herbs great and small, the licorice and ginger and many a clove and nutmeg to put in ale, whether fresh or old, or to put away in a box. The birds sang, in good sooth, that it was a joy to hear; the sparrow-hawk and the popinjay, the throstlecock made his ditty, and the wood-dove on the branch sang full loud and clear.

Sir Thopas fell in love-longing when he heard the singing of the throstle, and spurred on like a madman; his fair steed sweated so with the spurring that men might have wrung out water, and all bloody were his sides. Sir Thopas too was so weary from riding over the soft grass, so fiery was his vigour, that he laid him down in that place and rested his charger and let him feed. 'Oh St. Mary, *benedicite!* What ails this love to bind me so sore? Perdy, I dreamed all the night long that an elf-queen shall be my love and sleep under my robe. An elf-queen will I verily love, for in this world is no woman worthy to be my mate; all other women I renounce, and betake me over dale and down to an elf-queen.'

Straight he climbed into his saddle and spurred over stile and stone to espy his elf-queen; till he found in a secret retreat the land of faerie so savage; for there was none other durst ride into that country. At length came a great giant, Sir Elephant by name, a man perilous of his deeds, and said, 'Young knight, by Mahound unless thou spurrest out of my haunt, with mace I will slay thy charger. Here dwells the queen of Faerie with harp, and pipe and tabor.'

The knight replied, 'As I hope for bliss, to-morrow will I meet thee when I am in armour. And I hope, by my faith, very bitterly shalt thou yet pay for it by this lance's point. Thy maw will I thrust through, I trust, ere prime of day; and here shalt thou be slain.'

Sir Thopas drew back apace. The giant cast stones at him from a fell staff-sling; but Child Thopas escaped, all through God's grace and his own fair port.

Still give ear to my song, lords, that is merrier than the nightingale, for I will whisper you how Sir Thopas, with his slender flanks, spurred over hill and dale and came to town again. His merry men he bade make glee and jollity, for needs must he fight a giant with three heads; all for the love and joyance of one who shines full fair. 'Call hither my minstrels, to recite tales whilst I arm me; and romances full royal, of popes and cardinals and also of love-longing!'

First they fetched him sweet wine and mead in a wooden bowl; royal spicery, gingerbread and licorice and cummin with sugar so fine. Next to his white flesh he donned breeches and shirt of fine clear lawn, and over his shirt a quilted tunic and over that a coat of mail to save his heart from piercing. Over that he wore a hauberk of strong plate, all of Jews' work, and his surcoat white as a lily. His shield was all of red gold, and bore a carbuncle and a boar's head. There he swore by bread and ale how that the giant should die, betide that might! His greaves were of full hard leather, the sheath of his sword of ivory, and his helmet bright and brazen, his saddle of whale-ivory, his bridle shone like the sun or as the moonshine. His spear was of fine cypress and boded war — no peace for him! — , with its head ground full sharp. His steed was dapple-gray and went a soft and gentle amble all through the land.

Lo, my lords, here is my first fit done! If you will have more, I will seek to tell it.

For charity's sake, now hold your tongues, knight and gracious lady, and hearken to my story. I will tell you anon of battle and knighthood and of ladies' love-longing. Men speak of noble romances, of Horn Child and of Ypotis and Pleyndamour, of Bevis and Sir Guy and Sir Libeaus. But Sir Thopas bears the flower of royal knighthood.

He bestrode his good steed and glided forth upon his way like a spark out of the burning. His crest was a tower with a lily therein. May God shield his body from harm! And because he was an adventurous knight, he would not sleep in a house, but lay without in his hood; his bright helm was his pillow and his charger grazed beside him upon the herbage fine and fresh. Himself drank of water of the spring, like Sir Percival the knight, that was so worthy under his weeds; till on a day —

The Host's Interruption of Sir Thopas

'No more of this, for God's dignity!' quoth our Host; 'you so weary me by your very silliness that mine ear ache with your rubbish-prate, God so bless my soul! To the Devil with such a rhyme, well may men call it doggerel!'

'Why so?' said I. 'Why will you stop me in my tale more than another, since it is the best rhyme I know?'

'By heaven,' quoth he, 'because, to speak plainly, your stinking rhyme is not worth a curse; you do naught but waste time. Sir, flatly, you shall rhyme no longer. Let us see whether you can tell us aught in worthy poetry, or at least somewhat in prose, in which there may be some mirth or instruction.'

'Gladly,' said I, 'in God's name! I will tell you a little thing in prose that ought to please you, I trust; else truly you are hard to please. It is an edifying moral tale, though it be told in sundry ways by sundry folk, as I shall show you. As thus: you well know that each evangelist who tells of Jesu Christ's passion tells not everything as his fellows tell it; but nevertheless their substance is all true, and all accord in their substance, albeit their telling differs. For Mark and Matthew, John and Luke, some say more and some less when they tell of his piteous passion; but doubtless their meaning is all one. Therefore, lordings all, I pray, if you think I vary in my speech, as thus, — though I tell somewhat more proverbs in this little treatise to enforce my matter with than you have heard other folk tell, and though I say not the same words that you have heard before, yet I pray you all blame me not. For in my meaning you shall not find much variance from the meaning of that little treatise after which I make this pleasant tale. Therefore I crave of you to hearken to what I shall say, and let me tell my tale through.'

The Tale of Melibeus

A young man called Melibeus, mighty and rich, had of his wife, who was called Prudence, a daughter who was called Sophia. Upon a day it befell that he went into the fields to disport him. His wife and daughter he left within his house, of which the doors were fast shut. Three of his old foes espied it, and set ladders to the walls of his house and entered by the windows, and beat his wife and wounded his daughter with five mortal wounds in five sundry places (that is to say, in her feet, in her hands, in her ears, in her nose, and in her mouth), and left her for dead and went away.

When Melibeus was returned into his house and saw all this mischief, like a madman he began to rend his clothes, and to weep and cry. Prudence his wife, as far as she durst, besought him to cease his weeping; but notwithstanding he began to cry and weep more and more.

This noble wife Prudence remembered the wise words of Ovid, in his book called *The Remedy of Love*, where he says, 'he is a fool that would hinder the mother to weep at the death of her child for a certain time, till she have wept her fill; but then a man ought to do his diligence to comfort her with sweet words, and pray her to cease her weeping.' For which reason this noble wife Prudence suffered her husband to weep and cry for a certain space; but when she saw her time, she spoke to him in this wise. 'Alas, my lord,' quoth she, 'why make you yourself to be like a fool? In sooth it fits not a wise man to show such sorrow. Your daughter, by the grace of God, shall recover and escape. And even were it so that she were now dead, for her death you ought not to destroy yourself. Seneca says, "the wise man shall not be too comfortless for the death of his children, but certes he should suffer it in patience, even as he awaits the death of his own proper person." '

This Melibeus answered anon and said, 'What man should cease his weeping, who has so great a cause to weep? Jesu Christ our Lord Himself wept for the death of Lazarus, His friend.'

Prudence answered, 'Certes, well I know that moderate weeping is not forbidden to him that is sorrowful, and amongst folk in sorrow, but rather it is fully granted him to weep. The apostle Paul writes unto the Romans, "a man shall rejoice with them that make joy, and weep with such folk as weep." But though moderate weeping be granted, over-violent weeping is forbidden. Temperance in weeping should be considered, after the instruction of Seneca, "when thy friend is dead, let not thine eyes be too moist with tears, nor yet over-dry; although the tears come to thine eyes, let them not fall." And when you have lost your friend, do your diligence to get another friend; and this is more wisdom than to weep for your friend whom you have lost, for therein is no help. And therefore, if you govern yourself by sapience, put away sorrow out of your heart. Remember you that Jesus the son of Sirach says, "a man to be joyous and glad in heart, it conserveth him flourishing in his age; but soothly a sorrowful heart maketh his bones dry." He says also thus, that "sorrow in heart slayeth full many a man." Solomon says, that "right as moths injure garments, and the small worms the tree, right so sorrow injureth the heart." Wherefore we ought, as well at the death of our children as at the loss of our temporal goods, to have patience. Remember the patient Job, when he had lost his children and his temporal substance, and in his body received and endureth full many a grievous tribulation; yet he said thus, "our Lord hath given it to me, our Lord had bereft it from me: blessed be the name of our Lord!" '

To these aforesaid things answered Melibeus unto his wife Prudence, 'All your words are true, and also profitable; but truly my heart is troubled with this sorrow so grievously that I know not what to do.'

'Summon,' quoth Prudence, 'all your true friends and your kinsmen who are wise; tell them your case, and hearken to what counsel they say, and govern you after their sentence. Solomon says, "work all thy doings by counsel, and thou shalt never repent." '

Then by the counsel of his wife Prudence this Melibeus summoned a great congregation of folk, such as surgeons, physicians, old folk and young, and some of his old enemies reconciled in semblance to his love and his grace. And therewith came some of his neighbours that did him reverence more for fear than for love, as haps often. There came also full many subtle flatters, and wise advocates learned in the law.

And when these folk were assembled together, this Melibeus in sorrowful wise showed them his case; and by the manner of his speech it seemed that in heart he bore a cruel ire, ready to do vengeance upon his foes, and desired that war should speedily begin. Yet nevertheless he asked their counsel upon this matter.

[The greater part of the tale, consisting of the advice of Melibeus' wife and friends, is here omitted.]

And when that dame Prudence saw her time, she enquired and asked her lord Melibeus what vengeance he thought to take on his adversaries. To which Melibeus answered and said, 'Certes, I think and purpose fully to disinherit them of all that ever they have, and to send them into exile forever.'

'Certes,' quoth dame Prudence, 'this were a cruel sentence, and much against reason. For you are rich enough, and have no need of other men's goods; and you might lightly in this wise get you a covetous name, which is a vicious thing and ought to be eschewed of every good man. For according to the saying of the apostle, "covetousness is the root of all evils". And therefore it were better for you to lose so much goods of your own than to take of their goods in this manner. For better it is to lose goods with honour than to win goods with baseness and shame. And every man ought to do his diligence to get him a good name. And he ought also not only to busy himself to keep his good name, but also to strive ever to do somewhat by which he may refresh his good name, for it is written that "the old good praise or good name of a man is soon gone and past when it is not renewed or refreshed". And as touching that saying, that you will exile your adversaries, methinks that is much against reason and beyond moderation, considering the power that they have given you upon themselves. And it is written that "he is worthy to lose his privilege that misuseth the might and the power that is given him". And even supposing you might enjoin for them that punishment by right and by law (which I believe you may not do), I say peradventure you could not put it in execution; and then were it likely to return to war as it was before. And therefore if you will that men should yield you obedience, you must judge more courteously; that is to say, you must give easier sentences and judgments. For it is written that "he that most courteously commandeth, him men most obey". And therefore I pray you that in this necessity you contrive to overcome your own heart. For Seneca says that "he that overcometh his heart overcometh twice"; and Tullius says, "there is naught so commendable in a great lord as when he is benign and meek, and is easily appeased". And I pray you that you will forbear now to do vengeance, in such a manner that your good name may be kept and conserved; and that men may have cause and matter to praise you for your pity and your mercy; and that you may never have cause to repent you of any thing which you have done. For Seneca says, "he overcometh in an evil manner that repenteth him of his victory". Wherefore, I pray you, let mercy be in your mind and in your heart, to the effect and intent that God almighty may have mercy on you in His last judgment. For St. James says in his epistle, "judgment without mercy shall be done to him that hath no mercy of another person".'

When Melibeus had heard the great reasons and arguments of dame Prudence, and her wise instructions and teachings, his heart began to incline to the will of his wife, reflecting on her faithful meaning; and he conformed him anon, and assented fully to work after her counsel, and thanked God, from Whom proceeds all virtue and all goodness, that had sent him a wife of so great discretion. And when the day came that his adversaries should appear in his presence, he spoke unto them full kindly, and said in this wise: 'Albeit that of your pride and presumption and folly, and of your carelessness and ignorance, you have misconducted yourselves and trespassed against me; yet, forasmuch as I see and behold your great humility, and that you are sorry and repentant for your guilts, it constrains me to grant you grace and mercy. Therefore I receive you to my grace, and forgive you utterly all the offences, injuries and wrongs that you have done against me and mine; to this effect and to this end, that God of His endless mercy will at the time of our dying forgive us our guilts in which we have trespassed against Him in this wretched world. For doubtless, if we be sorry and repentant of the sins and guilts in which we have trespassed in the sight of our Lord God, He is so liberal and so merciful that he will forgive us our guilts, and bring us to His bliss that has no end. Amen.'

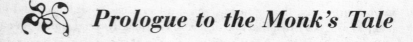

Prologue to the Monk's Tale

When I had ended my tale of Melibeus and of Prudence and her goodness, our Host said, 'As I am a faithful creature, and by the precious *corpus Madrian*, I would give a barrel of ale so my dear good wife had heard this story! She has no such patience as had Melibeus' wife. By God's bones! when I beat my lads, she brings me great clubbed staves and cries, "Slay every one of the dogs! Break them, back and every bone!" And if any neighbour of ours will not make a reverence to my wife in church or is so bold as to offend against her, she ramps in my face when she comes home and cries, "False coward, avenge your wife! By *corpus* bones, you shall have my distaff and go spin, and I will have your knife!" Day and night she will be saying, "Alas that I was ever born to wed a coward-ape and a milksop, who is put upon by every creature! You dare not stand up for your wife's rights!" This is my life, unless I will pick a quarrel with my neighbours; I must take myself out at the door or I am lost, unless I were foolhardy in her quarrel as a wild lion. I wot well that some day she will make me kill some neighbour and then flee for my life, for I am a dangerous man with my knife in hand, albeit I dare not resist her, for she is big of arms, in faith, as he shall find who injures her in word or act. But let us pass this matter by.

'My Lord Monk, be merry of cheer, for in faith you shall tell a tale. Lo, Rochester stands hard by there. Ride forth, mine own lord, spoil not our sport. But by my troth, your name I know not, whether to call you my lord Sir John, or Sir Thomas, or else Sir Alban. Of what convent are you, in heaven's name? You have a full fair skin, I vow to God; it must be a noble pasture, that where you feed: you are no penitent or ghost! On my faith, you are some kind of officer, a noble sacristan or cellarer, for by my father's soul I deem you must be a master at home, no poor cloister-monk nor novice neither, but a governor, wise and wily; and a comely-looking person withal, for brawn and bones. May God bring him to confusion who first brought you to the religious life! Alas, why wear you so wise a cope? Had you leave, as you have the might, you would have begotten many a fair creature. God bless me, but an I were pope, not you only, but every mighty man, though he were shorn full high on his pate, should have a wife. All the world is lost; religion has taken up all the best, and we lay-folk are but shrimps. Of feeble trees come feeble scions; therefore be our heirs so slim and feeble that they cannot well engender. This makes our wives to make assay of religious folk. — But be not worth, my lord, that I make merry thus; full often in jest I have heard a sooth told.'

This worthy Monk took all in patience, and said, 'I will do my diligence, as far as tends to virtue, to tell you a tale, or two or three of them. And if you list to hearken hither, I will tell you the life of St. Edward; or else I will first relate certain tragedies, of which I have a full hundred in my cell. A tragedy means a certain story, as the old books tell us, of him who stood once in great prosperity and falls out of high estate into misery and ends in wretchedness. They are commonly in verses of six feet, which men call hexameters. Many are indited in prose, and also in many a sundry metre. Lo! this description should suffice. Now hearken if you please to hear. But first I beseech you to excuse my ignorance if I tell not these things in order, be it of popes, kings, or emperors, according to their times, as they are found written, but put some before and some behind, as they come now into my remembrance.'

 ## *The Monk's Tale*

In the manner of tragedy I will bewail the misfortune of them that stood in high estate and so fell that no remedy could bring them out of their adversity. For when Fortune will flee, none can detain the course of her. Let no man trust in blind good fortune; be warned by these old and true ensamples.

Lucifer
At Lucifer, though he were an angel and not a man, I will begin. For though Fortune cannot harm an angel, yet for his sin he fell down from his high degree into hell, where he now is. O Lucifer, brightest of all angels, now art thou Satan and canst never depart out of that misery into which thou art fallen.

Adam
Lo, Adam was created in the plain of Damascus by God's own finger and not uncleanly begotten of man's loins, and of all paradise was he lord, saving one tree. Never man on earth was of so high estate till for sin he was driven from his high prosperity to labour, misfortune, and hell.

Samson
Behold Samson, who long ere his birth was announced by an angel and consecrated to almighty God, and stood in high honour as long as he had his eyes. Was never such another as he for strength and hardihood. But he told his secret to his wives, wherefore he slew himself for misery.

This noble almighty champion slew a lion and rent him all in pieces with no weapon save his two hands, as he walked on his way to his wedding. His false wife so cajoled and entreated him till she knew his counsel and treacherously revealed it to his foes, and forsook him and took another mate. In wrath he took three hundred foxes, and bound their tails together and knit a burning brand to every tail and so set the foxes' tails afire. They burnt up all the corn in that land and also all their olive-groves and vines. He slew a thousand men with no weapon but an ass's cheek-bone. When they were slain, he was so athirst that he wellnigh perished; and prayed God to pity his pains and send him drink, or else he must die. From a molar-tooth in the ass's dry jaw-bone there rushed anon a spring, from which he drank his fill. Thus God helped him, as *Judges* tells.

At Gaza on a night by main force, in spite of the Philistines in that city, he tore up the gates of the town and carried them on his back high upon an hill for men to see. O noble almighty Samson dear, hadst thou not told thy secret to women, in all this world would have been nowhere thy match.

This Samson never took strong drink nor wine, nor did ever razor or shears come upon his head, by precept of the divine messenger, for all his strength lay in his hair. Full twenty winters, year by year, had he the governance over Israel. But soon must he weep full bitterly, for women brought him to ruin. He told his mistress Delilah that all his strength lay in his hair, and she falsely sold him to his foemen, and whilst he slept in her lap on a day, she had his hair clipped and sheared and let his enemies detect his secret. When they found him in this plight, they bound him fast and put out his eyes. Before his hair was clipped or shorn no bond could bind him, but now he was imprisoned in a cave and made to grind at a hand-mill. O noble Sampson, strongest of men, once a judge in glory and wealth, now mayst thou weep with thy blind eyes, since thou art fallen from weal into wretchedness. The end of the poor creature was this. On a day his foemen made a festival and set him to play the fool before them. And this was in a splendid temple. But at last he wrought dread ruin; for he shook two pillars and made them fall; down fell temple and all, and there it lay, and it slew him and all his foemen, the princes every one, that is to say, with three thousand bodies besides.

I say no more of Samson. Be warned by this old and simple ensample, that men tell not their secret to their wives if it touch life or limb.

Hercules

His own deeds sing laud and high renown of Hercules, the sovereign conqueror, the flower of strength in his time. He slew the lion and took his skin, and laid low the Centaur's boast. He slew the Harpies, the cruel fell birds, and robbed the dragon of his golden apples. He brought away Cerberus the hell-hound. He slew the cruel tyrant Busiris and gave him to his horses to devour, flesh and bones. He slew the fiery venomous serpent, and broke one of the two horns of Achelous, and Cacus he slew in a rocky cave, and the giant Antæus, the strong, and the grisly boar, and carried heaven upon his neck for many days. Was never creature since the world was made that slew so many monsters. For his strength and high virtues, throughout this wide world ran his name, and he travelled to see every realm. He was so strong that no man could say him nay. At both ends of the world, says Trophee, he set pillars for a bourne.

This noble champion had a sweetheart, Dejanira by name, fresh as the May, and, as these clerks note, she sent him a shirt, fresh and fine. Alas this shirt, out upon it! It was envenomed so subtly that ere he had worn it half a day, his flesh all fell from his bones. But natheless some clerks excuse her, and blame one Nessus who made it. Be that as it may, I will not accuse her; but he wore the shirt upon his naked back till his flesh blackened with the venom. And when he saw there was no help, he raked up for himself a bed of hot coals, for he deigned not to die with any poison. Thus died this worthy, mighty Hercules. Lo, who can trust long on Fortune? He who follows the ways of this crowded world is often laid full low before he is ware. Wise is he who knows himself. Beware, for when Fortune chooses to flatter, she watches to overthrow her man in such way as he would least imagine.

Nebuchadnezzar

The mighty throne and precious treasure, the glorious sceptre and royal majesty of King Nebuchadnezzar can scarce be described by tongue. Twice he won Jerusalem, and carried off the vessels of the temple. At Babylon was his sovereign seat, and there he enjoyed his glory and delight.

The fairest children of the royal blood of Israel he made his eunuchs and thralls. Amongst others was Daniel, the wisest child of all; for he expounded the king's dreams when there was no clerk in Chaldæa who knew to what end his dreams pointed. This proud king had a golden statue made, sixty cubits long and seven broad, to which he commanded both young and old to bow and pay veneration, or be burned in a furnace full of red flames. But never would Daniel and his two young fellows consent to that act. This king of kings, proud and lifted up, deemed that God who sits in majesty could not bereave him of his high station. But suddenly he lost it, and became like a beast, and ate hay as any ox and lay under the sky and walked in the rain with wild beasts, till a certain time was revolved. His hair grew as an eagle's feathers, his nails were like a bird's claws, till God released him from certain years of punishment and gave him back his wit. And then with many a tear he thanked God, and ever in his life was in dread to do amiss or trespass further, and until he was laid on his bier he knew that God was mighty and full of grace.

Belshazzar

His son, Belshazzar, who held the throne after his father's day, could not beware by his father, for he was proud of heart and sumptuous of life, and ever an idolater. His high estate made him feel secure in his pride. But Fortune cast him down, and suddenly divided his kingdom.

Upon a time he made a festival to all his lords and bade them be blithe; he called his officers, 'Go,' quoth he, 'bring forth the vessels which my father, in his day of greatness, took from the temple of Jerusalem, and thank we our high gods for the honour that our elders left with us.' His wife, his lords and his concubines drank out of these noble vessels sundry wines as long as they would. And this king cast his eye upon the wall and saw an armless hand writing, for fear of which he quaked and sighed sore. This hand which made Belshazzar so sore aghast wrote, *Mane, techel, phares*. In all that land was no magician who could expound these letters; but Daniel expounded it anon and said, 'King, God lent to thy father glory and honour, dominion, treasure, and revenue. And he was proud and in no wise feared God, and therefore God sent upon him heavy vengeance and bereft him of his kingdom. He was cast out from the company of man, his habitation was with asses, and he lay like a beast in wet and dry, till he knew by grace and reason that the God of heaven has dominion over every realm and every creature. And then God had compassion of him and restored to him his kingdom and his own form. Now thou, his son, art proud also, and knowest all these things. Thou art rebel to God, and art his foe. Thou has drunk from his vessels boldly; and also thy wife and thy wenches drank sinfully sundry wines from the same vessels, and cursedly thou praisest false gods. Therefore great pains are decreed for thee. This hand that wrote on the wall *Mane, techel, phares*, was sent from God, believe me. Thy kingdom is departed, thou weighest naught, thy kingdom is divided and shall be given to the Medes and Persians.' And the same night the king was slain and Darius occupied his station, though he had no lawful right thereto.

Lordings, you may take warning hereby, how there is no security in lordship. For when Fortune will forsake a man, she bears away kingdom, and wealth, and friends, great and small. What friends a man has in good fortune, mishap will make enemies. I believe this proverb is full true and full general.

Zenobia

Zenobia, Queen of Palmyra, as the Persians write concerning her glory, was so valorous and so bold in arms that no other passed her in hardihood, nor in lineage nor in other nobleness. She was descended from the blood of Persian kings; I say not that she was fairest of all women, but her form could not be amended. From her childhood I find that she fled to the wood from woman's office. With her broad arrows she spilled many a wild hart's blood; she was so swift that she seized them anon. When she was older she would kill lions and leopards, and rent bears in pieces and in her arms dealt with them at will. She durst seek wild beasts' dens and roam over the mountains all night and sleep under a bush. For very strength she could wrestle with any young man, were he never so active. Naught could stand against her arms. She kept her maidenhood against every person and deigned to be bound to none. At length her friends married her to Odenatus, a prince of that country, albeit she delayed them long. (And ye shall understand that he had even such fancies as she.) But nevertheless, when they were knit together, they lived in joy and felicity, for each held the other dear. She had two sons by this Odenatus, whom she brought up in virtue and learning. But now return we to our tale. I say so worshipful a creature, so wise withal and liberal without prodigality, so active and resolute in war, so courteous as well, was nowhere to be found in all this world. Her rich array as well of vessels as of clothes could not be declared; she was all clad in gems and gold. She spared not, for any hunting, to gain full knowledge of sundry tongues when she had leisure, and to learn books was all her delight, and how she might spend her life in virtue.

And, to treat shortly of this story, so doughty were she and her husband that they conquered and held with strong hand many great kingdoms and many a fair city in the orient which had belonged to the majesty of Rome. Never could their foemen put them to flight whilst Odenatus' days lasted. Whoso list to read of her battles against Sapor the king and others, and how all these events fell out, why she made her conquests and what title she had thereto, and afterward of her woe and mischance, how she was besieged and taken, let him go to my master Petrarch, who writes enough of this, I believe. When Odenatus died, she held the realm with her own mighty hand and fought so fiercely against her foes that there was no king nor prince in all that region but was glad if he found such grace that she warred not upon him. With her they made treaty and alliance to live in peace and let her ride and sport at will. Neither Claudius the emperor of Rome nor Gallienus before him, nor any Armenian or Egyptian, Syrian or Arabian, was so courageous as to dare fight with her in the field, lest she slay them with her own hands or put them to flight with her troops.

Her two sons went in regal habit as heirs of all their father's realms; and Hermanno and Thymalao were their names in Persian. But ever Fortune mingles gall in her honey; this mighty queen could endure no long time; Fortune made her fall from her kingdom into wretchedness and mischance.

Aurelian, when the governance of Rome came into his hands, planned to do vengeance upon this queen, and took his way with his legions toward her land; and, to tell it shortly, made her flee, and at last seized and bound her in fetters with her two children, and won the land and went back to Rome. Amongst other things that he won, this Aurelian, the great Roman, took with him her chariot all wrought with gold and gems, that men might see it. Zenobia walked before his triumphal car with gilt chains hanging from her neck, crowned according to her station, and her habit loaded with gems. Alas, Fortune! she that was once dreadful to kings and emperors, upon her all the rabble gape. Alas! she that was helmed in steel in stern onslaughts, and won strong towns and towers by force, shall now, as it were, have a helm of glass upon her head. She that bore a splendid sceptre shall, in turn, bear a distaff.

Peter, King of Spain

O noble worthy Peter, Spain's glory, whose majesty Fortune held so high, in truth men ought to mourn thy piteous death. Thy brother made thee flee thine own land, and afterwards in a siege by subtlety thou wert betrayed and led to his tent and there slain by his own hand; and he succeeded to thy kingdom and revenues. He who bore for arms the field of snow, with a black eagle therein, caught by the rod coloured as flame, brewed all this sin and cursedness; and the Wicked Nest was a worker of this extremity. He was no whit like Charlemagne's Oliver, who ever heeded fidelity and honour, but a Ganelon of Armorica corrupted by a bribe, who brought this worthy king into such a snare.

Peter, King of Cyprus

O worthy Peter, King of Cyprus, thou who wonnest Alexandria by noble generalship, thou broughtest woe to many an heathen. For this thine own lieges bore malice to thee and on a morning murdered thee in thy bed, for naught but thy knighthood. Thus Fortune rules and guides her wheel, and brings man from joy to sorrow.

Bernabo of Lombardy

Great Bernabo Visconti of Milan, the god of pleasure and scourge of Lombardy, since thou climbedst to such high estate, why should I not recount thine ill fortune? Thy brother's son, allied to thee doubly, both nephew and son-in-law, caused thee to die in his prison. But why or how thou wert slain I know not.

Ugolino, Earl of Pisa

No tongue, for pity, can tell of the languishing of Earl Ugolino of Pisa. But a little out of Pisa stands a tower in which he was imprisoned with his three little children, the eldest scarce five years old. Alas! it was great cruelty to put such birds in such a cage! In that prison he was forced to die, for Roger, Bishop of Pisa, had made on him a false accusation, wherefore the people rose against him and put him in prison, in such wise as you have heard; and of meat and drink he had so little that it could scarce suffice, and that little poor and bad withal. On a day it befell that at the hour when his meat was wont to be brought, the gaoler shut the tower-doors. He heard it well, but spoke not; and in his heart a thought came that they would have him die of hunger. 'Alas!' he said, 'that I was made!', and the tears fell from his eyes. His young son, three years old, said to him, 'Father, why weep you? When will the gaoler bring us our pottage? Have you no morsel of bread? I cannot sleep for hunger; would God I might sleep forever! Hunger would not then creep into my belly; I long more after naught, save bread.'

Thus day by day this child cried till he lay down in his father's arms and said, 'Farewell, father, I die,' and kissed his father and died the same day. When the woful father saw him dead, for sorrow he began to bite his two arms, 'Alas, Fortune, alackaday!' he said. 'All my woe I blame on thy false wheel!' His children deemed that he gnawed his arms for hunger, and not for grief, and said, 'Father, do not so, alas!, but eat rather our flesh. Our flesh you gave us —, take our flesh from us, and eat enough.' Thus they said to him, and then within a day or two they laid them in his lap and died. Himself also died of hunger in despair; thus ended this mighty Earl of Pisa, cut away from his high estate by Fortune. And here enough of this tragedy. Whoso would hear more of it, let him read the great poet of Italy called Dante, for he will relate it all from point to point, and not lack one word.

Nero

Although Nero was as vicious as any fiend lying low in hell, yet, as Suetonius tells us, he had this wide world in subjection, east and west, north and south. His habit was all decked with rubies, sapphires and white pearls, for in gems he had great delight. Never was emperor more dainty or proud or sumptuous of array; that robe which he had worn once he would never see again. Many a net of gold thread he had, to fish in the Tiber when he would divert him. All that he wished to do he made lawful by decree, and Fortune obeyed him as his friend. He burned Rome for his amusement, and upon a day slew the senators to hear how men would weep and cry. He slew his brother, and deflowered his sister. He put his mother in piteous plight, and cut her open; alack that he recked so little of his mother! No tear fell from his eye at that sight, but he said, 'A fair woman she was.' It is marvel how he could be critic of her dead beauty; he only commanded wine to be brought and drank anon. When might is joined to cruelty, alas, too far will the harm go.

In youth this emperor had a master, to teach him learning and courtesy, the flower of moral wisdom, if the books lie not. Whilst he was under this master he was made so intelligent and so gentle that it was long before tyranny or any other vice durst attack his soul. Nero had great awe of this Seneca, because he would ever discreetly chide him for his vices. 'Sir,' he would say, 'an emperor must needs be virtuous and hate tyranny.' Wherefore Nero made him to bleed to death from both his arms in a bath. This Nero had had a custom in youth to rise in presence of his master, but this became in time a great vexation to him, and therefore he made him die thus. This wise Seneca chose to die in a bath thus rather than have other torments; and thus Nero killed his dear master.

Now it befell that Fortune would no more cherish the haughty pride of Nero. Though he were strong, she was stronger. She thought, 'I am too foolish, in faith, to set in high degree a man so full of vice, and call him emperor; I will drag him from his seat, — when he least expects, he shall fall.' On a night the people rose against him for his crimes, and when he was aware of it he betook him out at his door alone and knocked hard at a door where he looked for friendship; the more he cried the faster they shut the doors. Then he knew well that his hope had misled him, and called no longer, but went his way. The people shouted and muttered roundabout, so that he heard them with his own ears, 'Where is this false tyrant, this Nero?' For fear he was almost out of his wits, and prayed piteously to his gods for succour, but it availed not. He wellnigh died for terror, and ran into a garden to hide him. There he found two churls sitting by a great glowing fire, and to them he began to pray to slay him and strike off his head, that men might not know his body and do it shame. He slew himself, he knew no better say, at which Fortune laughed and made sport.

Holofernes

No king's captain put more realms in subjection, nor in his time was mightier in every wise in the field, nor of greater renown, nor more magnificent in high arrogance than Holofernes. Fortune ever kissed him wantonly and led him up and down, till his head was off before he knew it. Not only all men held him in awe lest they forfeit riches or liberty, but he made every one to deny his own faith. 'Nebuchadnezzar was god and none other god should be adored,' he said. No person durst trespass against his behest, save in Bethulia, a strong city, where one Eliachim was priest. But take heed of Holofernes' death. On a night he lay drunk amid his host within his tent, great as a barn, and yet for all his pomp and power, Judith, a woman, smote off his head as he lay on his back sleeping, and stole privily from his tent to the town with his head.

King Antiochus

What need to tell of the high royal majesty of King Antiochus, of his lofty pride and evil works? Nowhere was such another. Read what he was in the book of Maccabees, and his proud words, why he fell from high well-being and how he died wretchedly upon an hill. Fortune had so advanced him in glory that verily he thought he could reach the stars and weigh each mountain in the balance and restrain all the floods of the sea. God's people he most hated, and would slay them in torment, weening that God could never abate his ride. And because they had mightily vanquished Nicanor and Timotheus, he so hated the Jews that he bade straightway prepare his chariot and swore full savagely he would go back to Jerusalem and cruelly wreak his ire upon it. But he was soon hindered in his purpose. For his threats God smote him so sore with an invisible, incurable wound, that it cut and bit his guts till he could not bear his pains. Verily the vengeance was just, for he had wounded many a man's guts. Yet for all his pain he would not cease his cursed and damnable purpose, but he bade array his host. Suddenly, before he was aware, God daunted all his pride and brag; for he fell so hard from his chariot that his limbs and flesh were rent and he could neither walk nor ride, but was borne about in a chair all bruised in back and side. God's vengeance smote him so cruelly that evil worms crawled through his body, and withal he stank so horribly that, whether he slept or woke, none of all his household could endure the stench of him. In this mischief he wailed and wept, and knew God to be Lord of every creature. To himself and to all his host the stench of his carrion was full loathsome; none could carry him to and fro. And in this stink and horrible pain he died wretchedly upon a mountain. Then had this robber and homicide, who had made many a man weep and lament, the reward due unto arrogance.

Alexander

The story of Alexander is so widespread that every person of discretion has heard somewhat or all of his fortune. In brief, he won by force this wide world; or else folk were fain, by reason of his high renown, to send to him for peace. He laid low the pride of man and beast wherever he came, even to the ends of the world. Never yet could comparison be made betwixt him and another conqueror. All this world quaked for dread of him, he was the flower of knighthood and liberality, Fortune made him inheritor of her honours, and save wine and women, naught could blunt his high purpose in arms and labours, he was so full of lion-like spirit. What praise were it to him if I told of Darius and an hundred thousand more, kings, princes, earls, bold dukes whom he conquered and brought to woe? I say the world was his so far as man can walk or ride; what more can I say? For though I wrote or talked evermore of his knighthood, it would not suffice. He reigned twelve years, says *Maccabees*, and was son of Philip of Macedon, who was the first king in the land of Greece. O worthy noble Alexander, alas that ever such a thing should befall! Thou wert poisoned by thine own talk. Fortune diced with thee and turned thy six into an ace, and yet wept never a tear! Who shall give me tears to lament the death of high blood and of nobility, of him who wielded the world and yet thought it not enough, so full was his spirit of high emprise? Alas, who shall help me to arraign false Fortune and execrate that poison, both of which I blame for all his woe?

Julius Cæsar

By wisdom, manhood and great labour Julius the Conqueror rose from humble birth to royal majesty, and won all the occident over land and sea by the strength of his hand or by treaty, and made it tributary to Rome. And afterwards he was emperor, till Fortune became his adversary. O mighty Cæsar, in Thessaly thou didst war against Pompey, thy father-in-law, who controlled all the chivalry of the orient as far as dawn of day, and by thy knighthood thou didst capture and slay all save a few folk who fled with him. Thus thou didst put the orient in awe, thanks to Fortune that sped thee so well. But now I will bewail this Pompey a little while, this noble governor of Rome, who fled in this battle. One of his men, I say, a false traitor, smote off his head and brought it to Julius to win his favour. Alas, Pompey, conqueror of the orient, that Fortune should have brought thee to such an end!

Julius repaired to Rome in his triumph, crowned high with laurel. But on a time, Brutus Cassius, who ever bore ill-will to his high estate, made a secret subtle conspiracy against him, and chose the place where he should die by poniards, as I will tell you. Upon a day, as he was wont, this Julius went to the Capitol, and there this false Brutus and his other foes seized him anon and wounded him with many a wound, and there let him lie. And he never groaned except at one stroke, or else two, unless the books are false. So manly of heart was this Julius, and so well he loved comely dignity, that with all his deadly sore wounds he cast his mantle over his hips, that none should see his nakedness. Thus, as he lay tranced and a-dying, and knew verily that his life was spent, yet had he thought of dignity.

Lucan, I commit this story to thee, and to Suetonius, and Valerius also, who wrote beginning and end of it, how to these two great conquerors at first Fortune was friend and then their foe. Let no man trust long to have her favour, but evermore be watchful of her. Be warned by these mighty conquerors.

Crœsus

This rich Crœsus, once the king of Lydia, albeit he was sorely dreaded by Cyrus, yet was he caught in the midst of his pride and led to the fire to be burned. But such a rain poured from the welkin that it slew the fire and let him escape. Yet he had not grace to beware till Fortune made him hang, mouth open, upon the gallows.

When he was escaped, he could not refrain from beginning a new war again. He deemed well, since Fortune sent him such hap as to escape by help of the rain, that he could never be killed by his foes; and also he dreamed a dream upon a night; of which he was so fain and proud that he set his whole heart upon vengeance. He was upon a tree, he dreamed, and Jupiter washed him, back and sides, and Phœbus brought a fair towel to dry him. With this he was all puffed up, and bade his daughter, who stood beside him and he knew abounded in high learning, to tell what it signified. She began right thus to expound his dream: 'The tree,' quoth she, 'betokens the gallows, and Jupiter betokens the rain and snow, and Phœbus with his clean towel, they are the beams of the sun. You shall be hanged, father, in sooth; the rain shall wash you and the sun dry you.' Thus flat and plainly she warned him, his daughter, hight Phania. So Crœsus, the proud king, was hanged; his royal throne availed him not.

Tragedy is no other thing than to cry and bewail in song Fortune's attacks and unware strokes upon proud thrones. For when men trust her, then she fails them and covers her bright face with a cloud.

Prologue to the Nun's Priest's Tale

'Ho, good sir, no more of this,' quoth the Knight. 'What you have told is enough, in truth, and much more, for a little heaviness goes far with most folk, I believe. As for me, it is a great distress to hear of the sudden fall of folk who have been in great ease and wealth, alas! And the contrary is joy and delight, as when a man who has been in poor estate climbs up and waxes prosperous and there abides. Such a thing is gladsome and goodly to speak of.'

'Yea, by St. Paul's bell,' quoth our Host, 'you say sooth. This monk claps his tongue on high; he told how "fortune covered with a cloud" — I wot never what, and also you heard right now of a "tragedy"; and yet there is no help, perdy, in bewailing or complaining what is done, and also it is grievous, as you have said, to hear of heaviness. Sir Monk, no more of this, for the love of heaven. Your tale distresses this whole party; such talk is not worth a butterfly, for therein is no jollity nor sport. Wherefore, Sir Monk, or Sir Piers by your name, tell us of somewhat else, I pray you heartily; for in truth, were it not for the clinking of your bells, hanging over all your bridle, by heaven's King, I should have fallen down for slumber ere this, though the slough had been never so deep. Then would your tale have been told in vain! For truly, as these clerks say,

> "Whene'er a man can find none audience,
> It helpeth not to speak his wit or senses."

I know how to understand a good tale well told, I believe. Sir, tell somewhat of hunting, I prithee.'

'Nay,' quoth the Monk, 'I list not to make sport. Let another tell, as I have told.'

Then our Host, with rude and bold speech, said forthwith to the Nun's Priest, 'Come nearer, thou priest, thou Sir John, come hither and tell of somewhat to gladden our hearts. Be blithe, though you ride upon a nag. What though your horse be foul and lean! If he serve you, reck not a peascod. Look that your heart be evermore merry.'

'Yea, sir,' quoth he, 'yea, Host, in faith if I be not merry, you may chide me well.' And forthwith he broached his tale and spoke thus to us all, this goodly man, this sweet priest, Sir John.

The Nun's Priest's Tale

A widow, poor and somewhat on in years, dwelt once in a little cottage that stood in a dale beside a grove. Since the day she was last a wife, this widow of whom I tell this tale had lived full patiently and simply; for her goods and earnings were but small. By husbanding what God sent, she kept herself and her two daughters; she had three large sows and no more, three kine and a sheep named Molly. Her bower and hall were full sooty, where she ate many a slender meal; she needed never a bit of pungent sauce, nor did dainty morsel ever pass her throat; her diet matched her gown. Surfeiting never made her sick, her only physic was a temperate diet, with exercise and heart's content. It was not the gout kept her from dancing, nor did the apoplexy molest her head. Neither red wine nor white drank she; her board was served for the most with white and black, of which she found no want, milk and brown bread, with broiled bacon and at times an egg or two, for she was a kind of dairy-woman.

She had a yard enclosed all about with sticks and a dry ditch, and herein she had a cock, Chanticleer. In all the land was not his match for crowing; his voice was merrier than the merry organ, that goes in church on mass-days. More trusty was his crowing in his yard than a clock or an abbey horologe; he knew by nature each revolution of the equinoctial in that longitude, for when each fifteen degrees were ascended, then he crew, that it could not be bettered. His comb was redder than fine coral, and indented like a castle-wall. His black bill shone like jet; like azure were his legs and toes, his nails whiter than the lily-flower, and his hue like burnished gold. This noble cock had in his governance seven hens, to do all his pleasure, his sisters and paramours, and wondrous like him in looks; of which the fairest hued on her throat was named fair Demoiselle Partlet. She was courteous, discreet, debonair and companionable, and bore herself so fairly since she was seven nights old that truly she held the heart of Chanticleer all locked, and herself bore the key; he loved her so that well was him. But such a joy as it was to hear them sing in sweet accord when the bright sun began to rise,

'My lief is faren in londe!'

For at that time, as I have made out, beasts and birds could sing and speak.

Now it so befell, one dawning, as Chanticleer sat on his perch amongst his wives in the hall, and next him this fair Partlet, that he began to groan in his throat as a man grievously troubled in his dream. When Partlet heard him thus roar, she was aghast, and said: 'Oh dear heart, what ails you to groan thus? A fine sleeper you are; fie, for shame!'

And he answered, 'Madame, take it not amiss, I pray you; 'tis God's truth, I dreamed right now that I was in such mishap that my heart is yet sore affrighted. Now God bring my dream to good, and keep my body from foul prison! I dreamed how I roamed up and down within our yard, and saw there a beast like a hound, who would have made arrest upon my body and killed me. He was betwixt yellow and red in colour, his tail and ears tipped with black, unlike the rest of his coat; his snout was slender and his two eyes glowing. For fear of his looks I almost die even now. This caused my groaning, doubtless.'

'Avaunt!' quoth she; 'fie upon you, faint heart! Alas! for by that God in heaven you have now lost my heart and love. In faith, certes, I cannot love a coward. Whatsoever any woman will say, all of us desire to have husbands bold, wise, and liberal, trusty with secrets, not a niggard nor a fool, nor aghast at every weapon, nor yet a boaster, by the heaven above us! How durst you, for shame, say to your dear that aught could make you afraid? Have you not a man's heart, yet have a beard! Alas, can you be aghast at dreams? There is naught in dreams but vanity, God wot. Dreams are engendered of surfeit and often of fumes and of folks' temperaments, when his humours are too abundant in a person. Truly this dream which you have dreamed comes from a superfluity of your red choler. This causes folk in their dreams to have dread of arrows and of fire with red blazes, of huge beasts, that they will bite them, of fighting, and great and small whelps; even as the melancholy humour causes full many a man to cry out in sleep for fear of black bears or black bull, or also black devils will catch him. I could tell also of other humours that work woe to many a man in sleep. But I will pass on as lightly as I may. Lo Cato, who was so wise! said he not thus, "Take no heed of dreams"? Now sir,' quoth she, 'for the love of heaven, when we fly down from these rafters, do take some laxative. On peril of my life and soul, I lie not and counsel you for the best, that you purge you both of choler and of melancholy; and, that you delay not, though there be no apothecary in this town, I will myself direct you to herbs that shall be for your health and weal; and I shall find the herbs in our yard which have the natural property to purge you beneath and also above. Forget not this, for God's sake! You are full bilious of temperament. Beware lest the sun as he climbs up find you replete with hot humours. And if he do, I dare lay a groat that you will have a tertian fever, or an ague that may be the death of you. For a day or two you shall have a light diet of worms ere you take your laxatives, — your spurge-laurel, centaury, and fumitory or else hellebore, that grows there, your caper-spurge or buck-thorn berries, or herb-ivy growing in our yard, and pleasant to take. Peck them right up growing and eat them in. By your father's soul, husband, be merry and dread no dreams. I can say naught else.'

'Gramercy for your lore, madame! But nevertheless,' quoth he, 'as to Sir Cato, who has such a name for wisdom, though he bade fear no dreams, by God, men may read in old books of many a man of more authority than ever Cato had, who says all the reverse of his opinion, and has well found by experience that dreams are significant as well of joy as of tribulations that folk endure in this present life. There needs no argument for this; very experience shows it.

'It is told by one of the greatest authors that men read that once two companions went in full pious mood on a pilgrimage, and it so happed they came into a town so full of people and so scant of lodgings that they found not so much as one cottage where they could both be lodged. Wherefore they needs must part company for that night, and each went to his quarters as chance assigned them. One was lodged in a stall far off in a yard, with plow-oxen; the other was well enough housed, as was his chance or his fortune, that govern all of us. It so befell that long ere dawn this man dreamed, as he lay in his bed, that his friend began to call upon him, saying, "Alas! for I shall be murdered in an ox's stall this night. Now help me, brother dear, ere I die; come to me in all haste." This man started out of his sleep for fear, but when he had waked he turned over and took no heed of this, thinking his dream but vanity. Thus he dreamed twice in his sleep. And at the third time his fellow seemed to come to him and say, "I am now slain. Behold my wounds, deep, wide and bloody. Arise early in the morn, and at the west gate of the town thou shalt see a dung-cart in which my body is privily hid; stay that cart boldly. In sooth, my gold caused my murder." And he told him every point, how he was slain, with a pale pitiful face. And trust well, his fellow found the dream full true, for on the morrow, at earliest day, he betook him to his fellow's lodging, and when he reached the ox-stall, he began to shout after him. The inn-keeper answered forthwith, "Sir, your fellow is gone. At daybreak he left the town." This man began to fall into suspicion, remembering his dream, and forth he went without tarrying to the west gate of the town, and found a dung-cart, ready to dung a field, and in such shape as you have heard the dead man say. And with a bold heart he began to call for vengeance and justice upon this felony. "My fellow is murdered this very night and lies gaping in this cart on his back. I cry out upon the magistrates who should rule and keep the city. Help! alas! here my fellow lies slain!" Why more of this tale? The people rushed out, cast the dung-cart over, and in the middle of the dung they found the dead man, all freshly murdered. O blessed God, faithful and just! Lo, how Thou ever reveal-est murder! Murder will out, that we see daily. Murder is so horrible and abominable to the God of justice and reason that He will not suffer it be covered up. Though it lie hid for years, murder will out, this is my conclusion. And right anon the magistrates seized the carter and tortured him so sore, and also the inn-keeper, on the rack, that they soon acknowledged their wicked-ness and were hanged by the neck-bone.

'By this may men see that dreams are to be feared. And certes I read in the same book in the very next chapter following (I lie not, as I hope to be saved), of two men that for a certain cause would have passed over the sea into a distant land, if the wind had not been adverse, and made them to tarry in a city standing pleasantly on a haven-side. But on a day, at evening, the wind changed and blew even as they would. Merry and glad they went to rest, and planned to sail early. But a great marvel befell one man as he lay asleep, who dreamed toward day a wondrous dream. He thought a man stood beside his bed and bade him tarry; "if thou go to-morrow, thou shalt be drowned; my tale is done." He woke and told his fellow his dream, and prayed him to give up his journey. His fellow, who lay by his bed's side, began to laugh and sore mocked him. "No dream can so affright my heart that I will stay my business; I set not a straw by thy dreamings, for dreams are but vanity and humbug. Men are ever dreaming of owls or apes and also of many a bewildering thing; they dream of things that never were nor shall be. But since I see that you intend to tarry here and thus of your free will lose your chance by sloth, God wot it grieves me, but have good-day." Thus he took his leave and departed. But ere he had voyaged over half his course, I know not why, nor what mischance ailed it, but by some mishap the ship's bottom was rent, and ship and man went down in sight of other ships hard by, that had sailed at the same time. Therefore, fair Partlet so dear, you may learn by such old ensamples that no man should reck too lightly of dreams, for I tell you that without doubt many a dream is to be dreaded full sore.

'Lo, I read in the life of St Kenelm, the son of Kenulph, the noble king of Mercia, how he dreamed a dream; on a day a little before he was murdered, he saw his murder in a vision. His nurse expounded all his dream and bade him beware of treason; but he was no more than seven years old, and paid little heed to any dream, so holy he was of spirit. By heaven, I would give my shirt that you had read his legend as I have! I tell you truly, Dame Partlet, that Macrobius, who wrote the vision of the noble Scipio in Africa, affirms dreams to be fore-warnings of things that men see afterward.

'Furthermore, I pray you look well in the Old Testament and see if Daniel held dreams to be a vanity. Read of Joseph also and there you will find whether dreams be sometimes (I say not always), warnings of future things. Look at the king of Egypt, Sir Pharaoh, and at his baker and his butler, whether they felt no virtue in dreams! Whoso will turn to the chronicles of sundry realms may read many a wondrous thing about them. Lo Crœsus, once king of Lydia! Dreamed he not that he sat upon a tree, which signified that he should be hanged? Lo Andromache, Hector's wife! She dreamed the very night before that the life of Hector should be lost if he went that day to battle; she warned him, but it availed not, for he went none the less to fight, and anon was slain by Achilles. But that tale would be all too long to tell, and I must not tarry, for it is high day. In short, I conclude that I shall have adversity after this vision; and I say, moreover, I set no store by laxatives. They are poison, I wot it well; I defy them, I like them not a whit.

'Now let us speak of mirth, and stint all this. In one thing, Madame Partlet, as I hope for joy, god has greatly blessed me; for when I see how scarlet-red you are about your eyes, and the beauty of your face, all my fear dies away. For as true as the Gospel, *Mulier est hominis confusio*; madame, the meaning of this Latin is that woman is man's whole bliss and joy! For when I feel your soft side at night, though I cannot draw closer, because our perch is so narrow alas!, I am so full of joy and comfort that I defy all dreams and visions.'

And with that, down he flew from the rafter, and with him all his hens, for it was day. He began to call them all with a *chuk*, for he had found a grain of corn lying in the yard. He was royal, he was afraid no longer; twenty times ere prime he clasped Partlet; he looked as it were a grim lion, and roamed up and down on his toes, he deigned not to set his foot to ground. He chucked when he came upon a grain of corn, and his wives ran to him. Thus royal, like a prince in his hall, I will leave this Chanticleer in his feeding-ground, and afterward I will say what befell him.

The month in which the world was made, March, when God first created man, was complete, and there had passed two and thirty days more. It befell that Chanticleer in all his glory, with his seven wives walking beside him, cast his eyes to the bright sun, which had sped through one-and-twenty degrees and somewhat more in the sign of Taurus; and by nature and not education he knew that it was prime, and he crew with joyous voice. 'The sun,' he said, 'is climbed up the heavens one-and-forty degrees and more. Madame Partlet, my world's bliss, hearken to the happy birds how they sing, and see the fresh flowers springing up; mine heart is full of comfort and revelry.' But suddenly a sorrowful case befell. For the latter end of joy is ever woe, God wot; joy of this world is soon gone, and an orator that could indite fairly might safely put it in a chronicle for a profound truth. Now let every wise man hearken; this story is every whit as true, I dare be bound, as the book of Lancelot of the Lake, which women hold in great reverence. Now will I return to my text.

A coal-fox, sly and unrighteous, who had dwelt three years in the grove, by decree of almighty Providence burst through the hedges that same night into the yard whither stately Chanticleer was wont to repair with his wives, and there lay quietly in a bed of herbs till it was past eleven of the clock, awaiting his time to fall upon Chanticleer, as all these homicides are fain to do that lie in wait to murder men. False murderer, lurking in thy lair! Thou new Iscariot, new Ganelon, false dissimulator, even as the Greekish Sinon that brought Troy utterly to woe! Accursed be that morn, O Chanticleer, on which thou flewest from thy rafter into the yard! Well thou wast warned by thy dreams that this day was perilous to thee. But what God foresees must needs come to pass, according to certain clerks; as witness any perfect clerk that there is great altercation in the schools and great disputing about this matter, and ever has been amongst an hundred thousand men. But I cannot sift it to the chaff, as can the holy doctor Augustine or Boethius or Bishop Bradwardine; whether God's glorious foreknowing compels me of necessity to do a thing, (by necessity I mean absolute necessity), or else whether I am granted free choice to do or not that same thing, though God foreknew it long before; or whether His knowing constrains not at all except by a conditional necessity. With such matters I will not have to do. My tale is all of a cock, as you may hear, who took his wife's counsel (out upon it!) to walk in the yard that morning, after he had dreamed his dream of which I told you. Women's counsels are oft baneful. Woman's counsel brought us first to woe and made Adam depart from Paradise where he was at ease and full merry. But because I know not whom I might vex if I should upbraid women's counsel, let us pass it over, for I said it but in sport. Read what authors, who treat of such matters, say of women. These be the cock's words and not mine; I cannot imagine harm of any woman.

Fairly lay Partlet in the sunshine with all her sisters by, to bathe her merrily in the sand, and the gallant Chanticleer sang merrier than the mermaid in the sea; for *Physiologus* in truth says that they sing merrily and well. And it so befell, as he cast his eye upon a butterfly amongst the herbs, that he was aware of this fox who lay hidden. He had no mind then to crow, but cried anon, 'cok cok!' and started up like a man affrighted in his heart. For by instinct a beast is fain to flee from his natural enemy if he sees it, though he had never cast eye upon it before.

This Chanticleer, when he first espied him, would have fled, but that the fox straightway spoke, 'Alas, gentle sir, where will you go? Are you afeard of me, your own friend? Now certes I were worse than a fiend if I desired harm or indignity to you. I am not come to spy upon your privacy, but in truth only to hearken how you sing. For truly you have as merry a voice as any angel in heaven, and more feeling in music than Boethius had, or any singer. My lord your father (God rest his soul!), and your mother too, of her courtesy, have been in my house, to my great content; and you, sir, I would fain please, certes. And speaking of singing, I must say, — may I be struck blind if I ever heard man, save you, sing as did your father in the morning. Certes, all that he sung was from the heart. And to make his voice the stronger he took such pains that he must needs shut both his eyes, so loud he cried, standing on tip-toe withal and stretching forth his long, slender neck. And also he was of such discretion that there was no man in any land who could pass him in song or wisdom. I have indeed read in the life of Burnel the Ass, amongst the verses, about a cock, who, because a priest's son, when he was young and foolish, gave him a rap on his leg, in after years made him to lose his benefice. But certainly there is no comparison betwixt his wisdom and subtlety and discretion and your father's. Now sing, sir, for sweet charity's sake. Let see, can you imitate your father?'

This Chanticleer began to flap his wings; he could not espy the cozenage, so ravished he was by the flattery. Alas! ye lords, many a false flatterer and parasite is in your courts, who please you more, in faith, than he who says you sooth. Read of flattery in *Ecclesiasticus*, and beware their treachery.

This Chanticleer stood high on his toes, stretching his neck and shutting his eyes, and began to crow loudly for the nonce. Up started Sir Russel the fox forthwith, seized Chanticleer by the throat and bore him on his back away toward the wood, for as yet no man gave chase.

O destiny that mayst not be eluded! Alas that Chanticleer flew down from the rafters and that his wife recked not of dreams! And all this mischance fell on a Friday! O Venus, goddess of pleasance, why wouldst suffer Chanticleer to die upon thy day, who was thy servant and did all within his might in thy service, more for delight than to multiply the world? O Geoffrey de Vinsauf, dear sovereign master, that when thy noble king Richard was slain by shot, didst mourn his death so sore, why have I not now thy learning and thy pen to chide the Friday as thou didst! (For truly it was on a Friday he was slain.) Then I would show you how I could mourn Chanticleer's dread and torment. Not when Ilium was won and Pyrrhus had seized King Priam by the beard and slain him with his naked sword, as *Æneid* says, was ever such cry and lamentation made by ladies as by the hens in the yard, when they saw this sight of Chanticleer. Above all Dame Partlet shrieked, louder than Hasdrubal's wife when her husband perished and the Romans had burned Carthage; who was so full of torment and frenzy that she leapt into the fire and burned herself with a steadfast heart. O woful hens, even so ye cried as the senators' wives when Nero burned the city of Rome and their husbands all perished, slain guiltless by this Nero.

But now I return to my tale once more. This poor widow and her two daughters heard these hens cry and lament, and started out at the door forthwith and saw the fox make toward the wood, bearing the cock away on his back. 'Out! alas! help!' they cried. 'Ho! ho! the fox!' and after him they ran, and many another person with cudgels. Ran Colle, our dog, and Garland and Talbot, and Malkin with her distaff in hand; ran cow and calf and the very hogs, so afeared they were for the barking of the hounds and the shouting of the men and women. They ran till they thought their hearts would burst, they yelled like fiends in hell, the ducks quacked as if they were being slaughtered, the geese in fear flew over the tree-tops, a swarm of bees came out of the hive; so hideous was the noise, ah *benedicite!*', certes Jack Straw and his rabble never made shouts half so shrill when they were slaughtering a Fleming, as were made this day after the fox. They brought horns of brass, of wood, of horn and bone, and blew and bellowed in them, and so shrieked and whooped withal till it seemed as if the heavens would drop. Now, good men, I pray you all hearken.

Lo, how Fortune suddenly overturns the hope and arrogance of her foe! This cock, lying upon the fox's back, in all his fright spoke to the fox and said, 'Sir, if I were as you, so may God help me, I should say, — "Turn back, all ye proud churls! A very pestilence fall on you! Now that I am come to this wood's edge, the cock shall abide here, in spite of your teeth. I will eat him, in faith, and that at once." '

'In faith, it shall be done,' answered the fox. And as he spoke that word, nimbly the cock broke away from his mouth and flew high upon a tree. And when the fox saw him gone, 'Alas! Chanticleer!' quoth he; 'alas! I have done you wrong to affright you, when I seized and brought you out of the yard. But, sir, I had no ill intent; come down and I shall make you see it. I shall say the sooth to you, so may God help me!'

'Nay then,' quoth the cock, 'I beshrew both of us, and first I beshrew myself, both blood and flesh, if you beguile me more than once. No more shall your flattery make me sing and shut my two eyes. For he who wilfully shuts his eyes when he should see, God let him never thrive!'

'Nay,' quoth the fox, 'but God give him evil fortune who is so indiscreet as to prate when he should hold his peace!'

Lo, such a thing it is to be negligent and heedless and trust upon flattery! But you who hold this tale foolishness, of naught but a fox and a cock and a hen, take the moral, good sirs. For St. Paul says that all that is written is written for our doctrine, in sooth. Take the fruit and leave the chaff. And now may the good God, if His will be so, as says my lord archbishop, make us all good Christians and bring us to His heavenly bliss. — Amen.

Epilogue to the Nun's Priest's Tale

'Sir Nun's Priest,' said our Host, 'blessings on your breech for this merry tale of Chanticleer! By my troth, if you were a secular man, a right hearty fellow you would be with dames. See what brawn and what a neck this gentle priest has, and what a chest! He looks with his eyes like a sparrow-hawk. He needs not dye his colour with brasil nor Portugal-red. Now may fair befall you for your tale, sir!'

And after that, with a merry look, he said to another as you shall hear.

The Physician's Tale

There was a knight, as Titus Livius tells, called Virginius, full of honour and nobility, strong in friends and in wealth. One daughter he had by his wife, and never another child. The maid was fair and excellent of beauty above every creature; for Nature had wrought her with singular diligence, and so excellently as though she would say, 'Lo! I, Nature, when I will, can thus form and colour a creature; who can imitate me? Not Pygmalion, though he ever forge and hammer or carve or paint, for I dare aver that Apelles and Zeuxis would toil in vain if they presumed to carve or paint, forge or hammer, and counterfeit me. For He that is the chief Shaper has made me His vicar-general to form and paint earthly creatures even as I will; and each thing under the waxing, waning moon is in my care. And I ask counsel of none; my Lord and I are in full accord, and in honour of Him I made her, as I make all my other creatures, whatsoever their hue or form.' Thus Nature would say, methinks.

This maid was fourteen years old, in whom Nature took such joy. Even as she paints a lily white and a rose red, so upon the gracious limbs of this noble

119

creature, before she was born, did Nature paint these colours where such colour should be. And Phœbus did dye her great tresses like to the streams of his burning heat. And if her beauty was excellent, a thousand-fold more was she virtuous; in her there lacked no quality which discreet folk can praise. She was chaste, as well in spirit as in body, wherefore she bloomed in virginity with all humility and abstinence, temperance and patience, and with measure in her bearing and adornment. She was ever discreet in replying. Though I dare to say she was as wise as Pallas and her speech as ready as any woman's, she had no artificial terms to seem wise. She spoke according to her degree, and all her words, great and small, were full of virtue and good breeding. She was shamefast with a young maiden's shamefastness, constant in heart and ever busy to drive out sloth. Bacchus had no mastery over her mouth, for wine and youth foster Venus, as fire when men cast oil or grease therein. For very virtue and of her own motion, she often feigned her sick, to flee company where folly was like to be talked of, as at feasts, revels and dances, that be occasion of wantonness. Such things make children too soon mature and bold, which has ever been perilous. All too soon may the child learn to be bold when she has waxed a wife.

And you elderly duennas, who have the governing of lords' daughters, take not my words amiss, but remember that you are set over them only for one of two reasons; either because you have kept virtue, or because you have fallen into frailty, and, having wholly forsaken such misconduct for evermore, know well the old game. Therefore, for Christ's sake, look that you be not slack to teach them virtue. A poacher of venison, who has forsworn his old greed and cunning, can keep a forest the best of any. Now watch over them well, for you can if you will. Look well that you assent to no slip, lest you be condemned for your evil mind, for whoso does is a traitor, of a surety. And take heed of this; of all treason the most pestilent and hellish is when a person betrays innocence. You fathers and mothers also, who have children one or two, yours is all the surveillance over them, whilst they are under your care. Beware that by the ensample of your life or by your negligence in correcting they perish not, for if they do, I dare truly say you shall dearly pay for it. Under a soft and negligent shepherd, the wolf has torn many a sheep and lamb. Let this one ensample suffice here, for I must return to my tale.

This maid of whom I tell so kept herself that she needed no duenna, for in her life maidens might read, as in a book, every good word and act that befits a virtuous maid; so prudent was she and kind. On every side spread the fame of her beauty and goodness, so that throughout that land all who loved virtue praised her; except envy alone, that is ever sorry for other men's weal and glad of their sorrow and sickness (the doctor Augustine so describes it).

Upon a day this maid went toward a temple in the town, with her dear mother, as is the manner of young maids. Now in this town was a justice, who was the governor of this region, and so befell that he cast his eye upon this maid, noting her well as she came past where he stood. Anon his heart and thought were changed, so was he caught with her beauty, and he said privily to himself, 'This maid shall be mine in spite of any man.' Anon the fiend slipped into his heart, and showed him right soon how by cunning he might win the maiden to his purpose; neither by force nor bribe, he thought, could he speed, for she was strong in her friends and confirmed in such extreme goodness that well he knew he could never win her to evil. Wherefore after great deliberation he sent for a churl in that city whom he knew to be both bold and cunning. To him this judge told his tale in secret wise and took his assurance to tell no creature; and if he did, he should lose his head. When this cursed plan was agreed to, the judge was glad, and made him great cheer and gave him rich and precious gifts.

When the conspiracy was planned from point to point, how his sin should be full subtly performed, as you shall soon hear plainly, home went the churl, whose name was Claudius. This false judge, who was called Appius (so was his name, for this is no fable but a notable historical thing, — the substance of it is true without any doubt), — this judge went about to hasten his joy all that he might. And so befell soon after, as the book tells us, that he was sitting in his consistory, as he was wont, and giving out his judgments upon sundry cases. This false churl came rushing in and said, 'So please you, lord, do me right upon this piteous bill of complaint against Virginius. And if he shall say it is not true, I will prove it and find good witnesses, that my bill tells the truth.'

The judge answered, 'Unless he be here I cannot give a final sentence. Let him be called, and after that I will listen gladly. You shall have all justice here, and no wrong.'

Virginius came to know what the judge would have, and forthwith the cursed bill was read, the effect of which you shall hear: 'To you my dear lord, Sir Appius, showeth your poor servant Claudius how a knight, called Virginius, against the law and all equity, and expressly against my will, holds my servant, my rightful thrall, who one night was stolen from my house whilst she was full young. This will I prove by witness, lord, so please you. She was never his daughter, whatsoever he may say. Wherefore I petition you, my lord the judge, so please you, yield me my thrall.' Lo, this was the substance of his bill.

Virginius began to stare upon the churl; but ere he could tell his tale (which he would have proved as a knight should, and have certified by many a witness, that it was false which his adversary said), this cursed judge would not wait at all nor hear a word more from him, but gave his judgment thus: 'I decree that this churl shall have his thrall forthwith; you shall keep her in your house no longer. This is my award; go bring her forth and put her in our keeping; this churl shall have his thrall.'

When the worthy knight by the justice's sentence must perforce give his daughter to the judge, to live in sin, he went home and sat him down in his hall, summoned his dear daughter, and with a face deathlike as cold ashes gazed upon her humble face with a father's pity striking through his heart, albeit he would not turn from his purpose. 'Daughter,' quoth he, 'Virginia, there are two ways, death or shame, which you may go, alas that I was born! For never have you deserved to die by blade or sword. O ender of my life, daughter dear, whom I fostered up with such joy that you were never out of my remembrance! O daughter who are my last woe and last joy of my life, oh gem of chastity, take your death in patience, for this is my doom. For love and not for hate you must die. My merciful hand must smite off your head. Alas that ever Appius saw you! This false judgment has he given on you to-day.' And he told her all the case as you have heard; it needs not tell it more.

'Mercy, dear father,' quoth the maiden, and laid her two arms about his neck, as she was wont; the tears burst from her two eyes as she said, 'Good father, must I die? Is there no help?'

'No, dear daughter mine,' said he.

'Then give me space,' quoth she, 'my father, to bewail my death a little; for Jephthah certes gave his daughter time to lament ere he slew her, alas! And God wot that she had no guilt except that she ran to meet her father first to welcome him with great honour.' And with that word she fell down in a swoon. When her swoon was past, she rose up and said to her father, 'Blessed be God, I die a maid. Give me my death ere I have dishonour. Do your will with your child, in the name of God!'

And then she prayed him oft to smite gently with his sword, and then she swooned again. Her father, with sorrowful heart and will, smote off her head, and holding it by the hair, went to display it to the judge where he still sat in consistory. When the judge saw it, the book tells, he bade take him and hang him straightway. But anon a thousand people burst in to save the knight, of their pity and ruth. For this false iniquity was known; the people anon had suspicion, by the manner of the churl's challenge, that it was by Appius's consent; they well knew that he was lascivious. Wherefore they came anon against this Appius and cast him into prison, where he slew himself. And Claudius, the servant of Appius, was condemned to be hanged upon a tree; but that Virginius, of his clemency, so prayed for him that he was exiled, or else of a surety he had been made an end of. The remnant were hanged, great and small, who were of consent in this cursedness.

Here may men see how sin has its deserts. Beware, for no man knows a whit whom God will smite, nor how the worm of conscience may tremble at a wicked life, though it be so privy that none wot of it but the sinner and God. For be he ignorant or learned, he knows not how soon he shall be made afraid. Therefore I counsel you, receive this warning: forsake sin ere sin forsake you.

The words of the Host to the Physician and the Pardoner

Our Host began to swear like mad. 'Out! Alas! By the holy rood, this was a false churl and a false justice! As shameful a death as heart can think come to these judges and their advocates! But all the same, this poor maid is slain, alas! She bought her beauty too dearly; wherefore I say, as men may see, fortune's or nature's gifts ever cause death to many a creature. Her beauty was her death I say. Alas, how pitifully she was slain! From both these gifts I spoke of now, men often have more harm than profit. But truly, my own dear master, this is a piteous tale to hear. But natheless it is no matter, pass it over; I pray God save your gentle body, and your Hippocrateses and your Galens, and your jugs and vessels and every box full of your syrops. God bless them and our Lady Saint Mary! As I live, you are a proper fellow and like a prelate, by Saint Ronan. Said I not well? I cannot speak like a scholar, but I know well that you made my heart so ache that I have wellnigh caught a spasm. 'Sblood! Unless I take physic, or else a draught of musty and malty beer, or hear a merry tale forthwith, my heart is done for, in pity for this maid. You there, you Pardoner,' he said, 'tell us at once some mirth or sport.'

'By Saint Ronan, it shall be done,' quoth he, 'but first I will drink and eat a bit of bread here at this ale-house.'

But straightway the gentlefolk began to call out, 'Nay, let him not tell ribaldry; tell us some moral thing that we may learn some wisdom, and then we will gladly hear.'

'I agree, certainly,' quoth he, 'but I must have time to think up some virtuous thing while I drink.'

Prologue to the Pardoner's Tale

'Lordings,' quoth he, 'when I preach in churches, I strive after a high-resounding voice, and I ring it out as round as a bell, for I know by rote all that I say. My theme is and ever was one and the same, — *Radix malorum est cupiditas*. First I pronounce whence I come, and then I show my bulls, one and all, but first the seal of our liege lord the king upon my patent, — that I show first to secure my body, lest any man, priest or clerk, be so bold as to disturb me in Christ's holy labours. After that I say forth my say, and show bulls of popes and cardinals and patriarchs and bishops, and in Latin I speak a few words to give a savour to my preaching and to stir men to devotion. Then I show forth my long crystal boxes, crammed full of clouts and bones; all the folk ween that they are holy relics. I have a shoulder-bone set in latten which came from an holy Jew's sheep. "Good men," I say, "mark my words; wash this bone in any spring, and if a cow or calf or sheep or ox swell up that has been stung or bitten by any serpent, take water from this spring and wash its tongue and it will be whole anon. And moreover, every sheep that drinks a draught from this spring shall be whole of pox or scabs or sore. And mark what I say. If the goodman that owns the beasts will drink, fasting, a draught from this spring every week ere cock-crow, as this holy Jew taught our fore-fathers, his beasts and his stock shall multiply. And sirs, it will cure jealousy also; though a man be fallen into a jealous fury, only make this pottage with this water and he will nevermore mistrust his wife, though he know the very truth of her fault, — though she had taken two or three priests.

' "Here too is a mitten. He that will put his hand in this mitten shall see his grain multiply, be it wheat or barley; so he offer pence, or else groats.

' "But, good men and women, of one thing I warn you; if any person is now in this church who has done a horrible sin and dares not be shriven of it for shame, or if any woman, old or young, has made her husband a cuckold, such folks shall have no power or grace to make offerings here to my relics. But whoso knows him to be free from such fault, let him come up and offer in the name of God, and I will assoil him by the authority granted me by bull."

'With this trickery I have won a hundred marks, year by year, since I have been a pardoner. I stand like a cleric in my pulpit, and when the lay folk are sat down I preach as you have heard and tell a hundred false cozening quips beside. Then I take pains to stretch out my neck and bob my head east and west over the people, like a dove perched upon a barn. My hands and tongue go so briskly that it is a joy to see my diligence. All my preaching is of avarice and such cursedness, to make them large in giving their pence and especially to me. My aim is all for gain and not at all for correction of sin. I reck not, when they are underground, though their souls go a-blackberrying! Certes, many a sermon arises from an ill intent, how to please and flatter folk and to aim for promotion through hypocrisy, now from vain glory and again from hate. For when I dare not otherwise have it out with a man, then I sting him with my bitter tongue as I preach, so that he cannot escape being falsely defamed, if he have trespassed against me or my brethren. For though I tell not his name, men shall know whom I mean by hints and other circumstances. Thus I requite folk who do us ill-turns, and thus I spit out my venom under the guise of holiness, seeming holy and faithful. I say again, in few words, I preach for no motive but avarice; wherefore my theme is and ever was, *Radix malorum est cupiditas*. Thus can I preach against that same vice which I practice, covetousness. But though myself be guilty of it, I can make other folk depart from avarice and repent full sore. But that is not my chiefest purpose, I preach for naught but covetousness; and this should suffice for this matter.

'Then I tell them many an ensample from old stories of long ago. For simple people love old tales; such things they can well remember and repeat.

'What! — believe you so long as I can preach and gain gold and silver by discoursing, that I shall live in poverty willingly? Nay, nay, truly I never thought of it! I will preach and beg everywhere I go; I will not labour with my hands nor make baskets to live by, only because I will not be an idle beggar. I will intimate none of the apostles. I will have wool, wheat, cheese, and money, were it given by the poorest lad or widow in a village, though her children pine and starve! I will have a merry wench in every town and drink liquor from the vine.

'But hearken, lordings, in conclusion. Your will is that I tell a tale. Now that I have drunk a good draught of malty beer, by the Lord I hope I shall tell you a thing that ought by reason to be to your liking. For though myself be a vicious man, yet I know how to tell you a moral tale which I am wont to tell in my money-getting homilies. Now hold your peace, and I will begin.'

The Pardoner's Tale

Once there dwelt in Flanders a company of young folk who followed after folly, as riotous living and gaming in stews and taverns, where with harps, lutes and citterns they danced and played at dice day and night, and ate and drank inordinately. Thus they did service to the Devil in cursed fashion within those Devil's temples by abominable superfluity. Their oaths were so great and so damnable that it was grisly to hear them swear; they rent our blessed Lord's body in pieces anew (as if the Jews had not rent him enough!), and each laughed at the others' sins. And anon came dancing girls, graceful and slim young fruit-wenches, singers with harps, bawds and confectioners, who are all very officers of the Devil to kindle and blow that fire of lust that is near allied to gluttony. I take Holy Writ to witness that in wine and drunkenness are excess and lust. Lo, how drunken Lot sinned against nature, not knowing what he did; he was so drunk he knew not what he wrought. Herod (let any one look up the history), when he was full of wine at his feast, gave command at his own table to slay the Baptist John, guiltless. Seneca also of a surety says a good word; he says he can find no difference betwixt a man that is out of his mind and him who is drunken, except that madness, when it attacks an ill-conditioned fellow, endures longer than drunkenness. Oh cursed gluttony, first cause of our undoing, origin of our damnation, until Christ redeemed us with His blood! Only think how dearly was this cursed sin paid for; this whole world was ruined by gluttony! Our father Adam and his wife in verity were driven from Paradise to labour and woe for that vice. For whilst Adam fasted I read that he was in Paradise, and when he ate of the forbidden fruit of the tree, he was cast out to woe and pain. O gluttony, well may we accuse thee! If a man but knew how many maladies follow from gluttony and excess, he would be more moderate of his diet as he sits at table. Alas! for the tender mouth and the short throat, east and west and south and north men labour in the earth and air and water to get dainty meat and drink for a glutton. On this, O Paul, well canst thou discourse. 'Meat unto belly and belly unto meat, — God shall destroy both,' as Paul says. Alas! foul is it to say, by my faith, but fouler is the act, when a man drinks so of the white and red that he makes a jakes of his throat through this accursed excess. The apostle, weeping, says piteously, 'There walk many of whom I have told you, and I say it now weeping and with a piteous voice, they are enemies of the cross of Christ, their end is death, their god is their belly. O belly, foul bag, full of corruption! what labour and cost to provide for thee! How these cooks pound and strain and grind, and turn substance into accident, to satisfy all thy greedy taste! Out of the hard bones they knock the marrow, and cast away naught that may go through the gullet soft and sweet. Of spicery and bark, root and leaf, is made the glutton's delicious sauce, to get him ever a new appetite. But he that follows after such delights, certes, is dead while he lives in those vices.'

Wine is a lecherous thing, and drunkenness is full of wretchedness and of contention. O drunken man, thy face is disfigured, thy breath is sour, thou art foul to clasp in arms, and the sound through thy drunken nose seems as if thou saidest ever, 'Sam-soun, Sam-soun!' And yet Samson drank never wine, God wot. Thou fallest like a stuck pig, thy tongue is lost and all thy care for honest things, for drunkenness is the very sepulchre of man's wit and discretion. He over whom drink has dominion can keep no counsel, of a surety. Now keep you from the wine white and red, and chiefly from the white wine of Lepe for sale in Fish Street, or Cheapside. This Spanish wine subtly creeps through other wines growing hard by, and such fumes arise therefrom that after two or three draughts, though a man deem himself to be at home in Cheapside, he is even at the town of Lepe in Spain, not at Rochelle nor at Bordeaux; and then he will say. *'Sam-soun, Sam-soun!'*

But hearken to one word, I pray you, lordings all; the supreme acts of victory in the Old Testament, I dare be bound, were done through the help of the true omnipotent God in prayer and abstinence. Look into the Bible and there you may see it. Look too at Attila, the great conqueror, who died in shame and disgrace, bleeding at his nose in a drunken sleep. A great captain should live soberly. And moreover, consider right carefully what was commanded to Lemuel, — not Samuel, I say, but Lemuel; read the Bible and find it expressly set down as to giving wine to them that have oversight of justice. But no more now, for this may suffice.

Now that I have spoken of gluttony, I will forbid you gaming, which is the very mother of lies, deceit, and cursed for forswearing, of blasphemy of Christ, manslaughter and waste of money and of time; and furthermore, it is a disgrace and against all honour to be known as a common gamester. And ever the higher a man's estate, the more abandoned he is held to be. If a prince practise hazard, by all temperance and public policy common opinion will hold him the lower in reputation. Stilbon, the wise ambassador, was sent to Corinth in great pomp from Lacedaemon to make an alliance; and when he came he chanced to find all the greatest men of that land playing at hazard. Wherefore, as soon as might be, he stole home again to his country and said, 'I will not lose my good name there, nor will I take on me such a shame as to ally you to gamblers. Send other wise ambassadors; for by my troth I would rather die than ally you with gamesters. For you who be so glorious in honours shall not be allied with gamesters by my will, or treaty of my making.' Thus spake this wise philosopher. Look also how the king of the Parthians, as the book tells us, sent in scorn a set of golden dice to King Demetrius because he had practised gambling; wherefore he held at no value his glory and renown. Lords may find other kinds of virtuous diversion to pass the day with.

Now I will speak a work or two of false and great oaths that old books treat of. Violent swearing is an abominable thing, and false swearing is yet more to be blamed. The high God, as witness Matthew, forbade swearing at all; but especially the holy Jeremy says of swearing, 'Thou shalt say thine oaths in sooth, and not lie, and swear in righteousness and judgment.' But idle swearing is a cursedness. Behold how in the first table of the high God's glorious commandments the second commandment is, 'Take not my name amiss or in vain.' Lo, He forbids such swearing earlier than He forbids homicide or many other cursed things. I say that it stands in this order, as any one knows who knows the commandments, how that is the second commandment. And moreover I tell you flatly that vengeance will not depart from the house of him who is too outrageous of his oaths. 'By God's precious heart and by the nails of His cross, by the blood of Christ in the abbey of Hales, my chance is seven; yours is five and three. By God's arms, if you play falsely, this dagger shall go through your heart!' This is the fruit that comes of the two dice-bones, forswearing, ire, falseness, murder. Now for the love of Christ Who died for us, forsake your oaths, great and small. But, sirs, I will now tell on my tale.

These three rioters of whom I speak, long before any bell had rung for prime, were set down in a tavern to drink. And as they sat, they heard a bell tinkle that was carried before a corpse to his grave. One of them called to his boy, 'Off with you, and ask straightway what corpse it is passing by; and see you report his name aright.'

'Sir,' quoth the boy, 'it needs not. It was told me two hours before you came here; he was an old fellow of yours, perdy, and he was slain suddenly in the night, as he sat very drunk on his bench. A privy thief men call Death, that slays all the people in this country-side, came with his spear and smote his heart in two, and went his way without a word. He has slain a thousand in this pestilence; and master, ere you come before him, methinks you were best be warned of such an adversary. Be ready to meet him ever; thus my mother taught me, I can say no more.'

'The child speaks truth, by St. Mary,' said the taverner, 'for over a mile hence, in a large village, he has slain both woman, child, churl and knave. I believe his habitation be there. It were great wisdom, a man to be on his guard lest he do him a hurt.'

'Yea, God's arms!' quoth this reveller, 'is it such peril to meet with him? I vow to God's bones I will seek him in the highways and the byways. Hearken, fellows, we are all as one; let each of us hold up his hand and become the others' brother, and slay this false traitor Death. He shall be slain ere night that slays so many, by God's dignity!'

These three plighted their troth together, each to live and die for the rest as he were their sworn brother, and up they all started in this drunken fury, and forth they went toward that village of which the taverner had spoken; and many a grisly oath they swore, and Christ's blessed body they rent to pieces, — 'Death shall be dead if they can but catch him.'

When they had gone but a little way, even as they were treading over a stile, an old man and poor met them, and greeted them full meekly, and said, 'Now, lordings, God be with you!'

The proudest of these three revellers answered, 'What, churl, bad luck to you! Why are you all wrapped up save your face? Why live you so long and so decrepit?'

This old man began to peer into his visage, and said, 'Because I cannot find a man, though I walked from hence to India, in hamlet or in city, who will exchange his youth for mine age. And therefore I must keep mine old age as long as it is God's will. Alas, death will not take me! Thus I walk, a restless caitiff, and thus morn and night I knock with my staff upon the ground, which is my mother's gate, and say, "Dear mother, let me in. Lo, how I vanish away, flesh and skin and blood! Alas, when shall my bones be at peace? Mother, I would exchange my chest with you, which has been long time in my chamber, yea, for an hair-cloth shroud to wrap me in!" But still she will not do me that favour; wherefore my face is full pale and withered. — But sirs, it is not a courteous thing to speak churlishly to an old man, unless he trespass in act or word. You may read yourselves in Holy Writ, "Before an old hoary-head man ye shall arise;" wherefore I counsel you, do no harm now to an old man, no more than you would that it were done to you in your old age, if you abide so long. And now God be with you, wherever you go or be; I must go whither I have to go.'

'Nay, old churl, not so fast, by God,' said this second gamester straight-away. 'By St. John, you part not so lightly! You spoke even now of that traitor Death who slays all our friends in this country-side. By my troth, you are his spy! Tell where he is, or by God and the Holy Sacrament you shall pay for it. Truly you are of his consent to slay us young folk, false thief.'

'Now sirs,' quoth he, 'if you are so fain to find Death, turn up this crooked path; for by my faith I left him in that grove under a tree, and there he will tarry, nor for all your bluster will he hide him. See you that oak? There you shall find him. May God, Who redeemed mankind, save you and amend you!' Thus spoke this old creature.

And each of these revellers ran till he came to that tree, and there they found wellnigh eight bushels, as it seemed to them, of florins coined of fine round gold. No longer sought they then after Death, but each was so glad at the sight of the precious hoard that they sat them down by the fair shining florins. The worst of them spoke the first word. 'Brethren,' he said, 'heed what I say; though I jest oft and make sport, I have a pretty headpiece. Now Fortune has given us this treasure that we may live the rest of our lives in mirth and jollity, and lightly as it comes, so we will spend it. Eh! God's precious dignity! Who would have weened to-day that we should have so fair a grace! Could this gold be but carried hence to my house or else to yours, — for you know well all this gold is ours, — then were we in high felicity. But truly it may not be done by day. Folk would call us sturdy thieves and hang us for our own treasure. It must be carried by night, as wisely and slyly as may be. Therefore I advise that we draw cuts amongst us all, and he that draws the shortest shall run with a blithe heart to the town and that forthwith, and privily bring us wine and bread. And two of us shall cunningly guard this treasure, and at night, if he delay us not, we will carry it where we all agree is safest.'

One of them brought the cuts in his fist and bade them look where the lot should fall. It fell to the youngest of them and he straightway went forth toward the town. So soon as he was gone, the second said to the third, 'You well know you are my sworn brother, and now I will tell you somewhat to your advantage. Here is gold great plenty, to divide amongst the three of us; and you know well our fellow is gone. Now if I can shape it so that it be divided among the two of us, had I not done you a friendly turn?'

'I wot not how that may be,' the other answered, 'he knows the gold is left with us two. What shall we do? What shall we say to him?'

'Shall it be a secret?' said the first villain. 'I shall tell you in few words what we shall do to bring it about.'

'I assent,' said the other, 'not to betray you, by my troth.'

'Now,' quoth the first, 'you know well we be two and that two shall be stronger than one. Look when he is set down; do you arise and scuffle with him as in sport, and I will rive him through the two sides, and look that you do the same with your dagger. And then shall all this gold be shared betwixt you and me, dear friend. Then may we both fulfill all our lusts, and play at dice at our own pleasure.' And thus were these two villains accorded to slay the third as I have said.

The youngest, going to the town, revolved full often in his heart the beauty of those bright new florins. 'O Lord,' quoth he, 'if so be I could have all this treasure to myself, no man living under God's throne should live so merry as I!' And at last the fiend, our enemy, put it into his thought to buy poison with which to slay his two fellows; for the fiend found him in such a way of life that he had leave to bring him to perdition, for utterly his full purpose was to slay them both and never to repent. And forth he went without delay into the town to an apothecary, and prayed him to sell him some poison that he might kill his rats; and also there was a pole-cat in his yard, he said, which had killed his capons, and he would fain wreak him upon the vermin that ruined him by night. 'And you shall have such a thing,' answered the apothecary, 'that, so may God save my soul, no creature in all this world can eat or drink of this compound the amount of a grain of wheat, but he shall die anon. Yea, he shall die the death, and that in less time than you can walk a mile, this poison is so violent.'

This cursed man gripped the box of poison in his hand, and then ran into the next street to a shop and borrowed three large bottles. Into two of them he poured his poison, but the third he kept clean for his own drink, for he planned to labour all night long carrying away the gold. And when this reveller, the Devil take him!, had filled his three great bottles with wine, he repaired again to his fellows.

What need to discourse about it more? For as they had planned his death, even so they slew him, and that anon. When this was done, one of the two said, 'Now let us sit and drink and make merry, and then we will bury his body.' And with that word he chanced to take one of the bottles where the poison was, and he drank and gave his fellow to drink also. Wherefore anon they both died. And certes Avicenna wrote never in any canon or any chapter more wondrous signs of empoisoning than these two wretches showed ere they died. Thus ended these two murderers, and also the false poisoner also.

O cursed sin, full of cursedness! O treacherous homicide! O gluttony, lust and gaming! Thou blasphemer of Christ with insult and great oaths habitual and proud! Alas mankind, how may it be that to thy Creator Who made thee, and redeemed thee with His precious heart's blood, thou art so false and unkind, alas!

Now, good men, God forgive you your trespasses and guard you from the sign of avarice. My holy pardon will cure you all, so you offer nobles and other sterling coin, or else silver rings, brooches, spoons. Bow your heads, bow them under this holy bull! Come up, wives, offer of your yarn! See, I enter your name here in my roll; you shall enter into heaven's bliss; I assoil you by mine high power, you that will make offerings, as clear and clean as when you were born – (lo sirs, thus I preach). And may Jesu Christ, our soul's physician, grant you to receive His pardon; for that is better than mine, I will not deceive you.

But sirs, one word I have forgot to say. Here in my wallet I have relics and indulgences as fair as any man's in Britain, that were given me by the pope's own hand. If any of you of devotion will make an offering and have mine absolution, come forth now and kneel down here and take meekly my pardon; or else take pardons all new and fresh as you go along, at every town's end, so you ever anew offer nobles and pence which be good and sound. It is an honour to every person here to have a competent pardoner to absolve you as you ride through the lonely country, in case of misadventure which might befall. Peradventure one or two may fall down off their horses and break their necks in two. Look what a security it is to you all that I fell into your company, who may assoil you all, high and low, when the soul shall pass from the body! I counsel that our Host here be the first, for he is most enveloped in sin. Come forth, Sir Host, and offer first, and you shall kiss all the relics, yea, for a groat; straightway, unbuckle your purse!

'Nay, nay, may I have Christ's malison if I do,' quoth he. 'Let be; it shall not be, on my soul. You would make me kiss your old breech and swear it were a saint's relic, be it never so foul! But by the holy cross and St. Helen, I would I had your guts in my hand instead of relics or halidom; pull them out, I will help you carry them. They shall be shrined in a hog's belly!'

This Pardoner answered not a word; so wroth he was, he would not speak.

'Now,' quoth our Host, 'I will not talk with you longer, nor with any other angry man.'

But anon when the worthy Knight saw all the people laughing, he said, 'Enough, no more of this. Sir Pardoner, be of merry cheer, and I pray you, Sir Host, that are so dear to me, kiss the Pardoner. And Pardoner, I pray you draw near again, and let us laugh and make sport as we did before.' And forthwith they kissed and rode on.

Prologue to the Wife of Bath's Tale

'Experience, though no authority were in this world, were quite sufficient for me, to speak of the woe that is in marriage; for, lording, since I was twelve years old, — God be thanked, Who lives forever, — husbands five have I had at church-door (for so oft have I been wedded); and all were worthy men of their degree. But in truth it was told me not long ago that since Christ went never but once to a wedding, in Cana of Galilee, by that same ensample he taught me that I should not be wedded but once. Lo! hearken what a sharp word for the nonce spake Jesus, man and God, beside a well, in reproof of the Samaritan woman; quoth he, "Thou hast had five husbands; and that man which hath thee now is not thine husband." Thus said he, certainly. What he meant thereby I cannot say; but I ask, why the fifth man was no husband to the Samaritan woman. How many might she have in marriage? As yet never in my life have I heard definition of the number. Men may divine and interpret up and down, but well I wot, of a surety, God expressly bade us to wax and multiply; that noble text I can well understand. Likewise well I wot he said also that my husband should leave father and mother and take me. But he made mention of no number, of bigamy or of octogamy. Why should men speak abuse of them?

'Lo, Sir Solomon the wise king! I believe he had more than one wife, and would to God it were lawful for me to be refreshed half so oft! What a gift of God had he in all his wives! No man has such, who lives now in this world. God wot this noble king, to my thinking, had a merry life with each of them, so joyous was his lot! Blessed be God that I wedded five! And they were the best that I could pick out, both of their bodies and of their coffers. Divers schools make perfect clerks, and much practise in many sundry employments verily makes the perfect workman. Of five husbands I am the scholar. Welcome be the sixth, whenever he shall come! In sooth, I will not keep me chaste wholly; when my husband is departed from the world, anon some other Christian man shall wed me. For then, the apostle says, I am free, a God's name, to wed where I list. He says that it is no sin to be wedded; better it is to be wedded than to burn. What reck I thought folk speak shame of cursed Lamech and his bigamy? Well I wot Abraham was an holy man and also Jacob, so far forth as I know, and each of them had more wives than two, and also many another holy man. When saw you that in any time high God by express word forbade marriage? Tell me, I pray you. Or where commanded he virginity? You know as well as I, out of doubt, that the apostle, when he speaks of maidenhood, says that thereof he had no precept. Men may counsel a woman to be single, but counselling is not commanding; he put it in our own judgment. For had God commanded maidenhood, then with that word had he condemned marrying. And certes, if no seed were sown, whence then should virgins spring? Paul durst not command a thing for which his master gave no behest. The prize is set for virginity; win it who can, let see who runs best. But this word is not to be taken by every person, but only where Almighty God lists to give the grace. The apostle was a maid, I wot well, but nevertheless, though he wrote that he would every creature were even as himself, all that is but counsel to virginity; and he gave me leave and indulgence to be a wife. So likewise, without shame and without charge of bigamy, may I wed again if my mate die. It were good, he said, to touch no woman, for it is peril to bring together fire and tow; you know what this ensample may mean. This is the sum of it all, — the apostle held virginity more perfect than the marrying of the frail; I call them frail unless man and wife would lead all their life in continence.

'I grant it well, I have no malice though maidenhood be set above bigamy. Them it pleases to be clean, body and soul; of mine own estate I will make no boast. For you well know a lord has not every vessel in his house made of gold; some be of wood, and do their lord service. God calls folks to him in divers manners, and each one has of God his own gift, — one this, one that, as it pleases God to allot. Virginity is a great perfection, and also devout continence. But Christ the fount of perfection, bade not every person go sell all that he had and give to the poor, and in such wise follow him and his footsteps. He spake this to such as would be perfect; and by your leave, lordings, such am I not. I will bestow the flower of my life in the acts and fruits of marriage.

'But I say not that every-one is bound to go and wed. Then should men take no heed of chastity. Christ was chaste though formed as a man, and many a saint since the beginning of the world; yet they lived in perfect chastity ever. I will have no malice toward virginity. Let virgins be bread of purified wheat-seed, and let us wives be called barley-bread; and yet, as Mark can tell, our Lord Jesu refreshed many a man with barley-bread. I will persever in such estate as God has called us to; I am not queasy. I will not retire; a husband I will have, who shall be my debtor and thrall, and have his tribulation upon his flesh, whilst I am his wife. As long as I live I have the power over his own body, and not he. Right thus the apostle told it me, and bade our husbands love us well. All this saying well pleases me.'

Up started the Pardoner, and that straightway; quoth he, 'Now dame, by God and St. John, you are a noble preacher in this matter! I was about to wed a wife; alas! why should I pay for it so dearly upon my flesh? Rather I would wed no wife this year.'

'Abide! my tale is not yet begun,' quoth she. 'Nay, you shall drink out of another barrel ere I go, that shall savour worse than ale. And when I have told forth my story to you, of the scourge that is in marriage, in which I have been expert all my life — that is to say, I myself have been the scourge — then you may choose whether you will sip of that same tun that I shall broach. Be mindful, ere you come too nigh; for I shall tell half a score of ensamples. Whoso will not be warned by other men, by him shall other men be warned; these same words writes Ptolemy; read his Almagest.'

'Dame,' said this Pardoner, 'I would pray you, if it were your pleasure, tell forth your tale as you began, spare for none, and teach us young men of your experience.'

'Gladly,' quoth she, 'if it please you. But I pray all this fellowship, if I speak after my fancy, take it not amiss. For mine intent is but to make sport. Now, sirs, I will tell on. May I never see another drop of ale or wine, if I say not sooth of my husbands; and three of them were good, and two of them were bad. The three men were good, rich and old, and by my faith, I set no store by them. They had given me their gold and their treasure; I needed no longer do my diligence to win their love or do them honour. They loved me so well that I set no value on their love. A wise woman ever alike will set her to win love where she has none; but since I had them under my thumb and had all their land, why should I take heed to please them, unless it were for my profit and pleasure? I ruled them so, by my faith, that many a night they sang "alack-a-day!" Not for them, I believe, was fetched the bacon that some men win at Dunmow in Essex. I governed them so well by my rules that each of them was full blissful and fain to bring me gay things from the fair. They were full glad when I spake friendly to them, for God wot, I chid them without mercy.

'Now hearken, you wise wives who can understand, hearken how craftily I bare me. Thus shall you speak, and thus you shall put them in the wrong, for there is no man can swear and lie half so boldly as a woman. I say this for the behoof of prudent wives when they have a little stepped aside from prudence.

A prudent wife, if she know how to stand her own friend, shall make a man believe that the chough is mad, and shall take witness of her own maid in confirmation. But now hearken how I spake: —

' "Sir old dotard, is this how you would have things? Why is my neighbour's wife so fine? She is honoured everywhere she goes, whilst I have no trim array and must sit at home. Are you in love? What do you at my neighbour's house? Is she so fair? What whisper you with our maid? *Benedicite!* Let be your japes, old sir lecher! And if I have innocently a friend or a gossip, and I walk to disport me at his lodging, you chide as a fiend. You come home as drunk as a mouse and sit on your bench preaching, Devil take you! You say to me, it is a great evil to wed a poor woman, for the cost; and if she be rich, of high kin, then you say that it is a torment to suffer her pride and her vapours. And if she be fair, you say that every rake will have her, you very knave! She who is assailed upon every hand cannot abide long in chastity. You say that some folk desire us for our wealth, some for our figure, some for our beauty, some because we can sing or dance, some for our manners and mirth, and some for our hands and slim arms. Thus all goes to the Devil, by your account. You say that a castle-wall may be so long assailed from every side that none can keep it. And if a woman be foul, then you say that she covets every man she sees, and will leap on him like a spaniel, till she find some man to chaffer for her. You say no goose so grey goes in the lake but will be after a mate, and that it is a hard matter to manage a thing that no man would willingly have at all.

' "Thus you say, old losel, when you are going to bed; and that no wise man need marry, nor any man who has a mind to heaven. With a wild thunder-dint and fiery lightning-bolt may your withered neck be snapped in two! You say that dripping houses, and also smoke, and chiding wives, make men flee out of their own homes. Ah, *benedicite!* What ails such an old man to chide thus? You say that we wives will cover our vices till we be fast-tied, and then we show them. That is a villain's proverb! You say that oxen, asses, horses, hounds are proved at some time, ere men buy them, and so be basins, lavers, spoons, stools, pots, cloths and attire and all such household stuff; but folk make no assay of wives till they be wedded. Old rascally dotard! And then, you say, we will show our vices.

' "You say also it mislikes me unless you praise my beauty and pore ever upon my face and call me 'fair dame' everywhere; and unless you make a feast on the day I was born, and dress me gay and freshly; and unless you do honour to my nurse, and to my maid in my bower, and to my father's kins-folk — all this you say, old barrel full of lies!

' "And yet you have caught a false suspicion of our apprentice Jankin, for his crisp hair shining like fine gold, and because he squires me back and forth. I would not have him, though you should die tomorrow! But tell me this — bad luck to you! — why hide you away from me the keys of your chest? Perdy, they are my goods as well as yours! Why think you to make a fool of the mistress of your house? Now by my lord St. James, however you may rage, you shall not be master both of my body and of my goods; one of them you must forego, maugre your eyes.

' "Why must you needs inquire after me or spy upon me? You would lock me in your chest, I believe! You should say, 'Wife, go where you will, take your pleasure, I will believe no tales; I know you for a true wife, Dame Alice.' We love no man who takes note or care whither we go; we would have our freedom. May he be blessed of all men, that wise astrologer, Sir Ptolemy, who says this proverb in his book Almagest,

> 'His wisdom is the highest in the land,
> Who never recks who hath the world in hand.'

You are to understand by this proverb — so you have enough, why need you reck how merrily other folk fare? For in sooth, old dotard, you shall have all you will of me. He who will forbid a man to light a candle at his lantern is too great a niggard; perdy, he should have never the less light. So you have enough, you need not complain.

' "You say also that if we make us gay with clothing and with costly dress, it is peril to our chastity; and yet, plague take you!, you must confirm it with these words of the apostle: 'Ye women shall apparel you in a habit made chastely and shamefastly, and not with tressed hair and gay gems and pearls, nor with gold, nor rich clothes.' I give not a fly for your text or your rubric. You said also I was like a cat; for a cat, if a man but singe its skin, will dwell ever at home; but if she be sleek and gay of her fur, she will not remain in the house an hour, but ere any day dawn, will forth to show her skin and go a-caterwauling. This is to say, sir rogue, if I be fine, I will run out, to show my rig.

' "Sir old fool, what ails you to spy after me? Though you pray Argus to be my sentry with his hundred eyes as best he can, in faith he shall not keep watch over me unless it like me. Still could I pull the wool over his eyes, by my thrift!

' "You say also that there be three things the which trouble all this world, and that no person can endure the fourth. Oh, dear sir rascal, Jesu shorten your life! Still you preach and say a hateful woman is reckoned for one of these adversities. Be there no other manner of similitudes that you may liken your parables to, unless an unlucky woman be one of them?

' "You liken woman's love to hell, or to barren land where no water can lie. You liken it also to wildfire; the more it burns, the more it lusts to consume everything that can be burned. You say that even as worms destroy a tree, right so a wife destroys her husband; this they know that are tied to women."

'Lordings, right thus I would stoutly affirm in my guile, to mine old husbands, that they said in their drunkenness; and all was false, yet I took witness of Jankin and also of my niece. O Lord! the pain and woe I did them, and full guiltless, by the rood! For I could bite and whine like a horse. I knew how to complain, though I were the culprit; else oftentimes had I been undone. He who first comes to the mill, first grinds; I complained first, and thus our war was ended. They were right glad to excuse themselves full hurriedly of things that they never had done in all their lives. I would accuse mine old husband of wenches, when he could scarce stand for sickness; yet it tickled his heart because he thought that I had so great fondness for him. I swore that all my walking abroad by night was to espy wenches whom he made merry with. Under colour of that I had many a privy jest at him; for all such wit is given to us when we are born. Deceit, weeping, and spinning has God given to women by nature, so long as they live.

'And thus I boast me of one thing; in the end I had the better in every way, by cunning, or by force, or by some manner of device, such as continual murmur or grumbling. And chiefest at night had they ill fortune; then would I scold and grant them no ease, till they had paid their ransom to me, whatever I would have. And therefore I tell this to every man: let him win who can, everything has its price. With empty hand men may lure no hawks. For the sake of gain I would give them their way, and make me a feigned willingness; and yet I never had pleasure in bacon, from Dunmow or elsewhere. And so I would be ever chiding them; though the pope had sat beside them, by my troth, I would not spare them at their own board. I paid them word for word; so may the Almighty Lord help me, though I made my testament right now, I owe them never a word that is not paid. By my wit I wrought it so that they were fain to give it up, else had we never been at peace. For though mine husband looked like a mad lion, yet should he fail of his end.

'Then would I say, "Good dear, take note how meekly looks Wilkin our sheep; come near, my spouse, let me buss your cheek. You should be all patient and mild, and have a sweet tender conscience, since you thus preach of the patience of Job. Endure ever, since you can preach so well; and unless you do, in faith we must e'en teach you that it is pleasant to have a wife in peace. Verily one of us two must bend to the other; and since a man is more reasonable than a woman, you must be the one. What ails you to grumble and groan thus? Is it because you would have me all to yourself? Why, take all, have every bit! Peter! I beshrew you, but ye love it well! If I would sell my love, I could go as fresh as a rose, but I will keep me for you only. You are to blame, I say the truth to you." Such manner of words had we; but now will I speak about my fourth husband.

'He was a reveller, that is, he had a paramour. And I was young and full of frolic, strong and stubborn, and jolly as a magpie. Well could I dance to a little harp, and sing like any nightingale, when I had taken a draught of sweet wine. Metellius, the hog, the foul churl, who with a staff bereft his spouse of her life, because she drank wine, should not have frighted me from drink, had I been his wife. And after wine I must needs think on Venus; for so surely as cold engenders hail, a lickerous mouth is mother to lechery. In a tippling woman is no denial, as lechers know by experience. But Lord, Lord! when I mind me of my youth and mirth, it tickles me about the root of my heart! To this very day it does my heart good that I have had my fling in my time. But alas! age, that envenoms all things, has bereft me of my pith and my beauty. Let them go. Farewell! the Devil go with them! The flour is gone, and no recall; now as best I may must I sell the bran. But even now will I strive to be right merry.

'Now will I tell of my fourth husband. I say I had great despite in my heart that he had pleasure in any other. But by the Lord and Saint Joce, he was quit! I made a rod of the same wood for his back; not with my body, in any foul manner, but truly I made folk such cheer that for anger and very jealousy I made him fry in his own grease. I was his purgatory on earth, by the Lord, — wherefore I hope that his soul is in glory now. For God wot, he sat full oft and sang, when his shoe pinched him right bitterly. No creature wist, save God and he, how sore I wrung him in many a wise. He died when I returned home from Jerusalem, and lies buried under the rood-beam, albeit his tomb is not quite so curiously wrought as the sepulchre of Darius that Apelles so cunningly made. It had been but a waste to bury him preciously! Farewell to him; he is now in his grave and in his chest, God rest his soul!

'Now will I speak of my fifth husband — God let his soul never come in hell! And yet he was the most villainous to me, as I feel yet on my ribs all on a row, and ever shall to my ending day. But he was so fresh and merry, and could wheedle so well, that though he had beaten me on every bone, anon he could win my love again. I believe I loved him best, because he was chary of his love. To say the sooth, we women have an odd fantasy of this matter; look what thing there be which we cannot lightly win; and thereafter will we crave and cry ever. Forbid us a thing, and that we desire; press on us hard, and then we will flee. Slight us, and we will set forth all our wares; a great press at market makes dear merchandise, and too cheap is held at small value. This every wise woman knows.

'My fifth husband — God bless his soul! — which I took for love and not for riches, was sometime a clerk of Oxford; and he had left school, and went to board with my gossip, who dwelt in our town — God have her soul! Her name was Alison. She knew my heart and my privity better than our parish priest, by my soul! To her I bewrayed all my counsel. For had my husband spat on a wall, or done a thing that would have cost him his head, I would have told his secret every bit to her, and to another worthy wife, and to my niece, whom I loved well. And full often so I did, God knows, which oftentimes made his face red and hot for very shame, and he would blame himself for telling me so great a privity.

'And so befell that once, in Lent, (so ofttimes I got me to my gossip, for ever yet I loved to be merry, and to walk from house to house in March, April, and May, to hear sundry tales) that Jankin the clerk, and dame Alice my gossip, and I myself, walked into the fields. All that Lent my husband was in London; I had the better leisure to play, and to see and to be seen of lusty folk. What wist I where my good lot was next ordained to be cast? Therefore I made my visits to vigils and to processions, likewise to preachings and to these pilgrimages, to miracle-plays and to weddings, and wore my gay scarlet gowns upon me. These worms and these moths and mites ate them never a whit, upon my peril! And wot ye why? because they were used well. Now will I tell forth what happed to me. I say that we walked in the fields, till in sooth we had such jollity together, this clerk and I, that in my foresight I spake to him, and told him how he should wed me, were I widowed. For, I speak it not in boast, certainly never yet was I without provision for marriage — nor for other things also. I hold that mouse's heart to be not worth a leek which has but one hole to jump to, and if that fail, then all is over. I made him to believe that he had enchanted me; my dame taught me that craft. And I said also I dreamed of him all night; he would have slain me as I lay on my back, and my whole bed was full of very blood; but yet I hoped that he should bring good fortune to me, for blood betokens gold, as was taught me. And all was false; I dreamed not a whit of it, save as in this I ever followed my dame's teaching, as well as in other things besides. But now, sir, let me see; what shall I say now? Aha! By God, I have it again. When my fourth husband lay on his bier, I wept ever and made doleful countenance, as wives must, for it is the custom; and I covered my visage with my kerchief. But since I had purveyed me a new mate,

I wept but little, I vow. In the morning my husband was borne to church by the neighbours, who made dole for him, and our clerk Jankin was one of them. So may God help me, when I saw him go after the bier, methought he had so clean and fair a pair of feet and legs that I gave all my heart into his power. He was twenty winters old, I believe, and if I am to tell the truth, I was forty. But I had ever a colt's tooth. I was gap-toothed; I bore the print of Saint Venus' seal, and that well became me. I was a lusty one, and fair, and rich, and youthful, and merry of heart, so may God help me. For certes, I am all of Venus in feeling, and my heart is Martian. Venus gave me my love for pleasure and my wantonness, and Mars my sturdy hardihood. Mine ascendent was Mars in Taurus. Alas, alas! that ever love was sin! I followed ever my bent by virtue of my constellation. That made it that I could not withhold my chamber from any good fellow. Yet I have the mark of Mars upon my visage and also in another place. For as I hope to be saved, I loved never discreetly, but ever followed mine appetite, were he short or tall, black or fair; I took no heed, so he pleased me, how poor he was, nor of what station.

'What should I say but at the end of a month this jolly clerk Jankin, that was so debonair, wedded me with great splendour? And I gave him all the land and fee which I had ever been given; but afterwards I repented me full sore, for he would suffer nothing that I desired. By God, he smote me once on the ear! That was because I rent a leaf out of his book, and my ear waxed all deaf because of the blow. I was as stubborn as a lioness, and a very chatterbox with my tongue, and I would walk as I had done before from house to house, though he had sworn I should not. Wherefore he would oftentimes make homilies and tell me about old Roman histories; how Simplicius Gallus left his wife and forsook her for all his days, for naught save that he saw her one day looking out of his door with head uncovered. He told me the name of another Roman who forsook his wife also because without his knowledge she was at a summer-game. And then he would seek in his Bible that proverb of the Ecclesiast where he commands and firmly forbids that a man should suffer his wife to go roll about. Then indeed he would say right thus,

> "Whoso buildeth his house all out of sallows,
> And spurreth his blind horse over the fallows,
> And suffereth his wife to go seek hallows,
> Is worthy to be hanged upon the gallows."

But all for naught; I cared not an acorn for his proverbs or his old saw, and I would not be chidden by him. I hate him who tells me my faults; and God wot, so do more of us that I! This maddened him against me, but I would never forbear for him.

'Now by Saint Thomas, I will tell you the sooth, why I rent a leaf out of his book, for which he smote me so that I became deaf. He had a book which he would be still reading, night and day, for his disport. He called it Valerius and Theophrastus; at this book he would ever be laughing consumedly. And also there was once a clerk at Rome, a cardinal, hight Saint Jerome, composed a book against Jovinian; and besides this in my husband's book there were Tertullian, Chrysippus, Trotula, and Heloise, that was abbess not far from Paris, and also the Parables of Solomon, Ovid's Art of Love and many a book; and all these were bound in one volume. And every night and day, when he had leisure and freedom from other outside occupation, it was his habit to read in this book about wicked women; of them he knew more lives and legends than there are of good women in the Bible. For trust well, it is an impossibility that any clerk will speak well of women, unless it be of the lives of holy saints; but of any other woman never the more for that. Who painted the Lion, tell me? By God, if women had written histories, as have clerks in their oratories, they would have written about men more evil than all the sons of Adam could redress. The children of Mercury and the children of Venus be full contrarious in their deeds; Mercury loves wisdom and knowledge, and Venus riot and prodigality. And, by reason of their diverse temper, each is depressed in the other's exaltation; thus Mercury is depressed in Pisces, where Venus is exalted, and Venus is depressed where Mercury is exalted. Therefore no woman is praised of any clerk. When the clerk is old and all unable to serve Venus worth his old shoe, then sits he down and in his dotage writes that women cannot keep their marriage vow!

'But now to my tale, why that I was beaten for a book, perdy, as I told you. Upon a night Jankin, our goodman, sat by the fire and read in his book, first of Eva, for whose wickedness all mankind was brought to misery, for which Jesu Christ Himself was slain, Who redeemed us with His heart's blood. Lo! here you may read expressly about woman, that she was the perdition of all mankind. Then he read to me how Samson lost his hair in his sleep; his doxy cut it with her shears, through which treason he lost both his eyes. Then I tell you he read me about Hercules and his Dejanira, who caused him to set fire to himself. Nor did he any wise forget the penance and woe which Socrates had with his two wives, how Xantippe cast foul water on his pate; this blameless man sat still as a stone, wiped his head, and durst say no more than, "Ere thunder ceases, comes the rain." Of his cursedness he found a relish in the tale of Pasiphaë, queen of Crete; fie! speak no more of her horrible lust and desire — it is a grisly thing. He read with full good devotion about Clytemnes- tra, that for her wantonness treacherously cause her husband's death. He told me also for what cause Amphiaraus perished at Thebes; my husband had a legend about his wife Eriphyle, who for a brooch of gold privily informed the Greeks in what place her husband hid him; wherefore he met a sorry fate at Thebes. He told me of Livia and Lucilia, who both caused their husbands to die, the one for hate, the other for love. Livia, late one evening, empoisoned her husband because she had become his foe; Lucilia, concupiscent, so loved her husband that she gave him a love-drink, that she might ever be in his mind, but of such a sort that he was dead ere morning. And thus in one way or the other husbands come to grief. And then he told me how one Latumius lamented to Arrius, his fellow, how there grew in his garden such a tree on which, he said, his three wives had hanged themselves with desperate heart. "Oh dear brother, give me a slip from this same blessed tree," quoth this Arrius, "and it shall be planted in my garden!" He read about wives of later date, that some have murdered their husbands in their sleep, and embraced their gallants whilst the corpse lay all night flat on the floor. And some have driven nails into their husband's brains whilst they slept, and some have given them poison to drink. He spake more evil than heart can devise.

'And therewithal he knew more proverbs than in this world grow blades of grass. Quoth he, "It is better to have thy dwelling with a lion or a foul dragon, than with a woman wont to chide." "Better it is," quoth he, "to dwell high in the roof, than down in the house with an angry woman; they are so wicked and contrary, they ever hate what their husbands love." He said, "A woman casts her shame away when she casts off her smock"; and again, "A fair woman, but she be also chaste, is like a gold ring in a sow's nose."

'None could think or dream the woe and fury in my heart. And when I saw that he would never leave reading all night in this cursed book, all suddenly I plucked three leaves out of his book, even as he read, and also I so took him on the cheek with my fist that he fell down backward into our fire. And he started up like a mad lion, and smote me on the head with his fist so that I lay as dead on the floor. And he was aghast when he saw how still I was, and would have fled on his way, till at last I came out of my swoon. "Oh, hast thou slain me, false thief, and hast thou murdered me thus for my land?" I said. "Ere I die, yet will I kiss thee." And he came nearer and kneeled down fairly and said, "Dear sister Alison, so God help me, I shall never smite thee again! Thou thyself art to blame for what I have done. Forgive it me; and that I beseech thee." — And yet again I hit him upon the cheek, and said, "Thief, thus much I am revenged. Now I will die; I can speak no more."

'But at last with great pain and grief, we fell into agreement betwixt ourselves. He gave into my hand all the bridle, to have the governance of house and estate, and over his tongue and hands to boot. And I made him burn his book then and there. And when I had got unto myself all the sovereignty, through a master-stroke, and when he said, "Mine own faithful wife, do as you will the rest of your days; be you the guard of your honour, and of my dignity also," — we had never dispute after that day. God help me so, I was as loving to him as any wife betwixt Denmark and India, and also as true; and so was he to me, and I pray to God, Who sitteth in glory, so bless his soul, of His sweet compassion! Now I will relate my story, if you will hearken.'

The Friar, when he had heard all this, laughed and said: 'Now, dame, so may I have joy, this is a long preamble of a tale!' When the Sumner heard the Friar make outcry, quoth he, 'Lo! God's two arms! A friar will evermore be meddling. Lo, good men! a fly and also a friar will fall into every dish and every affair. Why speak you of preambulation? What! amble or trot, or hold your peace and go sit down! You hinder our sport thus.'

'Yea, will you so, sir Sumner? Now by my faith,' quoth the Friar, 'I shall tell, ere I go, such a tale or two of sumner that all the folk here shall laugh.'

'Now, Friar, I beshrew your face,' quoth this Sumner, 'and I beshrew myself, except I tell stories, two or three, of friars before I come to Sittingbourne, shall make your heart grieve. For well I wot your patience already has left you."

'Peace, and that straightway!' cried our Host; and said, 'Let the woman tell on. You fare like folk drunk with ale. Do, dame, tell on; that is best.'

'All ready, sir, even as you will,' quoth she, 'if I have license of this worthy Friar.'

'Yes, dame,' quoth he, 'tell forth your tale, and I will listen.'

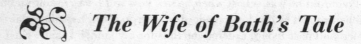

The Wife of Bath's Tale

In the old days of King Arthur, of whom Britons speak great glory, this land was all filled with fairy power. The elf-queen danced full oft, with her merry company, in many a green mead; this was the belief of old, as I find in books. I speak of many hundred years ago; but in our times no man can see elves any more. For now the great charity and the prayers of limiters and of other holy friars, who reach every land and every brook, as thick as motes in a sunbeam, blessing halls, towers, chambers, kitchens, cities, burgs, castles, thorps, dairies, barns, stables, bowers — this brings it to pass that there be no elves. For where a fairy was wont to walk, there walks the limiter himself now, of mornings or of afternoons, and says his matins and his holy things as he goes in his mendicancy. Women may go up and down in safety; in every bush, under every tree, save him, there is none incubus — and he will do them nought but dishonour.

And so befell that this King Arthur had a lusty young knight in his court, who on a day came riding from the river; and it happed that he saw a maid walking ahead alone as she was born, and her he ravished. For this violation there was such clamour and such appeal unto King Arthur, that the knight was condemned by course of law to die; and peradventure, such was the statue then, he would have lost his head, but that the queen and other ladies so long prayed the king for grace, till he granted him his life thereupon, and gave him over to the queen's will, to choose whether she would save him or let him die.

The queen thanked the king right heartily; and after this, upon a day when she saw her time, she spake thus to the knight: 'You stand yet,' quoth she, 'in such case that you have even now no assurance of your life. I grant you life, if you can tell me what thing it is that women desire most. Beware, and guard your neckbone from iron! And if you cannot tell it forthwith, I will give you yet leave to go for a twelvemonth and a day, to search out and learn an answer sufficient for this point. And ere you depart, I will have security that you will yield up your body in this place.'

Woe was this knight, and he sighed sorrowfully. But what! He might not do even as he list. And at last he chose to go and come again even at the year's end, with such reply as God should purvey him; and he took his leave and went his way forth.

He sought every house and place where he hoped to find such luck as to learn what women chiefly love. But he could arrive at no coast where he could find two creatures agreeing together on this thing. Some said that women best love riches; some said honour; some said mirth; some, rich array; some, lusty husbands, and to be widowed and wedded often. Some said that our hearts are most eased when we be flattered and gratified. They came full nigh the truth; a man shall best win us by flattery, I will not deny it, and by attentiveness and diligence we are caught, both great and small. And some said how we love best to be free and to do even as we will, and that no man reprove us for our faults, but say that we be wise and never foolish at all. For in sooth there is none amongst us, if any man claw us on a sore place, that will not kick, because he tells us the truth. Try, and he shall find it out who does so. For be we never so sinful within, we would be held for wise, and clean of evil-doing.

And some said that we have great delight to be accounted stable and also trustworthy and steadfast in one purpose, and never bewraying what men tell us. But that tale is not worth a rake-handle, perdy! We women can conceal nothing, as witness Midas; will ye hear the tale?

Ovid, amongst other small stories, says that Midas had two ass's ears growing upon his head under his long hair, which blemish he hid full cunningly from every man's sight, as best he could, so that none wist of it save his wife. He loved her most and trusted her; and he prayed her to tell of his disfigurement to no creature. She swore to him, 'Nay, nor to gain all the world she would not do that villainy and sin, to bring her husband so foul a name; for her own honour she would not do it.' But nevertheless she felt she should die, to hide a secret so long; it swelled so sore about her heart, it seemed to her, that some word must needs burst from her. And since she durst tell it to no human creature, she ran down to a marsh hard by; her heart was ablaze till she came there. And ever as a bittern bumbles in the mire, she laid her mouth down unto the water: 'Thou water, bewray me not with thy sound,' quoth she; 'I tell it to thee, and to none else. Mine husband hath two long ass's ears. Now my heart is whole and well again; now it is out. In very truth I could keep it in no longer.' By this you may see that though we bide a time, we can conceal no secret forever; it must out. If you will hear the remnant of the tale, read Ovid; there you may learn it.

This knight, of whom is my tale chiefly, when he saw he could not come by it — that is to say, what women most love — full sorrowful was the spirit within his breast. But home he went, he might not tarry; the day was come when he must turn homeward. And as he went, deep in care, it befell that he rode under a forest-side, where he saw four-and-twenty ladies and yet more go on a dance. Full eagerly he drew toward this dance, in hope of learning some piece of wisdom. But in truth, ere he fully came there, the dance was vanished — where, he wist not; and he discerned no living creature, save that he saw sitting in the green an old wife, a fouler creature none could imagine. At the approach of the knight this old wife arose and said, 'Sir knight, by this way lies no path. Tell me, by your faith, what seek you? Peradventure it may be the better for you; these old folk know many a thing.'

'My dear mother,' quoth this knight, 'in truth I am but a dead man, unless I can say what thing it is that women desire most. Could you instruct me, I would well pay you your reward.'

'Plight me your troth,' quoth she, 'on my hand here, that you will do the first thing that I require of you, if it lie in your power; and ere it be night I will tell it you.'

'Take my pledge here,' said the knight, 'I agree.'

'Then,' quoth she, 'I dare be bound your life is safe; for upon my soul I will stand to it that the queen will say as I do. Let see the proudest kerchief or caul of the whole court, who dare say nay to what I shall teach you. Let us go on, without further words.'

Then she whispered a word in his ear, and bade him be glad and have no dread.

When they were come to the court, this knight said 'he had kept his day, as he had promised, and ready was his answer.' Then were assembled to hear his answer full many a noble wife, and many a maiden, and many a widow, — because they be wise; and the queen herself sat as justicer. And then this knight was summoned. Silence was commanded to every person, and the knight was bidden tell in full audience what thing mortal women most love. This knight stood not like a dumb beast, but anon answered the question with manly voice, that all the court heard it. 'My liege lady,' quoth he, 'over all this world women wish to have sovereignty over their husbands as well as over their lovers, and to be in mastership above them. This is your chiefest desire, though you slay me for the word; do as you list, I am here at your will.'

In all the court there was neither wife not widow to gainsay what he replied, but all declared he was worthy to have his freedom. And at that word, the old woman started up whom the knight had seen sitting on the green.

'Your favour, my sovereign lady!' quoth she. 'Do me justice, ere your court break up. I taught the knight this answer, for which he plighted me his faith that he would do the first thing I should require of him, if it lay in his power. Before the court, then, I pray you, sir knight,' quoth she, 'that you take me to wife, for you well know that I have saved your neck. If I speak falsely, say me nay, upon your faith!'

This knight answered, 'I wot full well that such was my promise, alas and alack! But for the love of God, pray choose another request! Take all my goods; let my body go.'

'Nay, then,' answered she, 'I beshrew us both. For though I be foul, poor, and old, I would none of all the metal or ore that is buried under the earth or lies upon it, but I were thy wife, and thy love also.'

'My love!' quoth he, 'nay, my damnation! Alas that any of my kindred should be so foully mismated!'

But all this was for nought. This is the conclusion, that he was constrained, and needs must wed her. And he took his old wife and went to his chamber.

Now peradventure some men would say that of my negligence I take no care to tell you all the rejoicing and pomp which was at the celebration that day. To which thing I shall briefly answer, and say there was no joy nor celebration at all; but only heaviness and much sorrow. For he wedded her privily on a morn; and such was his woe, hid him all day after like an owl, his wife looked so ugly.

Great was his misery when he was alone with his wife; he tossed about and turned to and fro. His old wife lay evermore smiling, and said, 'Ah, *benedicite*, dear husband! fares every knight thus with his wife as you do? Is this the way of King Arthur's household? Is every knight of his so distant? I am your own love and your wife also, and I have saved your neck, and certes, I have never yet done you a wrong. Why do you so this first night? You fare as a man who has lost his wit. What is my guilt? Tell it me, for the love of God, and if I have the power, it shall be amended.'

'Amended!' quoth this knight. 'Alas, nay, nay; it cannot be amended forevermore! You are so loathly and so old, and also come of so low a lineage, that it is small wonder though I toss and turn. Would God my heart would burst!'

'Is this the cause of your unquiet?'

'Yea, certainly, and no wonder,' quoth he.

'Now, sir,' she replied, 'I could amend all this ere three days were gone, if I list, so you bear yourself toward me well.

'But when you speak of such gentility as is descended from ancient wealth, so that therefor you knights are men of breeding, — such arrogance is not worth a hen. Look who is ever most virtuous, openly and privily, and ever most inclines to do what gentle deeds he may; take him for the gentlest man. Christ wills that we claim our gentility from him, not from our ancestors' ancient wealth. For though all their heritage, by reason whereof we claim high station, descend to us, yet they cannot at all bequeath to any of us their virtuous living, which made them to be called gentle men and to bid us follow them and do in like manner. The wise poet of Florence, who is named Dante, has a noble saying on this matter; lo, in such rhyme is Dante's saying: —

> "Seldom into the branches of the tree
> Mounts worth of man, for He that gives it to us

Wills that of Him we claim nobility."

For we may claim naught as from our ancestors save temporal things which men may injure and impair. Every person also knows this as well as I, that if nobility were planted by nature in a certain family all down the line, then would they never cease to do the fair offices of nobility, both privately and before the world; they could never do villainy or sin. Take fire and bear it into the darkest house betwixt here and the mount of Caucasus, and let men shut the doors and go thence, nevertheless the fire will burn and blaze as fairly as though twenty thousand men beheld it; on peril of my life, it will hold to its natural office till it die! Here you may well see how nobility hangs not from ancient possessions, since folk perform not alway its works, as does the fire, lo! according to its nature. For, God wot, men may full often see a lord's son do shame and baseness; and he that will have esteem for gentility because he was born of a noble house and had virtuous and noble ancestors, and yet himself will not perform the deeds of gentility nor follow after his gentle ancestor who is dead, he is not noble, be he duke or baron; for base sinful deeds make a churl. For gentility then were but renown of your ancestors for their high worthiness, which is full extraneous to your person. Your gentility comes only from God. Then comes our true gentility of divine grace, and was in no wise bequeathed to us with our earthly station.

'Think how noble was that Tullius Hostilius, as Valerius tells, who rose out of poverty to high nobility. Read Seneca, and Boethius also; there you shall see expressly that he who does noble deeds is noble. And therefore, dear husband, I conclude thus: albeit mine ancestors were untutored, yet may the high God — and so I hope — grant me grace to live virtuously. Then I am noble, when I begin to live virtuously and to abandon evil.

'And you reproach me for poverty; but the high God on whom we believe chose freely to live in poverty. And certes every man, maid or wife, may well know that Jesus, King of Heaven, would not choose an ill manner of living. Verily, cheerful poverty is an honourable thing, so will Seneca say and other clerks. Whoso holds him content with his poverty, I count him rich, though he have not a shirt! He who covets is a poor creature, for he would have that which is not within his power. But he that has naught, nor covets to have, is rich, albeit you count him but a serving-lad. True poverty, it sings by nature. Juvenal says merrily, concerning poverty: —

> "The poor man as he strides along
> Before the thieves may sing a song."

149

Poverty is a hateful good, and a full greater ridder from cares, I believe, and also a great teacher of wisdom to him that takes it in patience. All this is poverty, though it seem wretched; and a possession which no-one will challenge. When a man is humbled, full often poverty makes him to know his God and himself also. Poverty methinks is a perspective glass through which he may see who are his true friends. And therefore, sir, I pray, so I grieve you not, upbraid me no more for my poverty.

'Now, sir, you reproach me for mine old age. And certes, sir, though there were no authority in any book to tell you so, yet you honourable gentlefolk say that men should do courtesy to an old creature, and for your gentle manners call him Father. And I could find authorities for this, I believe. Now you say I am old and foul — then dread you not to be a cuckold. For ugliness and age, on my life, are great wardens over chastity. But nevertheless, since I know what it is you would have, I shall fulfil your worldly will.

'Choose,' quoth she, 'one of these two things, to have me foul and old till I die, and to you a true, humble wife, never in all my days displeasing you; or else to have me young and fair, and take your adventure of the resorting to your house — or mayhap to some other place — which there will be for my sake. Now choose yourself which you will have.'

This knight took counsel with himself and sighed sore; but at last he spake after this manner: 'My lady and love, and my dear wife, I put me in your wise governance. Do you choose which may be greatest pleasure and greatest honour to you and me also; I care not which of the two, for it suffices me as it pleases you.'

'Then have I got the mastery over you,' quoth she, 'since I may make choice, and control as I list?'

'Yea, certes, wife,' quoth he; 'I hold that for the best.'

Quoth she, 'Kiss me, we be angered no longer. For by my faith I will be both unto you — that is to say, both fair, yea, and good. I pray to God that I may die mad, but I be as good and faithful as ever wife was since the world was new. And except I be in the morn as fair to see as any lady, queen or empress, betwixt the east and the west, do with my life and death as you will. Cast up the curtain, look how it is.'

And when the knight saw verily that she was so fair and likewise so young, he clasped her in his two arms for joy, his heart bathed in a bath of bliss. A thousand times together he kissed her.

And she obeyed him in all which might cause him delight or pleasure. And thus they lived in perfect joy to the end of their lives. And may Jesu Christ send us husbands meek, young, and lusty, and grace to overlive them that we wed. And also I pray Jesu to shorten their days that will not be ruled by their wives. And old, angry niggards of money, God send them betimes a very pestilence!

Prologue to the Friar's Tale

This noble Friar, this worthy limiter, was casting ever a kind of lowering cheer upon the Sumner, but as yet, for manners' sake, he spoke no ill word to him. But finally he said to the wife, 'Dame,' quoth he, 'may God give you joy! So may I prosper, you have here touched upon a great difficulty and a matter for the schools. You have said many a thing and right well, I aver. But, dame, as we ride by the way here, it needs not speak save of mirth; and in God's name leave quoting of authorities to preachings and also to the schools of learning. But if it please this company, I will tell you a jest about a sumner. Perdy! by the very name you may well know that no good may be spoken of a sumner — I pray none of you be ill-pleased. A sumner is a runner up and down with summons for fornications, and is beaten at every town's end.'

Then our Host spake: 'Ah, sir, you ought to be courteous and gentle, a man of your station. We will have no brawling in company. Tell your story, and let the Sumner be.'

'Nay,' quoth the Sumner, 'let him say whatsoever he lists. When it comes my turn, by God, I shall repay him every whit. I shall tell him how great an honour it is to be a flattering limiter, and I shall tell him what his office is, in good sooth.'

'Peace, no more of this,' quoth our Host. And then he said to the Friar, 'Tell on your tale, master mine.'

The Friar's Tale

Once there dwelt in my country an archdeacon, a man of high estate, who did bold execution in punishing fornication, witchcraft and pandering, slander, and adultery; offences of church-wardens, breaches of wills and contracts, neglect of the sacraments, and also many another manner of offence, which it needs not rehearse at this time; and also usury and simony. But certes, he brought greatest woe to lechers. They must sing, if they were caught! And those in arrears in their tithes were roughly handled, if any parson would make complaint on them. He missed never a chance to punish by fine. He made the people sing piteously for too small offering and scant tithes; for they were in the archdeacon's book ere the bishop caught them with his crozier. And then his jurisdiction gave him power to visit them with penalties. He had ready to his hand a sumner, there was no slyer boy in England; for he had his subtle crew of spies who told him of whatever might be to his profit. He could well spare one or two lechers to direct him to four-and-twenty more. For though this sumner were mad as a March hare, I will not refrain from telling of his rascality. For we are beyond his power; they have no jurisdiction over us friars, nor shall they ever, to the end of their lives.

— Quoth the Sumner, 'Peter! so are the women of the brothels put out of my power.'

'Peace, the black Devil take you!' thus said our Host. 'Let him tell his story. Now tell on, mine own dear master, and spare not, though the Sumner make outcry!' And then the Friar went on: —

'This false thief, this sumner, ever had bawds as ready to his hand as any hawk in England to come to the lure, and they told him all the secrets that they learned. For there was naught new in their acquaintance with him; they were his privy agents, and he drew great profit thereby, his master knew not alway how much. He could summon ignorant men on pain of excommunication, and they were glad to fill his purse and make him great feasts at the ale-house. And right as Judas had a little purse of his own and was a thief, even such a thief was he; his master had but half what was due him. He was, if

I shall give him his full praise, a thief, and a sumner, and a bawd. He had wenches also at his call, who told it in his ear whether Sir Robert or Sir Hugh or Jack or Ralf were with them, or whoso it might be. Thus were the wench and he oft in partnership. And he would fetch a feigned mandate and summon both of them before the chapter, and fleece the man and let the wench go. Then he would say to him, "Friend, for my love to you I will have you stricken out of our black books; you need have no more trouble in this matter. I am your friend, wherever I can aid you." Verily, he knew of more manners of extortion than I could tell in two years. For there is no hunting dog in this world that can tell a hurt deer from a sound better than this sumner knew a sly lecher or an adulterer or a paramour. And because that was the best of all his income, therefore he set all his mind to it.

And so befell upon a time that this sumner, ever watching for his prey, rode to summon a widow, an old beldame, feigning a case, because he would rob her. And it happed that he saw riding before him under a forest-side a gay yeoman. He carried a bow, and bright, sharp arrows; he wore a cape of green, and on his head a hat with black fringes.

'Sir,' quoth this sumner, 'hail, and well overtaken!'

'Welcome,' answered this yeoman, 'and every good fellow too! Where ride you under this green shaw? Will you far today?'

'Nay,' this sumner replied; 'here hard by is my purpose to ride, to raise a payment that pertains to my lord's dues.'

'Then are you a bailiff?'

'Yea,' quoth he. He durst not, for the very filth and shame of the word, say that he was a sumner.

'*Depardieux!*' quoth this yeoman. 'Dear brother, you are a bailiff and I am also. I am not known in this land. I would pray you of your acquaintance and brotherhood as well if it please you. I have gold and silver in my chest; if you hap to come in our shire, all shall be yours, even as you will have it.'

'Gramercy, by my faith,' said this sumner. And each pledged his troth in the other's hand, to be sworn brethren till death. And they rode on their way in pleasant converse.

This sumner, who was as full of prate as butcher-birds of spite, and always inquiring into all things, — 'Brother,' said he, 'now where is your dwelling, if I should seek you another day?'

This yeoman answered him in a mild voice: 'Brother,' quoth he, 'far in the north country, where some time I shall see you, I hope. Ere we part I shall so well direct you that you shall never miss my house.'

'Now brother,' spake this sumner, 'I prithee, whilst we ride by the way, since you are a bailiff as I am, teach me some subtle fetch and tell me faithfully how I may win most in mine office. And spare not for conscience or sin, but tell me, as a brother to me, how do you?'

'Now by my troth, dear brother,' said he, 'I shall tell you a faithful story. My wages be right small and strait. My lord is hard and stern to me, and my office is full laborious; and therefore I live by extortions. In sooth I take all that I can get; at least all that I spend I gain from year to year by cunning or by violence. Truly, I can tell it no better.'

'Now certes, so I do also,' quoth this sumner, 'I spare not to take, God knows, unless a thing be too heavy or too hot. What I can get privily, I have no manner of conscience in that. Without my extortion I could not keep body and soul together; nor will I be shriven for such japes, I beshrew these shrift-fathers, every one of them. By God and Saint John, we be well met! But, dear brother, tell me your name then,' quoth this sumner.

And in the meantime this yeoman began to smile a little. 'Brother,' quoth he, 'would you learn it? I am a fiend, my dwelling is hell. And I ride here about my pickings, to see whether men will give me anything. My pickings are all my income. Lo! how you ride for the same purpose, to win goods, you reck never how. Even so do I; for I would ride now to the end of the world for a prey.'

'Ah, *benedicite!* what say you! I thought you were truly a yeoman,' quoth this sumner. 'You have a man's shape as well as I. Have you then a determinate figure in hell, where you are in your natural state?'

'Nay, certainly,' quoth he, 'not there. But when we list, we can take a shape upon us, or else make it seem to you that we have one, sometimes like a man, or sometimes like an ape or like an angel; I can ride or walk in any form. It is no marvel that it be so; a lousy juggler can deceive you, and I know more craft than he, perdy!'

'Why,' quoth the sumner, 'ride you or walk in sundry shapes, then, and not alway in one?'

'Because,' he answered, 'we will make us such forms as are most fit to capture our prey.'

'Why take you all this labour?'

'For many a cause, dear sir sumner,' said this fiend. 'But there is a fit season for everything. The day is short, and it is past prime now, and yet this day I have won nothing. I would give my mind to gain, if I can, and not to explain our subtleties. For though I told them you, your wit is all too bare to understand them, brother mine. But yet, you ask why we labour; sometimes we be God's instruments and means to do His commands upon His creatures, when it pleases Him, in divers ways and shapes. Verily, we have no might without Him, if it please Him to resist us. And sometimes at our prayer we have leave to hurt the body only and not the soul. Witness Job, on whom we wrought woe. And sometimes we have power over both, that is to say, over soul and body also. And sometimes we be suffered to try a man, and bring disquiet to his soul and not to his body; and yet all is for the best. When he resists our tempting, it is cause of his salvation, though it were our intent to seize him, and not that he were saved. And sometimes we are servants to man, as to Saint Dunstan, the archbishop. And also I was servant to the apostles.'

'Yet tell me faithfully,' said the sumner, 'make you always new bodies thus out of the elements?'

The fiend answered, 'Nay; sometimes we feign, and sometimes we arise with dead bodies in divers manners, and speak as reasonably and fairly as Samuel did to the Witch of Endor. And yet some will maintain that it was not Samuel; I care not for your theology. But of one thing I forewarn you, I mock you not. You wish by any means to know how we be shaped; hereafter you shall come where you will not need to learn of me, my dear brother. For out of your own experience you shall be able to lecture from a pulpit on this subject better than Virgil, whilst he was alive, or Dante either. Now let us ride quickly; for I will keep company with you, till so be you forsake me.'

'Nay,' quoth this sumner, 'that shall not happen. I am a yeoman, as all men know, and I will hold my troth to you. For though you were the devil Sathanas, I will hold my troth to my brother, as I am sworn, and each of us is sworn, to be faithful brethren in this matter. And we both are going about our pickings. Take you your part, whatsoever men will let you have, and I shall take mine. Thus we may both live. And if either of us have more than the other, let him be loyal, and share it.'

'I agree, by my faith,' quoth the devil.

And with that word they rode forth upon their way. And even as they entered the outskirts of the town whither this sumner planned to go, they saw a cart laden with hay, which a carter was driving forth on his road. Deep was the mire, wherefore the cart was at a standstill; and the carter smote, and cried like mad, 'Come up! Brock! Scot! Spare not for the stones! The fiend fetch you, flesh and fell, as sure as ye were foaled! Such woe as I have had with you! Devil take all, horses, cart, and hay!'

This sumner said, 'Here shall we have sport,' and he drew near the fiend privily and negligently, and whispered in his ear, 'Hearken, brother; by your faith, hearken. Hear you not how the carter says? He has given it you, seize it forthwith, hay and cart and also his three nags.'

'Nay,' quoth the devil, 'never a bit, God wot; that is not his meaning, trust me. If you believe me not, ask him yourself, or else wait a while and you shall see.'

This carter patted his horses upon the crupper, and they began to stoop and pull. 'Up, now!' quoth he. 'Jesu Christ bless you, and all his handywork, great and small! That was well pulled, my own grey boy! I pray God and Saint Giles save thee! Now my cart is out of the slough, perdy!'

Quoth the fiend, 'Lo, brother, what said I? You may see here, the churl spoke one thing, but thought another. Let us go forth upon our journey. Here I shall gain no quitclaim payment.'

When they came out of the town somewhat, this sumner began to whisper his brother; 'Brother,' quoth he, 'there dwells here an old crone who had almost as lief lose her neck as give a penny of her goods. I will have twelve pence, though she go out of her wits, or I will summon her to our office, though I know no fault of her, God wot. But since you know not how to gain your living in this country, here take ensample from me.'

This sumner knocked at the widow's gate.

'Come out, thou old hag,' he cried. 'I believe thou hast some friar or priest with thee.'

'Who knocks?' said this widow. '*Benedicite!* God save you, sir, what is your sweet pleasure?'

Quoth he, 'I have here a bill of summons. On pain of excommunication look thou be before the archdeacon's knee tomorrow to answer for certain matters before the court.'

'Now,' said she, 'may the Lord Christ Jesu, King of kings, so verily help me, as I cannot! I have been sick, and that many a day,' quoth she; 'I cannot ride or walk so far, or it will kill me, so it pricks in my side. May I not ask for a bill of the indictment, sir sumner, and answer there through my proctor to such thing as men will charge me with?'

'Yes, pay me here on the spot,' quoth this sumner, 'let see, — twelve pence, and I will clear thee. I shall have but small profit therefrom, my master has the profit, not I. Haste thee, give me twelve pence, and let me ride away quickly; I can bide no longer.'

'Twelve pence!' quoth she. 'Now may my lady Saint Mary so surely help me out of care and sin, I have not twelve pence in my possession though I should gain this wide world. You well know that I am a poor caitiff and old. Show you charity on me!'

'Nay, then,' quoth he, 'the foul fiend fetch me if I excuse thee, though thou perish for it.'

'Alas!' she replied, 'I am not guilty, God knows.'

Quoth he, 'Pay me; or by the sweet Saint Mary I will bear away thy new pan for the debt thou hast long owed me, what I paid for thy penalty when thou madest thine husband cuckold.'

'By my salvation, you lie!' she cried. 'Never in all my days, wife or widow, was I summoned unto your court ere now; nor was I ever aught but faithful of my body! I give your body, and my pan also, unto the Devil black and rough!'

And when the devil heard her curse so upon her knees, he said, 'Now Mabely, mine own dear mother, is this that you say your wish in earnest?'

'May the Devil,' quoth she, 'take him, ere he did, and pan and all, unless he repent him!'

'Nay, old cob, that is not my mind, to repent me for aught that I have had of thee,' replied the sumner. 'I would that I had thy smock and all thy clothing.'

'Now, brother, be not wroth, but in all fair dealing your body and this pan,' quoth the devil, 'be mine by right. You must to hell with me to-night, where you shall know more of our secrets than a master of divinity.' And with that this foul fiend seized him; body and soul he went with the devil to the place where sumners have their heritage.

And God, Who made mankind after His likeness, save us and guide us one and all, and grant this Sumner to become a good man! And lordings (quoth this Friar), if this Sumner here would grant me the leisure, I could have told you, after the text of Christ and Paul and John and of many an one of our other doctors, such torments that your hearts might shudder; albeit, though I might speak for a thousand winters, no tongue can fully describe the pains of that same cursed house of hell. But, that we be saved from that cursed pit, watch, and pray Jesus for his grace so to guard us from Sathanas, the tempter. Listen to this word, and beware. The lion lies in wait ever to slay the innocent, if he can; dispose your hearts alway to resist the fiend, who will make you thralls and bondmen. He may not tempt you above your power for Christ will be your knight and champion against him. And pray that these sumners repent them of their misdeeds ere the fiend seize them.

Prologue to the Sumner's Tale

The Sumner stood up high in his stirrups. Against this Friar his heart was so maddened that he quaked with wrath like an aspen leaf. 'Lordings, I ask but one thing,' he said. 'I beseech you of your courtesy, since you have heard this false Friar lie, to suffer me to tell my tale! This Friar boasts that he knows about hell, and it is small wonder, God wot. Friars and fiends are but little apart. For you have ofttimes heard, perdy, how a friar's spirit was once carried off to hell in a vision, and as an angel led him about to show him all the pains there, not a friar saw he in all the place; of other folk in woe he saw plenty. Then spake the friar to this angel, "Now, sir," quoth he, "have friars such a fair fortune that none of them shall come to this place?"

' "Yes, many a million!" quoth this angel, and led him down unto Sathanas. "Now, Sathanas," said he, "hath a tail broader than the sail of a barge. Rise up, thou Sathanas," he cried, "let the friar see where the nest of friars is in this place!" And ere a man could walk half a furlong, even as bees swarm out of an hive, so there drove from out the place where the Devil sat twenty thousand friars all in a throng, and swarmed about through all hell, and came back again as fast as they could, and crept every one back whence they came; and he clapped himself down and lay full quietly. When this friar had looked his fill on the torments of this sorry domain, God of his mercy restored his spirit unto his body, and he awoke; but nevertheless he yet quaked for dread, so was the Devil's lair ever in his mind as his natural heritage. God save you all — save this cursed friar; and thus I end my prologue.'

The Sumner's Tale

Lordings, I believe there is in Yorkshire a marshy country called Holderness, about which went a limiter to preach and also to beg. And so befell that this friar had preached on a day at a church after his fashion; and especially and above all in his preaching he stirred up the people to pay for trentals, and for God's sake to give toward the building of holy houses, 'where divine service is honoured, not where holy church's goods are wasted and consumed, nor where alms are not needed, as amongst these endowed clergy, who may live, God be thanked, in weal and abundance! Trentals deliver from pains your friends' souls, young and old,' said he; 'yea, even when they be sung without any pause betwixt. A priest may keep merry and spruce, even though he sing more than one mass a day. Deliver out their souls forthwith; it is full hard to be clawed with awls or flesh hooks, or to burn or bake. Now for Christ's love, speed you fast.'

And when this friar had said all his mind, after *Qui cum Patre*, and after folk in church had given him what they would, he tarried no longer, but went his way, his frock tucked high and with scrip and a tipped staff. He began to peep and pry into every house, and beg meal and cheese or else wheat. His fellow had a staff tipped with horn, a pair of tablets of ivory and a style neatly polished, and as he stood, ever wrote the names of all the folk that gave him aught, as if he would pray for them. 'Give us a bushel of wheat, malt, or rye, a God's cake, or a morsel of cheese, or else what you will, we may not be choosers; a God's ha'penny or a mass-penny, or give us of your swine's flesh, if you have some; a strip of your blanket, dear dame, our dear sister! So, I write your name here; bacon or beef or such thing as you may have.'

A sturdy ruffian went ever behind them, who was their convent servant; and he bore on his back a bag in which he carried whatever folk gave them. And anon when the friar was out of the door, he scraped away every one of the names that he had written in his tablets; he served them with fables and mockeries.

—'Nay,' cried the Friar, 'there you lie, you Sumner!'

159

'Peace,' quoth our Host, 'for the love of Christ's dear Mother! Tell forth your story and spare not.'

'On my life,' quoth this Sumner, 'and so I shall.' —

He went from house to house so long till he came to a house where he was wont to be refreshed more than in an hundred other places. The goodman of the house lay sick, bedridden down upon a couch. *'Deus hic!* O Thomas, my friend, good day!' quoth this friar softly and courteously. 'Thomas (God reward you!), full often I have fared right well here; upon this bench I have eaten many a merry meal.' And off the bench he drove the cat and laid down his hat and staff, and scrip also, and seated himself softly. His fellow had walked on to town with his knave, to the hostelry where he planned to lie that night.

'O master dear,' quoth the sick man, 'how have you fared since the beginning of March? I have not seen you this fortnight or more.'

'God wot,' quoth he, 'I have laboured full diligently; and especially have I said many a precious orison for your salvation, and for our other friends, God bless them! I have been at your church to-day at mass, and after my simple understanding said a sermon, not entirely after the text of Holy Writ; for that is hard to you, I believe, and therefore I am willing to teach you all the interpretation thereof. Glossing is certainly a full glorious thing; for the letter slays, so say we clerks. I taught them there to be charitable, and to spend their goods where reason is. And I saw our dame there; ah! where can she be?'

'I believe she be in the yard yonder,' said this man; 'she will come straightway.'

'Eh, master! by Saint John, ye be welcome!' said this wife. 'How fare ye, truly?'

The friar arose full courteously and embraced her tight in his arms and sweetly kissed her, and chirped with his lips like a sparrow. 'Dame,' quoth he, 'right well, and as he who is every whit your servant. God be thanked, Who gave you both soul and body, I saw not this day in all the church so fair a wife, so God save me!'

'Yea? God amend defects, sir!' quoth she. 'At all events ye be welcome, in faith.'

'Gramercy, so I have ever found. But of your great goodness, dame, and by your leave, so it vex you not, I would speak with Thomas a little time. These curates are right negligent and slothful to search a conscience tenderly. My diligence lies in shrift, and in preaching, and in study of Paul's words and Peter's; I walk and fish for Christian men's souls, to yield Jesu Christ his due returns. All my mind is set upon spreading his word.'

'Now, by your leave, O dear sir, chide him well,' she said, 'for the love of the holy Trinity. Though he have all he can wish, he is as angry as a pismire. Though I cover him well at night and keep him warm, and lay mine arm over him, he groans like our boar, lies in our sty. I have no other profit of him at all; I cannot please him in any manner.'

'O, Thomas! *Je vous dis*, Thomas! Thomas! This the fiend does, this must be amended. Ire is a thing forbidden by the high God and thereof now I will speak a word or two.'

'Now, master, ere I go,' quoth this wife, 'what will ye dine on? I will go about it.'

'Now dame, *je vous dis sans doute*,' quoth he, 'if I had nought but the liver of a capon and only a bit of your soft bread, and after that a roasted pig's head (except that I would that no beast were killed for me), then had I homely sufficiency with you. I am a man of small sustenance. From the Bible my spirit draws its nourishment; my body is ever so ready and painful in watchings that my stomach is destroyed. I pray you, dame, be not vexed though I show you my counsel so, as to a friend. By God, I would tell it to but few.'

'Now, sir, but a word ere I go,' quoth she. 'My child died within these two weeks, soon after you went from this town.'

'I saw his death by revelation, at home in our dormitory,' said the friar. 'So God be my guide, I dare well say that within half an hour after his death I saw him borne to bliss in my vision, and so did our sacristan and our infirmarer. (They have been faithful friars this fifty year, and they may now make their jubilee and walk alone, God be thanked for his grace!) And with many a tear trickling on my cheeks, I rose up, and all our convent, without any noise or bells clattering; our song was *Te Deum*, and none other, save that I said an orison to Christ, thanking him for his revelation. For trust me right well, sir and dame, our prayers are more effectual and we see more of Christ's secrets than lay-folks, though they were kings. We live our lives in poverty and abstinence, and lay-folks in riches and profusion of meat and drink and in their foul delights. We hold in scorn all this world's pleasures. Lazarus and Dives lived diversely, and thereby had diverse guerdons. Whosoever will pray, must fast and be pure and fatten his soul and make lean his body. We fare as the apostle says: clothing and food suffice us, though they be not full fine. The cleanness and fasting of us friars makes Christ to accept our orisons.

'Lo, forty days and forty nights Moses fasted, ere the high and mighty God spake with him in the mount of Sinai. With empty belly, having fasted many a day, he received the law that was written with God's finger. And Elias, well you know, fasted long and was in contemplation on Mount Horeb, ere he had any speech with high God, Who is our life's physician. Aaron, who had governance of the temple, and also every one of the other priests, when they should go into the temple to pray for the people and do God service, they would never drink any manner of drink which might make them drunken; but there they would watch and pray in abstinence, lest they died. Take heed what I say. If they be not sober who pray for the people, — heed what I say! But no more, it suffices! Our Lord Jesu, Holy Writ records, gave us ensample of prayer and fasting. We mendicants, we blameless friars, therefore are wedded to poverty and chastity, to charity, humility, and abstinence, to persecution for righteousness' sake, to weeping, mercy and cleanness. And therefore our prayers, — I speak about us, we friars, we mendicants, — you may see are more acceptable to the high God than yours, with your feasts at the board. To speak the very truth, man was first chased *out* of Paradise for his gluttony; and in sooth man was chaste *in* Paradise.

'But, Thomas, hearken now. I have no text for it, I grant, but I find it in a kind of gloss, that our sweet Lord Jesu especially spake this concerning friars, when he said, "Blessed be they that be poor in spirit." And so on through all the gospel you may perceive whether its teachings be liker our profession or theirs that swim in endowments. Fie on their pomp and gluttony, and for their ignorance I despise them! Methinks they be like Jovinian, waddling as a swan and fat as a whale, vinolent like a bottle in the buttery, and worthy of all reverence are their prayers, good sooth! When they say the psalm of David for souls, lo, they say, "buf! *cor meum eructavit!*" Who save we follow Christ's gospel and footsteps, who are humble and chaste and poor, workers of God's word, not hearers only? Therefore even as a hawk springs up into the air with one soar, so the prayers of charitable and chaste, busy friars soar to God's two ears. Thomas! Thomas! On my life and by that lord that is called Saint Ives, were you not our brother you should never prosper! To Christ we pray day and night in our chapter, to send you speedily strength and health, that you may have the uses of your body once more.'

'God wot,' quoth he, 'I feel nothing therefrom! So Christ help me as I have spent upon divers kinds of friars full many a pound in a few years. Yet I fare never the better. Certainly I have almost consumed my goods; farewell my gold, it is all gone!'

'O, Thomas, do you so?' answered the friar. 'Why need you seek divers friars? He who has a perfect leech, why need he seek other leeches in the town? Your inconstancy is your ruin. Hold you me, then, or our convent, insufficient to pray for you? Thomas, that jape is not worth a mite; your malady comes because we have had too little. "Ah, give half a quarter of rye to this convent!" "Ah, give four-and-twenty groats to that convent!" "Ah, give a penny to that friar, and let him go!" Nay, nay, Thomas, it may not in any wise be thus. What is a farthing worth if it be parted in twelve? So, everything which is all united is stronger than when it is dispersed. You shall not be flattered of me; you would have our labour all for nothing, Thomas! The high God, who has wrought all this world, says that the labourer is worthy of his hire. Thomas, I would have nought of your treasure for myself, but because all our convent is ever so diligent to pray for you, and to build Christ's own church. Thomas, if you would but learn to help at building up of churches, you may find whether it be good to do, in the life of St. Thomas of India. You lie here, full of anger and ire, with which the Devil sets your heart blazing, and chide this blameless innocent here, your wife, who is so patient and meek. And therefore, Thomas, for your own good, if you will believe me, strive not with your wife. And carry this word away with you now; lo, what the wise man says touching this matter, "Be thou no lion within thine house; oppress not thy subjects, and cause not thine acquaintance to flee from thee." And Thomas, yet again I charge you, take heed of her that sleeps in your bosom. Beware of the serpent that creeps so slyly under the grass, and subtly stings. Hearken patiently, my son, and be warned that twenty thousand men have perished by striving with their wives and their mistresses. Now, Thomas, since you have so holy and meek a wife, why need you have contention? Verily there is no serpent so cruel nor half so fell when a man treads upon his tail, as a woman when wrath has caught her. Vengeance is then all that they desire. Ire is a sin, one of the great ones of the seven sins, abominable unto the high God; and it is destruction unto a man's self. This every ignorant vicar or parson can tell you, how ire engenders manslaughter. In sooth, ire is pride's instrument. I could tell so much evil of ire that my tale should last till to-morrow. And therefore I pray God day and night, may He never grant power to an ireful man. It is great harm and great pity to set an ireful man in high station.

'Once there was an ireful potentate, as Seneca tells; and during his rule, upon a day two knights rode forth, and, as Fortune willed, one came home, and not the other. Forthwith the knight was brought to the judge, who said thus, "Thou hast slain thy fellow; wherefore I condemn thee to the death." And he commanded another knight, "Go, lead him to the death, I charge thee." And it happened, as they went their way toward the place where he should die, that the knight returned whom men thought dead. Then they deemed that it was the best course to lead them both to the judge again. They said, "Lord, the knight hath not slain his fellow; here he standeth alive and whole." "By my soul," quoth he, "ye shall die, both one, and two, and three."

And to the first knight he said, "I condemned thee; thou must die in any case. And because thou art the cause why thy fellow dieth, thou also must needs lose thine head." And he spake to the third knight, — "Thou hast not done that which I commanded." And thus he caused all three of them to be slain.

'The wrathful Cambyses was also a drunkard, and ever took delight to be wicked. And so befell that a lord of his household, who loved virtuous morality, spake right thus on a day when they were alone together, "A lord, if he be vicious, is lost; likewise a repute for drunkenness is foul for any man, and chiefest for a lord. There is full many an ear and eye watching after a lord, — and he knoweth not where. For God's love, drink more temperately! Wine maketh a man miserably to lose his mind and also the power of all his limbs." "Thou shalt straightway see the contrary," quoth he, "and make proof by thine own experience that wine doth folk no such harm. No wine robbeth me of my power over hand or foot, or over the sight of mine eyes." And of his malice he drank much more by an hundred times than he had done aforetime. And straightway this cursed, wrathful wretch caused this knight's son to be brought, and commanded him to stand before him; and straightway he took his bow, and pulled the string up to his ear and slew the child with an arrow. "Now, have I a sure hand or no?" quoth he; "be all my might and mind gone? Hath wine robbed me of mine eyesight?" Why should I tell the knight's answer? His son was slain; there is no more to be said. Beware therefore how you jest with lords. Sing *Placebo*; and so shall I, whenever I am able, unless it be to a poor man. To a poor man we should show his faults, but not to a lord, though he be going to hell.

'Lo ireful Cyrus, that Persian, how he destroyed the river of Gysen, because a horse of his was drowned therein, when he went to conquer Babylon! He made that river so little that women could wade across it everywhere.

'Lo, what said he who knows so well how to teach? "Be no fellow to an angry man, nor walk by the way with a madman, lest it repent thee." There is no need to say more. Now leave your wrath, Thomas, dear brother; you shall find me as just as a square. Hold not the Devil's knife ever at your heart; your wrath wounds you all too sorely; but show me all your confession.'

'Nay,' quoth the sick man, 'by Saint Jude! I have been shriven this day by my parson. I have told him my condition fully. There needs speak of it no more, unless I list out of mine own humility.'

'Give me, then, of your gold for the building of our holy house,' quoth the friar, 'for, to erect it, many a mussel and many an oyster have been our food, whilst other men have fared delicately. And yet, God wot, the foundation is scarce finished, and as to the pavement, there is not a tile yet within our walls. By God, we owe forty pound for stones! Now, Thomas, help, for the sake of Him Who harrowed hell! Else we must sell our books, and if you lack our preaching, then the whole world will go all to destruction. For whoso would rob the world of us, so God save me, and by your leave, Thomas, he would steal the sun out of this world. For who can teach and work like us? And that is not only of late,' quoth he, 'but since Elias was, or Eliseus, there have been friars with their charity, our Lord be thanked! — that I find recorded. Now help, Thomas, for holy charity's sake!' And down he went on his knee anon.

This sick man waxed nigh mad with wrath. He would that the friar were in the flames, with his false dissimulation.

The household, which had heard this affray, came leaping in and chased out the friar. And forth he went with full angry cheer, and fetched his companion where he was with that day's winnings. He looked as it were a wild boar; he ground his teeth, he was so wroth. At a sturdy pace he went to the manor-house, where dwelt a man of great station, to whom he was ever confessor. This worshipful man was lord of that village. This friar came, as if he were in a frenzy, to where this lord sat at meat. Scarce could the friar speak a word, till at last he said, 'God save you!'

This lord looked up and said, *'Benedicite!* What, friar John! How are the times with you! I see well somewhat is amiss. You look as if the forest were full of thieves. Sit down now, and tell me what your grievance is, and if I have the power, it shall be amended.'

'I have suffered an insult this day, may God requite you!' quoth he, — 'down in your village; there is not in this world a lad so lowly that he would not abhor what I have received in your town. And yet nought grieves me so sore as that this old churl with his grizzled locks has likewise blasphemed our holy convent.'

'Now, master,' quoth this lord, 'I beseech you, tell me.'

'Not "master," sir,' quoth he, 'but servitor, — though in the schools I have had that honour. It pleases not God that men call us Rabbi, either in the market or in your great hall.'

'No matter,' he answered, 'but tell me all your grievance.'

'Sir,' quoth this friar, 'this day an odious mischief is befallen mine order and me, and so, *per consequens*, each rank in holy church, — God remedy it soon!'

'Sir,' said the lord, 'you know what is to be done. Discompose you not. You are my confessor; you are the salt of the earth and the savour. For God's love, keep your patience! Tell me your vexation.'

And forthwith he told him all. The lady of the house sat quiet all through, till she had heard all the friar's tale. 'Eh, God's mother!' quoth she, 'blessed maid! Tell me truly, is there aught else?'

'Madame,' quoth he, 'what think you hereon?'

'How think I?' she asked. 'So God prosper me, I say a churl has done a churl's deed. What should I say? God never let him prosper! His sick head is full of empty fancies; I hold him in a measure crazed.'

'Madame,' he answered, 'before God, I lie not; unless I may be avenged in another way, I shall defame him everywhere I speak, this false blasphemer, — the fiend have him!'

The lord sat as still as if he were in a trance, and revolved it in his heart; 'How had this churl the imagination to offer such a problem to the friar. Never until now have I heard of such. I believe the Devil put it into his mind. Eh, the villainous proud churl, I beshrew his face! Whoever heard of such a thing! What! lo, my churl! lo, how cursedly he spake to-day unto my confessor! Of a truth, I hold him a demoniac. Now eat your meat, and leave the churl to his sport. Let him go hang himself, in the Devil's name!'

Prologue to the Clerk of Oxford's Tale

'Sir Clerk of Oxford,' said our Host, 'you ride as quiet and demure as a maid newly espoused, sitting at the board. This day I have not heard one word from your tongue, I believe you are in a study over some sophism; but "everything hath its time," even as Solomon says. For God's sake, be of merrier countenance, it is no time now to study; tell us some merry tale, by your faith. For what man is entered into a game, he needs must assent to the rules of the game. But preach not, like friars in Lent, to make us bewail our old sins, nor let not your tale put us to sleep. Tell us some merry happening — store away your terms and colours of rhetoric and figures, keep them in reserve till so be you are composing in high style, as when men write to kings. I prithee speak so plainly now that we may understand what you say.'

This worthy clerk answered benignly, 'Host, I am under your rod. You have now the governance over us, and therefore I bind me to do obedience to you so far as reason asks. I will tell you a tale which I learned at Padua of a clerk, and a right worthy, as is shown by his words and deeds. He is now dead and nailed in his coffin, — I pray God rest his soul! Francis Petrarch, the laureate poet, is the name of this clerk, whose sweet rhetoric illumined all Italy with poetry, as John of Lignano did with philosophy and law and other learned arts. But death, which will not suffer us to dwell here but as it were a twinkling of an eye, has slain them both, and will yet slay all of us.

'But to tell on as I began of this worthy poet who taught me this tale: I say that first, ere he comes to the body of his tale, he endites a poem in a high style, in the which he describes Piedmont, and the country of Saluzzo, and speaks of the Apennines, the high hills that be the bounds of West Lombardy; and especially he speaks of Mount Vesulus, where the Po out of a small spring takes its first source and rising, and ever grows in its course eastward toward the Emilia, Ferrara and Venetia; all which were a long thing to describe. And truly to my judgment it seems an irrelevant thing, save that he would convey this knowledge. But this is his tale, which you may hear now.'

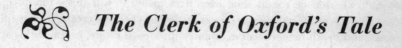 # The Clerk of Oxford's Tale

On the western side of Italy, down at the root of Vesulus the cold, there is a lusty plain, abounding in food-stuff, where you may behold many a tower and town founded in the time of the old fathers, and many another delectable sight. This noble country is called Saluzzo, whereof whilom a marquis was lord, as were his worthy ancestors before him, and his lieges great and small were all obedient and ready to his hand. Thus he lived in delights, and had done of yore, through favour of Fortune, beloved and feared both by his lords and his commons. And to speak of lineage, to boot, he was of the gentlest birth of Lombardy, a fair person and strong and young, and full of honour and courtesy, discreet enough to guide his country, save that he was blamable in certain things. And this young lord's name was Walter.

I blame him in this, that he considered not what might befall him in time to come, but put all his thought on present delight, such as hawking and hunting on every side. Wellnigh all other cares he let slip, and, what was worst of all, he would not wed a wife, for aught that might betide. This point only his people bare so sorely that on a day they went to him in troops, and one of them, who in lore was wisest, or else from whom the lord would take it least ill that he told him what his people thought, or else who could well expound such a matter, — he said thus to the marquis: —

'O noble marquis, your humanity gives us confidence and hardihood, as oftentimes as need is, to tell you our heaviness. Now, lord, of your nobility, accept the complaint which we lay before you with piteous heart, and let not your ears disdain my voice. Although I have naught more to do in this matter than any other man here, yet, my beloved lord, forasmuch as you have always showed me favour and grace, I dare the more to ask of you a little time of audience, to show our request, but only so as you, my lord, shall do fully as you list. For certes, lord, so we delight in you and in all your work, and ever have done, that we could not devise for ourselves how we might live in greater felicity.

'Save for one thing, lord, so we displease you not: that it might be your will to be a wedded man; then your people were in supreme hearts' rest. Bow your neck under that blissful yoke of sovereignty, not of service, which men call spousal or wedlock. And think lord, amongst all your prudent thoughts, how our days pass away from us in sundry wise; for though we sleep or wake, or though we ride or roam, time ever flees away, it will tarry for no man. And though your fresh youth be yet in flower, ever age creeps in, as still as stone, and death menaces all ages and smites each estate, and none escapes. And even as certainly as we each one of us know that we shall die, so uncertain are we of that day when death shall fall on us. Accept, then, our loyal meaning, who never yet refused your behest, and, lord, if you will assent, we will in short time choose you a wife born of the noblest and greatest of all this land, at the least, such that it ought to seem to God's honour and yours, as well as we can judge. Deliver us out of this anxious fear, and for the sake of the high God take a wife. For if so befell, as God forbid, that through your death your line should fail, and that a strange successor should take your heritage, ah, woe were us alive! Wherefore we beseech you to wed quickly.'

Their meek prayer and piteous countenance struck pity into the marquis's heart. Quoth he, 'Mine own dear people, you would constrain me to that which I never once thought of. I have rejoiced in my liberty, which is seldom found in marriage; where I was free, I must now be in servitude. But I see your loyal meaning, nevertheless, and trust your wisdom, and have ever trusted it.

Wherefore of my free will I will assent to wed, as soon as I ever am able. But as to the offer which you have made to-day to choose me a wife, I release you from that choice, and pray you to offer it no more. For, God wot, children are often unlike their worthy elders before them. Goodness comes all from God, not from the strain of which they were begotten and born. I trust in God's goodness, and therefore my marriage and well-being and peace I commit to Him; He may do as pleases Him. Let me alone to choose my mate; that charge I will bear upon mine own back. But I pray you and charge you upon your lives that whatsoever wife I take, you give me assurance to honour her, whilst her life may last, in word and deed here and everywhere, as if she were an emperor's daughter. And furthermore you shall swear this, that you will neither grumble nor strive against my choice. For since I am to forgo my liberty at your request, upon my soul I will wive where my heart is set. And except you will assent to this, speak no more of this matter, I pray you.'

With hearty will they swore and assented to all this thing, and no-one said nay; beseeching him ere they went that of his grace he would set for their sake a certain time for his espousals, as soon as ever he could. For still the people somewhat feared ever lest this marquis would not after all wed a wife. Such a day as pleased him, on which he would verily be wedded, he granted them, and said that he did all this only at their request. And with humble and submissive minds and reverently kneeling upon their knees they all thanked him; and thus they had achieved their desire, and all went their way home. And thereupon he commanded his officers to purvey the feast; and gave to his privy knights and squires such charge as he list; and they obeyed his commandments, and each did all his diligence to provide for a stately festival.

II

Not far from that illustrious palace where this marquis prepared for his marriage, stood a thorp in a pleasant site, where poor folk of that place had their huts and beasts, and drew their sustenance from their own labour, according as the earth yielded them its plenty. Amongst these poor folk dwelt a man held as poorest of all the village; but high God can sometimes send his grace into a little ox's stall. This man was named Janicula amongst the men of that thorp. He had a daughter named Griselda. This young maiden to the eye was fair enough; but to speak of beauty of virtue, in this she was one of the fairest under the sun. She was bred up in poverty, and through her heart ran no wanton desire; she drank oftener of the spring than of the cask, and because she would be pleasing in the sight of virtue, she knew labour well, but no idle ease. And though she were tender of age, yet in the breast of her virginity was enclosed a mature and staid temper, and she cherished her old poor father in great reverence and love. Spinning in the field, she watched a few sheep, and would never be idle until she slept. And when she came homeward, she would oftentimes bring worts or other herbs, which she shredded and seethed for their sustenance. And no soft bed was hers. She ever maintained her father's life with all the diligence and obedience that child could show to a reverend father.

Upon Griselda, this poor maid, the marquis set his eye full often, peradventure as he rode a-hunting; and when it so fell that he could see her, he cast his look upon her not with wanton glances of folly, but would often consider her countenance in sober wise, commending her womanhood in his heart, and also her virtue, surpassing any person of so young age as well in look as in deed. For though the common people have no great insight into virtue, he considered right well her goodness, and purposed that he would wed her only, if ever he should wed.

The day of the wedding came, but no-one could tell who the woman was to be; for which marvel many a man wondered, and said when they were in private, 'Will not our lord leave his vanities yet? Will he not wed? Alas the day! Why will he so beguile us and himself?'

But nevertheless for Griselda's sake this marquis had had brooches and rings made of gems set in gold and azure; and by a maid like to her in stature he had had the measurement of her clothing taken, and also of all other furnishings that pertain to such a wedding. The morning drew toward noon on the day when this wedding should be, and the palace was put all in array, hall and chambers, each according to its use. There you might have seen the offices stuffed plenteously with as dainty fare as could be found as far as Italy stretches. This royal marquis richly arrayed, the lords and ladies in his company who had been bidden to the feast, and the young knights of his retinue with the sound of mingled melody held the straight way to the thorp of which I have spoken. Griselda, full innocent of this, God wot, that all the array was made for her, was gone to fetch water at a spring, and came home as soon as ever she could. For indeed she had heard tell that the marquis was to wed that same day, and if she could she would fain have seen some of that sight. She thought, 'I will stand in our door, with other maidens my fellows, and see the marchioness; and therefore I will strive to do as soon as may be the labour which I must do at home. And then at leisure I may see her, if she hold this way to the castle.'

And as she was about to pass her threshold, the marquis came and began to call her. And straightway she set down her water-vessel in an ox's stall beside the threshold, and fell down upon her knees, and remained kneeling with sober countenance till she heard the lord's will. This thoughtful marquis spake to this maid full gravely and said, 'Where is your father, Griselda?' And she answered with reverence and humble cheer, 'Lord, he is ready at hand.' And she went in without longer stay and fetched her father to the marquis.

He then took this old man by the hand, and when he had him aside, spake thus, 'Janicula, I cannot longer hide the pleasure of my heart. If you vouchsafe it, whatever betide, ere I depart I will take your daughter for my wife as long as she lives. You love me, and are born my faithful liegeman, I wot well, verily; and I dare well say, all that pleases me pleases you. And especially, therefore, resolve me that point I have even now spoken of; if you will incline unto that thing, to take me as your son-in-law?'

These sudden words so astonied the old man that he waxed red and abashed and stood all quaking. Scarce said he a word save only this; 'Lord,' quoth he, 'my will is as your will; and against your pleasure I will nothing. You are my very dear lord. Rule this matter even as you list.'

'Yet I would,' quoth this marquis softly, 'that in your chamber I and you and she have a parley. And know you why? Because I would ask if it be her will to be my wife, and to rule herself after my wishes. And all this shall be done before you; I will not speak out of your hearing.'

And whilst they were in the chamber about their treating, of which you shall afterwards hear, the people came to the house without and marvelled how worthily and attentively she maintained her dear father.

But well might Griselda entirely marvel, for never before saw she such a sight; it is no wonder if she were astonied to see so great a guest come there, such as she never was accustomed to; she gazed at him with a full pale face. But briefly to hurry forth this tale, these are the words which the marquis spake to this true gentle faithful maid: 'Griselda,' he said, 'you shall understand well that it pleases your father and me that I should wed you; and also it may stand so, as I suppose, that you will grant it. But these questions I ask first. Since it is to be done in so hasty wise, will you now assent, or consider further? And this I ask: are you ready inclined with good heart to all my pleasure, that I may freely cause you to laugh or to grieve as seems to me best, and that you never shall murmur against it day or night, and also that when I say "yea," you never say "nay," neither by word nor frowning cheer? Swear this, and here I swear our alliance.'

Wondering at these words and trembling for fear, she said: 'Lord, undeserving and unworthy am I of that honour which you offer me. But as yourself will, even so will I. And here I swear that willingly I shall never disobey you in deed or thought, though I die for it; and yet I were loath to die.'

'This is enough, my Griselda,' quoth he.

And he went forth with a full grave countenance out at the door, and she came after. And to the people he said, 'This is my wife who stands here. Whosoever loves me, honour and love her, I beg. There is no more to say.'

And because she should bring into his house nought of her old gear, he bade that women should unclothe her even there. These ladies were not right joyous to handle her clothes wherein she was clad; but nevertheless from foot to head they clothed afresh this maiden bright of hue. Then they combed her hair, which lay untressed full rudely, and with their slender fingers placed a crown on her head, and covered her with gemmed ornaments, great and small. Why should I make a long tale of her array? When she was transformed into such richness, the people scarce knew her for her beauty.

This marquis espoused her with a ring brought for that purpose, and then set her upon a horse snow-white and gentle-paced, and conveyed her to his palace amid joyful people who led her and met her. And thus they spent the day in revel till the sun went down.

And to drive forth this tale quickly, I say that God of His grace sent such favour to this new marchioness that none would have believed she had been rudely born and fostered, as in a cot or ox-stall, but rather in an emperor's palace; in the eyes of every-one she waxed so worshipful and beloved that folk where she was born, who had known her year by year from her birth, scarce believed that she was daughter to Janicula, of whom I have spoken; but durst have sworn she was quite another creature. For though she had ever been full of worth, she increased in excellence of precious virtues rooted deep in good-ness of nature. She was so discreet and fair of speech, so benign and so worthy of reverence, and knew so well how to hold fast the people's hearts, that each person who looked upon her face loved her. The nobility of her fame was published not only in the town of Saluzzo, but in many a region thereabout. If one said well, another said likewise. So spread the report of her high goodness that men and women, young and old, went to Saluzzo to look upon her.

Thus Walter, wedded lowly, — nay, royally, with good fortune and honour, — lived at home well at ease and in God's peace and had outward weal sufficient. And because he had seen that under lowly degree is virtue often hid, the people held him a prudent man, and that is full seldom seen. This Griselda through her natural wit not only knew all the acts of wifely domesticity, but also when the case required it, she could amend the public weal. There was no discord, rancour nor heaviness in all that land which she knew not how to appease, and wisely to bring all those in trouble into rest and satisfaction. Though her husband were absent, if men of gentle birth or others of her country were wroth, anon she would reconcile them. Such wise and mature words she had, and judgments of such equity, that men thought her sent from heaven to save people and to redress every wrong.

Not long time after this Griselda was wedded, she bore a daughter, though she had liefer have borne a man-child. At this the marquis was glad, and the folk. For if a maid-child came first, she might by likelihood attain unto a man-child, since she was not barren.

III

It befell, as happens more times than one, that when this child had sucked but a little while, this marquis so longed in his heart to try his wife, and to know her steadfastness, that he could not cast out of his heart this marvellous desire to assay his wife. Needlessly, God wot, he thought to affright her. He had assayed her enough already, and found her ever good. What need was there to tempt her, and ever more and more? Though some men praise it for a subtle mark of wit, as for me I say that it ill befits to test a wife when there is no need, and to put her in anguish and fear. To this end the marquis wrought thus; he came along by night to the place where she lay, and said thus, with stern face and full troubled cheer: 'Griselda, that day when I took you out of your poor condition and put you in estate of high nobility, — you have not forgotten that, I trust. I say, Griselda, I trust this present dignity in which I have placed you makes you not forgetful that I took you in poor, lowly estate; in spite of any present weal, you must know yourself. Take heed of every word I say, for there is no creature hears it but we two. You know well yourself how you came here into this house, it is not long since; and though you be lief and dear to me, you are no wise so to my gentles. They say it is great shame and woe to them to be subjects and to be in servitude to you, who were born in a little village. And, in truth, especially since your daughter was born, they have spoken these words. But I desire to live my life in quiet and peace with them as aforetime. I cannot be regardless in this. I must act for the best with your daughter; not as I would, but only as my people will. And yet I am full loath to do this thing, God wot. And without your knowledge I will not act; but this I desire, that you give me your assent in one thing. Show now in your action the patience you promised me and swore in your cot, that day when your marriage was made.'

When she had heard all this, she changed neither in word nor face nor bearing; it seemed even as if she were not grieved. She said, 'Lord, all lies in your pleasure. My child and I with hearty obedience are all yours, and you may save or destroy your own possession; act after your own will. May God to save my soul, nought can please you that can displease me; I desire to have nothing, and fear to lose nothing, save only you. This mind now is in me, and shall be ever. No length of time or death can destroy it, or change my heart to another place.'

Glad was this marquis of her answer, yet he feigned as if he were not. His cheer and his look were full dreary when he went from the chamber. Soon after this he privily told all his purpose unto a trusty man, and sent him to his wife. This man was a kind of officer, whom he had oft found faithful in weighty matters; such folk can discreetly execute things bad as well as good. The lord well knew he loved and feared him. And when this officer knew his lord's will, he stole into the chamber.

'Madame,' he said, 'though I do a thing to which I am constrained, you must forgive me. You are so wise that you know full well that lords' behests must be done without feigning. They may well be bewailed or lamented; but men must needs obey their pleasure, and so I shall. There is nothing more to say. I am commanded to take this child,' — and he said no more, but caught up the child pitilessly and made as though he would have slain it before he departed. Griselda must suffer all and comply in all, and sat meek and quiet as a lamb and let him do his will. Ominous was the ill-fame of this man, ominous his face, ominous also his words, ominous the time in which he wrought this. Alas! her daughter whom she loved so, she thought he would have slain it even then. But still she neither wept nor sighed, consenting to what the marquis willed. But at last she began to speak, and meekly prayed the officer that as he was a worthy man and of gentle stock, she might kiss her child ere it died. And with full calm face she laid this little child in her bosom and kissed it and lulled it, and then made on it the sign of the cross; and said in her gentle voice, 'Farewell, my child, I shall never see thee more. But since I have marked thee with the cross, mayst thou be blessed of that Father Who died for us on a cross of wood. Thy soul, little child, I commit to Him, for this night thou shalt die for my sake.'

I believe that to a nurse it had been hard to see this rueful act; well might a mother have cried, 'Alas!' Yet she was so steadfast-calm that she endured all adversity, and meekly said to the officer, 'Have here your little young maid again. Go now, do my lord's behest,' she said. 'But of your grace I will pray you one thing, that unless my lord forbade you, at least you bury this little

174

body in some spot where no beasts nor birds may tear it.' But to that he would speak no word, and took the child and went his way.

This officer came back to his lord and told him Griselda's words and cheer, from point to point, in short and plain, and presented him with his sweet daughter. This lord felt some ruth, after his fashion, but nevertheless, as lords do when they will have their way, held still to his purpose, and bade this officer that he should privily wind and wrap this child full softly and tenderly in all points, and carry it in a coffer or wrapping; but, upon pain of having his head struck off, he should let no man know his purpose, nor whence he came nor whither he went. And he should take it to the lord's dear sister at Bologna, who at that time was countess of Panigo, and should show her this matter, beseeching her to do her diligence to foster this child in all gentle breeding. And whose child it was he bade her hide from everyone, for aught that might happen. And the sergeant went, and carried out this thing.

But now return we to this marquis. For now he went full intently searching whether he could see by his wife's bearing, or perceive by her speech, that she was changed. But he never could find her but ever steadfast and gentle. In every wise she was as glad, as humble, as busy in service and also in love to him as she was wont to be, nor spake she a word of her daughter. No chance sign of any affliction she felt was seen in her, nor ever mentioned she her daughter's name, in mirth or sadness.

IV

In this manner passed four years, ere she was with child again; but now, as God willed, she bore by this Walter a man-child, full gracious and fair to see. And when folk told it to his father, not only he but all his land was merry for this child, and thanked and praised God. When it was two years old and parted from the breast of its nurse, on a day the desire seized the marquis to assay his wife yet again, if he could. Ah, needless was the test! But wedded men know no measure, when they find a patient person.

'Wife,' quoth this marquis, 'ere this, you have heard that my people ill endure our marriage, and especially is it worse than ever in our lives now since my son is born. The murmuring slays mine heart! For the voice comes to mine ears so bitterly that it wellnigh destroys my spirit. They say thus now: "When Walter is gone, then shall the blood of Janicula succeed and be our lord, for we have none other." Such words of a surety my people say. Well ought I to take heed of such murmuring, for in truth I dread it, though they speak not plainly in my hearing; I would live in peace, if I could. Wherefore I am fully resolved to serve him privily by night as I served his sister. I warn you of this, lest you suddenly start out of yourself for any woe; be patient, I pray you.'

Quoth she, 'I have said thus, and ever shall, that I wish nothing and refuse nothing, in sooth, save as you list. I grieve not at all though my daughter and son be slain, so it be at your command. I have had no part in my two children save sickness first, and then woe and pain. You are our lord, do with your own even as you list. Ask no counsel of me, for even as I left at home all of my clothing when I first came to you, so I left my will and all my freedom, and took your clothing. Wherefore, I pray you, do your pleasure; I will obey your will. And certes, if I had prescience to know your desire ere you told it me, I would do it without neglect. But now that I know your desire and what you will, I hold firmly to all your pleasure. For if I wist that my death would do you pleasure, I would die right gladly to please you. Death can hold no comparison to your love.'

And when this marquis saw the constancy of his wife, he cast down his two eyes, and marvelled that she could suffer all this ordinance in patience. And forth he went with dreary countenance, but in his heart was full great gladness. This ill-favored officer, even as he seized her daughter, in the same wise or worse, if a man could contrive worse, caught up her son so fair. And ever alike she was so patient that she made no heavy countenance, but kissed her son and crossed him. Save only this: she prayed the man that, if he could, he should bury her little son in the earth, to save his tender limbs from fowls and beasts. But she could get no answer of him; he went his way as if he recked not. But he brought the child right tenderly to Bologna. This marquis more and more wondered at her patience; and if he had not verily known aforetime that she loved her children perfectly, he would have thought that she had endured this with calm visage out of some subtlety, and from cruelty or malice. But in verity he knew that next himself she loved her children best of all the world.

But now I would fain ask of women if these assays should not have sufficed. What more could a harsh husband contrive to test her wifehood and steadfastness, whilst he ever continued in his harshness? But there be folk of such disposition that, when they have taken a certain course, they cannot stint, but even as if they were bound to a stake, they will not remit that first purpose. Right so this marquis purposed fully to test his wife, as he was first minded. He watched to see by word or bearing if she were changed toward him, but never could find variance; she was ever the same in heart and visage. And ever the older she grew, the truer in love she was to him, if that were possible, and the more assiduous. It seemed that in the two there was but one will, for as Walter would, the same was her pleasure also. And, God be thanked, all fell out for the best. She well showed that for no disquiet on earth should a wife will aught, save as her husband would.

The ill-report of Walter spread often and widely, that of cruel heart he had wickedly murdered both his children in secret, because he had wedded a poor woman. Such murmur was general, and no wonder, for no word came to the people's ears save that they were murdered. Wherefore though his people before had loved him well, the scandal made them to hate him. To be a murderer is a hateful report! But nevertheless he would not stint of his cruel purpose for weal or woe; all his mind was set upon testing his wife.

When his daughter was twelve years of age, he sent his messenger to the court of Rome, which had been informed of his will already in subtle wise, commanding them to contrive such bulls as should answer his cruel purpose: how the pope, as if for the quiet of his people, bade him wed another if he would. I say he bade they should counterfeit the papal bulls, making mention that he had leave to abandon his first wife, as if by the pope's dispensation, to stint rancour and strife betwixt his people and him; thus said the bull, which they made all public. The common people, and no wonder, weened full well that it were so. When these tidings came to Griselda, I believe her heart was full sad; but she, this humble creature, evermore alike constant, was all ready to endure the adversity of Fortune, awaiting ever his desire and pleasure, to whom, heart and all, she was given as to her true earthly sufficiency.

But, to tell this story shortly, the marquis wrote a special letter in which he showed all his mind, and despatched it secretly to Bologna. He especially prayed the earl of Panigo, who had wedded his sister, to bring his two children home again all openly in honourable state. But he prayed him one thing above all, that though men should ask, he should tell no creature whose children they were, but say that the maiden was to be wedded anon to the marquis of Saluzzo. And this the earl did even as he was prayed. For on the day set he went on his way toward Saluzzo, and many a lord in a rich company, to escort this maiden; her young brother riding beside her. This blooming maid was arrayed against her marriage with many a clear gem; her brother, seven years old, was arrayed also full freshly as befitted him. And thus with great pomp and glad cheer they rode from day to day on their journey, shaping their course toward Saluzzo.

V

During all this and after all his wicked behaviour, to test his wife yet more, to prove her disposition to the utmost, and fully to learn whether she were as steadfast as formerly, on a day in open audience this marquis full roughly spake these words to her. 'Certes, Griselda, I have had pleasure enough in having you to wife, for your goodness, loyalty and obedience, not for any lineage or wealth of yours. But now, when I well reflect, I know in very truth that in great lordship is great servitude in sundry wise; I have not the freedom of every ploughman. My people cry day by day and constrain me to take another wife. And the pope also, to allay rancour, consents to this. And in sooth this I must tell you, that my new wife is on her way. Be strong of heart, and void her place. And the dower that you brought me, take it again, I grant you that grace. Return to your father's house. No man may have prosperity alway. I counsel you to endure the stroke of Fortune or of chance with steady heart.'

And she returned answer patiently, 'My lord, I know, and knew alway, that no man may make comparison between your magnificence and my poverty; no man can say that nay. I never held myself worthy in any wise to be your wife, no, nor your chamber-maid. And — I take high God for witness, and may He so surely gladden my soul — in this house where you made me lady I never held myself lady or mistress, but humble servant to your honour, above every earthly creature; and so I shall ever be whilst my life may last. That you of your kindness have so long held me in honour and dignity whereof I was not worthy, for that I thank God and you, and I pray Him reward you, there is no more to say. Gladly will I return to my father, and dwell with him to the end of my life. Where I was fostered from a child, I will lead my life till I die, a clean widow in body, in heart and all. For since I gave you my maidenhead, and am your undoubted loyal wife, God forbid that such a lord's wife take another man as husband or mate. And with your new wife God of His grace grant you weal and prosperity; I will gladly yield her my room where I was wont to be happy, for since it pleases you that I shall go, my lord, who were once all my heart's repose, I will go when you desire.

'But as for your proffer of such dowry as I first brought, it is well in my mind that it was but my wretched uncomely clothing, which now were hard to recover. — O good God! How noble and kind you seemed by your speech and visage that day when our wedding was made! But sooth is said, — at least I find it sooth, for it is proved on me, — love old is not as it was new. But certes, lord, though I die, for no adversity shall it ever be that I shall repent in word or deed of giving you my heart with full purpose. My lord, you know that you had me stripped of my poor weeds in my father's home, and of your grace clad me richly. Verily I brought nought else to you, save faithfulness and nakedness and maidenhead. And here I return my clothing forevermore, and also my wedding-ring. The remnant of your jewels, I dare assure you, are ready within your chamber. Naked I came out of my father's house, and naked I must return. All your pleasure I fain would follow, yet I hope it be not your will that I go out of your palace smockless. You could not do so unseemly a thing as permit that body in which lay your children to be seen all bare before the people as I walk. Wherefore, I pray you, let me not go like a worm by the wayside. Recall, mine own lord so dear, I was your wife, though unworthy. In reward of my maidenhead, therefore, which I brought and bear not away again, vouchsafe to give me as meed only such a smock as I was wont to wear, that I may cover the body of her who was your wife. And here, lest I vex you, I take my leave of you, mine own lord.'

Quoth he, 'The smock which you have on your back, let it there remain and bear it forth with you.' But for ruth and pity he could scarce speak these words, and must needs go out.

Before the folk she divested herself, and went forth toward her father's house in her smock, with her head and feet all bare. The folk follow her weeping, and ever as they go they curse Fortune. But she kept her eyes dry of tears, and in all this time spake no word. Her father, who anon heard these tidings, cursed the day and hour that nature shaped him to be a living being; for in sooth this old poor man was ever suspicious of her marriage, and ever since the first he deemed that when this lord had accomplished his desires, he would think it a disgrace to his estate to descend so low, and would discard her as soon as ever he could. He went quickly to meet his daughter, for by the noise of the folk he knew her coming, and weeping full sorely he covered her with her old coat, as well as might be. But he could not bring it on her body, for rude was the cloth and more worn by many days than at her marriage.

Thus for a certain time dwelt this flower of wifely patience with her father, in such wise that neither by her words nor by her countenance, before the folk or in their absence, showed she that injury had been done her. Nor seemed she to have any remembrance of her high estate. And no wonder was it; for in her great estate her spirit had ever been in deep humility; hers had been no tender mouth or delicate heart or pomp or semblance of royalty, but ever she was full of benign patience, discreet, humble, always honourable, and meek and constant to her husband. Men speak of Job, and most of all for his humility, as clerks can well indite when they list to speak concerning holy men. But in truth, though clerks praise women but little, no man can acquit himself in humility as woman can, nor can be half so loyal as women be, — unless it have happened very lately.

From Bologna was come this earl of Panigo, whereof the report spread amongst great and small. And also it was known in the ears of all the people that he brought with him a new marchioness in such pomp and splendour that never had the eye of man seen so noble an array in all west Lombardy. The marquis, who planned and knew all this, ere the earl came, sent his messenger to this same simple poor Griselda. And she came at his behest with humble heart and glad visage and with no swelling thoughts in her heart, and set her on her knees, and greeted him reverently and discreetly.

'Griselda,' quoth he, 'it is fully my will that this maiden, who shall be wedded to me, be received to-morrow in my house as royally as it is possible; and also that every person according to his degree shall have his proper place in seating and in service and in high pleasure, as best I can devise. In sooth I have no women able to array the chambers in order after my pleasure; and therefore I fain would that all the oversight thereof were yours. You know also of old all my pleasure. Though your garb be ill provided and poor to look upon, do you your devoir, at the least.'

Quoth she, 'Not only, lord, am I glad to do your pleasure now, but in all things I desire also to serve you and to please you in my degree without fainting, and shall evermore. Never, for weal or woe, shall the spirit in my heart cease to love you best with all my loyal purpose.'

And with that word she began to prepare the house and to set tables and make beds, and strove to do all she could, praying the chambermaids for God's sake to haste them and busily shake and sweep. And she, the most active of them, arrayed the hall and every chamber.

About midday this earl alighted, and with him these two noble children, whose array, so richly furnished, the folk ran to gaze upon. And then first they said amongst themselves that Walter was no fool though he pleased to change his wife, for it was for the best. For, as they all judged, she was fairer than Griselda, and of more tender years; and fairer fruit and more pleasing should spring of them, for her high lineage. Her brother also was so fair of face that the people joyed to see them, commending now the marquis' course.

Author. 'O stormy people! changeable as a vane, unstable, ever faithless, indiscreet, delighting ever in new rumour! Ye ever wax and wane like the moon. Ever full of prate, dear enough at a farthing! your judgment is false, your constancy turns out ill, a full great fool is he who trusts you.' Thus said discreet folk in that city, when the people all over were at gaze, because they were glad, only for the novelty, to have a new lady of their town. No more now make I mention of this; but I will address me again to Griselda, and tell of her constancy and zeal.

Full busy was Griselda in all that pertained to the feast. Not at all was she abashed for her clothing, though it was rude and also somewhat rent. But with glad countenance she betook her to the gate with the other folk, to greet the marchioness, and after that continued her tasks. And she received the guests with such glad cheer and discernment, each after his degree, that none perceived any fault; but ever they wondered what she might be, who was in such poor attire, and yet so well understood stately ceremony, and worthily they praised her prudence. Meanwhile she ceased not to commend so well this maid, and also her brother, with all her heart and full gracious temper, that none could have praised them better.

At last, when these lords went to sit down to meat, the marquis called Griselda as she was busy in his hall.

'Griselda,' quoth he, as it were in mirth, 'how like you my wife and her beauty?'

'Right well, my lord,' she answered; 'for in good faith I never saw a fairer. I pray God to give her prosperity, and pleasure enough to you both to your life's end. One thing I beseech you and warn you also: that you prick not this tender maiden with any tormenting, as you have others. For she has been fostered more tenderly, and, to my thinking, she could not bear adversity as could a creature fostered in poverty.'

And when Walter saw her patience, and glad cheer without any malice, though he had so often afflicted her, and how she was ever staid and constant as a wall, continuing ever her innocence, — this stern marquis began to incline his heart to take pity upon her wifely steadfastness.

'This is enough, Griselda mine. Be no more aghast,' quoth he, 'nor troubled. I have tested your loyalty and your kindness both in great station and in poverty, as well as ever woman was tested. Now I know, dear wife, your steadfastness,' — and he took her in his arms and began to kiss her. And she in her wonder heeded it not; she heard not what thing he said to her. She fared as if she had but just started out of a sleep, till she came out of her amazement. 'Griselda,' quoth he, 'by God Who died for us, you are my wife, nor have I another, nor ever had, so God save my soul! This is your daughter whom you supposed to be my wife; the other, in faith, shall be mine heir, as I have ever purposed. You bare him verily in your body. I have kept them privily at Bologna; but take them back, for now you cannot say that you have lost either of your two children. And folk that have said otherwise of me, I warn them well that I have done this deed out of neither malice nor cruelty, but to test your womanhood; not to slay my children — God forbid! — but to keep them privily till I knew all your mind and will.'

When she heard this, she fell down in a swoon for piteous joy, and after her swooning she called both her young children to her; and, piteously weeping, embraced them in her arms and tenderly kissed them, full like a mother, with her salt tears bedewing their hair and their faces. Ah what a pitiful thing it was to see her swooning and to hear her humble voice! 'Gramercy, lord,' quoth she, 'I thank you that you have saved me my dear children. Now reck I not though I die right here; since I stand in your love and grace, no matter when my spirit departs. O, my tender, dear young children! Your sorrowful mother believed full well that cruel hounds or some foul vermin had eaten you; but God in his mercy, and your benign father, have caused you to be tenderly guarded.' And in that same moment all suddenly she fell to the ground. And in her swoon she held her two children so firmly in her embrace that only with much cunning and trouble they tore the children from her arms. Ah, many a tear trickled down many a pitying face amongst them that stood hard by; scarce could they remain about her.

Walter cheered her and soothed her sorrow; she rose up from her trance abashed, and every creature made joy and festival toward her, till she commanded herself once more. Walter so earnestly strove to please her that it was rare to see the cheer betwixt the two, now they were joined again. These ladies, when they saw their time, took her and went into a chamber and stripped off her rude garments, and in cloth of gold that shone bright, with a crown of many rich stones upon her head, they led her into the hall, where she was honoured as was her due. Thus came this piteous day to a joyous end, for every person strove to spend the day in mirth and revel, till the stars' light shone in the welkin. Far more splendid in every man's sight was this feast, and of greater cost, than was the revel at their wedding.

These two lived full many a year in high prosperity, concord and quiet. The marquis married his daughter richly unto a lord, one of the worthiest of all Italy. And he kept his wife's father in rest and peace at his court, till the soul crept out of his body. Griselda's son, after his father's day, succeeded to his inheritance in quiet and peace, and was fortunate in marrying, though he put not his wife to grievous test.

This world is not so strong as it has been in times of yore, there is no gainsaying that; and therefore hearken what mine author says. This story is told, not because wives should follow Griselda in humility, for it were intolerable if they should; but because every person in his estate should be firm in adversity, as Griselda was. For this cause Petrarch wrote this story, which he indited in lofty style. For since a woman was so patient toward a mortal man, much more ought we to receive in meekness all that God sends us; for there is great reason that He should test what He has made. Tempt He will no man whom He has redeemed, as Saint James says, if ye read his epistle; but without doubt He tests folk all the time, and suffers us full often to be beaten in sundry wise with sharp scourges of adversity, not to learn our temper, for certes He knew all our frailty ere we were born, but only for our discipline. And all His rule is for the best; therefore let us live in virtuous endurance.

But hearken to one word, lordings, ere I depart; it were full hard nowadays to find in a whole town three Griseldas, or even two. For if they were so tested, the gold of them is now so ill alloyed with brass, that though the coin be fair to the eye, it would break in two rather than bend. And so for love of the Wife of Bath, — whom and all her kind may God maintain in high mastery, it were pity else, — with heart fresh and lusty I will say you a song to gladden you, I trust; and let us cease from earnestful matters. Listen to my song, which runs thus: —

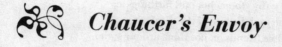 ## Chaucer's Envoy

Griselde is dead, and all her sufferance,
And buried in a green Italian vale;
Wherefore I cry in open audience,
No wedded man so hardy be to assail
His own wife's patience, in the hope to find
Griselda's, or for certain he shall fail.

O noble wives, full of high sapience,
Let no humility your clappers nail,
And let no clerk have cause or diligence
To write of you so wonderful a tale
As of Griselda, patient, meek and kind,
Lest Chichevache gulf you in her entrail.

Follow Echo, goddess of impudence,
That answers up the hill and down the dale;
Be never cozened for your innocence,
But sharply take on you the governaille.
Print in your mind this lesson on mankind
For common profit, and it will avail.

Ye archwives, ever stand on your defence,
Since ye are strong as elephant or whale;
Suffer not puny man to do offence.
Ye slim wives, frail and splenetic and pale,
Bite as a snake in Afric or in Ind,
And rattle as a windmill in a gale.

Dread ye not men, do them no reverence,
For though your husbands armèd be in mail,
The arrows of your crabbed eloquence
Shall pierce their breast and make their top to vail
And also with jealousy your husbands bind,
And ye shall make them couch as doth a quail.

If thou be fair, go where is dalliance,
And show thy stomacher and farthingale;
If thou be foul, be free of thy dispense,
To win thee friends let not thine ardour stale.
As leaf in tree-top be thou light of mind,
And let him chafe and weep and wring and wail.

Prologue to the Merchant's Tale

'Weeping and wailing, care and sorrow, I know enough,' quoth the Merchant, 'at morn and at eve, and so do others that be wedded, I believe; well I wot it is so with me. I have a wife, the worst possible; for though the Fiend were coupled to her, I dare well swear she would overmatch him. Why should I rehearse to you all points of her great malice? She is an evil creature in all things. There is a long and large difference betwixt Griselda's meekness and the surpassing cruelty of my wife. Were I unbound, never again would I come into the snare, by mine head! We wedded men live in care and sorrow; try it who will, he shall find, by Saint Thomas of India, that I say sooth, — as to the greater part, I speak not of all; God shield it should be so! Ah, good sir Host! I have been wedded these two months, and not more, perdy! And yet I believe that he who has all his life been wifeless could in no wise, though men would rend him to the heart, tell so much sorrow as I could tell now here of my wife's cursedness!'

Quoth our Host, 'Now, Merchant, so may God save your soul, since you know so much of that gear, I pray you full heartily, tell us a part thereof.'

'Gladly,' he replied, 'but of mine own hurt, for sorry heart I can tell no more.'

The Merchant's Tale

Once there dwelt in Lombardy a worthy knight, born in Pavia, in which town he lived in great prosperity; and for sixty years he was wifeless and ever pursued his carnal pleasure on women where his appetite was fixed, just as these fools do that be laymen. And when he was past sixty years, this knight had such a mind to be a wedded man — were it from holiness or dotage, I cannot say — that he did all he could, day and night, to espy where he might wed him; praying our Lord to grant him once to know that same blissful existence that is betwixt husband and wife, and to live under that holy bond with which God first bound man and woman.

'No other way of life,' said he, 'is worth a bean. For wedlock is so easy and pure that it is paradise on earth.' Thus spake this old knight, who was so wise.

And of a certainty, as true as God is King, it is glorious to take a wife, especially when a man is old and hoar; then a wife is the jewel of all his treasures. Then he ought to take a young wife and a beautiful, on whom to beget him an heir; and lead his life in joy and bliss, whilst these bachelors sing 'alas!', when they find any reverse in their affairs of love, which are but childish vanity. And in sooth it is fitting that bachelors have pain and woe oft; they build on brittle ground, and find brittleness when they look for certainty. They live but as a bird or a beast, in freedom, under no restraint, whilst a wedded man in his degree lives a life blessed and ordered, secured under the yoke of marriage; well may his heart abound in all gladness and bliss. For who obeys as a wife? Who is so faithful as his mate, and also so attentive to care for him, sick and well? For weal or for woe, she will not forsake him. She is not weary to love and serve him, though he lie bedridden till he die. And yet some clerks deny it, of whom Theophrastus is one. But what matter though Theophrastus is pleased to lie? He says, 'Take no wife, for the sake of thy thrift, to spare expense in thine household; a faithful servant is more diligent than thine own wife to keep thy goods. For all her days she will claim a half part. And if thou be sick, God is my witness, thy true friends or a faithful lad will care for thee better than she that ever waits, and has waited many a day, after thy goods.' This evil saying, and an hundred more evil, writes this man, — may God curse his bones! But heed no such vain opinions; reject Theophrastus and hearken to me.

Verily, a wife is God's gift. All other manner of gifts, such as lands, rents, pasture, commonage, or movable property, are all gifts of Fortune, I declare boldly, which pass away as a shadow upon the wall. But without doubt, and to speak plainly, a wife will last and abide in your house (longer than you would wish, peradventure). Marriage is a full great sacrament; he who has no wife, I hold him a lost man, who lives helpless and desolate, — I speak of lay folk. And hearken why — (I say not this lightly); it is because woman was wrought to be man's help. The high God, when he had made Adam, and saw him all alone, and belly-naked, — God of his great goodness said, 'Let us now make an helper for this man, like to himself.' And then he made Eve for him. Here you may see and prove hereby that a wife is man's help and comfort, his terrestrial paradise and his diversion. So obedient and excellent she is that they cannot but live in unity. They be one flesh; and one flesh, I apprehend, has but one heart in weal and woe.

A wife! ah, Saint Mary! *benedicite!* How could a man feel any mischance who has a wife? Certes, I cannot say. The bliss that is betwixt them two no tongue can tell or heart think. If he be poor, she helps him labour; she keeps his goods and wastes never a bit. All that her husband desires, well pleases her. She says not once 'nay' when he says 'yea.' Says he, 'do this'; she answers, 'all ready, sir.' O, blessed order, precious wedlock, thou art so pleasant and virtuous and so highly commended and approved, that every man who holds himself to be worth a leek ought all his days upon his bare knee to thank his

God that has sent him a wife, or else pray God to send him a wife to last until he dies. For then is his life set in security. He cannot be deceived, I believe, so he work after his wife's counsel; wives are so faithful and discreet that he may hold his head up boldly. Therefore, if you will be as the wise, do ever as women counsel you.'

Lo, how Jacob by the good counsel of Rebecca his mother, as these clerks read, bound the kid's skin about his neck, and thus won his father's benison. Lo, Judith, as the history tells; she by wise counsel guarded God's people and slew Holofernes whilst he slept. Lo, Abigail, how she by good counsel saved her husband, Nabal, when he was to have been slain. And look also how Esther by good counsel delivered the people of God from woe, and made Mardocheus to be advanced by Ahasuerus.

There is nothing superlative in degree, as Seneca says, above an humble wife. Suffer your wife's tongue, as Cato bids. She shall command, and you shall permit it, and yet of her courtesy sometimes she will obey. A wife will guard your household-thrift. Well may the sick man lament who has no wife to keep his house. I want you, if you will act wisely love your wife well, as Christ loves His church. If you love yourself, you will love your wife; no man hates his own flesh, but all his days he fosters it, and therefore I bid you cherish your wife, or you shall never prosper. However men mock and jest, of all mortal folk husband and wife hold the safest road. They are so knit no harm can happen, — and especially from the wife's side.

Wherefore in the days of his age, this January of whom I speak meditated on the lusty life, the virtuous quiet, in honeysweet marriage. And on a day he sent for his friends, to tell them all his mind.

With grave countenance he told his tale, and said, 'Friends, I am hoar and old, and, God wot, almost on the brink of the grave; now must I consider my soul somewhat. I have wasted my body on folly, but blessed be God! that shall be amended; for I will be a wedded man, and that forthwith, of a surety, in all possible haste. I pray you, help me to plan for my speedy marriage unto some fair maiden tender of years, for I will not tarry; and on my side, I will try to seek out to whom I may be quickly wedded. But inasmuch as you are more numerous than I, you rather than I should be able to study out such a thing, and where it were best for me to mate.

'But of one thing, my dear friends, I warn you: by no manner of means will I have any old wife. In sooth, she shall not be over twenty years of age; I full fain would have old fish and young flesh. Better is a pike than a pickerel, and better the tender veal than old beef,' quoth he. 'I will have no woman thirty years of age; such are but bean-straw and coarse fodder. And also, God wot, these old widows, — they know so much of Wade's boat, so many arts and troublous tricks when they would use them, that I should never live in peace with a widow. For a change of divers schools makes subtle clerks; and woman is half a clerk of many schools. But of a certainty men can guide a young thing, just as men can mold warm wax with the hands. Wherefore I tell you in short and plain, I will have no old wife, for this very reason. For if it fell out so ill that I could have no joy of her, then should I lead a life of adultery and go straight to the Devil when I die. And I should get no children of her; yet I tell you all, I had rather hounds should eat me than that my heritage should fall into strange hands. I dote not, I know the reason why men should wed, and furthermore I know that many a man speaks of wedlock who knows no more than my page for what reasons man should take a wife. If he cannot live chaste all his days, let him take a wife in piety, for the sake of procreating children, to the honour of God in heaven and not only for love and passion; and because they should shun lechery and yield their debt when it is due; or that each of them should help the other in misfortune, as a brother shall a sister, and live holily in continence. But, sirs, by your leave, I am not such; for, God be thanked, I feel my limbs strong and sufficient to play all a man's part. I know best what I can do. Though I be white on my head, I fare like a tree that blossoms ere it yield fruit; a blossoming tree is not dry or dead. I feel myself hoar only on my hair; my heart and limbs are as green as the laurel is throughout the year. And since you have heard all my mind, I pray you assent to my will.'

Divers men told him diversely many old ensamples about marriage. In sooth, some blamed it, some praised it; but in the end, to speak briefly, as altercation every day befalls betwixt friends in dispute, there fell a strife betwixt his two brethren, of whom the first was called Placebo, the second Justinus.

Placebo said, 'Brother January, right small need had you, my lord so dear, to ask counsel of any one present, save that you are so sapient that of your high prudence you list not turn aside from the word of Solomon. This word he said to us, "Do all things by counsel and then thou shalt not repent thee." But though Solomon spake such words, mine own dear lord and brother, I hold your own counsel the best, so may God save my soul! For, brother mine, take this from me: I have been a courtier all my life now, and God wot, though I be unworthy, I have stood in high place about lords of full great estate; yet I never had strife with any of them. Verily, I never withstood them. I wot well my lord knows more than I; what he says I hold to be sound, and say the same, or things similar. Any counsellor who serves a lord of high degree is a full great fool, if he dare take upon himself, or even think that his counsel should surpass his lord's wisdom. Nay, by my faith, lords be no fools; you yourself have showed here to-day so holily and well such lofty wisdom, so devoutly and well, that I approve and confirm all your words and your opinion every whit. By the Lord, there is no man in all this town nor in all Italy who could have spoken better; Christ is well pleased with this counsel. And in truth it shows a high spirit in any man who is advanced in age, to take a young wife; by my father's soul, your heart hangs on a jolly pin! Do in this even as you will, for in conclusion I hold it best.'

Justinus, who sat ever quiet and hearkened, answered Placebo in this wise: 'Now, brother mine, be patient, I prithee; since you have spoken, hearken to me. Seneca, amongst his other wise words, says that a man ought right well to consider to whom he gives his land or his goods. And since I ought to bethink me well to whom I give my goods away, much more ought I to bethink me to whom I give my body; for right well I warn you it is no child's play to take a wife without due thought. A man must inquire, I hold, whether she be rich or poor, wise and sober, or bibulous and proud, or otherwise a bad lot, — a chider, a waster of goods, and a termagant. Albeit no man shall find or imagine any in this world that trots perfectly in all, neither man nor beast, nevertheless it should suffice that any wife have more good traits than ill vices. And all this demands leisure to inquire into. For, God wot, I have wept full many a privy tear since I have had a wife. Let whoso will praise the life of a wedded man, in sooth I find in it only cost and trouble, and observances bare of all bliss. And yet, — God wot, my neighbours around me, and especially many a troop of women, say I have the most steadfast and meekest wife living. But I know best where my shoe wrings me. But for all of me, you may do even right as you will; you are a man of years, consider how you enter upon marriage, and especially with a young wife and a fair. By Him that made water, air, earth, and fire, the youngest man in all this company has enough to do to have his wife to himself, trust me. Not for three years can you wholly content her; a wife demands right much respectful ministration. But I pray you be not ill-pleased with me.'

'Well; have you done your speech?' quoth this January. 'A straw for your Senaca and your proverbs; I care not two blades of grass for your school-terms. Wiser men than you have assented to my plan, as you have heard even now. Placebo, what say you?'

'I say,' quoth he, 'that is is verily a cursed man who hinders matrimony.' And at these words they straightway arose and fully agreed that he should wed when he list and whom he would.

High imagining and careful thought about his marriage began to occupy January's soul from day to day, and night by night many a fair shape and many a fair visage passed through his heart. Whoso should take a well-polished mirror and should set it in the general market-place, then should he see many a form pass across his mirror;. and in the same wise January began to consider in his thoughts the maidens who dwelt nigh him. He wist not where his thoughts should settle. For if one had beauty of countenance, another stood so highly in the people's grace for her steadiness and kindness that she most had the general approval. And some were rich, and had a bad reputation. But nevertheless, betwixt sport and earnest, at last he fixed on one, and let all the others pass out of his heart, and of his own motion chose her; for love is ever blind. And when he was laid in his bed, in his heart and mind he portrayed her fresh beauty and tender age, her small middle, her long and slim arms, her wise demeanor, her steadiness, her good breeding and her womanly bearing. And when his choice was fixed upon her, it seemed to him that it could not have been bettered; for when he was resolved, he thought every other man's wit so poor that none could reply against his choice; this was his fancy.

He sent to his friends with urgent request and prayed them to do him that pleasure to come to him speedily. He would relieve them, one and all, of their labour (he said), and there was no more need for him to walk or ride about, for he had appointed where his choice should rest.

Placebo came straightway, and also all his friends. And first of all January begged of them the grace that none of them should offer argument against the purpose which he had taken; which course was pleasing to God, and a sure foundation for his well-being. He said there was in the town a maiden who had a great name for beauty, though she were of low degree; but her youth and her beauty sufficed him. Which maiden, he said, he would have, to lead all his life with her in ease and holiness; and he thanked God that he might have her entirely, (that no creature should share his bliss, and prayed them to do their diligence that he failed not of success; would they do this, his spirit were at rest. 'Then,' quoth he, 'there is nothing to mar my bliss, save that one thing pricks in my conscience, the which I will rehearse to you here. Full long I have heard it said,' quoth he, 'that no man can have two perfect joys, that is, on earth and also in paradise. For though he avoid the seven sins and also every branch of that tree, yet is there such perfect felicity and ease and joy in marriage, that now in mine old age I am every aghast that I shall now lead so merry a life, so delicious, without woe and contention, that I shall have my heaven now on earth. For since the true heaven is bought so dearly with tribulation and great penance, how should I, then, who shall live in such happiness as all wedded men have, come to the bliss where Christ lives eternally? This is my dread, and do you, my two brethren, resolve me this question, I pray.'

Justinus, who despised his folly, answered forthwith in his mockery; and to abridge his long tale he would cite no authority, but said, 'Sir, so there be none obstacle other than this, God may work so high mercy and marvel for you that, ere you have the due offices of Holy Church, you may repent of a wedded man's life, in which you say there is no woe or contention. And God forbid else, that he send not a wedded man grace to repent well oftener than to a single man! And therefore the best counsel I know is, despair not, sir, but have in your memory that peradventure she may be your purgatory. She may be God's instrument and God's scourge; then shall your soul skip up to heaven swifter than an arrow out of a bow. I hope to God that hereafter you shall learn that there is no such felicity in marriage, and never shall be, as to hinder your salvation, so you solace yourself with your wife temperately, as is just and reasonable, and please her not too amorously, and keep you from other sin also. My tale is done, for my wit is thin, but be not aghast at this, my brother. But let us wade out of this matter. The Wife of Bath has declared full well in little space, if you have understood, upon marriage, which you have in hand. And now fare you well, and God have you in His grace!'

And after these words Justinus and Placebo each took leave of him and each other. And when they saw it must needs be, by discreet and wise negotiation they wrought so that this maiden, who was named May, should be wedded to this January as soon as ever she could. I believe it would delay you too long if I told you of every bond and document whereby she was enfeoffed in his estates, or of all rich preparation. But finally the day was come when they both betook them to the church to receive the holy sacrament. Forth came the priest with stole over his shoulders, and bade her be like Rebecca and Sara in faithfulness to marriage vows and in discretion; and said his orisons as is wonted, and signed them with the cross and prayed God bless them, and made all secure enough with holy rites.

Thus were they wedded with all ceremony, and at the feast he and she sat upon the dais with other honorable folk. All full of joy and happiness was the palace, and full of instruments of music and of viands the most dainty in all Italy. Before them stood such instruments of music that Orpheus nor Amphion of Thebes made never such melody. With every course came such bursts of minstrelsy that Joab never trumpeted half so clear to men's hearing, nor Thiodamas at Thebes, when the city was in dread. Bacchus poured out the wine for them on every side, and Venus laughed upon every one of them, for January was now her knight and would make trial of his spirit as well in marriage as in freedom; and with her torch in her hand she danced about before the bride and all the company. I dare right well say this, of a sooth, that Hymen, who is god of marriage, saw never in his life so merry a wedded man. Thou poet Martian, who describest to us that merry wedding of Philology and Mercury, and the songs that the Muses sang, hold thou thy peace; too small are both thy pen and thy tongue to describe this wedding. When tender youth weds stooping age, there is such mirth that it cannot be written; try it yourselves, and then shall you know whether or not I lie in this.

May, who sat with so benign a countenance, to look upon her seemed enchantment; so meek was her look, Queen Esther never looked with such eyes upon Ahasuerus. I cannot describe to you all her beauty, but thus much I may tell, that she was like the bright morn of May filled to the full with all beauty and joy.

This January was ravished into a trance every time he beheld her face. 'Now would God it were become night,' he thought, 'and that the night would last forever! Would that all these people were gone!' And finally he did all he could, saving his honour, to hasten them in crafty wise from the feast. And time came when it was in reason to rise. And after that, folk danced and drank deep, and cast spices all about the house, and every man was full of joy and happiness. All but a squire, called Damian, who full many a day had carved before the knight. He was so ravished with his lady May that for the very pain he was wellnigh mad; he almost fainted and swooned where he stood, so sore had Venus wounded him with her brand as she bore it in her dancing. And quickly he got to his bed, — and I speak no more of him as at this time, but there let him weep and lament his fill, until fresh May will have pity on his pain.

Auctor. O perilous fire, that breeds in the bedstraw! O household foe that proffers this service! O traitor servant, false appearance of domestic faithfulness, like to the sly faithless serpent in the bosom, — God shield us all from knowing you! O, January, drunken in joy of marriage, see how thy Damian, thine own squire and thy man born, has in mind to do thee dishonour. God grant thee to spy out thine household foe. For there is no worse pestilence in this world than an household for ever before thee. —

The sun had run his diurnal arc; his body could no longer sojourn on the horizon in that latitude; night with his dark rough mantle began to overspread the hemisphere. Wherefore all this lusty throng parted from January, with thanks on every side. Home to their houses they rode in all lustihood, where they did their things even as pleased them, and went to rest when they saw their time. Soon after, this impatient January would go to bed, would tarry no longer. He drank punches, cordials and sweet wine of Italy with stinging spices, and many a full choice syrop, such as the cursed monk Constantine has written of in his book *De Coitu*; he was no whit backward to partake of all of them. And to his close friend he said, 'For God's love, in courteous wise let the house be emptied as soon as may be.' And they did even as he desired. Men drank, and anon drew the curtain. The bride was brought to bed as still as a stone; and when the bed had been blessed by the priest, every creature betook him out of the chamber.

When the day began to dawn January took a sop of bread in fine cleared wine and sat upright in his bed and sang full loud and high, and kissed his wife and made wanton cheer. He was all coltish, and as full of sportiveness and jargoning as a flecked magpie. The slack skin about his neck shook whilst he sang, so chanted and croaked he. But God knows what May thought in her heart, when she saw him sitting up in his shirt and nightcap, with his lean neck' she valued him not a bean. Then he said, 'I will take my rest; now the day has come, I can watch no longer.' And down he laid his head and slept until prime. And afterwards in due season up rose January, but fresh May, as the good custom is for wives, kept her chamber up to the fourth morning. For all must have repose sometime, or else they cannot long endure, — no living creature can, be it man or beast, or fish or bird.

Auctor: Now will I speak of the wretched Damian, who, as you shall hear, is languishing for love, and therefore I speak to him thus, and say, 'O hapless Damian, alas! Answer my demand now, how shalt thou tell thy woe to thy lady, the fresh May? She will say "no," and also if thou speak, she will reveal thy sorrow. May God be thy help! I can say no better.' —

This sick Damian so burned in the flames of Venus that he was dying of desire, wherefore he could endure no longer in this state, but put his life in hazard, and secretly he borrowed a pen-case, and wrote all his pain in a letter, in the style of a complaint or a lay, unto his fair fresh lady. And he put it into a purse of silk which hung over his shirt, and laid it next his breast.

The moon, which on that noon when January wedded fresh May was in the second degree of Taurus, was now glided into Cancer; thus long had May abode in her chamber, as is the custom amongst these nobles; a bride shall not eat in the hall till four days, or three at the least, be gone; then let her go to the banquet. The fourth day being completed from noon to noon, when the high mass was ended, this January sat in the hall, with May as fresh as a bright summer's morning. And so befell, this good man bethought him of his squire and said, 'Saint Mary! how is it that Damian attends not upon me? Is he still sick, or how is it?'

His squires, who stood beside him, made excuse for their fellow because his sickness hindered him from his duties; none other cause could keep him away.

'That grieves me; he is a gentle squire, by my faith!' quoth this January. 'Were he to die, it were harm and pity; he is as wise, discreet and secret as any man of his degree that I know, and also manly and ready to serve, and likely to prosper in his life. After meat, as soon as I can, I myself and also May will visit him, to do him all the comfort I know how.'

And for these words every man blessed him, that of his noble kindness he would thus comfort his squire in sickness; for it was a gentle deed.

'Dame,' quoth this January, 'after meat when you are come to your chamber out of this hall with your women, mind that you all go see this Damian; make him some entertainment, he is a man of gentle blood, and tell him that I will visit him when I have but rested me a little. And haste you, for I will abide till you come to me again.' And after these words he called to him a squire, who was marshal of his hall, and told him certain things, what he would.

This fresh May with all her women held her way straight to Damian. Down by his bed-side she sat, comforting him in as goodly way as she could. This Damian, when he saw his time, put into her hand secretly his purse and also his missive in which he had written his desires, without more ado than that he sighed wondrous deep, and softly said to her, 'Your grace to me, and I pray that you expose me not. I am dead if this thing be known.'

This purse she hid in her bosom and went her way; ye get no more of me on this meeting. And now she came to January, and sat full softly upon his bed-side. He took her and kissed her full often, and laid him down to sleep. She made excuse to leave the room, and when she had read through this billet, at last she rent it all to bits and privily cast them away in a safe place.

Who thinks hard now but fair fresh May? She came back to the side of old January, who slept till the cough awaked him. But lest over-nice folk be wroth with me, I dare not let you know whether it seemed to her paradise or hell; and here I leave them till evensong rang and they must arise.

Were it by destiny or chance, were it by some mystic influence or by nature or through the constellations, — that the heavens stood in such array that the time was fortunate (for as these clerks say, everything has its time) to give a billet in the service of Venus to any woman, to get her love, — as to all this I cannot say; but great God in heaven, who knows no act is without cause, let Him judge of all, for I will hold my peace. But the truth is that this fresh May received that day such an impression of pity for this sick Damian that she could not drive from her heart the thought of bringing him ease. 'In truth,' she thought, 'I care not whom this thing may annoy, for here I warrant him to love him best of any creature, had he no more than his kirtle.'

Lo, pity runs quickly into a gentle heart! Here you may see how excellent a generosity there is in women, when they take counsel well. There may be some tyrant, indeed there be many, with hearts as hard as any stone, who would have let him die in the place rather than have granted him favour; and would rejoice in their cruel pride, and care not though they did murder.

This gentle May, full of pity, made a letter with her own hand, in which letter she granted him her full favour; nought lacked but only day and place where she might meet him, for it should be even as he would have it. And upon a day, when she saw her time, May went to visit this Damian, and craftily thrust this letter down under his pillow; let him read it if he will! She took him by the hand and wrung it hard, but so secretly that there wist no creature of it, and bade him be all well soon, and went forth to January, when he sent after her.

Up rose Damian next morning; all his sickness and sorrow were gone. He combed his hair, he preened and pranked him, he did all that his lady could wish; and also he was as docile toward January as ever was hunting-dog. He was so pleasant to every one (for cunning is all, whoever knows how to use it), that every creature was fain to speak well of him; and fully he stood in his lady's favour. And thus I leave Damian going about his business, and I will proceed with my tale.

Some clerks hold that highest felicity consists in pleasure; and if this be so, in sooth this noble January shaped his course by all his power to live in the highest happiness, in honourable wise as beseems a knight. His house and all his manner of life were made as honourable and befitting his degree as a king's. Amongst others of his seemly appurtenances, he made a garden, all walled with stone; so fair a garden I wot of nowhere. For out of doubt, I believe verily, he who wrote the Romance of the Rose could not well describe the beauty of it; nor would Priapus, though he be god of gardens, be sufficient to tell the beauty of the garden and of the spring under an ever-green laurel. Full oftentimes Pluto and his spouse Proserpina, and all elfdom, disported them and made melody about that pool, and danced, as men told. This aged knight, noble January, took such pleasure in walking and diverting him there that he would suffer no person save himself to bear the key; for he carried ever a little silver key to the small wicket, with which, when he list, he opened it. And in the summer season, when he would solace him with his wife, he would go thither with May his wife and none but they two. And in this wise this

January and his blooming spouse lived many a merry day. But earthly joy lasts not ever, for January or any creature.

Auctor. O sudden chance, O thou fickle Fortune, so deceitful like the scorpion, that with thine head flatterest when thou wilt sting; they tail with its venom is death. O brittle joy! O sweet, strange venom! O monster, that canst paint thy gifts so craftily, under guise of steadfastness, that thou deceivest both great and small! Why hast thou thus deceived January, who hadst taken him as thy full friend? And now thou has robbed him of both his eyes, for sorrow of which he would fain die. —

Alas! this noble, lordly January, amidst all his prosperity and lustiness, is waxed blind, and that suddenly. He wept and wailed sore, and therewith, lest his wife should fall into some folly, the fire of jealousy so burned his heart that he would fain some man had killed both him and her. For he desired not that either in his lifedays or after his death she should be loved or wedded, but ever live as a widow in black clothes, solitary as the turtle-dove that has lost her mate. But at the last, sooth to say, his sorrow began to assuage after a month or two; for when he wist that it could be no otherwise, he took his adversity in patience, save that he could not forego to be evermore jealous. Which jealousy was so inordinate that neither in the hall nor in any house else, nor in any other place, would he suffer her to walk or ride, unless he had evermore his hand on her. Wherefore this fresh May wept full often, who loved Damian so warmly that either she must soon die or else she must have him. She looked ever for the day when her heart should break.

Upon the other side Damian was become the most sorrowful creature that ever was, for neither by day nor by night could he speak a word to fresh May upon his subject, or upon any such matter, unless January were to hear it, who had hand upon her evermore. But notwithstanding this, by writing to and fro and by privy signals, he knew her mind; and she knew also whither his purpose tended.

Auctor. O January, what boots it though thou couldst see as far as ships sail? As well be deceived when blind as be deceived when a man can see. Lo Argus with an hundred eyes, much as he could pry or pore, yet was he hoodwinked; and, God wot, so be others that ween verily that it be not so. But to pass over all that is a pleasure, and I say no more. —

This fresh May, that I have been speaking of, pressed into warm wax the little key, which January carried, of the small wicket through which he often went into his garden. And Damian, who knew all her plan, privily counterfeited the key. There is no more to say, but there shall soon betide some marvel through this key, which you shall hear, if you will tarry.

Auctor. O noble Ovid, God wot thou sayest full truly! What sleight is so long and painful that a lover will not find out in some way? Men may learn from Pyramus and Thisbe; though they were watched everywhere full long and strictly, they had an understanding, whispering through a wall; none could have described such a trick. —

But now to my tale. Ere eight days were passed, ere the month of July, it befell that through the urging of his wife January caught so great an appetite to divert him in his garden, with none but they two, that upon a morning he said to this May, 'Rise up, my wife, my noble lady, my sweeting; the turtle's voice is heard, my sweet dove; the winter is gone, with his drenching rains. Come forth, now, with thy dovelike eyes! How fairer be thy breasts than wine! The garden is enclosed all around; come forth, my white spouse; of a surety thou hast wounded me in mine heart, O wife! I have known no blemish in thee. Come forth, and let us take our disport. I chose thee for my wife and my solace.'

Such old words of folly he used. To Damian she made a sign that he should go before with his key. This Damian then opened the wicket and in he darted, and that in such wise that none could see or hear it, and anon he was sitting quietly under a bush. This January, as blind as a stone, holding May by his hand and with no one else, went into his fresh garden, and quickly clapped the wicket to.

'Now wife,' quoth he, 'here is none but you and I, — you, who are the creature I love best. For by that Lord That sits in high heaven, I had liefer die on a sword than harm you, dear faithful wife! For God's sake, think how I chose you, not for any covetousness, in verity, but only for the love I bore you. And though I be old and see not, be true to me, and I shall tell you wherefore. Three things you shall win thereby, certes: first, Christ's love; and honour for yourself; and all my heritage, town and tower. I give it you, make out the charters as you list; this shall be done to-morrow ere the sun go down, so surely may God bring my soul to heaven. First I pray kiss me in sign of covenant, and though I be jealous, blame me not. You are so deeply imprinted in my thought, that when I consider your beauty and therewith my old unpropitious age, certes, though I die for it, I cannot suffer to be out of your company, for very love; and this is very truth. Now wife, kiss me, and let us roam about the garden.'

This fresh May, when she heard these words, answered January mildly; but first of all she began to weep. Quoth she, 'I have a soul to guard as well as you, and also mine honour, and that tender flower of my wifehood, which I secured to your hand when the priest bound my body to you. Wherefore I will answer thus, by your leave, my dear lord: I pray to God, never dawn the day that I die not, as foully as woman can, if I ever do that shame to my kindred, or so smirch mine honour, as to be false. And if I do that fault, let me be stripped and put in a sack, and drowned in the nearest river. I am a gentlewoman, and not a wench. Why speak you thus? But men ever be faithless and women ever have fresh reproach from you; you have no other pretext, I believe, than to speak of distrust and reproach to us.'

And at that word she saw where Damian sat in the bush, and she began to cough and made signs with her finger that Damian should climb up a tree which was laden with fruit; and up he went. For verily he knew all her purpose, and every sign that she could make, far better than January, her own husband. For she told him all of this matter in a letter, how he was to act. And thus I leave him sitting up in the pear-tree, and January and May roaming pleasantly.

Bright was the day and the firmament blue; Phœbus sent down his beams of gold, to gladden every flower with his warmth. At that time he was in Gemini, I believe, but little removed from his depression in Cancer, which is the exaltation of Jupiter. And so befell, this bright morning-time, that in the further side of that garden was Pluto, who is the king of fairyland, and many a lady with him, following his wife, Queen Proserpina, one after another, straight as a line. (Ye may read the story in Claudian, how he fetched her away in his grisly chariot, whilst she was gathering flowers in the meadow.) This king of fairyland then sat him down upon a bank of turves green and fresh, and forthwith he said thus to his spouse: 'My wife,' quoth he, 'no person can say nay, experience proves ever the treason which women do to men. I can tell ten hundred thousand notable stories about your infidelity and frailty. O Solomon, wise, richest in wealth, filled with sapience and earthly glory, thy words be full worthy to be remembered of every creature that knows wit and reason. Thus he praises the goodness of man: "Amongst a thousand men still I found one good, but of all women I found none." These be the words of the king who knows your wickedness. And Jesus the son of Sirach, I believe he but seldom speaks respectfully of you. A wild-fire and corrupt pestilence fall upon your bodies to-night! See you this honourable lord? Alas, because he is old and blind, his own man shall make him a cuckold. Lo here in the tree he sits, the profligate! Now of my royal power I will grant to this old, blind, worthy knight that he shall recover his vision, when his wife would do him wrong. Then he shall know all her looseness, both to her dishonour and of others besides.'

Quoth Proserpina, 'You shall, if you so wish; but by the soul of my mother's sire I swear that I shall grant to her to return a sufficient answer, and for her sake to all women after; that, though they be overtaken in any guilt, they shall excuse themselves with bold face, and bear down those who would call them to account. None of them shall die for lack of an answer. Although a man had seen somewhat with both of his eyes, nevertheless we women shall face it boldly out, and weep, and swear, and craftily chide, so that you men shall be as ignorant as geese. What care I for your authorities? I wot well this Jew, this Solomon, found many a fool amongst us women. But though he found no good woman, yet many another man has found women full faithful, good and virtuous. Witness them that dwell in Christ's house; they proved their steadfastness by their martyrdom. Also the Roman histories make mention of many a true faithful wife. But, sir (and be not wroth), albeit he said he found no good woman, I pray you take the man's meaning; he meant thus, that in sovereign goodness there is none but God, That sitteth in Trinity. Eh, for the love of the one true God! Why make you so much of Solomon? What though he builded a temple, God's house? What though he were glorious and rich? So likewise he made a temple to false gods; how could he do a thing more forbidden? Perdy! fairly as you plaster his name, he was a lecher and an idolater, and in his old age he forsook the true God. As the Bible says, if God had not spared him for his father's sake, He would have rent the kingdom away earlier than He did. I care not a butterfly for all the dishonour that you men write of women. I am a woman, I must needs speak or else swell till my heart burst. For since he said we be praters, so surely may I keep all my tresses whole, as I spare not out of any courtesy to speak harm of him who would wrong us.'

'Dame,' quoth this Pluto, 'be wroth no longer, — I give it up. But since I swore mine oath that I would grant him his sight again, I warn you that of a truth my word shall stand. I am a king, it is not fitting that I should be false.'

'And I,' quoth she, 'a queen of the fairies. She shall have her answer, I undertake. Let us have no more words hereof. In sooth I will oppose you no longer.'

Now return we to January, who was in the garden with his fair wife, and sang more merrily than a popinjay, 'Thee I love best, and ever shall, and none other.' So long he wandered amongst the alleys until he came by the pear-tree where this Damian sat on high, right merry amongst the fresh green leaves. This fresh May, so bright and fair, began to sigh, and said, 'Alas my side! Now sir, for aught that may hap, I must have some of the pears that I see, or I must die, so sorely I long to eat of the small green pears. Help, for the love of our

Lady in heaven! I tell you of a truth, a woman in my situation may have so great an appetite for a fruit that she may die unless she have it.'

'Alas!' quoth he, 'that I have not here a boy that could climb! Alas, alas, that I am blind!'

'Yea, sir,' quoth she, 'no matter; but if you would vouchsafe, for love of heaven, to clasp that pear-tree within your arms (for I well know you distrust me); then, so I might set my foot on your back, I could climb up well enough.'

'Certes,' quoth he, 'there should be nothing wanting here, if I could help you even with my heart's blood.'

He stooped down, and she stood on his back and caught hold by a branch and went up. Ladies, I pray you be not wroth; I cannot gloss, I am a rough man. And forthwith this Damian received her.

And when Pluto saw this great wrong, he restored his sight to January and made him see as well as he ever could. And when he had his sight again, never was there man so fain of anything. But his thought was evermore on his wife, and he cast his two eyes up into the tree, and saw Damian with his wife. And he set up such a roar and a cry as the mother does when the child is dying: 'Out! help! alas!' he began to cry. 'O rude, bold lady, what do you?'

And she answered, 'Sir, what ails you? Have patience and reason in your mind. I have helped you in both your eyes. On peril of my soul, I lie not; it was taught me that to heal your eyes there was nothing better than to stand with a man up in a tree. God knows, I did it with a full good intent.'

'With a man up in a tree!' he said. 'God grant that you both die a shameful death! It was worse than that; I saw it with mine eyes, else let me be hanged by the neck!'

'Then,' quoth she, 'my medicine is all false; for certainly, if you were able to see well, you would not say these words to me; you have some glimmerings, but you have not perfect sight.'

Quoth he, 'I see with both of mine eyes as well as I ever could, God be thanked! And by my troth, methought it was as I said.'

'You are bewildered, good sir, bewildered,' quoth she. 'This thanks I have because I have given you your sight! Alas that ever I was so kind!'

'Now, dame,' quoth he, 'let us forget all of it. Come down, my love, and if I have spoken amiss, God so help me as I am sorry for it.'

'Yea, sir,' quoth she, 'you may think as you will; but, sir, a man that wakes out of his sleep cannot speedily take good heed of a thing or see it perfectly, till he be thoroughly used to the daylight. Even so a man who has been blind a long time cannot straightway see so well, when his sight is newly restored, as he who has seen for a day or two. Till your vision be settled for a time, full many a sight may beguile you. Be careful, I pray you; for by the Queen of heaven full many a man thinks to see a thing, and it is all otherwise than it seems. He who misapprehends, misjudges.'

And with that she leaped down from the tree. Who was glad but this January? He kissed her and embraced her full often and gently stroked her, and led her home to his palace. Now, good men, I pray you be ever of good cheer. Thus ends my tale of January, and God bless us, and his mother, our Lady!

Epilogue to the Merchant's Tale

'Eh! God's mercy!' said our Host. 'Now I pray God keep me from such a wife! Lo what sleights and wiles be in women! They be ever as busy as bees to deceive us simple men, and they will ever swerve from the truth, it is well proved by this Merchant's tale. I have a wife as true as steel, without doubt, though she be otherwise a poor one; but she is a blabbing shrew with her tongue and has an heap of other faults. — No matter about that, let such things pass. But, know you what? Be it said secretly, sorely I rue that I am tied to her. But if I were to reckon up every fault of hers, of a certainty I were too foolish; and I say this with good reason, for it would be reported to her by some one of this company; by whom, it needs not to state, since it is women know how to move out such gear. And also my wit suffices not to tell all. Wherefore my tale is ended. Squire, draw nearer, if you will vouchsafe, and tell us somewhat about love; for, certes, you know as much of that as any man.'

'Yea, sir,' quoth he, 'and I will tell you with hearty good-will as much as I am able. For I will not rebel against your desire; I will tell a tale. Hold me excused if I speak amiss; my intention is good. Lo, this is my tale.'

❧ *The Squire's Tale*

There dwelt a king at Sarray, in the land of Tartary, who made war upon Russia, through which many a doughty man died. This noble king was named Cambuscan, who was so renowned in his time that nowhere, in any region, was there a lord so excellent in every wise. He lacked nought that befits a king. He kept the faith of the religion to which he was born and pledged by oath; and in addition he was brave, wise, rich, and true of his word, and ever alike merciful and just, benign, honourable, and as steadfast of his nature as the centre of the earth; young, lusty and strong, ambitious in arms as any young knight of all his court. He was fair of person and blessed by Fortune, and ever maintained his royal station so well that there was nowhere such another. This noble king, Cambuscan the Tartar, had by his wife Elpheta two sons, of whom the eldest was named Algarsyf and the second Cambal. This worthy king also had a daughter named Canacee, who was the youngest. But it lies not in my tongue or in my cunning to tell you all her beauty; I dare not undertake so lofty a task, and also mine English is insufficient; it must be an excellent master of rhetoric, who should know the colours of style which pertain to that study, if he were to describe her every feature. I am not such, I must speak as I am able.

And so befell that when this Cambuscan had borne his diadem twenty years, he had the feast of his nativity proclaimed throughout his city of Sarray on the last Ides of March, according to the year's course, as he was wont to do, I deem, from year to year. Phœbus the sun was full merry and bright, for he was nigh his exaltation in the face of Mars, and in the house of Mars in Aries, the choleric, hot sign. Full lusty and mild was the weather, wherefore the birds, in the bright sunshine, what with the season and the young green things, sang their loves full loudly; they had got them protection, they thought, against the keen, cold sword of winter.

This Cambuscan, of whom I have told you, in royal vestments and with his diadem, sat full high upon the dais in his palace-hall and held his feast, so ceremonious and so rich that never was the like in all this world. Whereof if I should tell you all it would occupy a summer's day. And also it needs not describe the order of the service at every course; I will not tell of their strange pottages, of their swans or young herons. And also in that land, as old knights relate, certain meats are esteemed right dainty which in our land men hold in but low esteem. No man could relate all. I will not delay you, for it is prime, and we should gain nought, but let the day slip by; so I will return to the process of my tale.

It so befell that after the third course, whilst this king sat thus in his state, listening to his minstrels play their things deliciously before him at the board, all suddenly in at the hall-door there came a knight on a brazen steed, and in his hand a broad glass mirror. A gold ring he had upon his thumb, and by his side hung a naked sword. And up he rode to the high table. There was spoken never a word in all the hall, for marvel of this knight; young and old watched full eagerly to see him.

This strange knight, who came so suddenly, all armed full richly save his head, saluted king and queen, and all the lords by order as they sat in the hall, with such deep reverence and obeisance as well in speech as in bearing, that though Gawain with his antique courtesy were come again out of fairyland, he could not have corrected this knight in a word. And then before the high table he spake his message on a manly voice, after the form used in his language, without fault in syllable or letter; and, that so his story should seem the more acceptable, his cheer accorded with his words, as the art of speech teaches them that learn it. Albeit I cannot follow his style, nor climb over so high a stile, yet to the general understanding I say this, which was the purport of all that ever he said, if so be I have it in memory: 'The king of Araby and Ind, my liege lord, saluteth you on this festal day as he best can, and in honour of your feast sendeth you by me, who am ready to your command, this steed of brass, that easily and well can bear your body whithersoever your heart willeth to go, without harming you, through foul or fair, in drought or rain, in the space of one natural day, that is, four-and-twenty hours; or if you list to fly in the air as high as an eagle when he lists to soar, this same steed shall bear you, ever without hurt, till you be where you desire, though you repose or sleep on his back; and he will come back again, at the turning of a pin. He who wrought it understood full many a craft; he watched after many a constellation ere he had done this work, and knew full well many a seal and bond of magic.

'This mirror also which I have in my hand, hath such a might that men can see in it when any adversity shall befall your realm or yourself, and plainly who is your friend or foe. And above all this, if any bright lady hath set her heart on any manner of man, she shall behold his treason, if he be false, his new love, and all his craftiness, and so openly that naught shall be hidden. Wherefore against this lusty summer season he hath sent this mirror and this ring here before you to your excellent daughter here, my lady Canacee. The virtue of the ring is this, if ye will listen; that, if it please her to wear it upon her thumb or to carry it in her purse, there is no bird that flieth under the heavens whose voice she shall not well understand; and shall plainly and fully know his meaning, and answer him again in his language. And every grass that hath root she shall likewise know, and whom it will heal, though his wounds be never so deep and gaping.

'This naked sword which hangeth beside me hath such virtue that, whatsoever man you smite, it will bite and cut all through his armour, were it as thick as a branched oak; and whatsoever man is wounded by the blow shall never be whole till it please you in mercy to stroke him with the flat in that place where he is hurt; this is as much as to say that you must stroke him again with the flat of the sword on the wound, and it will close. This is the very truth, without all colouring; it will not fail whilst it is in your possession.'

And when this knight had thus said his say, he rode out of the hall and alighted. His steed, which shone like the sun, stood still as a stone in the courtyard. This knight anon was led to his chamber and unarmed and set at meat. The presents, that is to say, the sword and the mirror, were full royally fetched and borne into the high tower by certain officers appointed; and the ring was solemnly borne to Canacee, where she sat at the board. But verily, without any falsehood, the brazen horse could not be removed, and stood as if it were glued to the ground. No man could draw it out of its place by any contrivance of windlass or pulley; and with good reason, they knew not the secret. Therefore they left it in the place till the knight taught them the manner to remove it, which you shall hear afterwards.

Great was the press that swarmed to and fro to gape on this horse that stood thus; for it was as high and broad and long and as well proportioned for strength as if it were a Lombard steed; and therewith so like a perfect horse, and so quick of eye, as if it were a noble Apulian courser. For certes, from its tail to its ear neither nature nor art could better it in any way, as all the people deemed. But ever their greatest wonder was how it could go, and was of brass. It was of fairy craft, so the people thought. Divers folk judged diversely; as many heads, so many wits. They murmured like a swarm of bees, and made explanations out of their fantasies, rehearsing these old poems, and said it was like the Pegasus, the horse which had wings for flying; or else it was like the horse of Sinon the Greek, which brought Troy to destruction, as men may read in these old histories. Quoth one, 'My heart is afeared evermore; I believe some armed men be in there, who plot to win this city. It were right good that all such things were looked into.' Another whispered low to his fellow and said, 'He lies. It is rather like an appearance made by some magic, as jugglers contrive at these great feasts.' Thus they prated and talked of sundry fears, even as ignorant people are wont to deem of things that be made more cunningly than they in their ignorance can comprehend. They are fain to judge toward the worser side.

And some of them marvelled about the mirror, which had been carried up into the keep, how men could see such things therein. One answered and said that it might well be in a natural way, through arrangements of angles and of cunning reflections, and said there was such an one in Rome. They spake of Alhazen and Vitello and Aristotle, who wrote of curious mirrors and of perspective glasses, as they know who have heard their books.

And others wondered about the sword that would pierce through everything; and fell in speech of King Telephus, and Achilles with his wondrous spear, for he could both heal and harm with it, even in such wise as men could with the sword of which you have just heard. They spake of sundry methods of hardening metal, and also of sundry drugs, and of how and when it should be hardened; all which is unknown, to me at least.

Then they spake of Canacee's ring, and all said they never had heard of such a wondrous contrivance in rings, save that Moses and King Solomon had the name of skill in such craft. Thus said the people, and drew into groups. But nevertheless some said it was wondrous to make glass out of fern-ashes, and yet glass is not like fern-ashes; but because men have known that art so long, therefore their talking and wonderment have ceased. And some marvel as greatly at the cause of thunder, at ebb and flood tides, at gossamer, at mist, at all things, till the cause is known. Thus the people prated and gave opinions and explanations, till the king arose from table.

Phœbus had left the meridian, and the royal beast, the noble Leo with his Aldiran, was yet ascending, when this Tartar king Cambuscan rose from the board where he sat aloft. Before him went the loud minstrelsy, as he proceeded to his presence-chamber, where they sounded divers instruments till it was like heaven to listen. Now danced lusty Venus' dear children, for their lady sat full high in Pisces and looked on them with friendly eyes.

This noble king sat upon his throne, and forthwith the stranger knight was fetched to him, and went on the dance with Canacee. Here was jollity and revel which a dull man cannot describe; he must be acquainted with love and his service, and be a festive man fresh as May, who could describe such gear. Who could tell you the manner of the dances, such rare and lusty demeanour, such crafty glancing and dissimulation for fear jealous men might see? No man but Sir Lancelot, and he is dead. Therefore I pass over all this merriment; I say no more, but leave them at this sport till they betook them to supper.

Amid all this melody the steward bade hasten the spices and also the wine. The ushers and the squires have gone. The wine and the spices come forthwith. They ate and drank; and when this was ended, they went to the temple, as was but right. The service done, they supped, still by daylight. What need to relate all the furnishing? Each man wot well that at a king's feast there is plenty for great and small, and more dainties than I have knowledge of.

After supper this noble king went to see the horse of brass, with all the company of lords and ladies after him. Such wonderment there was at this horse of brass, there never was such since the great siege of Troy where also men marvelled at a horse. But finally the king asked this knight as to the virtue and powers of this charger and prayed him to tell the management thereof. The horse began to trip and dance as soon as ever this knight laid hand upon the rein; and he said, 'sire, there is no more to say save that when you list to ride you must turn a pin which stands in his ear, which I shall tell you of alone. You must name to him also to what place or to what country you list to ride. And when you come to the place where you wish to stop, you must bid him descend, and turn another pin, for in this lies the root of the whole contrivance, and he will descend and do your will and abide quietly in that place. Though all the world should swear otherwise, he shall not be drawn or borne thence. Or if you list to bid him go thence, turn this pin, and immediately he will vanish out of the sight of every man, and come again, whether it be by day or night, when it shall please you to summon him back, in such manner as I shall anon tell you betwixt you and me alone. Ride when it may please you, there is no more to be done.'

When the king was instructed by that knight, and in his mind had properly comprehended the manner and the form of all this contrivance, thus glad and blithe this noble, doughty king repaired to his revel as before. The bridle was carried to the tower and guarded amongst his most precious jewels. The horse vanished out of sight, I know not how; you get no more out of me! But thus I leave this Cambuscan holding celebration for his lords in merriment and jollity well-nigh till day began to spring.

II

The nurse of digestion, Sleep, blinked on them and bade them take heed that much drink and labour call for rest; and with yawning mouth he kissed them all and said it was time to lie down, for blood was dominant. 'Cherish blood, nature's friend,' quoth he. Yawning they thanked him, and by twos and threes every person drew to his repose, as Sleep bade; they took it to be best. Their dreams shall not be told by me; their heads were full of the fumes of wine, which cause dreams which have no significance. They slept till it was high prime, the greater part, except Canacee. She was full temperate, as women are wont to be; for she had leave of her father to go to rest soon after it was evening. She list not to become pallid, nor to look jaded in the morn. And she slept her first sleep, and awoke; she changed colour twenty times with the joy which she had in her heart, both for her curious ring and for her mirror. And in her sleep, even for the impression which the mirror had made upon her, she had dreamed a dream. Wherefore, ere the sun began to glide up, she called to her duenna beside her, and said she list to rise. Her duenna, one of these old women who would fain be deemed right prudent, answered her anon and said, 'Madame, whither will you go thus early? For the folk be all a-bed.'

Quoth she, 'I will arise, for I list to sleep no longer, but to walk about.'

Her duenna called a great rout of women, fully ten or twelve, and up they rose. Up rose the fresh Canacee herself, as ruddy and bright as the young sun when he is advanced four degrees into the Ram; no higher was he when she was ready. And she walked forth at an easy pace, lightly arrayed for the lusty, sweet season, to amuse herself and walk afoot, and with her but five or six of her following. And she went forth in the park down an alley. The vapour which glided up from the earth made the sun seem broad and ruddy; but it was so fair a sight that it made all their hearts to bound, what with the season, and the morn, and the fowls which she heard sing; for straightway she knew what they meant and all their minds, even by their singing.

If the end why every tale is said be delayed till the appetite be cold of them that have long hearkened after it, the savour passes away ever more and more for the fulsomeness of its prolixity. Wherefore methinks I should come to the point, and quickly make an end of their walking.

Full high over her head, as Canacee was rambling and diverting her, in a tree all dry and white as chalk there sat a falcon, which cried so with a piteous voice that all the wood resounded with her cry. She had beaten herself so piteously with both her wings that the red blood ran down the tree where she was perched. And ever alike she cried and shrieked, and so tore herself with her beak that there is no tiger or beast so cruel dwelling in either wood or forest that would not have wept for pity of her, if weep he could, she ever shrieked so loudly. For never yet was man living, if I could but well describe a falcon, who heard of such another for fair plumage and nobility of form and all that could be noted. She seemed peregrine falcon from a strange land; and evermore as she perched there she swooned now and again for loss of blood, till she well nigh fell from the tree.

This fair princess, who bare on her finger the curious ring, through which she understood all that any fowl could say in his language, and could answer him again therein, comprehended what this falcon said and well nigh died of pity. And she went full quickly to the tree, and looked pityingly on the falcon and held out her kirtle, for well she wist the falcon must fall from the branch when next it swooned for loss of blood. A long while she abode to watch it, till at last she spake to the hawk in this manner, as you shall now hear.

'What is the cause, if it may be told, that you are in this furious hell-torment?' Thus she spake to the hawk in the tree. 'Is this for sorrow at some death, or for loss of love? For, as I believe, these be the two things that oftenest cause woe unto a gentle heart. It needs not speak of other causes of sorrow; for you are avenging yourself upon yourself, which well proves that either love or fear must be the cause of your cruelty, since I see that no other creature is hunting you. For the love of God, pray spare yourself, or what can be your help? For never before now, north or south, saw I beast or fowl use himself so piteously. You slay me with your sorrow in sooth, I have so great compassion of you. For God's love, come down from the tree; and, as I am a true king's daughter, I wist verily the cause of your trouble, if it lay in my power I would amend it ere it were night, so help me the great God of nature. And I shall find herbs full plenty, to heal your hurts with speedily.'

Then this falcon shrieked more piteously than ever she did, and anon fell to the ground and lay in a swoon as if dead, like a stone, whilst Canacee took her in her lap, till she awoke from her swoon. And after she had revived, she spake thus, even in her hawk's speech: 'That pity runs soon into a gentle heart, seeing its own likeness to be in bitter pains, is proved every day, as men may witness as well in fact as by authority; for a gentle heart manifests gentle deeds. I see well, my fair Canacee, that of your true womanly benignity which nature has set in your disposition you have compassion on my distress. And for no hope to fare the better, but only to be obedient unto your generous heart, and to make others beware through me, as the lion is warned through the chastisement of the dog, — for that very reason and purpose, whilst I have time and leisure, I will make confession of my hurt ere I go.'

And ever, whilst the one told her sorrow, the other wept as if she would turn to water, till the falcon bade her be still. And sighing she spake her mind right thus: 'Where I was bred and fostered (alas the time!) in a rock of grey marble, so tenderly that nothing ailed me, I knew not what adversity was, till I could fly full high under the heavens. Then a tercelet dwelt hard by me that seemed fountain of all nobility; albeit he was full of treason and falseness, it was so cloaked under humble bearing, colour of truth and pleasing behaviour and zealous devotion, in such manner that no creature could have deemed he could feign, so deep and fast did he dye his colours. Even as a serpent hides him under the flowers till he can see his time to sting, so this god of love, this hypocrite, performed his ceremonious attentions, and, in seeming, all the observances that accord with the nobility of love. As in a tomb all the fairness is without, and underneath is the corpse in such guise as you know, such was this hypocrite; seeming hot and truly cold, in this wise he served his purpose, so that none save the Fiend knew his real mind.

'So long had he wept and made complaint, and feigned his service to me for many a year, that my heart, too pitying and too simple, all innocent of his crowned malice, fearful of his death, as methought, upon his oaths and assurances granted him love, on this condition, that my honour and good name should be preserved evermore, both privily and openly; that is to say, in accordance with his desert, I gave him all my heart and thought, — on no other terms, as God knows and he, — and took his heart in exchange for mine forever. But sooth is said, many a day since, "an honest man and a thief think not alike." When he saw the thing gone so far that I had granted my love fully in such wise as I have now said, and had given him my loyal heart as utterly as he swore he gave his heart to me, forthwith this tiger, full of all duplicity, fell on his knees with such humble devotion and such deep reverence, and in his bearing so like a gentle lover, so ravished with bliss, as it seemed, that never Jason, nor Paris of Troy — Jason? — certes, nor any man else since Lamech was, who first of all men began to love two, as write folk of old, nor never man since the first man was born, could imitate the sophisms of his artfulness by one twenty-thousandth part; nor as to doubleness or feigning were worthy to unbuckle his shoe, nor could thank a creature as he did me! His manner was a heaven for any woman to behold, were she never so wise, so he painted and combed at point-device his words as well as his bearing. And I so loved him for his dutiful attention and for the faith I deemed to be in his heart that, if so were I knew that anything pained him, were it never so little, methought I felt death wring my heart. And in short, this thing went so far that my will was the instrument of his will; that is to say, my will obeyed his in everything, so far as was reason, ever keeping the bounds of my honour. And never held I a thing dearer than he, nor so dear, God wot, and never more shall.

'This went on more than a year or two, that I imagined naught but good of him. But finally thus it stood at last, that Fortune would that he must depart out of that place where I was. Whether I was woful, that need not be asked; I cannot describe it. For one thing I dare say boldly I know thereby what the pain of death is, such grief I felt that he could not remain. So on a day he took leave of me, he so sorrowful also that I verily believed that he had felt as much grief as I, when I heard him speak and saw his aspect. But nevertheless I thought him so faithful, and also, sooth to say, that he should return within so little while, and also reason demanded that he should go, for his honour's sake, as often happens, that I made a virtue of necessity and took it well, since it must be. I hid my sorrow from him as best I could, and took him by the hand and swore by Saint John and said thus to him, "Lo, I am all yours; be such as I have been to you and shall be." What he answered it needs not repeat; who can speak better than he, who can do worse? When he had spoken everything fairly, then he wrought his deeds. "Therefore it behooveth him have a full long spoon who shall eat with a fiend," — thus have I heard tell. So at last he must forth upon his way, and forth he flew till he came where he would. And when it pleased him to abide, I believe he had in mind that text, that "everything, returning to its own nature, is rejoiced;" thus folk say, I believe. Men love newfangledness by their very nature, as does a bird that men feed in a cage. For though night and day you take care of it and strew its cage fairly and soft as velvet and give it milk and bread, sugar, honey, yet even so soon as its door is open, it will spurn down the cup with his feet, and will to the wood and eat worms, so newfangled be they as to their food, and of their proper nature love novelties. No nobility of blood can keep a bond upon them. So this tercelet fared, alas the while! For though he was of gentle birth, and gay and fresh, goodly to see, and humble, and generous, upon a time he saw a kite flying, and straightway he so loved this kite that all his love clean departed from me, and in this wise has he broken his faith. Thus the kite has my love in her service, and I am lost without remedy!' And with that word the falcon shrieked, and swooned again in Canacee's lap.

Great was the lamentation for the falcon's pain which Canacee made, and all her women. They knew not how they might gladden the falcon. But Canacee bore her home in her garment, and softly wrapped her in plasters, where she had hurt herself with her beak. Now could Canacee do nought but dig herbs out of the ground and make new salves out of herbs rare and fine of hue, with which to heal this hawk; from morn to night she did all the diligence she could. And she made a cage by her bed's head, and covered it with blue velvets in sign of the loyalty that is found in women. And on the outside all the mew was painted green and all these false birds were painted, as be these wrens, tercelets and owls; and pies, to cry and chide at them, were painted near in scorn.

Thus I leave Canacee caring for her hawk; I will speak of her ring no more now, till the time comes to say how this falcon regained her lover, repentant, as the story tells, through the mediation of Cambalo, the king's son, of whom I have told you. But from here I shall proceed in my tale to speak of such battles and such chances that never yet were heard so great marvels. First I will tell you of Cambuscan, who in his time won many a city; then I will speak of Algarsyf, how he won Theodora as his bride, for whom he was full oft in great peril, had he not been holpen by the brazen steed; and after that I will speak of Cambalo's combat in the lists with the two brethren for Canacee, ere he could achieve her. And I will begin again where I left off.

III

Apollo whirled up his chariot so far, till the house of Mercury, the sly god —

The Words of the Franklin to the Squire

'In faith, Squire, you have quit yourself well, and like a gentleman. I praise your wit highly, considering your youth,' said the Franklin. 'I commend you, sir, so feelingly you speak! To my mind there is none in this company shall be your peer in eloquence if you live. God give you good fortune, and send you continuance in virtue, for I have great delight in your speaking. I have a son, and by Saint Trinity I had rather he were a man of such discretion as you, than have twenty pounds' worth of land, though it were fallen to me even now. Fie on possessions unless withal a man's self be worth somewhat! I have chidden my son, and yet shall chide him, because he will not incline to virtue; but his wont is to play at dice and to spend and to lose all that he has. And he had rather talk with a page than commune with any person of gentle birth where he might properly learn gentle manners.'

'A straw for your gentle manners! What, Franklin!' quoth our Host; 'well you know, perdy, that each of you must tell at least a tale or two, or break his word.'

'That I well know, sir,' quoth the Franklin. 'I pray you hold me not in scorn though I speak a word or two to this man.'

'Tell on your tale, without more words.'

'Gladly, sir Host,' quoth he. 'I will obey your will. Now hearken to what I tell you. I will not oppose your wish in any way, so far as my wits shall suffice. I pray God my tale may please you; then I shall well know that it is good enough.'

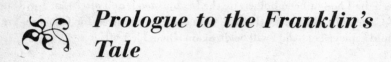

Prologue to the Franklin's Tale

'These old gentle Britons in their time made lays about divers happenings, rhymed in their early British tongue; which lays they sang to their instruments of music, or else read them, for their pleasure. And one of them I have in mind, which I will relate with good will as best I can. But, sirs, I am a rude man, and at the beginning I pray you to hold me excused for my homely speech. In sooth, I learned never rhetoric; a thing that I speak must be plain and bare. I slept never on the mount of Parnassus, nor learned Marcus Tullius Cicero. Colours of speech I know none, of a surety; only such colours as grow in the mead, or else such as men dye or paint. Colours of rhetoric be too curious for me, my spirit has no feeling in such matters. But if you list you shall hear my tale.'

🌿 *The Franklin's Tale*

In Armorica, which is called Brittany, there was a knight who loved and served a lady in the best manner he could. And he wrought many a labour, many a great emprise, ere he gained her. For she was one of the fairest women under the sun, and also come of so high kindred that this knight scarce durst for fear tell her his woe and his pain and distress. But at last she took such pity upon his pains, because of his worthiness and chiefest for his humble attentiveness, that privily she agreed to take him for husband and lord, in such lordship as men have over their wives. And that they might live in the more blessedness, he swore to her as a knight, of his own free will, that never at any time in all his life should he take upon him any sovereignty against her will, nor show jealousy toward her, but obey her and follow her will in all things, as any lover shall do toward his lady; save only the name of sovereignty, — that he would have for the honour of his station.

She thanked him, and said with full great humility, 'Sir since of your noble mind you offer me so free a rein, God forbid that of my guilt there were ever war or contention betwixt us two. Sir, I will be your true humble wife till my heart break; take here my pledge.'

Thus they were both in quiet and peace. For one thing, sirs, I dare safely say, — friends must comply with one another, if they would hold company long. Love will not be constrained by mastership; when mastery comes, forthwith the god of love beats his wings, and farewell, he is gone! Love is as free as any spirit. Women by their nature desire liberty, and not to be under constraint as a thrall; and so do men, if I shall say sooth. Look who is most patient in love, he has the advantage over all. Patience is a high virtue, of a certainty; for, as these clerks say, it conquers things that rigour could never attain to. Men should not chide or complain at every word. Learn to endure, or else, on my life, ye shall learn it, whether ye will or no. For certainly there is none in this world but sometimes he does or speaks amiss. Wrath, sickness, the stars, wine, woe, changing humours, full often cause a man to act or speak amiss. A man may not be avenged of every wrong; according to the occasion in every person who knows how to rule his life, there must be moderation. And therefore, that he might live at ease, this wise worthy knight promised forbearance toward her, and she full seriously swore to him that there never should be lack in her. Here men may see a humble and wise agreement; thus she took her servant and her lord, — servant in love, and lord in marriage. Then he was in both lordship and bondage. Bondage? — nay, but on high in lordship, since he has both his lady and love; certes, his lady, and also his wife, who accepted that law of love. And in this happy state he went home with his wife to his country, not far from Penmark, where was his dwelling, and where he lived in happiness and comfort. Who, unless he had been wedded, could tell the joy, the comfort, and well-being betwixt husband and wife?

This blessed condition lasted a year and more, till the knight of whom I speak, who was called Arveragus of Kayr-rud, laid his plans to go and dwell a year or two in England, which also was called Britain, to seek worship and honour in arms. For he set all his pleasure on such toils. And he dwelt there two years; the book says thus.

Now I will leave Arveragus, and will speak of Dorigen his wife, who loved her husband as her heart's blood. For in his absence she wept and sighed, as these noble wives do (when they will). She mourned, watched, wailed, feasted, lamented; desire for his presence so distracted her that she cared nothing for all this wide world. Her friends, who knew her heavy thoughts, comforted her in all they could. They preached to her; day and night they told her that she was slaying herself without cause, alas! And with all diligence they comforted her all they could, to make her leave her heaviness.

By process of time, ye all know, men may grave in a stone so long that some figure will be imprinted on it. So long they comforted her, that with the aid of hope and reason she received the imprint of their consolation. Wherefore her great sorrow began to assuage; she could not abide ever in such frenzy. And also whilst she was in all this sorrow, Arveragus had sent home to her letters of his welfare, and that he would soon return; else this sorrow had slain her heart. Her friends saw her sorrow began to slacken, and on their knees prayed her for God's love to come and roam about with them, to drive away her dark fantasies. And finally she agreed, for well she saw that it was best.

Now her castle stood hard by the sea, and for diversion she often walked with her friends high upon the shore, whence she saw many a ship and barge sailing upon their course, wherever they would go. But then became that a part of her grief. For full often she said to herself, 'Alas! Is there no ship of so many that I see, will bring home my lord? Then were my heart all cured of its bitter, bitter pains.'

Another time she would sit there and ponder, and from the shore cast her eyes down. But when she saw the grisly black rocks, her heart would so quake for very fear that she could not hold herself on her feet. Then she would sit down on the green and piteously look into the sea, and with sorrowful, cold sighs say right thus: 'Eternal God, who through Thy providence guidest the world by sure government, Thou makest nothing in vain, men say. But, Lord, these grisly, fiendly, black rocks, which seem rather a foul disorder of work than any fair creation by such a perfect, wise, and unchanging God, — why hast Thou wrought this irrational work? For by this work is fostered neither man nor bird nor brute, south or north, east or west. It does not good, to my seeming, but harm. Seest Thou not, Lord, how it destroys mankind? Rocks have slain an hundred thousand bodies of men, although they be not in my memory; which mankind is so fair a part of Thy work that Thou madest it like to Thine own image. Then it should seem Thou hadst a great fondness toward men; but how then may it be that Thou createst to destroy them such means which do no good, but ever harm? I wot well that clerks will say as they please by arguments that all is for the best, though I cannot understand the manner. But may that God that made the wind blow guard my lord! This is my conclusion; I leave all disputation to clerks. But would to God that all these black rocks were sunk into hell, for his sake! These rocks slay mine heart for fear.'

Thus she would speak to herself, with many a piteous tear. Her friends saw that it was no diversion for her, but only a disquiet, to walk by the sea, and devised for her sports in other places. They led her by rivers and springs and also in other delectable places; they danced and they played at chess and backgammon. So on a day in the morning-time, they went to divert them all the long day in the garden hard by, in which they had made their provision of food and other things. And this was on the sixth morning of May, and May with his soft rains had painted this garden full of leaves and flowers. And truly the craft of man's hand had so curiously arrayed this garden that never was a garden of such beauty, unless it were paradise itself. The odour of flowers and the fresh sight would have gladdened any heart that ever was born, unless too great sickness or too great sorrow distressed it; so full was it of delight and beauty. After dinner they began to dance and sing, save only Dorigen, who ever made complaint and moan, because she saw not him go on the dance who was her husband and also her love. But nevertheless she must abide for a time and with good hope let her sorrow pass.

Upon this dance, amongst other men, there danced before Dorigne a squire who was fresher and gayer of apparel than is the month of May, I believe. He sang and danced to surpass any man who is or was since the world was made. He was, to boot, if a man should describe him, one of the best endowed men alive; young, strong, rich, prudent, full of high qualities, well beloved and holden in great honour. And in short, if I am to tell the truth, this servant to Venus, this lusty squire, who was called Aurelius, had loved Dorigen, all without her knowledge, more than any creature two years and more, as was his chance; but never durst he tell her his woe. He drank all his penance without cup. He was in despair, he durst say nothing save that in his songs he would reveal his woe somewhat, as in a general complaining; he said he loved, and was nowise beloved. Of such matter he made many lays, virelays, songs, complaints, and roundels, how he durst not utter his sorrow, but languished like a fury in hell; and die he must, he said, as did Echo for Narcissus, who durst not tell her woe. In other manner than this which I speak of he durst not reveal his passion to her; save that, peradventure, sometimes at dances, where young folk perform their respects, it may well be that he looked upon her face in such wise as a man who asks for favour; but she knew nothing of his meaning.

Nevertheless it befell, ere they went thence, that because he was her neighbour and a man of worship, and she had known him of old, they fell into speech; and Aurelius drew more and more toward his matter, and when he saw his time, he said thus: 'Madame, by God That made this world, so I knew it would gladden your heart, I would that the day when your Arveragus went over the sea, I Aurelius had gone whence I never should have returned; for I well know that my service is in vain, my guerdon is but breaking my heart. Have pity upon my bitter pains, madame, for with a word you may slay me or save me — would God that I were buried here at your feet! I have now no time to say more; have mercy, sweet, or you will cause me to die!'

She looked at Aurelius: 'Is this your desire?' quoth she. 'Say you thus? Never before knew I what was in your mind; but now, Aurelius, I know it. By that God that gave me breath and soul, never in word or deed shall I be an untrue wife, so far as I have my senses. I will be his to whom I am bound. Take this for my final answer.' But in sport after that she said thus: 'Aurelius, by the high God in heaven, yet would I consent to be your love, since I see you so piteously lamenting; look what day you remove all the rocks, stone by stone, all along Britanny, that they hinder not ship or boat to go, — I say, when you have made the coast clear of rocks that there is no stone to be seen, then I will love you best of all men. Take here my pledge, so far as my power reaches.'

'Is there no other mercy in you?' he said.

'No,' quoth she, 'by that Lord that made me! For I well know that shall never happen. Let such follies pass out of your heart. What delight should a man ever have to go loving another man's wife, who has her ever at his will?'

Aurelius gave many a sore sigh. Woe was him when he heard this; and with a sorrowful heart he answered, 'Madame, this were impossible! Then I must die of a quick, dreadful death.' And with that word he turned back.

Then many a one of her other friends came roaming up and down in the paths, and knew naught of this affair, but speedily began new revel; till the bright sun lost his hue, and the horizon had bereft him of his light (this is as much as to say, it was evening). And they went home in joy and contentment, save, alas, wretched Aurelius alone! He went to his house with sorrowful heart; he saw that he could never escape death, and felt his heart grow cold. Up to the heaven he held his hands and set him down on his bare knees, and raving said his orison; for very woe he was out of his wits and knew not what he spake. With piteous heart he began his plaint unto the gods, and first to the sun: —

'Apollo,' he said, 'lord and ruler of every plant, herb, tree, and flower, who givest to each of them his times and seasons, according to thy declination, as thy lodging changes toward north or south; lord Phœbus, cast thy merciful eye upon wretched Aurelius, who am but lost. Behold, lord, my lady has sworn my guiltless death, unless thy benignity have some pity upon my dying heart. For well I wot, lord Phœbus, that thou mayst help me best of all save my lady, if thou wilt. Now vouchsafe to hear me tell thee in what wise I may be holpen Thy blessed sister, Lucina the bright, chief goddess and queen of the sea, though Neptunus have his godhead in the sea, yet is she empress over him; thou well knowest, lord, that even as it is her desire to be quickened and lightened by thine orb, wherefore she follows thee eagerly, right so the sea desires of its nature to follow her, being goddess both in the sea and in rivers great and small. Wherefore, lord Phœbus, this is my prayer, — do this miracle or break my heart; that now at this next opposition, which shall be in the sign of the Lion, pray her to bring a flood so great that it shall overtop by at least five fathom the highest rock in Armorican Britain, and let this flood last two years. Then, certes, I may say to my lady, "Keep your promise, the rocks be gone." Lord Phœbus, do this miracle; pray her that she go no faster course than thou; I say, pray thy sister that these two years she go no faster course than thou. Then shall she ever even at full, and the spring flood-tide last day and night. And, unless she vouchsafe to grant me my dear sovereign lady in such manner, pray her to sink every rock into her own dark region under the ground where Pluto dwelleth, or nevermore shall I gain my lady.

Barefoot I will go a pilgrimage to thy temple at Delphi. Lord Phœbus, see the tears on my cheeks, and have some pity on my pains.'

And with that he fell down in a swoon and long time lay in a trance. His brother, who knew his trouble, caught him up and brought him to his bed. In this care and torment I let this woeful creature lie despairing. He may choose, for all of me, whether he will live or die.

Arveragus was come home, with other valiant knights, in health and great honour as the flower of chivalry. Oh! now art thou happy, Dorigen, who hast in thine arms thy lusty husband, the vigorous knight, the valiant warrior, who loves thee as his own heart's life. Never thought he to be suspicious whether any creature had spoken to her of love whilst he was gone; he had no fear of that. He gave no heed to any such matter, but danced, jousted, and made great cheer toward her. Thus I leave them in happiness and bliss, and will tell of the sick Aurelius.

Two years and more lay wretched Aurelius in languor and mad torment, ere he could walk a step on earth; and no comfort had he in this time, save from his brother, a clerk, who knew of all this woful matter. For in truth he durst say no word thereof to any creature. He carried it under his breast more privily than Pamphilus his love for Galatea. His breast was whole, to outward view, but ever in his heart was the keen arrow. And ye well know that in surgery the cure of a wound healed without is perilous, unless men could touch the arrow or get at it.

His brother wept and wailed privily, till at last it came to his mind that whilst he was at Orleans, in France, — as young clerks who are desirous of studying curious arts seek in every nook and corner to learn this special lore, — it came to his mind that, upon a day whilst he studied at Orleans, he saw a book of natural magic, which his fellow, who was then a bachelor of law, had privily left upon his desk, though he were there for a different study; which book spake much of the celestial influences touching the eight-and-twenty mansions which belong to the moon, and such folly as is not worth a fly in our day. For Holy Church's faith which is in our Credo will not suffer any illusion to harm us. And as soon as he remembered this book his heart began to dance for joy, and he said privily to himself, 'My brother shall be cured speedily; for I am sure there be arts by which men create divers apparitions, such as these cunning jugglers feign. For often at feasts, I have heard tell, within a large hall these jugglers have made water and a barge come in and row up and down in the hall. Sometimes a grim lion has seemed to come, and sometimes flowers spring as in a meadow, sometimes a vine, with grapes white and red, sometimes a castle of lime and stone. And when they list, straightway they caused it all to pass out; thus it seemed to every man's sight.

'Now then, I conclude thus, that if I could find some old comrade at Orleans who is acquainted with these mansions of the moon, or other natural magic besides, he should well cause my brother to possess his love. For by means of an illusion a clerk may make it appear to a man's sight that all the black rocks of Brittany be every one removed, and that ships come and go along the shore, and that this continue a day or two in such form. Then were my brother all cured. Then she must needs keep her promise, or else at least he shall shame her.'

Why should I make a longer story? He came to his brother's bed and gave him such encouragement to go to Orleans, that he started up at once, and went on his way forth in hopes to be relieved of his care. When they were almost come to that city, about two or three furlongs away, they met a young clerk roaming by himself who greeted them discreetly in Latin, and then said a marvellous thing. 'I know the cause of your coming,' quoth he. And ere they went a foot further, he told them all that was in their minds. This clerk of Brittany asked him of the companions whom he had known in old days, and he answered him that they were dead; for which he wept many a tear. Aurelius alighted anon from his horse and went forth home to his house with this magician, who made them well at ease; no victual wanted that might give pleasure. A house so well appointed Aurelius had never seen in his life.

Ere he went to supper, the magician showed him forests, and parks full of wild beasts; there he saw harts with their lofty horns, the largest that eye ever saw. He beheld an hundred of them slain by dogs, and some bleeding from bitter arrow-wounds. When these wild deer vanished, he saw falconers upon a fair river, slaying the heron with their hawks. Then he saw knights jousting on a plain. And after this, the magician did him the pleasure to show him his lady on a dance, in which he himself was dancing, as seemed to him. And when this master who wrought the magic saw that it was time, he clapped his hands, and farewell! all our revel was gone. And yet whilst they saw all this marvellous sight, they stirred never out of the house, but sat still in his study, where his books were, and no creature but they three.

This master called his squire to him, and said thus: 'Is our supper ready? It is almost an hour, I will be bound, since I bade you make our supper, when these honourable men went with me into my study, where my books be.'

'Sir,' quoth this squire, 'when it please you it is all ready, though you would have it even now.'

'Go we to supper, then,' quoth he, 'that is best. These folk in love must take repose sometime.'

After supper they fell into talk over the sum which should be this master's guerdon for removing all the rocks of Brittany and also from the Gironde to the mouth of Seine. He raised difficulties and swore, so God save him! he would not have less than a thousand pound, and he were not right fain to go for that sum,

Auelius answered straightway, with joyous heart, 'Fie on a thousand pound! This wide world, which men say is a ball, would I give, if I were lord of it. This bargain is done, for we be agreed. You shall be paid faithfully, by my word. But look now that you delay us here no longer than to-morrow, for any negligence or sloth.'

'Nay,' this clerk said, 'take here my faith in pledge to you.'

To bed went Aurelius when he would, and had repose well-nigh all that night. What for his labour and his hope, his woeful heart had relief from suffering. On the morrow, when it was day, they took the straight road to Brittany, Aurelius and this magician, and dismounted at the place where they would be. And, as books remind me, this was the cold, frosty season of December. Phœbus waxed old and of hue like latten, who in his hot declination shone with his bright beams like burnished gold; but now he was descended into Capricorn, where he shone full pale, I dare well say. The bitter frosts, with sleet and rain, have destroyed the green in every yard. Janus with his double beard sits by the fire and drinks the wine out of his ox-horn; before him stands brawn of the tusked boar, and every lusty man cries, 'Noël!'

Aurelius did his master all the cheer and reverence he could, and prayed him to do his diligence to bring him out of his bitter pains, or with a sword he would slit his own heart. This cunning clerk so pitied this man that he sped him all he could, day and night, to watch after a fitting time to work his problem; that is to say, to create an appearance, by such an illusion or crafty sleight — I have no terms of astrology — that she and every person should think and say that the rocks of Brittany were gone, or else sunk under the earth. So at last he found his time to work his japes and his sorry feats, performance of such a cursed superstition. He brought forth his Toledo tables, full well corrected; there lacked naught, neither his tables of *anni collecti* nor of *anni expansi*, nor his roots, nor his other gear, such as his centres, and his arguments, and his tables of proportional parts for his equations. And for his calculations he knew full well how far Alnath in the eighth sphere was pushed from the head of that fixed Aries above, which is reckoned to be in the ninth sphere; full cunningly he calculated by means of all this. When he had found his first mansion, by proportion he knew the remnant, and he well knew the rising of his moon, in which planet's face and term, and all the rest. And he knew full well the moon to be in a mansion favourable to his enterprise, and knew also the other matters to be observed for working such illusions and such cursed practices as heathen folk used in those days. For this reason he no longer tarried, but through his magic it seemed for a week or two that all the rocks were away.

Aurelius, who was still despairing whether he should have his love or fare amiss, waited night and day after this miracle. And when he knew that there was no hindrance, but that every rock was gone, he fell down at his master's feet forthwith and said, 'I, Aurelius, woeful wretch, thank you, lord, and Venus my lady, that have helped me from my cold cares.' And he took his way forth to the temple where he knew he should see his lady. And when he saw his time, anon he saluted his dear sovereign lady with timid heart and full humble face. Quoth this woeful man, 'Mine own lady, whom I most fear and love as best I know how, and whom of all this world I were loathest to displease, — were it not that I have such distress for you that anon I must die here at your feet, I should never tell you how I am encompassed with woe. But certes I must either die or make complaint. Guiltless, you slay me, for very pain. But though you have no pity for my death, consider ere you break your pledge. For the sake of God in heaven, repent you ere you slay me because I love you. For well you know what you promised, madame; not that I challenge anything of you as of right, my sovereign lady, but only of your grace. Nevertheless, in a garden yonder, at such a spot, you wot right well what you promised me, and you plighted your troth in my hand, to love me best; God wot, you said so, though I be unworthy thereof. Madame, I speak it for your honour, more than to save my heart's life; I have done as you bade, and if you will, you may go and see. Do you list; remember your promise, for, quick or dead, you shall find me right in that garden. It all lies with you, to make me live or die. — But well I wot the rocks are gone.'

He took his leave, and she stood astonied with not a drop of blood in all her face. She thought never to have come into such a trap. Quoth she, 'Alas that ever this should befall! For I never deemed that such a prodigy or marvel could betide, by any possibility. It is against the course of nature.'

And home she went a sorrowful creature; scarce could she walk for very fear, and for a whole day or two she wept and wailed and swooned, that it was pitiful to behold. But why it was she told no-one, for Arveragus was gone out of town. But with pale face and full sorrowful cheer she spake to herself, and said thus in her plaint as I shall tell you. Quoth she, 'Alas! I complain on thee,

Fortune, who hast bound me unawares in thy chain, from which to escape I know no help save only death or dishonour; one of these twain it behooves me to choose. But neverthelesss I had rather forfeit my life than have shame of my body, or lose my fair repute, or know myself false. And by my death, of a surety, I may escape.

'Alas, has not many a noble wife and many a maiden slain herself before this, rather than trespass with her body? Yea, certes; lo! these histories testify it. When the thirty tyrants, full of cursedness, had slain Phidon at a feast in Athens, of their malice they commanded men to arrest his daughters and bring them before them all naked, to fulfil, their foul pleasure, and they made them dance in their father's blood upon the pavement, — God give them ill fortune! Wherefore these woful maidens, in fear of this, privily leaped into a well and drowned themselves, rather than lose their maidenhood; so the books relate. They of Messenia had fifty maidens of Lacedæmonia sought out, with whom they would work their lechery; but of all that band there was none who was not slain, and with good will chose not rather to die than consent to be robbed of her maidenhood. Why should I, then, fear to die?

'Lo also the tyrant Aristoclides. He loved a maiden named Stymphalis, who, when her father was slain on a night, went straightway to Diana's temple, and laid hold of the image with her two hands, and would never let go. No person could tear her hands from it, till she was slain in that very place. Now since maidens have had such scorn to be defiled with man's base pleasure, methinks a wife ought indeed rather slay herself than be defiled.

'What shall I say of Hasdrubal's wife, who slew herself at Carthage? For when she saw that the Romans had won the city, she took all her children and skipped down into the fire, and chose rather to die than that any Roman dishonoured her. Did not Lucrece slay herself at Rome, alas, when she was violated by Tarquin, because she deemed it shame to live when she had lost her honour? The seven maidens of Miletus also for very fear and woe slew themselves rather than the folk of Gaul should violate them. I could tell now more than a thousand stories, I believe, touching this matter. When Abradates was slain, his dear wife slew herself and let her blood flow into Abradates' deep, wide wounds, saying, "My body, at least, no creature shall defile, if I can hinder it."

'Why should I cite more ensamples hereof, since so many have slain themselves rather than be defiled? I will end thus, that it is better for me to slay myself than so to be defiled. I will be true to Arveragus, or slay myself in some wise, as did the dear daughter of Demotion, because she would not be defiled. O Scedasus, it is full great pity to read how thy daughters died, who slew themselves for the same cause, alas! It was as great pity, or indeed greater, for the Theban maiden that slew herself even for the same grief, to escape Nicanor. Another Theban maiden did likewise; because one of Macedonia had violated her, she redressed her maidenhood by her death. What shall I say of the wife of Niceratus, who for a like cause took her life? How true also was his love to Alcibiades, and chose rather to die than to suffer his body to be unburied! Lo, what a wife was Alcestis! What says Homer of Penelope the good? All Greece knows of her chastity. It is written thus of Laodamia, in sooth, that when Protesilaus was slain at Troy, she would live no longer after his days. I may tell the same of noble Portia; she could not live without Brutus, to whom she had given all her whole heart. The perfect wifehood of Artemisia is honoured through all heathenesse. O queen Teuta! thy wifely chastity may be a mirror to all wives. The same thing I say of Bilia, of Rhodogune and also of Valeria.'

Thus Dorigen made her plaint a day or two, ever purposing to die. But nevertheless Arveragus, this worthy knight, came home the third evening, and asked her why she wept so sore. And she began to weep ever more bitterly.

'Alas that ever I was born! Thus I said,' quoth she, 'this was my oath,' — and she told him what you have already heard; it needs not rehearse it more.

This husband, with cheerful countenance and in friendly wise, answered and said as I shall tell you; 'Is there aught else but this, Dorigen?'

'Nay, nay,' quoth she, 'so may God help me; God forbid there were more; this is too much.'

'Yea, wife,' he replied; 'leave sleeping that which is quiet. It may yet be well to-day, peradventure. You shall keep your pledge, by my faith! For may God so surely have mercy on me, for the very love I have to you I had far rather be stabbed to the heart, than you should not hold your pledge. Truth is the highest thing that a man may hold.' But with that word he burst out weeping forthwith, and said, 'I forbid you, on pain of death, ever whilst your life lasts, to tell this matter to any creature I will endure all my woe as best I can, and make no such heavy countenance that folk might deem or guess harm of you.'

And he called forth a squire and maid, and said, 'Go forth straightway with Dorigen and bring her to such a place.' They took their leave and went their way, but they wist not why she went thither. He would tell his mind to no-one.

Peradventure in sooth many of you will hold him a foolish man herein, that he would put his wife in jeopardy; hearken to the tale, ere you exclaim upon her. She may have better fortune than you look for; and when you have heard the tale, judge.

This squire Aurelius, who was so amorous of Dorigen, happened by chance to meet her amidst the town, even in the busiest street, as she was bound by the straight way for the garden where she had promised to go. And he also was bound gardenward; for well he ever espied it when she would go out of her house to any place. But thus they met, by chance or good fortune; and he saluted her with joyous mood, and asked whither she went.

And she answered, as if she were half crazed, 'To the garden, as my husband bade, to keep my promise, alas! alas!'

Aurelius wondered at this thing, and in his heart had great compassion of her and her lament, and of Arveragus, the worthy knight who had bidden her hold all she had promised, so loath was he that his wife should break her pledge. And he had great ruth in his heart over it, and he considered on all sides what were best, that he would refrain from his desire rather than to do so high a churlish wretchedness against nobility and all gentle manners. Wherefore he said thus in few words: 'Madame, say to Arveragus, your lord, that since I see his great nobility to you (and also I well see your distress), that it seemed better to him to suffer shame — and that were pity — than you should break your troth to me, I had rather suffer perpetual woe, than part the love betwixt you. Into your hand, madame, I release, cancelled, every assurance and every bond that you have made to me heretofore from the time when you were born. I plight my troth that I shall never reproach you on the score of any promise. And here I take my leave, of the best and truest wife that in all my days I ever yet knew. But let every woman beware what she promises; let her at least think of Dorigen.' Thus of a surety a squire can do a gentle deed, as well as can a knight.

She thanked him upon her bare knees, and went home to her husband and told him all, even as you have heard me say it. And be ye sure, he was so well pleased that I could not tell how much; why should I indite further of this matter? Arveragus and his wife Dorigen led forth their days in sovereign bliss. Never again was there vexation betwixt them. Evermore he cherished her as though she were a queen, and she was true to him. Concerning these two folk ye get no more from me.

Aurelius, who had forfeited all the expense, cursed the time when he was born. 'Alas! alas!' quoth he, 'that I promised a thousand pounds' weight of refined gold unto this philosopher! How shall I do? I see nothing more but that I am undone. I must needs sell mine heritage and be a beggar. I cannot abide here and shame all my kindred hereabout, unless I may obtain better grace of him. But nevertheless I will seek of him to let me pay at certain times year by year, and will thank him for his great courtesy. I will keep my word, I will not be false.'

With sore heart he went to his coffer and brought to this clerk gold of the value of five hundred pounds, I believe, and besought him of his noble courtesy to grant him certain days to pay the remnant, and said, 'Master, I dare well boast that I never failed of my word as yet. For verily my debt shall be paid you, whatever befall me, though I go a-begging in my bare kirtle. But would you vouchsafe, upon security, to respite me for two or three years, then it were well with me. For otherwise I must sell mine heritage. There is no more to say.'

This philosopher answered gravely and said thus, when he heard these words, 'Have I not kept my covenant with you?'

'Yea, certes, well and truly,' quoth he.

'Have you not had your lady even as you desired?'

'No, no,' quoth he and sighed sorrowfully.'

'What was the cause? Tell me, if you can.'

Aurelius began his tale anon, and told him all, as you have heard, it needs not rehearse it again. He said, 'Arveragus of his nobility would rather have died in sorrow and woe, than that his wife were false to her troth.' He told him also the sorrow of Dorigen, how loath she was to be a wicked wife, and that she had rather have died that day, and that it was through innocence she had sworn her oath. 'She never heard tell before of magic illusion; that made me have pity upon her. And even as freely as he sent her to me, so freely I sent her back to him. This is every whit; there is no more to say.'

This philosopher answered: 'Dear friend, each of you did a gentle deed toward the other. You are a squire, he is a knight. But God in his blessed power forbid but a clerk may verily do a gentle deed as well as any of you. Sir, I release you your thousand pound, as freely as if you were but now crept out of the earth and had never known me ere now. For, sir, I will not take a penny of you for all my art and all my labour. You have paid well for my subsistence. It is enough. And farewell, have good day.' And he took his horse and forth he went upon his journey.

Lordings, I would ask you this question now: Which, think ye, was the most generous? Now tell me, ere ye go farther. I can no more; my tale is finished.

Prologue to the Second Nun's Tale

'That minister and nurse unto sin which in the English tongue men call Idleness, portress of the gate of voluptuousness, well ought we to do all our endeavour to eschew and to put her down by her opposite, that is to say, by lawful activity, lest the Fiend through our idleness catch us. For he who continually watches to ensnare us with his thousand sly cords can so lightly catch a man in his trap, when he can espy him in idleness, that till a man be seized right by the skirt, he is not aware that the Fiend has him in his grasp. We ought indeed to work and to withstand idleness. And though men never feared to die, yet they well see, by unshaken reason, that idleness is rotten sloth, of which there never comes any good fruit. And men see that sloth holds her in a leash, only to sleep and eat and drink and to devour all that others get by labour. And to put from us such idleness, which is cause of so great ruin, I have here faithfully done my endeavour in translating, after the Legend, thy glorious life and passion, O thou with thy garland wrought of roses and lilies; I mean thee, Saint Cecilia, maid and martyr!

'And on thee at my beginning, who art the flower of all virgins, of whom Bernard loved so well to write, on thee I first call. Thou comfort of us wretches, help me to relate thy maiden's death, who through her merit won eternal life and victory over the Fiend, as man may read in her legend hereafter. Thou maid and mother, daughter of thy Son, well of mercy, thou healer of sinful souls, in whom God of His goodness chose to dwell, thou meek one and high above every creature, thou didst so far ennoble our human kind that the Maker of nature had no disdain to clothe and wrap His Son in flesh and blood. The eternal Love and Peace, whom earth and sea and sky ever praise without ceasing, who is Lord and Guide of that threefold compass, took man's shape within the blessed cloister of thy body. And thou, spotless virgin, bore of thy body the Creator of every creature, and remainedst a pure maiden. In thee is united magnificence with mercy, goodness, and such pity that thou, who are sun of excellence, not only helpest them that pray to thee, but ofttimes of thy kindness, ere men beg thy help, thou goest before full freely, and art their life's physician.

'Thou meek and blessed fair maiden, help me now, a wretched exile in this desert of gall. Think on the woman of Canaan, who said that whelps eat of the crumbs that drop from their master's table; and though I, an unworthy son of Eve, be sinful, yet accept my faith. And since faith is dead without works, give me wit and time so to work that I be quit of that darkest place of all. O thou mother of Christ, dear daughter of Anne, so fair and full of grace, be mine advocate in that high presence where *Hosanna* is sung without ceasing! And illumine by thy light my imprisoned soul, which is troubled by the contagion of my body, and also by the weight of earthly desire and lying loves. O haven of refuge, O salvation of them that be in sorrow and distress, now help me, for I will turn to my labour.

'Yet I pray you that read my words to forgive me though I do no diligence to endite this story cunningly; for I have both words and thought from him who wrote the story in reverence for the saint, and I follow her legend; and I pray you that where need is ye will amend my work.

'First I would expound to you the name of the saint, as men may read in her history. It signifies, as men would say in English, *heaven's lily*; her name was *lily* for the pure chasteness of her virginity; or because she had the whiteness of honour and the green of conscience and the sweet savour of good fame, was she called a lily. Or Cecilia is as if one should say *the way for the blind*, because she was an ensample through her good teaching. Or else, as I see in the books, the name Cecilia is compounded by a manner of joining from *heaven* and *Leah*; and here by a figure *heaven* is put for meditation upon holiness, and *Leah* for her ceaseless activity. Cecilia may also be interpreted *lacking blindness*, for her great light of sapience, and for her shining virtues. Or else, lo! this maiden's bright name comes from *heaven* and *leos*; because men may well rightly call her, ensample of all good and wise works, *heaven of people*, for *leos* signified *people* in English. And even as men can see in the heaven the sun and the moon and everywhere the stars, even so may men see spiritually in this noble maiden the magnanimity of faith, and also the perfect clearness of sapience, and sundry bright and excellent works. And even as these philosophers say that heaven is swift and round and burning, so was the fair white Cecilia ever full swift and diligent in good works, and round and perfect by perseverance in good, and ever burning full brightly with love. Now have I declared to you what was her name.'

The Second Nun's Tale

This maiden bright Cecily, as her life says, was come of Romans, and of a noble family, and from her cradle up fostered in the faith of Christ and bare his gospel in her mind. As the books say, she never ceased to pray and to love and fear God, beseeching him to protect her virginity. And when this maiden was to be wedded unto a man, who was called Valerian, of age full young, and the day of her wedding was come, full devout and meek of spirit she had clad her in an hair-shirt next her flesh, and under her robe of gold that so fairly clothed her; and whilst the organ made melody, thus she sang in her heart to God alone: 'O Lord, keep my soul and also my body unspotted, lest I be confounded.' And for the love of Him who died upon a tree she fasted every second or third day, ever praying full earnestly in her orisons.

The night came, and she must needs go with her husband, as is the usage; and anon she said to him privily, 'O sweet, dear, well-beloved spouse, there is a secret which I would tell you right gladly, if you would hear it, if so be you will swear not to betray me.'

Valerian swore to her solemnly that he would nevermore betray her, for any reason or anything that might betide. And not till then she said to him, 'I have an angel that loves me, and is every ready to guard my body with great love, whether I wake or sleep. And of a surety if he perceive that you touch me or love me ignobly, forthwith he will slay you on the spot; and thus you should die in your youth. And if you protect me in clean love, he will love you as he loves me, for your purity, and show you his joy and his brightness.'

Valerian, chastened as God willed, answered again, 'If I am to trust you, let me behold and see that angel. And if it be a very angel, then I will do as you have prayed me. And if you love another man, in sooth I will slay you both right with this sword.'

Cecily answered anon right in this wise, 'That angel you shall see, if you list, so you believe on Christ and be baptized. Go forth to the Appian Way,' quoth she, 'which lies but three miles from this town, and to the poor folk that live there say right thus as I shall tell you. Say to them that I, Cecily, sent you to them, to show you the old good Urban, for a secret necessity and good purpose. And when you see Saint Urban, tell him the words which I told you; and when he has purged you from sin, then you shall see that angel, ere you depart.'

Valerian went to the place, and even as he was taught anon he found this holy old Urban lurking amongst the graves of the saints. And forthwith, without tarrying, he gave his message. And when he told it, Urban held up his hands for joy, and dropped tears from his eyes. Quoth he, 'O Almighty Lord, Jesus Christ, Sower of chaste counsel, Shepherd of us all, take to Thyself the fruit of that seed of chastity which Thou hast sown in Cecilia! Lo, like a busy bee, without guile, Thine own thrall Cecily ever serveth Thee. For that very spouse, whom but now she took, full like a fierce lion, she sendeth here to Thee, as meek as ever was any lamb!'

And with that word anon appeared an old man, clad in white shining garments, a book in his hand with letters of gold, and he stood before Valerian, who fell down as dead for fear when he saw him. And the aged man caught him up, and right thus he read out of his book: 'One Lord, one faith, one baptism, one God alone and Father of all, above all and over all everywhere;' these words were all written in gold.

When this was read, this old man spake, 'Believest thou this thing, or not? Say yea or nay.'

'I believe all this,' quoth Valerian, 'for I dare well hold that no creature under heaven can think of a truer thing than this.' Then the old man vanished, whither Valerian knew not; and Pope Urban christened him in that very place.

Valerian went home and found Cecily standing in his chamber with an angel; this angel bore in his hands two crowns of lilies and roses. And first he gave the one to Cecily, as I read, and then the other to Valerian, her husband. Quoth he, 'Ever guard these crowns well, with pure body and unspotted thought; I have fetched them to you from Paradise. Never more shall they decay, believe me, or lose their sweet savour; and never shall any person behold them with his eyes, unless he be chaste and hate baseness. And thou, Valerian, because thou also hast so quickly assented to good counsel, say what thou wouldst have, and thou shalt have thy boon.'

'I have a brother,' he answered, 'and I love no man so in this world. I pray thee that my brother may be granted grace to know the truth, as I do here.'

The angel said, 'Thy request is pleasing to God, and ye shall both come unto his blessed feast with the palm of martyrdom.'

And at these words Tiburce his brother came. And when he perceived the savour cast by the roses and lilies, he began much to marvel in his heart, and said, 'I wonder whence comes at this season of the year that sweet savour of roses and lilies that I smell. For though I held them in my two hands, the savour could go no deeper in me. The sweet perfume which I feel in mine heart has changed me into another nature.'

Valerian said, 'We have two crowns, snow-white and rose-red, clear-shining, which your eyes have no power to behold. And as you smell them through my prayer, so shall you see them, dear brother, if so be, without sloth, you will believe aright and know the true faith.'

Tiburce answered, 'Say you this to me in very truth, or hear I in a dream?' 'Surely in dreams,' quoth Valerian, 'have we been up to this time, my brother. But now first our dwelling is in truth.'

'How know you this, in what wise?' asked Tiburce.

'That I shall tell you,' answered Valerian. 'The angel of God has taught me the truth. You shall behold him, if you will renounce the idols and be pure; and else not.'

— And of the miracle of the two crowns Saint Ambrose vouchsafes to speak in his preface; solemnly this noble, beloved doctor celebrates it and says thus: To receive the palm of martyrdom, Saint Cecilia, filled with the gift of God, abandoned the world, and even the marriage-chamber; and of this testifies the confession of faith by Valerian and Tiburce, to whom God of his bounty deigned to grant two crowns of well-smelling flowers, and sent them by his angel. The maiden brought these men to heavenly happiness. Verily, the world has learned of what price is devotion to chastity. —

Then Cecily showed him in clear and open words that all idols are but a vain thing, for they be dumb, and also deaf; and she charged him to leave his idols.

'Whosoever believes not this, to speak it plainly, he is a beast,' quoth Tiburce then.

And she, hearing this, began to kiss his breast and was full glad that he could discern the truth. 'I take you this day for mine ally,' said this beloved, blessed, fair maiden, and then spake as you may hear: 'Lo, even as the love of Christ made me your brother's wife, in that same manner I here forthwith take you for mine ally, since you will scorn your idols. Go now with your brother, and be baptized and make you clean, that so you may see the angel's face of which your brother told.'

Tiburce answered and said, 'Dear brother, first tell me whither I shall go, and to what man.'

'To whom?' quoth he. 'Come, with right good cheer I will lead you to Urban the pope.'

'To Urban?' quoth Tiburce. 'Brother mine Valerian, will you lead me thither? Methinks that were a marvellous thing. Mean you not that Urban who has been so oft condemned to die, and ever abides in one nook and another, and dares not once put forth his head? If he were found, or if men could spy him out, they would burn him in such a red fire! — and us also, to bear him company. And whilst we seek the Divinity that is privily hid in heaven, at all events we shall be burned in this world!'

To whom Cecily boldly answered, 'Men might well fear, and with reason, to lose this life, mine own dear brother, if this were the only life, and there were none else. But there is a better life elsewhere, fear not, which never shall be lost, of which God's Son through His mercy has told us. That Father's Son created all things; and all that are created with reasonable intelligence the Spirit, That proceeded from the Father, has verily endued with souls. By words and by miracles God's Son, when He was in this world, declared that there is another life where men may dwell.'

To whom Tiburce answered, 'O dear sister, said you not but now that there is but one God, in truth the Lord? And how can you now bear witness of three?'

'That I shall tell ere I go,' she said. 'Even as a man has three faculties, memory, imagination and also understanding, so in one divine being there may right well be three Persons.' Then she full earnestly preached to him of Christ's coming, and taught him of His pains and many points of His passion; how God's Son was lodged in this world to bring full forgiveness to mankind, which was bound in sin and cold cares. All this she expounded to Tiburce.

And after this with earnest mind he went with Valerian to pope Urban, who thanked God, and with a light and glad heart christened him, and there made him perfect in his knowledge, and God's knight. And after this Tiburce had such favour that every day he saw the angel of God, in time and space. And every manner of prayer that he made to God, it was sped anon.

It were full hard to tell in order how many miracles Jesu worked for them. But at last, to speak briefly and plainly, the officers of the town of Rome sought them out and fetched them before Almachius the prefect, who questioned them and knew all their mind, and sent them to the image of Jupiter and said, 'Whoso will not sacrifice, strike off his head. This is my sentence.'

Straightway one Maximus, who was an officer to the prefect, and his clerk, seized these martyrs of whom I tell; and when he led forth the saints, himself wept. And when he had heard the saints' instruction, he got him leave of the executioners, and led them straightway to his house; and by their preaching, ere it was evening, they rooted out the false faith from the executioners, and from Maximus and from all of his folk, and made them believe in God alone. When it waxed night, Cecily came with priests, who baptized them all together. And afterwards, at daybreak, Cecily said to the two with a full grave cheer, 'Now, Christ's own beloved knights, put away all the works of darkness, and arm you in the armour of light. In truth you have fought a great battle, your course is finished, you have preserved your faith; go to the unfading crown of life. The righteous Judge whom you have served shall give it to you, as you have won it.'

And when she had said this, men led them forth to do sacrifice. But when they were brought to the place to tell the event briefly, they would by no means offer sacrifice or incense, but with humble hearts and steadfast devotion went on their knees, and there lost their heads, both Valerian and Tiburce. Their souls went to the King of grace.

Anon this Maximus, who saw this thing, with piteous tears told that he had seen their souls glide to heaven with angels all bright and shining. And with his words he converted many, wherefore Almachius caused him to be so beaten with whips of lead that he lost his life.

Cecilia took him and anon buried him gently beside Tiburce and Valerian, in her burial-place, under the stone. And then Almachius instantly bade his ministers to fetch Cecily openly, that she might do sacrifice before him and incense Jupiter. But they, converted by her wise teaching, wept full sore and gave full credence to her word, and cried once and again, 'Christ, God's Son without inequality, Who has so good a servant to serve Him, is very God; this is our full judgment, this we believe with one accord, though we die.'

Almachius, who heard of this happening, bade fetch Cecily that he might see her. And lo! this was his first demand, 'What manner of woman are you?' quoth he.

'I am a gentlewoman born,' she answered.

'I ask you,' quoth he, 'though it displease you, of your religion and your belief.'

'You have begun your question foolishly,' quoth she, 'who would call for two answers to one demand. You asked like an ignorant man.'

To that similitude Almachius answered, 'Whence comes this your so saucy answering?'

'Whence?' quoth she to that question. 'From conscience and pious faith unfeigned.'

Almachius said, 'Take you no heed of my power?'

And she answered him this: 'Your power is right little to be feared; for the power of every mortal man is verily but like a bladder, full of wind. For when it is blown up, all the boast of it may be laid full low by a needle's point.'

'Full wrongfully you began,' quoth he, 'and still in wrong you persever. Know you not how our mighty noble princes have commanded and made ordinance that every Christian creature shall suffer penalty unless he renounce his Christianity; and shall go all quit if he renounce it?'

'Your princes err,' quoth Cecily then, 'as your nobility do; with a mad judgment and against the sooth you make us guilty. For you who well know our innocence impute to us blame and also of crime, because we pay honour to Christ and bear a Christian name. But we who know how potent is that name, cannot deny it.'

Almachius answered, 'Choose one of these two: do sacrifice, or renounce Christianity, that so you may escape.'

At which the fair, holy, blessed maiden began to laugh, and said to him, 'O Judge, confounded in your folly, would you have me renounce innocence, to make me a wicked person? Lo his dissimulation here before all the people! He stares and demeans him like a madman as he looks about.'

To whom Almachius: 'Know you not, unhappy wretch, how far my power may go? Have not our mighty princes given me both power and authority, yea, of life and death? Then why speak you to me so proudly?'

'I speak but steadfastly,' quoth she, 'not proudly. For I say, for my part, we have deadly hatred for that sin of pride. And if you fear not to hear a truth, I will show openly and justly that you have uttered a full great untruth. You say your princes have given you power both to slay a person and to give him life; you that can only bereave of life, you have none other power or warrant! You have the right to say that your princes have made you a minister of death; but if you speak of more, you lie, for your power is full naked.'

'Away with your boldness,' Almachius said then, 'and sacrifice to our gods, ere you depart. I care not what insult you lay on me, for I can suffer them like a philosopher; but the insults which you speak of our gods, them I cannot endure.'

Cecily answered, 'O foolish creature, you have said no word whilst you have spoken with me that has not betrayed to me your folly, and that you are in all things an ignorant officer and a vain judge. There lacks nothing of blindness in your bodily eyes, for a thing which we all see to be stone, as men may easily perceive, that same stone you will call a god. I counsel you, since you see not with your blind eyes, let fall your hand upon it, and grope over it well, and you shall find it stone. It is a shame that the people shall so make a mock of you and laugh at your folly, for men everywhere and universally wot well that mighty God is in His high heavens; and these images can profit naught to you nor to themselves, you may easily see, for in effect they are not worth a mite.'

These words and other such she said, and he waxed wroth and bade men should bring her home to her house, 'and there,' quoth he, 'burn her right in a bath of red flames.'

And as he bade, so it was done. For they shut her fast in a bath, and day and night maintained a great fire beneath. Through the long night and also a day, for all the fire and the heat of the bath, she sat all cold and felt no pain; it made her not even to sweat a drop. But in that bath she must lose her life; for Almachius with evil mind sent his order to slay her there. He smote her three strokes on the neck — that executioner, but in no wise could he smite her neck all asunder. And because there was a law at that time that none should do a man that pain to smite the fourth stroke, hard or soft, this executioner durst do no more; but he went his way and left her lying there with her neck cut, half-dead.

The Christian folk about her caught the blood full fairly with sheets. Three days she lived in this torment, and never ceased to instruct them in the faith. Those whom she had fostered therein, to them she still preached, and to them she gave her effects and her goods. And then she committed them to the pope Urban, and said, 'I asked this of the heavenly King to have respite of three days and no more, that I might commend these souls to you, lo! ere I depart; and that of my house I might have a church made to endure perpetually.'

Saint Urban with his deacons privily fetched the body and buried it by night honourably amongst his other saints. Her house is called Saint Cecilia's Church. Saint Urban hallowed it, as he well had the power; and there, unto this day, in worthy manner men do service to Christ and his saint.

Prologue to the Canon's Yeoman's Tale

When the life of Saint Cecilia was finished, ere we had ridden fully five miles, at Boughton-under-Blean there overtook us a man clad in black garments, and underneath he had a white surplice. His hackney, a dapple-grey, so sweated that it was a marvel to behold; it seemed he had spurred hard for three miles; and also the horse that his yeoman rode sweated so that it could scarce walk. The foam lay full thick about the breast-harness, and the rider was all flecked with foam like a magpie. A bag doubled-over lay on his crupper; it seemed he carried little clothing. This worthy man rode lightly clad, as if for summer. In my heart I began to wonder what he was, till I observed how his cloak was sewed to his hood; from which, when I had long considered, I deemed him to be some canon. His hat hung down at his back by a string, for he had ridden faster than a walk or trot; he had spurred ever like mad. He had a burdock-leaf under his hood against the sweat, and to save his head from the sun. But it was a joy to see him sweat! His forehead dripped like a still, full of plantain and pellitory.

And when he had reached us, he began to call out, 'God save this merry company! I have spurred fast after you,' quoth he, 'because I would overtake you, to ride in this pleasant company.'

Also his yeoman was full of courtesy, and said, 'Sirs, but now in the morning-tide I saw you clatter out of your hostelry, and warned my lord and sovereign here, who is full fain to ride with you for disport; he loves dalliance.'

'Friend, God give you good fortune for your warning,' said our Host then, 'for certes it would seem your master were a good judge, and so I well believe. I will be bound also he is full jocund. Can he perhaps tell a merry tale or two, to gladden this company?'

'Who, sir? My lord? Yea, and no mistake; he knows more than enough about mirth and jollity. Also, sir, trust me, if you knew him as well as I do, you would marvel how well and craftily he can work, and that in sundry matters. He has taken on him many a great emprise which were full hard for any man here to achieve, unless they learn it of him. Homely as he rides amongst you, it would be to your advantage if you knew him. I dare stake all that I own, you would not forego his acquaintance for much riches. He is a man of high discretion; I warn you well, he is a superior man.'

'Well,' quoth our Host, 'I pray you then tell me, is he a clerk, or not? Say what is he?'

'Nay, he is greater than a clerk, of a certainty,' said this yeoman, 'and in a few words, Host, I will show you somewhat of his craft. I say my lord knows such subtlety (but from me you cannot know all his cunning, and yet I help somewhat in his work) that he could turn clean upside-down all this ground on which we be riding till we come to Canterbury-town, and could pave it all with silver and gold.'

And when this yeoman had said to him thus, our Host said, '*Benedicite!* This thing is a wondrous marvel since your master is of such high wisdom, wherefore men ought to reverence him, that he needs so little his own worship. Verily, his cloak is not worth a mite, for such a man. By mine head, it is all foul and all torn also. Why is your master so sluttish, I pray you, since he is able to buy better clothes, if his performance accord with your words? Tell me, and that I beseech you.'

'Why? Wherefore ask you me?' quoth this yeoman. 'So God help me, he shall never prosper! (But I would not publish what I tell you, therefore prithee keep it secret.) In faith, I believe he is too wise. What is overdone will come to no good issue; as clerks say, it is a fault. Wherefore I hold him ignorant and foolish therein. When a man has too great a wit, full often it chances that he misuses the same; so does my lord, and it sorely grieves me. God amend it, and that is all!'

'No matter for that,' quoth our Host. 'But good yeoman, since you know of the cunning of your lord, I pray you heartily, tell us how he does, since he is so subtle and skilful. Where dwell you, if it may be told?'

'In the outskirts of a town,' quoth he, 'lurking in corners and blind alleys, where these robbers and these thieves naturally hold their privy timorous dwelling, as they are who dare not shew their presence. So fare we, to tell the truth.'

'Now,' quoth our Host, 'let me talk to you. Why is your face so discolored?'

'Peter!' he answered; 'bad luck to it! I am so used to blow in the fire, that it has changed my colour, no doubt. I am not wont to peer into any mirror, but toil sore and learn multiplying. In our art we grope continually onward, and pore over the fire, but for all that we fail of our end, for it ever turns out amiss. We delude many folk, and borrow gold, be it a pound or two, or ten or twelve, or many more sums, and make them think that at least of one pound we can make two. Yet it is false. But ever we have good expectation to do it and grope after it. But that art is so far ahead of us that we cannot overtake it, though we had sworn to do so, it slides away so fast. In the end it will make us beggars.'

Whilst this yeoman was talking thus, this canon drew nearer, and heard everything the yeoman spake; for this canon was ever suspicious of what men said. For Cato says that he who is guilty verily believes everything to be said of him. This was the cause that he drew so nigh his yeoman, to hear all his speech. And then he said to his yeoman, 'Hold your peace, speak not a word; if you do, you shall pay for it dearly. You slander me here before these folk, and also reveal what you should hide.'

'Yea, tell on, whatever befall,' quoth our Host. 'Care not a mite for all his threatening!'

'In faith, no more I do, but little,' he replied.

And when this canon saw that it would not be, but his yeoman would tell all his secrets, he fled away, for very sorrow and shame.

'Ah!' the yeoman said, 'here comes sport. I will tell now anon all that I know, since he is gone — the foul Fiend strike him! For never hereafter, I promise you, will I have to do with him, for penny nor for pound. He who first brought me to that game, sorrow and disgrace to him ere he die! For by my faith it is bitter earnest to me; I feel that well, whatso men say. And yet for all my pain and sorrow, labour and mischief, I could never in any wise leave it. Now would God my wit might avail to tell all that belongs to that craft! But yet I will tell you part; since my lord is gone I will spare not, such things as I know I will tell.'

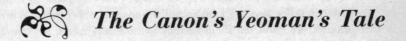

The Canon's Yeoman's Tale

With this canon I have dwelt seven year, and of all his wit I am never the better; thereby I have lost all that I had, and, God wot, so has many another besides. Where I was wont to be bright and gay in clothing and other goodly gear, now I am fain to wear an old stocking on my head; and where my colour was fresh and ruddy, now it is wan and leaden. Whosoever practises it shall rue it sorely. And with all my toil the wool is pulled over my eyes till they water. Lo the gains of multiplying! That slippery science has made me so bare that wherever I turn I have not a penny; and into the bargain I am so in debt thereby, for gold that I have borrowed, that in sooth I shall never pay it whilst I live. Let every man take warning by me forevermore! Whatever manner of man inclines thereto and continues in it, I hold his thrift done with. So God help me, he shall gain naught but to empty his purse and thin his wits. And when through his madness and folly he has lost his own goods through this hazardous game, then he incites other folk to it, to lose their goods as he had done. For it is a joy and comfort to scoundrels to have their fellows in pains and distress; thus a clerk taught me once. No matter for that, no I will tell of our art.

When we be where we practise our elfish craft, we seem wondrous wise, our terms be so book-learned and outlandish. I blow the fire till my heart faints. Why should I tell each proportion of things we work on, as five or six ounces, it may well be, or some other quantity of silver; and busy me telling you the names of orpiment, burnt bones, iron sheets, that be ground into full fine powder? And how all is put in an earthen pot, and salt put in, and pepper also, before these powders that I speak of, and well covered with a glass plate, and many another thing which there was? And of the cementing of pot and glasses that no part of the air should pass out? And of the moderate or the smart fire which was made, and of the care and woe which we had in the sublimation of our matters, and in the amalgaming and calcining of quicksilver, called crude mercury? For all our sleights, we fail of our end. Our orpiment and sublimated mercury, also our litharge ground on a porphyry slab, of each of these a certain number of ounces, naught helps us, our labour is vain. Nor the ascension of vapours, nor the solid bodies that lie fixed at the bottom, can help us aught in our operation. For all our labour and travail is lost, and all the cost which we lay out upon it is gone also, the Fiend take it!

There is also many another thing appertaining to our craft; though I cannot rehearse them in order, because I am an unlearned man, or set them according to their nature, yet I will tell them as they come to my mind; as Armenian clay, verdigris, borax, and sundry vessels of earth and glass, our urinals and descensories, vials, crucibles and vessels for sublimation, flasks, and also alembics, and other such-like things, dear enough at a farthing. It needs not rehearse each of them, reddening waters, bull's gall, arsenic, sal-ammoniac and brimstone; and many an herb I could tell you, as agrimony, valerian, moonwort, and other such if I list to tarry; our lamps burning day and night to bring about our end, if we ever could; also our furnace for calcining, alb-ification of waters, unslaked lime, chalk, white of egg, divers powders, ashes, dung and the like, clay, waxed bags, saltpetre, vitriol, and divers fires of coal or wood, salt of tartar, alkali, prepared salt, matters combust and coagulate, clay mixed with horses' or men's hair, and oil of tartar, alum, glass, yeast, unfermented beer, crude cream of tartar, red orpiment; and of the absorbing and incorporating of our matters, our citronizing of silver, our cementing and fermentation, our moulds, assaying vessels and many another thing.

I will also tell you in order, as was taught me, the four spirits and the seven bodies, as I oft heard my lord name them. The first spirit is called quicksilver, the second orpiment, the third sal-ammoniac, and the fourth brimstone. Also the seven bodies, lo here they are! The sun is gold, the moon we hold to be silver, Mars iron, Mercury we call quicksilver, Saturn is lead, Jupiter tin, and Venus is copper, by my father's soul!

Whosoever will practise this cursed craft, however rich he be, shall not be rich enough; for all the goods he spends about it he shall lose, I have no doubt of that. Whoso list to display his folly, let him come forth, and learn multiplying; and every man who has aught in his strong-box, let him come forth now and wax a philosopher. Peradventure you deem that craft light to learn? Nay, nay, God wot! Be he monk or friar or priest or canon or any other, though he sit at his book night and day learning this uncanny foolish lore, all is in vain, and worse perdy! And to teach this subtlety to an unlearned man — fie! speak not thereof, it will not be! Know he book-learning, or know he none, in the end he shall find it all the same. For, by my salvation, both learned and unlearned end alike well in multiplying, when all is done; that is to say, both fail.

Yet I forgot to make rehearsal of corrosive waters and of metal filings, of fusible metal, of mollification of bodies and also of their induration, oils and ablutions, — to tell all would exceed any Bible that is anywhere; therefore it is best I should desist from all these names. For I believe I have told you enough already to raise a fiend, look he never so savage.

Oh nay! Let be! The philosopher's stone, called elixir, we all seek after hard; for had we that, we should be secure enough. But I declare to the God of heaven, for all our craft and all our sleight and when we have done everything, it will not come to us. It has made us spend much gold, the loss whereof nigh drives us mad, save that good hope creeps into our hearts, and makes us ever to trust, for all our pains, to be relieved by finding it. But such trusting and hoping bring discipline full sharp and hard; I warn you well, it is ever to seek. That future tense, in trust thereto, has caused men to part from all that ever they had. Yet of that art they never think they have had enough, for it is bitter-sweet to them; thus it seems. For if they have but a sheet to wrap them in by night, and a rough cloak to walk in by day, they would sell them to spend on this craft; they can never stint till naught remain. And wherever they go, men may know them evermore by the smell of brimstone. They stink for all the world as a goat; their savour is so hot and rammish, trust me, that though a man be a mile from them, the savour will infect him. Lo, thus by their smell and their threadbare array men may, if they list, know these folk. And if a man privily ask them why they be clothed so scurvily, anon they will whisper in his ear and say that if they were espied, men would slay them, for their art. Lo, thus they betray the innocent.

Pass we over this; I go to my story. Ere the pot be placed on the fire, my lord, and none but he, compounds metals with certain quantities of other matters, — now he is gone, I dare speak boldly, — for, as men say, he is cunning at his craft, at least I wot well he has such a repute, and yet full oft he runs into blame. And know you how? Full often it happens that the pot breaks to pieces, and farewell, all is gone! These metals be so violent that our walls cannot resist them, unless they are wrought of stone and lime. They pierce so, and go through the wall, and some parts sink into the earth — thus at times we have lost many a pound —, and some are scattered all over the floor, and some leap into the roof; without doubt, though the Fiend show him not in our sight, I believe he is with us, the knave! In hell, where he is lord and master, is not more woe or rancour or ire. When our pot is broken, as I have told, every man chides and deems himself abused. One will say that it was all along of the building of the fire; one says nay, it was the blowing (then I was afeared, for that was mine office). 'A straw for that,' says a third, 'you are a pack of fools! It was not mixed as it ought to be.'

'Nay,' says the fourth, 'stop, and hear me; because our fire was not made with beech-wood, that and none other is the cause, by mine head!'

I cannot tell what it was along of, but well I know we have great strife. 'What!' quoth my lord, 'there is no more to do now, and another time I will beware of these perils; I am right sure the pot was cracked. Be that as it may, be not confounded. As we are wont, let the floor be swept anon, and pluck up your hearts and be glad and blithe.'

The rubbish is swept on an heap and a canvas spread on the floor, and all this rubbish thrown into a sieve and many times sifted and picked over.

'Perdy,' quoth one, 'there is yet here somewhat of our metal, though not all. Though the thing have miscarried this time, it may go well enough another time. We must venture our wealth. A merchant, trust me, cannot always remain in prosperity, perdy! One time his merchandise is drowned in the sea, and another time it comes safe to land.'

'Peace!' quoth my lord. 'Next time I will try to bring our craft to another issue. And unless I do, sirs, let me bear the blame. Well I wot there was a defect somewhere.'

Another says the fire was too hot; but hot or cold, I vow we end evermore amiss. We fail of what we would get and ever rave in our madness. And when we be all together, every man seems a Solomon. But all that shines like gold is not gold, as I have heard tell. Nor is every apple good that is fair to the eye, howsoever men prate. Lo, even so it is amongst us; he that appears the wisest is the greatest fool, by the Lord, when it comes to the test, and he that seems the truest man is a thief; that you shall know, ere I leave you, by the time I have made an end of my tale.

II

Amongst us there is a religious man, a canon, who would infect a whole town, though it were as great as Nineve, Rome, Alexandria, Troy, and three more as well. His sleights and his infinite falseness no man could write, I believe, though he lived a thousand year. His like for falsehood lives not in all this world, for he would so involve himself in his cunning terms and speak his words so slyly, when he would commune with a man, that he would make him dote anon, unless it were a fiend, as he is himself. He had beguiled full many a man, and will more, if he lives a time longer. And yet men ride and walk many miles to seek him and have his acquaintance, knowing naught of his false manners. And if you list to hear me, I will tell of this.

But, worshipful religious canons, deem not that I slander your order, though my tale be of a canon. In every order is some rogue, and God forbid a whole company should pay for the folly of one man. It is nowise my intent to slander you, but only to chide what is amiss. This tale is told not only for you but for others besides. You wot well how amongst Christ's twelve apostles there was no traitor except only Judas. Then why should all the guiltless remnant have reproof? As to you I say the same, save only this, if you will hear me: if any Judas be in your convent, remove him betimes, if there be fear of shame or loss, I counsel you. And be not displeased, I crave, but hearken to what I shall say.

In London dwelt many years a priest, an annualer, who was so pleasant and serviceable to the goodwife where he was at board that she would suffer him to pay naught for victual or clothing, went he never so fine. And he had spending-money a-plenty. No matter about that; I will now proceed and tell my tale of the canon who brought this priest to ruin. One day came this false canon to this priest's chamber where he dwelt, beseeching him to lend him a certain sum of gold, and he would repay it him. Quoth he, 'Lend me a mark for three days only, and on my day I will pay it you. And if so be you find me false, the next time have me hanged by the neck!'

This priest handed him a mark, and that straightway, and this canon thanked him again and again and took his leave and went his way forth; and on the third day brought his money back, whereat this priest was wondrous fain.

'Certes,' quoth he, 'it annoys me not a whit to lend a man a noble, or two or three, or whatsoever I may have, when he is so faithful of nature that he will nowise exceed his time. To such a man I can never say nay.'

'What!' this canon said. 'Should I be untrusty? Nay, that were a new thing! Faith is a thing that I will hold ever, to the day when I shall creep into my grave; and God forbid else! Believe this as sure as your creed! I thank God, and in good time be it said, that there never yet was man ill-content for gold or silver that he loaned me; and never was falsehood in my heart. And sir,' quoth he, 'since you have been so kind and shown me such courtesy, I will show you somewhat of my secret knowledge, in order to require your kindness somewhat; and, if you list to learn, I will teach you fully how I can work in philosophy. Take good heed, you shall well see with your eyes that I will do a master-stroke ere I leave you.'

'Yea?' the priest said. 'Yea, sir, and will you so? Marry! I heartily pray you for that.'

'At your commandment, sir, in truth,' the canon replied; 'God forbid else!'

Lo how this thief could proffer his service! It is full sooth that such proffered service stinks, as these old sages testify. And full soon I will prove it by this canon, root of all treachery, who evermore delights, such fiendish thoughts press into his heart, to bring Christ's people to mischief. God keep us from his false dissembling!

This priest knew not with whom he dealt, and saw naught of his harm to come. O guileless priest, poor innocent! Anon thou shalt be blinded by thy covetousness. O luckless creature, full blind is thy wit, thou art no wise aware of the deceit which this fox has planned for thee. Thou canst not escape his wily tricks. Wherefore, unhappy man! to come to the consummation of thy ruin, I will hasten me forthwith to tell thine unwit and folly, and also the falseness of that wretch, so far as my cunning may go.

You think this canon was my lord? In faith, and by heaven's Queen, it was not he, but another canon, that knows an hundred-fold more subtlety, sir Host. He has betrayed folk full often; it dulls me to rhyme of his falseness. Ever when I speak of it, my cheeks wax red with shame for him, at least they begin to glow, for redness have I none in my visage; for sundry fumes of metal, which you have heard me rehearse, have consumed and wasted my redness. Now take heed of this canon's cursedness!

'Sir,' quoth he to the priest, 'let your man go for quicksilver, that we may have it straightway, and let him bring two or three ounces. And when he comes, anon you shall see a marvellous thing, which you never saw ere this.'

'Sir,' quoth the priest, 'it shall be done without fail,' and he bade his servant fetch this thing, and he was ready at his word, and went forth and straight returned with this quicksilver, sooth to say, and handed these three ounces to the canon. And he laid them down and bade the servant to bring coals, that he might go anon at work.

The coals were fetched forthwith, and this canon took a crucible out from his bosom and showed it to the priest. 'This instrument which you see,' quoth he, 'take it in your hand and do you put therein yourself an ounce of this quicksilver; and begin here to wax a philosopher, in the name of Christ! There be full few to whom I would offer to show thus much of my knowledge. For you shall see here, by experience, that I shall mortify this quicksilver anon, right in your sight verily, and make it as good silver and as pure as any in your purse or mine or elsewhere, and make it malleable. And else hold me as false, and unfit to show my face amongst folk forevermore. I have here a powder, which cost me dear, and shall make all good; for it is the ground of all my cunning which I shall show you. Send your man out and let him be outside and shut the door, whilst we be about our secret, that no man may spy us whilst we work upon this craft.'

All that he bade was done; this servant straight went out and his master shut the door, and they went speedily to their labour. This priest, at the bidding of this cursed canon, anon set this thing upon the fire, and blew the fire and busied himself full diligently. And this canon cast into the crucible a powder, I wot not whereof it was made, either of chalk or of glass or somewhat else, that was not worth a fly, with which to blind the priest; and he bade him hasten and bed the coals all above the crucible; 'for,' quoth this canon, 'in token that I love you, your own two hands shall do all which shall be done here.'

'Gramercy,' quoth the priest, light of heart, and heaped the coals as the canon bade. And whilst he was busy, this fiendish wretch, this false canon, the foul Fiend have him! took out of his bosom a beechen coal, in which an hollow had been made full craftily with an ounce of silver filings therein; and the hole was securely stopped with wax to keep the filings in. And understand that this false contrivance was not made there but earlier. And hereafter I shall tell of other things which he brought with him. Ere he came there, he thought to beguile the priest, and so he did, ere they parted; he could not cease till he had skinned him. It dulls me to speak of him; if I wist how, I would fain avenge me of his falseness. But he is here today, gone to-morrow; he is so variable, he abides nowhere.

But now take heed, sirs, for God's love! He took his coal and held it privily in his hand. And whilst the priest busily bedded the coals, as I told you, this canon said, 'Friend, you do amiss. This is not bedded as it should be, but I shall soon amend it. Now let me take a hand in it for a little, for I pity you, by Saint Giles! I see how you sweat, you are right hot, take a cloth here, and wipe away the wet.' And whilst the priest wiped his face, this canon — bad luck to him! — took his coal and laid it above, over the middle of the crucible, and then blew hard till the coals began to burn well.

'Now give us drink,' quoth the canon; 'all shall be well soon, I warrant. Sit down and make merry!'

And when this canon's beechen coal was burned, all the filings anon fell out of the hollow and down into the crucible; and so it must needs in reason, since it was placed so exactly above. But alas! the priest wist nought thereof; he deemed all the coals alike good, for he perceived nothing of the trick. When this alchemist saw his time, he cried, 'Rise up, sir priest, and stand by me. Go, step out and bring us a chalk-stone, for I know well you have no mould; and if I have good fortune, I will make a thing shaped even as a mould. And bring with you also a bowl or a pan full of water, and then you shall well see how our business shall prosper and stand test. And yet, that you shall have no distrust nor wrong conceit of me in your absence, I will never leave you, but go and come back with you again.'

To tell it briefly, they opened and shut the chamber-door, and went their way, carrying the key with them, and came again without pause; why should I linger the day long? He took the chalk and fashioned it as a mould, as I shall tell you. I say, he took out of his own sleeve a thin plate of silver, which was but an ounce in weight. And take heed, now, of his cursed wile — ill may he prosper! He shaped his mould in length and breadth after this plate so slyly that the priest noted it not; and he hid the plate again in his sleeve. Then he took his matters off the fire and put them into the mould with merry cheer, and cast it into the water-vessel when he was ready, and straightway bade the priest, 'Look what is there; put your hand in and grope. You shall find silver there, I believe. — What the Devil of hell should it be else? A shaving of silver is silver, perdy!'

This priest put his hand in, and took up a strip of fine silver. And glad in every vein was this priest when he saw it was so. 'God's blessing, and his mother's and all hallows' may you have, sir canon!' quoth he; 'and I their malison, if I become not your man in all I am able, if you vouchsafe to teach me this noble craft and this subtlety!'

Quoth the canon, 'Yet I will make assay a second time, that you may watch well and be expert in this, and another time if need be, try in my absence this study and this skilful science.' Then he said, 'Get another ounce of quicksilver, without more words, and do therewith as before with that other which is now silver.'

This priest busied him as best he could to do as this canon, this cursed man, bade him, and blew the coals hard that he might achieve his desire. And meantime this canon was all ready to beguile the priest again; and for a show he held in his hand a hollow stick (take heed and beware!), in the end of which was put an even ounce of silver filings, as in his coal before; and the end was well stopped with wax to keep in his filings every whit. And whilst this priest was at his work, this canon with his stick anon betook him thither and cast in his powder, as before, — I pray God the Devil may flay him out of his skin for his falsehood, for in thought and deed he was ever false! And with the stick, which was ordained with that false contrivance, he stirred the coals above the crucible, until the wax melted in the fire, as every man, but he be a fool, knows very well it must, and all that was in the stick poured out and fell straight into the crucible. Now, good sirs, what would you have better than well enough? When this priest was beguiled again, and suspected naught but good faith, he was so glad that I can in no wise describe his mirth and his gladness. And once more he offered body and goods to the canon.

'Yea,' quoth the canon, 'though I be poor, you shall find me skilful; I warn you there is more behind. Is there any copper here?' he asked.

'Yea, sir,' quoth the priest, 'I believe there be.'

'Else go buy us some, and that straightway. Now go your way, good sir, and hasten.'

He went out and returned with the copper, and his canon took it in his hands, and weighed out an even ounce of it. My tongue is too simple a minister of my wit to express the duplicity of this canon, root of all cursedness. To them that knew him not he seemed friendly, but he was fiendish in heart and mind. It wearies me to tell of his falsehood and yet I will express it, to the end that men may beware thereby, and truly for no other reason.

He put his ounce of copper in the crucible, and straightway set it on the fire and cast in powder, and made the priest blow and bend over in his work as he did before; and it was all a fetch. He made the priest his dupe, even as he would.

And afterwards he cast it into the mould and at last put it into the pan of water and thrust in his own hand; and he had a strip of silver in his sleeve, as you have heard me tell before. He slyly took it out, the priest all unwitting of his false art, and left it in the bottom of the water-pan, and he rumbled to and fro in the water, and wondrous privily took up the copper plate also — this priest perceiving naught — and hid it, and caught him by the breast and spake to him and thus said sportively, 'Stoop down; by God, you be to blame! Help me now as I did you the other time. Put in your hand and look what is there.'

The priest took up this strip of silver forthwith, and then said the canon, 'Let us go to some goldsmith with these three strips which we have made, and see if they be aught. For in faith I lay my hood that they be pure, fine silver; and that shall straight be tested.' They went to the goldsmith with the three strips, and assayed them with fire and hammer; no man could gainsay that they were as they ought to be.

This besotted priest! who was gladder? Never was bird gladder of dawn, never was there nightingale in the season of May list better to sing, never lady delighting to carol or to speak of love or womanly virtue, never a knight to do a bold deed of arms so as to stand in the grave of his dear lady, than this priest to learn this sorry craft. And he spake thus to the canon, 'For the love of God Who died for us all, if I may deserve it of you, how much shall this receipt cost? Tell it, now!'

'By our Lady,' the canon said, 'I warn you well, it is dear; for there can be no man in England work it, save myself and a friar.'

'No matter,' quoth he. 'Now, sire, for God's sake, what shall I pay? Tell me, I beg.'

'In truth I say it is full dear,' he replied. 'Sir, in a word, if you desire it, you shall pay forty pound, so God save me! And were it not for the friendly act that you did me a while ago, you should pay more in sooth.'

Anon this priest fetched the sum of forty pounds in nobles, and handed them all to the canon for this receipt; yet all his operation was but fraud and cozenage.

'Sir priest,' he said, 'I care to have no praise for my skill; I would it were kept close. Keep it secret, as you love me. For if men knew all my secret lore, by God, they would have so great malice to me for my philosophy that they would kill me without fail.'

'God forbid!' quoth the priest. 'What say you! I had rather spend all the goods I have (else may I lose my head!) than you should fall into such mischance.'

'For your good will, sir,' quoth the canon, 'right good luck to you; and so gramercy and farewell!'

He went his way, and the priest never saw him after that time. And when, at such time as he would, this priest came to make trial of this receipt, farewell, it would not be! Lo, thus he was gulled and beguiled. Thus that canon insinuates himself, to bring folk to ruin.

Consider, sirs, how in every station there is such strife betwixt men and gold that scarce any gold remains. This multiplying blinds so many that in good faith I believe it is the greatest cause of such scarcity. Philosophers speak with such misty terms in this craft that men cannot take hold of it by any wit that they have now. They may well chatter like jays, and put all their delight and pains on polishing up their terms; but they shall never attain their end.

But a man may lightly so learn multiplying that he shall bring his goods to naught, if he have any! Lo, such lucre is to be gained in this lusty sport! It will turn a man's joy to anger and grief, and also empty great and heavy purses, and win the malison of them that have lent their goods thereto. Oh fie, for shame! cannot those who have been burned flee the fire's heat, alas! You that follow this craft, I counsel you leave it, lest you lose all. For better than never is late; never to thrive were too long a period. Though you prowl far and wide, you shall never find your object. You are as bold as blind Bayard the horse, who blunders forth and thinks of no peril; he is as bold to run against a stone as to pass beside it in the way. So fare you that multiply. If your eyes cannot see well, look that your mind lack not its sight. For though you stare and look never so widely, you shall not gain a mite in that business, but lose all that you can borrow, beg, or steal. Withdraw the fire, lest it burn too hot; I mean, meddle no more with that craft, for if you do, your thrift is clean gone.

And I will here tell you straightway what philosophers say on this matter. Lo, thus says Arnold of the New Town in his Rosary; in good sooth he says right thus, 'No man can mortify mercury except it be with the aid of its brother.' And he says how that he who first said this thing was Hermes, father of philosophers; he tells how the dragon dies not, in sooth, except he be slain by his brother; and that is to say, by the dragon he understood mercury and naught else, and by his brother, brimstone, that were drawn out of *sol* and *luna*. 'And therefore,' said he, 'take heed to my saw, let no man busy him in this art, unless he can understand all the mind and speech of philosophers; if he do, he is a foolish man. For this knowledge and this cunning is of the secret of secrets, perdy!'

Also there was a disciple of Plato who on a time said to his master, as his book Senioris will testify, and made this demand of him in sooth, 'Tell me the name of the secret stone.'

'And Plato forthwith answered him, 'Take the stone which men call Titanos.'

'Which is that?' quoth he.

'The same is Magnesia,' quoth Plato.

'Yea, sir, and is it so? This is to interpret *ignotum per ignotius*. I pray you, good sir, what is Magnesia?'

'It is a water, I say, that is made of four elements,' quoth Plato.

'Tell me,' he said then, 'the principle of that water, if it be your will.'

'Nay, nay,' quoth Plato, 'that I will not, certainly. The philosophers were all sworn never to discover it to any, or in any wise write it in any book. For to Christ it is so precious and dear that He would not that it be discovered, save where it pleases His Godhead to inspire man, — and also to forbid whom He will. Lo this is all.'

Then I conclude thus; since the God of heaven will not that the philosophers name how a man shall come by this stone, I deem it to be the best counsel to let it go. For whoso makes God his adversary, to work anything against His will, certes, he shall never thrive, though he multiply to the day of his death. And here I stop, for my tale is done. God send every honest man weal for his bale. Amen.

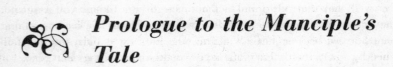

Prologue to the Manciple's Tale

Know you not where there stands a little village called Bob-up-and-down, under Blean forest on the Canterbury road? There began our host to jest and to make mirth and said, 'What! sirs, Dun is in the mire! Is there no man who for prayer or pay will awaken our companion here behind? A thief might full easily tie and rob him. See how he nods! see, for cock's bones, as if anon he would fall from his horse. Is that a London cook, — plague take him! Make him come forth, he knows his penance, for he shall tell a tale, although it be not worth a bottle of hay, by my faith! Awake, you Cook, God give you sorrow! what ails you to sleep in the morning? Have you had fleas all night, or had ado with some quean, or are you drunk, so that you cannot hold up your head?'

This Cook, who looked full pale, said to our Host, 'So God bless my soul, there is fallen on me such heaviness, I wot not why, that I had rather sleep than have the best gallon of wine in Cheapside.'

'Well,' quoth the Manciple, 'if it may do ease to you, sir Cook, and annoy no person who rides here, and if our Host is willing, of his courtesy, I will excuse you of your story for now; for your visage is full pale, your eyes also look dazed, methinks, and I well know your breath stinks full sour, which well shows you are indisposed; good faith, you shall never be flattered by me! Lo, this drunken creature. See how he yawns as though he would swallow us right anon. By your father's soul, man, keep your mouth shut, the Devil of hell set his foot in it! Your cursed breath will infect us all; fie, stinking swine! fie, ill hap to you! Ah! take heed, sirs, of this lusty fellow. Now, will you joust at the quintain? Methinks you are in a noble state for that, sweet sir! I believe you have drunk ape-wine, and that is when men play with a straw.'

At this speech the Cook waxed wroth, and began to nod vehemently upon the Manciple for lack of speech, and down the horse cast him, where he lay till men picked him up. This was a fair bit of horsemanship for a cook! Alas that he had not kept to his ladle! And great was the shoving to and fro to lift him up, and much the care and woe, ere he was once more in the saddle, so unwieldy was this sorry, wan ghost.

'Because drink had dominion over this man,' then said our Host to the Manciple, 'I believe by my salvation that he would tell his tale but lewdly; for were it wine or old ale or musty that he has drunk, he speaks through his nose and puffs hard and also he has a cold in his head. He has also more than enough to do to keep himself and his nag out of the slough. And if he fall from his nag again, then we shall all have enough to do to lift up his heavy drunken carcass. Tell on your tale, no matter for him. But nevertheless, Manciple, you are too unmannerly, in faith, thus openly to twit him with his fault. Peradventure another day he will stop your high-flying and bring you down as a hawk to the hand. I mean he will glance at sundry small matters, as to find fault with your reckonings, which, if it came to proof, were not for your credit.'

'No,' quoth the Manciple, 'that were a great mischief; so he could lightly bring me into the trap. Yet I had rather pay for the mare which he rides on than have him at strife with me; I will not anger him, by mine head! What I spake, I said in jest. And what think you? I have in a gourd here a draught of wine, yea, of a ripe grape, and anon you shall see a merry jest. This Cook shall drink thereof, if I can make him, and he will not say me nay, I stake my life.'

And of a truth, to tell it all, the Cook drank deep out of this vessel, alas! What need had he? Already he had drunk enough. And when he had pooped in this horn, he handed the gourd back to the Manciple, and of this drink he was wondrous fain and thanked him in such wise as he was able.

Then our Host began to laugh marvellous loud and said, 'I well see we must needs carry good drink with us wherever we go; for that will turn rancour and vexation into accord and love, and appease many a wrong. O thou Bacchus, blessed be thy name, that so canst turn earnest to sport. Worship and thanks to thy godhead! But of that ye get no more of me! Tell on your tale, Manciple, I pray you.'

'Well, sir,' quoth he, 'now harken.'

The Manciple's Tale

When Phœbus dwelt down here on this earth, as old books make mention, he was the lustiest young knight in all this world, and also the best archer. He slew Python, the serpent, on a day as he lay sleeping in the sunshine; and he wrought many another noble worthy achievement with his bow, as men may read.

He could play on every manner of instrument, and so sing that it was heavenly melody to hear the sound of his clear voice. Certes Amphion, king of Thebes, who walled that city by his singing, could never sing half so well as he. And also he was the seemliest man that is or was since the world was made. What need to describe his features? For no man so fair lived in this world. And therewith he was full of gentle manners, of honour and of perfect worthiness.

This Phœbus, flower of all young men alike in chivalry and in generosity, for his sport and also in sign of his victory over Python, as the history tell us, was wont to bear a bow in his hand. Now this Phœbus had in his house a crow, which he fostered long time in a cage and taught to speak, as men teach a jay. This crow was white as a snow-white swan, and when he would say his say, could speak as well as any man by counterfeiting. And withal no nightingale in all this world could sing by an hundred thousandth part so wondrous merrily and well.

Now this Phœbus had in his house a wife whom he loved more than his soul, and was ever busy night and day to please her and do her reverence, save only, if I am to tell the truth, he was jealous and solicitous to guard her well; for he was loath to be duped. And so is every person in such case, but all in vain; it avails not. A good wife, clean in deed and thought, should not be watched, in sooth; and truly the labour is in vain to watch an evil one, that will not be kept. This hold I as very folly, to waste labour in watching wives; thus write old clerks.

But now to my theme, as I first began. This worthy Phœbus did all he could to please her, deeming that with such pleasance and with his manhood and fair demeanour none should put him from her grace. But this, God wot, no man can compass, — to constrain a thing which Nature has placed in a creature's very being. Take any bird, put it in a cage, and set your mind and heart all on fostering it tenderly with meat and drink, with all dainties you can fancy, and keep it as cleanly as you can; though his cage be never so gay with gold, yet this bird had twenty thousand times rather go eat worms and such wretchedness in a forest cold and rude. For he will do his diligence ever to escape from his cage, if he can; this bird ever desires his liberty. Take a cat, and foster him well with cream and tender meat and make him a silken couch; and let a mouse run by the wall. At once he forgets cream and flesh and every dainty in that place, such appetite has he to eat a mouse. Lo, here desire has his dominion, and appetite banishes discretion. A she-wolf also has a villainous low nature; at the time when she list to have a mate, she will take the scurviest wolf she can find, or the one least of honour.

All these ensamples I speak concerning these men that be untrue, — and never a bit of women! For ever men have a wanton appetite to take their pleasure with lower creatures than their wives, be they never so fair, never so true and meek. Flesh is so eager after novelty, Devil take it!, that not for long can we find pleasure in aught which accords with virtue.

This Phœbus thought of no guile, and was deceived for all his goodliness; for under him she had another, a man of small reputation, worth naught in comparison to Phœbus, — more was the pity! Thus it often haps, and much harm and woe comes therefrom. And so befell when Phœbus was away that his wife sent anon after her seducer. Seducer? — this is a knavish word, certes; forgive it me, I pray you. The wise Plato says, as you may find in the books, that word and act must needs accord; if a man shall tell a thing as it is, the word must be cousin to the action. I am a rude man, I say right thus, that truly there is no other difference than this betwixt a wife of high degree that is dishonest of her body, and a poor wench, — if so be they both do amiss, — that the gentlewoman, high in estate, shall be called her paramour's lady-love; and because that other is a poor woman, she shall be called his wench or his doxy. And God wot, mine own dear friend, men abase the one as low as the other.

Right so betwixt an usurping tyrant and an outlaw or a roving thief, I say the same, there is no difference. This definition was told to Alexander, that, because the tyrant is of greater power by the force of his retainers to slay downright and to burn house and home and lay everything full low, therefore behold! he is called a captain; and because the outlaw has but a small band and cannot do so great harm nor bring a country to such mischief, men call him an outlaw or a bandit. But because I am not a bookish man, I will tell never a word more of saws from books, but I will go to my tale, as I began.

When this flighty wife of Phœbus had sent for her paramour, the white crow, which hung ever in the cage, beheld them, and said never a word. And when Phœbus the lord was come home, this crow sang 'Cuckoo! cuckoo! cuckoo!'

'What, bird!' quoth Phœbus. 'What song singest thou? Wert thou not wont to sing so merrily that it was a joy to mine heart to hear thy voice? Alas, what song is that?'

'By the Lord,' quoth he, 'I sing not amiss. Phœbus,' quoth he, 'for all thy worth, thy beauty and thy noble birth, for all thy sweet singing and all thy melody, and for all thy watching, thine eye is bleared by a man small and of no reputation, not worth a gnat alongside thee, by mind head!' What more would you have? Anon the crow told him, by trusty tokens and bold words, how his wife had sinned, to his great shame and reproach; and told him once and again that he had seen it with his eyes.

This Phœbus turned away; it seemed to him his sorrowful heart would burst in twain. He bent his bow and set an arrow therein, and then in his ire he slew his wife. This is the conclusion, there is no more to say. And for sorrow of this he broke his instruments of music, harp and lute, gittern and psaltery; and he broke also his arrows and bow. And after that he spake thus to the bird: 'Traitor,' quoth he, 'with a scorpion's tongue thou hast brought me unto confusion. Alas that I was wrought! Why am I not dead? O dear wife, gem of delight, who wert so constant to me and so faithful, now liest thou dead with face pale of hue, full guiltless, that I dare verily swear! O rash hand, to do so foul a wrong! O turbid wit, O reckless ire, that heedlessly smitest the guiltless! O distrust, full of false suspicion, where was thy wisdom and discernment?

Let every man beware of rashness, believe naught without strong testimony; smite not too soon, ere ye know why, and consider soberly and well ere in wrath ye execute aught upon suspicion. Alas! rash ire has fully fordone a thousand folk, and brought them to the dust. Alas! I will slay myself for sorrow!'

And to the crow he said, 'O false thief, forthwith I will requite thee for thy false talk! Thou sangest once like a nightingale; now, false thief, thou shalt forego thy song and also all thy white feathers, and never in all thy life shalt thou speak again. Thus shall men be avenged on a traitor; thou and thine offspring shall ever be black, and shall never make sweet noise but every cry before tempest and rain, in tokening that through thy fault my wife is dead.'

And he rushed upon the crow, and that anon, and plucked out every one of his white feathers and made him black, and bereft him of his song and also of his speech, and slung him out at the door to the Devil, to whom I commit him! And for this cause all crows be black.

Lordings, by this ensample I pray you to take heed, and mark what I say: never whilst you live tell a man of his wife's frailty; of a sooth he will mortally hate you. Sir Solomon, as wise clerks say, teaches a man to guard his tongue well; but as I said, I have no book-lore. Yet thus my dame taught me: 'My son, in God's name think on the crow! My son, hold thy tongue and hold thy friend. A bitter tongue is worse than a fiend; my son, men may bless themselves against a fiend. My son, God of His endless goodness walled a tongue about with teeth and lips also, that man should consider well what he speaks. My son, full oft for too much speech has many a man been undone, as clerks tell; but evermore for little speech and well-advised is no man harmed. My son, thou shouldst restrain thy tongue at all times, save when thou dost thy diligence to speak of God in worship and prayer. The first virtue, son, if thou wilt learn it, is to restrain and well guard thy tongue; thus learn children of tender age. My son, there comes great harm of much speech and ill-advised, where less speech had been enough; thus was told and taught me. In much speaking sin is not wanting. Knowest thou the operation of a rash tongue? Even as a sword cuts and carves an arm in two, so, my dear son, a tongue cuts friendship in two. A prater is abominable to God; read Solomon so worthy and wise, read David in his psalms, read Seneca. My son, speak not, but nod with thine head. Make as if thou wert deaf, if thou hear a prater speak of perilous matters. The Flemings say, mind it if thou wilt, that little prating causes much rest. My son, if thou hast said no ill word, thou needst not fear to be betrayed; but he who has spoken ill, I aver, can in no wise recall his words. What is said, is said; forth it goes, though it repent a man, though it be lief or loath to him. He is his slave to whom he has spoken a thing for which he is sorry now. My son, beware, and be no new author of tidings, be they true or false. Wheresoever thou goest, amongst gentle or simple, guard thy tongue well, and think on the crow.'

Prologue to the Parson's Tale

By the time the Manciple had finished his tale, the sun was descended so low from the south line that, to my sight, his altitude was not nine-and-twenty degrees. It was then four of the clock, as I reckon; for my shadow there was eleven foot, or a little more or less, if I judge my height to be six foot. Withal the moon's exaltation, I mean Libra, was still ever ascending, as we were entering the edge of a thorp. Wherefore our Host, even as in this matter he was wont to govern our fair company, said in this wise, 'Lordings all, now there lack us no tales more than one. My judgment and my decree is accomplished; I believe we have heard from all sorts and conditions of you, and all my plan is almost fulfilled. I pray God, fair befall him who tells this tale to us lustily. Sir priest,' quoth he, 'are you a vicar, or are you a parson?' Say the sooth, by your faith! Be what you may, break not our game, for save you every man has told his tale; unbuckle, show us what is in your bag. For truly methinks by your cheer you should knit up some great matter indeed. Tell us a tale straightway, for cock's bones!'

This Parson answered straightway, 'You get no fabulous matter out of me! For Paul, writing unto Timothy, reproves them that depart from that which is soothfast and tell fables and such wretchedness. Why should I sow chaff out of my fist when I can sow wheat if I will? Wherefore I say, if you list to hear morality and edifying matter, and if you will lend attentive ears, I will full fain do you such lawful pleasure in reverence to Christ as I am able. But know well I am a Southern man, I cannot tell a tale — *rum, ram ruf* — hunting the letter; and God wot, I hold rhyme to be wellnigh as bad. And therefore I will humour no man, but if you list I will tell you a merry tale in prose, to knit up all this holiday story-telling and make an end. And Jesu of His grace grant me wit to show you on this journey the way of that same perfect and glorious pilgrimage, which is called Jerusalem the celestial. And, if you vouchsafe it, forthwith I shall begin my tale; wherefore I pray, tell your desires now, I can say no more. But nevertheless I put this meditation ever subject to the correction of clerks, for I am not versed in texts; I take but the sense, believe me. Therefore I protest that I stand subject to correction.'

Upon these words we assented straight, for it seemed to us a fit thing to do, to give him opportunity and hearing, and to end with some edifying matter. And we bade our Host to tell him that we all prayed him to tell his tale. Our Host spake for all of us. 'Sir priest,' quoth he, 'now fair befall you! Say what you list, we will gladly hear;' and to that word he added, — 'Tell your meditation,' quoth he. 'But haste you, the sun will down. Be fruitful, and that in short time, and may God send you His grace to do well!'

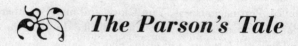 # The Parson's Tale

Our sweet Lord God of heaven, Who would have no man to perish, but will that we all come to the knowledge of Him, and to the blessed life which is perdurable, admonishes us by the prophet Jeremy, who says in this wise: 'Stand upon the ways, and see and ask for the old paths (that is to say, the old counsels), which is the good way; and walk in that way, and ye shall find refreshment for your souls,' etc. Many be the spiritual ways that lead folk to our Lord Jesu Christ, and to the Kingdom of glory. Amongst which ways there is one full noble and full meet, which cannot fail man or woman who through sin has gone astray from the right road to the celestial Jerusalem; and this path is called Penance, about which a man should gladly hearken and inquire with all his heart; to know what Penance is, and whence it is called Penance, and in how many ways be the actions or operations of Penance, and how many species of Penance there be, and what things appertain and are needful to Penance, and what things hinder Penance.

The Seven Deadly Sins

Now is it a needful thing to tell which be the deadly sins, that is to say, captains of sins; they all run in one leash, but in divers manners. Now they are called captains, forasmuch as they are chief, and the sources of all other sins. At the root then of these seven sins is Pride, the general root of all evils; for from this root spring certain branches, as Wrath, Envy, Accidia or Sloth, Avarice (or Covetousness, to the common understanding), Gluttony, and Lechery. And each of these chief sins has its branches and its twigs, as shall be declared in their chapters following.

On Pride

And though so be no man can entirely tell the number of the twigs and of the evils that come from Pride, yet will I show a part of them, a you shall perceive. There are Disobedience, Boasting, Hypocrisy, Scorn, Arrogance, Impudence, Swelling of heart, Insolence, Elation, Impatience, Strife, Contumacy, Presumption, Irreverence, Pertinaciousness, Vain Glory, and many another twig that I cannot declare. Disobedient is he who out of dislike disobeys the commandments of God and of his rulers and of his ghostly father. Boaster is he who boasts of the evil or of the good that he has done. Hypocrite is he who avoids showing him such as he is, and shows him such as he is not. Scornful is he who has disdain of his neighbour, that is to say, of his fellow-Christian, or scorns to do that which he ought to do. Arrogant is he who thinks that he has those good things in him which he has not, or weens that he should have them according to his deserts; or else he deems that he is that which he is not. Impudent is he who of his pride has no shame for his sins. Swelling of heart is when a man rejoices at evil which he has done. Insolent is he who despises in his judgment all other folk, in comparison with his own worth, his cunning, his speech, and his bearing. Elation is when he can endure to have neither master nor equal. Impatient is he who will not be taught or reproved of his sin, and by strife wars against truth wittingly, and defends his folly. Contumacious is he who through his indignation is against every authority or power of them that be his rulers. Presumption is when a man undertakes an emprise that he ought not to do, or else that he cannot do; this is called Surquidry. Irreverence is when men pay not honour where they ought to pay it, and expect to be reverenced. Pertinaciousness is when a man defends his folly and trusts too much in his own wit. Vain Glory is to have pomp and delight in his temporal dignity, and to glorify himself in this worldly state. Prating is when men speak too much before folk, and clatter on like a mill, and take no heed of what they say.

And there is yet a kind of privy Pride, that waits to be saluted first ere he will salute, although he be of less honour than that other is, peradventure; and also he expects or desires to sit, or else to take the wall of him in the street, or to kiss the pax, or be incensed, or go to the offering before his neighbour, and such similar things; peradventure contrary to his duty, but that he has in his heart and intent such a proud desire to be magnified and honoured before the people.

Now there be two kinds of Pride; one of them is within the heart of man, and the other is without. Of a truth these aforesaid things, and more than I have said, appertain to pride that is within the heart of man; and the other kinds of pride be without. But nevertheless the one of these species of pride is a sign of the other, just as the gay arbour at the tavern-door is a sign of the wine that is in the cellar. And this is in many things: as in speech and bearing, and in exorbitant array of clothing; for certes, if there had been no sin in attire, Christ would not have noted and spoken of the clothing of that rich man in the gospel. And Saint Gregory says that precious clothing is blame-worthy for the costliness of it, and its softness and its choiceness and elaboration, and for the superfluity and the inordinate scantness of it. Alas! may men not see, in our days, the sinful costly array of clothing, and especially in too great superfluity or else in too inordinate scantness?

As to the first sin, that is in superfluity of clothing, which makes it so dear, to the harm of the people; not only the cost of embroidering, the modish notching or striping, waving, paneling, winding, or bending, and like waste of cloth in vanity; but there is also costly furring in gowns, so much punching of holes, so much slitting with shears; further, the excessive length in the aforesaid gowns, trailing in the dung and in the mire, on horse and also on foot, men's as well as women's, so that all that which trails is verily in fact wasted, consumed, threadbare and rotten with dung, instead of being given to the poor; to the great loss of the aforesaid poor folk. And that in sundry wise: this is to say, the more that cloth is wasted, the more it costs the people for scarcity of it; and furthermore if so be they would give such punched and slit clothing to the poor folk, it is not fitting for them to wear in their estate, nor sufficient to answer their necessity, to protect them from the inclemency of the firmament. On the other hand, to speak of the horrible, inordinate scantness of clothing, as be these short-cut jackets or kirtles, which through their short-ness cover not their hinder parts, which fare as it were the hinder parts of a she-ape in the full of the moon; and moreover, with all of their persons which they show by their modish dress, in striping their hosen into white and red, it seems as if half their persons were flayed. And if so be they divide their hosen into other colours, as white and black, or white and blue, or black and red, and so forth; then it seems by the variation in colour that the half part of them were corrupt by Saint Anthony's fire, or by cancer, or by other such ill. As to their hinder parts, it is full horrible to see. For certes that foul part they show to the people proudly, in despite of seemliness, which seemliness Jesu Christ and his friends took heed to show in their lives. Now as to the exorbitant array of women, God wot that though the visages of some of them seem full chaste and meek, yet they give notice of wantonness and pride through their array of attire. I say not that seemliness in the clothing of man or woman is unfitting, but certes superfluity or inordinate scantness of clothing is reprovable. Also the sin of excess in adornment or of equipage appears in things that appertain to riding, as in too many dainty horses which be kept for pleasure, which be so fair, fat, and costly; and also in too many vicious serving-men that be kept because of them; also in too curious equipment as in saddles, cruppers, breast-pieces and bridles, covered with precious cloth and rich, bars and plates of gold and of silver. For which God says through Zachary the prophet, 'I will confound the riders of such horses.' These folk take little heed of the riding of the Son of the God of heaven, and of His equipage when He rode upon the ass, and had no other equipment but the poor clothes of His disciples; nor read we that He ever rode upon other beast. I speak this of the sin of excess, and not of reasonable seemliness, when reason requires it. And further, certes, pride is greatly manifested in the keeping of great households, when they be of little profit or of no profit at all; and especially when such a household is felonious and baneful to the people, through the insolence of high lordship or through subordinates. For certes, such lords then sell their lordship to the Devil of hell, when they support the wickedness of their households; or else when these folk of low degree, as those who keep hostelries, support the theft of their hostlers, and that appears in many kinds of deceits. Such manner of folk be the flies that seek out the honey, or the hounds that seek out the carrion. Such folk aforesaid spiritually strangle their dominion; for which thus says David the prophet, 'May an evil death come upon such rulers, and God grant that they may descend all down into hell; for in their houses be iniquities and wickednesses,' and not the God of heaven. And certes, unless they amend them, even as God gave his benison to Laban through the service of Jacob, and to Pharaoh through the service of Joseph, so will God give his malison to such rulers as support the wickedness of their servants, unless they amend them. Pride of the table also appears full often;

for certes, rich men be bidden to feasts and poor folk be put away and rebuked. Also in excess of divers meats and drinks; and especially such manner of baked-meats and pottages, with burning spirits, dishes decorated and castellated with paper, and such-like waste, that it is a scandal to think upon. And also in too great preciousness of vessels and curiosity of minstrelsy, by which a man is the more incited to wanton pleasures; if so be he set his heart the less upon our Lord Jesu Christ, verily it is a sin; and verily the delights might be so great in this matter that by them a man might lightly fall into deadly sin. The varieties of sin which arise from Pride, truly when they arise from wickedness thought of, devised and forecast, or else from habit, are deadly sins without doubt. And when they arise from frailty sudden and unadvised and speedily are repressed again, though they be grievous sins, I conceive that they be not deadly. Now might men ask whence Pride arises and springs; and I say, sometimes it springs from the gifts of nature, sometimes from the gifts of fortune, and sometimes from the gifts of grace. Certes the gifts of nature consist either of bodily gifts or gifts of the soul. Certes, bodily gifts are health of body, as strength, activity, beauty, gentle birth, privilege. Natural gifts of the soul be good wit, sharp understanding, subtle ingenuity, natural power, good memory. Gifts of fortune be riches, high degrees of lordship, the praises of the people. Gifts of grace be knowledge, power to suffer spiritual travail, benignity, virtuous contemplation, withstanding of temptation and such-like things. Of all which aforesaid gifts certes it is a full great folly for a man to pride himself upon any. Now to speak of natural gifts, God wot sometimes we have them in our nature as much to our hurt as to our profit. As, to speak of health of body; certes, it passes away full lightly, and also it is often occasion of the sickness of our soul; for God wot, the flesh is a full great enemy to the soul; and therefore the more the body is in health, the more we be in peril of falling. Also for a man to pride himself on his strength of body, it is an high folly; for certes, the flesh lusts against the spirit, and ever the stronger the flesh is, the sorrier may the soul be: and, over all this, strength of body and worldly boldness full often bring many a man into peril and mischance. Also to pride himself upon his gentle birth is full great folly; for ofttimes the gentility of the body destroys the gentility of the soul; and also we be all of one father and of one mother, and we all be of one nature, rotten and corrupt, both rich and poor. In sooth, one kind of gentility is to be praised, which adorns man's temper with virtues and moral excellencies, and makes him Christ's child. For trust well, that over whatsoever man sin has mastery, he is a very serf to sin.

Now there be general tokens of gentility; as the eschewing of vice and ribaldry and service of sin, in word, deed and look; and the practising of virtue, courtesy and purity; and to be liberal, that is to say, generous in moderation, for that liberality which passes measure is folly and sin. Another token is that a man remember the kindness that he has received from other folk. Another is to be benign to those under him who be good; wherefore, as says Seneca, 'There is nothing more seemly in a man of high estate than graciousness and mercy. And therefore these flies that men call bees, when they make their king, they choose one that has no prick wherewith he can sting.' Another is that a man have a noble heart and a diligent, to attain to high excellent things. Now certes, for a man to pride him upon the gifts of grace is also an inordinate folly; for those gifts of grace that should have turned to goodness and medicine for him to turn to venom and confusion for him, as says Saint Gregory. Certes also whoso prides him upon the gifts of fortune, he is a full great fool; for sometimes a man is a great lord in the morning who is a poor caitiff and a wretch ere it be night; and sometimes the wealth of a man is cause of his death; sometimes the pleasures of a man cause the grievous malady through which he dies. Certes the commendation of the people is sometimes full false and full brittle to trust; this day they praise, to-morrow they blame. God wot, desire to gain commendation of the people has caused death to many an unquiet man.

Now since it is so that you have understood what is pride, and which are the species of pride, and whence it grows and springs, now shall you understand what is the remedy against the sin of pride, and that is humility or meekness. That is a virtue through which a man has true knowledge of himself, and sets no store or value by himself in regard to his deserts, considering ever his frailty. Now there be three kinds of humility; humility in heart, and another humility in mouth; the third is in his deeds. The humility of heart is of four kinds: one is when a man holds himself as worth naught before God of heaven. A second is when he despises no other man. The third is when he cares not though men hold him worth naught. The fourth is when he is not sorry for his humiliation. Also humility of mouth consists in four things: in moderation of speech, in humbleness of speech, and when he acknowledges with his own mouth that he is such as he thinks he is in his heart; another is when he praises the goodness of another man, and belittles nothing thereof. Also humility in works is of four kinds. The first is when he puts other men before himself. The second is to choose the lowest place everywhere. The third is gladly to assent to good counsel. The fourth is to abide gladly by the award of his rulers, or of him who is of higher degree; certes, this is a great deed of humility.

Then shall men understand what is the fruit of penance; and, according to the word of Jesu Christ, it is the endless bliss of heaven, where joy has no contrary state of woe or trouble, where all evils of this present life be passed; where is security from the pain of hell; where is the blessed company that rejoice evermore, each of the others' joy; where the body that once was foul and dark is brighter than the sun; where the body that once was sick, frail, and feeble and mortal, is immortal, and so strong and hale that nothing can harm it; where is neither hunger, thirst nor cold, but every soul is replenished with the sight of the perfect knowledge of God. This blessed realm men can gain by spiritual poverty, and the glory by meekness; the fulness of joy by hunger and thirst, and the rest by toil, and the life by death and mortification of sin.

Chaucer's Retraction

Now pray I all them that hearken unto this little treatise or read it, that if there be anything in it that pleases them, thereof they thank our Lord Jesu Christ, from Whom proceeds all wit and all goodness. And if there be anything that displeases them, I pray them also that they ascribe it to the defect of my uncunning and not to my will, which would full fain have said better if I had had cunning. For our Book says, 'All that is written is written for our instruction,' and that is mine intent. Wherefore I beseech you meekly, by the mercy of God, that you pray for me, that Christ have mercy on me and forgive me my guilts: — and especially for my translations and enditings of worldly vanities, which I revoke in this my retraction: as is the book of Troilus; the book also of Fame; the book of the Nineteen Ladies; the book of the Duchess; the book of Saint Valentine's day of the Parliament of Birds; the tales of Canterbury, those that tend to sin; the book of the Lion; and many another book, if they were in my remembrance; and many a song and many a lecherous lay; — that Christ of his great mercy forgive me the sin. But for the translation of Boethius De Consolacione and other books of legends of saints, and homilies, and books of morality and devotion, for that thank I our Lord Jesu Christ and His blessed mother, and all the saints of heaven; beseeching them that they from henceforth unto my life's end send me grace to bewail my guilts and to study the salvation of my soul; and grant me the grace of true penitence, confession and satisfaction to be done in this present life; through the benign grace of Him That is King of kings and Priest over all priests, That bought us with the precious blood of His heart; so that I may be one of them that shall be saved at the day of doom: *Qui cum patre, etc.*

The Minor Poems

✿ *An ABC*

ALMIGHTY, all-merciful Queen, to whom all this world fleeth for succour, to have release from sin, sorrow and trouble, glorious Virgin, flower of all flowers, to thee I flee, confounded in error! Thou mighty, gracious lady, help and relieve me, pity my perilous malady! My cruel adversary hath vanquished me.

BOUNTY hath so fixed his tent in thy heart that well I wot thou wilt be my succour; thou canst not reject him who with pious mind asketh thine aid. Thine heart is ever so bounteous, thou art the liberal giver of full felicity, haven of refuge, of quiet and rest. Lo how the seven thieves pursue me! Help, bright lady, ere my ship go to pieces!

COMFORT is there none, save in thee, dear lady, for lo! my sin and confusion, which ought not to come into thy presence, have brought against me a grievous suit, founded on strict justice and my despair. And in justice they might well maintain that I were worthy of condemnation, were it not for thy mercy, blessed queen of heaven.

DOUBT is there none that thou, queen of misericorde, art source of grace and mercy on earth. Through thee God vouchsafed to be reconciled with us. For certes, dear, blessed mother of Christ, were the bow of justice and wrath bent now in such wise as it was at first, the righteous God would hear of no mercy; but through thee we have favour, as we desire.

EVER hath my hope of refuge been in thee, for in divers manners thou hast received me into misericorde heretofore full oft. But grant me favour, lady, at the Great Assize, when we shall come before the high Judge! So little fruit shall be found in me then that, unless thou well chasten me before that day, by strict justice my work will destroy me.

FLEEING I come to thy tent for succour, to hide me from the tempest full of terror, beseeching thee, though I be wicked, that thou withdraw thee not. Ah, help me yet in this need! Though I have been a beast in will and in act, yet, lady, clothe me with thy grace. Take heed, lady, thine enemy and mine is in point to pursue me unto my death.

GLORIOUS maid and mother, who never in earth or heaven wast bitter, but ever full of sweetness and mercy, help, that my Father be not angry with me. Speak thou, for I dare not behold Him! Alack the while! I have so done on earth that certes, unless thou be my succour, He will exile my spirit to eternal stench.

HE vouchsafed, tell Him, to become a man, to have a kinship with us, as was His will; and with His precious blood He made the writ upon the cross as general release for every penitent that believeth in Him. And therefore, bright lady, pray for us! Then thou shalt both still all His displeasure, and snatch his prey from our foe.

I WOT it well, thou wilt verily be our succour, thou art so full of bounty. For when a soul falleth into sin, thy pity goeth and haleth him back again. Then thou makest his peace with his Lord and bringest him out of the crooked path. Whoso loveth thee shall find he loveth not in vain, as he leaveth this life.

KALENDARS and illuminated texts be they in this world who be lighted with thy name; and whoso talketh to thee by the straight path need not fear to be maimed in soul. Now, queen of comfort, since thou art she from whom I seek my medicine, let my foe more re-open my wound; I commit my health all into thine hand.

LADY, I cannot portray the sorrow thou hadst beneath the cross, nor His grievous suffering. But by the pains of both I pray you, let not the foe of us all make his boast that he hath vanquished in his fatal lists what ye both have bought so dearly. As I first said, thou ground of our being, continue to keep thy pitiful eyes upon us!

MOSES, who saw the burning bush with red flames, of which was never a stick consumed, saw the sign of thine unspotted maidenhood. Thou art the bush which Moses deemed had been a-fire, on which descended the Holy

Ghost; and this was in symbol. Now, lady, defend thou us from the fire which shall last eternally in hell.

NOBLE princess, who never hadst peer, certes, if there be any comfort for us, cometh from thee, thou beloved mother of Christ; none other melody or song have we to rejoice us in our adversity, none other advocate who will and dare so pray for us; and that for so small hire as thou, who helpest us for an Ave-Marie or two.

O TRUE light of blind eyes, O true delight of them in labour and trouble, O treasurer of grace to mankind, thou whom for thine humility God chose as mother! From His hand-maiden He made thee mistress of heaven and earth, to offer up our petition. This world ever waiteth upon thy goodness, for thou never failest any person in need.

PURPOSE I have sometime to seek out why the Holy Ghost sought thee, when Gabriel's voice came to thine ear. He worked not such a marvel to make war upon us, but to save us whom afterwards He redeemed. Then we need no weapon to save us; but only needful penance, when we have not done it, and to ask and receive mercy.

QUEEN of comfort, yet when I consider that I have sinned toward both Him and thee, and that my soul is worthy to sink, alas, caitiff whither can I go? Who shall be my mediator to thy Son? Who but thyself, who art fount of pity? More ruth than any tongue in this world can tell thou hast on our adversity.

REFORM me, mother, and chasten me, for verily my Father's chastening I dare in no wise abide, so hideous is His just reckoning. Mother, from whom all mercy to man hath ever sprung, be thou my judge and also my soul's leech. For ever in thee pity bounds to each who will beg thee for pity.

SOOTH is it that God granteth no mercy without thee; for God of His goodness forgiveth none unless it please thee. He hath made thee vicar and mistress of all the world and also empress of heaven; and He represseth His justice after thy will, and in token of that He hath crowned thee is so royal wise.

TEMPLE of devotion, where God hath His abode from which misbelievers be proscribed, to thee I bring my penitent soul. Receive me; I can flee no further!

O queen of heaven, with those venomous thorns for which the earth was accursed full long ago I am so wounded, as thou mayst well see, that I am almost lost; it paineth so grievously.

VIRGIN so splendid in apparel, who leadest us into a high tower of Paradise, counsel and guide me, how I may obtain thy grace and thy succour, although I have been in error and foulness. Lady, do thou summon me to that court that is called thy bench, O fresh and blooming! where mercy shall ever abide.

XRISTUS thy Son descended into this world to suffer His passion upon the cross, and also that Longinus should pierce His heart and let His heart's blood run down; and all this was to save me. I am false and unkind to Him, and yet He desireth not my damnation, — For this I thank thee, succour of all men.

YOUNG ISAAC was verily type of His death, who so obeyed his father that he recked not to be slain; even so thy Son list to die as a lamb. Now lady full of mercy, since He measured out His mercy so liberally, I entreat thee be thou not scant; for we all sing and say thou art ever our shield against vengeance.

ZACHARY calleth thee the open spring to wash the sinful soul from its guilt. Therefore I ought well to read this lesson, that we are lost were it not for thy tender heart. Now, lady bright, since thou canst and wilt be merciful to the seed of Adam, bring us to that place that is raised for penitents who are deserving of mercy. Amen.

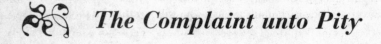

The Complaint unto Pity

Pity, that I have sought so long with sore heart and with gnawing pain that there was never in this world one so woeful who died not! To speak the sooth, my purpose was to complain unto Pity of the cruelty and tyranny of Love, who slays me for my faithfulness. And when through the length of certain years I had continually sought a time to speak, I ran to Pity, all wet with weeping, to pray her to avenge me on Cruelty. But, ere I could break out with a word, or tell any of my bitter pains, I found Pity dead, and buried in an heart. When I saw the lighted bier I fell down, dead as a stone whilst the swoon lasted. I arose with colour all changed, and pitiously turned mine eyes on her, and pushed my way nearer the corse and began to pray for the soul. I was a lost man; that was the end.

Thus I am slain, since Pity has died. Alas! that ever that day should come! What manner of man dare hold up his head now, on whom shall any heart call in sorrow? Now Cruelty has prepared to slay each one of us, folk with vain hopes, without counsel in our pains; to whom shall we complain, now that she is dead? Yet this fresh wonder increases in me, that no creature but I knows that she is dead, out of all the men who have known her in her time. And yet she died not so suddenly. I have ever full diligently sought her since I first had wit or man's mind; but she was dead, ere ever I could come upon her.

About her bier there stood cheerily, without any woe as me-thought, perfect Bounty, well and richly armed, and fresh Beauty, Jollity and Pleasure, Assured Manner, Youth, Honour, Wisdom, High Estate, Dignity and Fair Demeanour, confederated both by bond and by kinship. I had a written complaint in my hand, to have put up to Pity as a petition, but when I found all this company there, who rather would ruin all my cause than give me help, I held my complaint quiet; for certes without Pity no petition can avail with that folk. Then I left all these virtues, save Pity, watching over the corse, as you have heard me say; all confederate by the bond drawn by Cruelty, and all of one consent that I should be slain. And I put away my complaint, for I durst not show to my foes my petition, the import of which in few words runs thus: —

The Petition

Humblest of heart, most worthy of reverence, benign flower, crown of all virtues, showeth thy servant, if I durst so call myself, his mortal hurt unto thy royal honour; and not only for his evil plight, but for thy renown, as he shall declare. It standeth thus: thy foe Cruelty, under guise of womanly Beauty, that men should not know her tyranny, is allied against thy royal estate with Bounty, Nobility and Courtesy, and hath now deprived thee of thy station, which is called Beauty-Lives-with-Kindness. For by nature and by thy true inheritance thou art ever allied unto Kindness; and verily thou oughtest to use thy power to help Truth in his adversity. Thou art also the crown of Beauty. And certes, if thou art wanting in these twain, the world is lost; and that is all. Also what availeth Demeanour and Nobility without thee, benign creature?

Shall Cruelty be thy mistress? Alas! what heart may long suffer it? Wherefore unless thou the sooner take care to break that perilous alliance, thou slayest them that be obedient to thee. And further, if thou suffer this, thy renown is fordone in a little season; there shall no man well know what thing is Pity. Alas that thy renown should ever sink so low! Thou art then cast down from thine heritage by Cruelty, which occupieth thy station; and we be in despair who seek after thy favour. Thou queen over Furies, have mercy on me who have sought thee so tenderly and long; let some beam of thy light shine on me, who ever more and more love and fear thee. For in sooth the sorrow is mine; and though I be not cunning in my lament, for God's love have mercy on my pains! My pain is this, that whatsoever I would, that have I not, nor aught like it; and ever Desire sets my heart a-flame. Also on the other hand, wheresoever I go, I have everywhere hard by, unsought, whatever thing can increase my pains. Naught is wanting save my death and then my bier. What need to show any part of my pain, since I suffer every woe that heart can think, and yet I dare not lament to thee? For well I wot, though I wake or sleep, that thou carest not whether I sink or swim. But nevertheless, as shall be seen, I will maintain my faithfulness till my death. That is to say, I will be thine ever; though thou slay me through Cruelty, thy foe, still my spirit shall never part from thy service, for any pain or grief. Since thou art dead — alas that ever it should be! — I may well weep thus for thy death and make lament, with heart sore and full of gnawing pain.

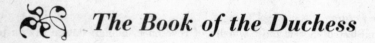

The Book of the Duchess

By this heaven, I wonder greatly how I live, for I can scarce sleep at all, day or night; I have so many an idle fantasy only for lack of sleep, that, by my troth, I heed naught, how it comes or goes, and naught is either sweet or bitter to me. All is alike — joy or sorrow, whatsoever it be, — for I have no feeling, but am, as it were, a thing stunned, ever in point to fall down; for sorry fantasies are ever wholly in my mind. And ye well know it were against nature to live in this wise; for nature would not suffer any earthly creature to abide long time without sleep, and to be in sorrow; and I cannot sleep, night or morn. And thus melancholy and dread of dying, and default of sleep and heaviness, have so slain my spirit of life, that I have lost all lustiness. Such fantasies be in my head that I wot never what is best to do.

But men might ask me why I cannot sleep, and what is ailing me. Nevertheless who asks this, in truth, wastes his asking. Myself cannot tell why it is thus; but in sooth, I believe, I hold it to be a sickness that I have suffered these eight year, and yet my remedy is never the nigher. For there is but one physician that can heal me. But that is past. Pass we over until another time; what will not be, must needs be left; it were good to hold to our first matter.

So when I saw I could not sleep the other night, I sat up till late upon my bed, and bade one reach me a book, a romance, and he gave it me to read and pass the night away; for methought it better sport than to play at either backgammon or chess. And in this book were written fables, which clerks and other poets in old days had put into rhyme, to read and to remember as long as men loved the law of nature. This book spake only of such matters as the lives of ancient queens and kings, and many other little histories. Amongst all this I found a tale that methought was marvellous.

This was the tale: There was a king who was named Ceyx, and he had a wife, the best that could live; and this queen was called Alcyone. It so befell ere long that this king would fare across the sea. To tell it shortly, when he was thus at sea, such a tempest arose that it broke the ship's mast and made it fall, and made a breach in their ship and drowned every man, so that, as the book tells, never was found board or man or aught beside. Even thus the king Ceyx met his death.

Now to speak of his wife: This lady who was left at home marvelled that the king came not back, for he had been gone for long. Anon her heart began to grieve bitterly; and because evermore it seemed to her that it was not well that he so tarried, she longed so after her husband that it were a piteous thing, certes, to tell the heartfelt sorrow of this noble queen, alas!, for she loved him best of all. Anon she sent north and south to seek him, but they found naught.

'Alas!' quoth she, 'Alas that ever I was born! And is my lord and my love dead? Certes, I make a vow here to my god that I will never eat bread unless I can learn tidings of my lord!' Such was the sorrow of this lady that in very sooth I who have writ this book had such pity and ruth to read of her woe, that, by my troth, I fared the worse all the morrow after, to think of her pains.

So when she could learn no tidings that any man could find her lord, she swooned full oft and said, 'Alas!' For sorrow she was wellnigh mad, and knew no counsel but one; anon she set her down on her knees and so wept that it was pitiful to hear.

'Ah mercy, sweet dear lady!' quoth she to her goddess, Juno. 'Help me out of this distress, and give me grace to see my lord soon, or to know where he is or how he fares or in what state, and I shall do sacrifice to thee, and with good will become wholly thine, body, heart, and all. And except thou wilt do this, sweet lady, send me grace to sleep and to dream in my sleep some faithful dream, through which I shall know of a surety whether my lord be alive or no.'

And with that word she hung down her head and fell into a swoon, as cold as stone. Her women caught her up straightway, and unclad her and carried her to bed. And she, worn out with weeping and watching, was weary; and thus, ere she knew it, the dead sleep fell upon her, from Juno, who had heard her prayer and caused her quickly to sleep. For as she prayed, so it was done in fact. For Juno anon called her messenger to do her errand; and when he was come near, she commanded him thus: 'Haste thee,' quoth Juno, 'to Morpheus, — thou knowest him well, the god of sleep. Now understand well and heed! Say thus on my behalf, that he go quickly into the great sea; — and bid him by any means to take up the body of Ceyx the king, which lies full pale and all bloodless. Bid him creep into the body and cause it to go to Alcyone the queen, where she lies alone, and tell her in brief how it was verily drowned the other day. And let the body speak even as it was wont to speak whilst it was alive. Go now quickly, and hie thee!'

This messenger took leave, and went his way and never stopped till he came to the dark valley that stands between two cliffs, where never yet grew corn or grass or tree, or anything that served for aught, nor beast or man or aught else; save that there were a few springs came running down from the cliffs, and made a dead, sleepy sound, and ran down past a cave that was digged wondrous deep under a rock amid the valley. There lay these gods and slept, Morpheus and Eclympasteyre, who was heir to the god of sleep, who slept and did none other toil. This cave was as dark everywhere about as the pit of hell. They had good leisure to snore in rivalry, — who were the soundest sleeper! Some hung chin on breast and slept standing upright, their heads hidden; and some lay a-bed and slept the long day through.

This messenger came flying swiftly and cried, 'O ho! Awake, and that anon!' It was in vain; none heard him. 'Awake!' quoth he. 'Who is it lies there?' And he blew his horn right in their ears, and cried wondrous loud, 'Awake!'

This god of sleep opened one eye and asked, 'Who calls there?'

'It is I,' quoth this messenger. 'Juno bade thou shouldst go,' — and he told him what he was to do, as I have told you before; it needs not rehearse it again. And when he had spoken, he went his way.

Anon this god of sleep started out of his slumber, and went and did as he had been bidden; he took up the drowned body straightway, and bore it forth to the wife, queen Alycone, where she lay, a little before dawn. And it stood even at the foot of her bed, and called her by her very name, and said, 'My sweet wife, awake! Let be your sorrowful course, for in your sorrow lies no profit. For certes, sweet, I am dead; thou shalt never more see me alive. But, good sweet heart, look thou bury my body, what time thou mayst find it beside the sea. And farewell, sweet, my world's joy! I pray God relieve thy sorrow; our happiness lasts too short while here on earth!'

At that she opened her eyes and saw naught. 'Alas!' quoth she for sorrow, and died before the fourth morn. But what more she said in that delirium I may not tell you now, it were too long delay. I will tell you of my first matter, for which I have told this thing of queen Alcyone and Ceyx.

For thus much I dare well say, I should have been dead and all buried, even for default of sleep, if I had not read and noted this tale. And I will tell you wherefore; because for weal or woe I could not sleep ere I had read this tale of this drowned Ceyx the king and of the gods of sleep. When I had well read this tale and looked all through it, a wonder it seemed to me if it were true; for I had never heard tell before of any gods that could cause men to sleep or wake. For I never knew any god but one. And jesting I said anon, — and yet I list full little to make mirth, — 'Rather than die thus through default of sleep, I would give to that Morpheus, or his goddess, dame Juno, or anyone else, I reck not who, to make me sleep and have some repose, — I will give him the very best gift that ever he looked for in his life. And here into his keeping, now straightway, if he will grant me a little sleep, I will give him a feather-bed of the down of pure white doves, right well enveloped in fine black satin from overseas and striped with gold, and also many a pillow, with every pillow-case of cloth of Rennes, to sleep on softly; he need not turn and turn. And I will give him all that behooves to a chamber; and with pure gold I will have all his halls painted, and covered with many a fold of tapestry of one pattern. This he should have (knew I where his cave is), if he could make me sleep forthwith, as the goddess did Alcyone. And thus may this god Morpheus win from me greater pay than ever he won. And Juno, who is his goddess, I shall so requite that I she shall hold herself content.'

Scarce had I said that word, even thus as I have told it you, when suddenly, but how I knew not, such a lust to sleep seized me anon that I fell asleep right over my book, and even therewith I dreamed a dream so rarely sweet, so wonderful, I trust never yet had man the wit to tell the interpretation thereof; no, verily, not Joseph of Egypt, he who so interpreted the dream of king

Pharaoh, no more than could the least one of us; nor scarce Macrobius, he that writ all the vision that king Scipio dreamed, that noble man, Africanus — such marvels befell then. — I believe could justly interpret my visions. Lo thus it was, this was my dream.

Methought thus: it was May, and about dawn where I lay in my bed all naked, in my dream I looked forth, for I was awakened by a great crowd of small birds which had startled me out of sleep through the sound and sweetness of their song; and I dreamed they sat all the while upon the roof of my chamber outside all about upon the tiles, and they sang in tune, each in his own wise, the most solemn service that ever man heard, I believe; for some of them sang low, some high, and all in accord. To tell shortly and in brief, never was heard so sweet a voice, unless it had been from some heavenly thing, so merry a harmony, so sweet strains, that certes I would not have failed to hear them for all the town of Tunis; for my whole chamber rang through the harmony of their singing. For nowhere was ever heard instrument or melody yet half so sweet, or of half so meet accord. For there was none of them that only feigned to sing, but each of them strove to find out merry, cunning tones, and they spared not their throats.

And, sooth to say, my chamber was full well covered with paintings, and all the windows were well glazed with glass full clear, and not a hole broken, that it was a great delight to behold. All the story of Troy was wrought in the glazing — of Hector and King Priam, of Achilles and Laomedon, of Jason and Medea, of Paris and Helen and Lavinia. And all the walls were painted in fine colours with all the Romance of the Rose, both text and gloss. My windows were all shut, and through the glass the sun shone upon my bed with bright beams and many glad, golden rays; and the sky was full beauteous, and the air blue, bright and clear, and right mild it was in sooth, neither cold nor hot. And in all the sky was not a cloud.

And as I lay thus, methought I heard a hunter blow his horn wondrous high and clear, to try it and learn whether it were clear or hoarse in tone.

I heard men, horses, hounds and other creatures going to and fro; and all men spake of hunting, how they would have mightily slain the hart, and how far the hart at length had plunged into the thicket, — I know not what it was. Straightway when I heard that, how they would go a-hunting, I was right glad and anon was up, and went forth from my chamber, and took my horse, and never stopped till I came to the field outside. There I overtook a great rout of hunters and foresters, with many relays of hounds and dogs in leashes, and they hied them quick to the forest, and I with them. So at the last I asked one that led a dog in a leash, 'Tell me, fellow, who shall hunt here?' quoth I. And he answered, 'Sir, the emperor Octavian; and he is hard by here.' 'In God's name, well met,' quoth I, 'go we fast!' and began to ride on. When we came to the forest-side, every man did anon as it behooves to do in hunting. Anon the master of the hunt, hot-foot, blew three notes on a great horn, at the uncoupling of his hounds. In a little the hart was lighted on, hallooed, and headed back long time; at last this hart fetched a compass and stole away from all the hounds by a secret course. The hounds had all outrun the scent, and were at fault; upon that the hunter at last blew a recall wondrous loud.

I was gone walking away from my tree, and as I went there came by and fawned upon me as I stood a whelp that had followed the chase but was untrained. It came and crept up to me as humbly as if it had known me, held down its head and laid back its ears, and laid its hair down all smooth. I would have caught it, and anon it fled and was gone from me. I followed it, and it went forth down by a flowery green path right thick with grass, soft and sweet with many flowers, fair under the foot, and little used, it seemed. For both Flora and Zephyr, they two that make flowers to spring, I believe had fixed their dwelling there; for it was, to behold it, as if the earth should strive to be gayer than the sky, to have seven times more flowers than the sky has stars. It had forgotten the woes of winter and the poverty which he had made it suffer with his cold morns; all was forgotten, as men could see. For all the wood was waxed green; the sweetness of dew had made it grow.

There needs not ask whether the place stood thick with trees, so full of leaves, with many a green spray. And each tree stood by itself full ten or twelve feet from the others. So great trees, of such huge strength, and forty or fifty fathoms high, and clean without bough or stick up to the tops, broad and also so thick — they were not an inch asunder — that everywhere below there was shadow; and many a hart and hind was both before me and at my back. The wood was full of fawns, young horned deer, bucks, does, and many a roe, and many squirrels that sat full high in the trees, and ate, and made festival in their manner. In brief, it was so full of beasts that though Argus, the noble computer, set to reckoning on his abacus, and reckoned with his ten figures — by which figures all mankind, if they be skilful, may reckon and count and tell the number of everything, — yet he would fail to reckon exactly the wonders that I dreamed in my dream.

But forth the beasts roamed down the wood wondrous fast; and at last I was ware of a man in black who sat and leaned against a huge oak. 'Lord!' I thought, 'who may that be? What ails him, to sit here?' Forthwith I approached, and found sitting up straight a wondrous fine-looking knight, — by his bearing methought so, — of good height and young, four-and-twenty years of age; there was but little hair in his beard, and he was clothed all in black. I walked softly up behind him, and stood there as still as anything, so that truly he saw me not, because he hung his head down. And with a deathlike sorrowful voice he rhymed to himself ten or twelve verses of a complaint, the most piteous, the most rueful, that ever I heard; for, by my troth, it was a great marvel that nature could suffer any living being to have such sorrow and not die. Full piteous, pale and bloodless, he recited a lay, a kind of a song, but without note or tune; and this was it, for I can well rehearse it. It began right thus: —

> 'I am with sorrows overrun,
> Happiness get I never none,
> Now that I see my lady bright,
> That I have loved with all my might,
> Hath died and is forever gone.

> 'Alas, O death, what aileth thee
> That thou wouldst not have taken me,
> When that thou tookst my lady dear;
> That was so fair, so fresh, so free,
> So good that every man may see
> For all goodness she had no peer?'

When he had made his lament thus, his sorrowful heart began to grow very faint and his spirits dead. For very fear the blood fled down to his heart, to warm it – for well it felt that the heart was sore afflicted, — also to learn why so horridly it shook its disposition, and to gladden it. For it is the principal member of the body, and that caused all his hue to change and wax green and pale, because no blood was seen in any limb of his.

Thereat anon, when I saw how ill he fared there, I went and stood right at his feet and greeted him; but he spake not, but reasoned with his own thought and in his mind earnestly debated whether and why his life should hold out — his sorrows were so painful, and lay so cold on his heart. So his sorrow and heavy thought suffered him not to hear me; for he had well-nigh lost his mind, though Pan, whom men call the god of nature, were never so wroth against him for his melancholy. But at last, in truth, he became aware of me, how I was there before him and doffed my hood, and greeted him as best I knew how. Gently and softly he said, 'I prithee be not wroth; truly I heard you not, sir, nor saw you not.'

'Ah, good sir,' quoth I, 'no matter. I am right sorry if I have at all disturbed you out of your thought. Forgive me if I have trespassed.'

'Yeah, the amends are light to make,' quoth he, 'for none are needed; there is none offence in word or deed.'

Lo how goodly this knight spake, as if it had been another than he that I had troubled. He was neither over-forward nor over-distant. And I saw that, and began to consider him, and found him very ready to talk, right marvellous discreet and reasonable, as methought, for all his woe. Anon I began to devise talk with him, to look whether I could in any wise know more of his mind. 'Sir,' quoth I, 'this sport is over, I believe this hart is gone; these hunters can find him nowhere.'

'I care not therefore,' quoth he, 'my mind is never a whit on that.'

'By our Lord,' quoth I, 'I well believe you; even so methinks by your cheer. But, sir, will you hear one thing? Methinks I see you in great sorrow, but certes, sir, if you will at all discover your woe to me, I would amend it if I have the power, so may God help me! You can prove it by trial, for, by my troth, I will use all my power to make you whole. And tell me of your bitter sorrows; peradventure it may ease your heart, which seems full sick in your breast.'

With that he glanced at me aside, as who should say, 'Nay, that can never be.' 'Gramercy, good friend, I thank you,' quoth he, 'that you have such a desire, but it can never the more be done. No man can gladden my sorrow, which causes my fresh look to droop and fade, and has so ruined mine understanding that woe is me that I was ever born! Nothing can make my sorrows pass; not the Remedium of Ovid, nor Orpheus god of melody, nor Dædalus with cunning devices; nor can physician heal me, not Hippocrates or Galen. Woe is me that I live a day! But whosoever would make assay of himself, whether his heart can have pity of any sorrow, let him see me. I wretch, whom death has made naked of all bliss that was ever, who am become most miserable of all men, who hate my days and my nights! My life, my pleasures, are loathsome to me, for all welfare and I are at odds. Death itself is my enemy; though I would die, it will not so. For when I follow, it flies from me; I would have it, it will not have me. This is my cureless torment, ever dying, and never dead; so that Sisyphus lying in hell knows no more sorrow. And, by my troth, whosoever knew all my bitter sorrows, if he had not compassion for them, must have a fiendish heart. For whoso sees me first in the morn, may say he has met with sorrow, for I am sorrow, and sorrow is I.

'Alas! I will tell thee why; my song is turned into lamentation, and all my laughter to weeping, my glad thoughts to heaviness, mine ease and also my rest into travail; my weal is woe, my good is evil; and evermore my sport is turned into ugly pain and my delight into mourning; my health is turned into sickness, all my security into dread; all my light is become darkness, my wit is folly, my day is night, my love is hate, my sleep is waking, my mirth and eating are fasting, mine aspect is foolishness and is all confounded whereso-ever I am; my peace is turned into contention and war. Alas! how could I fare worse? My boldness is turned into abasement, for false Fortune has played a game of chess with me, alack the day! The traitress false and guileful, who promises everything and performs nothing, she walks upright, yet she walks lame; she looks foully and askew, yet shows fair looks; the cruel gracious one, who scorns many a creature! An image she is, falsely portrayed; for she will quickly swerve aside. She is the monster's head, covered; as filth strewn over with flowers. Her greatest glory and flower of honour is to lie; for that is her nature. Without faith, law or restraint, she is false; and ever laughing with one eye and weeping with the other. That which is set aloft, she puts all down. I liken her to the scorpion, a false, flattering beast; for with his head he makes cheer, but amid all his flattery he will sting and envenom with his tail, and so will she. She is the envious charity that is ever false, and seems goodly; so she turns her false wheel about, now to one side the hall, now at the other, for it is never steadfast. Full many a man has she thus blinded. She is a delusion of enchantment, which seems the same and is not — , the false thief!

'What has she done, believe you? By our Lord, I will tell you. She played at chess with me; with her divers false moves she stole upon me and took my queen. And when I saw my queen gone, alas! I could play no longer, but said, "Farewell, sweet, in truth, and farewell all that ever there is!" Therewith Fortune said, "Check!" and then "Checkmate!" in the middle of the board, with a roving pawn, alas! She was more skilful at play than Attalus — so he was named —, who first made the game of the chess. But would God I had once or twice known and understood the problems that the Greek Pythagoras knew! Thereby I had played the better at chess, and the better had guarded my queen. And yet to what end? Truly I hold that wish not worth a straw. It had been never the better for me. For Fortune knows so many a fetch that there be but few who can beguile her. And also for another cause she is the less to blame; before God, I myself would have done likewise, had I been in her place; she ought the more to be excused. For this I say, had I been God and could have had my will, when she captured my queen, I should have made the same move; for, so God save my soul, I dare well swear she took the best!

'But I have lost my bliss through that move; alas that I was born! For evermore, I truly believe, in spite of my will, my pleasure is wholly at an end; but yet what is to be done? By our Lord, it is to die quickly! In spite of all I give not up the thought, but live and die therein. There is no planet in the firmament, or element in the air or earth, that gives me not the gift of weeping, when I am alone. For when I consider well, and bethink me how nothing is owing me in mine account with sorrow; and how there remains no gladness which may gladden me in my distress, and how I have lost content and have no pleasance left; then I may say, nought remains at all. And when all this falls into my mind, alas! then I am overwhelmed! For what is done is still not to come. I have more sorrow than Tantalus.'

When I heard him tell this tale so piteously as I have told you, scarce could I abide longer, it did my heart so much grief. 'Ah, good sir!' quoth I, 'say not so. Have some pity on that nature which makes you a living man! Remember Socrates; for he cared not three straws for aught that Fortune could do.'

'No,' quoth he, 'I cannot do thus.'

'Why so, good sir?' quoth I. 'Perdy! say not so, for in sooth, though you had lost the twelve pieces, if you murdered yourself for sorrow, you should be condemned in this case as justly as Medea was, who slew her children for Jason (and Phyllis also hanged herself for Demophon, alackaday! because he broke his appointed time to come to her). Another frenzied lover was Dido, queen of Carthage, who slew herself because Æneas was false. Ah! what a fool she was! And Echo died because Narcissus would not love her; and even so has many another wrought folly. And Samson, who slew himself by means of a pillar, died because of Dalilah. But there is none alive on earth who would make this woe for a queen at chess!'

'Why?' quoth he. 'It is not thus. You know full little what you say. I have lost more than you ween.'

'Lo, sir,' quoth I, 'how can that be? Good sir, tell me all wholly in what wise, how, why, and wherefore you have thus lost your bliss.'

'Blithely,' quoth he, 'come sit down. I tell you upon the condition that with all your understanding you give your whole mind to hearken to it.' — 'Yes, sir.' — 'Pledge your faith thereto.' — 'Gladly.' — 'Keep to it then.' —

'So may God save me, I shall right blithely hear you, as well as I can, with all the whole wit I have.'

'In God's name!' quoth he, and began: 'Sir,' quoth he, 'from my youth, since first I had any manner of wit or natural understanding to comprehend in my own wit what love was in any wise, without fail I have ever been wholly subject to love, and have paid tribute with devoted mind, and by reason of his pleasantness have become his vassal with good will and body, heart and all. All this I put in his service, as to my lord, and did homage, and full devoutly prayed him that he should so bestow my heart that it were pleasance to him and worship to my dear lady. And it was long ago that I did this and knew not why, and many a year before my heart was fixed anywhere; I believe it came to me of nature. Peradventure I was ready for that impressure as a white wall or a tablet; for it is ready to catch and receive all that men will put thereon, whether they will portray or paint, be the works never so curious. And at the time I did so, I was able to have learned and understood another art or book-lore, peradventure, as well as love or better. But because love came first into my mind, therefore I forgot it not. I chose love for my first craft therefore it remains with me; because I received it when I was so young that evil had not then turned my mind to be nothing worth through learning too much. For then Youth, my mistress, ruled me in idleness; for it was my first youth, and I then knew full little good. All my acts were volatile, and all my thoughts varying; all that I knew then was alike good to me. But thus it was.

'On a day it happed that I came into a place where truly I saw the fairest company of ladies that ever man had seen with eye together in one spot. Shall I call it hap or grace that brought me there? Nay, but Fortune, who is full prone to lie, the false, perverse traitress! Would God I might call her by a fouler name! For now she makes me full sad; and I will tell why ere long. Amongst all these ladies I saw one, in sooth, that was like none other in the whole company; for I dare verily swear that as the summer's shining sun is fairer, clearer, and has more light for all the world than any planet which is in the sky, — the moon, or the seven stars, so she surpassed them all in beauty, in demeanor and comeliness, in stature, in seemly gladness, so well endowed with goodliness, — in brief, what more shall I say? By God and His holy apostles, it was my sweet one, her very self! She had such a steadfast aspect, such a noble port and demeanour! And Love, who had heard my prayer, had cast his eye on me thus soon; anon she was so fixed in my mind, and so suddenly, that I took no manner of counsel but from her look and from my heart; because her eyes, I believe, looked in such gladness on my heart that mine own mind only said it were better to serve her for naught than to stand well with another. And it was true, for I will straightway tell you why, every whit.

'I saw her so comely on the dance, so sweetly carol and sing, laugh and sport so girlishly, and look so gently, speak so amiably and well, that certes I believe nevermore was seen so blessed a treasure. Every hair on her head, sooth to say, was not yellow, or red, or brown; methought it was most like gold. And what eyes my lady had! Gentle, good, glad, steadfast, simple, of good size, not too wide; and also her look was not sidelong nor askance, but so simply direct that it drew and quite took up all that looked upon her. Anon her eyes seemed as if she would have mercy; fools thought it; but it was never the more so. It was no feigned thing, but her very own manner of looking, that the goddess, dame Nature, had made them open not too much, and gently close; for were she never so glad, her gaze was not spread wide in folly; nor wildly, though she were in mirth. But methought her eyes ever said, "By God, my wrath is all given over!"

'She had also such joy in life that dullness was afraid of her. She was not too grave nor too glad; never creature, I believe had more measure in all things. But she hurt many an one with her glance, and that oppressed her heart full little, for she knew naught of their thoughts; but whether she knew or not, at all events she cared for them not a straw. He who dwelt at home was no nearer to get her love than he who was in Ind; the foremost was alway in the rear. But good folk she loved before all, as a man may love his brother; of which love she was wondrous liberal, in places where reason would have it so.

'And what a visage she had! Alas, mine heart is wondrous woful that I cannot describe it! I want both the language and the wit to portray it perfectly, and also my spirits be dull to describe so great a thing; I have no wit sufficient to comprehend her beauty. But thus much I dare say, that she was ruddy, fresh and lively of hue, and her beauty renewed itself every day. Her face was nigh the best feature of all; for certes Nature had such delight to make that fair, that truly my love was her chief pattern of beauty and chief ensample and type of her work; for however dark it be, evermore methinks I see her. And moreover, though all those that ever lived were now alive, they should not have discerned one evil sign in all her face; for it was grave, simple and kind.

'And what a goodly soft language had that sweet physician of my life! — so friendly, so wise, so firmly based upon all reason and so inclinable to all virtue, that I dare swear by the rood that never was found such a sweet-sounding fluency of speech, nor truer-tongued, nor less scornful, nor more healing, so that I durst swear by the mass, though the pope sang it, that never was man or woman greatly hurt through her tongue; as for her, all trouble hid from her. Never was less flattering than in her words, so that her simple testimony was found as true as any bond or as the pledge of any man's hand. And she could not chide a whit; that all the world knows full well. And such a fair neck had that sweet one that no bone or blemish was to be seen that misbecame her. It was white, smooth and straight, without hollow; and collar-bone to all seeming had she none. Her throat, as I can recall, seemed a round tower of ivory, of proper size, not too great.

'And good, fair *White* she was called; that was my lady's very name. She was both fair and bright, she had not her name wrongly. She had right fair shoulders, and long body and arms, every limb plump and round but not over-large; hands full white and pink nails, round breasts, a straight, flat back, and hips of good breadth. I knew no manner of defect in her, that her limbs were not all in accord, so far as I could know.

And she could disport herself so well when she would, that I say she was like to a shining torch, from which every man can have light in plenty, and it has none the less. In manner and comeliness even so was it with my dear lady; for any man, if he would and had eyes to behold her, might take joy enough in her bearing. For I dare swear if she had been amongst ten thousand, in the eyes of men that could judge she would have been at the least a chief glass of fashion of all the company, though they had stood on a row. For wheresoever folk made merry and out-watched the night, methought the fellowship barer without her, as I saw once, than a crown without gems. Truly to mine eyes she was the solitary phœnix of Araby, for there is never but one alive; and never knew I such an one as she.

To speak of goodness, truly she had as much gentleness as ever had Esther in the Bible, and more, if more could be. And therewithal in sooth she had a wit so broad, so wholly inclined to all virtue, that by the rood all her understanding was without malice and set upon joyous things; in addition, I never yet saw one less hurtful than she in her acts. I say not that she had no knowledge what evil was; else methinks she had had no ripe judgment.

'And verily, to speak of faithfulness, it had been pity if she had not had that! Thereof she had so full a share, I dare say it, and swear to it well, that Faith himself had chosen to set his principal manor, his abiding-place, in her above all others. Therewith she had the greatest gift of steadfast constancy and unconstrained temperate self-control that I ever yet knew, so wholly long-suffering was she, and so gladly would hear reason; it well followed that she knew how to rule her life, and loved to do well. This was her disposition, ever whit. Therewith she so well loved right she would do no wrong to any person; yet no person could do her shame, she loved so well her own fair repute. She would delude no honest man, nor by half word or look hold him in suspense, be sure; nor send a man into Wallachia, Prussia nor Tartary, Alexandria nor Turkey, and anon bid him strictly to go bareheaded to the dry sea and come home by the Carrenare; nor say, "Sir, see now that I hear worship of you, ere you come again." She gave rein to no such little freaks.

'But to what end tell I my tale? On this very one, as I have said, was all my love wholly placed; for certes, that sweet woman, she was my sufficiency, my pleasure, my life, my fortune, my health, and all my bliss, my worldly welfare and comfort; and I was entirely hers, every whit.'

'By our Lord,' quoth I, 'I well believe you! In faith your love was well bestowed; I wot not how you might have done better.'

'Better? No creature could have done so well!' quoth he.

'Perdy,' quoth I, 'I believe it, sir.'

'Nay, believe it well.'

'Sir, so I do; I well believe you that you truly thought she was the best and the very fairest to behold, for whosoever had looked with your eyes.'

'With mine? Nay, all that saw her said so, and swore to it. And though they had not, I should still have loved best my noble lady, though I had had all the beauty that ever Alcibiades had, and all the strength of Hercules; besides had all the worthiness of Alexander, and all the wealth that ever was in Babylon or Carthage or Macedonia, or in Rome or Nineve; and also, as I hope to be saved, had been as hardy as Hector, whom Achilles slew at Troy (and for that deed Achilles was slain also in a temple; for the two were slain, both he and Archilochus, for love of Polyxena, and so says Dares Phrygius); or had I been as wise for Minerva, I should ever have loved her, without doubt, for I must needs. "Needs!" Nay, I speak idly now; not "needs." I will tell why; it was because my heart desired it with its own free will, and also I was bound to love her as the fairest and best. She was as good as ever was Penelope of Greece, or Lucrece, the noble wife who was the best of wives — he tells thus, the Roman Titus Livius; she was as good as they, as I hope for salvation, and had no equal, though their stories be authentic; at least she was as faithful as Lucrece.

'But wherefore tell I how I first saw my lady? I was right young, sooth to say, and had full great need to learn; when my heart longed to love, it was a great emprise. But as my wit could best, after my young, childish understanding, I set it verily to love her in my best fashion, to do her such honour and service as I then could, by my faith, without feigning or sloth; for wondrous fain I was to see her. So much it relieved me that when I saw her first in the morn, I was healed of all my sorrow for the whole day thereafter, till it were eve; methought nothing could hurt me, were my sorrows never so bitter. And so she still holds my heart that, by my troth, I would not let my lady out of my thought for all this world; no, in truth!'

'Now by my troth, sir,' quoth I, 'methinks you fare as one who confesses without repentance.'

'Repentance!' quoth he; 'nay! fie! Should I now repent me of loving? Nay, certes; then I were worse than Achitophel, or Antenor, the traitor who betrayed Troy, as I hope for bliss! — or the false Ganelon, he that procured the betrayal of Roland and Oliver. Nay, whilst I am alive on earth I shall forget her nevermore.'

'Now, good sir,' quoth I, 'you have told it me already — there is no need to rehearse it again —, how you first saw her, and where; but if you would tell me the manner of your first words to her, for that I would beseech you; and how she first knew your mind, whether you loved her or no; and also tell me what you have lost, which I have heard you tell of.'

'Yea,' said he, 'you know not what you say. I have lost more than you ween.'

'What loss is that?' quoth I. 'Will she not love you? Is it thus? Or have you done aught amiss, so that she has left you? Is this it? For God's love, tell me all.'

'Before God, so I shall,' quoth he. 'I say even as I have said: all my love was placed on her. And yet long time she knew of it never a whit, believe me well; for be right sure, I durst not tell her my mind for all this world, nor would I have angered her, truly. Knowest thou why? She was ruler of my body; she held the heart, and he whose heart is held cannot escape.

'But to keep me from idleness, truly I busied myself in making songs, as best I knew how, and oftentimes sang them aloud. And I made many songs, though I could not make them so well, nor knew all the art, as could Tubal, Lamech's son, who first invented the art of song; for as his brother's hammers rang to and fro on his anvil, from that he took the first melody; but the Greeks say that Pythagoras was the first inventor of the art; Aurora tells so. But no matter for that, as to the two of them. At all events, thus I put my feeling into songs, to gladden my heart; and lo! this was the first — I know not whether it were the best: —

> ' "Lord! but mine heart it maketh light
> When I think on that sweetest creature,
> A comely one to see;
> And wish to God it might so be
> That she would hold me for her knight,
> My lady, fair and bright!"

'Now, I have told you my first song. Upon a day I bethought me what woe and sorrow I was suffering for her then, and yet she knew it not, nor durst I tell her my mind. "Alas!" thought I, "I know no remedy, and unless I tell her, I am but a dead man; and if I tell her, verily I am afeared she will be wroth. Alas! what shall I do then?" In this debate I was so woful, methought mine heart would burst in twain. So at last, I bethought me in sooth that Nature never formed in a living being so much beauty and goodness without kindness. In hope of that, I told my story, from necessity, and with sorrow, as if I should never have done so; maugre my head, I must needs tell her or die. I wot not well how I began; I can repeat it but ill. And also, so God help me, I believe it was on an unlucky day, as the days of the ten plagues of Egypt. For I missed many a word in my tale from pure fear lest my words were misplaced. With sorrowful heart and deadly wounds, timid and quaking from very fear and shame, and stopping ever and anon in my words for dread, my hue all pale, full often I waxed both pale and red; I bent my face down before her, I durst not once look at her, for wit and assurance all were fled. I cried "Mercy!" and no more. It was no sport, it was bitter pain.

'At last when my courage was returned, to relate my words shortly, I besought her with my whole heart to be my sweet lady; and swore and heartily promised her ever to be steadfast and loyal, and to love her ever afresh and anew, and never to have other lady, and to protect all her honour as best I could; I swore that to her, — "because yours for evermore is all that ever there is in me, my sweet heart! And never will I be false to you, unless in a dream — so surely may God help me!"

'And when I had finished my tale, God wot she counted it all not worth a straw, methought. To tell it briefly as it was, her answer in truth was this; I cannot now follow her words well, but this was the substance of her answer; she said "nay," utterly. Alack for the sorrow and woe I suffered then! Truly Cassandra, who so bewailed the destruction of Ilium and Troy, had never such sorrow as I that day. For very fear I durst say no more, but stole off. And thus I lived for full many a day, so that truly I had no need any day to seek for sorrow farther than my bed's head; I found it at hand every morn, because it was in no fickleness I loved her.

'It so befell, in another year I thought once I would try to make her know and understand my woe; and she well perceived that I desired naught but what was good and worshipful, and above all things to guard her good name and dread any dishonour for her, and that I was full eager to serve her; and it were pity I should die, since truly I desired no evil. So when my lady knew it, she gave me all wholly the noble gift of her favour, always saving her honour, certes, I mean no otherwise. And therewith she gave me a ring; I believe it was the first gift. But whether my heart was glad is no need to ask! So God help me, I was straightway raised as from death to life, of all haps the best, the gladdest and the most peaceful. For truly, that sweet creature, when I was in the wrong and she in the right, she would ever forgive me full graciously and kindly. In all my youth, in all hazard, she took me under her rule.

'Therewith she was alway so true, our joy was ever and alike fresh. Our hearts were so perfect a pair that never for any woe was the one counter to the other. In sooth they both felt alike one joy and also one sorrow; they were both alike glad or troubled; verily all was the same to both. And thus we lived many a year, — so well, I cannot tell how well.'

'Sir,' quoth I, 'where is she now?'

'Now!' he said, and stopped straightway. Then he waxed as deathlike to see as a stone, then said, 'Alas that I was born! That was the loss which I before told you I had suffered. Remember how I said before, "You know full little what you say; I have lost more than you ween." God wot, alas, it was she!'

'Alack, sir, and how? What are you saying?'

'She is dead!'

'Nay!'

'Yes, by my troth!'

'Is that your loss! By God, it is a grievous thing!'

And anon at that word the hunters began to range forth; it was all done, the hart-hunting, for that time.

Upon that, methought, this king rode homeward to a place hard by, but a little distance from us, a long castle with white walls, by Saint John! on a rich hill, as I dreamed; thus it was. Right thus I dreamed, as I relate it to you, — that there was a bell in the castle, which seemed to strike the twelfth hour.

At that I awoke, and found myself lying in my bed; and the book that I had been reading, of Alcyone and king Ceyx and of the gods of sleep, I found it even in my hand. Thought I, this is so rare a dream, that as the days go by I will strive to put it into rhyme as best I can, and that anon. This was my dream; now it is ended.

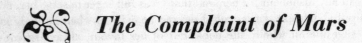

The Complaint of Mars

Rejoice, ye birds, at the grey dawn; lo Venus, arisen amongst yonder ruddy streaks! And ye fresh flowers, honour this day, for ye will open when the sun rises. But ye lovers that be in fear, flee, lest wicked tongues discover you. Behold the sun yonder, the candle of Jealousy! Stained with tears and with wounded heart, take your leave; and, by Saint John I adjure you, take comfort somewhat in your bitter sorrows; the time will come again when your woes shall cease. A heavy morn is not too great a price for a joyous night.

(Thus, Saint Valentine, I heard a bird sing upon thy day, ere the sun rose. And yet sang this bird: —)

Waken all, I counsel you. And ye who have not humbly chosen your mates betimes, make your faithful choice now. And ye who have chosen as I prescribe, renew your homage at least; confirm it, to last perpetually, and patiently accept what befalls you. For the honour of this high festival yet will I sing, in my bird's fashion, at least the import of the complaint which woful Mars made at parting from fair Venus, upon a morn when Phœbus, with his fiery red torches, came searching out every fearful lover.

Mars, the lord of the third heaven above, as well by the heavenly revolutions as by his deserts, won Venus his love, and she took him in subjection, and as a mistress taught him his lesson, commanding him he should never whilst he served her be so bold as to despise any lover. She forbade him all jealousy and tyranny, cruelty and arrogance. She made him so humble and docile to her pleasure that, when she deigned to look upon him, he patiently accepted her will, were it to live or die. And thus she bridled him after her wont, with no scourge but of her look.

Who reigns now in joy but Venus, with this worthy knight under her rule? Who sings now but Mars, that serves thus the fair Venus, giver of pleasance? He binds him to obey her perpetually, and she binds her to love him alway, unless his trespass should sever the bond. Thus were they knit, and reigned in the skies, gazing upon each other, until it fell upon a day that they set a time when Mars should glide as rapidly as might be into her nearest palace, there to tarry, walking slowly upon his course, until she should overtake him; and he prayed her for his love to haste her. Then he said, 'Sweet mistress of my heart, you well know mine evil case here; for verily till I meet with you my life stands all in Fortune's power. But when I see the beauty of your countenance, no fear of death can hurt me, for all your lustiness is a joy to mine heart.'

She had so great compassion upon her knight, dwelling alone till she should come, that wellnigh her mind was overborne with woe; for it so was that there was none then to counsel him or make him welcome. Wherefore she sped on her way almost as much in one day as he in two. And no tongue can tell the great joy betwixt them twain when they met once more. Without more ado they betook them apart, and thus I leave them in joy and bliss. This valiant Mars, fount of knighthood, folded the flower of beauty in his arms, and Venus kissed Mars, god of war.

Now this Mars of whom I read sojourned privily in a chamber in the midst of the palace for a certain time, till fear came upon him by reason of Phœbus, who was come quickly and boldly within the palace-gates, with torch in hand, of which the bright rays smote full brilliantly where lay this blooming queen, Venus, within her chamber, which was painted over with great white bulls. Venus knew, by the light which shone so brightly, that Phœbus came that he might burn them with his heat. This hapless Venus, drowned in wet tears, embraced Mars, and said, 'Alas, I die! The torch is come that will reveal all this world!'

Up started Mars, he list not sleep when he heard his lady so lament. But because tears were not in his nature, instead of tears fiery sparks burst for woe out from his two eyes. And he seized his hauberk which lay by him; flee he would not, nor could he hide him. He threw on his helmet of huge weight, and girt him with his sword; and in his hand he so shook his mighty spear, as he was wont in battle, that wellnigh it snapped. He was full heavy to walk over the land. No longer could he abide with Venus, but he bade her flee lest Phœbus spy her.

Woful Mars, what canst thou say, who art left behind in this perturbed palace, in peril to be slain, alas? And also thy penance is double, for she who has thy heart in hold is passed half beyond the beams of thine eyes. Well mayst thou weep and lament because thou art not swift.

In fear of Phœbus' light Venus now fled on her lonely course into the tower of Mercury. Alas, nor had she succour there, for she neither found nor saw any manner of creature, and there had but little power. Wherefore she fled into a cave within the gate, to hide her. Dark was this cave and smoky even as hell, and stood but two paces within the gate, and there I leave her in the dark for the space of one natural day.

Now I will speak of Mars, that for mad and furious sorrow would fain have seen his own heart's blood; since he must lose her company, he cared not a farthing for his life. So feeble he waxed for heat and woe, that he nearly died, he could scarce endure. He passed over but one step in two days; but nevertheless, and for all his heavy armour, he followed after her who was his life's balm, for whose departing he had more wrath and woe than for all his burning in the sun's fire. Slowly after her he walked, lamenting till it was piteous to hear. 'Oh, lady bright, Venus,' he said, 'alas that ever my course had so wide a compass! When shall I meet you, dear heart, alack! This twelfth day of April I endure this mischance, through Phœbus' malice.'

God help luckless solitary Venus! But as God willed, it happed that whilst Venus wept and made lament, Mercury, riding on his chase, could see his palace-tower from the sign Aries, and he saluted her, and made her welcome, and received her as his right dear friend.

Mars abode still in his adversity, ever lamenting her departure, and now I remember me of his lament. And therefore, on this lusty morn, I will say and sing it as best I can; and then I will take my leave. God give every person joy of his mate!

Mars's Lament

The law of laments requireth in reason that if a man shall make piteous plaint there must be cause therefor; or men may deem that he complaineth foolishly and causelessly. Alas, that is not my case! Wherefore, as well as my troubled wit can reach, I will rehearse the ground and cause of my pain; not to gain a remedy, but to make known the ground of my heaviness.

When I was first created, alas, and brought hither for certain ends by Him who ruleth over each intelligence, I gave my loyal service and my thought for evermore — how dearly I have paid for it! — to her who is of such excellent power that if any man cometh into her presence when she is wroth and will take no heed of him, he cannot long remain rejoicing in his love. This is no feigned matter that I relate. My lady is very source and spring of beauty, pleasure, generosity, and nobility; of rich array — how precious it is! —, of all friendly disport, of love and merriment, of benign humility, of the melody of all sweet instruments; and also she is so well endowed by fortune and virtue that her goodness is made manifest through the whole world. What wonder, then, though I have knit my service to such an one, who may devote me to weal or woe, since it lieth in her power? Therefore I have promised my heart to her forever; nor, truly, though I die, shall I cease to be her most loyal servant and her knight. I flatter not, as all may know. For this day I shall die in her service; unless I win mercy, I shall never again set eyes upon her.

To whom then shall I lament my distress? Who can help me? Who can cure my hurt? Shall I complain to my bountiful lady? Nay, certes! For she is in such heaviness from fear and sorrow that it will soon be her bane, I believe. Were she but safe, of me were no charge. Alas that ever lovers must endure so many perilous chances for love! For though lovers be as faithful as any metal newly forged, mischance oft betideth them. Sometimes their ladies will have no pity; sometimes, did jealousy but know it, they would lightly devote themselves to death; sometimes malicious folk with foul tongues defame them. Alas, whom can they please? Only the false lover hath comfort. But what availeth so long a sermon about, and about, the chances of love? I will return, and speak of my distress. What destroyeth my peace is this, that my true lady, my salvation, is in terror, and knoweth not to whom to make lament. O dear heart! O sovereign lady! Good cause have I to swoon and die away for your distress, though I felt none other hurt or fear.

To what end hath God enthroned on high created love or companionship beneath him, and constrained folk to love in spite of their teeth? And then, methinks, their joy lasteth not for the twinkling of an eye; and some never gain joy to the day of their death. What signifieth this? What is this mystery? To what end constraineth He His folk to desire a thing so eagerly, unless it should endure? Though he cause a lover to love a thing, and make it seem steadfast and lasting, yet he subjecteth it to such mishap that a man hath no repose with His gift. And that is a marvel, that so just a King doth such cruelty unto that which He hath created. Thus, whether love break or endure, in any wise he who hath to do with love hath sorrow oftener than the moon changeth. It seemeth that God hath enmity toward lovers, and, like a fisherman, as men may see any day, he so baiteth his hook with some delight that many a fish is crazed till he be seized therewith; and then first he hath all his desire, and at the same time all mischance; and though the line break, yet hath he pain, for he is wounded so sorely by the hook that he hath his pay for evermore.

The brooch of Thebes, so full of rubies and precious stones of Ind, was of such nature that every person who set eye on it thought he must go out of his mind; so sore would the beauty of it grip his heart, till he had it he thought he should die. And ever whilst it was his he should endure such distress of fear that he wellnigh would go mad. And when it went from his possession, then had he double passionate woe because he had foregone so fair a treasure. Yet, after all, this brooch was not the cause of this distraction; but he who wrought it endowed it so that every person who possessed it should have sorrow. And therefore the fault was in the craftsman, and in the foolish coveter. So fareth it with all lovers and with me. For though my lady be so fair that I was mad till I had won her favour, she caused not mine adversity, but He Who wrought her, Who set such beauty in her face that it made me covet, and to win mine own death. Him I blame that I perish; and mine own folly, that ever I climbed so high.

But ye bold knights of renown, since ye be of my clan (all be I unworthy so great a name, yet these clerks say I am your patron), therefore ye ought to have some compassion upon my distress, and take it not as sport. The proudest of you may yet be well tamed. Wherefore I pray you of your noble kindness ye lament my sorrow. And ye my ladies, made by nature true and steadfast, ye ought to have pity upon folk in pain. Now ye have cause to wear sable;

well ought ye to lament, since your glorious empress is desolate; now should your holy tears fall as rain. Alas, your empress and your boast, nigh dead with fear, faileth of her end. Likewise ye lovers, all together, lament ye for her who with unfeigned, meek demeanour was ever ready to come to your succour. Bewail her who ever held you dear; bewail beauty, bounty and courtesy; bewail her who endeth your toil; bewail that ensample of all honour, who never did aught but gentle deeds; show, therefore, some kindness toward her.

 # The Parliament of Birds

That life so brief, that art so long in the learning, that attempt so hard, that conquest so sharp, that fearful joy which ever slips away so quickly, — all this is love, which so sore astounds my feeling with its wondrous operation, that when I think upon it I scarce know whether I wake or sleep. For albeit I know not love myself, nor how he pays folk their wage, yet I have full often chanced to read in books of his miracles and his cruel ire; there, of a surety, I read he will ever be lord and sovereign, and his strokes be so heavy I dare say naught but — Ill luck to such a lord! I can say no more.

What for pleasure and what for learning I am wont to read books, as I have told you. But wherefore speak I of all this? Not yore ago I chanced to look at a book, written in antique letters, and therein I read full diligently and eagerly through the long day, to learn a certain thing. For, as men say, out of old fields comes all this new corn from year to year; and, in good faith, out of old books comes all this new knowledge that men learn. But now to my theme in this matter: it so delighted me to read on, that the whole day seemed to me but short. This book which I tell of was entitled thus, *Tully on the Dream of Scipio*. It had chapters seven, of heaven and hell and earth, and the souls that live therein; as to which I will tell you the substance of Tully's opinion, as briefly as I can.

First the book tells how, when Scipio was come into Africa, he met Masin-issa, who clasped him in his arms for joy. Then it tells their speech and all the joy that was betwixt them till the day began to fail; and then how Scipio's beloved ancestor Africanus appeared to him that night in his sleep. Then it tells how Africanus showed him Carthage from a starry place, and disclosed to him all his good fortune to come, and said to him that whatsoever man, be he learned or unlettered, loves the common weal and is virtuous, shall go unto a blessed place where is joy without ending. Then Scipio asked whether folk that die here have life and dwelling elsewhere; and Africanus said, 'Yea, without doubt,' and added that our space of life in the present world, whatsoever way we follow, is but a kind of death, and righteous folk, after they die, shall go to heaven.

And he showed him the Milky Way, and the earth here, so little in comparison with the hugeness of the heavens; and after that he showed him the nine spheres. And then he heard the melody that proceeds from those nine spheres, which is the fount of music and melody in this world, and the cause of harmony. Then Africanus bade him not to take delight in this world, since earth is so little and so full of torment and ill favour. Then he told him how in a certain term of years every star should come into its own place, where it first was; and all that has been done by all mankind in this world shall pass out of memory.

Then he prayed Africanus to tell him fully the way to come into that heavenly happiness; and he said, 'First know thyself to be immortal; and ever look that thou diligently labour and teach for the common weal, and thou shalt not fail to come speedily to that dear place which is full of joy and of bright souls. But breakers of the law, in sooth, and lecherous folk, after they die, shall ever be whirled about the earth in torment, till many an age be passed; and then, all their wicked deeds forgiven, they shall come unto that blessed region, to which God send thee His grace to come.'

The day began to fail, and dark night, which withdraws beasts from their activity, bereft me of my book for the lack of light; and I betook me toward my bed, full of brooding and anxious heaviness. For I both had that which I would not, and what I would that I had not. But at last, wearied with all the day's labour, my spirit took rest and heavily slept; and as I lay in my sleep, I dreamed how Africanus, in the selfsame guise in which Scipio saw him that time before, was come and stood even at the side of my bed. When the weary hunter sleeps, anon his mind returns to the wood; the judge dreams how his cases be sped, and the carter how his carts go; the rich dream of gold, the knight fights his foes; the sick man dreams he drinks of the tun, the lover that he has his lady. I cannot say whether my reading of Africanus were the cause why I dreamed that he stood there; but thus he spake, 'Thou hast done so well to look upon my old tattered book, of which Macrobius thought not a little, that I would requite thee somewhat for thy labour.'

Cytherea! thou sweet, blessed lady, who with thy fire-brand subduest whom thou wilt, and sentest me this dream, be thou my helper herein, for thou art best able. As surely as I saw thee in the north-northwest when I began to write my dream, so surely do thou give me power to rhyme it and endite it!

This aforesaid Africanus took me forthwith and brought me out with him to a gate of a park walled with mossy stone; and over the gate on either side, carved in large letters, were verses of right diverse sense, of which I shall tell you the full purport:

> 'Through me men go into that blessed place
> Where hearts find health and deadly wounds find cure,
> Through me men go unto the fount of Grace,
> Where green and lusty May shall ever endure.
> I lead men to blithe peace and joy secure.
> Reader, be glad; throw off thy sorrows past.
> Open am I; press in and hie thee fast.'

On the other side it said:

> 'Through me men go where all mischance betides,
> Where is the mortal striking of the spear,
> To which Disdain and Coldness are the guides,
> Where trees no fruit nor leaf shall ever bear.
> This stream shall lead thee to the sorrowful weir
> Where fish in baleful prison lie all dry.
> To shun it is the only remedy.'

These inscriptions were written, the one in gold, the other in black, and I beheld them for a season, for at the one my heart grew hardy, and the other ever increased my fear; the first warmed me, the other chilled me. For fear of error my wit could not make its choice, to enter or to flee, to lose myself or save myself. Even as a piece of iron set betwixt two loadstones of equal force has no power to move to or fro, — for as much as one draws the other hinders —, so it fared with me, who wist not which were better, to enter or not, until Africanus my guide caught and pushed me in at the wide gates, saying, 'Your doubt stands written on your face, though you tell it not to me. But fear not to come in, for this writing is not meant for you or for any, unless he be Love's servant. For in love, I believe, you have lost your sense of taste, even as a sick man loses his taste of sweet and bitter. Nevertheless, dull though you be, you can still look upon that which you cannot do; for many a man who cannot stand a bout is nevertheless pleased to be at the wrestling, and judges whether one does better or another. And if you have skill to set it down, I will show you matter to write of.'

With that he took my hand in his, whence I took comfort and quickly went in. But Lord, how glad and at ease I was! For everywhere I cast mine eyes were trees clad, each after its kind, with ever-during leaves in colour fresh and green as emerald, a joy to behold: the builder oak, also the hardy ash, the elm the pillar and the coffin for corpses, the boxtree for horns, the holm for whip-handles, the fir to bear sails, the cypress to mourn death, the yew the bowman, the aspen for smooth shafts, the olive of peace, the drunken vine, the victor palm, and the laurel for divination.

By a river in a green mead, where is evermore sweetness enough, I saw a garden, full of blossomy boughs, with white, blue, yellow and red flowers; and cold fountain-streams, no whit sluggish, full of small shining fishes with red fins and silver-bright scales. On every bough I heard the birds sing with the voice of angels in their melody. Some busied them to lead forth their young. The little coneys hasted to play. Further all about I espied the timid roe, the buck, harts and hinds and squirrels and small beasts of gentle nature. Stringed instruments I heard playing harmonies of such ravishing sweetness that God, Maker and Lord of all, never heard better, I believe. At the same time a wind, scarce could it have been gentler, made in the green leaves a soft noise which accorded with the song of the birds above. The air of that place was so mild that never was there discomfort for heat or cold. There grew every wholesome spice and herb, and no man could age or sicken. There was joy a thousand-fold more than man can tell. And it would never be night there, but ever bright day in every man's eye.

I saw Cupid our lord forging and filing his arrows under a tree beside a spring, and his bow lay all ready at his feet. And his daughter well tempered the arrow-heads in the spring the while, and by her cunning she piled them after as they should serve, some to slay, some to wound and pierce. Then anon I was ware of Pleasance and of Fair Array and Courtesy and Joy and that Art which has wit and power to cause a man to do folly, — she was disguised, I deny it not; and under an oak, I believe apart, I saw Delight, standing with Gentle Breeding. I saw Beauty without any raiment; and Youth, full of sportiveness and jollity, Foolhardiness, Flattery, Desire, Message-sending and Bribery; and three others — their names shall not be told by me.

And upon great high pillars of jasper I saw a temple of brass strongly stand. About the temple women a-plenty were ever dancing; some of whom were fair of themselves, and some gay in garb; only in their kirtles they went, with hair unbound — that was ever their office, year by year. And on the temple I saw many hundred pairs of doves sitting, white and beautiful. Before the temple-door sat Dame Peace full gravely, holding back the curtain, and beside her Dame Patience, with pale face and wondrous discreet, sitting upon a mound of sand. Next to her were Promise and Cunning and a crowd of their followers within the temple and without.

Inside I heard a gust of sighs blowing about, hot as fire, engendered of longing, which caused every altar to blaze ever anew. And well I espied then that all the cause of sorrows that lovers endure is of the bitter goddess, Jealousy. As I walked about within the temple I saw the god Priapus standing in sovereign place, his sceptre in hand, and in such guise as when the ass confounded him to confusion with its outcry by night. Folk were busily setting upon his head garlands full of fresh, new flowers of sundry colours.

In a privy corner I found Venus sporting with her porter Riches, that was full noble and stately in her bearing. The place was dark, but in time I saw a little light — it could scarce have been less. Venus reposed upon a golden bed till the hot sun should seek the west. Her golden hair was bound with a golden thread, but all untressed as she lay. And folk could see her naked from the breast to the head; the remnant, in truth, was well covered to my pleasure with a filmy kerchief of Valence; there was no thicker covering. The place gave forth a thousand sweet odours. Bacchus, god of wine, sat beside her, and next was Ceres, who saves from hunger, and, as I said, the Cyprian dame lay in the midst; to her on their knees two young folk were crying to be their helper.

But thus I left her lying, and further in the temple I espied how, in scorn of Dian the chaste, there hung on the wall full many a broken bow of such maidens as had first wasted their time in her service. And everywhere was painted many a story, of which I shall touch on a few, as of Callisto, and Atalanta, and many a maiden whose name I know not; and Semiramis, Candace, Hercules, Byblis, Dido, Thisbe and Pyramus, Tristram and Isolt, Paris, Achilles, Helen, Cleopatra, Troilus, and Scylla, and also the mother of Romulus, — all were portrayed on the other wall, and all their love, and in what plight they died.

When I was returned unto the garden that I spake of, so sweet and green, forth I walked to solace me. Then was I ware how there sat a queen who was exceeding fair over every other creature, as the brilliant summer sun passes the stars in brightness. This noble goddess Nature was set upon a flowery hill in a verdant glade. All her halls and bowers were wrought of branches after the art and measure of Nature.

Nor is there any bird that comes of procreation that was not ready in her presence, to hear her and receive her judgment. For this was Saint Valentine's day, when every bird of every kind that men can think on comes there to choose his mate. And they made an exceeding great noise; and earth and sea and the trees and all the lakes were so full that there was scarce room for me to stand, so full was all the place. And even as Alan, in the Complaint of Nature, describes Nature in her features and attire, so might men find her in reality.

This noble empress, full of grace, bade every bird take his station, as they were wont to stand ever on Saint Valentine's day from year to year. That is to say, the birds of prey were set highest, and then the little birds who eat, as nature inclines them, worms or other things of which I speak not; but water-fowls sat the lowest in the dale; and birds that live on seed sat upon the grass, so many that it was a marvel to see. There men could find the royal eagle, that pierces the sun with his sharp glance; and other eagles of lower race, of which clerks can tell. There was that tyrant with dun grey feathers, I mean the goshawk, that harasses other birds with his fell ravening. There was the noble falcon, that with his feet grasps the king's hand; also the bold sparrow-hawk, foe of quails; the merlin, that oft greedily pursues the lark. The dove was there, with her meek eyes; the jealous swan, that sings at his death, and the owl also, that forebodes death; the giant crane, with his trumpet voice; the thieving chough; the prating magpie; the scornful jay; the heron, foe to eels; the false lapwing, full of trickery; the starling, that can betray secrets; the tame redbreast; the coward kite; the cock, timekeeper of little thorps; the sparrow, son of Venus; the nightingale, which calls forth the fresh new leaves; the swallow, murderer of the little bees which make honey from the fresh-hued flowers; the wedded turtle-dove, with her faithful heart; the pea-cock, with his shining angel-feathers; the pheasant, that scorns the cock by night; the vigilant goose; the cuckoo, ever unnatural; the popinjay, full of wantonness; the drake, destroyer of his own kind; the stork, that avenges adultery; the greedy, gluttonous cormorant; the wise raven and the crow, with voice of ill-boding; the ancient throstle and the wintry fieldfare. What more shall I say? Men might find assembled in that place before the noble goddess Nature birds of every sort in this world that have feathers and being. And each by her command was diligent in tenderly choosing his mate.

But to the point: Nature held on her hand a formel eagle, the noblest in shape that she ever found amongst her works, the gentlest and goodliest; in her every noble trait so had its seat that Nature herself rejoiced to look upon her and to kiss her beak many times. Nature, vicar of the Almighty Lord, who has knit in harmony of exact number hot, cold, heavy, light, moist, and dry, began to speak in a gentle voice: 'Birds, take heed of what I say; and for your welfare and to further your needs I will hasten as fast as I can speak. Ye well know how on Saint Valentine's day, by my statute and through mine ordinance, ye come to choose your mates, as I prick you with sweet pain, and then fly on your way. But I may not, to win all this world, depart from my just order, that he shall begin who is most worthy.

'The tercel eagle, the royal bird above you in degree, as ye well know, the wise and worthy one, trusty, true as steel, which ye may see I have formed in every part as pleased me best — it needs not describe his shape to you —, he shall choose first and speak as he will. And after him ye shall choose in order, according to your nature, each as pleases you; and, as your hap is, ye shall lose or win. But whichever of you love ensnares most, to him God send her who sighs for him most sorely.' And at this she called the tercel and said, 'My son, the choice is fallen to thee. Nevertheless under this condition must be the choice of each one here, that his chosen mate agree to his choice, whatsoever he be who would have her. Ever from year to year this is our usage. And whoever at this time can win grace, in blissful time he came hither.'

The royal tercel, with bowed head and full humble cheer, spake and tarried not: 'For my sovereign lady, not for my mate, I choose, — and chose with will and heart and mind, — the formel of so noble shape upon your hand. Hers I am wholly and will serve her ever, let her do as she will, to let me live or die; beseeching her for mercy and grace, as my sovereign lady, else let me die here presently. For certes I cannot live long in torment; for in my heart every vein is cut. Having regard only to my faithfulness, dear heart, have some pity upon my woe. And if I be found untrue to her, disobedient or wilfully negligent, a boaster, or in time love elsewhere, I pray thee this be my doom, that I be torn to pieces by these birds, upon that day when she ever knows me untrue to her or by my guilt unkind. And since none loves her so well as I, though she never promised me love, she ought of her mercy to be mine; for I can fasten none other bond on her. Never for any woe shall I cease to serve her, however far she may roam. Say what thou wilt, my words are done.'

Even as the fresh red rose newly blown blushes in the summer sun, so grew the colour of this formel when she heard all this; she answered no word good or bad, so sore was she abashed; till Nature said, 'Daughter, fear not, be of good courage.'

Anon spake another tercel of a lower order: 'That shall not be. I love her better than thou, by Saint John, or at least I love her as well, and have served her longer, according to my station. If she should love for long being loved, to me alone should be the guerdon; and also I dare to say, if she find me false, unkind, a prater, or a rebel in any wise, or jealous, let me be hanged by the neck. And unless I bear me in her service as well as my wit enables me, to protect her honour in every point, let her take my life and all the wealth I have.'

Then the third tercel eagle said, 'Now, sirs, ye see how little time we have here, for every bird clamours to be off with his mate or lady dear, and also Nature herself, for the delay, will not hear half of what I would speak. Yet unless I speak I must die of sorrow. Of long service I boast not at all; but it is as like that I shall die of woe to-day as he who has been languishing these twenty winters; and it may well chance that a man may serve better in half a year, though it were no longer, than another man who has served many a year. I say not this concerning myself, for I can do no service to my lady's pleasure; but I dare say this, that I am her truest man, I believe, and fainest would please her. In short words, till death seize me I will be hers, whether I wake or sleep, and true in all that heart can think.'

In all my life since the day I was born never heard any man before me so noble a plea in love or any other thing, — if but a man had time and wit to rehearse their cheer and their words. And this discourse lasted from the morning till the sun drew downward wondrous rapidly. The clamour of birds to be released rung so loud — 'Have done and let us go!' — that I well thought the forest would be shivered. They cried, 'Make haste! Alas, ye will ruin us! When shall your cursed pleading have end? How should a judge believe either side for yea or nay, without any proof?'

The goose, cuckoo and duck so loudly cried, 'Kek, kek!', 'Cuckoo!', 'Quack, quack!', that the noise went through and through mine ears. The goose said, 'All this is not worth a fly! But hereof I can devise a remedy, and I will speak my verdict fair and soon, on behalf of the waterfowl, let who will smile or frown.'

'And I for the worm-eating fowl,' said the foolish cuckoo; 'of mine own authority, for the common welfare, I will take the office now, for it were great charity to release us.'

'Perdy, thou mayst wait a while yet,' said the turtle-dove. 'If thou be he to choose who shall speak, it were as well for him to be silent. I am of the fowl that eat seed, one of the unworthiest, and of little wit, that wot I well. But a creature's tongue were better quiet than meddle with such doings of which he knows nor rhyme nor reason. And whoso does, cumbers him right foully, for often office uncommitted does offence.'

Nature, that had ever an ear to the murmuring of folly at the back, said with ready tongue, 'Hold your peace there! And straightway, I hope, I shall find a counsel to let you go and release you from this noise. My judgment is that ye shall choose one out of each bird-folk to give the verdict for you all.'

The birds all assented to this conclusion. And first the birds of prey by full election chose the tercel-falcon to define all their judgment, and decide as he list. And they presented him to Nature and she accepted him gladly. The falcon then spake in this fashion: 'It were full hard to determine by reason which best loves this gentle formel; for each has such ready answers that none may be defeated by reasons. I cannot see of what avail are arguments; then it seems there must be battle.'

'All ready!' then cried these tercel-eagles.

'Nay, sirs,' quoth he, 'if I durst say it, yet do me wrong, my tale is not done. For, sirs, — take it not amiss, I pray —, it cannot go thus as ye desire. Ours is the voice that has the charge over this, and ye must stand by the judges' doom. Peace, therefore! I say that it would seem to my wit that the worthiest in knighthood, who has longest followed it, he highest in degree and of gentlest blood, were most fitting for her, if she list. And of these three she knows which he is, I believe, for that is lightly seen.'

The waterfowl put their heads together, and after short considering, when each had spoken his tedious gabble, they said verily, by one assent, how 'the goose, with her gentle eloquence, that so desires to speak for us, shall say our say,' and prayed God speed her. Then began the goose to speak for these waterfowl, and said in her cackling, 'Peace! Now every man take heed and hearken what argument I shall put forth. My wits are sharp, I love no delay; I counsel him, I say, though he were my brother, let him love elsewhere if she will not love him.'

'Lo here,' quoth the sparrow-hawk, 'a perfect argument for a goose, ill may she end! Lo, thus it is to have a wagging tongue! Now, fool, it were better for thee to have held thy peace than have shown thy folly, perdy! But to do thus lay not in her wit nor will; for it is truly said, "A fool cannot be silent." '

Laughter arose from all the birds of noble kind; and straightway the seed-eating fowl chose the faithful turtle-dove, and called her to them, and prayed her to speak the sober truth about this matter, and asked her counsel. And she answered that she would fully show her mind. 'Nay, God forbid a lover should change!' said the turtle-dove, and grew all red with shame. 'Though his lady be cold for evermore, let him serve her ever till he die. In sooth I praise not the goose's counsel, for though my lady died, I would have no other mate, I would be hers till death take me.'

'By my hat, well jested!' quoth the duck. 'That men should love forever, without cause, who can find reason or wit there? Dances he merrily who is mirthless? Who should care for him who is carefree? Yea, quack!' quoth the duck loud and long, 'God wot there be more stars than a pair.'

'Now fie, churl!' quoth the noble falcon. 'That thought came straight from the dunghill. Thou canst not see when a thing is well employed. Thou farest with love as owls with light; the day blinds them, but they see full well in darkness. Thy nature is so low and wretched that thou canst not see or guess what love is.'

Then the cuckoo thrust himself forward in behalf of the worm-eating birds, and said quickly, 'So I may have my mate in peace, I reck not how long ye contend. Let each be single all his life; that is my counsel since they cannot agree. This is mine instruction, and there an end!'

'Yea,' said the merlin, 'so this glutton have well filled his paunch, that should suffice for us all! Thou murderer of the hedge-sparrow on the branch, her that brought thee up, thou ruthless glutton! Live thou unmated, thou mangler of worms! It is no matter though thy tribe perish. Go, be thou a filthy fool so long as the world lasts!'

'Peace here, I command now,' quoth Nature. 'For I have heard the opinions of all, and yet we are never the nearer our end. But this is my final decision, that she herself shall have the choice of whom she list. Whoso be pleased or no, he whom she chooses shall have her straightway. For since it cannot here be debated who loves her best, as the falcon said, then will I grant her this favour, that she shall even have him on whom her heart is set, and he her that has fixed his heart on her. This judgment I, Nature, make; and I cannot speak falsely, nor look with partial eye on any rank. But if it be in reason to counsel thee in choosing a mate, then certes I would counsel thee to take the royal tercel, as the falcons said right wisely; for he is noblest and most worthy whom I wrought so well for mine own pleasure; that ought to suffice thee.'

The formel answered with timid voice, 'Goddess of nature, my righteous lady, true it is that I am ever under your rod, even as every other creature is, and I must be yours whilst my life may last. Therefore grant me my first boon, and straightway I will tell you my mind.'

'I grant it you,' quoth Nature; and anon this formel eagle spake in this wise; 'Almighty queen, until this year be ended I ask respite, to take counsel with myself; and after that to have my choice free. This is all that I would say. I can say no more, though thou slay me. In sooth as yet I will in no wise serve Venus or Cupid.'

'Now since it can betide no otherwise,' quoth Nature then, 'there is no more to be said here. Then I would these birds should go their way each with his mate, that they tarry here no longer.' And she spake to them thus as ye shall hear. 'To you I speak, ye tercels,' quoth Nature. 'Be of good heart, and continue in service all three; a year is not so long to wait. And let each of you strive after his degree to do well. For, God wot, she is quit of you this year; and whatsoever may betide afterwards, this interval is appointed you all.'

And when this work was all brought to and end, Nature gave every bird his mate by just accord, and they went their way. Ah, Lord! the bliss and joy that they made! For each of them took the other in his wings, and wound their necks about each other, ever thanking the noble goddess of nature. But first were chosen birds to sing, as was ever their custom year by year to sing a roundel at their departure, to honour Nature and give her pleasure. The tune, I believe, was made in France. The words were such as ye may here find in these verses, as I remember them.

> 'Welcome, summer, with sunshine soft,
> The winter's tempest thou wilt break,
> And drive away the long nights black!
>
> Saint Valentine, throned aloft,
> Thus little birds sing for thy sake:
>   Welcome, summer, with sunshine soft,
>   The winter's tempest thou wilt break!
>
> Good cause have they to glad them oft,
> His own true-love each bird will take;
> Blithe may they sing when they awake,
>   Welcome, summer, with sunshine soft,
>   The winter's tempest thou wilt break,
>   And drive away the long nights black!'

And with the shouting which the birds raised, as they flew away when their song was done, I awoke; and I took to me other books to read in, and still I read ever. In sooth I hope so to read that some day I shall meet with somewhat of which I shall fare the better. And so I will not cease to read.

A Complaint to His Lady

In the long night, when every creature should naturally take some rest, else his life cannot long hold out, then it falls most into my woful thoughts how I have dropped so far behind that save death naught can comfort me, so despair I of all happiness. This thought abides with me till morn, and forth from morn till eve. I need borrow no grief, I have both leisure and leave to mourn. There is no person will take my woe or forbid me to weep enough and wail my fill; the sore spark of pain destroys me.

This love has so placed me that he will never fulfill my desire; for neither pity, mercy nor grace can I find. Yet even for fear of death can I not root out love from my sorrowful heart. The more I love, the more my lady pains me; through which I see, without remedy, that I may nowise escape death.

Now in sooth I will rehearse her name. She is called Goodness-set-in-womanhood, Staidness-in-youth, and Beauty-without-pride, and Pleasure-under-control-and-fear. Her surname is Fair-ruthless, Wisdom-knit-to-fortune. Because I love her she slays me guiltless. Her I love best, and shall whilst I live, better an hundred thousand times than myself, better than all the riches and created beings of this world.

Now has not Love bestowed me well, to love where I shall never have part or lot! Alas! so is Fortune's wheel turned for me, so am I slain with Love's fiery arrow. I can but love her best, my sweet foe. Love has taught me no more of his art than ever to serve, and cease for no sorrow.

Within my true, care-worn heart there is so much woe, and also so little joy, that woe is me that ever I was born. For all that I desire I lack, and all that ever I would not have, that, in sooth, I ever find ready to my hand. And of all this I know not to whom to complain, for she who might bring me out of this recks not whether I weep or sing, so little pities she my pain. Alas! in sleeping-time I wake; when I should dance I tremble with fear.

This heavy life I lead for thy sake, though thou pay no heed thereto, my heart's lady, all my life's queen! For truly I durst say it, as I see it: meseems thy sweet heart of steel is now whetted against me too keenly. My dear heart, for best-beloved, why wilt though do me all this sorrow? What have I done or said to grieve thee, save because I serve and love thee and none else, and whilst I live will ever? Therefore, sweet, be not displeased. Thou art so good and fair, it were a right great wonder unless thou hadst suitors of all kinds, both good and bad; and the least worthy of all, I am he.

Nevertheless, mine own sweet lady, though I be unskilful and unfit ever to serve thine highness, even as best I knew how, yet this I swear, there is none fainer than I to do thy pleasure or to cure whatso I wist to distress thee. And had I as much power as will, then shouldst thou feel whether it were so or not; for in this world is none living who would fainer fulfill thine heart's desire. For I both love and fear thee so sore, and ever must and have done right long, that none is better loved, and never shall be. And yet I would only beg thee to believe me well and be not wroth, and let me continue to serve thee. Lo, this is all! For I am not so bold or mad as to desire that thou shouldst love me; for alas! well I wot that may not be; I have so little worth, and thou so much. For thou art one of the most excellent of the living, and I the most unlikely to prosper. Yet, for all this, know thou right well thou shalt not so drive me from thy service that I shall not ever serve thee faithfully, with all my five wits, what woe soever I feel. For I am so set upon thee that though thou never pity me, I must love thee and ever be as true as any man living can be.

The more I love thee, goodly and noble one, the less I find thou lovest me. Alas! when will that obduracy soften? Where now is all thy womanly pity, thy noble gentleness, thy graciousness? Wilt thou spend naught thereof on me? And so wholly as I am thine, sweet, and so great will I have to serve thee, if thus thou let me die, thou hast gained but little therefrom. For I believe I have given no cause. And this I beseech thee heartily, that if ever thou find, so long as thou livest, a servant more true to thee than I, then leave me and boldly slay me, and I will forgive thee all my death. And if thou find no truer man, why wilt thou suffer me to perish thus, and for no manner of guilt save my good desire? As good then be untrue as true.

But to thy will I submit my life and death, and with a right obedient heart I pray, do by me as is thy pleasure. Much rather had I please thee and die than to think or say aught to offend thee at any time. Therefore pity my bitter pains, sweet, and of thy grace grant me some drop; for else neither hope nor happiness may remain with me, nor abide in my troubled, careworn heart.

Anelida and Arcite

The Complaint of Fair Anelida and False Arcite

Thou fierce god of arms, Mars the red, who in the frosty country of Thrace art honoured as patron of the land within thy grisly, dreadful temple, be thou present, with Pallas, thy Bellona, full of grace, and continue and guide my song! Thus I cry to thee at my beginning. For it is sunk deep in my thought with pitiful heart to indite in English this old story, which I find in Latin, of Queen Anelida and false Arcite, which Eld, that frets and gnaws all things, has wellnigh devoured out of our memory as it has consumed many a noble tale. Also be thou favourable, thou Polyhymnia, who with thy blithe sisters on Parnassus, near Helicon, not far from Cirra, singest with memorial voice in the shade beneath the unwithering laurel; and let my ship come safe to the haven. First I follow Statius, and after him Corinna.

Then Theseus with long and arduous wars had overcome the fierce folk of Scythia, he came back to the homes of his country, crowned with laurel, in his car of beaten gold. At which the happy people one and all raised such a clamour that it rose to the stars, and did their utmost to honour him. Before this duke came trumpeters, in sign of high victory; and on his great banner was the image of Mars. In token of glory men might see many a load of treasure, many a bright helmet, many a spear and targe, many a lusty knight and many a joyous company, on horse, afoot, in all the plain about.

Hippolyta, his wife, the hardy queen of Scythia whom he had conquered, with her fair young sister, Emily, he brought with him splendidly in a chariot of gold; and she illumined all the ground about her car with the beauty of her face, full of all liberality and favour. With all his triumph and this laurel-crowned, in all the flower of Fortune's gift, I leave this noble prince Theseus riding on his way to Athens, and I will strive to bring in soon the story of the devious ways of false Arcite with Queen Anelida, of which I began to tell.

Mars, who through his furious wrathful course, to fulfill the ancient wrath of Juno, had set afire the hearts of the people of both Thebes and Greece to kill each other with bloody spears, rested never quiet, but thrust among them

304

both, now here, now there, and made them slay each other, so wroth were they. And when Amphiaraus and Tydeus and also Hippomedon and Parthenopæus were dead, and proud Capaneus was slain and also the two wretched Theban brethren, and King Adrastus gone to his home, Thebes stood so desolate and bare that no-one thereof knew any cure for his distress. And when the old Creon espied how the blood royal was brought down, he held the city by tyranny, and won the gentles of that country to be his friends and dwell in the town. So what for love of him, what for fear, the folk of noble blood were drawn to the town.

Amongst all these Anelida, Queen of Armenia, was dwelling in that town, fairer than the shining sun; throughout the world so spread her name that every creature had desire to look upon her; for in truth of all the women in this world's domain there was not her like. This queen was young, twenty years of age, of middle stature, and of such fairness that nature rejoiced to behold her; and to speak of her constancy, she surpassed Penelope and Lucrece. And, if she is to be comprehended in few words, nothing in her could have been bettered.

This Theban knight Arcite, sooth to say, was also young, and a lusty knight withal, but he was deceitful in love and nowise open, and more subtle than any in that art. With his cunning he won this bright lady; for so he assured her of his faithfulness that she trusted him above any creature. What should I say more? She so loved Arcite that, when he was absent any time, anon she felt her heart burst in twain. For in her sight he bare him humbly, so that she deemed she knew all his heart; but he was false. It was but feigned cheer, such artfulness as men have no need to learn. Nevertheless he had much ado ere he could win his lady, and swore he should die for distress, and should go out of his wits. Alack the while! For it was ruth and sin that she should pity his sorrows; but the false and the true think nowise alike.

Arcite found her generosity such that all that she had, much or little, was his, and to no creature made she cheer further than was pleasing to Arcite. There was no fault to find in her; she was so devoted to pleasing him that all that pleased him contented her. No manner of letter was sent her from any person touching love, but she showed it him ere it was burnt. So open was she, and did all she could to hide nothing from her knight, lest he upbraid her with any unfaithfulness; without tarrying she obeyed his behest. And he made him jealous over her, so that, when any man spake to her, anon he would pray her to swear what that word was, else he would be displeased. Then she thought to have gone out of her wits; but all this was only slyness and flattery. Without love, he feigned to be jealous. And all this she took so meekly that in every wish of his she found good reason, and ever more and more tenderly loved him, and honoured him as a king. With a ring was her heart wedded to him. So was her mind fixed to be faithful that wherever he went her heart went with him. When she should eat, her mind was so on him that she scarce heeded her meat, and when she was brought to her rest, she thought ever of him till she slept. When he was absent, she wept privily. Thus lived fair Queen Anelida for false Arcite, who did her all this evil.

In his lust for novelty, because she was so lowly and true to him, he took the less delight in her constancy, and saw another lady, a stranger and proud, and anon clad him in her colour — I wot not whether white, red or green —, and broke faith with the fair Anelida. Nevertheless it was no great marvel though he were false, for since the time of Lamech so long ago it has been the nature of men to be as false in love as ever he can be. Lamech was the first patriarch who loved two women, and lived in bigamy; and, unless men lie, he first invented tents. This false Arcite, when he became false, had to feign somewhat to cover his perfidy, like a horse that can both bite and whine. So he accused her of treachery, and swore he espied her double-dealing, and that all she declared to him was false. Thus swore this thief and went his way.

Alas! for pity and woe what heart could endure to tell her sorrow? Or what man has the cunning or wit? Or what man could abide in the chamber if I rehearsed to him the hell which the fair queen Anelida suffered for the false Arcite, who brought her all this pain? She wept and wailed and piteously swooned, and fell to the ground death-like as a stone, she writhed her limbs in knots, she spoke as if her wit were gone, and was all of ashen colour. She spoke no other word, great or small, than, 'Mercy, my cruel heart, Arcite!' And this lasted till she was so spent that she could not sustain her on her feet, but ever languished in this state.

Arcite at this had neither pity nor sorrow. His heart was elsewhere in new, blooming love, and deigned not to think on her woe; he recked not whether she swam or sank. His new mistress held him in so tightly by the bridle and under her lash that he feared every word as an arrow. Her coldness made him bow and bend, and turn or go as she list; for never in her life granted she him any grace of which he list to sing, but ever drove him on; scarce cared she to know that he was servant to her ladyship, and lest he be proud she kept him abased. Thus he served without fee or hire, and she sent him now on land and now by sea; and because she gave him his fill of coldness, she had him at her command.

All ye prudent women, take ensample here from Anelida and false Arcite; because she list to call him 'dear heart,' and was so meek, therefore he loved her little. The nature of man's heart is to delight in what is held back, so may God save me! For what he cannot have, that would he.

Now return we to Anelida, who day by day pined and languished. But when she saw that she gained naught, upon a day, full sorrowfully weeping, she thought to compose a complaint, and with her own hand she wrote it, and sent it to Arcite, her Theban knight.

The Complaint of Anelida the Queen upon false Arcite

The sword of sorrow, whetted with false pleasure, so pierces with the point of memory my heart, bare of bliss and black in hue, that all my dancing is turned into quaking, and my confidence into amazement, since it avails not to be loyal; for she who is truest shall rue it most, she that serves love and ever devotes her to one, and changes to no fresh love.

I know it myself as well as any; for with all my heart and might I love one an hundred thousand times more than myself, and called him my heart's life, my knight, and was all his, so far as was just. And when he was glad, I was blithe; and his misease was anon my death. And he in turn plighted me his troth, evermore to declare me his lady.

Now, alas! he is false, and without cause; and so pitiless of my woe that he deigns not once by a word to bring peace to my sorrowful heart, for he is caught in another leash. He laughs at my pain as he list, and yet I cannot withhold my heart to love him alway.

And for all this I know not to whom to lament. Alack, hard hour! Shall I complain to my foe, who wounded my heart and yet desires my harm be greater? Nay, certes! Further, I will never seek other help to probe my wounds. My destiny decreed all this full long ago; I will have none other medicine nor lore. I will ever be where I was once bound; what I have once said, be it said forever.

Alas, where is your noble gentleness, your words full of pleasance and humility, your devotion so lowly, your watchfulness and your attentiveness to me, whom you called your mistress, your sovereign lady here in this world? Alas, and vouchsafe you neither words nor kindly look for me in my heaviness? Alas, I buy your love all too dearly!

Now certes, sweet, though thus without cause you be the cause of my mortal adversity, your manly reason ought to refrain ere you slay your friend, and especially me, who never yet have in any wise wronged you, so surely as I hope He Who knows all things may save my soul from woe! But because I showed you, Arcite, all that men would write me, and, saving my honour, had such zeal to please you, was so meek, kind, and generous, — therefore you put blame on me, and reck not a mite of me, though through your cruelty the sword of sorrow bite my woful heart.

My sweet foe, why do you thus? For shame! And think you your repute will be bettered to take a new love and be faithless? Nay! and to put you now into scandal and blame, and bring adversity and grief on me, who (God well knows), ever love you best? Yet return some day and be honest again, and then shall this that is now all wrong turn to mirth and be all forgiven so long as I live.

Lo, dear heart, all this means, — shall I make petition, or lament? Which is the way to make you true? For either I must have you in my chain, or you must part us two by death; there are no other new courses betwixt these. For so many God have pity on my soul, as you verily are slaying me with pains; that may you perceive from my hue without deceit. For so far have I gone toward my death, I murder myself with my privy brooding. I weep, wake, fast, for piteous sorrow over your cruelty. Naught avails; I forsake all joys that I care for, I avoid company, I flee from gladness; who may vaunt her better of heaviness than I? And into this plight you have brought me guiltless, — for that I need no witness.

And should I petition you, and cast aside womanhood? Nay, rather death than do so foul a deed and, innocent, ask mercy! What need of that? And if I lament my wretched life, you reck not; that I know, without doubt. And if I proffer you mine oaths to excuse me, a mock shall be my reward. Your manner flowers, but seeds not; full long ago I should have seen that.

For though I had you back to-morrow, I might as well withhold April from rain as hold you to make you steadfast. Almighty God, Sovereign of truth, where is the truth of men? Who has slain it? Who loves them shall find them as secure as a rotten mast in a tempest. Is that a tame beast that is fain ever to run away when he is least affrighted?

Now have mercy, sweet, if I speak amiss; have I spoken ill, I pray? I wot not; my wit is gone. I fare as the song *Chaunte-pleure;* for now I lament, and now I am mirthful. I am so astonied that I die. Arcite has carried away the key to all my world and my good chance. For in this world is no waking being in more discomfiture than I, none endures more sorrow. And if I sleep a little time, then methinks your figure stands before me, clad in the azure of constancy, to proffer again a new assurance of faithfulness and to pray me for mercy.

This wondrous vision I have through the long night, and in the day I die of fear. And of all this you reck not a whit, in sooth. Nevermore are my two eyes dry, and I call upon your pity and your faith. But alackaday! they be too far to fetch! Thus my destiny keeps me a caitiff. And my wit is so weak, it cannot stretch to direct or guide me out of this fear.

Then, since I can do no more, I end thus, and give it up now and forever. For I shall never more put my security in the scales, or learn the lore of love. But as the swan, I have long heard tell, sings in his pains before his death, so sing I here my destiny or lot, how Arcite has pierced Anelida so sore with the point of memory.

When Anelida, this woeful queen, had written in this wise with her own hand, she fell into a swoon, her face as if dead, betwixt pale and green. And then she arose and with a sorrowful visage vowed a sacrifice unto Mars within his temple, which was fashioned as ye shall now hear.

[*Unfinished*]

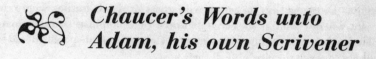

Chaucer's Words unto Adam, his own Scrivener

> Adam my scribe, if thee it ever befall
> Boece or Troilus to write anew,
> Under thy locks mayst thou have scab and scall,
> Unless after my lines thou copy true.
> So oft a day thy work I must renew,
> And criticise and rub and scrape and waste;
> And all is through thy negligence and haste.

The Former Age

A blissful life, peaceful and sweet, the peoples led in the former age. They held them content with the fruits they ate, which the fields were wont to give them. They were not pampered with excess. Unknown were the quern and the mill;

they fed on nuts, haws and such mast, and drank water from the cold spring. As yet the ground was not wounded by the plough, but corn sprang up not sown by man's hand; this they rubbed to meal, and ate not half they desired. No man had yet seen the soil turned in furrows, nor found the fire in the flint; the vine lay unpruned and uncultivated, no man as yet ground spices in a mortar to put in wine or sharp sauces. No dyer knew madder, weld or woad, the fleece remained in its first hue; no flesh knew the attack of knife or spear; man new no coin, good or bad; no ship yet cut the green and azure waves; no merchant yet fetched foreign wares.

Folk knew no trumpets for the wars, no high towers and walls square or round. Of what avail to make war? There lay no profit, there was no booty. But cursed was the time, I dare well say, when men first did their sweaty diligence to grub up metal which lurks in the dark, and first sought gems in the rivers. Alas! then sprung up all the accursed covetousness which first brought in our sorrow. These tyrants are not fain to put them in the press of battle, as Diogenes says, to win a wilderness or a few bushes where dwells poverty, where victual is so scarce and poor that naught is there but mast or apples. But where are money-bags and fat victual, there they will go and spare for no sin to assail the city with all their host.

As yet were no palace halls or chambers. In caves and woods sweet and soft slept these blessed folk in perfect peace, on grass or leaves, protected by no walls. Down of feathers, and bleached sheets, were not known to them, but in security they slept. Their hearts were as one, with no spot of soreness, and each kept his faith to other. The hauberk and the plate-mail were yet unforged. The lamb-like people, void of all sin, had no fantasy to contend against each other, but each cherished another tenderly. No pride was there, or envy, avarice, lordship, tyrannical taxation, but humility, peace, and good faith, the empress of all virtues. Jupiter the wanton, first father of delicate living, was not yet come into the world; nor had Nimrod, with lust of rule, built his lofty towers. Alas! alas! Well may men now weep and lament. For in our days is naught but covetousness and doubleness, treason and envy, poisoning, manslaughter and many a sundry murder.

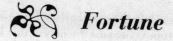 # *Fortune*

I

The Plaintiff against Fortune

This wretched world's mutability, as weal or woe, from poverty to honour, is governed by wayward Fortune, without order or wise discernment. Nevertheless, though I die, the lack of her favour shall not make me sing,

> 'T'ay tout perdu mon temps et mon labour.'

For, once for all, Fortune, I defy thee!

Yet there is left me the light of reason, whereby I may know friend from foe in thy mirror; so much thy whirling around, down and up, have taught me to know in little time. But, in sooth, no matter for thy rigour to him who has the mastery over himself. My self-sufficiency shall be mine aid: for, once for all, Fortune, I defy thee!

O Socrates, steadfast champion, she could never break thee! Thou never dreadedst her tyranny, nor foundest pleasure in her fair cheer. Thou knewest well the deceit of her fine hues, and that she prides her most in lying. I too know her to be a false dissembler: for, once for all, Fortune, I defy thee!

II

Fortune's Reply to the Plaintiff

No man is wretched, unless he deem himself so; and he who has himself has sufficiency. Why then sayst thou I am so harsh to thee, who hast thyself free from my control? Say thus, 'Gramercy for the abundance which though has lent ere this.' Why wilt thou strive? What knowest thou, how I may yet advance thee? And also thou has thy best friend yet living!

I have taught thee to know a friend in deed from a friend in appearance. Thou needst no gall of the hyena, which cures dim eyes of their pains; already though seest clearly; who wert in darkness. Still thine anchor holds, and still thou mayst come to that port where bounty carries the key to my riches: and also thou has thy best friend yet living!

How many have I refused sustenance whilst I have cherished thee in thy pleasant life! Wilt thou, then, enact a statute against me thy queen, that I shall ever be at thy command? Thou art born under my realm of variability, and thou with others must whirl around the wheel. In my teaching is more good, than evil in thine affliction. And also thou hast thy best friend yet living!

III

The Plaintiff's Reply to Fortune

I condemn thy teaching; it is but bitterness. Thou canst not rob me of my best friend, blind goddess; but that I know my fair-weather friends, for that I thank thee. Take them back, let them be put away; their niggard wealth is augury that thou wilt assail their fortress. A corrupt appetite ever goes before sickness. Everywhere this rule shall hold.

Fortune's Reply to the Plaintiff

Thou chidest my mutability, because I lent thee a drop of my riches and now am pleased to withdraw me. Why shouldst thou reproach my lordship? The sea may ebb and flow, more and less; the sky has the right to shine, rain or hail; even so may I show mine instability. Everywhere this rule shall hold.

Lo, the execution of that majestic Providence which oversees all things in righteousness, that same thing ye call *Fortune*, ye blind ignorant beasts! Heaven by nature is stable, this world is ever in restless travail; thy last day is the end of my part in thee. Everywhere this rule shall hold.

Fortune's Final Words

Princes, I pray you of your noble courtesy, let not this man thus chide and cry out upon me, and I will reward you for your trouble at my request, be there three of you or two. And, unless you list to relieve him, pray his best friend of his nobleness to help him to some better estate.

Merciless Beauty: A Triple Roundel

I

Your two bright eyes will slay me suddenly,
The beauty of them I cannot sustain,
So keenly strikes it through my heart and brain.
Unless your word will heal right speedily
Mine head's confusion and mine heart's sore pain,
 Your two bright eyes will slay me suddenly,
 The beauty of them I cannot sustain.

Upon my troth I tell you faithfully,
You of my life and death are sovereign,
And by my death the world shall see it plain, —
 Your two bright eyes will slay me suddenly,
 The beauty of them I cannot sustain,
 So keenly strikes it through my heart and brain.

II

 So has your Beauty from your bosom chaséd
 Pity, that it avails not to complain;
 For Pride fetters your Mercy in his chain.

To death all guiltless thus am I abaséd, —
I say the sooth, I have no need to feign;
 So has your Beauty from your bosom chaséd
 Pity, that it avails not to complain.

Alas that Nature in your visage placéd
Beauty so great that no man shall attain
To Mercy, though he perish for the pain!

So has your Beauty from your bosom chaséd
Pity, that it avails not to complain;
For Pride fetters your Mercy in his chain.

III

Since I from Love escapéd am so fat,
I think no more to be in prison lean;
Since I am free, I count him not a bean.

He may reply, and say or this or that;
I reck not on't, I speak right as I mean, —
   Since I from Love escapéd am so fat,
   I think no more to be in prison lean.

For evermore Love has abjured me flat,
And he for evermore is stricken clean
Out of my books, as he had never been.
   Since I from Love escapéd am so fat,
   I think no more to be in prison lean;
   Since I am free, I count him not a bean.

 ## *To Rosamond: A Ballade*

Madame, you are the shrine of all beauty, far as circles the map of the world, for you shine glorious as crystal, and your round cheeks be like ruby. Withal you are so blithesome and jocund, that when I see you dance at a merry-making, it is an ointment to my wound, though you do no dalliance to me.

For though I weep a tub full of tears, yet that woe cannot astony my heart; your seemly voice, that flows out so softly, fills my thought with joy and blessedness. So courteously I move, so bound by love, that I say to myself in my pains, it suffices me to love you, Rosamond, though you do no dalliance to me.

Never was pike so wallowed in spicy sauce as I am wallowed and immersed in love; wherefore right often I suspect myself to be true Tristram the second. My love can never cool or founder. I ever burn in amorous pleasure. Do as you list, I will be ever known your thrall, though you do no dalliance to me.

Tregentil   *Chaucer*

 # Truth

Flee from the press and dwell with truth. Let your goods suffice you, small though they be, for a hoard brings hate, and climbing insecurity, crowds bring ill-will, and everywhere prosperity brings blindness. Lust after no more than behooves you to have. You that counsel other folk, work well yourself; and truth shall make you free, doubt it not.

Be not in a tempest to make straight all that is crooked, trusting Fortune that turns like a ball. Little anxiety means great repose, and beware also of kicking against the pricks; strive not as the jug against the stones. Control yourself, who control the deeds of others; and truth shall make you free, doubt it not.

Receive submissively what is sent you; wrestling to win the world invites an overthrow. Here there is no continuing home; here is but wilderness. Forth, pilgrim, forth! Forth, beast, out of your stall! Know your true native land, look up, thank God for all things; hold the highway, let your spirit lead you; and truth shall make you free, doubt it not.

Therefore, brute-beast, leave to the world your old sorry ways; cease now to be a slave. Cry Him mercy Who of His own high goodness made you from nothing, and draw to Him most of all; pray for a common heavenly meed for you and also for others. And truth shall make you free, doubt it not.

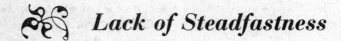

Gentilesse

What man claims to be noble must tread in the steps of Him Who was the first stock and father of nobility, and set all his wit to follow virtue and to flee vices. For unto virtue belong dignities, and not, I dare safely hold, unto iniquity, although he wear mitre, crown, or diadem.

This first stock of nobility was full of righteousness, true of His word, calm, pitiful, generous, clean in spirit, and loved honourable diligence and not the vice of sloth; and unless, like Him, His heir love virtue, he is not noble, though he seem rich, and though he wear mitre, crown, or diadem.

Vice may well be the heir to ancient wealth, but, as men may well perceive, no man can bequeath to his heir his virtuous nobleness, which is peculiar to no station, save to the Father, foremost in majesty, Who makes that man His heir who can please him, although he wear mitre, crown, or diadem.

Lack of Steadfastness

Sometime this world was so steadfast and stable that a man's word was sufficient bond; now it is so false and deceitful that, in effect, word and deed be no wise alike, for the whole world is so turned upside-down by wilfulness and corruption that all is lost for the lack of steadfastness.

Why is this world so variable, save that folk rejoice in dissension? Amongst us now a man is held for impotent unless by some conspiracy he can wrong or oppress his neighbour. What save wretched wilfulness causes all to be lost for the lack of steadfastness?

Truth is put down, reason is esteemed a fable; virtue has now no dominion,

316

pity is exiled, no man is merciful, through covetousness discernment is blinded. The world has made transmutation from right to wrong, from fidelity to instability, so that all is lost for the lack of steadfastness.

Final Words to King Richard

O prince, desire to be honourable, cherish thy folk, hate extortion! Suffer no thing to be done in thy domains that may be a reproach to thine office. Show forth thy sword of chastisement, fear God, execute the law, love fidelity and worth, and wed thy people again to steadfastness.

Chaucer's Envoy to Scogan

Shattered are the high statutes of heaven, which were created to endure eternally; for I see that the seven shining gods can wail and weep and suffer, even as a mortal creature on earth. Alas! whence can this thing come? I die almost with fear at this aberration. By the eternal word it was determined of yore that not a drop of tears should escape down from the fifth circle; but now Venus so weeps in that her sphere that she will drown us on earth.

Alas! Scogan, this is for your offence, you are cause of this pestilential deluge. Have you not said, blaspheming this goddess, through pride or extreme rashness, such things are as forbidden in love's law? That, because your lady looked not upon your pain, you gave her up therefore at Michaelmas? Alas, Scogan! never before, by man or woman, was Scogan blamed for his tongue! in scorn you called Cupid to witness for those rebellious words you spoke, wherefore he will no longer be your lord. And, Scogan, though his bow be not broken, he will not be avenged with his arrows on you, or me, or any of our figure; of him we shall have neither hurt not cure.

Yet now certes, friend, I fear ill fortune for you, lest for your guilt the vengeance of Love go forth upon all them that be hoar and round of figure, — who be folk so likely to speed in love! Then we shall have no reward for our labour.

But I well know you will answer and say, 'Lo, old Greyhead is pleased to rhyme and be merry!' Nay, Scogan, say not so, for I pray you hold me excused, God help me so! Nor, by my faith, think I ever to wake my muse into rhyme, who sleeps even as my sword rusts peacefully in my sheath! Whilst I was young I put her forth in the press. But all shall pass away that men prose or rhyme; let every man take his turn in his day.

Scogan, who kneel at the source of the stream of grace, of all honour and excellence, at the end of this stream am I, dull as if dead, forgotten in solitary wilderness. Yet, Scogan, think on Tully's *Friendship*, make mention of your friend there where it may fructify! Farewell! And look that you never again flout Love!

Chaucer's Envoy to Buckton

The Counsel of Chaucer touching Marriage, which was sent to Buckton

My master Buckton, when it was demanded of Christ, our Lord, what is truth or soothfastness, he answered not a word; as who should say, 'I know no man is all true.' Therefore, though I promised to describe the sorrow and woe that is in wedlock, I dare write no evil of it, lest I fall myself into such dotage again. I will not say how it is the chain of Satan, on which he ever gnaws, but I dare to say that, were he out of his torment, he would never again willingly be bound. But that doting fool who had rather be chained again than crawl out of prison, God let him never part from his woe, and no man bewail his case, though he weep!

Yet take a wife, lest you do worse. It is better to wed than to burn in worse manner. But all your days you shall have sorrow upon your flesh and be your wife's thrall, as wise men say. And if Holy Writ be not enough, perchance experience shall teach you that it were better to be taken prisoner in Friesland than again to fall into that trap of marriage.

This little writ, proverb or allegory, I sent you; heed it, I counsel you. He is unwise who cannot bear prosperity. If you are safe, put not yourself in jeopardy. I pray you read the Wife of Bath on this matter that we have in hand. God grant you to lead your life in freedom; full hard it is to be a bondman.

 # The Complaint of Venus

No solace is so to my mind, when I am in heaviness, as to have leisure to remember the manhood and worth, the fidelity and steadfastness, of him whose I am entirely so long as I live. No creature ought to blame me, for every creature praises his nobility.

In him is goodly kindness, wisdom, self-control, far more than any wit can devise; for good fortune has willed to advance him so far that he is the perfect treasure of knighthood. Honour itself honours him for his nobility, and Nature withal has formed him so well that I assure him I am his forever; for every creature praises his nobility.

And notwithstanding his excellency, his noble heart is so humble toward me in word, in deed, in cheer, and so diligent is he to serve me, that I am in all security. Thus I ought indeed to bless my fair fortune, since it pleases him to serve and honour me; for every creature praises his nobility.

II

Now certes, Love, it is right fitting that a person should buy thy noble gift full dearly, as by lying awake of nights, fasting at table, weeping in laughter, singing whilst lamenting, with downcast glance and visage, oft changing colour and look, lamenting in sleep, dreaming in the dance, — all the reverse of heart's content.

Jealousy be hanged by a cord! She would fain know all things by spying! A man may do naught, be it never so reasonable, but she deems it all to be evil. Thus pay we dear for love and his gifts, which oft he gives inordinately, as enough of sorrow and little delight, — all the reverse of heart's content.

A little time is his gift joyous, but full burdensome is the use of it; for subtle Jealousy, the deceitful, brings oftentimes disquietude. Thus be we ever in dread and pain, in uncertainty we languish and suffer, and right often have many a hard mischance, — all the reverse of heart's content.

III

But certes, Love, I speak not thus because I am minded to escape from thy net; for I have served thee so long that I am fain never to cease. No matter though Jealousy torment me; it suffices to see him when I can, and therefore, certes, to my ending-day I shall never repent of loving him best.

And certes, Love, when I consider all estates of men, I feel that through thy noble generosity thou has made me choose the best that ever walked on earth. Now, heart, love well, look thou never leave it. Let the jealous learn by trial that for no pains will I ever say nay; I shall never repent of loving him best.

Heart, it ought to suffice thee that Love has sent thee so high a grace, to choose the worthiest of all, the most of kin to mine own soul. Seek no further, in highway or byway, since I have found mine heart's content. Thus I end this my pensive lay; I shall never repent of loving him best.

Princess, receive in good part this complaint, addressed unto your excellent benignity after my little wit. For age has dulled my spirit, and well-nigh bereft my mind of all its subtlety in enditing; and also it is a great penance to me, since rhymes be so scarce in English, to follow word by word the curious art of Granson, the flower of poets in France.

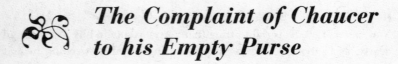

The Complaint of Chaucer to his Empty Purse

To you, my purse, and to none other creature
Lament I, for you are my lady dear.
I am so sorry now that you are light!
Certes, unless you make me heavier cheer,
I may as well be laid upon my bier.
Wherefore unto your mercy thus I cry —
Be heavy again, else certes I must die.

Vouchsafe this day, ere ever it be night,
That I the blessed chink of you may hear,
Or see your colour like the sunshine bright,
That never yet for yellowness had peer.
You are my life, mine heart you only steer,
Queen of content and of good company,
Be heavy again, else certes I must die.

Now, purse, who are to me my life's one light,
My life's one saviour, down in this world here,
Help me out of this city through your might,
Since you refuse to be my treasurer.
For I am clipped like priest or monk austere.
But yet I pray you of your courtesy
Be heavy again, else certes I must die.

O conqueror of the isle of Albion,
Who, through thy lineage, art King thereon,
And our free choice, this song to thee I sent;
Have mind, thou who canst all our woes amend,
Upon this little flower from Helicon.

 ## *Proverbs of Chaucer*

I

Why these garments manifold?
Lo this heat of summer day! —
After great heat comes the cold;
No man cast his furs away!

II

Of all this world the mighty space
Will not go in my short arms twain;
He who too much will embrace,
Little thereof he shall retain.

 ## *Against Inconstant Women*

Madame, in your love of novelty you have banished many a lover from grace. I take leave of your unsteadfastness, for well I wot so long as you live you cannot love for a full half-year in one place. Ever sharp is your appetite after new things; thus instead of blue you may wear naught but green.

Even as no image can be fixed upon a mirror, but lightly as it comes, so passes it, likewise is your love, so your deeds bear witness. No fidelity can clasp your heart, but you fare like a weathercock which turns his face with every wind, and that is manifest. Instead of blue you may wear naught but green.

For your fickleness you should be put in a pillory rather than Delilah, Criseyde or Candace; for your only constancy is in changing. That vice none can root out of your heart. If you lose one lover, you can easily acquire twain. All lightly clad for summer, — you well know what I would say —, instead of blue you may wear naught but green.

 ## *An Amorous Complaint made at Windsor*

I, who am the sorrowfullest man that ever yet lived in this world, who least know a remedy for myself, thus begin my mortal lament against her who can bring me either life or death, but has no mercy or pity on her truest lover, and slays me for my fidelity.

I can do or say naught to please you. For alack alackaday! certes it pleases you to laugh when I sigh, and thus you banish me from all my bliss. You have cast me on that pitiless isle whence never man alive can escape. This I have for loving you, dear heart. True it is, well I know by likelihood, that were it possible to estimate your beauty and goodness, I ought not to wonder though you cause me woe; since I, the unworthiest man walking on earth, durst ever place my thoughts so high, what wonder though you show me no favour!

Alas, thus is my life finished! My death, I see, is the end of it all! Well may I sing,

> 'In sorry time I spend my life!'

— bad luck to that song! For all my deadly plight, it was your old pity and mercy and mine own deep feeling that made me in all my sorrow to love you so dearly. And this in despair, I live in love, — nay but in despair I die! But shall I thus forgive you my death, who without cause torture me so? Yea, certes, I! For she is no cause of my folly, though she be cause of my death. It is not by her will that I serve her! Then since I am cause of mine own sorrow, and endure this without her wish, then right briefly in a word I may say it is no blame to her womanhood though such a wretch as I perish for her.

Yet it is ever two things slay me; her beauty, and mine eyes. So notwithstanding she is the very root of my dismay and of my death. For with one word she might heal me, if she would vouchsafe to do so. Why then joys she in my misery? It is her wont to find pleasure in seeing her servants die for her sake! But certes, then my wonder is, since she is the fairest creature that ever lived, to my wit, the benignest and also the best that nature has wrought or shall so long as the world may last, why she has left pity so behind her. It was, in sooth, a great fault in Nature. Yet, perdy, this is no defect in my lady; I would sorely blame only God or Nature. Though she show me no pity, I ought not despise my lady's sport, since she does likewise to other men. It is her pastime to laugh when men sigh; and I assent to all that gives her pleasure.

Yet, so far as I dare, I would with sorrowful heart beseech your gentle womanhood, that I might now venture to make known by words my sharp, bitter sorrow, that for once you would read my complaint, who have been right fearful lest through mine uncunning I here have said any word to displease you. As I hope for God's salvation, to me it were of all things most hateful to say a thing which might anger you. And to that day when I shall be laid in my grave you shall never find a truer servant. Though I have complained against you, forgive it me, mine own dear lady! I have ever been, and ever shall be, howsoever I journey on, either to life or to death, your humble, true man. You are to me my beginning and end, the sun which illumines the bright and shining star of love. By God and my troth, it is mine intent ever and anew to love you freshly. Live or die, I will never repent of it!

This complaint, this woful song and complaint, on Saint Valentine's day when every bird shall choose his mate, I write to her whose I am wholly and ever shall be; who never yet would receive me to mercy. And yet I will serve her for evermore and love her best, though she let me perish.

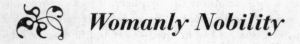

Womanly Nobility

My heart has so caught in its memory your complete beauty and steadfast self-control, all your excellencies, and your high nobility, that all my pleasure is set in serving you. So delight I in your womanly bearing, your blooming feature, your comeliness, that my heart has fully chosen you as mistress so long as I live, in true constancy, never to change for any manner of grief. And since I shall pay you this homage all my life without any grudging, serving you with all diligence, hold me somewhat in your memory. My woeful heart is in great hardship. See how humbly, with all singleness of mind, I conform my will to your ordinance, that as pleases you best you may heal my pains. Consider also how I hang in the balance in your service — lo, such is my lot! — awaiting grace, when your nobleness may be pleased to alleviate my woe, and through your pity promote me somewhat and fully abate my heaviness. And deem it to be in reason that womanly nobility should not seek to inflict extremities where it finds no disobedience.

Source of gentle breeding, lady of delights, sovereign of beauty, flower of womanhood, regard not mine ignorance, but of your kindness receive this, bethinking you that I have caught in my memory your complete beauty, your steadfast self-control.

Troilus and Criseyde

Book I

To tell the double sorrow in his love that Troilus had, son of King Priam of Troy, how his lot passed from woe to weal and afterwards to woe again, this is my purpose ere I part from you. Tisiphone, help thou me to endite these dolorous verses, that drop like tears from my pen; to thee I call, goddess of anguish, cruel Fury, ever sorrowing in pain; help me, the sorrowful instrument, that as well as I can help lovers to wail. For fitting is a dreary comrade to a woeful creature, and a sorry cheer to a sorrowful history. For I, the servant of Love's servants, dare not pray Love to speed me, though I die, so unpleasing am I, so far in the dark distance from him. But if my verse may bring gladness to any lover and avail him with his lady, to me be the travail and to him the thanks. But ye lovers that bathe in bliss, if any drop of pity be in you, remember your own past heaviness, and other folk's adversity, and think how ye too have felt Love's displeasure (or ye won him too easily), and pray for them that be in the case of Troilus, as ye shall hear, that Love may bring them to the heaven of fruition; and pray also for me to dear God that I may have might to show in Troilus' luckless lot somewhat of such pain and woe as Love's folk endure. And pray also for them that be in despair and may never be healed, and for them that be hurt by slanderous tongues, pray God of His mercy to grant them soon to pass out of this world that are in despair of Love's grace. And pray for those in joy, that God grant them ever good continuance and might so to please their ladies that it be honour and pleasure to Love's deity. For so I hope best to profit my soul, praying for Love's servants, writing their woe and living in charity, and having pity on them as if I were their own brother. Now hearken with good will, for now I go straight to my matter, where ye may hear the double sorrows of Troilus' love for Criseyde, and how in the end she forsook him.

It is well known how the valiant Greeks went armed toward Troy in a thousand ships, besieged the city nigh ten years, and wrought all their harm in diverse ways but with one intent, to avenge the ravishment of Helen done by Paris. Now it befell that there dwelt in the town a lord of great authority, a great seer named Calchas, so expert in wisdom through the replies of his god, Lord Phœbus, or Delphic Apollo, that he foreknew Troy must be destroyed. So when this Calchas knew by reckoning and also by answer of Apollo that the Greeks should bring such a force as should overthrow the city, he laid his plan to leave it anon; for well he knew by divination that Troy should be destroyed. Wherefore this prophetic sage took full purpose to depart in secret, and stole away privily to the Greeks' host, and they in courteous wise received him worshipfully and humbly, in hope that he had cunning to counsel them in every peril which they had to fear.

A clamour rose through all the town, when this was first perceived, and it was everywhere said that Calchas was fled as a traitor and allied with them of Greece; and men thought to be avenged on him that had thus falsely broken his faith, and said that he and all his kin together were worthy to be burned, skin and bone. Now in these straits and all unknowing of his false and wicked deed, Calchas had left his daughter, in much trouble, sore in dread for her life, not knowing what to do; for she was a widow and without a friend to whom to make her moan. Criseyde was this lady's name; to my belief, in all Troy-town was none so fair, for so surpassing and angelic was her beauty that she seemed a thing immortal, a heavenly perfect creature sent down in scorn of earthly nature. This lady, that heard all day in her ear of her father's shame, falseness and treason, was well-nigh out of her wit for dread and sorrow, and in her flowing widow's habit of brown samite she fell on her knees before Hector, and with piteous voice and tender weeping made her defence and begged his grace. Now this Hector was pitiful of nature, and seeing how wo-begone and fair she was, of his benignity he cheered her and said: 'Forget your father's treason, a plague on it!, and you yourself, while you list, dwell here with us in joy; and all the honour shall you have that men could do you if your father dwelt here still; and your body shall ever be protected, as far as my knowledge may go.' She thanked him with humble cheer, and would have thanked him more if he had suffered her; took her leave and kept herself quietly at home, with such household as behooved her station. As long as she dwelt in that city she observed her dignity, and was full well beloved and spoken of by young and old. But whether she had children or not I cannot learn from my books, wherefore I pass that over.

Events fell betwixt the Greeks and Trojans as they do in war; for one day they of Troy paid dearly, and another day they of Greece found the Trojans no whit soft, and thus both in turn, up and down, Fortune whirled on her wheel. But to tell all this, and how the town came to destruction, is not in my purpose; it were a long digression from my matter and would delay you too long. The events about Troy, how they befell, whosoever can may read in Homer or in Dares or in Dictys.

But though the Greeks shut in them of Troy and besieged their city all about, yet they would not leave their old usages in devoutly honouring their gods. And in especial honour they held a relic called Palladium, that was their trust above every other. And so befell in the time of April, when the mead is clothed with the new green of lusty Ver the spring, and with sweet-smelling flowers white and red, in sundry wise the folk of Troy did their old observances, as I read in the book, and held the feast of the Palladium, and to the temple went solemnly many a person to hear the service of the relic; and especially went many a lusty knight, and many a bright lady, and fair maiden high and low, full well arrayed, both for the season and the feast. Amongst other folk was Criseyde; in black widow's habit, but none the less, even as the first of our letters is now an A, so stood she first, matchless in beauty. Her goodly looks gladdened all the throng; never was seen thing more to be praised, nor under a black cloud so bright a star as was Criseyde; so said all folk that beheld her in her black weeds. And yet she stood alone behind others, full low and still, in little space and nigh the door, ever bashful and gentle, simple of attire, yet confident in eye and manner. Now Troilus, as he was wont, with his young knights, was going around and about in that broad temple ever beholding the ladies of the town; for no devotion had he to any, to lose sleep for her, but praised and censured whom he would, and as he walked about he watched keenly if any knight or squire of his retinue would sigh or let his eyes feed on any woman. Then he would smile and hold it folly, and say, She sleeps sweetly, God wot, whilst you roll and turn! Perdy, I have heard tell of your lovers' lives and your moonish devotion, and what labour you have to win love and what perplexity to keep it, and when your prey is lost, woe and dolour! You very fools, fond and blind; not one can beware by others!'

And with that word he turned up his face as if to say, 'Lo! is not this wisely said?' At which the God of Love began to lower for very ire, and planned to be avenged; and anon he showed indeed that his bow was not broken, for suddenly he hit him squarely. And still, oh blind world and purpose of man! can he pluck as proud a peacock. How often falls the event contrary to overweening and foul presumption, for caught is the proud and caught is the humble! This Troilus has climbed aloft, and little weens that he must come down. But ever fail fools' thoughts. When proud Bayard feels his corn, he skips out of the road, till the long lash hits him, and then he thinks, 'though I prance ahead first in the traces, full fat and newly clipped, yet I am but a horse, and I must endure a horse's lot and tug with my fellows.' So fared this fierce proud knight, though he were son to a noble king and deemed naught could stir his heart against his will; yet with a look his heart blazed up, so that he who but now was most lifted up with pride suddenly grew most subjected to love. Therefore, all ye wise and proud and noble, take example by this man not to scorn Love, that can so soon enthrall to him the freedom of your hearts. For ever it was and ever will be that Love can bind all things, and no man can annul the law of Nature. This ye all know, that men read of none that have had greater wit than they who have been most subdued by Love, and the strongest and highest of degree have been overcome by him. This ever was so, and is, and men shall ever see it, and truly it fits well to be so; for the wisest of all have rejoiced in love, and they most in woe have been most comforted, and often love has appeased the cruel heart and made the noble nobler of repute and caused them to dread vice and infamy. Therefore, since Love cannot well be withstood but can bind you as he will, and since he is so virtuous of nature, refuse not to be bondman to him. The staff is better than bends than that which breaks.

But to leave other collateral things, I mean to tell on my tale especially of this king's son, both of his joy and of his cold cares, and of all his deeds in this affair. This Troilus was going forth about the temple in his sport, looking now on this lady, and now on that, whether she were of the town or of the country-side, and it fell by chance that his eye pierced through a crowd and lighted on Criseyde, and there it stopped. Suddenly astonied, he began to behold her better and more carefully. 'O God-a-mercy,' thought he, 'where have you dwelt before that are so fair and goodly to see?' Therewith his heart began to swell, and he sighed, softly lest men should hear him, and then he put on again his first sportive air.

She was not among the smallest of her stature, but all her limbs answered so well to womanly perfection that never creature seemed less masculine. The very manner of her moving let a man guess her high estate and womanly nobility. Wondrous well Troilus began to like her movements and her bearing, which was a little scornful, for she let her look fall a little on one side as if to say, 'what! may I not stand here?' And after that her face brightened a little, till it seemed as if he had never seen so good a sight. There began to quicken in him so great a desire that the fixed impression of her began to fasten in his heart's bottom, and though before he had let his eye rove, he was fain then to let his horns shrink in till he scarce knew how to look. Lo! he that thought himself so wise, and scorned them that suffer love's pains, was full unaware that Love dwelt within the subtle beams of her eyes, until with her look he seemed suddenly to feel the spirit die in his heart. Blessed be Love than can thus convert men! Thus he stood to behold her in her black garb, nor made a sign nor said a word to tell his desire or why he stood thus. To maintain his former air he sometimes cast his look on other things, and then once more on her, as long as the service lasted, and afterwards, wellnigh confounded, he went softly out of the temple repenting that he had ever jested at Love's folk, lest the load of mockery should fall on himself; but he hid his woe, lest it should be known on any side.

When he had thus gone from the temple, he straight returned to his palace, shot through with her look as with a dart. Yet still he feigned joyousness, and brightened all his visage and speech, and ever smiled at Love's servants, saying, 'Lord! how joyously you lovers live! As often woe as weal betides the cunningest of you, that serves most attentively. Your hire is paid you; but how, God wot! Not well for well, but scorn for good service. In faith, your order is nobly ruled. All your rites may prove in vain, save for a few pitiful matters; and yet no faith demands such devotion as yours, you know full well. And that is not the worst, by my troth, but if I told you the worst point, however truly I spoke you would chide at me. But consider this, whatever with the best intent you do or leave undone, full often your lady will misconstrue and take it ill. If she be wroth, for any reason, you will have a groaning-time. Ah, happy is he that can be one of you!'

But for all this talk he held his peace when he could; love began so to lime his feathers that he was scarce able to feign to his retinue that he was oppressed by other cares. He knew not what to do for woe, and bade his men go where they would. When he was alone in his chamber, he sat down upon his bed's foot, first sighed and then groaned, and thought so constantly on her that, as he sat there broad awake, his spirit dreamed he saw her in the temple, and began newly to consider the manner of her looking, and thus he began to make a mirror of his mind in which he saw all her form. He found it in his heart to grant that it was a happy fortune for him to love such a one, and if he strove to serve her he might win her grace or at least be among her followers. And so he reflected that neither travail nor vexation, borne for so goodly a lady, could be thrown away or shame him, even though it were known, but he should be honoured and exalted by all lovers more than before. Thus he reasoned at the beginning of his love, all unaware of his woe to come; and thus he took his purpose to follow love's trade, but at first to keep his work privy and hide his desire from every living being, unless he might be advanced by letting it be known some time, remembering that love too widely blown abroad yields bitter fruit, though the seed be sweet. And he thought of much more, — what to speak, what to hold in, and how to bring her to love him. So he straightway began to indite a song, and to triumph over his sorrow, and with good hope he fully assented to love Criseyde and not repent. I will give every word of his song, save for the difference of our tongues, not only the substance, as mine author Lollius does; and whoso will hear it may find it in these next verses.

> If Love is not, ah God! what feel I so?
> And if Love is, what manner of thing is he?
> If Love be good, from whence then comes my woe?
> If he be ill, wondrous it seems to me
> That every torment and adversity
> Which comes of him I can so joyous think;
> For ever I thirst, the more from him I drink.
>
> And if 'tis in mine own delight I burn,
> From whence then comes my wailing and complaint?
> Rejoicing, why to tears do I return?
> I wot not, nor, unweary, when I faint.
> Oh living death, oh sweet harm strange and quaint!
> How can this harm and death so rage in me,
> Unless I do consent that it so be?
>
> And if I do consent, I wrongfully
> Bewail my case; thus rolled and shaken sore
> All rudderless within a boat am I
> Amid the sea and out of sight of shore,
> Betwixt two winds contrary evermore.
> Alas, what is this wondrous malady?
> For heat of cold, for cold of heat, I die.

To the god of Love he said with devout voice, 'Lord, now thine is my spirit, as it ought to be. I thank thee, Lord, that hast brought me to this. Whether she be a woman or a goddess that thou makest me serve, verily I know not, but as her man I will ever live and die. Thou standest mightily in her eyes as in a place fit for thy power. Wherefore, Lord, if my service or I may please thee, be gracious to me; for my royal estate here I resign into her hand and full humbly become her man and make her my lady.'

The fire of love (God save me from it!) deigned not to spare his royal blood, his might or his prowess, but held him low in thralldom, and burned him so ever anew in sundry wise that sixty times a day he grew pale. Day by day so grew his delight in thinking of her that he set at naught every other care, and full often, thinking to allay his heat, he would strive to see her goodly face. But ever the nearer he was, the more he burned; the nearer the fire, the hotter, as all this company knows. But far or near, by night or day, for wisdom or folly, I promise you, his heart, which was the eye of his mind, was ever on her, who was fairer to see than ever his Helen or Polyxena. Not an hour of the day passed that he said not to himself a thousand times, 'Goodly one whom I labour to serve as best I can, now would to God, Criseyde, you would pity me before I die. Alas, dear heart! my health and cheer and life are lost unless you pity me.'

All other fears were fled from him, both of the siege and for his own safety, and no other desires bred in him but tender yearnings to that one object, that she should have compassion on him and he might be her man for life; lo, herein stood his life! The fell deeds of arms of Hector or his other brethren moved him not at all, and yet wherever men went he was found among the best and remained the longest where peril was, and did such feats of arms that it was a marvel to think of, till as he thus won renown in arms all the Greeks dreaded him like death. Yet all this was not for hatred to the Greeks, not yet for the defence of the town, but only that his fame might please her the better. From this time love bereft him of his sleep and made his meat his foe, and his pains so increased that, if one noted him well, they showed in his face. Lest men should divine that the fire of love was burning him, he feigned other sickness and said he had a fever and it went hard with him. How it was I cannot say, whether his lady understood not all this, or feigned she did not, one of the two; but at all events I find in the book that she seemed to reck not of him nor of his pain or what was in his mind. This Troilus felt such woe that he was wellnigh mad, for his dread was ever this, that she so loved some other man that she would never take heed of him, for which he seemed to feel his heart bleed. Nor durst he tell a word of his woe, even to win all the world. When he felt a little lightening of his grief, full often he would lament thus with himself, 'O fool! now you are in the snare, who used to mock at love's tortures. Now you are caught; you may gnaw your own chains. You were wont to reproach lovers for a thing from which you cannot defend yourself. If this be known, what will every lover say of you except ever to laugh you to scorn behind your back, and say, "There he goes, that sapient sir that held us lovers in such low esteem! Now, God be thanked, he goes in the dance of those whom Love will promote but little." But ah, woful Troilus! since you are ordained to love, would God that you had lighted on one who might know all your woe, though she had no pity; but your lady is as cold in love toward you as frost beneath a winter moon, and you melt away like snow in fire. Would God I were already arrived in the port of death, to which my sorrow will bring me; Lord, it were a comfort to me! Then I should be quit of languishing in fear. For if my hidden sorrow should be blown abroad, I shall be mocked a thousand-fold more than any fool on whose folly men make rhymes. But now God help me, and you too, sweet, by whom Love has caught me, — yes, never man so fast. Mercy, dear heart! save me from death, for more than my life I will love you to the end. Cheer me with some friendly look, though you may never promise aught else.'

These words he spoke and full many another, and ever in his complaint called on her name, till he nigh drowned in salt tears; but all was for naught, she heard not his lament, and when he thought on the folly of such doings, his woe multiplied a thousand-fold.

Once, whilst he was thus bewailing himself alone in his chamber, a friend of his that was name Pandarus came in unawares, and heard him sigh and saw his distress. 'Alas!' quoth he, 'who is the cause of all this to-do? Merciful God! what evil has happened? Have the Greeks made you grow lean as soon as this? Or have you some remorse of conscience and are fallen into devoutness and bewail your sins, and are frightened into an access of attrition? What an honour to the besiegers of our town, that they can pack away the jollity of our lusty folk, and bring them to holiness!' These words he said to anger him, that anger might drive out his sorrow for the time, and arouse his spirit, for well he knew that the ends of the earth was not a man greater hardihood nor more desirous of honour.

'What chance,' quoth Troilus, 'has guided you to see me languishing here, rejected by every creature? But for the love of God, hear my request and go away, for in faith the sight of my dying will pain you, and die I must; therefore go away. But if you fancy that I am thus sick out of fear, mock me not, for it is not so. It is another thing, far more than the Greeks have done, which makes me grieve and pine to death. Be not wroth though I tell it not right now; I hide it for the best.'

This Pandarus, nigh melting for sorrow and pity, said full often, 'Alas! what may this be? Now, friend,' quoth he, 'if ever love or faith had been betwixt you and me, be not so cruel as to hide so great a care from your friend. Know you not that it is I, Pandarus? If I can do you no comfort, at least I can share your pain with you, as it is a friend's right to do with pain and pleasure. I have loved you all my life through wrong and right, and ever shall through true or false report. Then hide not your woe from me, but tell it straightway.'

Then began this sorrowful Troilus to sigh, and 'God grant it be best,' he said, 'to tell it you; for since you wish it so, tell it I will, though my heart burst. Well I wot you can give me no ease, but lest you deem that I trust you not, hearken, friend, for thus it stands. Love, against which stoutest defence least avails, so sore assails me with despair that my heart is driving straight upon the rocks. Desire assails me so burningly that I would rather be slain than be king of Greece and Troy together. Let this that I have said suffice, my faithful friend Pandarus, for now you know my woe, which I have told to no other. For the love of God, hide well my cold care, for many a harm might follow if it were known. Do you live in gladness, and leave me to die to my distress, unregarded.'

'Why have you thus unkindly hidden this from me so long, fool that you are?' quoth Pandarus. 'Peradventure your longing may be for such a one that my judgment may help us.'

'That,' quoth Troilus, 'were a wondrous thing; you that could never guide yourself well in love, how, a Devil! can you bring me to bliss?'

'Yea, Troilus, now hearken,' quoth Pandarus; 'though I be foolish yet it often happens that one who through excess has come to grief by good counsel may keep his friend therefrom. I have seen a blind man walk safe, where he fell who could look afar. A fool can often guide a wise man. A whetstone is no carving-instrument, yet it sharpens them. Eschew that wherein I have gone astray, and learn wisdom in my school, for so will your wit be well employed. All things are understood through their contraries. For how could the sweet ever have been known by him who had never tasted the bitter? No man may be truly glad, I believe, that was never in distress. White set by black and same by honour, each shows forth more, as all men know. Then since so much may be learned from contraries, I, that have so often fared grievously in love, ought to know how to counsel you in your dismay. Nor should you be ill-pleased though I desire to bear with you your heavy load, — it will hurt the less. Well I know that it fares with me as a shepherdess named Œnone wrote to your brother Paris in a lament; you saw the letter she wrote, no doubt?'

'Nay, never yet,' quoth Troilus.

'Now hearken,' said Pandarus, 'it was thus. "Phœbus, that first invented the art of medicine, knew remedies of herbs for every man's hurt; yet for himself his cunning was all barren, for love toward the daughter of King Admetus had so bound him in a snare that all his craft could not remedy his sorrow." So fare I, alack for me! I love one best, and win nothing but dole. Yet perchance I can counsel you, though not myself; twit me no more. I have no cause to soar and sport like a hawk, yet I can tell somewhat for your help. And of one thing you may be right certain, that I shall never betray you, though I die upon the rack; nor, by my troth, care I to dissuade you from your love, though I knew it were for your brother's wife Helen. Be she what she may, love her still. Therefore trust me fully as your friend, and tell me plainly your affair and final cause of woe. Fear not at all that my intent now is to reprove you, for no creature may forbid a man to love till he list to leave it. Know well that each is an error, to mistrust all and to confide in all, but to take the mean is wisdom; for to trust some one will test and prove his fidelity, and therefore I would fain correct your wrong conceit, and make you trust some person and tell him your woe. Therefore tell me, if you will. The wise man says, "Woe to him that is alone, for if he falls he has none to help him rise." Since you have a friend, tell him all. For the most helpful way to win love, in verity, as wise men will tell you, is not to wallow and weep like Queen Niobe, whose tears can yet be seen in marble. Leave your dreary weeping and let us lighten your woe with other talk, that your woeful hours may seem shorter. Delight not to search woe for more woe, like these fools in ill luck who add to their sorrows by other sorrow and care not to seek for cure. Men say misery loves company; that we ought to grant, for both you and I complain of love. So full of sorrow am I that no more ill luck can perch on me, because there is no room for it. God grant you be not afraid of me, lest I beguile you of your lady! You wot well whom I love as best I can, long time past. And since you know I speak from no wiliness, and since I am he whom you most trust, tell me somewhat. You know all my woe.'

Yet for all this Troilus spoke not a word, but for long lay still as if he were dead; then he started up with a sigh and lent his ear to Pandarus's voice, and rolled up his eyes till Pandarus feared lest he should fall into madness or die on the spot.

'Awake,' cried Pandarus sharply; 'what! are you slumbering in a lethargy, or are you like an ass at the sound of a lute, that hears when men ply the strings but no melody can sink into his mind to gladden him, because he is so dull in his beastly nature?'

With that Pandarus ceased his talk, but Troilus as yet answered not a word, for it was not his intent to tell any man for whose love he fared so ill. For it is said, 'a man often makes the rod with which he is beaten,' as these wise men discourse, especially in telling one's counsel in affairs of love that ought to be secret. Of itself it will come out soon enough unless it be warily guarded, and sometimes it is a good craft to seem to flee that which in truth a man eagerly hunts. All this Troilus turned over in his heart. But nevertheless, when he heard him cry 'Awake!', he began to sigh sore, and said, 'Friend, though I lie

336

still I am not deaf. Now peace, and no more shouting! I have heard your words and your lore, but suffer me to bewail my ill hap, for your proverbs cannot help me, nor know you any other cure for me; and I wish not to be cured, I wish to die. What know I of the queen Niobe? Let be your old ensamples, I beg.'

'Yea,' quoth Pandarus, 'therefore I say fools delight to bewail their woe and care not to seek remedy. Now I know that your reason fails you. But tell me, if I knew who she were for whom you have all this misadventure, durst you that I told her your woe in her ear, since you dare not yourself, and besought her to have some pity on you?'

'Why, no,' quoth he, 'by my troth!'

'What!' quoth Pandarus, 'not though I did it as earnestly as though I thought mine own life lay at stake?'

'No, brother, certes,' said Troilus.

'And why?'

'Because you should never speed.'

'Know you that well?'

'Yea, that is beyond a doubt,' said Troilus; 'for all that ever you can do she will not be won for such a wretch as I.'

'Alas, how can this be,' quoth Pandarus, 'that you are thus causeless in despair? What, is not your lady still alive? *Benedicite!* How know you that you can have no grace? Such trouble is not always beyond hope! Why, make not your cure thus impossible, for things to come are often uncertain! I grant that you endure as sharp a woe as Tityus in hell, whose stomach the fowls called vultures evermore tear, as we read in books. But I cannot endure that you remain in so unreasonable a thought as that there is no cure for your woe. With your coward heart and ire and foolish wilfulness, your despair will not even suffer you to tell of your smart, or so much as help yourself by giving a reason, but you lie as one indifferent to all the world. What woman can love such a wretch? If you die thus and she know not why it is, what can she deem but that you have given up the ghost through fear because the Greeks besiege us? Lord, much thanks you will win in this way! "The wretch is dead," she will say, and all the town to boot, "the Devil have his bones!" You may weep here alone and cry and kneel twenty winters. Give a woman love that she knows not of, and she will give you a reward that you shall not feel. Unknown is unkissed, unsought is lost. What! many a man has paid full dearly for love that his lady has known of, yea, for twenty winters, and never yet has he kissed his lady's mouth. What! should he fall into despair for this, or be a recreant, or slay himself, be she never so fair? Nay, nay! ever alike he shall be fresh and gay for the service of his dear heart's queen, and think that only to serve her is a guerdon a thousand-fold more than he merits.'

And of that word Troilus took heed, and anon thought of his folly and how Pandarus spoke sooth, that in slaying himself he could gain naught, but only do an unmanly act and a sin, if his lady knew naught of the cause; for full little of his woe she knew, God wot! With that thought he sighed and said, 'Alas, what is best for me to do?'

To which Pandarus answered, 'So please you, the best is that you tell me all your troubles; and by my troth, unless you find that I can medicine you before many days, you may have me torn in pieces and afterwards hanged!'

'Yes, so you may say,' quoth Troilus, 'but alas! that makes it not true, God wot. It is full hard to help a man when Fortune is his foe. All the men that live and breathe cannot withstand the harm wrought by her cruel wheel, for as she list she plays with bond and free.'

Quoth Pandarus, 'You are wroth, and so blame Fortune; now I begin to understand. Know you not that every manner of person is subjected to Fortune in some degree? And yet you have this comfort, that as her joys must pass, so must her sorrows; for if her wheel ceased one moment to turn, anon she should cease to be Fortune. Now how know you, since her wheel may not tarry, that her mutability will not do by you as you desire, or she may not be about to help you? Perchance you have cause for singing! Know you, then, what I counsel you? Let be your woe and downcast looks, for he who will have healing must first reveal his wound unto his leech. Though your grief were for my own sister, may I be tied forever to Cerberus in hell but she should be yours to-morrow if she were mine to give. Look up, I say, and tell me anon who she is, that I may go about your business. If I know her at all, I shall hope to speed the sooner. As you love me, tell me if I do.'

Now began Troilus' vein to bleed, for he was hit. 'Aha! here begins some sport,' said Pandarus, when he saw him wax all red for shame; and with that word he began to shake him. 'Thief, you shall tell her name.'

Troilus began to tremble as though men were leading him to hell. 'Alas!' said he, 'my sweet foe, the wellspring of my grief, is named Criseyde!' And with that word he wellnigh gave up the ghost for dread.

When Pandarus heard her name, Lord! he was glad. 'Dear friend,' said he, 'this goes well! In Jove's name, Love has placed you well. Be of good cheer! For good name, discretion and fair demeanour, she has enough of them, and of gentle blood. If she be fair, you know yourself, I dare say! A more bounte-ous I never saw for one of her station, nor a gladder, nor of speech friendlier, nor one who had more of Heaven's grace for doing well, or had less need to seek what to do; and as for honour, to crown it all, as far as her might may go, a king's heart seems by hers a wretch's. And therefore look you be of good comfort, for certainly in a noble and well-regulated temper the first point is this, — that a man should have peace with himself. In truth you ought to have, for there is nothing but good in loving well a worthy object. You ought to call it chance, but the grace of God. And also gladden yourself by thinking that since your lady has all virtues, she must have some pity amongst them; but see also that you seek nothing which is against her fair repute, for virtue stretches not itself as far as to shame.

'But right glad I am that I have lived to see your love bestowed so well, for by my troth I durst have sworn that never so fair a grace in love would have betided you. You were wont to check at Love in scorn and call him "Saint Idiot, Lord of all fools." How often have you prated and said that Love's servants, for folly, were verily God's apes, and some would take to their solitary beds, and munch their meat groaning, and another had the green-sickness, and you would pray God that he might die of it! And some of them, for the cold in bed, would put over them more than they needed, so you would often say; and some would often feign and tell how they had watched when in truth they had slept full sweetly. Thus they strove to rise, yet were underneath at last; so you would say in your japing; and that for the more part these lovers will be ever speaking, and that a sure safeguard against failing is to try everywhere. Now I can jape on you as much as I will; but I will go to the stake on it that you were none of these last ones! Now beat your breast and say to your god, "Grant me thy grace, Lord, for now I am in love, and repent me if I ever spoke ill." Thus you must say with all your heart.'

'Ah, Lord!' quoth Troilus, 'I consent, and pray that thou forgive my gibes, and I will do so no more whilst I live.'

'Well said,' quoth Pandarus, 'and now I hope you have appeased the god's wrath; and since you have wept many a drop and spoken to your god's pleasure, would to God you might be relieved! Trust well that she from whom all your woe arises may hereafter be your comfort also. The same ground that bears ill weeds bears also these wholesome herbs, and next the foul nettle, rough and thick, waxes, sweet and smooth and soft, the rose; next the valley is the hill on high, next the dark night the glad morrows, next the end of grief is joy. Hold your bridle even loose enough and let things go their natural course, or all our labour is thrown away.

> "He hasteth well that wisely can abide."

Be diligent, faithful and privy, be merry, liberal and persevering in your service, and all will be well. But he that is distributed into every place, as wise clerks write, is whole nowhere. What wonder if such a one speed not? Some love fares as if one should plant a tree or herb and pull it up straightway on the morrow. No wonder that it never thrives. Since the god of love has bestowed you in a place equal to your own worth, stand fast; you have sailed into a good port. Have ever good hope, in spite of the heaviness of your spirits; for, unless over-haste or your low spirit spoil our work, I hope to make a good end of this. Know you why? I am the less afraid to treat of this matter with my niece because I have heard from old clerks that there was never man or woman begotten yet that was not ready to suffer love's heat, either celestial or natural. Therefore I hope to find grace for you. As to her, with her beauty and youth, it fits her not yet, though she could and would, to be celestial; but right well it fits her to love and cherish a worthy knight. If she did it not, I hold it for a fault. Therefore I am now and ever ready to strive to do you this service; hereafter I hope to have the thanks of both of you for it, for you both are prudent and can so keep counsel that no man shall be the wiser, and so we all three may be gladdened. By my troth, now I have formed a good conceit of you in my wit! Since Love, of his goodness, has converted you from your sin, you shall be the best pillar of all his faith, I believe, and most harass his foes. See as an ensample now these great clerks that err most deadly against the faith, and are converted from their wicked deeds, through the grace of God that draws them to Him, — then are they the most God-fearing of folk, and strongest in faith, and can better than others withstand error.'

When Troilus had heard Pandarus consent to help him in winning Criseyde's love, his woe left tormenting him, and hotter waxed his love; and then he said, with sober face though his heart danced, 'Now may blessed Venus so help that before I die I may deserve some thanks of you, Pandarus! But, dear friend, how shall my woe be less till this is finished? And tell me this, what will you say of me and my pain? Most of all I dread lest she be wroth and will not hear or believe it.'

'You have a full great care,' quoth Pandarus, 'lest the churl should fall out of the moon! Lord, but I hate your foolish going-on! Why, attend to your own part of it! For God's love, I bid you one boon, and that is to let me alone; you will fare the better!'

'Why friend,' quoth Troilus, 'now do as you will! But hark to one word, Pandarus; I would not that you should suspect me in any such wantoness as that I would desire of my lady aught that tends to evil or baseness. For, believe me, I would rather die than she should fancy of me aught but what might tend to virtue.'

Then laughed this Pandarus, and answered anon, 'And I your surety? Fie, every lover speaks thus! Would that she had been standing by and had heard how you spoke! But farewell; I will go. Adieu, and be glad. God speed us both! Give me this anxious task, and of my success be the sweet fruit yours.'

Then Troilus fell on his knees and caught Pandarus tightly in his arms. 'Now fie on all the Greeks!' he said. 'Soon or late, God will help us, and, if my life hold out, before God some of them shall smart. And yet I am right sorry that this vaunt has escaped me. Now, Pandarus, I can say no more; but you are wise, — you know, you have the power, you are my all. All my life and death I lay in your hand! Help me now!'

'Yes, by my troth,' quoth Pandarus.

'God reward you, friend! And this especially,' said Troilus; 'keep me in her mind who may command me to the death.'

This Pandarus, all zealous to aid his dear friend, said, 'Farewell, and be assured I will deserve your thanks; and that you shall see, and here I pledge my troth.' And so he went his way, thinking how he might best beseech her for grace, and how he might find a time therefore. For a creature that has a house to build runs not to begin the work with hasty hand, but will bide a while, and send out his heart's line to measure how to begin upon his plan. All this thought Pandarus in his heart, and laid out his work full prudently ere he began it.

But as for Troilus, no longer he lay flat; anon up on his bay steed to play the lion in the field, till woe was the Greek who met him that day! And in the town thenceforth so goodly was his manner, and got him so much favour, that every one loved him that looked on his face. For he became the friendliest man, the gentlest and also the most generous, the most prudent, and in a word one of the best knights that lived. Dead was his cruel mocking, his high port and haughty manner, and each fault he exchanged for a virtue. And so let us leave Troilus for a season, who fares like a man sore hurt, who is somewhat relieved of the aching of his wound, but is healed none the more for that and abides the instruction of him who goes about his cure. So thus he awaits what may betide.

Book II

O wind, O wind, the weather begins to clear, and carry our sail out of these black waves. For in this sea my boat labours so that my cunning scarce can guide it. This sea I call the tempestuous despair that Troilus had been in, but now begin the Calends of hope. O lady mine Clio, be my Muse and my speed henceforth to rhyme well this book till I have done it! I need here none other art but thine. And so I excuse me to every lover; for I indite this out of no strained sentiment of mine own, but turn it out of Latin into mine own tongue. And so for all this work I desire neither thanks nor censure, but I pray you meekly to hold me free if any word be lame, for as my author said, even so say I. And though I speak of love without due feeling, it is no wonder, for it is nothing new that a blind man cannot judge in colours. You know too that in a thousand years there is a change in the forms of speech, and words which then were words of price seem to us now wondrous trivial and strange; yet they spake them so, and they sped as well in love then as men do now. And in sundry ages and lands sundry are the usages to win love. And therefore if it happen that any lover in this place hear how the story describes Troilus' coming into his lady's favour, and thinks, 'not so would I procure love,' or wonders at his speech or his doings, — I know how it may be, but to me it is no wonder. Every person who goes to Rome holds not one and the same road. In some lands all the sport were spoiled if men in love did even as men do here, as, for instance, in frank conduct or looks, in visiting, in the forums they follow, or in saying their say. Therefore men say each country has its own usages. And even in this place there are scarce three who have said and done quite alike in love; this way may please that man, that may please this. Yet there is naught that may not have been said by one or another, even as one graver may choose to grave in wood, and one on a stone wall, as it may betide. But since I have begun, I will go on and follow mine author as well as I can.

In May, the mother of glad months, when fresh flowers that winter killed are quickened again, blue, red and white, and balmy breaths float over every mead, when Phœbus from the white Bull lavishes his bright beams, — it so betided, as I shall sing, on the third day of May, that Pandarus too, for all his wise speech, felt his share of love's keen shots, which made his hue full pale, preached he never so well on love. That day a reverse in love befell him, for which he went to bed in woe and tossed and turned full oft ere day. When morning came the swallow Progne began to make her lament with a sorrowful lay, how she was metamorphosed; and ever lay Pandarus a-bed half in slumber till she made her chattering so nigh him, how Tereus carried her sister away, that with the noise he awoke, and called out and prepared to rise. He remembered his errand and his undertaking for Troilus; he knew that the moon was in a propitious place for his emprise, and he made his plan and took his way anon to his niece's palace hard by. Janus, god of entrance, guide him!

When he came thither, 'Where is my lady?' said he to her folk. They told him, and in he went and found her sitting with two other ladies in a paved parlour; they three were hearing a maiden read them the romance of the siege of Thebes.

'Madame, God save you,' quoth Pandarus, 'with your book and all the company.'

'Eh, uncle! welcome now heartily,' said she, and up she rose and took him quickly by the hand, and said, 'Last night I dreamed thrice of you — may it turn to good!,' and with that word she set him down on a bench.

'Yea, niece, you shall fare the better for it all this year, please God,' said Pandarus. 'But I am sorry I have stayed your listening to the book that you honour thus. For God's love, what says it? Tell us now, is it of love? Let me learn some good from you.'

'Uncle,' said she, 'your mistress is not here,' whereat they all began to laugh; and then she said, 'This romance that we read is of Thebes; and we have heard how King Laius died through Œdipus his son, and all those deeds; and here we stopped at these red letters, where the book tells how the bishop Amphiaraus fell through the ground to hell.'

'I know about all that,' quoth Pandarus, 'and all the siege of Thebes and all the woe, for thereof is a poem written in twelve books. But let be all this, and tell me how you do. Put off your wimple and show your face bare; put away your book and rise up, and let us dance and do some honour to May.'

'Eh, God forbid!' said she; 'are you mad? Is that a life for a widow? You make me fearful for you, you talk so wildly that you must be raving! It would fit me better to pray ever in a cave and read holy saints' lives. Let maids dance, and young married folk!'

'And yet,' said Pandarus, 'I could tell you a thing to make you dance.'

'Now, uncle dear, tell it for God's love; is the siege over? I am so afeared of the Greeks that I die of it.'

'Nay, nay,' said he, 'it is something better than five such.'

'Yea? Holy God!' said she, 'what thing is it then? What, better than five such? Eh, no, surely! For all this world I cannot fancy what it should be. Some mock, I believe. Unless you tell me yourself my wit is all too thin to guess it. God help me so, I wot not what you speak of.'

'But I pledge you my word, never shall this thing be told you, for all me.'

'And why so, uncle mine? Why so?'

'By God,' quoth he, 'that will I tell you anon. It is because, if you knew it, there would be no prouder woman alive in all the town of Troy, — as I hope to be saved, I jest not.'

Then she began to wonder a thousand-fold more than ever, and cast down her eyes, for never since she was born desired she so much to know a thing. But at last with a sigh she said, 'Now, uncle mine, I will not displease you, nor vex you with asking;' so with many lively words and friendly tales and merry cheer they talked of this and that, and went far away into many a rare matter, merry or deep, as friends do when they have met; till she came to ask him how Hector fared, the bulwark of the town and scourge of the Greeks.

'Full well, I thank God,' answered Pandarus, 'save that he has a little wound in his arm; and so does his lusty brother Troilus. He is a wise and worthy second Hector, full of all virtues, fidelity and nobility, prudence, honour, generosity and valour.'

'In good faith, uncle,' said she, 'I am glad to hear that they fare well. God save them both! Truly it is a great joy to see a king's son doing well in arms, and of good traits besides. For great power and moral virtue are seldom seen in one person on this earth.'

'In good faith, that is sooth,' answered Pandarus. 'But by my troth the king has two sons, Hector and Troilus, who are as void of vices as any men under the sun. Their mightiness is full widely known. It needs tell naught of Hector; in all this world is no better knight than he who is well of all worthiness. And he has yet more virtue than strength, and that many a wise and worthy person knows. And the same praise can I give Troilus. So may God help me, I know not such another pair!'

'By God, that is true of Hector,' quoth she, 'and of Troilus I can well believe the same; for men tell that he does so valiantly in arms day by day, and bears himself so gently here at home to every creature, that he has all praise of those by whom it were liefest to me to be praised.'

'You say right sooth,' said Pandarus, 'for whoso had been with him yesterday might have wondered at Troilus. For never yet flew so thick a swarm of bees as the Greeks that fled from him. Throughout the field in every man's ear was no cry but "There is Troilus!" Here, there, he hunted them so hard there was naught but Greek blood and Troilus! This one he hurt, that one he overthrew, and so it was wherever he went. He was their death and our shield and life. That day, so long as he grasped his bloody sword, none durst withstand him. And add to all this, he is the friendliest man of great station that ever I saw in my life, to such as he thinks likely to deserve honour.' And with that word Pandarus took his leave, — 'I will go hence.'

'Nay, then, I must be to blame,' said she then; 'what ails you to be so soon weary, and especially of us women? What will you? Nay, sit you down! By God, I have something more to say to you, to ask your counsel ere you go.'

Then every person about who heard that began to withdraw a little, whilst they two said their say. And when their talk was ended, of her plight and her conduct, Pandarus said, 'Now it is time I went. But yet, I say, arise and let us dance, and cast your widow's habit to the Devil! Why will you thus disfigure yourself, since so glad a chance has betided you?'

'Ah, well thought of' quoth she. 'For the love of God, am I not to know what you mean concerning this?'

'No, this thing needs leisure,' said he, 'and also it would grieve me much if I told it and you took it amiss. It were better for me to hold my tongue than say a sooth that should be against your liking. For by the goddess, Minerva, niece, whom I serve, you are the woman living in this world who, I believe verily, aside from passion, I best love and am loathest to grieve; and that you know yourself, I think.'

'Gramercy in truth, mine uncle,' said she, 'I have ever felt your friendship. To no man am I so bound as to you, and have repaid so little. By the grace of God, to the extent of my wit, I shall never knowingly offend you; and if I ever have, I will reform! But I beseech you, for the love of God, as you are he whom I most trust and love, let be your distant manner of speech, and say to me your niece what you have in mind.'

And with that word anon her uncle kissed her and said, 'Gladly, sweet dear niece; and do you take well what I shall say to you here.' With that she began to cast down her eyes, and Pandarus to cough a little, and he said, 'You know, niece, that after all, however some men may please to endite their tales with subtle art, the tales are meant for some clear end. And since the force of every tale is in its end, and since this matter is so advantageous, why should I colour it highly or draw it out at length to so faithful a friend as you?' And with that word he began right intently to gaze on her face and said, 'Now fair fortune on such a mirror!'

Then he thought, 'If I frame my tale in hard terms, or make a long story, she will find but little savour in it, and will believe I mean to beguile her. Tender wits fancy all things to be wily which they cannot plainly understand. So I will strive to suit my tale to her wit.'

She saw that he gazed upon her earnestly, and said, 'Lord! how hard you stare! Saw you me never before this! What say you! No?'

'Yes, yes,' quoth he, 'and shall better yet before I leave! But by my troth, I was only thinking whether fortune loves you, for now men shall see it. For to every man some goodly adventure is ordained at some time, if he can receive it; but if he will pay no heed to it when it comes, but wilfully slights it, why, it is neither chance nor fortune that deceives him, but only his own sloth and wretchedness. Such a creature is to blame, by my soul! You, fair niece, have full lightly found such a good adventure, if you are able to receive it. For the love of God, and of me, catch at it straightway, lest opportunity pass! Why should I make a longer tale of it? Give me your hand; for, if you but will, there is not in this world a creature so favoured. Since I am speaking with good intent, as I have told you, already, and love your honour and fair name as well as any creature born in this world, — by all the oaths that I have sworn to you, if you are wroth at this, or fancy I lie, I will never see you again. Be not aghast and tremble not! Why should you? Change not colour so for fear, for in truth the worst is over! And though my tale now seem strange, have good trust that you shall always find me faithful. Were it a thing I thought unfitting, I should bring you no such tidings.'

'Now, my good uncle, for God's love I pray you,' quoth she, 'make haste and tell me what it is, for I am both aghast to know what you will say, and beside myself with longing. Whether it be well or be amiss, say on! Let me not stay forever in this fear!'

'So I will; now hearken and I shall tell. Now, my niece, the king's dear son, the good, the prudent, the valiant, the lusty, the generous, that mirror of well-doing, the noble Troilus, so loves you that unless you help him it will be his death. Lo, this is all! What more can I say? Do what you will, let him live or die; but if you let him die, I will die too; here is my pledge that I lie not, though I should have to cut my throat with this knife!' With that the tears burst from his eyes, and he said, 'If you will make us both die thus guiltless, a fair fishing you have made! How mend you your own fortune if we both miscarry? Alas! that loyal man, my own dear lord, that noble gentle knight, who asks for nothing but a friendly look from you, I see him slowly dying as he walks about, and making all speed to be slain, if fortune will but grant it. Alas, that God sent you such beauty! If you are in truth so cruel that you reck no more of the death of so true and worthy a man than of the death of a wretch or a mocker, if you are such, your beauty cannot make amends for so cruel a deed. It were well to consider ere the pinch comes. Woe worth the fair gem without virtue, and the herb that can cure nothing! Woe worth ruthless beauty, and the creature that treads all others down; and you that are top and root of beauty, if there be no truth in you as well, by my troth you were better dead.

'But believe me, this is no crafty lure. I had liefer that you and I and he were hanged so high that all men might look on us, than that I should be his bawd. I am your uncle; the shame were to me as well as to you should I abet or assent to his hurting your honour. Now understand. I ask not that you should bind yourself to him by any promise, but only that you receive him with more joyous entertainment than before, so that at least his life be saved. This is all, and all we hoped for. So may God help me, I never meant aught else. Neither is this request more than reason, nor is there reasonable fear from it. Suppose the worst; you are afraid folk may wonder to see him come and go. Thereto I answer that any person but a natural fool will deem it but a friendly affection on his part. What! who will deem, when he sees a man go to a temple, that he eats the images! Think also how well and wisely Troilus conducts himself, never incautiously, so that everywhere he wins praise and gratitude. And besides, he will come here so seldom, what matter were it though all the town saw? Such friendly affection is common enough throughout this town, so evermore veil yourselves in that mantle; so be God my salvation, you were best do that. But, good niece, in any case to stint his woe, sugar your sour reserve a little, that you be not to blame for his death.'

Criseyde, who had heard all to the full, thought, 'Now I will test what he really means. — Now, uncle,' she said, 'what think you truly I should do in this case?'

'Well said,' quoth he; 'in sooth the best is that you love him in return for his love, as love for love is a reasonable reward. Think how in each of you every day age lays waste a part of your beauty, and therefore, before age clean devour you, go love. Old, no man will have you. Learn lore from this proverb: "Too late aware, says Beauty when she is gone." Old age in the end subdues pride. When the king's fool thinks a woman bears herself too high, he is wont to call at her, "So long may you and all proud dames live until crows' feet be grown under your eyes, and may you then have a mirror to pore over a-mornings!" I can wish you no more grief!'

With that he ceased, and bent his head down. She began to burst out weeping, and said, 'Woe, alas! Why am I alive? All the faith is gone out of this world. Alas! what will strangers do to me when he that I thought my best friend counsels me to love, who should warn me against it? Alas! I should have trusted faithfully that, if through my ill stars I had loved him or Achilles, Hector or any male creature, you would have had no mercy or moderation toward me, but would have held me in eternal reproach. Who may trust this false world? What, is this all the joy that I was to celebrate? Is this your counsel, and my blissful chance, and the prize that you promised me? Was all your coloured story told only for this end? O Lady Pallas, guide me in this dreadful case, for I am so astonied that I die!' And with that she began to sigh full sorrowfully.

'Ah, is there hope of nothing better?' quoth Pandarus. 'Before God, I shall come here no more this week, that am mistrusted thus. I see well that you care full little for him or me or for our death. Alas, what a woful wretch am I! Might he but live, no one would reck of my life. O cruel god, pitiless Mars, and ye three furies of hell, I call on you; let me never come out of this house if ever I meant shame or harm. But since I see my lord must needs die, and I with him, here I shrive me and say that it is your grievous sin to cause us both to die. But since it pleases you that I should die, by Neptune, god of the sea, from this day forth I will eat no bread till I see mine own heart's blood, for in verity I will die as soon as he!'

Up he started and dashed away, till Criseyde caught him by the kirtle. She was the fearfullest creature that ever was, and well-nigh died for fear when she heard him and saw his sorrowful earnest; and seeing naught amiss in his prayer, and the greater harm that might befall, she began to melt and sorely to fear, and thought, 'Unhappy chances betide every day for love, and in such cases men are cruel and wicked against themselves. If this man slays himself here in my presence, it will be no merriment! What men would think about it I cannot fancy; — I must play full cautiously.' So she cried thrice with a sorrowful sigh, 'Ah, Lord! what a sorry chance has befallen me! For my well-being lies in jeopardy, and mine uncle's life is in the balance. But with God's help I shall so act as to save mine honour and his life. Of two harms the less is to be chosen. I had rather receive your friend kindly, in all honour, than lose mine uncle's life! You say you require naught else of me?' And with that she ceased to weep.

'No, in truth, mine own dear niece,' he said.

'Well,' said she; 'then I will try. I will constrain my heart against my liking, save that I will not delude him with false hopes. I know not how to love a man, and cannot against my will, but otherwise I will strive from day to day to please him, saving my honour. To such a thing I would not once have said nay, except for my fanciful dread; and now, cease cause, cease malady. But here I make an attestation that, if you go deeper into this thing, certainly for no saving of you, though you both die the death, and though all the world turn against me on one day, never will I have more and other pity on him than I have said.'

'I agree, by my troth,' said Pandarus. 'But can I verily trust to you that you will truly hold to me the thing which you have promised me here?'

'Yes, without a doubt,' said she, 'my dear uncle.'

'— So that I shall have no cause in this matter to complain, or to preach to you again?'

'Why no, perdy! What need of more words?'

Then they fell into other cheerful talk, till at last, 'Oh, good uncle!' said she, 'for the love of Him that made us both, tell me how you knew first of his woe. Knows any man of it but you two?'

'No,' he replied.

'Can he talk well on love? Tell me, I pray, that I may the better prepare.'

Then Pandarus began to smile a little, and said, 'By my troth, I will tell you. The other day, not a long while ago, he and I were full half the day in the palace garden by a fountain, speaking of a means how we might repulse the Greeks. Soon after that we began to leap, and to throw the dart, till at last he said he would sleep, and laid him down on the grass, and I began to roam to and fro at a distance, till as I walked I heard how he began to groan full wofully, and I stalked him full softly from behind. As I can call to memory, thus he made his complaint to love; he said, "Lord, have ruth upon my pain. Though I have been a rebel, *mea culpa*, I repent me. O God, that at Thy good pleasure ordainest the end of every creature by just providence, accept my humble confession favourably, and send me such penances as liketh Thee, but of Thy kindness shield me from despair which may part my soul from Thee. For certes, Lord, so sorely has she that stood there in black wounded me with the looking of her eyes that it has sounded my heart's bottom, through which I know that I shall die. The worst is that I may not reveal it; and the hotter glow the coals if men cover them with pale ashes."

'With that he smote down his head and began to mutter I know not what. I stole away and made as though I had known nothing, and anon came again, stood by him and said, "Awake, you sleep all too long! It seems not that you pine for love, since you sleep so that none can wake you! Who ever saw so dull a fellow before?" "Yes, friend," said he, "let your head ache for love, and let me live as I may." Pale and wan for love as he was, he put on as fresh a look as if he should have led a new dance.

'This went on till it fell, only this other day, that I came strolling all alone into his chamber and found him lying upon his bed. Never heard I man groan so sore. What it was that he moaned out I know not, for as I was coming suddenly he left his complaint, at which I caught a suspicion and came nearer and found that he was weeping sore. So God save me as I never felt more truth for anything! Scarcely by cunning or by counsel could I restrain him from his death, so that even now I feel my heart weep for him. God wot, never since I was born was I so busy with preaching, and never swore such deep vows before he told me who might be his physician! Unless you would see me swoon, ask me not to rehearse all his words; only to save my life, and for no harm to you, am I brought to say thus much. For the love of the God that made us, make him such cheer that he and I may save our lives. Now have I fully shriven my heart to you. You know that my intent is pure; take heed of it. And now I pray God bless you that without net have caught such game! If you are wise as you are fair, well is the ruby set in the ring. Never were two so well brought together as you, and God grant us to see that hour when you are all wholly his as he is yours!'

'Aha!' quoth she; 'nay, I spoke nothing of that! God help me so, you spoil all.'

'Eh, mercy, dear niece!' he answered hastily. 'Whatsoever I spoke, I swear by steel-helmed Mars I meant no ill. Now be not wroth, my dear niece, mine own blood.'

'Well, well!' said she, 'you are forgiven.'

With that he took his leave and went home, — Lord, how happy and content! Criseyde tarried not, but arose and went straight into her closet, where she sat her down as still as a stone, and turned over in her mind every word that he had said as it came back to her, and was somewhat astonied for the very newness of it all. But when she had fully considered, she found naught perilous, why she ought to fear; for it is possible that a man may love a woman till his heart splits, and she not love in return unless she will.

Thus as she sat alone and thought, a clamour arose about a skirmish without the walls, and men cried in the street, 'See, Troilus has right now put the Greek troop to flight!' At that all her household began to shout, 'Ah, let us go and see! Cast up the lattice! He will ride through this street to the palace, there is no other way from the Gate of Dardanus, where the chain is open!'

Then came he and all his men, riding at an easy pace in two troops, even as his happy day would have it, which (men say) betides of necessity and may not be disturbed. Troilus, all armed full richly save for his helm, sat on his bay steed, which was wounded and bled, wherefore he rode at a full soft pace. But Mars, the god of battle, were not so knightly a sight to look upon as he! So like a man of arms and a knight he was, so full of high prowess; for he had both the frame and the strength to do those deeds, as well as the hardihood, and to see him in all his gear, so fresh and young and powerful; it was heaven to look on him. His helm, hanging behind his back by a lace, was hewn open in twenty holes; his shield was all crushed with maces and swords, and one might see it in many an arrow which had pierced the horn and sinew and hide of it; and ever the people cried. 'Here comes our hero, next his brother the mainstay of Troy!' At this, when he heard the people cry out over him, he waxed a little red for shame, so that it was rare sport to see how soberly he cast down his eyes.

Criseyde all the time took in his look, and let it softly sink into her heart, till she said, 'Who has given me a potion?' At her own thought she waxed all red, remembering in her own mind, 'Lo, this is he who my uncle swears is sure to die unless I have mercy and pity.' And, abashed only with the thought, she pulled in her head, and that quickly, whilst he and all the people passed by. She cast over in her mind his excellent prowess, his station, his renown, his wisdom, his form, and his nobility; but what most won her was that his distress was all for her, and she thought it were pity to slay such a one, if his intent were faithful.

Now some malicious person may prate thus, 'This was a sudden love! How might it be that she so readily loved Troilus even at the first sight?' Yea, verily! Whosoever says so, may he never flourish! Everything must needs have a beginning, before it be full grown. I say not that she so suddenly as this gave him her heart, but only that she began to incline to like him at first, and I have told you why; and after that his manhood and his longing for her made love to drive its mines within her heart. Wherefore by degrees and by good service he got her love, and not suddenly. And also blessed Venus was even then sitting in her seventh house of heaven, well placed among the stars and with benign aspects, to help poor Troilus out of his woe; and to say the sooth she had been right favourable to him at his nativity. The better he sped for that; God wot!

Now let us for a season leave Troilus riding on, and turn forthwith to Criseyde, that sat alone with bent head, and debated what resolutions she should take at last, if so be her uncle should not leave to press Troilus upon her. And Lord! how she argued back and forth in her heart, now warm and now cold, and how she folded and unfolded what were best to eschew and what to do! Of what she thought I shall write somewhat, as mine author sets it down.

She thought first how well she knew Troilus' person by sight, and also his nobleness; she thought, 'It will not do to grant him love, yet it were an honour to me in my station, and also for his well-being, to have to do with such a lord in honest mirth. And well I wot he is my king's son, and peradventure, since he so joys to see me, if I should utterly flee his company he might have me in despite, through which I might stand in worse case than ever. Now were I wise to procure needless hate for me, where I may stand in favour? There is measure in all things, I wot. Though a man forbid drunkenness, I trust he will not demand that every creature be drinkless forever. Since I know his distress is for me, I ought not to despise him for that, if so be his intent is good. I know his virtues of long time past, and that he is not a fool, and that men say he is no braggart and is too wise for so mean a vice; and besides I will never make so much of him that he shall have any cause to boast of me, — he shall never hold me in such a bond. Now suppose the worst, that men may guess that he loves me, — what dishonour to me is this? Can I hinder him? All the time men love women without their leave; when they are weary of it, let them cease! I wot well he is worthy to have the best of women in this world, saving her honour, for except only Hector he is out and out the worthiest knight. And yet now his life lies in my power! Such is love, and my good chance.

'It is no wonder that he should love me; so God speed me, though I would not any man knew of my thought, I am one of the fairest and goodliest women here, and so men say throughout this town. What wonder though he take delight in me? Thank God, I am mistress to myself, well at ease for one in my station, right young, and at liberty in a lusty pasture, untroubled by jealousy or such strife. No husband can say to me "Checkmate!" (All husbands are either full of jealousy, or masterful, or love novelty.) What shall I do? To what end live I as I am living? Shall I not love if I will? What! I am not a nun; and though I give my heart to this worthy knight, if I keep my honour and my fair repute, by rights it can be no shame to me.'

But even as in changeful March the sun shines bright, and then a cloud is driven by the wind and overspreads the sun for a season, a cloudy thought passed through her soul and overspread all her bright thoughts, till she wellnigh dropped with fear. That thought was, 'Since I am free, alas! shall I now love, and jeopardize my security and enthrall my liberty? How durst I think of such a folly! Can I not note in other folk in love their joy full of fear, their thralldom, their pain? No woman is in love but has cause to lament it. Love is of itself the most stormy life that ever was, ever is some distrust in love, or foolish strife, some cloud is over that sun. And when we wretched loving women are in trouble, all we can do is sit thinking and weeping; all the revenge we can have is to drink up our own woe. And wicked tongues are so ready to speak harm of us! And men are so faithless that, as soon as their desire is satisfied, love ceases, and forth to a new love! Harm done is done, whosoever rue it. Though these men at first tear themselves for love, a sharp beginning often has a weak end. How many times it has been known, the treachery done to women! What such love is for, I cannot see; or what becomes of it when it is gone. No-one will break his shins against it! That which at first was naught turns into naught again. And then, if I give myself to love, how anxious and busy I must be to cajole those who prate and gossip about love, and to silence them, that they say no harm of me; for though there be no cause, yet they fancy evil when folk but please their friends. Who can stop every wicked tongue, or the reverberation of ringing bells?'

And then her thoughts began to clear, and she said, 'He who undertakes nothing, willy-nilly achieves nothing.' And then with the next thought her heart began to quake; hope went to sleep and dread awoke; now she was hot, now cold. Thus betwixt the two, she rose up, and went out to divert her.

Down the stair she went into the garden with her three nieces, and up and down they took many a turn in their sporting, she and Phlexippe, Tarbe and Antigone, so that it was a joy to look on them, and a great throng of her other women followed her in the garden all about. The yard was large, well shaded with green boughs full of blossoms, and with turved banks and sanded alleys railed off, in which she walked arm in arm betwixt her nieces; till Antigone the fair began to sing a Trojan song, that it was a heaven to hear her clear voice.

'O Love,' she sang, 'to whom I have ever been and shall be humble subject, true in mine intent as I best can be, to thee, Lord, for evermore I give my heart's joy in tribute. For never yet thy grace sent to any person so blissful cause as I have to live her life in all security and joy. Blessed god, thou hast so well bestowed me in love that no living creature could imagine how it could be better; without jealousy or strife I love one the most devoted to good service that ever was, without weariness or feigning, nor stained with the least spot. He is the well of worthiness, ground of fidelity, mirror of goodliness, rock of security, Apollo in wit, root of virtue, discoverer and head of delight, through whom all sorrow has died in me; he loves me best, and so love I him; now blessings on him wherever he be! Whom should I thank but thee, God of Love, for all this bliss in which I bathe? And thanks to thee that I myself love. This life that I am in is the perfect life, to drive away all manner of sin and vice, and so to strive after virtue that day by day my will betters itself. Whoso says that to love is a fault or a bondage, he is either envious or right foolish, or so wicked that he cannot love. Such manner of folk I believe defame Love as know naught of him; they speak of him, but they never bent his bow. What, is the sun the worse though a man for feebleness of his eyes cannot endure to look on it? Or Love the worse though wretches cry out on him? He is worthy of no weal that can endure no sorrow; and therefore let him who has a head of glass beware of the flying stones in battle. But I with all my heart and strength will love to the end my dear heart, mine own knight; upon whom my heart has grown so firm, and his on me, that they will last forever. Though I feared at first to begin to love him, now I wot well there is no peril in it.'

There she ceased her song, and thereat said Criseyde, 'Now, niece, who made this song?'

'Madame,' answered Antigone, 'the goodliest maid of great estate in the town of Troy, that led her life in most bliss and honour.'

'In sooth,' said Criseyde, and began to sigh, 'so it seems by her song. Lord! is there such happiness amongst these lovers as they say so fairly?'

'Yea, certes,' said the white Antigone. 'All the folk that have been or are alive cannot describe the bliss of love. But deem you that the perfect bliss of love is known to every wretch? Nay, nay! They ween that any hot desire is love; away with them, they wot nothing of it! Men must ask saints if it is fair in heaven and fiends if it is foul in hell.'

Criseyde answered her nothing thereto, but said, 'In faith, it will be night directly.' Yet every word that she had heard from her she began to imprint fast in her heart, and ever love terrified her less than it did at first, and began to sink into her heart, till she was almost ready to be converted.

The glory of the day, the eye of heaven, the foe of night (all this means the sun!) had sped his day's course and was fast westering and dropping downward; and white things began to wax dun in the dimness, and the stars to appear, when she and her folk went in together. So when she was ready to go to rest, and all but her women had left the chamber, she said that she would sleep, and they brought her anon to bed. When all was hushed she lay still and thought of all this thing; how, I need not rehearse to you, for ye are wise! Upon a green cedar, under the chamber-wall where she lay, a nightingale sang full loud in the face of the bright moon; peradventure, in his bird's manner, a lay of love that made her heart glad. She hearkened to him so long that at last dead sleep took her. And as she slept, anon she dreamed how an eagle with feathers as white as bone set his long claws under her breast, and anon rent out her heart and put his own heart into her breast, at which she felt no fear or pain; and so, with heart left for heart, forth he flew.

Now we will let her sleep and hold forth our tale of Troilus, that is ridden to the palace from the skirmish I told of. He sat in his chamber waiting, till two or three of his messengers had gone for Pandarus, and sought so diligently that at last they found and brought him. Pandarus came bounding in and began to jape, 'Who has been well drubbed to-day with swords and sling-stones but Troilus? Who is all heated up? Lord, but you sweat! But arise,' he said, 'and let us sup and go to rest.'

'We will do as you list,' answered Troilus.

With all the seemly haste they could they sped them from supper and to bed, and every other person betook him out at the door and away. And now Troilus, whose very heart seemed to bleed for woe until he heard news, said, 'Friend, now am I to weep or sing?'

'Be still,' said Pandarus, 'and let me sleep, and put on your night-cap! Your needs are sped; now choose if you will dance or sing or leap! In few words, you are to trust in me. Sir, my niece will do well by you and love you best, by God and by my faith, unless sloth or lack of pursuit hinder! So far have I begun your work that this morning I gained for you her love, as of a friend, and thereto has she pledged her faith. At all events, a foot of your sorrow is cut off!' Why should I make a longer discourse of it? He told it all to him as you have heard before.

Even as flowers, closed through the cold of night, and bent low on their stalks, erect themselves in the bright sunshine, and stand spreading and blooming in rows, — so did Troilus revive, and threw up his eyes and said, 'O beloved Venus, praised be thy might and grace!' And to Pandarus he held up both his hands and said, 'Lord, all that I have is yours. I am all whole now, my bonds are broken. Whoever should give me a thousand Troys one after another would not gladden me so; oh my heart! it spreads so for joy, surely it will fly to pieces! But how shall I do? Lord! how shall I live? When shall I next see my dear heart? How can I go through this long time till you go to her from me again? You may answer, "Wait, wait!" but he that is hanging by the neck waits in great uneasiness!'

'Easily, easily, now, for the love of Mars!' cried Pandarus. 'There is a time for everything. Wait till the night is gone, for as sure as you are lying here by me I will be there at prime. Pray do somewhat as I tell you, or lay your charges on someone else. God wot, I have ever yet been ready to serve you; up to the present night I have never feigned to you, but to the extent of my wit have done all your pleasure, and ever will. Do now as I say and bear yourself with reason, — if you will not, you may blame yourself for your troubles; they are not my doing. I wot well that you are wiser than I a thousand-fold; but if I were as you, God help me so as I should this moment write her a letter with mine own hand in which I should tell her how ill I fared and beg her pity. Help yourself now, and neglect not out of sloth. I myself will go to her with the letter, and when you know that I am with her, do you mount a horse, — yea, in all your best gear, and ride by the place as it were about some other purpose; and if I may contrive it, you shall find us sitting at some window looking into the street. If you will, then you may salute us, but see that you look most upon me, and for your life beware of tarrying at all, God shield us! Ride on your way and hold yourself in! When you are gone, we shall speak somewhat of you, I promise you, to make your ears glow! As to your letter, you are wise enough to know how to write it. I know you will not write haughtily nor too artfully, or argue pertinaciously, or compose a letter as if you were a scrivener. And blot it with your tears a little. And if you think of some goodly tender word, good though it be, repeat it not over-often; for if the best harper alive, with the best-sounding and merriest harp and the best-pointed nails, should touch ever one string and ever play one descant, every creature's ears would grow dull to hear his glee and his sounding strokes. And see that you jumble in no discordant thing, as thus, to use terms of physic amongst love-terms. Let your matter have always its proper form, and let it be ever alike. If a painter should paint a fish with asses feet, and head it like an ape, it would not accord with itself; it were a mere jest.'

This counsel pleased Troilus well, but like a timid lover he said, 'Alas! dear brother Pandarus, I am ashamed to write lest in my simplicity I might speak amiss, or in anger she might reject my letter. If she did, naught could save me from death!'

'If you will,' answered Pandarus, 'do as I say and let me go with it. By the Lord that formed the east and the west, I hope anon to bring an answer right from her hand. If you will not do it, let it be then, and sorry be his life that ever again tries to help you against your will!'

Quoth Troilus, 'In God's name, I assent; I will arise and write if you wish. And I devoutly pray blessed God to speed the letter I shall write, and the sending of it. And do thou, fair Minerva, give me wit to devise the letter!' And therewith he sat him down and wrote in this wise.

First, he called her his very lady, his heart's life, his joy, the leech of his sorrow, his bliss, and by all those other terms that in such cases ye lovers search for. Then full humbly he recommended him to her grace, but to tell just how were to spend overmuch time. And then lowly he prayed her not to be wroth though in his folly he made bold to write to her, and he said that love caused him to do so, and otherwise he could not live, and piteously he cried her mercy. Then he said (and lied in his throat!) that he was worth little, and knew less, and that she was to excuse him for his lack of wit; he told how he feared her, and ever accused his own unworthiness, and he told his woe, which was infinite for ever and ever, and how he would ever hold his faith. Then he made his adieux, and folded the letter. With salt tears he bathed the ruby in his signet and set it hastily upon the wax, and a thousand times before he left off he kissed the letter that he was sealing, and said, 'Letter, a blissful destiny is ordained for thee, — my lady shall see thee.'

Betimes on the morrow Pandarus was up with it, and sped to his niece's palace, and said, 'Are you still asleep, at prime?' Then he began to jest, 'Ah my heart! so fresh it is, for all love's torments, I can never sleep of a May morning. I have a jolly woe and a lusty grief'

When Criseyde heard her uncle, with her heart full of timidness and desire to hear why he had come, she answered, 'Now on your faith, my dear uncle, what manner of wind has blown you hither? Tell us of your penance and your jolly woe. How far have you gone through love's dance?'

'By God!' quoth he, 'I hop always at the after end.' As she laughed as if her heart would burst, he went on, 'Look that you always find sport in my hood! But now please to listen. — There has but now come into town a stranger, a Greek spy, who has news to tell, about which I have brought you tidings. Let us go into the garden, and you shall hear a long discourse about this privately.'

With that they went arm in arm down from the chamber into the garden, and when they had gone so far that no man could hear what he spoke, he plucked out the letter and said, 'Lo, he who is wholly yours commends him humbly to your favour and sends you this letter by me; read it advisedly when you have time, and provide you some goodly answer, or, to speak plainly and as God sees me, he cannot live longer in such pains.'

She stood still then in fear, and took it not, but all her modest aspect began to grow more firm, and she said, 'Billet or note bring me none that touches such matters, for the love of God; and also, dear uncle, I pray you have more regard to my condition than to his desires. What more can I say? Consider now if this be reasonable, and shrink not, for partisanship or laziness, to admit the truth. Were it agreeable to my condition to take this letter, or so to have compassion on him as to bring harm or reproach on myself? Carry it back, in the name of Him in whom you believe!'

Pandarus began to stare upon her, and said, 'Now this is the greatest wonder that ever I saw. Let be these foolish doings! May I be smitten to death by lightning if I would bring you a letter to harm you, for all the city that spreads yonder! What are you trying to do? But thus you do, wellnigh all of you; he that most desires to serve you, you reck the least what happens to him, or whether he lives or dies. But, if I ever deserved anything from you, refuse it not,' and with that word he seized her and thrust the letter down into her bosom, saying, 'Now cast it from you straightway, that folk may see and gape at us!'

'I can abide till they be gone,' quoth she, and began to smile. 'Uncle, I pray you provide such an answer yourself as you will, for in truth no letter will I write.'

'No?' said he. 'Then I will, if you will dictate.'

Thereat she laughed and said, 'Let us go and dine.'

He began to jest at himself, and said, 'Niece, I am so pining for love that every second day I fast,' and he so flung out his best quips that she thought she should die of laughter at his mad folly.

When she was come into the hall, 'Now, uncle,' quoth she, 'we will dine anon,' and called some of her women and went straight to her chamber; and amongst her other matters this doubtless was one — privily to read the letter. She considered every line and every word, and found no defect, and thought in truth he knew good manners. Up she put it, and as she went in to dinner found Pandarus standing in a muse. Ere he was aware she caught him by the hood, and said, 'You were caught before you knew it.'

'I grant it,' quoth he; 'do as you list.'

Then they washed and sat them down to eat. After dinner and noon were passed, Pandarus slyly drew toward the window on the street and said, 'Niece, who has thus arrayed yonder house that stands over against us?'

'Which house?' said she, and came to look and told whose it was; and then they fell into talk of small matters, and both sat down in the window.

When Pandarus saw his time and that her folk were gone, 'Now, niece,' he said, 'tell on. How like you the letter? Knows he how to write one? By my torch, I wot not!'

Thereat she waxed all rosy, and began to hum and said, 'I believe so.'

'Requite him well, for the love of God,' said he, 'and to repay you I myself will sew up your letter.' Then he held up his hands and fell on his knee. — 'Now, good niece, however small it be, give me the task to fold and sew it.'

'Yea,' quoth she, 'for I am such a writer! And besides I wot not what I should say to him.'

'Nay, niece,' said he, 'say not so! At the least I beg you to thank him for his good-will, and let him not die. Now for the love of me, refuse not my prayer this once!'

'God grant all be well!' said she. 'So God help me, this is the first letter that ever I wrote, — yea, whole letter or even a part.' And she went alone into a closet to consider it more carefully, and began to unfetter her heart a little out of the prison of Disdain, and sat her down and began to write; and I mean to tell the substance in brief, so far as I can learn it. She thanked him for all his good intent towards her, but she could not delude him, not bind herself to love; yet she would gladly ease his heart by kindness as of a sister. She closed the letter and went back to Pandarus where he sat looking into the street; and down she sat her by him on a gold-embroidered cushion upon a stone of jasper, and said, 'So may the great God help me, I never did a thing with more trouble than this to which you constrain me!' Then she gave it him.

He thanked her and said, 'God wot, of a loath beginning comes often a good ending. And, my niece Criseyde, by yonder heavens, he has reason to be glad that you are now hard to win, for men say,

"Impressions light
Are light for flight."

But it is nigh too long that you have played the tyrant, and your heart has been hard to grave; now cease this (even though you keep the appearance of reserve), and haste you to grant him some joy; for trust me, hardness too long kept up full oft causes pain to turn to anger.'

Even as they were discoursing thus, right at the end of the street came Troilus riding slowly in his troop of ten, and passed along toward them as his way was to his palace. Pandarus espied him and said, 'Niece, see who comes riding this way. — Ah, fly not in! He sees us, no doubt, and he might think that you shun him!'

'Nay, nay!' said she, and waxed ruddy like a rose. With that Troilus humbly saluted her with a timid look, often changed colour, and cast a look up courteously, nodded to Pandarus and passed on his way. I leave it to you if he sat well on his horse and was goodly to look on that time and like a manly knight. Why should I be tedious, or tell about his accoutrement? In a word, Criseyde, who saw all, liked all, his person, his array, his look, his expression, his goodly manner and his nobleness; and liked them so well that never had she such ruth for his pain. However hard she had been aforetime, I hope in God she has now caught a thorn which she will not pull out in the next week. God send her more such thorns to pluck at!

Pandarus, as he stood by, felt the iron hot and began to smite. 'Niece, I pray you heartily,' he said, 'tell me what I ask you. A woman that should be to blame for his death, without guilt of his but only for her lack of pity, — were it well done?'

'Nay, by my troth,' quoth she.

'So God help me,' said he, 'you say the sooth now! You feel yourself that I lie not. See, how nobly he rides yonder!'

'Yea,' said she, 'so he does.'

'Well, as I have thrice told you,' said he, 'let be your false shame and your folly, and ease his heart by speaking with him. Let not silly scruples hurt you both.'

But here was a laborious task for Pandarus! 'Considering all things, it might not be. And why plead for speech with him? It were too soon to grant him such a privilege yet.' Her full intent, as she said, was to love him unknown to any, if she could, and reward him only with the sight of her.

But Pandarus thought, 'It shall not be so. If I have any power, she shall not hold this caprice any two years!' But why make a long discourse of it? He must assent to this resolution for the time; and when it drew toward night, and all was well, he took his leave, and sped homeward, his heart bounding for joy. Troilus he found alone in bed, lying, as do these lovers, in a trance betwixt hope and dark despair. Pandarus came in singing, as if to say, 'I bring you somewhat! Who is this buried in his bed so early?' he cried.

'It is I, friend,' replied the other.

'Who? Troilus? Nay, so help me the moon,' quoth Pandarus, 'you must arise and see a charm that was sent you but now and can heal you of your attack, if you do your diligence and help yourself.'

'Yea, through the mighty blessing of God,' said Troilus.

Then Pandarus handed him the letter, and said, 'Perdy, God has helped us! Make a light here, and look on all these black marks!'

Lord, how often did the heart of Troilus rejoice and quake whilst he read the letter, as the words gave him hope and fear! But at last he took for the best what she wrote him; for he saw somewhat on which his heart might repose, though she covered her words under a shield. Thus he held to the better side of it, so that, what with his own hope and Pandarus' promises, his chiefest woe at least he gave up.

But, as we may every day see ourselves, the more wood or coal there is, the greater the fire; even so, as hope of aught increases, so does the longing. Or even as an oak grows out of a little shoot, so through this letter began desire to increase and burn him. Therefore, I say, day and night hope kindled in Troilus more desire than he had before, and he did all he could to press on, by Pandarus' lessoning, and to write to her of his sore griefs. From day to day he let not opportunity grow cool, but sent some note or message by Pandarus, and did his other observances that behoove a lover in such case. According as the dice turned up for him, he rejoiced or said Alas!, and ever he pursued his fortunes, and, according to the answers which he received, his days were sorry or joyous. To Pandarus was ever his recourse, and piteously he lamented to him and asked counsel or succour. Pandarus, who saw his mad torment, waxed nigh dead for pity, and cast about with all his heart to slay some of his woe straightway.

'Lord and friend and brother dear,' he would say, 'God wot that your pain is pain to me. Yet if you will but lighten this woful visage, by my troth, before two days are gone I shall devise it that you shall come to a certain place where you can yourself pray her for favour. And certainly, I wot not if you know it, but those who are expert in love say that one of the things that further a man most is to have a good opportunity himself to press his suit and a safe place to reveal his woe. In a kind heart it must kindle some pity to see and hear the guiltless in pain. Perchance you are thinking, "Though so be natural feeling may make her begin to have a sort of pity on me, reserve will say, Nay you shall never win me; her heart's spirit so rules her within that though she may bend, yet she grows firmly on her root. What can all this do to cure me?" '

'Think, on the other side, that, when the sturdy oak has been hacked at for a long time and at last receives the lucky blow which fells it, its great mass causes it to come down all at once, like a rock or a mill-stone; for heavy things come down with a swifter force than light things do. The reed that bows with every blast will arise again full lightly when the wind ceases, but so will not an oak it is overthrown. — But I need not parable you forever. A man shall rejoice the more over a great emprise achieved well and enduringly, the longer he has been about it.'

'But now, Troilus, if you please, tell me somewhat which I shall ask you, — which of your brothers do you love best in your very heart of hearts?'

'Why, my brother Deiphobus,' said Troilus.

'Ere four-and-twenty hours,' quoth Pandarus, 'he shall relieve you without knowing it himself. Now leave me alone to work as I can.'

To Deiphobus he went then, who had ever been his good lord and friend, and whom he loved more than any save Troilus; and (to be brief) he said, 'I pray you be friend to a cause which touches me nearly.'

'Yea, perdy!' said Deiphobus; 'you well know in all that ever I can I am readier to serve you than any man save him that I love most, my brother Troilus. But say wherefore it is. Since the day I was born I never was, and never shall be, against anything, so I grieved you thereby.'

Pandarus thanked him and said, 'Lo, sir, I have a lady in this town, my niece, named Criseyde, whom some men would fain opress, and wrongfully have her possessions. Wherefore, and this is all, I beseech you of your lordship to be our friend.'

'Ah,' Deiphobus answered him, 'is not this lady, whom you speak of so distantly, Criseyde, my friend?'

'Yea,' he said.

'Then in truth,' replied Deiphobus, 'there needs no more of this, for trust well that I will be her champion with shaft and spear, and I care not though all her foes heard it. But you know about this matter, — tell me how it may be done to most avail?'

'Now let see,' quoth Pandarus; 'if you, my dear lord, would do me this honour and pray her to come to you to-morrow and relate her troubles, her adversaries would tremble to hear of it. And if I durst ask more, and charge you with so great a trouble as to have some of your brothers here with you who might help in her cause, then I wot well she should never fail to be helped, through your urgency and her other friends' managing.'

Deiphobus, who was by nature ever ready for all acts of honour and generosity, answered, 'It shall be done. And I can think of still a greater help. What say you if I should send for Helen to speak about this? I believe that is the best, for she can lead Paris as she will. As to my Lord Hector, my brother, it needs not pray him to be her friend, for once and again I have heard him speak such honour of Criseyde that he could say no more; she stands so well with him it needs not crave his help more, for he will be even such as we would have him. But speak you also to Troilus on my behalf, and pray him to dine with us.'

'Sir, all this shall be done,' Pandarus said, and took his leave, and never stopped till as straight as a line he came to his niece's house. He found her but just arisen from meat, and sat him down and spoke in this wise.

'Lord, how I have run! See you not how I sweat, niece? Yet I know not whether you are the more grateful to me! Are you not aware how false Polyphetes is about to go to law again and bring you new trouble?'

'I? No!' she said, and changed colour. 'What? Goes he about to harass and injure me more? Alack, what shall I do? I should not care for him were it not for Antenor and Æneas, who stand his friends in these things. But for the love of heaven, no matter, — let him have all he is after at once; I have enough for ourselves without that.'

'Nay,' said Pandarus, 'it shall never be so, for I have been even now with Deiphobus and Hector and others of my lords, and in short, set each of them against him; so that, as I hope to be saved, he shall never prevail against you, whatsoever he may try.'

As they were considering what were best to do, Deiphobus of his courtesy came himself to pray her to bear him company on the morrow at dinner, to which she assented in goodly manner. He thanked her and went his way; and after him Pandarus departed quietly to Troilus, and told him word for word how he had hoodwinked Deiphobus. 'Now is your time; bear yourself well to-morrow, and all is won. Now speak, now pray, now bewail piteously, neglect it not for false shame or fear or sloth. Sometimes a man must tell his troubles for himself. Believe this, and she will show you pity; you shall, in truth, be saved by your faith. But I see clearly you are afraid at this moment, and I lay a wager I can tell why! You are thinking, 'How can I do all this? By my very look folk will see that it is for her love that I fare so ill. Rather than that I would die for sorrow unknown." Think not so, do no such folly; for I have just found a cunning device so that folk need not see your face. You shall go straightway for overnight to Deiphobus' house, as it were to amuse yourself and drive away your malady (for indeed you seem sick). Soon after you are to go to bed, and say you can no longer endure to be about; and lie right there and await your fortune. Say that your fever is wont to take you about that time and to last till the morrow; and let us see now how well you can feign, for he that is in sorrow is sick. Go now, farewell! And now before Venus I trust that if you hold to this purpose, she shall fully confirm her favour to you.'

'In faith,' said Troilus, 'you need not counsel me to feign me sick, for I am sick in earnest, nigh unto death.'

'You will the better bewail you, then,' quoth Pandarus, 'and have the less need to counterfeit. Him that men see sweat they will readily deem hot! Hold close to your trist, and I will drive the deer to your bow.'

Therewith he quietly took his leave; Troilus went straight to his palace, gladder than ever before in his life, and took Pandarus' advice and went at night to Deiphobus' house. What need to tell you of all the cheer that his brother made him, or of his feigned attack, or his sick look, how they loaded him with coverlets when he was laid a-bed, and how they tried to cheer him? All their efforts were for naught; he held to the course that Pandarus had counselled him. But it is known that, ere Troilus was a-bed, Deiphobus had prayed him to be a friend and helper to Criseyde. God wot he agreed anon to be her full friend with all his might; as much need to pray him for that as to bid a madman to run wild!

The morrow came and the time of dinner approached; the fair queen Helen was to be an hour after prime with Deiphobus, whom she would not fail, but came to dinner quietly as his sister, suspecting naught. But God and Pandarus knew what this was all about! Criseyde came also, all innocent of this, and Antigone and her sister Tarbe also. Now let us flee prolixity, for the love of God, and go speedily to the outcome, without a longer tale of how all these folk were assembled there, and let us pass over their salutations!

Deiphobus did them all honour, and fed them with all that might please them; but evermore his refrain was, 'Alas! my good brother Troilus still lies sick,' and therewith he would sigh; and then he would strive to make good cheer and to entertain them as best he could. Helen also lamented his sickness so heartily that it was pitiful to hear; and everyone for the nonce became a leech, and said, 'Thus and thus men cure folk,' — 'This or that charm I will tell you.' And all the time one sat there who said nothing, but thought, 'Yet I could be his leech better than any!' After bewailing him they began to praise him, as folk will do still, when someone has begun to praise a man; then the rest fell to and exalted him a thousand-fold higher than the heavens! 'There be few lords who are and can do as much as he.' And Pandarus forgot not to confirm all they could say in his praise. All this Criseyde heard well enough, and laid it up in her memory, whilst her heart bounded within her; and who would not glorify her who had the power of life and death over such a knight? But I pass over all this, lest I keep you too long; all that I tell is only for the outcome of it.

When the time came to rise from dinner, they talked of this and that for a season. But shortly Pandarus broke off this speech and said, 'Will you speak now, as I prayed you, of the necessities of Criseyde?'

Helen, who was holding her by the hand, first spoke; 'Let us do so quickly,' she said, looking kindly upon Criseyde; 'ill luck and short life to him who would harm her, and to me if I do not all I can to make him rue it!'

'Do you tell your niece's case,' said Deiphobus to Pandarus, 'for you can tell it best.'

'My lords and ladies,' he began, 'it stands thus, — why should I delay you by a longer tale?' And then he rung them out an account of her foe, Poly-phetes by name, so villainous that one would spit on it! At this each one exclaimed more indignantly than the last, and all cursed Polyphetes: 'Such a man should be hanged, though he were my own brother, and so he shall be without fail!' Why should I tarry longer over this account? They all at once fully promised to be her friends in all that ever they could.

Helen then said, 'Pandarus, knows my lord my brother about this, — I mean Hector? Knows Troilus of it?'

'Yea,' he answered, 'but listen to me now; since Troilus is here, methinks it were good, if you assent, that she herself should tell him all this before she goes. Because she is a lady, he will have her grief more at heart. By your leave I will now but run in and let you know whether he sleeps, or will hear about this.' In he darted and whispered to him, 'God have your soul! I am bringing your bier!' Troilus smiled, and Pandarus without more parley went out anon to Helen and Deiphobus, and said, 'If there be no long straying or more company, he would have you bring in my lady Criseyde here, and he will listen to her as well as he can. But you know well the chamber is small, and even a few people will quickly make it hot; look you, I will incur no blame by bringing in a company that might injure or discomfort him, no, not for my better arm! You who know what is best, consider whether she had better wait till another time. As for me, it seems to me best that no one should go in but you two, unless it were I also; for I can in few words rehearse her case better than she can; and after that she might pray him in short to be her good lord and then take her leave. This could not much disturb his quiet; and he need not forbear his ease for you, as he will for her, being little known to him, and then I know well he would tell you another thing that it behooves her not to hear, that is secret and for the profit of the town.'

So they, knowing naught of his purpose, went in to Troilus without more ado. Helen in her sweet and gentle wise began to salute and rally him, and said, 'Indeed you must be up soon, fair brother; now I pray you be all well!' And then she laid her arm over his shoulder, and tried with all her wit to encourage and divert him. After this she said, 'We beseech you, my dear brother Deiphobus and I, for the love of God, — and so does Pandarus also, — to be good lord and hearty friend to Criseyde, who has of a certainty had wrong usage, as Pandarus here knows, who can declare her case better than I.'

Then Pandarus began to polish his tongue, and anon rehearsed her case; and then shortly, when he was done, Troilus replied, 'By my troth, as soon as I can walk I will right fain with all my might be one of those to sustain her cause.'

'Now blessings on you for that!' said Helen the queen.

'If it were your pleasure,' said Pandarus, then, 'that she might take her leave before she went, — '

'Ah, God forbid otherwise,' he replied, 'if she would vouchsafe to do so! — But you two, Deiphobus and my dear sister, I must speak of one matter to you, to gain your counsel'; and as hap was he found at his bed's head a copy of a document and a letter from Hector, asking counsel whether such and such a man (I wot not who) were worthy of death; and in a grave manner he prayed them anon to consider it. Deiphobus very seriously began to unfold this letter, and as they strolled out, and down a stair, he and queen Helen earnestly looked upon it, and in a green arbour read the thing together, poring over it fully an hour.

And so we leave them reading, and turn to Pandarus, who pried about to see that all was well, and hastened out into the larger chamber and said, 'God save all this company! Come, my niece, my lady queen Helen awaits you, and also my two lords; arise and bring with you your niece Antigone or whom you will. Or no matter, in truth, — the less crowd the better. Come forth with me, and look that you humbly thank them all, and when you see a fair season take your leave of them, lest we bereave him of his rest too long.'

Criseyde, replied, all innocent of Pandarus' intent, 'Let us go, dear uncle,' and went in with him arm in arm, her mind all on what she should say and how demean her; whilst Pandarus said earnestly to the rest, 'I pray you all to remain here, and be not too noisy in your mirth; consider what folk are within here, and in what plight one of them is, God amend him!' And as he went in, he said, 'Niece, I conjure you, begin full softly; and in the name of Him who has given life to us all, slay not this man who suffers so for your love! Fie on the Devil! Think who the man is and in what plight he is lying. Haste you, and think that whilst you tarry, time is utterly lost; as you will both say when once you are one. And secondly, think that as yet none divines aught of you two. Hasten now, if you can; whilst folk are blinded, all the time is clear gain. As he pursues and you hesitate and tarry, the moving of a straw will set folk to guessing, so that, though afterwards you would have merry days, you will dare naught. And why? Because she and she spake such a word, and he and he cast such a look! I dare not deal longer with you, lest I lose time; so up with you, and bring him to health!'

But now, ye lovers that are here, was not Troilus in a parlous state, that lay and heard them whispering, and thought, 'Ah Lord, now is my lot being cast, utterly to die or straightway to have comfort!' At this, the first time when he should entreat her for love, — ah, mighty God! what shall he say?

Book III

O blessed planet of which the clear beams adorn all the third fair sphere of heaven, O darling of the sun, dear daughter of Jove, giver of love's pleasance, goodly gracious one, ever ready to repair to gentle hearts, O very cause of weal and of gladness, praised by thy might and bounty! In heaven and hell, in earth and in the salt sea, is felt thy power; man and beast, bird and fish, herb and green tree, if I see clearly, in their due seasons feel thy heavenly exhalation. God loves, and will not forbid to love, and no living creature in this world without love is worth aught or can endure. Thou first didst move Jove to those joyous deeds through which all things live and are, and madest him amorous of mortal beings; and as thou wouldst thou ever gavest him in love content or adversity, and madest him to come down in a thousand forms for love on earth, and to take whom thou wouldst. Thou dost appease the ire of fierce Mars. As thou wilt thou makest hearts noble; those that thou wilt set a-fire, they abandon vices and dread shame, thou makest them to be courteous, lusty and benign, and to high and low, after a man's deserts, they might sends what joys they have. Thou holdest kingdom and house in unity, thou art the faithful cause of friendship. Thou knowest all those covert properties of things at which folk wonder so, when they cannot construe how it may come about that she loves him or he her, even as why this fish and not that comes to the net. Thou hast set a law for folk through all the world, and this I know from lovers, that whoso strives with thee hath the worse. Now, lady bright, of thy benignity teach me to describe in honour of those who serve thee, whose clerk I am, some of that joy which is felt in thy service. Pour feeling into my barren heart, and let me show thy sweetness! Calliope, be thy voice now present, for now is need! Seest thou not the strait I am in, how I must tell anon in Venus' praise the joy of Troilus? To which joy may God bring him who has need!

All this meanwhile lay Troilus repeating his lesson in this wise: 'My faith! I will say thus and thus; I will lament thus to my dear lady. This word is good, and thus and thus I will look. This and that I will be sure not to forget.' God grant him to do as he plans! And Lord, how his heart began to flutter and his sighs to come short, as he heard her come! Pandarus, leading her by the robe, approached and began to peep in at the curtain, and said, 'God work a cure on all the sick! See who is come here to visit you; here she is who is to blame for your death'; and thereat it seemed as if he wept almost.

'Ah, ah,' said Troilus ruefully, 'God knows that I fare ill enough! Who is there? In faith, I see nothing.'

'Sir,' Criseyde said, 'it is Pandarus and I.'

'You, dear heart? Alas! I am not able to rise to kneel and do you honour' and therewith he raised himself upright, and she at once put both her hands softly upon him.

'Ah, for the love of God, do not so to me,' said she; 'ah, what means this? Sir, I am come to you for only two causes, — first to thank you, and then to beseech you for continuance of your friendly lordship.'

When Troilus heard his lady pray him for lordship, he was between life and death for shame, nor could he have said a word in reply, though one had been about to smite off his head; and Lord, how ruddy he waxed all suddenly! And, sirs, the lesson that he thought he knew by heart to pray his lady with, was all run out of his memory.

Criseyde, who had a good wit, espied all this well enough and loved him none the less, though he were not malapert or pertinacious or over-bold, to sing a fool a mass. But what he said, when his shame had begun to go by, I will tell you as well as I can, as I find it in old books. The first word that escaped him was, twice, 'Mercy, mercy, dear heart!' And this he spoke in a voice changed and trembling for very fear, and his goodly bearing abashed, his hue now red, now pale, and his look downcast, humble and submissive. After these words he stopped a while, and his next words, when he could bring them out, were, 'God wot, so far as I have any wit at all, I have ever been all yours, and shall be till I am buried. Though I neither dare nor know how to make my lament to you, in faith I suffer none the less pain. Thus much I can utter now to the perfect woman whom I serve. If this displease you, right soon I will wreak it upon my own life, and do your heart a pleasure if my death can appease your wrath; for since you have once heard me say somewhat, I reck not how soon I die.'

Therewith to behold his manly sorrow might have melted a heart of stone. Pandarus wept as if he would turn to water, and ever poked his niece and said, 'It is true hearts that suffer! For the love of God, make an end of this thing, or slay us both at once in this place!'

'Why, what?' quoth she. 'By my troth, I wot not what you would have me say.'

'Why, then,' she said, 'I would pray him first to tell me his object and intent. I have never yet truly known what he means.'

'What I mean, sweet dear heart, goodly blooming noble one?' said Troilus. 'That you would sometimes look on me kindly with the beams of your clear eyes; and then agree that without hint of evil in any way I may be he always to do you faithful service, as to my own lady and chief delight, with all my wit and diligence; and that I should have, at your good pleasure and subject to your rod, comfort as great as my pain has been, and death if I break your commands; and that you deign to honour me so much as to lay any order upon me at any hour; and that I should be your true, humble, trusty servant, patient in my pains, evermore freshly desirous of diligent service, ready to receive your every desire with good will, however sorely I suffer: — this is my meaning, my own dear heart.'

'Lo, here is a hard request,' quoth Pandarus, 'reasonable for a lady to refuse! Now, my niece, were I a god you should die without mercy before the feast of Jove's birth, who have heard that this man desires naught but your honour, and see him wellnigh dying, and yet are so loath to suffer him to serve you.'

At that she began to turn her eyes on Troilus full simply and gently, whilst she considered with herself, and hastened not to fast with ever a word, but said soberly, 'Saving mine honour, and in such form as he has now said, I am truly willing to receive him fully to my service; beseeching him for God's love, and to the honour of faithfulness and nobility, that as I mean well to him so will he to me, and ever safeguard mine honour with prudence and diligence. And if from henceforth I can give him joy, in truth I will not fail. — Now be all whole again, and mourn no longer. But nevertheless I give you this warning, — king's son though you be, you shall have no more sovereignty over me in love than is right in such a case. If you do amiss, I will not forbear angering you; and whilst you serve me I will cherish you after your deserts. And in a word be glad, dear heart and all my knight, and be lusty and strong once more, and I will truly with all my power turn all your bitter into sweet. If I am she who may do you joy, for every woe you shall recover a felicity.' And then she took him in her arms and began to kiss him.

Pandarus fell on his knees, threw up his eyes to heaven and held his hands on high: 'Immortal god Cupid,' quoth he, 'of this thou mayst boast; and Venus, thou mayst make melody. For this miracle I seem to hear each bell in the town ring without hands! But stop, no more now of this; for these folk ere now will have read the letter and will be up anon. Hark! I hear them. But I conjure you, Criseyde, and you, Troilus, when you are able to walk, that you be in my house at my summons when I shall devise your coming. There you shall relieve your hearts right well, and we shall see which shall bear the palm in talking of love,' and therewith he laughed, 'for there you shall have leisure for it!'

'How long must I wait ere this be done?' quoth Troilus.

'When you are up and about,' he replied, 'this shall be done as I have said.'

With that Helen and Deiphobus were coming up even at the top of the stair. And Lord! how Troilus began to groan, to hoodwink his brother and sister! Quoth Pandarus, 'It is time for us to go. Take your leave of all three, niece, and let them speak together, and come forth with me.'

She took her leave of them full discreetly, as she well knew how, and they saluted her with all regard, I warrant you; and when she was gone, they commended her demeanour, her distinction and her wit, till it was a joy to hear them.

Now we will leave her on the way to her own house, and turn again to Troilus, who full lightly dismissed the letter that Deiphobus had seen in the garden, and would fain have been rid of Helen and of him. He said that he would fain sleep, and after all that talk have rest. Helen kissed him and took her leave betimes, and Deiphobus also; and everyone went home. Pandarus, as fast as he could, came back to Troilus, and all that joyous night he lay on a pallet by him to chat, and glad they were to be together.

When every other person was gone out and the doors were shut fast, to tell it shortly, Pandarus rose up and sat on the bedside, and began to speak soberly to Troilus as I shall tell you: 'My most loved lord and dear brother, God knows, and you know, how sore I grieved this year when I saw you so languishing more and more for love; so that with all my might and wit I have ever since done my diligence to bring you to joy, and I have now brought you to the state you wot of, so that through me you stand now in a fair way to thrive. Yet I say this for no boast, and know you why? Because (and a shame it is to say it) for your sake I have begun a sort of game which I will never do again for any man, though he were my brother a thousand-fold. That is to say, betwixt sport and earnest I am become for your sake such a go-between as brings women to men, — you know yourself what I mean. I have made my innocent niece so fully to trust your honour that all shall be even as you desire. But I take the all-wise God to witness that I never wrought this out of covetousness, but only to relieve that distress for which I thought you were wellnigh dying. So good brother, for God's love, since you have discretion, spare her fair name. You well know that amongst the people her name as yet is wellnigh sainted, for I dare to say that there never was man that ever knew her to do amiss. Woe is me that I who have caused all this new affair should know that she is my dear niece, and I at once her uncle and betrayer. Were it known that I had contrived to put the fantasy into my niece's head to do your pleasure and to be wholly yours, why! all the people would cry out upon it and say that I did the worst treachery in the world, she ruined and you profited nothing. Wherefore, ere I go a step further, I pray you again on your life that secrecy go with us in this affair, that is, that you never reveal it. Be not wroth though I often pray you to hold so high a matter secret, for my request you well know is reasonable. Think what woe has betided from making boasts, of old time as we read, and what mischances there are yet in this world from day to day for that same wicked offence. Wherefore these wise clerks that are dead have ever handed down such saws to us their posterity:

"The first of virtues is to hold thy tongue."

And were it not for diffuseness of speech, I could produce for you nigh a thousand old stories of women lost through men's false and foolish bragging. You know proverbs enough yourself against that fault of telling tales, even though men told truth as often as they lie. Alas, how often has one tongue made many a bright lady to say, "Alack the day that I was born!", and kept alive many a maiden's sorrow; and for the more part, if it were brought to the test, it is all untrue that men boast of. In the very nature of the thing, no braggart is to be believed. Vaunter and liar, both are one. Suppose thus: a woman grants me her love and says she will have none other, swears me to keep it secret, and afterwards I go and tell it to two or three; surely at the best I am a braggart, and a liar too, for I broke my promise. Look then if they are not to blame, such manner of folk, — indeed, what shall I call them?, — who make their boast of women, and name their names, who never yet promised them anything, nor knew them more than my old hat! It is no wonder, so God save me!, that women fear to deal with us men. I say not this for mistrust of you or of any wise man, but because of silly fools and the harm that comes in this world as much from folly as from malice. No woman, if she consider well, fears that fault in wise folk; for the wise are cautioned by the harm that fools run into.

'But now to the point. Dear brother, have all this that I have said in mind; keep your counsel and be of good cheer. In due season you shall find me faithful, and I will set your affair in such train that you shall be well content for it shall be right as you would have it. I know well that your intent is honest, and therefore I dare fully undertake this. You know what your lady has granted you; the day is set to draw up the charter! And now good-night, for I can no longer wake, but now that you are in bliss pray for me that God send me soon either death or relief!'

Who could tell half the joy and jubilation which the soul of Troilus felt when he heard Pandarus' promises? His old woe, that had made his heart faint, wasted and melted away in his joy, and all his store of sore sighs took wings at once, and he felt them no longer. Even as these hedge-rows and woods, that have been dead and dry through the winter, revest themselves in green when May is come and every lusty creature is gamesome, even so of a sudden was his heart full of rapture, and never was there a gladder man in all Troy. He cast up his look on Pandarus full gravely and friendly, and said, 'Friend, in April last you will remember how nigh death for woe you found me, and how busily you tried to learn from me the cause of my distress. You know how long I forbore to tell it, to you who are the man whom most of all I trust; yet there was no peril in revealing it to you, as I knew well. Tell me, if you please, how could I dare to tell others of this matter, who am of a tremble now, when no man can hear us? But nevertheless I swear to you by that God who governs all this world at His own pleasure, — and may Achilles with his spear cleave my heart, though my life were as eternal as it truly is mortal, if I swear falsely and if I late or soon would or durst or could reveal it, for all the wealth that God made under the sun, — I swear to you that I would rather die, come to my end in cruel King Agamemnon's prison, in the stocks amongst vermin and filth and wretchedness; and this I will swear to you to-morrow in all the temples of this town upon all the gods, if you wish to hear me. And I know well that you have done so much for me that I can nevermore deserve it, though I could die for you a thousand times a day. What more can I say than that I will serve you as your very slave, whithersoever you go, forever unto my life's end?

'But here I beseech you heartily that you never fancy in me such folly as this, — methought I saw in your speech your fear that I might deem what you are doing for me for friendship's sake to be the acts of a bawd. I am not mad, though I be unlettered; I know well the difference, perdy. He that goes on such a message for gold or riches, call him what you will; but this which you do, call it a gentle deed, and compassion and fellowship and trustfulness. All men know that distinctions must be made betwixt things that look alike. And that you may know I think not this service of yours to be a shame or scorn, here is my fair sister Polyxena, or Cassandra or Helen or any of the company; be she never so fair and shapely, tell me whichever of all you will have for yours, and let me alone to give her you! But since you have done me this benefit, to save my life and out of no hope of reward, now for the love of God perform this great emprise to the end, for now is greatest need, and I will ever obey all your behests, great and small. So now good-night, and let us both sleep.'

Thus was each of them well content with the other, so that all the world could not have made them more so. On the morrow, when they were up and arrayed, each went about his own affairs. But Troilus, though hope and pleasure made him burn in the sharp flame of desire, forgot not his prudent self-control, but restrained in many wise each hasty act and unbridled look, so that not a living person could have known by word or manner what was in his mind. His true thoughts were as far as the clouds from everyone, so well he could dissemble. And all this time that I am speaking of, this was his life: by day with all his power he served Mars in knightly arms, and for the most part he lay the long night and thought how he might best serve his lady and win her thanks. And though he lay full soft, I will not say that he was not somewhat discomforted in his thoughts, and that he turned not often on his pillows, and often longed not after the thing he lacked. In such cases, for aught I know, other men find it not all pleasure, any more than he did. But meanwhile, to come to the main thing, it certainly is written in the story that he saw his lady sometimes, and also that she spoke with him when she durst and would, and that they both considered full warily how they should proceed in everything in this matter. But they spoke so hurriedly and in such watchful dread lest any person should guess or overhear, that more than aught else they wished that Cupid would let them have their say out. But in the little that they spoke or did together, he was so heedful of all, that he seemed to her to know what she thought without a word from her, so that she had no need to ask him to do aught, or to forbid aught; wherefore it seemed to her that love, though it had come late, was opening to her the door to all joys. And, briefly to pass on in this tale, he so well employed his words and acts that he stood fully in his lady's grace, and twenty thousand times before she was done she thanked God that ever she had met with him; so well he knew how to bear himself in this lover's-service that no one in the world could have shown a better way. For she found him in all things so discreet, so secret and so compliant, that she felt he was to her a wall of steel, a shield against everything displeasing, so that she was no longer afraid to be under the governance of so prudent a man, I mean so far as the case required.

And to keep up this fire Pandarus was ever alike ready and diligent: all his thoughts were set on easing his friend, and ever he pushed on. He was sent to and fro, he fetched letters when Troilus was away. Never a man bore himself better to help his friend in time of need.

But now peradventure some man may look for me to rehearse every word or message, every look or smile of Troilus to his lady dear in all this time. I believe that were long to listen to, or to show all the words or every look of a man that stands in such a plight! In sooth I have never heard it done in any story, nor anyone here, I believe. I could not tell it all, though I would, for, as mine author says, there was one letter passed betwixt them that may well have contained a hundred verses, which he list not write of; how then should I endite a line of it?

But now to the consummation of it all. I say this, that, — whilst these two were in quiet and concord, as I have said, during this time that was so sweet, save only that they could not often come together or have leisure to say all they would, — Pandarus thought he had found a time for that which he had long striven for, to bring some time his fair niece and Troilus together at his house, where all this high matter of their love might be fully unraveled at leisure. Earnestly deliberating, he had foreseen and executed everything which might help his plan, and had spared no cost or labour. Let them come if they would, nothing should be lacking to them. And as to being espied there at all, that he knew to be impossible. Of a surety the wind was clear of every prating magpie and every spoil-sport; thus all was well, for all the world was blind to the thing. The timber is all ready to set up; naught is lacking but that we should know the hour in which she is to come.

Troilus, who knew fully of all this planning and watched it longingly, had founded his own plans upon it and devised his pretext, namely, that, if he were missed night or day whilst he was about his love-matter, he was gone to do sacrifice, and must watch alone at such and such a temple to receive an answer of Apollo, and to see him when the Greeks should flee. Therefore let no man hinder him (God forbid!), but rather pray Apollo to speed him!

Now there was little more to do; but Pandarus was up and at it, and (in brief) just after the changing of the moon, when the world is lightless a night or two, and when the heavens seemed preparing a rain, he went straightway on a morning to his niece, with what intent you have all heard. When he was come, he began to make sport as he was wont; and to make a mock of himself, and finally he swore by that and this that she should not evade him or make him longer gape at her, but she must certainly vouchsafe to come and sup in his house that evening. At which she laughed and made excuses, and said, 'It is raining, — why, how can I go?'

'A truce to this,' he replied; 'stand not thus debating! This must be done, and you shall soon be there.'

So at the last they agreed upon it; otherwise, as he softly swore to her in her ear, he would never come where she was again. And she began sportively to whisper him, and asked if Troilus were to be there. Nay, he swore to her, for he was out of town, and added, 'Supposing he were, niece, you need never have the more fear, for rather than folk should espy him there, I would die a thousand times.'

Mine author list not fully declare what she thought when he told her that Troilus was gone out of town, whether she thought he spoke truth therein or no; but he says that without more delay she agreed to go with him, since he begged her, and gave him due obedience as his niece. But nevertheless she besought him, though there were no real cause of fear, to beware the talk of goosish people, who fancy things that never were, and to consider well whom he brought to his house. 'Uncle, since I must trust you,' she said, 'look that all be well, for I am doing as you wish.' He swore this to her, by stock and stone and by the gods that dwell in heaven; or else, flesh and blood, he would abide with King Pluto as deep in hell as Tantalus! Why should I make a long story? When all was fixed, he arose and took leave.

That night she came to supper, with a certain attendance of her own men, and her fair niece Antigone and eight or nine other of her women. But who was glad now? Who but Troilus, think you, that stood and saw them through a little window in a closet where he was mewed up till midnight, unwitting to everybody but Pandarus? But now to our point. When she was come, with all joy and friendly greeting her uncle took her anon in his arms, and after, when the time came, one and all sat them down full quietly to the supper. God wot, there was no dainty needed to be fetched! After supper they rose, well content with the world, and with hearts lusty and glad. Happy was he who had the best device to please her, or who made her laugh! One sang, another played, one told a tale of Wade's boat. But at the last, as everything comes to an end, she must be going home, and took leave.

But ah, Fortune, executrix of destiny! Ah, influences of the high heavens! True it is that, under God, ye are our governors, though the manner be veiled from us beasts! This I say now, that Criseyde was about to hasten homeward; but all without her leave the gods' will was executed, wherefore she must remain. The bent moon with her pale horns, and Saturn and Jupiter, were conjunct in Cancer, so that such a rain came down from heaven that every woman there was in a very fright for that pounding rain; at which Pandarus laughed and said, 'Now were the time for a lady to get her hence! But, good niece, if I ever pleased you in anything, I beg you now to do my heart such a pleasure as to remain here all night with me; for niece, this is your own house, perdy! Now, by my troth, I say it not in sport, — for you to go now would shame me.'

Criseyde, who had as much prudence as half the world all together, took heed of his request, and since it rained so and all was a-flood, she thought, 'I may as well remain and agree gladly, with a friendly cheer, and win his thanks, as grumble and then remain; for as to going home, that may not be. — I will,' she said, 'sweet dear uncle; since you wish me, it is only reason, and I am right glad to remain here with you, and I was but jesting when I said I would go.'

'Gramercy, niece, verily,' he said. 'Whether you were jesting or no, I am right glad now that you will remain.'

Thus far all was well. And then again began new joy and festivity. But Pandarus would fain, if he could in manners, have hastened her to bed; and said, 'Lord, this is a huge rain, this is a storm to sleep through, and my counsel is that we soon begin to try! And, niece, know you where I shall lodge you? Right yonder in my little inner chamber, that you may hear no noise of thunder or of rain, and I alone in the outer house will be guardian of all your women. They shall all sleep soft and well in this middle chamber that you see here, and you shall be there within; and if you rest well to-night, come often, whatever weather is above you. — The wine anon! — Whenever you are ready, it is time to go to rest.'

There is nothing more to say but that straightway they drank their final draught, and drew curtains, and every person that had no more business there went out of the chamber. And evermore it rained and blew so marvellous loud that scarce could one hear another. Then her uncle Pandarus, as was fitting, with such of her women as were most privy with her, brought her full cheerily to her bed's side, and took his leave, bowing full low and saying, 'Without this chamber door and just across, lie all your women, so that you may call hither whom you will of them.' So when she was laid down in the inner chamber, and all her women in order a-bed as I have told, there was no more skipping or tramping about; but if any man were anywhere stirring he was bidden get to bed, Devil take him! and let those who were a-bed get to sleep.

But Pandarus, who knew well the old game and every point of it, when he saw that all was well so far, thought he would begin his work. He softly undid Troilus' closet door, sat down by him as still as a stone, and (to come briefly to the point) told him every word of all this thing, and said, 'Make you ready anon, for you shall go into the bliss of heaven!'

'Now Saint Venus,' quoth Troilus, 'send me grace, for never yet such need had I before, nor half the fear!'

'Fear never a bit,' said Pandarus, 'for it shall be even as you would have it. By my thrift, this night shall I make all well, or else cast all the gruel in the fire!'

'Yet do thou inspire me, blessed Venus,' quoth Troilus, 'as surely as I serve thee now and ever shall better and better till I die! And, O mirthful goddess, if I had evil aspects of Mars or Saturn when I was born, or thou wert combust or feeble, pray thy father of his grace to turn away all that harm, that I may go my way rejoicing, for the love of him whom thou didst love in the wood-shaw, I mean Adonis, that was slain by the boar. And help, Jove, for the love of fair Europa, whom thou in the form of a bull didst fetch away! Mars, with thy bloody mantle, hinder me not, for the love of the Cyprian dame! Phœbus, think how Daphne shut herself under the bark and for fear became a laurel-tree; yet for her love, help me now a this need! Mercury too, for the love of Herse, for which Pallas was wroth with Aglaurus, now help! And Diana, I beseech thee that this emprise be not hateful to thee! O three fatal sisters, who spun me my destiny ere any garment was shapen for me, now help this work that is beginning!'

'You wretched mouse's heart!' quoth Pandarus. 'Are you aghast that she will bite you? Why, don this furred cloak over your shirt and follow me. I will take the blame! — But abide, and let me go before a little.' With that word he began to undo a trap, and led Troilus in by the skirt of his garment.

The stern wind snorted so loud that no one could hear any other noise, and they who lay without the door were all safely asleep. Pandarus with a full sober cheer went anon to the door where they lay and softly shut it. As he was coming back privily, his niece awoke and asked, 'Who is walking there?'

'My dear niece,' quoth he, 'it is I. Wonder not at it, and fear not.' And he came close and said in her ear, 'Not a word, for the love of God, I beseech you! Let no creature arise and hear us talking.'

'Why, *benedicite*, what way came you in,' she asked, 'thus without their knowing?'

'Here at this little trap-door,' said he.

'Let me call someone,' she said then.

'Eh, God forbid that you should do such a folly!' quoth Pandarus. 'They might imagine what they have never once thought of. It is not good to wake a sleeping hound, nor to give any person cause for conjecturing. I will be bound your women are all asleep, and will be till sun-up, so that, for all them, men could mine the house. And when I have said all my say, I will go away unnoticed even as I came.

'Now, my niece, you must understand, as all you women will grant, that for a woman to hold a man long time in hand and let him call her "sweeting" and "dear heart," and then clap a coxcomb above his hood, I mean love another all this time, — she beguiles him and shames herself. Now why tell I you all this? You wot yourself as well as any that your love is fully granted to Troilus, the worthiest knight of this world, and you have thereto plighted your troth; so that, unless it were his fault, you should never be false to him whilst you live. Now it stands thus: since I left you, Troilus, to speak out flatly, has come in all this rain over a gutter by a secret route into my chamber, quite unknown to everyone save to myself, I swear by the faith I owe King Priam. And in such pain and distress he has come that, unless by now he is quite mad, he must speedily fall into madness, without God's help. And the cause why is this, — he says he has been told by a friend that you are said to love another, named Horastes, for sorrow at which this night is to be the end of all for him!'

Criseyde, when she heard all this strange talk, began to grow cold about her heart, and answered straightway with a sigh, 'Alas, I believed that, whoso told tales, my dear heart would not so lightly hold me false! Alas for mistaken fancies, what harm they do! Now I have lived too long! Horastes! And beguile Troilus! I know him not, so God help me! Alas, what wicked spirit told such a thing? Now certes, uncle, if I see him to-morrow, I will as fully acquit myself of that as ever woman did, if he will have me. Oh God!' she sighed, 'how worldly happiness, that clerks call false felicity, is mingled with many a bitterness! God wot, the condition of vain prosperity is full of anguish, for either joys come not together or else they will not last. Oh fickle weal, and unstable earthly joy! With whatsoever person thou showest thee merry, either he knows thou art changeful or knows it not; it must be one of the twain. Now if he knows it not, how can he say that he has true joy and bliss, who is ever in the darkness of ignorance? And if he knows that joy is fleeting, as every worldly joy must needs be, then every time he remembers this, the dread of losing joy keeps him from perfect happiness: and if he cares a farthing to lose his joy, it must seem that joy is worth full little. Wherefore I must conclude thus, that verily, for aught I can see, there is no true weal here in this world. But ah jealousy, thou wicked serpent, thou misbelieving envious folly, why hast thou made Troilus distrust me, who never yet wittingly offended him?'

'This matter has befallen thus, — ' Pandarus began.

'Why, uncle mine,' she cried, 'who told him such a thing? Alas! why does my dear heart thus?'

'You know, my niece, what it is,' said he. 'I hope all that is amiss shall yet be well; you can quench all this if you will. And I believe it is best that you do right so.'

'So I will to-morrow, in truth, before God,' she said, 'so that it shall suffice.'

'To-morrow? Alas, that were a fair deed!' he replied. 'Nay, nay, it may not stand so, for clerks write that peril goes with delay; nay, such dallying is not worth a bean. There is a time for everything, I dare avow. When a chamber or a hall is afire there is more need to save it promptly than to dispute and ask about, "How did that candle fall into the straw?" Ah, *benedicite!* in all this pother the harm is done, and — farewell, fieldfare! And now, my niece, take this not ill, but if you suffer him to be all night in this woe, so God help me, you never loved him; here betwixt you and me alone I am bold to say that. But I know well you will not do so, you are too wise to do so great folly as to jeopardize his life all night.'

'I never loved him? By heaven, I believe you never loved aught so well,' said she.

'By my thrift now,' quoth he, 'we shall see that. For since you make this comparison with me, if I would see him all night in sorrow for all the treasure in Troy-town I pray God I may never see happiness again! Look now, if you that are his love put his life in jeopardy all night for a thing of naught, by the God above us this delay comes not only from folly but from malice, and that I swear to. What! I tell you flatly, if you leave him in his pain it is neither a wise nor a gentle deed!'

'You may do one thing,' answered Criseyde, 'and therewith cure his distress. Take this blue ring and bear it to him, for there is nothing might better please him, save I myself, or more rest his heart. And tell my dear heart that his grief is causeless, and that he shall see to-morrow.'

'A ring?' quoth he. 'Yea, the hazel-woods shake! Ah, niece, that ring should have a stone that could make dead men live, and such a ring I believe you have not! Discretion is gone clean out of your head, that I can see, and more is the pity! Ah time lost, well thou mayst cure sloth! Know you not that a noble and high heart neither sorrows nor is calmed for a little thing? Were a fool in a jealous rage, I should not care a farthing for his sorrow, but should present him with a few soft words some day when I should chance to see him. But this thing stands in quite another fashion. This man is so noble and so tender of heart that he will wreak his sorrow on himself by his own death, for trust well, however he may suffer, he will speak no jealous word to you. And therefore before you break his heart, niece, speak yourself to him of this matter, for with a single word you can control his heart. Now I have told you his peril, and his coming is unknown to everybody, and there can be no harm or sin in it, perdy. I will be with you myself all the time. You know how he is your own knight and that by rights you ought to trust him; so I am all ready to fetch him when you say the word.'

All this tale was so piteous to hear, and sounded at first though so like a truth, and Troilus her knight was so dear to her, that, what with his privy coming and the security of the place, it is no wonder she granted him such a favour, since she did all in innocence. 'So God rest my soul,' she answered, 'as I am truly sorry for him! And if heaven grant me grace, I fain would do the best I can. But in faith, unless God send me better guidance, I am right at my wit's end on the *pons asinorum*, whether you stay or go for him!'

'Ah, niece, but listen,' quoth Pandarus; '*pons asinorum* is the bridge of asses; it seems hard that asses will never learn for very sloth and wilfulness. But this is only for those who are not worth two peas in any case; you are wise, and know that this cause of mine is neither hard, nor reasonable to withstand.'

'Well, uncle,' she replied, 'do herein as you will. But before he comes I will first arise; and for the love of God, since all my trust is on you two prudent men, now manage so discreetly that I may keep my fair name as well as he his happiness, for I am here in your power.'

'That is well said, dear niece,' he replied; 'blessings on that wise, gentle heart! But lie still, you need not spring up for him; receive him even here, and each of you for God's love relieve the other's pain! And ah! Venus, I praise thee, for I hope soon we shall be all merry.'

Full soon Troilus was on his knees even at her bedside, and full soberly in his best wise greeted his lady. But Lord! how red she waxed all suddenly! Nor, though men would have cut her neck asunder, could she have brought out a word, for his sudden coming. But Pandarus, whose feeling was so quick in every case, began anon to make sport, and said, 'Niece, see how this lord can kneel now to beg for your troth! Only see this nobleman now!' And with that word he ran for a cushion and said, 'Kneel now as long as you will! And may God soon bring your hearts to rest!'

If she let him kneel for a time, I cannot say whether sorrow made her forget, or whether she took it as only due from her suitor; but well I wot that she did him thus much pleasure, that she kissed him, though she was sighing sore, and then bade him sit down.

'Now you shall make a fair beginning,' quoth Pandarus. 'Now, good dear niece, make him sit within there upon your bedside, that each may hear the other better.' And at that he drew toward the fire, and took a light and showed himself busy at looking over an old romance.

Criseyde, who felt herself truly Troilus' lady and upon a clear ground of sureness, thought her servant and knight should not have fancied any falsity in her; yet nevertheless, considering his distress and that greatness of love is one cause of such folly, she spoke thus gently to him of his jealousy. 'Lo, my dear heart, it is the excellent glory of love, against which no man can or ought to make resistance, that drives me thus to take pity on your pain, and also because I know your heart to be all mine, and I have felt well and always seen your great fidelity and daily service and your constant goodness; for which, my dear heart and own knight, I thank you as far as my wit extends, though I cannot as much as were right. And to the extent of my knowledge and power I ever have been, and shall be whatever it may cost me, true to you and wholly yours with all my heart, and doubt you not that the test shall find it so.

'What this is all about, dear heart, I shall well say to you, so you grieve not though I complain to you of yourself; for thereby I mean to put a final end to the pain that holds your heart and mine in heavy case, and to redress every wrong. My own good knight, I know not why or how that wicked viper jealousy has crept into you so causelessly; I fain would do away the harm which he has wrought. Alas that he, or a piece of him, should make his haunt in so worthy a place, whence may Jove soon tear him out! But O Jove, author of nature, is it an honour to thy godhead that innocent folk suffer injury and he who is guilty goes quit? Ah! were it lawful to complain against thee, who permittest undeserved jealousy, I should cry out on thee. And all my woe is that now folk are wont to say, "Yea, jealousy is love," and would excuse a bushel of venom because one grain of love is dropped into it! But the great God in heaven knows if it be like love, or hate or anger! And thereafter it ought to have its name.

'But certain it is that one kind of jealousy is more to be excused than another; as when there is cause, or when the jealous fantasy is so well and duteously repressed that it scarce does or says aught amiss, but generously consumes all its own distress. Such jealousy I excuse for the nobleness of it. Some jealousy is so full of fury and despite that it surmounts all repression. But you, dear heart, are not in such case, as I thank God, wherefore this passion of yours I will but call an illusion wrought by abundance of love and busy anxiety, which causes your heart to endure this pain; for which I am right sorry, but I am not wroth. But now, to clear me and rest your heart, for the love of God let us test this suspicion, whether by ordeal or by oath, by casting of lots, or in whatever wise you will! If I am guilty, let me be slain! Alas, what more can I do or say?' With that a few bright fresh tears fell from her eyes, and she cried, 'O God! Thou knowest that never yet was Criseyde false to Troilus in act or thought!' And then she laid her head down in the bed, covered it with the sheet, sighing sore, and held her peace.

But now may God help to quench this sorrow, and so I trust He will, for He can best! I have often seen a full misty morrow follow a merry summer's day, and again green May follows after winter. Ever men see, and read in books, that after sharp conflicts come victories.

When Troilus heard her words, trust me, he cared not to sleep! It seemed to him no light chastisement to see his lady Criseyde's tears, but indeed, for every tear that escaped her, he felt the cramp of death creep and clutch him about the heart. In his mind he began to curse the time that ever he came there, or ever was born, for now was bad turned into worse, and all the labour which he had done already he deemed but lost, and himself lost as well. 'Ah Pandarus, alas!' he thought, 'your wiles serve for nothing, alack the day!' He hung down his head and fell on his knees and sorrowfully sighed. What could he say? He felt himself a dead man, for she was wroth who only could lighten his sorrows. But nevertheless, when he was able to speak, he faltered out, 'God knows that I am not to blame, when all is known, for this pleasant sport!' And then grief so shut up his heart that not a tear fell from his eyes; his spirits were so astonied and oppressed that they crushed his strength, till sorrow and fear and every feeling else faded away from him, and down he fell suddenly in a swoon.

It was no little sorrow to see this, but all remained quiet, for in a trice Pandarus was up and whispering, 'Not a word, niece, or we are lost! Be not afraid!' At last in spite of anything he cast him upon the bed, saying, 'Thief, have you a man's heart?' and rent off his mantle. 'Niece,' he said, 'unless you help now, your own Troilus is lost.'

'In faith,' she said, ' I would gladly if I but knew how, — alas that I was born!'

'Ah! my niece, if you would pull out the knife,' said he, 'that sticks in his heart, say "All is forgiven," and all the trouble will be over.'

'Yea,' she answered, 'grant me that, and take all the rest the sun goes round!' And thereat she vowed to him in his ear, 'Indeed, dear heart, I am not wroth, I pledge my word,' and she swore many another vow; 'now speak to me, for it is I, Criseyde.'

Yet none the more did he come to. They began to rub his wrists and the palms of his hands and to wet his temples; and to deliver him from his bitter bonds she often kissed him, and in a word she did all she could to revive him. At last he began to draw breath, and soon after that to come out of his swoon, and memory and reason to dawn upon him. When he was more fully awake, 'Oh mercy, God!' he cried, 'what is this?'

'This is pretty conduct!' quoth Criseyde. 'Is this a man's sport? What, Troilus, for shame! Will you do thus?' Therewith she laid her arm over him, oftentimes kissed him, and forgave him all. And he thanked her, and relieved his heart by talking to her, and she answered him, and with her goodly words diverted him, and comforted his sorrows.

Then said Pandarus, 'For aught I can see, neither I nor this candle serve any purpose here. Light is not good for sick folks' eyes! But now for the love of God, since you are brought into this goodly plight, let no heavy thought be hanging in your two hearts!' And then he carried his candle to the chimney.

And then, when she had taken of Troilus such oaths as she wished, though there were no need of them, she felt no fear or cause to bid him rise. In some cases a less thing than an oath may be enough, for every person who truly loves means naught but what is noble. But she wished to know of what man, and why, and on what occasion he felt this jealousy, since there was no cause; and she bade him tell her carefully the signs from which he conceived it, or otherwise certainly she averred that this was of malice, to test her. In a word, he must obey his lady's behest, and feign a cause to avoid a greater ill. He told her, 'when she was out at such and such a festival she might at last have looked at him,' — I know not what he said, somewhat not worth a farthing, having no fish for an excuse.

'Sweet, even were it so,' Criseyde answered, 'what harm was that, since I meant no evil? For, by that God who made us both, my intent is innocent in all things. Such talk is not worth a bean! Will you do as the childish jealous lover? Now truly you deserve to be beaten!'

Then Troilus began to sigh sorrowfully, and his heart died within him lest she should be wroth, and he said, 'Alas, my sweetest heart Criseyde, have mercy upon my sick fancies. If there be any wrong in those words that I said, I will trespass no more; do what you list, I hang on your grace!'

'For guilt, mercy,' answered Criseyde. 'That is to say, I forgive it all. And evermore you must remember this night, and be sure that you offend no more!'

'Nay, my dear heart, in truth,' quoth he.

'And now,' she said, 'forgive me that I caused you pain, my own sweet heart!'

This faithful, loving Troilus, taken by surprise with the bliss of it, put all in God's hand, as one who meant naught but good, and by a sudden resolve caught her to him fast in his arms. And there upon Pandarus benevolently quitted them, saying, 'If you be prudent, swoon no more now, lest more folk arise!'

What can the poor lark do when the sparrow-hawk has her in his foot? (— Though I tarry a year, some time I can do no less than follow mine author in telling of their joy as well as in telling their heaviness, whoever may find the tale sweet or sour!) Criseyde, as clerks write in their old books, began to quake like an aspen-leaf, when she felt him fold her in his arms. And Troilus, all whole after his cold cares, began to thank the seven bright gods. And thus sundry pains bring folk to paradise. So Troilus began to strain her in his arms, and said, 'Oh, sweet, as sure as I am alive now you are caught! Now there is none but we two! Now yield you, for there is no escape!'

And to that Criseyde answered, 'Had I not before this yielded myself, my sweet, dear heart, in truth I were not here now!'

Ah, truly it is said, and men may ever see, that to be healed of a fever or other great sickness men must drink full bitter drink; and to win gladness men oft must swallow pain and great woe. And here we see it, for this adventure after pain has won its cure. And now sweetness seems more sweet because bitterness was tasted before. Out of woe they are floating into bliss, such as they had never felt since they were born. Is not this better than that both should be lost? Let every woman take heed, for the love of heaven, to do thus when need comes!

Criseyde, all free now from dread and vexation, and with just cause to trust him, now that she knew his faithfulness and honest intent, made so much ado over him that it was a joy to see. As the sweet woodbine with many a twist twines about a tree, each wound arms about the other. And as the little abashed nightingale stops at first when she begins to sing, if she hear any herdsman's voice or any creature stirring in the hedge, and afterwards confidently lets her voice ring out, so Criseyde, when her fear was over, opened her heart and told all that was in it. And as a man who sees certain death before him, for aught that he can tell, and by a sudden rescue escapes, and out of death is brought into security, for all the world in even such present gladness was Troilus with his lady dear. — God grant we never meet with worse hap! –

Thus he began to delight himself in this heaven, and therewithal he kissed her a thousand times till he scarce knew what to do for joy.

'O Love, O Charity,' then he cried out, 'and thy mother, Cytherea the sweet, next after thee be she praised, Venus the benignant planet! And next I salute thee, Hymen! For never was man so beholden to you gods as I, whom ye have brought out of my cold cares. Benign Love, holy bond of all creatures whoso would have grace and will not honour thee, his desire attempts to fly without wings. All were lost, unless thy grace passed our deserts, unless thou of thy loving-kindness didst succour them that alway do for thee best labour and service. Me that have least desert amongst all that are admitted to thy grace, me thou hast helped where I was in point to die, and hast bestowed me in so high a station that no bliss can go beyond it. I can say no more, but reverence and laud be to thy kindness and thy might!' And thereat he kissed Criseyde, at which in truth she felt no discomfort!

'Now would to God, my sweetest heart,' he began again, 'I knew how I could please you! What man ever had so happy a lot as I, upon whom the best and fairest that ever I saw has deigned to rest her heart! Here men can see that mercy goes beyond justice. I am unworthy of you, lady bright; but I pray you of your benignity to think that, though I be unworthy, I must needs grow better in some wise through the virtue of your high service. And for the love of God, dear lady, as He has created me to serve you and wills that you should be my governor, to let me live, if you will, or die, teach me how to deserve your thanks, so that through my ignorance I may do naught to displease you. For certes I dare swear, blooming perfect woman, that all my life you shall find in me fidelity and devotion, and that I shall never break your command; and if I do, present or absent, for the love of God let me instantly be slain, if it so please your womanhood!'

'On this is all my trust,' quoth she; 'gramercy indeed, my own dear heart, my own heart's joy, my ground of comfort! But let us forget all this, for we have said enough. And finally, in one word, welcome, my knight, my peace, my sufficiency.'

One of the least of their joys it were impossible for my wit to tell. But ye who have been at such a feast of gladness, judge if they were glad! I can say no more but that this time, betwixt dread and security, these two felt the full worthiness of love. O blissful time, sought of them so long, how blithe thou wert unto them both! Why had I not bought such a time with my soul, yea, or the least joy that was there! Away, thou foul fear and thou coy disdain, and leave them dwelling in this heavenly bliss, which is so high that none can tell it! But though I cannot tell all, as mine author can with his goodly pen, yet, before God, I have ever told and shall tell the main part of his words. And if, in reverence of love, I have added in anything, I speak under your correction who have feeling in the art of love, and commit them wholly to your discretion, to increase or diminish what I have written; and to do so I beseech you. — But now to my former narrative.

These two that we left in each other's arms were so loath to go asunder that it would have seemed violent ravishment; or rather this was their chiefest fear, that all this might prove to have been a fond dream. Wherefore full oft each of them said, 'Sweet, am I holding you thus, or dream I it?' And Lord! with so goodly a look he gazed upon her that his eyes never moved from her face. 'Oh dear heart!' he said, 'can it be that you are really here?'

'Yea, my own heart, God be thanked for His goodness,' said Criseyde, and kissed him till for joy he knew not where his spirit was. Full often he kissed her two eyes, and said, 'Oh bright eyes, it was ye that wrought me this woe, ye humble nets of my dear lady! Though there be mercy written in your looks, God knows the text is full hard to read. How were ye able to bind me without cords?' And then once more he would take her strongly in his arms, and would sigh a thousand times; not such grievous sighs as men utter for woe, or when they are sick, but gentle sighs, such as give ease and show the feeling within. Of such sighs he could never heave enough.

And then soon they fell to speaking of sundry matters which had to do with their case, and in sport exchanged rings, of which I find nothing more in my books. But I know well that Criseyde gave him a brooch of gold and azure, in which was set a ruby like a heart, and stuck it on his garment.

Lord! Could a man believe that a covetous wretch, who blames love and thinks scorn of it, was ever yet granted such delight from all the pence that he can scratch together and hoard, as there is in one moment of perfect love? Nay, so God save me, no niggard can have such perfect joy. They will say yea, but Lord! how the anxious wretches lie in their throats, full of woe and fear! They call love a folly or madness, but it only befalls them to forego the wine of life both white and red, and to live in woe; may God give them ill chance, and promote every faithful lover! Would to God that these wretches who despise the service of love had ears as long as covetous Midas had, and had drunk as hot and strong a draught as Crassus drank for his evil lusts, to teach them that covetousness is sin, and love, for all that men hold it folly, is virtue!

These two of whom I am telling you were talking joyously in full trust of each other, and began to rehearse how and when and where each first knew the other, and every woe and fear that was over. All that heaviness, God be thanked, was turned to joy! When they came to speak of any woe of times past, ever the tale would break off in kissing and fall into a new joy; and since they were now one, they did all their might to recover their bliss and be at rest, and so countervail past woe with joy. Reason will not that I even speak of sleep, for it accords not with my matter. God wot, they thought of it full little! Lest this time so dear to them should in any wise escape in vain, it was passed in all eager and noble joy.

But soon the cock, the general time-keeper, began to flap on his breast and crow, and Lucifer, messenger of day, began to rise and throw out his beams, and eastward also rose Jupiter for any man to see, and then with sore heart Criseyde said to Troilus, 'Alas that I was born, my heart's life, my trust, my joy! What woe that day must sever us! For it is time for you to go hence, or else I am ruined forever. Alas, night, why wait thou not hover over us as long as when Jove lay with Alcmena? O black night, that wast created by God, as folk read in books, at certain times to hide this world with thy black weeds, that thereunder men may rest them, well may beasts complain and men chide thee, that when day is to break us with labour, thou fleest thus away and deignest not to give us rest. Too shortly thou dost thine office, thou hasty night! Because thou in malice so hastest thee downwards may God, author of nature, curse thee and bind thee to our hemisphere so that nevermore thou shalt revolve under the earth! For it is through thy rash hying out of Troy that I have so soon foregone my heaven!'

At those words Troilus seemed to feel bloody tears distill out of his heart; never yet had he felt such heaviness to grow out of such joy. He began to strain his lady dear in his arms, and said, 'Cruel day, accuser of the happiness that love and night have stolen and covered up, cursed be thy coming into Troy-town, for every little hole has one of thy bright eyes! Envious day, why wilt spy so? What hast thou lost? What seekest thou here? May God of His grace quench thy light forever! Alas, pitiless day, how have lovers offended thee? Thine be the pain of hell! Many a lover hast thou slain, and shalt slay! Thou pourest in and lettest them nowhere rest. Why dost thou proffer thy light here for sale? Go sell it to them that engrave little seals. We wish thee not, we need thee not!'

And he would chide Titan, the sun, and say, 'O fool, well may men despise thee, that hast Aurora all night by thy side, and sufferest her soon to rise up from thee, thus to plague lovers! What! Keep thy bed, thou and thy precious Morn! I pray God for ill luck to both of you!'

Then he sighed sore and said, 'My own lady, very root of my weal and woe, goodly Criseyde, must I be gone too? Must I, alas? My heart will burst in two! How shall I keep my life an hour, since with you is all the joy I have? What shall I do? I know not how or when I shall see the time to be with you again thus. God wot how it will fare with my life. Since longing for you even now so constrains me that I am dead unless I return, how can I remain long away from you? But, my own bright lady, if I knew utterly that your own servant and knight were as firmly enclosed in your heart as you in mine (which were more precious to me to know than to possess two such worlds as this), I should the better endure my pain.'

To this Criseyde answered with a sigh, 'Dear heart, in verity the game has now gone so far that sooner shall Phœbus fall from his sphere, and every eagle mate with the dove, and every rock move from his place, than Troilus shall fade from Criseyde's heart! You are so deeply graven upon my heart that, though I were to die upon the rack and even though I wished to turn you from my thoughts, so God save me, I could not! For the love of God who made us, let no other fancy creep into your brain and cause me to die! I beseech you to have me as fast in mind as I have you; if I verily knew that to be true, God could not increase my happiness a jot. Dear heart, be true to me, or else it were a rueful thing, for by heaven and by my troth I am yours! Be glad therefore, and live in trust; this I never said before, nor shall to another. If it were a great gladness to you to return after you are gone, I were as fain as you that you should, as surely as I hope for rest for my soul!' And then she took him in her arms and kissed him often.

Against his will, since it must needs be, Troilus rose up and prepared to go, and a hundred times took his lady dear in his arms; and sped on his way, saying in such voice as though his heart were bleeding, 'Farewell, dear sweet heart, God grant us safe and soon to meet!' To which she answered not a word for sorrow, so sore did their parting pain her, and Troilus went to his own palace as woe-begone, to say the truth, as she was.

So hard wrung him the pain of sharp desire to be again in bliss that it would not out of his remembrance. Returned to his royal palace, he crept softly to his bed, to sleep long, as he was wont. But all for naught; for all he lay and shut his eyes, sleep would not sink into his heart, for thinking how she for whom desire burned him was worth a thousand-fold more than he had believed. And in his mind he began to revolve up and down every word and look of her, and firmly to imprint in his thoughts even the least point of all that joy; and truly, from the very remembrance, longing burned him all newly, and the sweetness of love began to breed more than before, and yet there was naught that he could do.

Criseyde also, in the selfsame wise, was enclosing in her heart the worthiness of Troilus, his lustiness, his prudent acts, his nobility, and every point of their meeting; thanking Love that he had bestowed her so well, and longing to have her dear love again in such wise that she durst make him cheer.

In the morning came Pandarus to his niece and greeted her fairly, saying, 'All night long it rained so hard that, alas!, all my fear is lest you had little chance for sleep and dreams, sweet niece! All night the rain so kept me awake that some of us must have the headache, I believe!' Then he came nearer and said, 'How is it now, this bright morning? Niece, how do you fare?'

'Never the better for you,' Criseyde answered, 'fox that you are, bad luck to you! Before God, for all your innocent words it was you caused all these doings. Ah, one who first sees you knows you full little!' With that she covered her face with the sheet, and waxed red for shame.

Pandarus began to pry under it, and said, 'Niece, if I am to be slain, here is a sword; smite off my head!' With that he thrust his arm behind her neck, and at last kissed her.

I pass over all that which it needs not say. What! God forgives our sins, and she also forgave, and began to talk merrily with her uncle, for she had nothing else against him save this. But to make an end of this thing, when the time came she went home to her house. So now Pandarus has wholly gained his purpose.

Now let us turn again to Troilus, who lay full long a-bed restless, and privily sent after Pandarus to come to him in all haste. He came anon, full little did he refuse!, and greeted Troilus gravely and sat down upon his bed's side. With all the emotion of friendly love that heart can think of, Troilus fell on his knees before Pandarus, and before he would arise from the spot he thanked him earnestly a thousand times and blessed the day that Pandarus was born to bring him out of his trouble. 'Ah friend best of all friends that ever were,' he said, 'you have brought my soul to rest in heaven out of Phlegethon, the fiery flood of hell. Though I could give up my life a thousand times a day in your service, it would not avail a jot to pay my debt. The sun which sees all the world saw never yet, I dare stake my life, one so wholly fair and good as she whose I am wholly and ever shall be till I die. And that I am hers thus, thanks be to the high majesty of Love, and to your kind diligence! It is no little thing that you have given me, wherefore my life is your property forever. For it is through your help that I live, or else I had been dead now many a day!' And with that word he laid him down in his bed.

Pandarus listened full gravely till he had said all, and then answered, 'My dear friend, if I have done aught for you, God wot I am glad, as glad as a man could be of it, so God help me. But, — take not ill what I say, — for the love of God beware of this, that you yourself should bring to an end the joy into

which you are come. For of all fortune's sharp adversities the worst is this, —
for a man to have been in weal and to remember it when it is gone. You are
wise enough, therefore make no error. Though now you sit warm and safe, be
not too rash; if you are, of a surety it will ruin you. Now you are at ease; keep
yourself well in hand therein. For as sure as fire burns, it is as great a craft to
keep as to gain. Bridle your speech always, and your passions, for we hold
to worldly joy but by a wire, as we know well because it ever breaks so often.
Therefore we must needs be gentle with it!'

'Before God, my dear friend,' quoth Troilus, 'I hope I shall so bear me that
naught shall be lost through my guilt; nor shall I ever be so rash as to hurt her.
We need not always take thought nicely about this matter. If you knew my
heart well, Pandarus, in faith you would have small anxiety for this!'

Then he began to tell him about that happy time, and how at first he feared
that he had angered her. And then, 'Friend, as I am a true knight,' he said,
'and by the faith that I owe to God and to you, I had it never half so hot as at
this moment! And ever the more love stings me, the more it delights me. I wot
not certainly how it is, but now I feel a new quality in my love, yea, quite
another than I felt before now.'

'He that once has been in the joy of heaven,' answered Pandarus, 'I dare be
sworn ever afterwards feels otherwise than when he first heard tell of it.'

To say all in one word, Troilus was never sated with speaking of this
thing, with praising to Pandarus the goodness of his own dear lady and with
thanking and making much of him. This talk was ever new till night parted
them.

Soon after this, as Fortune would have it, came the blissful sweet time when
Troilus was forewarned that he should meet his lady again where they met
before, for which he felt his heart swim in joy, and duly praised all the gods.
Let us see now if he can be merry! The form and manner of her coming, and
of his, were observed as before, and need not be described; in joy and security
Pandarus brought the two together when they would, and left them in quiet
and peace. Now that they are met you need not ask me if they are blithe. If it
was well before, it now was better a thousand-fold, I need not tell you;
gone was every sorrow and fear, each sought only to please the other, and both
had and knew they had as much joy as heart may contain. This is no little
thing to say, it passes every wit to describe. It is not enough to call it that
perfect felicity which these wise clerks so commend. This joy cannot be writ-
ten with ink; this passes all that heart can conceive.

But (alas the while!) they began to see the well-known signs of day's
approach, for which they seemed to feel death's wound. They changed colour

for woe, and they began anew to revile day, calling it envious, traitor, and more evil names, and bitterly cursing the morning light. 'Alas!' quoth Troilus, 'now I see that Pyroeis and the three other swift steeds that draw the sun's car have gone by some short by-path in my despite, which makes it so soon day. And now because the sun so hastens to be up, I will never again do sacrifice to him!' But day needs must part them as before, and when their loving talk and endearments were over, they set a time for another meeting.

And many a time they did the same, and thus for a while Fortune left in bliss Criseyde and the Trojan prince. So in contentment, bliss and singing Troilus led his life. He spent, jousted, made festival, he gave freely on all sides and wore many a gay garment, and ever kept about him, as suited his estate, a world of folk the best and lustiest that he could find; so that such a report of him for honour and largesse spread throughout the world that it rang upwards to the gate of heaven! And as to his love, he was in such gladness that in his heart he deemed, I believe, that there was no lover in the world so well at ease as he. The goodliness or charm which nature had placed in any other lady could not untie so much as one knot of the net which Criseyde had woven about his heart. It was so closely meshed and knit that to undo it anywhere, — for aught that could betide that might never be. Full often he would lead Pandarus by the hand into a garden, and there make such a long and joyous tale of Criseyde and her womanhood and beauty that it was heaven to hear his words; and then he would sing, in this manner: —

'Love, that hath the rule of earth and sea, Love that hath set his behests in high heaven, Love, that with a saving bond holdeth the peoples joined as he will, Love, that frameth laws for true friendship and maketh wedded couples to dwell in virtue, may he make binding the harmony of which I tell! That the world with eternal fidelity holdeth his diverse times and seasons in concord; that the warring elements observe an ever-during bond; that Phœbus must lead forth his rosy day, and that the moon hath lordship over the nights, — all this is caused by Love, ever praised be his power! The sea, ever greedy to flow, constraineth his floods in a certain limit that they wax not fiercely to drown the earth and all things for evermore. And if Love ever relaxed his bridle, all that now loveth should leap asunder, and all were lost that now Love holdeth together. And so would to God, Who is the author of nature, that Love with his strong bond would encircle all hearts and so fast tie them that none should know the way out of his bondage! And to cold hearts I would that he should give a wrench, to make them love and have pity on sore hearts and protect them that be faithful.'

In all that the siege demanded he was foremost, ever the first to be clad in arms, and certainly, unless books err, most dreaded of any man save Hector. And this increase of hardihood came to him from love, to gain his lady's thanks, which so changed the spirit within him. In time of truce he would ride a-hawking or else hunt boar, lion or bear (the small beasts he let go!). When he came riding back to town, full often his lady, as fresh as falcon come out of the mew, was ready at her window to give him a goodly salute. His talk was most of love and virtue, and held all pitiful lowness in scorn, and there was no need, I promise you, to beg him to honour the worthy and relieve those in distress, and right glad he was when he heard that any lover was faring well. For he held everyone but lost, to say the sooth, unless he were in love's high service, I mean folk who might well be so. And besides all this, so well could he talk of love and order his array so richly, that every lover thought all well whatsoever he did or said. Though he were come of royal blood, yet he never cared out of pride to gird at anyone; to each one he was benign, which won him thanks on every side. Love (praised be his grace!) made him flee pride and envy, ire and avarice, and every other vice.

Thou bright lady, daughter to Dione, and also thy blind and winged son Dan Cupid, ye nine sisters that by Helicon on the hill Parnassus choose your abode, since ye must leave me now, I can say no more but praised be ye forever, without end! Through you I have told in my song fully the joyous course of Troilus' love, albeit there were some distress mingled in it, as mine author choose to describe. My third book thus I now end, and leave Troilus in joy and peace with Criseyde, his own dear heart.

Book IV

But all too little, alack the day!, lasts such joy; thanks to Fortune, who ever seems truest when she will beguile, and to fools can so attune her song that she catches and hoodwinks them, the common traitress! And when a person is thrown down from off her wheel, then she laughs and grimaces upon him. From Troilus she began to turn away her bright visage, and took no note of him, but clean cast him out of his lady's grace and set up Diomed on her wheel. Wherefore my heart begins to bleed even now, and my very pen to quake for fear of what I must write; for the matter of my book must henceforth be how Criseyde deserted Troilus, or at least how she was unkind, as folk write who have handed down the story. Alas, that they should ever know cause to speak ill of her, and if they slander her, in truth themselves should have the ignominy! O ye Erinnyes, Night's three daughters, that lament in endless torture, Megæra, Alecto, Tisiphone, — and also thou cruel Mars, father to Quirinus, — do ye help me finish this fourth book, that in it be fully showed Troilus' loss of life and love together.

Whilst the strong Greeks were lying about Troy-town in a host, as I have said before, and Phœbus was shining from the breast of Hercules' Lion, it befell that Hector with full many a bold baron planned to fight with the Greeks, as he was wont, to do them what harm he could. I know not how long it was betwixt the taking this purpose and the day they meant to sally forth; but upon a day Hector and many a worthy man issued through the gates in armour bright and fair, with spear in hand and big bows bent, and anon their foemen met them beard to beard in the field. With spears ground sharp, with arrows, darts, swords and fell maces they fought all the day long, and brought horse and man to the ground, and with their axes dashed out brains. But the last assault, to confess the truth, the folk of Troy conducted so ill that they had the worse and fled homewards at night. On which day Antenor was taken prisoner, in spite of the prowess of Polydamas or Mnestheus, Xanthippus, Sarpedon, Polymnestor, Polytes, or the Trojan Sir Riphæus, and such other lesser folk as Phœbuseus; so that for that blow the folk of Troy dreaded in great part to lose their safety. But nevertheless at their urgent asking a truce was made, and they began to treat for making an exchange of prisoners, and, for the over-plus which the Greeks had, gave large sums; and anon this plan was known in every street in town, and also in the camp, and amongst the first it reached Calchas' ear. When he had learned that this treating was to be carried through, he went and pressed into the consistory amongst the old Greek lords and sat him down where he was wont; and with a changed face begged a boon, and that for the love of God they should do him so much reverence as to cease from noise and give him a hearing.

'Lo, my lords,' then he said, 'I was once a Trojan, as it is doubtless known; and, if you so remember, I am Calchas, who first of all gave you comfort when you needed it, and informed you well how you should prosper. For doubt you not that after a season through your means Troy shall be burnt and beaten down to the ground. And in what manner you are to destroy this town and achieve all your will you have ere this heard me describe. This you wot, my lords, I believe. And because the Greeks were so dear to me, to teach you how in this case you were best do, I came myself in my proper person, having no regard to my treasure or my income, in comparison with your well-being.

Thus I left all my goods and came to you, my lords, deeming in this I should please you. All this loss brings me no regret; I am willing, as I hoped to be saved, for your sake to lose all that I have in Troy, — save a daughter whom I left at home asleep, alas!, when I fled out of the town. Cruel and harsh father that I was, how could I have had so hard a heart? Alas that I brought her not in her shift! For sorrow of this I will not live till to-morrow, unless you lords have pity on me. For because ere now I saw no way to deliver her, I have held my peace; but now, or never, I may have her right soon if it please you. Grant me help and grace! Amongst all this throng may some have compassion on this old caitiff in trouble, since it is for you that I have all this heaviness! You have now Trojans enough fettered in prison, and, if it be your will, my child may now be redeemed by one of them. Now for the love of God and of generosity, alas!, grant me one out of so many. What need to refuse this prayer, since you shall shortly have both town and people? On peril of my life, I lie not; Apollo has told it me faithfully, and I have also found it in the stars, and by divination and augury, and I dare to say that the time is hard at hand when fire and flame shall spread over all the town, and thus shall Troy turn to cold ashes. For it is certain that Phœbus and Neptune, who made the walls of the town, are so wroth with the folk of Troy that they will bring it to ruin even for anger with King Laomedon; because he would not pay them their hire, the town shall yet be put in flames.'

As this grey old man was telling his tale, humble in his speech and looks, the salt tears ran fast over his two cheeks. So long he begged them for succour that, to relieve his bitter sighs, they granted him Antenor without more pause. And who was glad but Calchas then! And full soon he laid his charges on them who should go on the embassy, and earnestly prayed them to bring back in return for Antenor King Thoas and Criseyde; and when King Priam had granted his safe-conduct, the embassadors went straight to Troy.

When the cause of their coming had been told, the aged King Priam summoned thereupon his whole parliament, whose decision was that the exchange of prisoners and all the requests pleased them well, and thereupon the embassadors proceeded inward.

Troilus was present when Criseyde was asked in place of Antenor, and wellnigh died to hear the words. His face changed full soon, but lest men should spy his feeling, he said not a word and with manly heart kept this sorrow under. Full of anguish and grisly fear he awaited what other lords should say. If they should grant the exchange of her (which God forbid!), then he thought of two things, — first to save her honour and then how best he might withstand the exchange. Full diligently he considered it. Love made him all eager to keep her and rather to die then let her go, but on the other side Reason said to him, 'Do not so without her assent, lest, if you resist it, she should become your enemy, and say that through your meddling your loves are blown abroad which before were unknown.' Wherefore he thought it best that, even though the lords would that she should go, he would let them decide as they wished, and tell it his lady first; and when she had told him her wish, then he would fall speedily to work, though all the world should strive against it.

Hector, when he heard how the Greeks would have Criseyde for Antenor, resisted it and answered gravely, 'Sirs, she is no prisoner. I wot not who laid this charge upon you, but for my part you may say to them, straightway that we are not wont here to have women for sale.'

An outcry straightway then arose as violent as the blaze of straw set a-fire; for their evil fortune would have it so that the Trojans demanded the cause of their own ruin. 'Hector,' they cried, 'what ill ghost inspire you thus to shield this woman and cause us to lose Antenor, so wise and bold a baron? You choose a wrong course. He is one of the greatest of our townsmen, and anyone may see we have need of folk. Hector, let be such fancies. King Priam,' they cried, 'we say this, that all our voice is to give up Criseyde and to deliver Antenor.'

Ah Lord Juvenal, true are thy sage words, that folk so little know what is to be desired that full often they find their ruin thus, blinded to their true advantage by the cloud of error. And lo here an ensample ready! This folk desires now to deliver Antenor, who brought them to mischance; for he was afterwards traitor to the town of Troy. Alas, they let free him too early; foolish world, behold thy discernment! Criseyde, who never did them harm, shall no longer bathe in bliss. Antenor shall come home, and she shall out, so everyone demanded. So the parliament pronounced that Criseyde should be yielded up for Antenor, and it was decreed by the president. Though Hector full often prayed against it, and whatever man withstood it, all was for naught; it must and should be, for the larger part of the parliament would have it so.

When the assembly had broken up, Troilus without a word sped to his chamber, all alone save for a man or two of his, whom he bade hie them out, for he would sleep, as he told them. And then he laid him upon his bed. As in winter the leaves drop away one by one till the tree is naked and naught but branch and bark, so lay Troilus bereft of all his welfare, bound in the black bark of misery, ready to start out of his wits, so sorely oppressed him the exchanging of Criseyde. This sorrowful man rose up and shut every door and window and then sat him down upon his bed's side, like a dead wan image.

Then the woe heaped up in his breast began to burst out, and he in his frenzy to fare as the wild bull when he is pierced to the heart, and plunges hither and thither and roars aloud in lament of his death. So Troilus flung himself about the chamber, ever smiting his breast violently with his fists, and beating his head upon the wall and his body on the ground to kill himself. His two eyes streamed out like two swift springs. His loud sobs so bereft him of speech that he scarce could say, 'O death, alas! why wilt thou not take me! Cursed be the day when Nature framed me to be a living creature!'

But when the fury which twisted and oppressed his heart by length of time began somewhat to assuage, he laid him down to rest on his bed. But then began his tears to burst out yet more, till it is wonder that a man's body could hold out against half this grieving. Then he said thus, 'Alas, the day! Fortune, what have I done, what is my guilt? How hadst thou heart to beguile me so? Is there no grace, must I perish? Must Criseyde away? How canst thou find it in thy heart to be so cruel to me? Have I not honoured thee all my life above all the gods, as thou well knowest? Why wilt thou take my joy from me? Troilus, what may men call thee now but the wretch of wretches, fallen from glory into misery, where I will lament Criseyde till breath fails me? Alack, Fortune! If my joyous life displeased thy foul envy, why didst not slay my father the king or my brethren or myself, — me, cumber-world, useless, ever dying yet never dead? If Criseyde alone were left me, I should not care whither thou didst steer. Yet it is she thou hast robbed me of. Yet this is evermore thy way, to bereave a man of what is dearest to him, thus to prove thy capricious violence. Thus am I lost beyond remedy. O Love, O true lord! Thou knowest best my heart and thoughts. Alas, O God! How shall my sorrowful life fare if forego what I have bought so dearly? Since thou hast brought Criseyde and me fully into thy grace, and sealed both our hearts with thy seal, how canst thou suffer it to be annulled? What shall I do? As long as I can last alive, I will bewail this cursed fortune in torment and cruel pangs, as solitary as I was born. Never will I see it rain or shine, but I will end my woful life, like Œdipus, in darkness.

'Ah, my weary spirit, that flickerest to and fro, why wilt not fly out of the wofullest body that ever walked on ground! Soul, lurking in this woe, unnest thee; fly from my heart and let it burst, and follow ever thy lady; thy rightful place is no longer here. Woful eyes, since your pleasure was all to see Criseyde's shining eyes, what shall ye do now but lie vainly still and weep out your sight? Since she is quenched that was wont to illumine you, in vain from this time forth have I two eyes, since your virtue is gone. O my Criseyde, sovereign lady of that woful soul that cries thus, who shall now give me comfort? When my heart is dead, receive in kindness the spirit that hastens to thee, for it shall ever be thy servant. Therefore no matter though the body may die! Lovers, that are set high upon the wheel of Fortune in good estate, God grant that ye ever find love of steel, and long may your life endure in joy! But when ye pass my sepulchre, remember your fellow rests there, for I, though unworthy, loved too. Unwholesome ill-living old man, Calchas I mean, alas! what ailed thee to become a Greek, since thou wast born Trojan? Calchas, that wilt be my bane, thou wast born in cursed hour for me! Would to blessed Jove that I once had thee where I would in Troy!'

A thousand sighs, hotter than coals, passed one after another out of his breast, mingled with the plaints which ever fed his woe and with his never-ceasing tears. In a word, his pains so racked him, and he grew so weak, that he felt at last neither joy nor suffering, but lay in a trance.

Pandarus, who had heard at the parliament what every lord and burgess said, and how the exchange had been decreed with one voice, began wellnigh to go out of his wits. Scarce knowing what he did, he rushed to Troilus. A knight, who at the time was keeping the chamber door, undid it anon, and Pandarus went softly into the dark chamber toward the bed, tenderly weeping and so dazed that he knew not what to say. With his face all drawn and arms folded he stood before Troilus and looked on his piteous face. But Lord! how chilled grew his heart to see his friend in woe! When Troilus was aware of his friend, he began to melt as the snow before the sun, for which Pandarus wept as tenderly as he; and for a space the two were speechless, and could not say one word for grief.

But at last Troilus, nigh dead for suffering, burst out in a groan, and said in a husky voice amid his sighs and sobs, 'Pandarus, I am dead without remedy. Heard you not at the parliament how my Criseyde is lost for Antenor?'

Pandarus, deadly pale, answered piteously, 'Yea, I know all how it is. Would it were as false as it is true! Merciful heaven, who would have believed it! Who would have believed that in so short a time Fortune would have overthrown our joy! For I deem that in this world there is no creature that ever saw stranger ruin wrought by chance than this. But who can divine all or eschew all? Such is the world! Wherefore my conclusion is, — let no person trust to gain from Fortune peculiar favour, for her gifts are common.

'But tell me, why are you so mad as to sorrow thus? Why like you so, since you have already had all your desire, have had your portion from Fortune? But I, that never in all my loves felt one friendly look or glance, — let me wail and weep thus till I die! And besides this, as you know well yourself, this town is full of ladies, and a fairer than ten such as she ever was, I believe, I shall find in some company, yea, one or two, without any doubt. Therefore be glad, dear friend; if she be lost, we shall find another! What! God forbid that all pleasure should be in one thing only and in none else! If one can sing, another can dance well; if one be goodly, another is merry and lightsome; and this one is fair and that one demeans her well. Each thing is prized for its peculiar virtue, this falcon for heron and that one for waterfowl. "The new love oft drives out the old," as writes Zeuxis, who was full wise. A fresh plight will have a fresh plan. Think too that you are bound to preserve your own life. Such a fire as yours must by nature grow cool in time, for since it is but chance pleasure, some chances will put it out of your remembrance. For as sure as day follows night, a new love, or labour or other trouble, or else seldom seeing the beloved ones, caused old affections to pass away. As for you, one of these you will have, to shorten your sharp and bitter pains; her absence will drive her out of your heart!'

These words he said only to help his friend, lest he should die for sorrow, and assuredly, so he stanched his woe, he recked not what sorry stuff he spoke. But Troilus gave little heed to it all. One ear heard it, and it went out at the other. But at last he answered, and said, 'Friend, this leechcraft, and to be healed thus, were very well if I were such a fiend as to betray her who is true to me. But I pray God, to the Devil with such counsel! May I die at once on this spot, ere I do as you would have me! She whom I serve, to whom my heart is given of right, shall have me as wholly hers till I die, whatsoever you say. What, Pandarus! Since I have promised her, I will be false to please no one, but as her man I will live and die, and never serve another creature. And when you say you will find another as fair as she, — let be, compare her not with any being formed here by nature. O my dear Pandarus, once and have done! You shall never convince me with all this. Therefore I beg you hold your peace, — you slay me with your words. You bid me let Criseyde go, and get me another fresh new love. It lies not in my power, dear friend, and though I could I would not. And if you can play at rackets with love to and fro, handy-dandy, now this, now that, then foul befall her that cares for your woe! You do by me, you Pandarus!, as one who comes a-walking to a man in pain and says, "Think not of pain and you shall feel none!" You must first transmute me into a rock and take from me all my passions, before you can so lightly take my woe from me. So long this sorrow may delve and sap under my breast that death may well take my life from it. But Criseyde's arrow will nevermore out of my soul, and when I am dead I will go dwell in pains with Proserpine, and there I will eternally lament this woe, and how we two are parted. And then you made here an argument how it should be a less pain to forego Criseyde because she has truly been mine and we were together in ease and felicity. Why prate you so, who once said to me, "It is worse for him who is thrown out of weal than if he had never known that weal"? But tell me this: since it seems to you so light a thing to change ever to and fro in love, why have you not done your best to exchange her who has caused all your trouble? Why not let her slip out of your heart? Why not love another sweet lady, who may set your heart at ease? If you have ever had misadventure in love, yet cannot drive it from your heart, I who have lived in lustiness and joy as much as any man alive, how should I forget it, and that so soon? Where have you been, cloistered so long, who argue with such formal logic? Nay, Pandarus, all your counsel is nothing worth, and finally, in spite of anything, I am doomed to death. Ah death, that art ender of every grief come now, since I have called thee so often; for kindly is death when, often called, he comes and ends pain. Well I know that, whilst I lived in peace, I would have paid hire ere death should slay me; but now his coming is so sweet that naught on earth I long after more. O death, do thou either quench with thy cold stroke this heat of sorrow, or else drown me anon in tears. Thou ever slayest so many in divers manners, unsummoned, against their will, do me this service at my prayer. Deliver the world now of the wofullest creature that ever was, for it is time that I die who am useless in the world!'

And then Troilus distilled in tears like liquor out of an alembic. Pandarus held his peace and cast his eyes upon the ground; but at last he thought, 'What, perdy! Rather than my comrade die I will say somewhat more to him! — Friend,' he began, 'since you are in such heavy case, yet are pleased to blame my arguments, why not gain redress yourself and by your own manhood stop all this vexation? Can you not carry her off? Shame on you! Either hold her here, or let her go and leave this foolish grief. Are you in Troy, yet have no hardihood to seize upon a woman who loves you and will herself be on your side? Now what a light-minded folly! Rise up and let be your weeping and show you are a man. Within this hour I will be dead or she shall remain with us!'

To this answered Troilus gently, 'Dear brother, of all this I myself have oft thought, and of more yet. But why it cannot be you shall hear; and when you have given me a hearing, then you may say all your mind. First, since the town has all this war for the violent ravishing of women, as you know, I should never be suffered to do so great a wrong. I should also be blamed of every person if I so resisted my father's decree, since she is exchanged for the town's good. I have thought also, so she would assent, to ask her of my father's grace; then I thought, this were to accuse her, and to no purpose, since I know well I cannot gain her thus. For since my father has sealed her exchange in so high a place as parliament, he will not take back his word for me. Most of all I dread to trouble her heart by violent acts if I do such a thing; if I should do it openly, it must be slander to her reputation, and I would rather die than defame her. God forbid that I should not hold her honour dearer than my life! Thus for aught that I can see, I am lost; for certainly, being her knight, I must hold her honour dearer than myself in every case. Thus I am pulled betwixt desire and reason; desire counsels me to trouble her, and reason and dread will not.' So, weeping as if he could never leave off, he said, 'Alas, how shall wretched I fare! I feel my love and the causes of my woe ever increase, Pandarus, and hope is ever less and less. Alack and alack! why will my heart not burst? In love is little heart's ease!'

'Brother, for all me,' quoth Pandarus, 'you may do as you will. But if I had it so hot, and were of your rank, she should go with me. Though all the town cried out on this thing in chorus, I should not care a groat for the noise. When men have shouted well, then let them whisper, for a wonder lasts never in town but nine nights! Consider not reasons so deeply and superfinely, but straightway help yourself. It is better that others weep than yourself, and most of all since you two are become one. Be found a little to blame rather than die here like a gnat, without any hurt. Rise up, — by my head, she shall not go! It is no ravishment nor a sin, in my mind, to detain her who loves you most of all. Peradventure she may hold you for a fool, thus to let her go to the Greek camp. Consider also, as you well know,

> "That Fortune helps the hardy in's emprise,
> And flees from wretches for their cowardice."

Though your lady might be a little vexed, hereafter full well you shall make your peace, but as for me I truly cannot believe that even now she could take it ill. Why then should your heart quake in fear? Think how Paris your brother has his love; then why should not you have yours?

'And, Troilus, one thing I dare swear to you. If Criseyde your beloved loves you as well as you love her, before God she will not take it ill though you bring remedy to this mischief. And if she is willing to pass forth from you, then she is false; so love her the less! Therefore take knightly heart, and think that for love every law is broken every day. Show now somewhat your courage and strength. Fear not, but have mercy on yourself. Let not this wretched woe gnaw upon your heart, but stake the world manly on the cast of the dice, and if you die as a martyr, go to heaven! I will stand by you myself in this act, though I and all my kin at once should lie in the street like dead dogs, stricken through with many a wide, bloody wound. In every case you shall find me a friend. But if you wish to die here like a wretch, adieu, and the Devil have him who cares!'

At these words Troilus began to come to life. 'Gramercy, friend,' he said, 'I agree. But, in truth and finally, though I should die otherwise, you cannot so spur me, nor pain so torment me, that I should plan to ravish her unless she herself wills it.'

'Be that as it may be,' answered Pandarus. 'But tell me then, you that have been grieving so, have you sounded her wishes?'

'Nay,' answered he.

'Whence this dismay then,' quoth Pandarus, 'when you know not that she will be ill-pleased to be carried off, since you have not been with her? Has some angel whispered it in your ear? Rise up, then, as if nothing were amiss, wash your face and go to the king, or he may wonder why you are thus absent. You must by your prudence hoodwink him and the rest, or perchance he may send after you ere you are aware. In a word, dear brother, be of good cheer and let me work in this affair. For I shall so shape it that somehow and sometime this night you shall come to privy speech with your lady, and by her words and by her looks you shall full soon learn all her mind, and what is best to do. And now farewell, for on this I rest.'

The swift Rumour, which reports things false and true equally, was flown on ready wing through Troy from man to man, ever freshly telling this tale, how Calchas' bright-faced daughter was to be exchanged for Antenor by decree of parliament. Which tale as soon as Criseyde had heard, caring nothing for her father at such a time, nor whether he lived or died, she heartily prayed Jupiter confound him who brought such a report! Anon she began to fear to ask any person about it, lest it might be true, for all her heart and mind she had so utterly given to Troilus that all this world could not loosen her love nor cast him out of her heart, but she must be his as long as life should last. Thus she was so burning betwixt love and fear that she knew not what to do.

But as men see in towns everywhere that women will ever be a-visiting their friends, so a flock of women began to come to Criseyde, thinking to please her, and sat them down with their pathetic joy and with their prating.

Said one first, 'I am truly glad for your sake, who are going to see your father.'

'In truth,' said another, 'so am not I, for it is too short a time that she has been with us.'

'I hope,' quoth the third, 'that she will bring in peace on both sides, and may God almighty conduct her when she goes!'

All this woman-like talk she heard no more than as if she were in another place. All the while, though her body sat amongst them, God wot her attention and her heart were elsewhere. Her soul was roaming after Troilus, and without a word she thought of him. And these women, thinking to please her, went on pouring out their tales about nothing. Such trivial things could bring no comfort to her who meanwhile was on fire with quite another feeling than they supposed; so that she felt her heart almost die within her for woe and for weariness of that company. Wherefore no longer could she restrain her welling tears, which gave signs of the bitter pain of her spirit, when she remembered from what heaven into what hell she was fallen, now that she must forego the sight of Troilus. When they heard her bitter sighs, those foolish women sitting about her supposed that she wept because she must leave that company, and never chat again with them that she had known so long. So when they saw her weep, they thought it kindness; and each of them began to weep too. Eagerly they began to comfort her for a thing of which, God wot!, she recked full little, and thought to divert her with their words and oft begged her to be of good cheer. Even so much comfort they wrought her therewith as a man is eased for an aching head by clawing him on the heel! And after all this empty folly they all took leave and went home.

Criseyde, full of piteous sorrow, went up out of the hall into her chamber and fell on her couch nigh dead, in full purpose never to rise thence; and she began to demean her as I shall tell you. The salt tears from her two eyes ran out as a shower in April. She beat her white breast, cried a thousand times after death, and held herself for a lost creature, because she must forego him who alone was wont to lighten her woe. She tore her wavy hair of sunnish hue, full often wrung her long and slender fingers, and prayed God of His mercy to cure her ills by death. Her pale hue, once so bright, bore witness of her woe and stress, and thus she spoke sobbing:

'Alas! woeful wretch, luckless being, born under a cursed constellation, I must go from this place and part from my knight. Woe worth that day when I first saw him with my two eyes, and above all else woe worth that evening; which cause me, as I him, all this pain! What will he do? What shall I do, how shall I live if I part from him? Dear heart that I love so, who shall do away the sorrow that thou art in now? O father Calchas, be this crime at thy door, and cursed be the day when Argiva bore me of her body to be a living soul! To what purpose live I in such sorrow? What is Criseyde worth apart from Troilus? How should a fish last without water, or a plant or other creature without its natural food? Wherefore full oft I have heard the byword, "Earthless, green things soon die." Thus I shall do: since I dare not handle sword or dart, for their cruelty, from that day I leave thee (if the sorrow of that kill me not) no meat or drink shall come in me, till my soul is unsheathed out of my breast, and thus I shall slay myself. And Troilus, all my vesture shall be black, in token that I who was wont to possess thee in peace, dear heart, am as one withdrawn from worldly life; and till death meet me, my convent-rules shall ever be sorrow, lament and abstinence. I bequeath my heart and the woful ghost therein to complain eternally with thy spirit, for they shall never part. Though on earth we two be parted, yet in those compassionate fields where Pluto reigns, and where is no torment, shall we be together, as Orpheus is with Eurydice his mate. Alas, dear heart, thus for Antenor I shall soon be given up! But how shalt thou fare in this woful case, — how shall thy tender heart support it? Forget this sorrow, my love, and me also; for in sooth, so thou farest well, I care not that I die!'

How could the plaints that she made in her distress ever be all read or sung? I wot not, and, as for me, if I could describe all her grief, my little pen should make it seem less than it was and childishly deface her noble sorrow. Therefore I pass it by.

Ye have heard me tell how it was agreed that Pandarus should be sent from Troilus to Criseyde; and so he came full secretly to tell his message, where she lay in torment and in frenzy, and using herself in piteous wise. He found her breast and face bathed full wet with her salt tears, her mighty tresses unbraided and her sunnish hair hanging all about her ears, which gave him a true sign of the torment of death that she was longing for. When she saw him, she began for shame to hide her tearful face in her arms, at which Pandarus was so woe-begone and so steeped in pity that he scarce could remain in the chamber. For if at first she had wailed bitterly, now she began to wail a thousand times more.

'Mine uncle Pandarus,' she began, betwixt her sobs, 'was the great first cause of many a joy to me, which is now transmuted into cruel woe. Am I now to welcome you or not, who first brought me into the service of love which, alas! is ending thus? Ends love, then, in woe? Yea, or men lie, and so does every earthly joy, methinks. Sorrow ever occupies the end of bliss, and whoso believes it not let him look on me, woful wretch, that hate myself and curse my birth, feeling myself pass from grief to desperation. Whoso sees me, sees at once sorrow and pain, torment, lament and woe; there is no harm lacking to my woful body, — anguish, cruel bitterness, languor, annoy, smart, dread, fury and sickness. I believe verily tears rain down from heaven in pity of my bitter suffering.'

'You my distressful sister,' quoth Pandarus, 'what think you to do? Have you no regard for yourself? Why will you destroy yourself, alas! Leave all this sorry work and take heed to what I shall say, and hearken meekly to the message which I bring from your Troilus!'

Criseyde turned her then, making such lament that it was death to behold. 'Alas! what words,' quoth she, 'can you bring? What can my dear heart say, whom I fear nevermore to see? Will he have a shower of tears from me before I go? I have enough, if it is that he sends after!'

She was such to look upon in her visage as one swathed and carried on a bier. Her face, once the image of Paradise, was now changed into quite another sort; the sportiveness, the laughter and every other joyous trait that men were wont to find in her were all fled, she lay deserted by them all. Her two eyes were encircled by purple rings, in true tokening of her pain, so that it was a deathly sight to behold. Wherefore Pandarus could not restrain his tears from pouring down. But nevertheless as best he could he repeated the message of Troilus.

'Niece, I believe well you have heard how the king with other lords have thought it best to make an exchange of Antenor and you, which is the cause of all our disquiet and woe. How this thing pains Troilus no man's tongue on earth can tell, for his final resolve is to die. Wherefore we have so grieved, he and I, that it has wellnigh slain us both, but through my counsel he has at last somewhat given over his tears; and I believe he would fain be with you this night, to devise a remedy in this, if there might be any. This, in short and plain, is the substance of my message as my wit can best express it, for you who are in such a frenzy of torment can attend to no long preamble. So hereto you may return an answer; — and for the love of God, dear niece, leave this woe ere Troilus come!'

'My woe is great enough,' said she, and sighed sorely as one in deadly sharp distress, 'and yet to me his sorrow is much worse, who love him better than he loves himself, I believe Alas! has he such heaviness for me, complains he so piteously for me? Now truly his sorrow doubles mine! God wot it is grievous to me to part, but yet harder it is to see him in such woe. Well I wot it will be my bane, and die I truly will! — But did him come,' she cried, 'before death that threatens me now drive out the spirit which flutters in my heart.' And with these words she fell prone on her two arms, and began to weep piteously.

'Alas!' said Pandarus; 'why do you thus when you know the time is hard by when he shall come? Rise up quietly, that he find you not thus tear-stained, unless you would have him fly out of his mind; for if he knew that you fare thus, he would kill himself, and if I expected all this gear, he should not come hither for all the wealth of Priam, for what purpose he would straightway form I know full well. Therefore I say again, let be this sorrow, or, flatly, he will die; and plan to diminish and not increase his sorrow, dear sweet niece. Heal him, wound him not more; by some prudent plan cure his sorrow. What boots it to weep a street-full, or for you both to drown in salt tears? A time of cure is ever better than a time of lament. This is what I mean: when I bring him hither, do you two wise ones with one accord devise how to upset this exchange, or for you to come again straightway after you have gone. Women are cunning at hasty planning. Let see how your wit shall serve you, and what I can do to help shall not be wanting!'

'Go,' quoth she, 'and truly, uncle, I will do my best to refrain my tears in his sight, and to cheer him I shall do all my best and search every nook of my heart. If salve may be found for this sire, it shall not be wanting through my fault, I promise you.'

Pandarus departed and sought for Troilus, till he found him all alone in a temple, caring no longer for life. He was making moan and praying full tenderly to each of the pitiful gods to let him pass soon out of the world. That there was no other favour for him he thought full well, and (to say it all in few words) he was so fallen in despair that he was utterly resolved to die. For thus was ever his argument; — he said, 'I am utterly lost, alack the while! For all things that hap, come by necessity; thus it is my destiny to be lost. For certainly I wot well that divine Providence has ever foreseen that I should lose Criseyde; since there is no doubt that God foresees all things, and ordains and disposes them to be as they have deserved to be.

'But nevertheless whom shall I believe, alas! For though there be many a great clerk that proves foreordination by arguments, some men say that naught comes of necessity; but that free choice is granted every one of us. Alackaday! So cunning are ancient clerks I know not whose opinion to hold. For some men say, if God foresees everything, — and God cannot be deceived, perdy! — then that must befall, though men had sworn it should not, which Providence has foreseen. Wherefore I say that, if from eternity He has known our thoughts and deeds, then even as these clerks declare we have no free choice. For other thoughts or deeds could never come to pass but such as infallible Providence has all-wisely foreseen. For if there might be a chance to twist our way out from God's foreknowledge, then there were no prescience in God, but rather only an uncertain expectation; and certes it were blasphemy to believe that God has no more perfect and clear knowledge than we men, who have doubtful conjecturings. But it were false and foul and wicked cursedness to fancy in God such a possibility of erring.

'Also this is an opinion of some whose crowns are shorn full high and smooth, that things come not because Providence has foreseen them, but that because things are to come, therefore Providence all-wisely foresees them. Therefore in this opinion the necessity passes in the opposite direction. For the necessity is not that what is foreseen must surely befall, but (as they say) that what befalls must all surely have been foreseen. Herein I am inquiring diligently which thing is the cause of which, — God's prescience the cause of the necessity of things to come, or the necessity of things to come the cause of the prescience. But though I strive not further to show in what order the causes stand, I know full well that things foreknown must certainly befall, even if it follow not therefrom that it was the foreknowledge which made the befalling necessary.

'For if a man be sitting yonder on a seat, then certes your belief that he is sitting must needs be true; and even as true must be the converse, that, if your belief be true because he is sitting, then he must needs be sitting. And thus there is necessity on either side, in him necessity of sitting and in you necessity of rightness. But, you may say, the man sits not because your belief that he is sitting is true; but, rather, because the man was already sitting, therefore your belief is true, in faith. And I say, though your belief be true because of his sitting, yet there is interchange of necessity between him and you.

'Thus in the same wise, as it seems to me, I may frame my reasoning on God's providence and on things to come; by which reasoning men may well see that those things which betide on earth come all by necessity. For although it be true that because a thing is to come it is foreseen, and not that it be to come because it is foreseen; yet nevertheless one of the two must be true, that a thing to come must needs be foreseen, or else a thing foreseen betides of necessity, which in truth suffices utterly to destroy our free choice. But now it is absurd to say that the befalling of temporal things is cause of God's eternal prescience; truly that were a false conclusion. What were such a thought but to believe that God foresees things to come only because they are to come, and that all things which have once befallen have been the cause of that sovereign providence which infallibly foreknows all things? Even as when I know there is a thing, that thing must needs be so, right so when I know a thing as coming, come it must. And thus the befalling of things known before the time cannot be escaped by any path.' And then he ended, 'Almighty Jove upon thy throne, who knowest the truth about all this, pity my sorrow and let me die straightway, or else bring Criseyde and me out of our trouble!'

Whilst he was in this heaviness, disputing with himself in this matter, Pandarus came in. 'O mighty God upon Thy throne!' quoth he: 'Eh! who ever saw a wise man demean him so! Why, Troilus! Have you such pleasure to be your own enemy, — what think you to do? Criseyde is not gone yet, perdy! Why allow fear so to destroy you that your eyes seem dead in your visage? Lived you not all your life before without her, and fared full well and at ease? Were you born for her and none other? Did Nature fashion you only to please her? Can you not think thus in your trouble, that as chances fall in dice, so there come and go pleasures in love? And this is my chiefest wonder, why you sorrow thus when you know not yet how her going shall be, nor have you yet tested her wit, whether she can herself avert it. It is time then for a man to sorrow at the hard necessity and to offer his neck, when his head must off.

'Therefore take heed what I say. I have been with her long a-talking, even as you and I agreed, and it has evermore seemed to me that she has somewhat in the privity of her heart wherewith, if I see aright, she can put a stop to all this thing of which you are in dread. Wherefore my counsel is that you go to her at night and make an end of this. Of her great might blessed Juno I hope will send her grace to us. My heart says, "Certainly she shall not go." Therefore let your heart repose a while and be constant; that is best.'

'You say right well,' Troilus answered, sighing sore, 'and I will do even so.' And then he said to him what more he would.

When it was time to go, he came alone full privily to her, as he was wont. And how they did I will tell you straightway. It is the truth that when they first came together, the sorrow so wrung their hearts that neither could salute the other, but could only embrace and softly kiss. Whichever had least woe knew not what to do nor could bring out a word, for woful sobbing. The tears which they let fall were as bitter, beyond the manner of tears, as aloes or gall. The woful Myrrha, as I find written in books, wept not through her bark tears so bitter; there is not so hard a heart in all this world that would not have felt compassion.

But when their two weary spirits returned to their proper seats, and by length of sobbing the pain began somewhat to grow dull, and the spring of bitter tears to ebb, and their swelling hearts to subside, Criseyde spoke thus, with broken voice all hoarse with crying: 'O Jove, I die! Mercy, I beg! Help, Troilus!' Therewith her woful spirit was on the point of flitting from its home, and she laid her face upon his breast and lost the power of speech.

Thus she lay with that hue all livid which once was the freshest and fairest ever seen; as he gazed upon her, calling her name, she lay as dead, answerless, her limbs all cold and her eyes rolled upward, and the sorrowful man could think of naught to do save often to kiss her cold mouth. God Himself knows that he was woful! He arose and stretched her out at length; for aught that he could find, there was no sign of life in her. Full often his song was, 'Alas!

Alas!' When he saw how she lay speechless, with sorrowful voice and joyless heart he said to himself that she was gone from this world. After he had bewailed her long, wrung his hands, said what he could not but say, and besprinkled his breast with salt tears, then he began to wipe his tears off full dry and with piteous devotion to pray for her soul, and said, 'Lord, upon Thy throne, have pity also on me for I must shortly follow her!'

She was all cold and without feeling, so far as he could tell, and he could feel no breath, which to him was a faithful sign that she was gone forth out of this world. And when he saw that there was no other resource, he disposed her limbs in such a fashion as men do for folk that are to be laid on bier. And then with stern and savage heart he plucked his sword out of its sheath to slay himself, whatever agony it might cost; so that his soul might follow hers where the decree of Minos should place it, since love and cruel Fortune would not that he should live longer in this world.

'O cruel Jove, and thou, hostile Fortune,' he said, filled with high scorn, 'I can say no otherwise than that ye have falsely slain Criseyde; and since ye can do no worse to me, fie on your might and your works so perverse! Ye shall never speed against me in so cowardly wise, — no death shall part me from my lady! For since ye have slain her thus, I will leave this world and hasten forth after her spirit. Never shall a lover say that Troilus durst not for fear die with his lady; in very truth I will bear her company. But since ye will not suffer us to live here, yet suffer our souls to be together. And thou, city, that I leave thus wofully, thou, Priam, and my mother and all my brethren, farewell, for I go! Atropos, make thou ready my bier! — And thou Criseyde, sweet dear heart, receive my spirit now — ,' he was about to say, his sword at his heart, all ready for death.

But, as God would have it, thereupon she awoke from her swoon, began to sigh, and 'Troilus!' she cried.

'Criseyde, my heart, live you yet?' he answered, and let his sword slip downward.

'Yea, my heart, thanks be to Cyprian Venus!' quoth she. And then she sighed sorely, and he began to comfort her as he could, took her in his two arms and often kissed her, and did all his best to cheer her; wherefore her spirit, which was fluttering at her lips, went again softly into her heart. At last, as her eye glanced around, she espied his sword lying bare, and cried out for fear and asked why he had drawn it. Troilus straightway told the cause and how he would have slain himself; for which Criseyde gazed upon him, and folded him fast in her arms, saying, 'Ah mercy, God! What an act! Alas, how nearly we were both dead! Then if I had not spoken, as good hap willed, you would anon have slain yourself?'

'Yea, without doubt,' quoth he.

'Alas! she answered, 'by the Lord that made me, I would not have lived an hour after your death, to be crowned queen of all the land the bright sun shines on, but with this very sword lying here I should have slain myself. — But stay,' she said, 'for we have had enough of this. Now let us rest ourselves together and speak of our trouble, for by the night-light burning there I see well that day is not far hence.'

When they were set down together, folded in each other's arms, it was not as at times before; each gazed piteously on the other as one that had lost all his joy, saying 'Alas that they were born!': till at last woful Criseyde said to Troilus, 'Lo! my heart, you well know this, that if a man be ever complaining his woe and seek not how to be helped, it is merely folly, and increase to his trouble. Since we two are come together here to find a remedy, it is time to begin straightway. I am a woman, you know full well; and as I have formed a plan suddenly, I will tell it you whilst it is hot! Methinks neither you nor I ought in reason to make half this to-do, for there are ways enough to redress what is amiss, and to slay this gloom. I suppose our woe is for nothing else than because we must part. Considering all, we shall find nothing else amiss. But what remedy is there here except that we lay our plans soon to meet again? This is the conclusion of the whole matter, dear sweet heart! Now that I shall guide things so that I shall return soon after I have gone, thereof I have no manner of doubt. Certainly within a week or two I shall be here; and that it can be so I will show you a multitude of ways in few words. I will not make a long discourse, for time lost can never be recovered, but I will go right to my conclusion. And forgive it me, for God's love, if I speak aught against your heart's repose, for truly I say it for the best; and I protest that this thing which I shall say is only to show you my purpose to find the best way to help us, and I beg you to take it no otherwise, for, in fine, what so you command me that I will do; of that there is no question.

'Now hearken: you know full well that my going is so fully decreed by parliament that I judge it cannot be annulled by all the world. And since no plan to hinder it can help us, let that pass out of mind, and let us devise a better way. True it is that our parting will trouble and cruelly distress us, but he that serves Love must sometimes have pains if he would have joy. And since I am to go no farther from the city than I can ride back in half a morning, it ought to cause us the less sorrow. I shall not be so mewed up that, since you well know there is now a truce, you shall not full well learn of my estate from day to day, my own dear heart. And before the truce is over I shall be here, and thus you will have won both Antenor and me also. Strive now to be of good cheer, and think, "Criseyde is gone now, but what! she will speedily return." '

'And when, alas!'

'Right shortly, by heaven. Before ten days, I dare be bound. And then straightway you will be so fain because we shall evermore be together, that the whole world could not tell our joy. Often, as we are now, to hide our secret, we have found it best that you speak not with me for a whole fortnight nor I with you, nor even see you in the street. Can you not then wait ten days in such a case to save my honour. If not, in faith you can bear little!

'You know too how all my kin are here, save only my father, and also all else that is mine, and especially you, dear heart, whom I would not cease to see for all this world, wide as it is! If this be false, may I never behold Jove's face in heaven! Why, believe you that my father so craves to see me thus, except for fear lest folk in this town despise me for his unhappy act? What knows he of the life which I lead? If he knew how well I fare in Troy, we should not be grieving over my departure.

'You see too that every day more and more men treat of peace, and it is supposed that men shall give back queen Helen, and that the Greeks shall amend that wherein they have injured us. So though there were no other comfort than that on every side men are proposing peace, you may dwell in the more ease of heart. For if there be peace, dear heart, of necessity men must commune together and ever be riding and walking to and fro as thick as bees fly from a hive, and every person have liberty to remain where he will, without leave. And though there be no peace, yet hither I must return; for whither should I go, or how (a plague!) should I remain there ever in fright amongst those men of arms? Wherefore, so may God me, I cannot see what you should fear.

'Here is another way, if so be all this suffice you not. My father is old, as you know well, and age is full of covetousness; and I have but now found a way to catch him without a net! Listen now, and see if you will assent. Men say, Troilus, that it is hard to have the wolf full and the wether whole; this is to say, men full oft must spend part to save the remnant. Ever with gold men may impress the heart of him that is set on covetousness. How I mean it I will tell you. I will take to my father the goods which I have in this town, and say they are sent in trust from a friend or two of his to save them; which friends fervently pray him to send in haste after more, whilst the town stands thus in jeopardy. And that shall be a huge amount, I shall tell him. But lest folk should espy it, this may be sent by none but me. I shall also show him how many friends I have near the court, if peace betide, to mollify the wrath of Priam and bring him back to grace.

'So, what for one thing and what for another, I shall so bespell him with my words, sweet one, that he shall dream his soul is right in heaven! For Apollo and the doctrine of his clerks avail not three haws! Desire of gold shall so dazzle his soul that I shall make an end as I list. And if he shall enquire by his augury if I lie, I shall verily contrive to disturb him and pluck him by the sleeve making his augury, or persuade him that he has not well understood the gods; for the gods speak in equivocations, and for one truth they tell twenty lies. And it was fear first invented gods, I suppose (this is what I shall say to him), and it was his coward heart made him construe the gods' text amiss when he fled from his Delphi in fear. If I make him not speedily to turn about, and do as I will within a day or two, I pledge myself to die!'

And truly, as I find it written, all this was said with sincerity and good intent, and her heart was true and loving towards him, and she nigh died for woe when she left him and purposed ever to be faithful; thus they write that knew of her deeds.

With eager ear and heart Troilus heard all this debated to and fro, and verily it seemed to him he was of the same mind; yet evermore his heart misgave him, as to letting her go. But finally he made shift so to turn his heart as to trust her and make the best of it. Wherefore the great fury of his pain was quenched with hope, and they began their old joyous endearments. As the birds, when the sun is bright, delight in their song amongst the green leaves, the words that they spoke together delighted them and cleared their hearts.

But nevertheless, in spite of all, the going of Criseyde would not out of his mind, and full often he prayed her piteously that he might find her true of heart. 'Certes, if you are unkind,' he said, 'and if you return not on the day set, I shall never again have health or honour or joy! For as truly as the sun rises in the morning, and so surely may God bring me, woful wretch, out of this cruel sorrow to rest, I will slay myself if you tarry! Though there be little to care about in my death, yet, rather than cause me to suffer so, remain here, my own dear heart! For truly the sleights that I hear you plan are full likely to fail altogether. Thus men say, 'the bear thinks one thing, but his leader quite another'! Your sire is wise, and it is said,

'Men may outrun but not outwit the wise.'

It is full hard to limp undetected before a cripple, for he understands the art!

In trickery your father is eyed as Argus, for albeit he is bereft of his goods, his old craft so remains with him that for all your woman's art you shall not blind him nor feign aught, and that is all my dread.

'I know not if peace will ever come. But peace or no peace, for jest or earnest since Calchas has once been on the Greek side and so foully lost his honour, he will dare come here no more for shame. Wherefore to hope that way, for aught that I can see, is but a fantasy. You shall see also your father will cajole you to marry, and he can preach so well, and will so commend and praise some Greek, that he will ravish you with his words or force you to do as he will. And Troilus, for whom he will have no pity, will die in his fidelity! Besides all this, your father will despise us all and say this city is as good as lost and that the siege will never be raised, because all the Greeks have sworn to maintain it till we are slain and our walls overthrown. Thus he will affright you, and ever I fear that you will remain. And also you will see so many a lusty knight amongst the valiant Greeks, and each will be so diligent with heart, wit and might to please you, that you will weary of the rudeness of us simple Trojans, unless pity sting you, or sense of fidelity. And that is so grievous a thought to me that it will send the soul from my breast. Of a surety I can look for naught but evil if you go. Your father's craft will ruin us. If you go, as I have told you already, think that I am a dead man, without help.

'Wherefore with heart piteous, true and humble I cry you mercy a thousand times. Pity my bitter pains and contrive to do as I would have you. Let us steal away, we two alone. Think how it is folly, when a man has his choice, to lose the substance for the show. I mean thus: since we can well steal off before day and be together so, what sort of wit were it to put it to the test, in case you should go to your father, whether you can return again or no? I mean it were a great foolishness to put this sureness into jeopardy. To speak in a homely wise of goods and wealth, we both can carry with us enough to live upon in honour and pleasure till the day of our death. Thus we can escape this fear; and whatever other way you can speak of, in truth my heart misgives me. Be assured you need dread no poverty, for I have elsewhere kin and friends, so that, though we came in our bare shirts, we should lack for neither gold nor goods, but be held in honour as long as we dwelt there. Let us go straightway, for in my mind this is the best, if you assent.'

With a sigh Criseyde answered him in this wise, 'Truly, my dear faithful heart, we may well steal away as you describe, or find such sorry new ways; but full sore shall we repent it afterwards. So may God help me in my hour of greatest need, as you suffer all this fear without cause. For on that day when I am false to you, my Troilus, my knight, for dread of my father or any other man, or because men cherish me or offer marriage or station or pleasure, may Saturn's daughter Juno by her power cause me, as mad as Athamas, to abide eternally in Styx, the pit of hell! And this I swear to you by every celestial god and every goddess, on every infernal deity, on every nymph and faun and satyr great and small (which be half-gods of the wilderness)! And let Atropos snap my thread of life if I be false! Now doubt me if you will! And thou, Simois, that like a clear arrow ever runnest through Troy downward to the sea, bear witness of this word, that, on that day when I am untrue to Troilus, my own noble heart, thou return backward to thy source, and I sink body and soul in hell!

'But as to what you speak of, to go away thus and abandon all your friends, God forbid you should do so for any woman's sake, and above all since Troy has now such need of help! Take heed of one thing, — if this were known, my life and your honour should lie in the balance. God shield us from such disaster! And if so be peace be made hereafter (as ever, after distress, comes mirth), — why, Lord! what sorrow and woe you would be in because you durst not for shame return! Ere you so jeopardize your honour, be not too hasty and eager in this business: sorrow is never wanting to the hasty man. What believe you the people all around would say of you? It is full easy to divine. They would say, and swear to it, that not love but voluptuous pleasure and coward dread drove you to this deed; thus your honour, which now shines so bright, were wholly lost, dear heart. And also think on my fair name, which still is green; how foully I should disgrace it, and spot it with what filth, if I should depart with you in this wise! Though I lived to the end of the world I should never win it back. Thus I were wholly lost, and that were pity and sin.

'Therefore put down all this heat by reason. "Patience conquers," men say. Be not penny-wise pound-foolish, but make a virtue of necessity. Be patient, and think that he is ever lord of Fortune that cares not a rush for her, and that she daunts no one but a craven. Trust to this, dear heart, that ere Phoebus' sister bright Lucina, which is now in the Ram, pass out of the Lion, I will be here, without any doubt. I mean, and so may Juno, queen of heaven, help me!, that the tenth day, unless death assail me, I shall see you.'

'And now,' quoth Troilus, 'if that be true, I will make a shift to suffer to the tenth day, since I see it must needs be. — But for the love of God, let us steal privily away, if it may be so, for ever alike my heart says it will be the best for us to live in quiet peace.'

'O mercy, God, what a life this is!' quoth she. 'Alas, you slay me for very grief! I see well now that you mistrust me, for by your words it is now clear. Now for the love of bright Cynthia and in pity for me, mistrust me not thus without cause, since I have plighted you my troth to be faithful. Think well that sometimes it is wisdom to let one occasion go, to gain another. I am not yet lost to you though we be a day or two apart! Drive out these fancies from your head, trust me and let go your grief, or by my troth I will not live till morning. For if you knew how sore it pains me, you would have done; God knows the very spirit in my heart weeps to see you weep that I love most, and because I must go to the Greek camp. Yea, were it not that I know a way to come again, I would die even here. But certes I am not so foolish a man that I cannot imagine a means to return the day that I have promised. Who can hold back what will away? Not my father, for all his cunning gear! By my thrift, my departure shall another day turn us all to joy.

'Therefore I beseech you with all my heart, if you list to do aught at my prayer and for the love with which I love you too, that before I leave you I may see you of so good cheer and comfort that you may put my heart at rest which is not a-bursting. And besides this, my own heart's true sufficiency, since I am wholly yours, I pray you that whilst I am absent no delight in another put me from your remembrance. I am ever afeared, for, as men declare,

'Love is a thing ay full of busy dread.'

For if you should be untrue (which God forbid!), no lady lives in this world who were so betrayed or woe-begone as I, who believe all faithfulness in you. Of a surety, if I believed otherwise, I were no better than dead. Unless you find cause, for God's love be not unkind to me!'

'God, from whom no thought is hidden, grant me joy,' answered Troilus, 'as surely as never, since the day I first cast these eyes on her, was I false to Criseyde or shall be till I die! In few words, well may you trust me! I can say no more, it shall be found indeed at the test.'

'Gramercy indeed, my best lover,' quoth she; 'and may blessed Venus let me never die till I may stand at a point of happiness to require him well who deserves so well! Whilst God leaves me my wit, I shall so act that honour shall be reflected back on me, I have found you so true! For trust well that neither vain delight, nor yet your royal estate, nor only your valour in war or martial tourney, nor your pomp or splendour, nobility or wealth, made me take pity on your distress, but your moral virtue, founded upon your faithfulness, — that was the cause why I first had pity on you. And your gentle heart and manhood, and that I believed you held in despite all that tended to ill, such as roughness and vulgar desires, and that your reason bridled your pleasures, — this gave me over to you more than to any other creature, to hold for life. And this may not be spoiled by length of years or changeful Fortune.

'But may Jupiter, who of his might can make the sorrowful glad, grant us the boon to meet here again ere ten days, that it may content your heart and mine. And now farewell, for it is time that you were up and away!'

After they had long lamented, and had often kissed and been folded in each other's arms, the day began to rise and Troilus prepared to go, and looked ruefully upon his lady, feeling the cold pains of death, and commended him to her grace. Whether he was woful I need not ask! For the mind of man cannot imagine, nor understanding consider, nor tongue tell, the cruel pains of his hapless lover, which passed every infernal torment. When he saw that she could not remain who was rending his soul out of his heart, without anything more he went from the chamber.

Book V

The fatal destiny was approaching which Jove has in his disposition and commits to you, angry Parcæ, sisters three, to execute: by which Criseyde must from Troy, and Troilus must dwell in pain till Lachesis twine his thread no longer. The golden-tressed Phœbus on high had thrice with his bright beams melted the snows and Zephyr had as often brought back the tender green leaves, since the son of Queen Hecuba had begun to love her, for whom all his sorrow was, that she must depart that morn.

As prime Diomed was full ready to lead Criseyde to the Greek host, for sorrow at which she felt her heart bleed, not knowing any remedy. Truly, as men read in books, never was woman known so full of care or so loath to leave a city. Troilus, at his wit's end, as a man that had lost all his joys, was ever awaiting his lady, the true blossom, and more, of all his former happiness. But, Troilus, farewell now to all of it, for never again shalt thou see her in Troy! It is truth that whilst he thus waited he hid his woe full manly, that it was scarce seen in his cheer. At the gate where she was to ride out he tarried with certain folk awaiting her, so woe-begone, though he would not lament, that he scarce could sit his horse. When Diomed mounted his horse, Troilus quaked for ire, so was his heart gnawed within him, and he said to himself, 'Alas! such a foul wretchedness, — why will I suffer it? Why will I not set it right? Were it not better to die at once than evermore to languish thus? Why should I not straightway give rich and poor enough to do, before she should go? Why not bring all Troy upon an uproar, why not slay this Diomed, or why not rather with the help of a man or two steal her away? Why endure I this, why not help to cure my own woes?'

I shall tell why he would not do so fell a deed; he had ever in heart a sort of fear lest Criseyde in the uproar might be slain. This was all his anxiety, and else he had surely done it.

When Criseyde was ready to ride, full sorrowful she sighed 'Alas!' But there was no help, forth she must, for aught that might befall, and she slowly rode onward. What wonder though it pained her, when she was foregoing her own dear heart? Troilus in courteous wise, with hawk on hand and a great troop of knights, rode far on to bear her company beyond the valley. And full fain he would no doubt have ridden farther, and woe was him to part so soon; but turn he must. And with that Antenor was come from the Greek host, at which every person was glad and made him welcome. Troilus, though his heart were not light, did his best at least to refrain from weeping, and kissed Antenor and made much of him. Then he must take his leave; he cast his eye piteously upon her and rode nearer, to speak to her and take her gravely by the hand. Lord, how tenderly she wept! And he said to her full softly and secretly, 'Now keep your day and kill me not!' Then with a pale face he turned his charge about, and spoke not a word to Diomed nor to any of his troop, and departed homeward.

Of this the son of Tydeus took heed, as one that knew more than the primer of love's craft; when he saw the folk of Troy departed, he took her by the bridle and thought, 'All my labour shall not be in vain, if I may help it; I will say somewhat to her, for at the worst it may beguile our journey. I have heard it said a score of times,

'He is a fool that will forget himself.'' '

Yet thus he thought well enough too, 'Of a surety I am about a wild-goose chase, if I am malapert or speak of love, for doubtless, if she have in her thought him that I guess, he cannot be put out of it so soon. But I shall find a way so that she shall not know yet what I mean.'

In due season Diomed, knowing full well what he was about, began to fall in speech of this and that, asked why she was in such distress, and besought her that if he could in any wise advance her pleasure, she should command it him, and he would do it, he said. And faithfully, as a knight, he swore her there was naught that could content her but he would do it with all his heart. He prayed her to appease her sorrow, and said, 'In faith, we Greeks can delight to honour you as well as folk of Troy. I wot it seems strange to you, he said also, ' — and no wonder, it is all new — , to exchange the acquaintance of these Trojans for folk of Greece, who are all foreign to you. Yet God forbid but you should meet amongst us all as kind a Greek as any Trojan is, and as true. And because even now I swore to you to be your friend and as helpful as I could, and I have had more acquaintance with you than any other Greek has had, from this time forth day and night I pray you to command me, whatsoever it may cost, in all that may please your heart, and to treat me as your brother, and not to scorn my friendship. Though your sorrow be for some great matter, I know not why, but my heart feels a joyous desire to put it away at once; and if I cannot set your troubles right, full sorry I am for your heaviness. For though you Trojans have been wroth with us Greeks many a day, yet in truth we all serve one god of Love; and for the love of God, my noble lady, whomsoever you may hate, be not wroth with me. For truly no man serving you can be half so loath to merit your wrath. And were we not so nigh the tent of Calchas, who may see us, I would tell you all that is in my mind. But all this shall be kept under seal till another day. Give me your hand; so may God help me, as I am and ever shall be whilst life shall last, your own above every creature. This I never said before now to any woman born, for as I hope for joy, I never loved a woman before, nor ever shall again. So for God's love be not my foe, dear lady, though I know not how to make my complaint to you aright, because I have yet to learn. Wonder not, my own bright lady, though I speak to you of love thus early; I have heard ere this of many a man has loved a lady whom he never saw in his life before, nor have I the power to strive against the god of Love, but I must ever obey him and pray you for mercy. Such worthy knights as there are in this host, and you so fair, every one of them will do his best to stand in your favour; but if so fair a grace should befall me that you would call me your servant, none of them will so lowly and so truly serve you as I shall till I die.'

Unto that talk Criseyde answered but little, being so oppressed with sorrow that in effect she heard not his tale except here and there a word or two. Her sorrowful heart seemed ready to burst, and when she espied her father from afar, she wellnigh sank down off her horse. But nevertheless she thanked Diomed for all his trouble and good cheer, and for offering his friendship; she would accept it in good part, and would gladly do what might please him, and would trust him, as well she might (so she said). And then she alighted from her horse. Her father took her in his arms, and twenty times he kissed her sweetly. 'Welcome, dear daughter mine,' he said. She too said she was fain that she might be with him, and stood forth mute, mild and gentle. — And here I leave her abiding with her father, and I will tell you forth of Troilus.

To Troy this woful man is returned, in sorrow bitter above all other sorrows, with fierce look and pitiless face. Abruptly he leaped down from his horse, and with a swollen heart stalked through his palace to his chamber; he took no heed of any one, nor for fear durst any speak a word to him. And there to the sorrows that he had held in he gave full issue, and cried out for death; and in his frantic mad throes he cursed Jove and Apollo, he cursed Cupid and Ceres, Bacchus and Venus, he cursed Nature, his own birth, himself, his fate, and every created thing save his lady. He went to bed, and there wallowed and turned like Ixion in hell, and in this state he remained till nigh day. Then his heart began a little to subside through the tears which began to gush upward, and piteously he cried upon Criseyde, and he spoke thus to himself:

'Where is my own dear lady? Where is her white bosom, where is it? Where are her arms and her clear eyes, which were with me yesterday at this time? Now I may weep many a tear alone, and grope about; but, saving a pillow, I find naught to embrace. How shall I do? Why have I let her go, when will she come again? I know not, alas! Would God I had then been slain! Oh my heart Criseyde, oh my sweet foe, oh my lady, whom alone I love, on whom I bestowed my heart forever! See how I die, and thou wilt not rescue me! Who sees thee now, my true loadstar, who sits or stands in thy presence, who can allay the war in thine heart now I am gone? To whom dost thou lend thine hearing, who speaks for me now in mine absence? Alas, that is all my grief, — no one, for well I know thou farest as ill as I. How should I endure ten full days of this, when the first night I have all this pain? Sorrowful creature, how shall she too fare, how shall her tender heart bear such woe for me? Piteous, pale, and wan for longing will be thy fresh womanly face before thou comest back hither!'

And when he fell into any slumber, anon he would begin to groan, and dream of the dreadfullest things that might be: as that he was in a solitary horrible place ever lamenting, or that he was amongst his enemies and fallen into their hands. And therewith his body would start, and with the start he would suddenly awake, and feel such a tremor in his breast that his body would quiver for fear. And he would make a sound, and feel as if he were falling far and low from on high, and then he would weep, and so dolorously pity himself that it was wondrous to hear his fantasy. Another time he would earnestly comfort himself, and say it was folly to suffer such dread so causelessly; and then his bitter pains would begin anew, so that any man would pity his sorrows. Who could tell aright or fully describe his woe, his lament, languor, and pain? Not all the men who are or have been on earth! Thou, reader, canst full well divine that my wit cannot depict such woe; in vain I should toil to write it when my wit is weary to think it!

The stars were still visible in heaven, though the moon was waxed full pale, and the horizon eastward began to whiten, and Phœbus with his rosy car soon after began to draw upwards, when Troilus sent for Pandarus. All the day before, Pandarus could not have come to see him, not if he had pledged his head, for all day he was with King Priam, so that it lay not in his liberty to go anywhere. But on the morrow he went to Troilus when he sent after him, for in his heart he could well divine that all night Troilus had been awake for sorrow; and that he wished to talk to him of his trouble Pandarus knew full well without book! Wherefore he made his way straight to the chamber, gravely greeted Troilus, and sat him down on the bed.

'My Pandarus,' quoth Troilus, 'I cannot long endure this grief. I believe I shall not live till to-morrow, therefore upon that chance I would devise to you the manner of my sepulture, and do you dispose of my goods even as seems best to you. As to the funeral-fire in which my body shall be burned to coals, and the feast and funeral games at my vigil, I pray you take good care that all be well done. And offer Mars my steed, my sword and helm; and, beloved brother, give my bright-shining shield to Pallas. The dust into which my heart shall be burned I pray you to take and conserve in a vessel of gold that men call an urn, and give it my lady whose I am and for whose love I die so piteously, and do me this grace to pray her keep it for a remembrance. For I feel clearly, by my malady and by my dreams now and of yore, that I certainly shall not live; and the owl, that men call Ascalaphus, has shrieked after me all these two nights. And, O thou god Mercury, do thou guide my soul and fetch it when thou wilt!'

'Troilus, my dear friend,' Pandarus answered and said, 'I have long told you that it is folly to sorrow thus and without a cause; wherefore I can say no more. But whoso will not trust counsel or instruction, I can see no help for him but to let him alone with his fantasy. But I pray you tell me now, Troilus, believe you that any man ere this was ever hotly in love as well as you? Yea, God wot! And full many a worthy knight has foregone his lady a month, and yet not made half your lament! What need have you to make all this woe; since day by day you can see yourself that men must needs part from their loves or from their wives? Yea, though he love her as his own heart, yet he will not thus contend with himself, for well you know, dear brother, that friends cannot always be together. How fare these folk that see their loves wedded and bedded with others through compulsion of friends, as betides full often? God wot, they take it discreetly, well and mildly, for good hope keeps up their hearts; and because they can bear a time of sorrow, as time hurts them a time cures them! So should you hold out, and let the time slip by, and strive to be glad and lightsome! Ten days is not so long to wait! Since she has promised you to return, she will not break her promise for any man. Fear not but she will find a way to return, I dare stake my life thereon!

'Your dreams and all such fancies, — drive them out and let them go to the Devil! They proceed from your melancholy, which causes you all this suffering in your sleep. A straw for all dreams and their significance, — so may God help me, I value them not two peas! No man knows aright what dreams mean. Priests of the temple say that dreams are the revelations of the gods; and they say as well that they are infernal illusions. And leeches say that they proceed from men's natural temperaments, or from gluttony or fasting. Others say that visions come through impressions, as when a person has held a thing fast in mind. Others say, as they read in books, that by nature men dream according to the time of year, and that the manner of it goes by the moon. Thus who knows, in truth, what they signify? Believe them not. It is these old wives find a relish in dreams, and also in auguries of birds (such as death-bodings of ravens or shrieking of owls), for fear of which folk expect to perish. To believe in them is both false and base. Alas, alas! that so noble a creature as a man should dread such filth!

'Wherefore I beseech you with all my heart that you spare yourself all this, and now arise without a word more and let us plan how this time may best be passed away, and how we may live lustily when she returns, which shall be right soon. So God help me, you were best do thus. Rise, let us occupy the time, and speak of the lusty life that we have led in Troy, and delight in the time to come that shall bring us our bliss now so quickly. Thereby we shall so forget or overcome the langour of these ten days that it shall scarce be a hardship. This town all about is full of lords, and all this time the truce is lasting; let us go to Sarpedon, who lives but a mile away, and divert ourselves in some lusty company. Thus you shall beguile the time until that blissful day when you are to see her who is causing your grief. Now rise, dear brother Troilus; certes it does you no honour to weep and crouch so in your bed. Believe me truly in one thing; if you lie thus a day or two, folk will say that you are feigning sickness out of cowardice, and dare not arise!'

'Brother mine,' answered Troilus, 'folk who have suffered grief know that it is no wonder if a man weep and make sorrowful cheer who feels a hurt and smart in every vein. I am no wise to blame though I ever lament or always weep, since I have lost the cause of all my happiness. But since of very necessity I must arise, I will do so as soon as I can. May God, to whom I offer my heart, send quickly the tenth morning! Never was fowl so fain of May as I shall be when she returns who is cause of both my torment and my joy. But where in all this town is it your counsel that we can best divert ourselves?'

'By heaven, my counsel is,' quoth Pandarus, 'that we ride to King Sarpedon to disport us.' This they talked of back and forth, till at last Troilus consented to rise, and they went forth to Sarpendon.

This Sarpedon, ever free-handed and noble of station, fed them day by day with every rich viand that could be served on table, whatever wealth it cost. Such splendour, so said great and small, was never known at any feast before that day. Nor is there any instrument delicious in sound of wind or touch of string, which tongue may tell of or hear remember, in all this world so far as men have travelled, that it was not heard in harmony at the feast. Nor was so fair a company of ladies ever seen before on the dance.

But what availed this to Troilus, who recked not of it for sorrow? Ever alike his piteous heart was seeking busily after his lady Criseyde. All that his heart thought was ever of her, now this, now that, so diligent in fancy that no festival could gladden him. Since his own lady was away, it was a sorrow to behold the ladies at the feast; or to hear instruments of music. When she was absent who bore the key of his heart, it was his fancy that none ought to make melody. Nor was there an hour in all the night or day, when he was where he could not be heard, that he said not, 'O bright and lovesome lady, how hast thou fared since thou wert here? Welcome indeed, my own sweet lady!'

But alackaday! Fortune was but deluding him, and meant to mock him even more.

The letters that she had sent him of old he would read over alone a hundred times betwixt prime and nones, refiguring within his heart her from and her womanhood, and every word and act that was past. Thus the fourth day wore through; and then he was for going home. 'Dear brother Pandarus,' he said, 'mean you that we shall remain here until Sarpedon shall dismiss us? It were more seemly that we took leave ourselves. For the love of heaven, let us take our leave this night and turn homeward, for truly I will not tarry thus!'

'Are we come hither to fetch fire and run with it home again?' Pandarus replied. 'God bless me, in very truth I cannot tell whither we could go where any man should be gladder of us than Sarpedon is. If we hasten away so suddenly, I hold it for churlishness, seeing we said we would remain with him a week; to take our leave the fourth day, truly he would wonder at it. Let us hold to our purpose, and, since we promised to remain, keep our agreement and then ride away.'

Thus with all the trouble in the world Pandarus made him remain, and at the week's end they took leave of Sarpedon and sped on their way. 'Now Lord grant me the grace at my home-coming,' quoth Troilus, 'to find Criseyde come!', and he began to sing.

'Yea, a likely story!' thought Pandarus, and said full softly to himself, 'God wot, this hot excitement may have time to cool ere Calchas send Criseyde back!' But nevertheless he chaffed and jested and swore his heart promised him that she would come as soon as ever she could. When they were come to Troilus' palace, they alighted and took their way to his chamber, and till night began to fall they talked of the bright Criseyde; and then when they would, they sped them from supper to rest.

On the morrow, when day began to brighten, Troilus started out of sleep and said full piteously to his dear friend Pandarus, 'For the love of God, let us go see Criseyde's palace; since as yet we can have no more gaity, let us at least see her palace!' And therewithal, to hoodwink his household, he devised a reason for going to town, and they took their way to Criseyde's house. But Lord! how woful was this poor Troilus! He felt his sorrowful heart would burst in two; for when he saw her doors all barred, he nigh fell down for sorrow, and when he saw how every window was shut, his heart grew cold as frost. With a changed and deadly pale face he passed by without a word, and rode so fast that no person observed his countenance. And then he said, 'Ah desolate palace, ah house once called the best of houses, empty and comfortless palace, lantern whose flame is quenched, palace that now art night, and once wert day and crown of all houses, illumined with the sun of all bliss, ah ring from which the ruby is fallen out, ah cause of woe as one of solace! Thou oughtest indeed to fall, and I to die, since she is gone who governed us both. Yet since I can do no better, I fain would kiss thy cold doors, if I durst before these folk. Farewell, shrine, from which the saint is gone!' And then with a changed face, piteous to see, he cast his eye upon Pandarus, and as he rode, when he could see his time, he told him his new sorrow and his former joys so pitifully and with so deadly a look that any one would have had compassion.

Then he rode up and down, and everything came to his memory as he rode by places in the city where aforetime he had enjoyed Love's pleasantness: 'Yonder I last saw my lady dance, and in that temple my sweet lady first caught me with her clear eyes; and yonder I have heard my dear heart laugh full merrily, and yonder she said to me once, "Now, good sweet friend, love me well, I pray!'; and yonder she looked on me in so goodly a manner that my heart is hers till death; and in that corner of that house, I heard my dearest lady sing so well with her womanly melodious voice, so goodly and so clear, that in my soul the blissful sound seems to ring yet! And in that yonder spot my lady first took me into her grace.'

Then he thought, 'O blessed lord Cupid, when I remember the history, how thou hast warred against me on every side, men might make a book of it like a tale. What need hast thou to seek a conquest on me, since I am thine, wholly at thy will? What joy is it to thee to destroy thine own folk? Lord, well hast thou wreaked thine ire on me, mighty god, deadly to offend! Show mercy now, O lord! Thou knowest well I crave thy grace above all dear pleasures, and will live and die in thy faith; in reward of which I ask but one boon, that thou send me back Criseyde speedily. Let her heart long to return as eagerly as mine to see her; then I wot well she will not tarry. Blessed lord, I pray thee be not so cruel to the blood of Troy as Juno was to Theban blood, for which the folk of Thebes had their destruction!'

After this he galloped to the gate where Criseyde had ridden out. Up and down there he made many a turn, and often said to himself, 'Alas, here my joy and bliss rode out! Would to the blessed God that I might see her come again into Troy! I conducted her to yonder hill, alas!, and there took leave of her; yonder I saw her ride on to her father, for sorrow of which my heart will split. And hither at evening I came home; and here I remain and ever shall, outcast from happiness, till I can see her again in Troy!'

And himself he imagined oft to be worn and pale and grown thinner than he was wont, and that men said secretly, 'What can it be? Who can guess the truth, why Troilus shows these heavy looks?' And all this, that he had these fancies, was only his melancholy. Another time he would imagine that every man passing along the street pitied him, and that they said, 'I am right sorry Troilus is dying.' And thus, as you have heard, he went through a day or two, living as one that stands betwixt hope and dread. Wherefore he took comfort in showing in verses as best he could the occasion of his woe, and in making a song in few words, somewhat to relieve his heavy heart. And when he was out of every man's sight, with a soft voice he would sing thus of his sweet lady as you shall hear:

> 'O Star which hast withdrawn from me thy light,
> With heart full sore I have good cause to wail,
> That ever dark, in torment night by night,
> Toward my death with wind astern I sail.
> Wherefore it by the tenth night I should fail
> To see thy guiding beams for but an hour,
> My ship and me Charybdis will devour.'

When he had sung this song, he would fall straightway to his old sighs, and every night he would stand beholding the bright moon, and telling her all his sorrow and would say: 'Of a surety, when thou art newly horned I shall be happy, unless all the world be false. I saw thine old horns the morning when my own sweet lady rode hence, who is the cause of all my torment. Therefore,

O bright Lucina, for the love of God, run fast about thy sphere; for when thy new horns begin to spring, my bliss shall return.'

Ever more and more the days seemed to him longer than they were wont, and the sun to go his course wrongly, by a longer way then before. 'Truly,' he said, 'I fear the sun-god's son Phaethon is returned, and drives his father's car amiss.' — He would walk long upon the walls and gaze over toward the Greek camp, and say to himself, 'Yonder is my noble lady; or else yonder, where the tents are! And thence comes this air, so sweet that in my soul I feel it restore me. And surely this wind which ever stronger and stronger blows in my face comes of my lady's deep and sore sighs! I know it because nowhere in all this town save only here feel I a wind which sounds so like pain; "Alas, why are we two parted?" it says.' Thus he wore through this long time till the ninth day was fully past, and ever beside him was Pandarus, striving his utmost to comfort and gladden him, and ever growing him hope that the tenth day she should come and stint his sorrow.

On the other side was Criseyde, with a few women, amongst the valiant Greeks. Many times a day she lamented: 'Alas that I was born! I have lived too long, well may my heart yearn for death. And I cannot amend things, alas! for now are they worse than ever I believed they could be. For aught I can do to please him, my father will not grant me the favour to return; yet if so be I outstay my time, my Troilus will think in his heart that I am false, as indeed it will seem. Thus I have small thanks on either hand. Alackaday that I was born! And if I jeopardize myself and steal away by night, and if so be I am caught, I shall be held to be a spy; or else, as I dread most, if I fall into the hands of some wretch, I shall be a lost woman, true though my heart may be! Mighty God, pity my sorrows!'

Full pale waxed her bright face and her limbs lean, as she stood all the day, when she durst, and looked on the place where she was born and had ever dwelt; and lay all the night weeping, alas! And thus the woful woman led her life, despairing of all help. Many times a day she would sigh distressfully, and went ever imagining to herself the great worthiness of Troilus, and recalling all his goodly words since the first day when her love began to spring. Thus she set her woful heart ablaze by the remembrance of what she longed for. There is not so cruel a heart in all this world that would not have wept at her bitter pains, if the ear had heard her tenderly weeping morn and eve; she needed borrow no tears! And the worst of her pain was that there was none to whom she durst lament. Ruefully she looked toward Troy, and beheld the high towers and roofs; 'Alas! the joy now is turned into bitterness, which I have often had within yonder walls! Troilus, what dost thou now? Lord! thinks he yet upon Criseyde? Alas that I trusted not his counsel and went not with him! My sighs had not then been half so bitter. Who could have said that I did amiss to steal away with such a one as he? But too late comes the physic when men bear the corpse toward the grave! Too late now to talk of that! Alas, Prudence! one of thy three eyes I ever lacked ere I came here; time past I well remembered, and could well see time present, but I could not foresee the future, till I was in the snare, and that brings now my bitterness. But nevertheless, betide what will, to-morrow night I shall steal at some point out of this host, and go with Troilus where he will. This is best, and this purpose I will hold. No matter for the prating of wicked tongues. Ever have wretches shown malice toward love! Whoso will pay heed to every word, or rule himself after every man's opinion, shall never prosper, of a surety. What some folk blame, others ever commend. For all such varying talk, happiness is enough for me! Wherefore, without more debate, I will to Troy; and there an end!'

But, God wot, before two full months she was right far from that intent. Both Troy-town and Troilus shall slip from out her heart with naught to stay them, and she shall resolve to abide.

This Diomed of whom I told you went about arguing within himself with all the craft that ever he knew, how he might best and soonest bring Criseyde's heart into his net. This purpose he never could leave, and laid out hook and line to fish for her. He believed well that she was not without a lover in Troy, for never since he brought her thence could he see her laugh in gladness. He could not think how he might best soothe her heart; 'but to make assay can do no harm, for he that assays naught achieves naught,' he would think. Again, upon a night he said to himself, 'Now am I not a fool, knowing well how her woe is for love of another man, hereupon now to go making trial of her? I might know it cannot profit me. Wise folk say in books,

'Men shall not woo a woman in heaviness.'

Ah! but whoso could win such a flower away from him for whom she mourns day and night, he might call himself a conqueror indeed!' And right anon, being a bold fellow, he thought in his heart, 'Hap as it may, I will seek after her heart, though I die for it; I can lose no more than my words!'

This Diomed, as books tell us, was prompt and courageous in his acts, with stern voice and mighty square limbs, hardy and headstrong, sturdy and knightly of deeds like his father Tydeus; some men say he was free of tongue; and he was lord of Calydon and Argos.

Criseyde was moderate of stature, and in form and face and expression there could be no fairer thing created. Offtimes it was her wont to go with her bright hair tressed down her back by her collar and bound with a thread of gold. Save that her eyebrows joined together, there was no blemish in aught that I can learn of. But to speak of her clear eyes, truly they that saw her wrote that Paradise stood formed in them; and evermore love strove within her with her rich beauty, as to which were the greater. She was grave and simple and discreet withal, the highest-bred and stateliest lady that could be, ever goodly of speech, charitable, generous, and gay; nevermore was pity wanting in her tender heart, which was somewhat unstable. Her age truly I cannot tell.

Troilus was well-grown in height, and so perfectly formed and proportioned that nature could not have bettered him; young, fresh, strong, bold as a lion, and true as steel in every point, one of the best-endued with virtues of all beings that ever were or shall be whilst the world lasts. And certainly it is found in the histories that he was never second unto any man of his time in the valour that belongs to a knight. Though a giant might pass him in strength, his heart stood equal to the first and best, to venture whatsoever he would.

But, to tell on of Diomed, it befell that on the tenth morning after Criseyde went out of the city, Diomed came, as fresh as a bough in May, to the tent where Calchas lodged, and feigned an affair with him. What was in his mind I shall tell you shortly. Criseyde welcomed him, and made him to sit down by her, and ready enough he was to tarry! Straightway men fetched forth the wine and spices to them, and they talked on of this and that, as friends do, and some of the talk you shall hear. First he fell into speech of the war betwixt them and the folk of Troy, and he besought her to tell him also what she thought about the siege. From that question he came to asking if the Greek customs and behaviour seemed strange to her; and why her father delayed so long to marry her to some noble person.

Criseyde, who was in strong pains for love of her own knight Troilus, answered him as well as she could, but as to what was in his mind it seemed as if she knew not.

Nevertheless Diomed began to gain boldness, and said, 'If I have taken heed of you aright, my lady Criseyde, methinks that, since I first laid hand on your bridle when you came that morning out of Troy, I have never been able to see you except in sorrow. I cannot say what the cause may be, unless it be the love of some Trojan; which would grieve me right sore, that you should ever spill a quarter of a tear for any man that dwells there, or should cheat yourself so piteously. Believe me, it is not worth your while. The folk of Troy, one and all, are as it were in prison, as you see yourself; nor could one of them come off thence alive for all the gold betwixt sun and sea. Trust me and understand me right well: not one shall come alive to mercy, were he lord of ten worlds! Before we go hence, such vengeance shall be taken on them for the carrying off of Helen, that the very Manes, gods of torment, shall be aghast for fear the Greeks may do them hurt, and henceforth unto the end of the world men shall dread to ravish a queen, so cruel shall our vengeance appear! And unless Calchas mislead us with sly double words, and equivocations, such as men call words with two visages, you shall know well that I lie not, and all this you shall see with your own eyes, and that anon, you could scarce believe how soon. Now take heed, for it shall be so! What! Believe you that your wise father would have readily given Antenor for you if he knew not that the city should be destroyed? Nay, nay, as I hope for joy! He knew well that not one Trojan shall escape, and for that great fear he durst not let you dwell there longer. What more will you, sweet lovesome lady? Let Troy and the Trojans pass out of your heart! Be of good cheer, drive out that bitter hope, and call the beauty of your face back again, which you so mar with salt tears. Troy is brought to such peril that now no remedy can save it. Think well that before to-morrow you may find amongst the Greeks a more perfect lover than any Trojan is, and more kind and more zealous to serve you. And if you vouchsafe, bright lady, I will be he to serve you, yea, rather than be lord of twelve Greeces!'

With those words he began to wax red, and his voice to tremble a little, and he somewhat turned away his face and was silent a while. Afterwards he recovered himself, and throwing a grave look on her, he said, 'I am, though you may care naught for it, as well-born as any in Troy. If my father Tydeus had lived longer, Criseyde, before now I should have been king of Calydon and Argos, and so I hope I yet shall be. But he was lacklessly slain at Thebes, all too soon, alas the pity!, to the harm of Polynices and many another. Since I am your man, and you the first, dear heart, whom I ever sought permission ardently to serve (as I ever shall do whilst I live), ere I leave this place I pray you grant me that I may to-morrow at better leisure tell you all my pain.'

Why should I tell all his words? He must have spoken enough for one day at least, for Criseyde granted him to have speech with her on the morrow, if he would speak no more of such matters. With her heart so fast set on Troilus that none could tear it away, she spoke to him haughtily: 'Diomed, I love that place where I was born, and may Jove of his grace deliver it soon from all its troubles! O God, of Thy might grant it prosperity! That the Greeks would wreak their wrath on Troy if they could, I know well; but, before God, it shall not befall as you say. I know my father is wise and ready of wit; and since he has brought me so dear, as you have told me, I am the more bounden to him.

That the Greeks are men of noble parts I know full well: but in truth men shall find within Troy-town as worthy folk, as perfect, wise, and gentle as are betwixt Ind and the Orcades! That you could serve your lady well, and win her thanks, I well believe. But, to speak of love, I had a lord to whom I was wedded, and to whom all my heart belonged till he died; and other love there now is not in my heart, nor ever was, so may Pallas help me. That you are of high and noble kindred I have indeed heard tell; and it is that gives me so great a wonder that you will so mock any woman! God wot, love and I are far apart; I am more disposed to lament wofully until my death. As yet truly I care not for mirth; what I shall do hereafter I cannot tell. Day by day now my heart is busy in tribulation, and you in arms. Perchance it may so happen hereafter, when you have won the town, and when I see what I never yet saw, that I shall do what I never yet did! This ought to suffice you. I will gladly talk with you to-morrow, so you speak not of this matter, and you may come here again when you list. Ere you go, thus much I will say: So help me bright-haired Pallas, if ever I take pity on any Greek, it shall be you, by my troth! I say not therefore that I will do it, nor say I no; and my last word is that as God sees me, I mean honestly.' With that she lowered her eyes and began to sigh, saying, 'O Troy-town, I pray God I may yet see thee in peace and quiet, or else let my heart burst!'

But, to speak in few words, this Diomed began freshly to press on again, and begged hard for her grace, and after this he took her glove, of which he was full glad; and finally, when the sun had set and all was going well, he rose and took leave.

Bright Venus had followed in the west and showed the way where broad Phœbus had gone down, and Cynthia the moon was urging on her chariot-horses to whirl out of the Lion if she could, and the Zodiac was showing its bright candles, when Criseyde withdrew to her rest within her father's bright fair tent; revolving round and about in her soul the words of this impetuous Diomed, his high station, the peril of the town, and how she was alone and had need of friends' help. And thus, to say the sooth, began to breed the causes why she took her full purpose to remain.

The morning came, and Diomed to Criseyde; and briefly, lest ye should interrupt my tale, he spoke so well for himself that he allayed all her sighs, and finally consoled her for the greater part of her grief. After this, the story tells us, she gave back to him the fair bay steed which he had won from Troilus; and she gave him a brooch (she need not have done that!) which Troilus had given her; and, to console his amorous sorrow, she made him to bear on his lance her sleeve as a pennon. I find elsewhere in the histories than when

Diomed was hurt through the body by Troilus she wept many a tear, seeing his wide wounds bleed, and that she took good care in nursing him. And, to heal him of his bitter grieving, men say — I know not — that she gave him her heart. But truly the history tells us that woman never made more lament than she, when she became false to Troilus.

'Alas!' she said, 'my name for fidelity in love is now clean gone for evermore! For I have betrayed one of the gentlest that ever was, and one of the worthiest. Alas! unto the world's end no good word shall be sung or written of me, so shall books reproach me. Ah, my name shall be tossed on many tongues, and throughout the world my knell shall be knolled, and women most of all shall hate me! Alas that such a case should betide me! They will say that, as much as in me lay, I have done them dishonour. Though I be not the first that has done amiss, how helps that to put away my blame! But since I see there is nothing better and that now is too late to repent, at least I will be true to Diomed. But, Troilus, since there is no help, and thou and I are thus parted, still I pray God to bless thee, as truly the noblest that ever I saw, for faithful service and watchful keeping of his lady's honour.' At those words she burst out weeping. 'And certes I shall never hate thee, but thou shalt ever have of me the love of a friend and my words of praise, though I should live forever! Truly I should be sorry to see thee in any adversity, and I know well I leave thee without guilt of thine. But all things shall pass away. And so I take my leave.'

How long it was before she forsook him for this Diomed, truly I believe no author tells it. Let every man now examine his books, and he will of a surety find no time set down; for though Diomed began betimes to woo her, yet there was more to do before he won her. Nor would I chide this unhappy woman farther than the history chides her; her name is published so far, alas!, that it ought to suffice for her guilt. And, because she was so sorry for her faithfulness, if I could in any wise excuse her, in truth I would do it yet for pity.

Troilus was living through the time, as I have told before, so well as he could. But often was his heart hot and cold, and chiefly that same ninth night, on the morrow after which she had promised him to come again. God wot, full little rest and no desire to sleep had he that night! The laurel-crowned Phœbus, as he went ever upward in his course, was beginning to warm the wet waves of the eastern sea, and Nisus' daughter the lark was singing with lusty spirit, when Troilus sent after his Pandarus; they went to divert them on the walls of the town, and to see if they could espy aught on Criseyde, and till it was nones they stood to watch who should be coming. Every sort of person coming from afar they said must be she, till they could see him clearly. Now was Troilus' heart dull, now light! And thus bemocked stood the two to stare after nothing.

'For aught I can think,' said Troilus, 'Criseyde surely cannot come into the town before nones. She has enough to do, I dare be bound, to escape from her old father at all. He will make her dine, too, before she goes, — a plague upon him!'

'It may well be, certainly,' Pandarus answered, 'and therefore let us dine, I beg you, and after nones you may return.'

Home they went without more words, and then returned. But long may they seek before they find what they gape after; Fortune meant to mock them both.

'I see well now,' quoth Troilus, 'that she has so long tarried with her old father that it shall be nigh eve before she comes. Come forth, I will to the gate. These porters are ever dull of wits, and I shall find some excuse to make them keep the gates open, even though she may come late.'

The day went fast, and evening came, yet no Criseyde came to Troilus. He looked forth past hedge, tree, and grove, and reached his head far out over the wall. At last he turned about and spoke: 'By heaven, Pandarus, I know her meaning now, but I was almost back in my old woe! This lady shows her wit, of a truth; she means to ride back privily, she will not have folk foolishly gape at her when she comes, but she thinks to ride softly into the town at night, and by my hood, I commend her wisdom! Think it not over long to wait here, dear brother, we have naught else to do. — And Pandarus, now will you believe me? By my troth, I see her! Yonder she is! Lift your eyes, man, can you not see?'

'Nay, by my honour,' Pandarus answered; 'all wrong, by heaven! Man, what say you? Where are your eyes? What I see yonder is only a travelling-cart!'

'Alas, you say the truth!' said Troilus. 'But surely it is not for nothing that I feel such joy in my heart now, my thoughts bode some good; I know not how, but never since I was made felt I such inner comfort. She comes to-night, I dare stake my life.'

'It may be, well enough,' answered Pandarus, and held with him in all that ever he said. But in his own heart he had his thoughts, and laughed softly, and then said full gravely to himself, 'All that you are waiting for here is in the moon! Yea, farewell all the snow of yester-year!'

The gate-ward began to call the folk who were without the gates, and bade them drive in their beasts, or else they must remain without all the night. And far on in the night Troilus turned his horse homeward with many a tear, for he saw it availed not to remain. But nevertheless he cheered him with the thought that he had reckoned the day wrongly, and said, 'I understood her amiss; for the night I last saw Criseyde she said, "I shall be here, if I can, sweet dear heart, before the moon now in the Ram pass out of the Lion." Wherefore she may yet keep all her promise.'

And on the morrow he went to the gate, and up and down on the walls, westward and eastward, he made many a turn. But all for naught, his hope ever deceived him. Wherefore at night he went home at last with sorrow and sore sighs. Hope fled clean out of his heart, he had nothing now whereon longer to rely, and so sharp and wondrous strong were his throes that his heart seemed to bleed for the pain. For when he saw that she broke her promise and remained so long, he knew not what to think thereof. The third, fourth, fifth, and sixth days after the ten days, his heart lay betwixt hope and fear, yet somewhat trusted still to her old promises. But when he saw she would not keep to her time, he could find no help except to plan soon to die. Thereat the wicked spirit (God bless us from him!), that men call mad Jealousy, crept into his heavy heart; and his melancholy and his desire to die made him to forsake eating and drinking, and to flee from every company. This was the life he led all this time. He was so wasted that scarce could a man know him; he grew so lean, so pale and wan and feeble, that he walked with a staff. Thus he wore himself out by his resentment. And whoso asked him where his trouble was, he said it was all about his heart. Full often Priam and his dear mother, and his brethren and sisters, asked him why he was so cast down and what was the cause of all his pain. But all for naught; he would not lament to them for the true cause, but said he felt a grievous malady about his heart, and fain would die.

So one day when he had laid him down to rest, it befell that in his sleep be seemed to be walking in a forest to weep for love of her who was giving him this pain. As he roamed up and down through the forest, he dreamed he saw a boar with great tushes lying asleep in the heat of the bright sun, and by this boar, folding it fast in her arms and continually kissing it, lay his bright lady Criseyde. For sorrow and rage at this sight he started out of his sleep, and cried aloud on Pandarus: 'Ah Pandarus! Now I know the beginning and end of it, and there is no more but that I am a dead man! My bright lady Criseyde, whom I trusted above every creature, has betrayed me; she has pleased her heart elsewhere! The blessed gods of their great power have showed it in my dream. Thus I beheld Criseyde in my dream — ,' and he told him the whole matter.

'Alas, my Criseyde! What subtlety, what new pleasure, what beauty or wisdom —! What cause have I given thee for anger? What guilt of mine, or what dread event, has taken thy thoughts from me, alas! O trust and faith and confidence! Who has torn Criseyde, all my joy, away from me? Alas! why have I ever let thee go, and wellnigh started out of my wits when thou wentest! Who will ever believe in oaths again? God wot, bright lady, Criseyde, I believed that every word thou spakest was gospel. But who can better beguile, if he will, than he whom men most trust? O my Pandarus, what shall I do? Now I fear so sharp a new pain, that since there is no help now, it were better I slew myself with my two hands than ever thus to weep. Death would put an end to the woe which every living day wears me away.'

'Alack the day that I was born!' cried Pandarus. 'Have I not said before that many a man is beguiled by dreams? Why? — because folk expound them amiss! How dare you for any dream say your lady is false, only out of your own fears? Let this thought be, you understand not the interpretation of dreams. When you dreamed of this boar, perchance it may signify that her old grey father is lying in the sunshine at the point of death, and that she is crying and weeping and kissing him as he lies on the ground. That is the true way to read your dream!'

'How can I do then to learn the truth,' said Troilus, 'were it never so little of it?'

'Now you speak like a wise man,' replied Pandarus; 'my counsel is, that since you can write well, you straightway send her a letter, which shall bring you certainty in place of doubtfulness. And see now why! For, I dare be bound, if she be untrue I cannot believe that she will write again; and if she write, you shall soon learn whether she has the power to come back, or else, if she is hindered, she will somewhere tell the cause. You have not written to her since she went, nor she to you. I dare wager, she may know such good cause that you yourself would readily agree that her tarrying is best for both of you. Now write her therefore, and you will speedily feel the truth of this; and that is all there is to do.'

The two lords agreed in this resolution, and that anon; and straightway. Troilus sat him down and turned it over and over in his mind how he could best depict his woe to his own dear lady. He wrote thus:

'Fresh flower, in whose service alone I have ever been and shall be, with heart, body, life, desires, thought, and all, I woful man recommend me to your noble favour, as steadily as matter fills space, and in every humble wise that tongue can tell or heart think. May it please you to remember, dear heart, as you well know, how long ago it was that you went away and left me in bitter pains. As yet I have had no remedy, but am ever from day to day more woe-begone, and so must remain so long as it please you that are spring of my weal and woe. Wherefore, as one driven by sorrow to write, with timid faithful heart I write to you of my woe, increasing newly every hour, and lament as much as I dare, or can express myself. For what is defaced herein, you may blame the tears which rain from my eyes, which themselves would speak and lament if they could.

'I first beseech you not to deem your clear eyes defiled if they look on this, and that you will vouchsafe to read through this letter. And if, because my cold cares are slaying my wit, aught amiss should escape me, forgive it me, my own dear heart! If any lover durst or might justly complain piteously upon his lady, I believe that I am he: considering this, that you have tarried these two months amid the Greek host, where you said you would abide but ten days. But in two months you have not returned. Yet forasmuch as I must needs be content with all that contents you, I dare complain no more; but humbly and with sad sick sighs I must write you of my grievous restless sorrows, desiring evermore from day to day to know fully, if it be your pleasure, how you have fared and done in this absence. May God so increase your welfare, dignity and health that they may ever unceasingly grow upward! I pray God to fulfil all your heart's desire, my lady, and grant that you may be pitiful to me as surely as I am true to you.

'And if it please you to learn of the estate of one crammed with every grief, whose woe no wit can depict, I can say no more but that at the writing of this letter I was alive, yet all ready to let my woful spirit flit; which I delay to do, and hold it yet in hand, until I see the tenor of your message to me. My two eyes, which still have the useless power of sight, are become founts of salt tears. My song if turned to lamentation for my adversity; my good into harm, my ease into hell, my joy into woe, — I can say no more, but every joy or pleasure is turned into its contrary, wherefore I curse my life. All which you can redress by coming home to Troy, and create in me joy a thousand times more than ever I had. For never yet was heart so blithe to be alive as I shall be so soon as I shall see you.

'And if no sort of compassion move you, yet think on your pledge. And if my guilt have deserved death, or if you list never again to see me, yet in reward of my past service I beseech you, my heart's lady, my true loadstar, for the love of God to write me hereupon, that death may end my struggle. If any other cause delay you, then recomfort me with your letter. Though your absence be a hell to me, I will bear my woe with patience and divert me with your letter of hope. Now, sweet one, leave me not thus lamenting, but write, and with hope or death deliver me from pain. I know of a surety, my own dear true heart, that when you next see me Criseyde will not be able to know me, so have I lost my health and colour. Daylight of my heart, my noble lady, so thirsts my heart ever to behold your beauty that I scarce hold my life.

'I say no more, though I have more to say to you than I can express. Whether you bring me life or death, I pray God send you a joyous life. So farewell, goodly fresh fair woman, who may order me to life or death! To your faithfulness I ever recommend me, in such a manner of health that unless you grant me health I shall have no health. In your power stands the day when my grave shall wrap me, whenever you will that it be so. In you is my life, in you is might to save me from the torture of all grievous pains. And now farewell, my own sweet heart.'

This letter was sent forth to Criseyde, and she wrote back in effect thus; she said piteously that so soon as she could she would indeed come and mend all that was amiss; yea, she would come, — but she knew not when. In her letter she made wondrous much of him, and swore she loved him best of all; all which assurances he found to be but hollow. Troilus, now thou mayst wear the willow and go whistle! So wags the world! God shield us from harm, and promote every person that means honestly!

Day and night increased the woe of Troilus for Criseyde's tarrying, and his hope and strength lessened. He laid him down in his bed, and neither ate, drank, slept, nor said a word, and wellnigh went out of his mind, ever imagining that she was faithless. The dream of which I told would never pass from his remembrance. He thought he had verily lost his lady, and that Jove in his watchful providence had showed him in sleep the symbol of her unfaithfulness and his misfortune, and that this boar was the figure thereof. Wherefore he sent for the Sibyl his sister, who was named Cassandra, and told her all his dream and begged her to resolve for him the mystery of that strong boar with stout tushes. Within a little while Cassandra expounded his dream to him thus. She first began to smile, and said:

'O brother dear, if you desire to learn the truth of this, you must learn certain old stories, how Fortune has overthrown ancient lords; by which you will shortly know this boar full well, and of what stock he is sprung, as men find in books. Diana was wroth because the Greeks would not do her sacrifice nor set incense afire upon her altar, and because they so neglected her she avenged herself wondrous cruelly. For she made a boar, as huge as a stalled ox, to devour all their corn and vines. To slay this boar all the folk of the country were raised, amongst whom there came to see the boar a maiden, one of the most renowned of this world; and Meleager, lord of that country, so loved this noble blooming maiden that he pursued this boar till he slew it by his manhood, and sent her the head. From this, as old books tell us, there arose a strife, and great ill-will; but how this Meleager died through his mother's deed I will not tell, for it were too long. And from this lord was Tydeus lineally descended, or else old books lie.'

She told also how Tydeus went to the strong city of Thebes to claim dominion over the city for his fellow Polynices, whose brother Eteocles held it full wrongfully; this story she told at large. She told also how Hæmonides escaped when Tydeus slew fifty stout knights. She told all the prophecies word by word, and how the seven kings with their host besieged the city all about; and told of the holy serpent, and the well, and the Furies, of Archemorus' burial and funeral games, and how Amphiaraus fell through the ground, how Tydeus, lord of the Argives, was slain, how Hippomedon was drowned and Parthenopæus died of his wounds, and how proud Capaneus was slain with a thunderbolt. She told him also how each of the brethren, Eteocles and Polynices, slew the other in a skirmish, and of the Argives' weeping and woe, and how the town was burnt. And so she came down from the old histories to Diomed, and thus she spoke: 'This same boar betokens the son of Tydeus, Diomed, who is descended from Meleager, who slew the boar; and wheresoever your lady is, in truth this Diomed has her heart, and she his. Weep if you will, or not! For of a surety Diomed is in, and you are out!'

'You say not the truth,' he said, 'you sorceress, with your false spirit of prophecy. You deem yourself a great diviner! Now but see this fanciful fool, that wearies herself to slander ladies! Away with you, Jove give you sorrow! Before another day you may be proved false. As well you might slander Alcestis, who of all creatures that ever were was the loyalest and the best, unless men lie; for when her husband was in jeopardy of death unless she would die, she chose to die in his stead and go to hell; and die she did, as the books say.'

Cassandra departed, and with savage heart he forgot his woe for anger at her words. He leaped from his bed, as though a leech had cured him, and day by day sought and inquired about with all diligence to learn the truth of this. And thus he endured his lot.

Fortune, to whom the permutation of things is assigned by the providence of high Jove, how sovereignty shall flit from folk to folk, or when a folk shall be smitten, began from day to day to pull away the bright joyous plumage of Troy till it was bare. During all this, the term of Hector's life was approaching wondrous fast. The Fates would that his soul should unbody, and had devised a means to drive it out, against which it availed him not to contend. On a day he went to fight, and there met his end, alas! And methinks every sort of man that practices arms ought to lament the death of one who was so noble a knight. For whilst he was dragging a fallen king by his hauberk, Achilles rove him unawares through the mail and through the body; and thus was this worthy knight brought to his death.

For him, as old books tell us, such lament was made that tongue cannot tell it, and most of all was the sorrow of Troilus, next to Hector, the chiefest fount of valour. And in this woe he remained until, what for sorrow and what for love and unrest, many times a day he bade his heart break. Nevertheless, for all his despair and dread that his lady was untrue, his heart ever repaired to her, and, as lovers do, he sought ever freshly to recover the bright Criseyde, and was excusing her in his heart, that it was Calchas caused her tarrying. Oftentimes he half resolved to disguise himself like a pilgrim, and go to see her. But he could not so transform himself as to be unknown to discerning folk, nor devise an excuse to serve if he should be known amongst the Greeks; for which he often wept many a tear. Oftentimes he wrote newly to her again, and full piteously, for no sloth withheld him; beseeching her that since he was true she would return and hold her troth to him. To all which matter upon a day Criseyde replied, out of pity (or so I take it), and wrote thus:

'Mirror of goodliness, Cupid's son, sword of knighthood, spring of nobility! How could a man in torment and in sickness and dread as yet send you gladness? I, without heart or health or joy, can neither send you heart not health, since I cannot deal with you nor you with me. My heart's pity has fully understood your letters, the paper all written over with laments and stained with tears, and how you require me to come again. As yet this may not be but why, I make no mention now for fear lest this letter should be found. God knows how grievous to me are your unrest and your urgency. You seem not to take for the best what the gods ordain; nor is aught else, methinks, in your mind but only your pleasure. But be not wroth, I beg you.

'The cause why I tarry is all wicked tongues. For I have heard much more than I deemed was known, how things have stood betwixt us two, which I shall amend by dissimulation. And — be not wroth now — I have understood also how you are at present but deluding me. But no matter for this now; I cannot believe aught to be in you but all truth and nobleness. Come I will; but I stand here amid such difficulties that I cannot appoint what day or what year that shall be. But in fine I pray you as heartily as I can for your good word ever, and for your friendship. And truly, whilst my life shall last, you may count me for a friend. I pray you further not to take it ill that I write you in few words. Where I am, I dare not make long letters, and I never yet could write well. Great matters men often express in little room. The intent is all,

435

and not the length of the letter. And now farewell, and may God have you in His grace!'

This letter Troilus thought altogether cold, when he read it, and sorrowfully sighed. It seemed to him to bode the beginning of change. But finally he could not believe that she would not keep what she had promised him, for he who loves well is full loath to give up love, even though it grieve him. Nevertheless men say that at last, in spite of anything, a man must see the truth. And right soon such a case befell, so that Troilus well perceived that she was not so loyal as she ought to be; and at last he knew certainly that all was lost that he had been about.

Troilus was standing one day in his melancholy, full of suspicion of her for whose love he felt himself dying. And so befell that a sort of tunic, emblazoned with an escutcheon, was being borne up and down throughout Troy, as was the custom, before Deiphobus as a token of his victory. This tunic, as mine author Lollius tells, he had torn the same day off Diomed. When Troilus saw it he began to take heed, observing the length and breadth and all the work-manship. As he beheld it, suddenly his heart grew cold; for he had found within on the collar a brooch which he had given Criseyde that morning when she had perforce left Troy, in remembrance of him and of his grief, and which she had pledged him her faith to keep. Now he knew full well that his lady was no longer to be trusted.

He went home and sent speedily after Pandarus, and told him beginning and end of this new chance and all about the brooch, complaining of her fickleness of heart, and of his long love and faithfulness and suffering. He cried aloud upon death to restore his peace to him. 'O Criseyde,' he cried, 'bright lady, where is thy pledge, where is thy promise, where is thy love, and thy faithfulness? Is Diomed now so dear to thee? Alas! If thou wouldst not stand firm in faith to me, I had trusted that at the least thou wouldst not thus have deceived me. Who now will ever believe oaths? I would never have believed ere now that thou, Criseyde, couldst so have changed, nor that, unless I had done amiss to thee, thy heart was so cruel as to slay me thus. Alas, thy name for faithfulness is now blotted out, and that is all my sorrow! Was there no other brooch that thou caredst to endow thy new love with, but that very brooch that I wet with my tears and gave thee for a remembrance of me? Thou gavest it, alas!, for no other cause but scorn, and because thou wouldst thus show utterly thy meaning. I see that thou hast cast me clean out of thy mind. And yet for all the world I cannot find it in my heart to cease loving thee for an hour. Alack! in a cursed time I was born; I love thee best in all the world, who hast given me all this woe! Now God send me the grace to meet with this Diomed! Truly if I have power and opportunity I shall yet make his sides bloody, I hope. O God, Who oughtest to take heed to advance fidelity and punish wrong, why wilt not wreak vengeance on this crime? Ah Pandarus, you who blamed me for trusting dreams and were wont to upbraid me, now if you will you may see yourself how true is your bright niece! In sundry forms, God wot, the gods show joy and grief in sleep, and by my dream this is proved. And certainly, for final resolution, henceforth as I can I will seek my own death upon the field, and I care not how soon be the day. But truly, Criseyde, sweet maiden, whom I have ever loved with all my might, I have not deserved that thou shouldst do thus!'

Pandarus, hearing all this and knowing that he spoke the truth, answered him not a word, sorry for his friend's sorrow and shamed for his niece. Astonied by these two causes, he stood speechless, as still as a stone. But at last he spoke: 'Dear brother, I can do no more for you. What should I say? Indeed I hate Criseyde! God wot, I shall hate her evermore. What you once besought me to do I did, having no regard to my honour nor to my peace. If I did aught to your pleasure, I am glad. And for this betrayal now, God knows it is a sorrow to me! Of a surety, to ease your heart I fain would amend this, if I knew how. I pray almighty God to deliver her soon out of this world! I can say no more.'

However great the sorrow and lamentation of Troilus. Fortune held ever on her course; Criseyde loved the son of Tydeus, and Troilus must weep in cold cares. Such is this world! In any station of life is but little heart's ease, whoso will look to it. God grant us to make the best of it!

In many a cruel battle was seen the knighthood and mighty strength of the noble Troilus, as men may read in these old books, and full cruelly day and night the Greeks must pay for his wrath. Most of all he sought after Diomed, and oftentimes I find they came together with bloody strokes and huge words, assaying how their spears were sharpened. Often in savage fury, God wot, Troilus beat upon Diomed's helmet. Nevertheless Fortune would not that either should die by the other's hand.

If I had undertaken to write of the prowess of this valiant knight, I would tell now of his battles. But forasmuch as I began first to write of his love, I have told of that as well as I could. Whoso would hear of his noble deeds, let him read Dares; he can tell them all together. And I beseech every bright-faced lady, and every noble dame, whatso she be, that they be not worth with me for Criseyde's guilt, though she were untrue. Ye may see her guilt in other books before mine; and more gladly I will write; if ye please to have me, of the faithfulness of Penelope and good Alcestis. Nor write I thus of faith and falsehood only for the sake of men, but most of all for those women who are betrayed through false folk. Those who through great subtlety and wit betray you, God give them sorrow, amen! It is this has moved me to write; and, in fine, I pray you all beware of men and hearken to what I say.

Go, my little book! Go, my little tragedy! Be not a rival of other poems, but be humble amongst them all, and kiss their steps wherever you see Virgil and Ovid go, and Homer, Statius, and Lucan. May God yet send thy maker power, before he die, to use his pen in some comedy! And because there is so great diversity in English and in the writing of our speech, pray also to God that none copy thee wrong nor mar thy metre through defect of his tongue. Wheresoever thou be sung or read, beseech God that thou be understood. But now back again to my story.

The Greeks paid dearly, as I began to tell you, for the wrath of Troilus, who was without any peer in his day save Hector, so far as I can learn. His hand slew thousands. But alack and alack (save that it was God's will)!, the fierce Achilles mercilessly slew him. And when he was slain thus, his freed spirit went full blissfully up into the eighth sphere of heaven, leaving all the elements in their spheres below him. Thence he gazed long upon the wandering stars, hearkening to the harmony of sounds full of heavenish melody, and then down upon this little spot of earth embraced by the sea; and then he began utterly to despise this wretched world, and held all to be vanity in comparison to the full felicity of heaven above. At length he cast his eyes down upon the spot where he was slain, and laughed within himself at the grief of them that wept so for his death, and condemned all our deeds who follow so hard after blind pleasures which cannot endure, when we should cast our whole heart on heaven. So on he went to the place where Mercury allotted him a dwelling. Thus ended Troilus for love, thus ended his worth and his royal station, thus ended his joyousness and his nobility; to such an end leads this false world's instability. Thus, as I have told, began his loving of Criseyde; and in this wise he died.

O young lusty folk, youths and maids, in whom love ever grows up with your age, get you home from worldly vanity! cast up the eyes of your heart to that God that made you after His image, and think that all this world is but a market-fair, and passes as soon as the sweet flowers. And love Him who for pure love, to redeem our souls, first died upon the cross, and rose again, and now sits on high in heaven. He will fail no creature, of that be sure, who will lean his heart wholly on Him. And since He is most gentle and best to love, what need to seek feigned loves?

Here in this book you may see the pagans' cursed old rites, and how little their gods avail. See here the end of this wretched world's desires! See here the end and reward for toil given by Jove, Apollo, Mars, and such rabble! And likewise the manner of old clerks' speech in poetry you may see here. O moral Gower, I address this book to thee, and to thee, philosophical Strode, that ye may vouchsafe to correct it, where need is, of your righteous zeal and benignity.

And now to that true Christ that died on the rood I pray with all my heart for mercy, and to the Lord I say thus: Thou One, Two, Three, eternally existing, that ever in Three, Two, One reignest uncircumscribed, yet circumscribest all, defend us from our foes, visible and invisible. And make us, Jesu, worthy of Thy mercy, for the love of Thy benign maiden-mother.

The House of Fame

Book I

God turn every dream to good for us! For to my wit it is wondrous, by the rood, what causes dreams by night or by morrow; and why some be fulfilled and some never, why this is a vision, and this a revelation, why this is one kind of dream, and that another, and not to every man alike; why this one is an illusion and that an oracle. I know not, but whosoever knows the causes of these prodigies better than I, let him divine; for I certainly wot naught thereof, and never think to trouble my wit too arduously to learn their kinds of significance, or the length of time to their fulfilment, or why this is cause of dreams rather than that; as whether folks' temperaments make them dream of what they have been thinking on; or else, as others say, over-enfeeblement of brain, from sickness or abstinence, imprisonment, frequently of stews, or great distress; or else disorder of Nature's customs, as when a man is too zealous in study, or melancholy, or so full of inward fear that no man may offer him relief; or else whether the devoutness and meditation of some often cause such dreams; or be it that the cruel, hard life which these lovers lead, who hope or fear overmuch, so that their mere fancies cause visions; or whether spirits have the power to make folk dream o' nights; or if the soul from its proper nature be so perfect, as men judge, that it foreknows what is to be, and warns one and all of each of their haps to come, by means of visions or figurings, but our flesh cannot understand these aright, because the warnings are too dark; — I know not what cause is. Good luck in this great clerks, who treat of this matter and others! For I will now make note of no opinion, but only pray that the holy cross turn every dream to good for us. For never have I since I was born, nor any man else before me, I firmly believe, dreamed so wonderful a dream as I did the tenth day of December; which, as I can now recall it, I will tell you in full.

But trust well, at my beginning I will anon make invocation, with special devoutness, to the god of sleep, who dwells in a cave of rock by a stream which comes from Lethe, which is a bitter river of hell; hard by a folk called the Cimmerians ever sleeps this mirthless god with his thousand sleepy sons, whose want is ever to sleep; and this god I tell of I pray to grant me success to tell my dream aright, if every dream be within his power. And may He who is Mover of all that is and was and ever shall be give them that hearken to it joy of all they dream this year; and to stand in the favour of their loves or in whatever plight they were faintest to stand in, and shield them from poverty and shame and mishap and every ill, and send all their desire to them that receive it well and scorn it not or misjudge it in their minds through malicious intent. And whosoever through presumption or hate or scorn or envy, through spite or mockery or wickedness, may misjudge it, — dream he stockings-on or stockings-off, I pray Jesus God that every ill that any man has had since the beginning of the world may befall him therefore ere he die, and that he may fully deserve it all, lo! with such a fulfilment as had Crœsus King of Lydia of his vision, who died upon a high gibbet! This prayer shall he have of me; no more charity have I than this! Now, as I have told you, hearken to what I dreamed ere I awoke.

The tenth day of December, when it was night, I lay down to sleep even where I was wont, and fell asleep wondrous soon, as one who was weary from walking a pilgrimage of two miles to the shrine of Saint Leonard, to make soft what had been troublous.

But as I slept I dreamed I was within a temple of glass, in which were more golden images standing in sundry niches, and more rich tabernacles, and more pinnacles of gemmed work, and more cunning picturings and rare manners of figures in old work than ever I had seen. For verily I knew never where I was, but well I knew, truly, that it was of Venus, this temple; for straightway I saw her figure pictured, floating naked in a sea; and also her rose-garland white and red, perdy, about her brows, and her comb to comb her hair; her doves, and Dan Cupid, her blind son, and Vulcan, full brown of his face.

But as I roamed about, I found a tablet of brass on a wall, where was written: 'I will now sing, if I am able, the arms and also the man, who, fugitive from Troy-country, first came through fate into Italy to the Lavinian strand with full great suffering.' And then anon began the story, as I shall tell you all. First I saw the destruction of Troy, through the Greek Sinon, who with his false oaths and his feigned cheer and his leasings made the horse to be brought into the city, through which the Trojans lost all their happiness. And after this, alas!, was graven how Ilium was assailed and won, the King Priam pitilessly slain and also Polites his son, by Sir Pyrrhus.

And next to that I beheld how Venus, when she saw the castle burning, descended from heaven and bade her son Æneas to flee; and how he fled and escaped from all the press, and took Anchises his father and bare him away on his back, crying, 'Alack and alackaday!' Which Anchises carried in his hands those gods of the country which were unburned. And next in all this company I saw Creusa, the wife of Sir Æneas, whom he loved as his soul, and her young son Iulus, and also Ascanius, fled with so heavy looks that it was piteous to see; and how at a turning of a path as they went in the forest Creusa was lost and died, alas!, but I know not in what wise; how he sought her, and how her spirit bade him to flee the host of the Greeks, and said he must to Italy without fail, as was his destiny; so that it was piteous to listen to her words when her spirit appeared to him, and how she prayed him to guard her son. There I saw also graven how he and his father and his household sailed forth with his ships towards the land of Italy, as straight as they could go.

There, cruel Juno, who art Lord Jupiter's wife, and hast hated ever all the Trojan blood, I saw thee run as a mad-woman, and call the Æolus, the god of winds, to blow out from all directions so wildly that he should drown lord and lady, serving-man and wench, of the whole Trojan nation without any rescue. There I saw arise such a tempest that every heart might shudder to see it painted on the wall. There, Venus, I also saw graven how thou, my lady dear, weeping with full woeful countenance, prayedest Jupiter on high, because the Trojan Æneas was they son, to save and guard his fleet. There saw I Jove kiss Venus and grant abatement of the tempest. There saw I how it ceased, and how Æneas proceeded with great toil and privily arrived in the country of Carthage; and on the morrow, how he and a knight called Achates met with Venus walking in rare disguise, as she had been an huntress, with the wind blowing through her hair; how Æneas, when he knew her, began to bewail his sufferings, and that his ships were sunk, or else lost, he knew not where; how she began to comfort him and bade him go to Carthage, where he should find his folk who had been left behind on the sea.

And, to pass over this thing shortly, she put Æneas so in grace with Dido, queen of that land, that, to tell it briefly, she became his love in heart and body. Why should I speak more artfully or strive to paint my words in speaking of love? It will also not be; I know nothing of that craft. And to tell the manner in which they became acquainted, it were a long story to tell, and would delay you over-long. There I saw graven how Æneas told Dido every chance that had happened to him on the sea. And after that was graven how she made of him, in brief and in a word, her love, her joy, her master, and did him all the reverence, and lavished on him all the wealth that any woman could, weening all had been as he had sworn her, and hereby deeming that he was good, for such he seemed. Alas! what evil is wrought by appearance when it is false to the truth of the case! For he was traitor to her, wherefore, alas! she slew herself. Lo! how ill a woman does to love him who is unknown! For lo, by heaven! it is not all gold that shines. For, on my life, many a cursed fault may be covered under goodly seeming; therefore be no man so foolish as to take a lover only because of aspect, speech or friendly manner; for this every woman shall find, that sometimes a man by his nature will appear outwardly the fairest, till he have gained what he desires, and then he will invent excuses, and swear that she is unkind or false or sly or two-faced. All this I am minded of by Æneas and Dido, and her foolish inclination, who loved a guest all too soon. Therefore I will say a proverb:

> 'Who knows the herb right perfectly
> May safely lay it to his eye.'

Without doubt this is true.

But let us speak of Æneas, how he betrayed her and left her full unkindly, alas! So when she utterly perceived that he would fail in his troth to her, and would turn from her to Italy, she began to wring her two hands. 'Alas!' quoth she, 'alas, woe is me! Is the troth of every man, that he will have a new one every year (if it will last that long), or else three peradventure? As thus: of one he would have fame in magnifying his reputation; another, he says, for friendship; and there shall be yet the third, that shall be taken, lo, for delight or some especial advantage.' In such words Dido bemoaned her great pain, as I dreamed; I cite none other author. 'Alas!' she said, 'my sweet heart, have pity on my bitter sorrows, and slay me not! Go not away! Ah woful Dido, alas!' Then she said to herself, 'O Æneas, what wilt thou do? Ah that neither thy love, nor thy pledge that thou hast sworn with thy right hand, nor my cruel death, may keep thee here with me still! Ah, have pity of my death! Surely, my dear heart, thou knowest full well that never yet, so far as my wit could stretch, have I wronged thee in thought or deed. Ah, have ye men such goodliness in speech, and never a bit of truth? Alas, that ever woman had pity on any man! Now I well see and can tell others that we wretched women have no subtlety; for certainly thus we be served every one, for the more part. However sorely ye men can groan, anon as soon as we have accepted you, in truth we are deceived; for though your love last for a season, watch for the conclusion, how for the more part ye will end. Alack that I was born! For through you my good name is lost, and all my deeds are read and sung over all this land, in every mouth. O Evil Report! for lo, there is nothing so swift as she is. Ah, true it is, everything is known, though it be wrapped deep in mist. And also, though I might live forever, I can never so retrieve what I have done, that, alas!, I shall not be said to have been shamed through Æneas, and that it shall not be judged of me thus: 'Lo even as she has done, she will of a surety do again.' Thus the people say privily.'

But what is done is yet to do; verily, all her lament and moan availed her not a straw. And when of a truth she knew that he was gone forth unto his ships, she went anon into her chamber and called her sister Anne and lamented to her, and said that she was the cause why she first loved Æneas, and had counselled her thereto. But what! When this was said and done, she rove herself to the heart and died of the bitter wound. But all the manner of her death and the words she said, whosoever would fain know it, let him read Virgil in the book of the Æneid, or the epistle in Ovid, which she wrote ere she died. And were it not too long to endite, by heaven I would put it here.

But alack for the harm and pity that have betided from such faithlessness, as men may often read in books, and see it still in deed every day, so that it is dolorous to think on! Lo Demophon, duke of Athens, how he forswore himself full falsely, and wickedly betrayed Phyllis, who was the king's daughter of Thrace, and falsely tarried past his appointed time; and when she knew he was false, she hanged herself by the neck because he had been so faithless to her. Lo! was not this a woe and a pity? Also, lo! how false and heedless was Achilles to Briseis, and Paris to Œnone, and Jason to Hypsipyle, and again Jason to Medea, and Hercules to Dejanira (for he left her for Iole, which brought him his death, perdy!). Also how false was Theseus, who betrayed Ariadne, as the story tells us, — the Devil be his soul's destruction! For he would have been all devoured, willy-nilly, had it not been for Ariadne. And because she pitied him, she helped him to escape from his death. And he played her a right false trick; for some time after this he left her sleeping alone on a desert isle amid the sea, and stole away and left her to shift for herself; and took her sister Phædra with him and went to his ship. And yet he had sworn to her by all that ever he could swear upon that, so she saved his life, he would wed her; for, as the book says, of a truth she desired naught else.

But to excuse Æneas full for him his great trespass, the book says that in truth Mercury bade him go into Italy and leave the region of Africa and Dido and her fair town.

Then I saw graven how Sir Æneas set sail for Italy; and how there arose a great tempest, and how he lost his steersman, whom the rudder, ere he took heed, smote overboard, lo! as he slept. And also I saw how the Sibyl and Æneas, hard by an isle, went down into hell to see his father, the noble

Anchises; how he found there Palinurus, and Dido, and also Deiphobus; and he saw every torment of hell, which were long to relate. Which whoever wishes to know, he must read many a line in Virgil or Claudian or Dante, who can tell it.

Then I saw graven all the arrival of Æneas in Italy, and his treaty with king Latinus, and all the battles that he was in and also his knights, ere he gained what he would have; and how he took Turnus' life and won Lavinia in marriage; and all the marvellous portents of the celestial gods; how, maugre Juno and all her arts and fetches, Æneas achieved all his emprise, for Jupiter took care of him at the petition of Venus, — whom I pray ever to save us and ever ease us of our sorrows!

When I had seen all these sights thus in this noble temple, I thought, 'Ah Lord that madest us! Never yet saw I such magnificence of figures and such wealth as I have seen graven in this church. But I wot not who had them wrought, nor where I am, nor in what land. But now I will go out even to the wicket, and see if I can espy any man stirring anywhere who can tell me where I am.'

When I came out at the doors I gazed about me diligently. Then I saw only a large field as far as I could see, without town or house or tree or bush or grass or ploughed ground; for all the field was sand, as fine as men may see yet lying in the desert of Libya. Nor saw I any manner of being that is formed by Nature, to instruct or direct me. 'O Christ, Who reignest in blessedness,' I thought, 'save me from phantom and illusion!' And devoutly I cast mine eyes to the heaven. Lo, at the last I was ware then how hard by the sun, as far up as I could discern with mine eyes, methought I beheld an eagle soar, only it seemed much greater than any eagle that I had ever seen. But verily this is as true as death, — it was golden, and shone so brilliantly that never man had seen such a sight, unless the heaven had gained another such all new and of gold; so brightly shone the eagle's feathers. And then it began somewhat to descend.

Book II

Now hearken, every manner of man who can understand English and list to learn of my dream; for now or never ye shall hear so wondrous a vision that neither Esaias nor Scipio nor King Nebuchadnezzar, Pharaoh, Turnus, nor Elcanor dreamed such a dream as this. Now, fair blessed Cyprian dame, be my helper in this task! And ye who dwell on Parnassus, by the pure fount of Helicon, help me to endite and rhyme! O Thought, that recorded all that I dreamed and locked it in the treasury of my brain, now shall men see if there be any power in thee to tell all my dream aright. Now make known thy power and craft!

This eagle that I have spoken of, that soared so far on high and shone as with feathers of gold, I began to behold more and more, and to see its beauty and the marvel of it all. But never was lightning-stroke, or that thing which men call the thunderbolt — which sometimes has smitten a tower to powder and burned it by its swift onslaught — that so swiftly descended as this bird, when it beheld me abroad in the field. And with his grim and mighty feet, within his long sharp claws, he caught me at a swoop as I fled, and soared up again, carrying me in his strong claws as easily as if I were a lark, — how high I cannot tell you for how I came up I knew not. For every faculty in my head was so astonied and stunned, what with his swift ascent and mine own fear, that all my sense of feeling died away, so great was mine affright.

Thus I lay long in his claws, till at last he spoke to me in human voice and said, 'Awake and be not so aghast; fie upon you!' And then he called me by name, and, to arouse me the better — so I dreamed — he said 'Awake!' to me, even in the same voice and tone that one whom I could mention uses; and at that voice, to tell the truth, my mind returned to me, for it was spoken to me kindly, — as it was never wont to be. And at this I began to stir, and he bore me on his talons till he felt that I grew warm and also felt my heart beating. Then he began to be mirthful with me and with words to comfort me, and said twice, 'Marry, you are troublesome to bear, and more than you need be, perdy! For, so God help me, you shall have no harm of this. This thing that has happened to you is for your instruction and your profit. Let see! dare you look yet? Be fully assured, I tell you plainly, I am your friend.'

And therewith I began to marvel within my mind. 'O God Who madest nature,' thought I, 'am I to die in none other way? will Jove stellify me, or what thing may this all mean? I am neither Enoch nor Elias nor Romulus — nor Ganymede, who, as books tell, was borne up to heaven by Lord Jupiter and made the gods' butler.'

Lo this was my fancy then! But he who carried me espied that I thought thus, and said, 'You think amiss in your own mind; for Jove is not minded — I dare well put you full out of doubt — to make a star of you as yet. But ere I bear you much farther I will tell you what I am, and whither you shall go, and why I came to do this, so you take good heart and tremble not for fear.'

'Gladly,' quoth I.

'Now that is well,' quoth he. 'First, I who have you in my feet, at which thing you fear and marvel, dwell with the god of thunder whom men call Jupiter, who sends me full often flying far to do all his commands. And for this cause he has sent me to you — now hearken, by your troth! he has pity of you, verily, because so long and attentively you have served his blind grandson Cupid and also the fair Venus, ever yet without reward; and nevertheless have set your wit — full small though it be — to making books, songs, ditties, in rhyme or in cadence, as you best know how, in worship of Love, and of his servants also, that have sought and seek his service; and strive to praise his art, although you had never a portion therein. Wherefore, so God bless me, Jove deems it great humility and also great virtue, that full often you will set your head to aching by night, so diligently enditing, and evermore of Love, in honour and praise of him and to the furtherance of his folk; and have set forth the whole of their matter, and despise neither him nor his folk, though you must needs go upon the dance with them he cares to promote but little. Wherefore as I said, in truth, Jupiter considers this and other things also, fair sir; that is, that you gain no tidings of Love's folk, whether they be glad or no, nor of anything else that God made; not only that no tidings come to you from far lands, but you hear neither this nor that of your very neighbours who dwell almost at your door; for when your labour is all ended and you have made all your reckonings, instead of rest and novelty you go home anon to your house, and as dumb as any stone you sit at another book till your eyes are all dazed. Thus you live like a hermit (though your abstinence be but small!).

'And therefore Jove of his kind favour wills that I should bear you to a place which is called the House of Fame, to give you some disport and diversion, as some recompense for your labour and devotion to Cupid the careless, — lo, ever without reward! And so this god will of his grace requite you with some manner of thing, if you will be of good heart. For trust well, when we be come where I say, you shall hear of more wondrous things, I dare wager, more tidings of Love's folk, both truthful sayings and lies; and more loves newly started, and more love's long labours won; and more loves that betide by chance, no man wot why, save as a blind man starts up an hare; and more jollity and goings-on, whilst they find love true as steel, as they think, and see joy and well-being everywhere; more discords, more jealousies, more murmurs, more changes, more dissimulations and feigned makings-up, and more wool pulled over folks' eyes and then fleeced off without razor or scissors in two hours, than there be grains of sand; and reward also more lovers falsely led on, and more renewals of old abandoned acquaintances, more lovedays and reconcilings, than there be strings on instruments of music; and also more exchanges of loves than ever were grains of corn in barns. Scarce can you believe all this?' quoth he.

'No, so surely may God help me!' I said.

'No? Why?' quoth he.

'Because to my wit it seems impossible, though Fame had all the magpies and all the spies in a whole kingdom, that she should yet hear all this, or they espy it.'

'Ah, yes, yes!' quoth he to me. 'That can I prove by reason worthy of credence, so you give heed to understand my words. First you shall hear where she dwells, as your own book relates it. As I shall tell you, her palace stands even in the very midst of the way betwixt heaven, earth and sea; so that, whatsoever is spoken privily or openly in all three of these domains, every sound must pass to it, or whatsoever comes from any mouth, be it read or sung or whispered, or spoken in security or fear, — certainly it must needs thither, that palace stands in so exact a spot, and the road thereto is so open.

'Now hearken well, for I will show you a right proper argument and a noble demonstration out of mine own imagining. Geoffrey, you know this right well, that everything there is in nature has a natural place where it is best conserved; toward which place everything is naturally inclined and moves to come thither when it is far away therefrom. As thus; lo, you may ever see that any heavy thing, as stone or lead, or something of weight, if you carry it never so high and let go your hand, it will fall down. Even so I say of fire or sound or smoke or other light things; they always seek to go upward on high. Whilst each is free, light things go up and heavy things down. And for this reason you perceive that every river, of its nature, tends to go to the sea, fish have their dwelling in river and sea, as I read, and trees also be in earth. And hence each thing has its proper mansion, to which it seeks to repair, and where it is ever at its best. Lo, this opinion is well known from the mouth of every philosopher, as Aristotle, and Lord Plato, and many another clerk.

'And, to confirm my interpretation, you know this well, that speech is sound, else no man could hear it. Now hearken to what I shall teach you. Sound is naught but broken air; and every speech that is uttered, aloud or privily, good or ill, is in substance nothing but air. For as flame is but lighted smoke, sound is broken air. But this be in many ways, of which I will tell you two; as sound that comes of pipe, or of harp. When a pipe is blown strongly, the air is twisted and rent with violence, lo, this is mine interpretation. And when men smite harp-strings, heavily or lightly, lo, the air breaks apart with the stroke. Even so it breaks when men speak; thus you have learned what speech is.

'Next now I will teach you how every word or noise or sound, though it were piped by a mouse, must needs through its multiplication come to the House of Fame. I prove it thus — take heed, now — by experiment; for if now you throw a stone into water, you know well that anon it will make a little round spot, like a circle, peradventure as broad as pot-lid; and right anon you shall see how that wheel will cause another wheel, and that, the third, and so forth, friend, every circle causing another wider than itself was. And thus from small circle to great, each circumscribing the other, each caused by the other's motion, but ever increasing till they go so far that they be at both brinks. Although you cannot see it from above, these circles spread beneath the water as well, though you think it a great marvel. And whoever says that I vary from the truth, bid him prove the reverse. And even thus, of a certainty, every word that is spoken, loud or privy, first moves a circle of air thereabout, and from this motion anon another circle is stirred. As I have proved of the water, that every circle causes a second, even so is it with air, my dear brother; each circle passes into another greater and greater, and bears up speech or voice or noise, word or sound, through constant increase, till it come to the House of Fame; take this in earnest or no — it is truth.

'Now I have told, if you can bear it in mind, how speech or sound by its very nature is inclined to draw upward; this I have proved, as you can perceive; and that the abode to which each thing is inclined has in truth its particular location. Then it is right plain that the natural abode of every speech and sound, fair or foul, has its natural position in the firmament. And since everything that is out of its natural place of a certainty tends to go thither, as I have before proved to you, it follows, perdy, that every sound naturally tends to go right up to its natural place. And this place which I tell of where Fame is pleased to live is set in the midst of these three, the sea, the sky, and the earth — as the place where sound is most readily received. Then this is the conclusion; every speech of every man, as I began first to tell you, moves up on high to pass to Fame's place, by its very nature. Tell me this faithfully, have I not thus simply made a proof without any subtlety of speech or great prolixity of philosophical terms or poetical figures or colours of rhetoric? Perdy, it ought to please you, for hard language and hard matter together are annoyous to hear; know you not this well?'

And I answered and said, 'Yes!'

'Aha!' quoth he. 'Lo! thus I can speak simply to a simple man, and show him such arguments that he can shake them by the beaks, they shall be so palpable. But tell me this, I pray you, what think you of my conclusion?'

Quoth I, 'It is a good argument, and like to be even so as you have proved to me.'

'Perdy,' quoth he, 'and as I believe, you shall yet, ere it be eve, have proof of every word of this argument by experience; and with your ears hear well that every word that is spoken, top and tail and every whit, certainly comes into Fame's house, as I have said. What would you further?' And with this word he began to soar higher, and said, 'By Saint James, now we will speak entirely of sport. How fare you?'

'Well,' quoth I.

'Now by your faith,' quoth he, 'see down yonder whether you know any town or house or any other thing. And when you recognize aught, look you warn me and straightway I shall tell you how far you now are therefrom.'

And then I looked down and beheld fields and plains, and now hills, now mountains, now valleys, now forests, and now (but scarce I saw them) great beasts; now rivers, now cities, now towns, now great trees, now ships sailing on the sea. But soon, after a while, he had flown so high from the ground that all the world seemed no more than a point to mine eyes; or else the air was so thick that I could discern naught. With that he spake to me anon and said, 'See you any town or aught that you know down yonder?'

I said, 'Nay.'

'No wonder is it,' quoth he, 'for Alexander of Macedon was not half so high as this, nor the king Sir Scipio, who in a dream saw every point of hell and earth and paradise; nor also luckless Dædalus, nor foolish Icarus his child, who flew so high that the heat melted his wings and he fell wet amid the sea and there drowned; for whom was made great lamentation. Now,' quoth he, 'turn your face upward and behold this large region, this air. But look you be not afeared of them that you shall see; for in this region, of a truth, dwells many a citizen, of which Sir Plato speaks. Lo, these be the aerial beasts.'

And so I saw all that multitude both walk and fly abroad.

'Now,' quoth he then, 'lift up your eyes; lo, see yonder the Galaxy, which men call the Milky Way, because it is white; and some, in faith, call it Watling Street. It was once burned with fire, when the red sun's son, called Phaethon, would at all hazards drive and guide his father's chariot. The chariot-horses knew well that he understood not their manage, and began to leap and plunge and to bear him now up now down till he saw the Scorpion, which is still a sign in heaven. And for fear of that he lost his wit, and let go the reins of his horses; and anon they mounted and descended till both air and earth burned;

till lo, Jupiter at last slew him and hurled him from the chariot. Lo, is it not great harm to let a fool have the management of a thing that he cannot control?'

And with this word, sooth to say, he began to soar steadily upward; and rejoiced me more and more, he spake to me with such friendly wisdom. Then I looked below me and beheld the aerial beasts, clouds, winds, mists, tempests, snows, hails, rains and their generation after their kind, and all the way over which I had come. 'O God that madest Adam,' quoth I, 'great is Thy power and Thy splendour!' And then I thought of Boethius, who writes, 'A thought may fly so high on the wings of Philosophy as to mount above every element; and when it hath gone so far, then the clouds may be seen behind its back,' and all of which I have spoken. Then I began to grow confused and said, 'I wot well that I am here, but whether in body or in spirit verily I wot not; but Thou, God knowest!' For not as yet had He sent me clear understanding. Then I thought on Martian, and also on the *Anticlaudianus*, and that their description of all the heavenly region was true, so far as I had experience thereof. Therefore I can now believe them.

And at this the eagle cried out and said, 'Let be your fancies. Will you learn aught about stars?'

'Nay, in very sooth,' quoth I, 'right naught. And why? because I am too old now.'

'Else,' quoth he, 'I would have told you the names of the stars, and all the signs of the heavens, too, and what they be.'

'No matter,' said I.

'Yes verily, it does matter,' quoth he; 'and knows you why? For you read in the poets how the gods have made stars of bird, fish, beast, or man or woman, as the Raven, or either Bear, or Arion's fine harp, Castor, Pollux, the Dolphin or the seven daughters of Atlas, — how all these are set in the sky. For though you often hear of them, yet you know not where they be.'

'No matter,' quoth I. 'It needs not; so God speed me. I believe them that write of this matter even as much as though I knew their places here; and also they shine so radiantly here, it would ruin all my sight to look on them.'

'That may well be,' quoth he. And so he carried me on a while, and then cried out so that I heard never a thing so loud. 'Now up with your head, for all is now well over. Lo, Saint Julian! a good hostelry! Behold, see here is the House of Fame. Can you not hear what I hear?'

'What?' I asked.

'The great sound,' quoth he, 'that rumbles up and down in Fame's House, full of rumours, both of fair words and chiding and of false and true compounded. Hearken well, it is not whispered, in faith! Hear you not the great murmur?'

'Yes,' quoth I, 'well enough, perdy.'

'And what sound is it like?'

'Peter!' quoth I, 'like the beating of the sea against hollow rocks, when tempest engulfs the ships, to a man who stands a mile thence and hears the roar. Or else it is like the last mutter after a thunder-clap, when Jove has smitten the air. But it makes me sweat for fear!'

'Nay,' quoth he, 'fear not thereat, it is naught that will bite you! Truly you shall have no harm.'

And at this word we were come as nigh the place as a man might hurl a spear. I knew not how, but he set me fairly on my feet in a road, and said, 'Walk on at your ease and take your chance or lot, whatever you shall find in Fame's place.

'Now,' quoth I, 'whilst we have time to speak, ere I go from you, for the love of God tell me, — in sooth I would fain learn it of you, — whether this noise that I hear be, as I have heard you tell, from folk that live down upon the earth, and comes here in that manner which I heard you describe but now; and whether there is not in all that house yonder a living creature that makes all this loud ado.'

'No,' quoth he, 'by Saint Clara, and so surely may God help me! But of one thing I will warn you at which you will marvel. Lo, you know how every speech comes to the House of Fame yonder; it needs not tell you again. But now understand this right well: when any speech is come up to the palace, anon it becomes like the same creature who spoke those words on earth, and in the selfsame garb; and has so the very likeness of him who spake the words that you would believe it were the same body, man or woman, he or she. And is not this marvellous?'

'Yes! by the heavenly King,' quoth I.

And at this word he said, 'Farewell, and here I will await you. And may the God of heaven send you grave to learn some good here.'

And anon I took leave of him and walked on to the palace.

Book III

Apollo, god of knowledge and light, through thy great power do thou guide this little last book! Not that I desire that poetical art be shown here in sign of skill; but, because the rhyme is light and uncrafty, yet make it somehow pleasing, even though some verse be wanting in a syllable, and though I seek to display no art, but only my meaning. And if, divine power, thou wilt help me to show now what is noted in my mind — lo, that is to describe the House of Fame — thou shalt see me go straightway to the nearest laurel that I can find and kiss it, because it is thy tree. Now enter straightway into my breast!

When I was gone from this eagle, I began to look about. And truly, before I proceed further, I will describe to you all the aspect of house and site; and all the manner how I approached this place, which stood upon so lofty a rock that in Spain there stands none higher. But I climbed up with great labour, yet notwithstanding I was attentive to see and to pore wondrous low at my feet, to find out if I could in any wise of what manner of stone this rock was; for it was like a thing made of glass, save that it shone much more brightly. But of what congealed matter it was, I wist not, of a truth. But at last I espied that it was every whit a rock of ice, and not of steel. Thought I, 'By Saint Thomas of Kent, this were a feeble foundation on which to build so lofty a place! He ought to boast but little who builds hereon, so God save me!'

Then I saw the whole side graven with many names of famous folk, who had lived in much weal and had their renown blown afar. But scarce could I make out any letters to read their names by; for in truth they were so nearly thawed away that one or two letters of every name were melted away, so unfamous was their fame grown. But men say, 'what may endure forever?'

Then I pondered in my heart how they were melted away by heat, and not worn away by storms. For on the opposite side of this hill, that lay to the north, I saw how it was written full of names of folk that had great renown of old time, and still they were as fresh as if men had written them there that very day or the very hour when I peered upon them. And well I knew the reason; all this writing which I saw was preserved by the shadow of a castle which stood on high; and the writing lay on so cold a spot that heat could not deface it.

Then I went up the hill and found on top an abode such that all the men alive would have no cunning to describe the beauty of it, nor could devise a plan to make such another, its match in beauty and so wondrously wrought; it still astonies my mind and makes all my wit labour, to think on this castle. The great art and beauty, the plan and curious workmanship, I cannot describe to you; my wit suffices not. Nevertheless all the substance thereof I have yet in my remembrance. For it seemed to me, by Saint Giles, all was of beryl, without piercing or joints; both castle and tower and hall and every chamber. I saw many subtle devices, gargoyles and pinnacles, tabernacles and imageries; and also it was as full of windows as flakes fall in great snowstorms. And also in each of the pinnacles were sundry niches, in which all about over the castle outside stood all manner of minstrels and tellers of tales both tearful and merry, of all that ministers to Fame. There I heard Orpheus playing full skilfully upon a harp which sounded clear and well: and hard by his side sat the harper Arion and Achilles' Chiron, and the Briton Glasgerion, and many another harper; and in seats below them sat small harpers with their glees and instruments, and stared up at them and counterfeited them like apes, or as art counterfeits nature. Then I saw standing behind them, far away and all by themselves, many scores of thousands, who made loud minstrelsy with bagpipes and shawms and many other kinds of pipes, and skilfully played both them of clear and them of reedy sound, such as be played at feasts with the roast-meat, — and many a flute and lilting-horn and pipes made of green stalks, such as these little shepherd-lads have who watch over beasts in the broom.

Then I saw there Atiteris, and Sir Pseustis of Athens, and that Marsyas who lost his skin, on face, neck, and body, because, lo, he would vie with Apollo, to pipe better than he. There I saw famous pipers of the German speech, both young and old, learning love-dances, springs, rounds and these foreign capers. In another part I saw standing in a large space certain of them that make bloody sounds with trumpet, clarion and horn; for they that fight and shed blood are fain to have clarioning. There I heard Misenus, of whom Virgil speaks; also I heard Joab trump there, Thiodamas, and others besides. And all them in Aragon and Catalonia, that were acquainted with the clarion, who were famous to hear of in their time, saw I trumpeting there.

On other seats I saw sitting there, playing upon sundry instruments which I cannot name, more folk than there be stars in heaven; of whom I will not now rhyme, considering your pleasure and the time that would be lost: for this you know, that time lost can in no way be recovered. There I saw jugglers playing, magicians, wizards and pythonmesses, charmeresses, old witches, sorceresses, who use exorcisms and also these mystic fumigations; and also clerks who well know all this natural magic, and who give their minds and their craft, in certain aspects of the ascendant, to making images, through which magic, lo, they may make a man sick or whole. There I saw thee, queen Medea, also Circe and Calypso; there I saw Hermes Ballenus, Lymote, and also Simon Magus. There I saw, and knew by name, those who by such arts gained men renown. There I saw Colle the juggler perform upon a table of sycamore a thing strange to describe; I saw him carry a windmill under a walnut-shell.

Why should I make a longer story, from now to doomsday, of all the people that I saw? When I had beheld all this folk, and found myself free and no whit withheld, and had again mused a long while upon these walls of beryl, which shone more brightly than glass, and made all things, in truth, to seem greater than they were, as is natural to Fame, I roamed on till I found on my right the castle-gate, which was so well carven that there was never such another; and yet the workmanship was done by chance as often as by pains. It needs not make you tarry too long, to tell you of the flourishes on this gate, nor of the curves, nor of the carvings, nor how they are terms in the art of masonry, as corbels full of imagery. But Lord, how fair it was to the eye, all pointed with beaten gold!

But in I went, and that anon, and there I met many an one crying, 'A largess! a largess! hold your hands out! God save our own noble lady Fame, the lady of this castle; and all them that desire to have renown of us!' Thus I heard them cry, and they came quickly out of the hall and threw down sterling coins, nobles and others. And some were crowned like kings-at-arms, with crowns wrought full of lozenges, and on their garments many ribands and fringes. Then at last I discovered that they were all pursuivants and heralds, who cry rich folk's praises; and every man of them, I can tell you, had thrown upon him a vesture which men call a surcoat, embroidered wondrous richly, although they were not alike. But, on my life, I will not go about to describe all the coats-of-arms which they thus wore on their surcoats, for it could not be done; men might make a bible on it twenty foot thick, I believe. For verily whosoever knew them might have seen there all the coats-of-arms of famous folk that have lived in Africa, Europe and Asia since knighthood first began. Lo! how should I tell all this now?

And what need like likewise to tell you of the great room of the castle, that every wall of it and floor and ceiling and all else was plated half a foot thick with gold, and that was not at all alloyed, but to every test as fine as a ducat of Venice (of which all too few are in my pouch)? And all was studded with bosses full of the finest fair stones, of which men read in the Lapidary, as thick as grasses grow in a mead. But it were all too tedious to recite the names; therefore I pass on. But in this rich, lusty place, which was called Fame's hall, there was not a very great press of folk, nor any crowding of too great a throng. But all on high, on a dais, sitting on an imperial throne made of an entire ruby, which is called a carbuncle, I saw eternally enthroned a being in woman's form; and never was seen such another formed by Nature. For, sooth to say, at the first methought she was so little that the length of a cubit was longer; but ere long she stretched out so wondrously that she reached to earth with her feet and with her head touched the sky, where shine the seven planets. And also, to my wit, I saw a still greater wonder, looking upon her eyes; but truly I never counted them; for she had as many eyes as there be feathers upon birds, or as were on the four beasts that did honour God's throne, as John writes in the Apocalypse. Her hair, which lay in waves and curls, shone before mine eyes like burnished gold. And, sooth to say, she also had as many projecting ears and tongues as there be hairs on beasts. And on her feet truly I saw partridge's wings growing.

But Lord, the gems and riches that I saw adorning this goddess! And Lord, the heavenly melody of songs full of concord that I heard sung about her throne, so that all the palace walls rang! So sang the mighty Muse, she who is called Calliope, and also her eight sisters, full gracious in their visages. And evermore and eternally the folk sang of Fame, as I heard then,

> 'Blessed be thou and thy name,
> Goddess of renown and Fame!'

Then, lo, at last I was ware, as I turned mine eyes upward, that this noble queen bore on her shoulders both the coat-of-arms and the name of them that had wide glory, — Alexander, and Hercules, who lost his life because of a shirt! Thus I found this goddess sitting in dignity, honour, and splendour; all which I will leave a while, to tell you of other things.

Then I saw standing on either side, straight down from the dais to the broad doors, many a metal pillar, which shone not very brightly. But though they were of no great splendour, nevertheless they were made for noble use and great significance; and folk honourable and reverend I saw standing upon the columns, of whom I will try to tell you.

Lo, first of all I saw stand on high upon a column of lead and fine iron, him of the school of Saturn, the Hebrew, the ancient Josephus, who told of Jewish history; and upon his lofty shoulders he bore up the fame of Jewry. And by him stood other seven wise and worthy to be named, helping him to bear the burden so great and so heavy. And because they wrote of battles as well as other old wonders, lo, therefore this column of which I tell you was made of both lead and iron. For iron is the metal of Mars, god of battle; and lo, the lead, of a truth, is the metal of Saturn, that turns in so large an orbit. Then on every row stood forth some whom I could recognize, though I tell them not in order, lest I make you tarry too long. These of whom I shall speak I truly saw standing there. Upon a strong iron pillar, stained all over with tiger's blood, was he of Toulouse who is named Statius, who bore up the renown of Thebes on his shoulders, and also the name of cruel Achilles. And in good sooth there stood beside him, wondrous high on an iron pillar, he, the great Homer; and with him Dares and Dictys in front, and also Lollius and also Guide de Columnis and the English Geoffrey also. And each of these was busy to bear up the fame of Troy, and so heavy was it that to bear it was no sport. But still I full well discerned that there was a little ill-will amongst them. One held that Homer's story was but a fable, and that he spake lies, and feigned in his poems, and that he favoured the Greeks.

Then I saw standing on a pillar of bright tinned iron that Latin poet Virgil, who long time has borne up the fame of pious Æneas. And next him on a pillar of copper was the clerk of Venus, Ovid, that has sowed wondrous broadly the name of the great god of Love. And there he well bore up his renown upon this pillar, as high as I could see; for this hall of which I speak was grown in highest, length and breadth, far greater, a thousandfold, than it had first been; that I saw well. Then I saw hard by on a column wrought of stern iron the great poet Sir Lucan; and he bore upon his shoulders, as high as I could see, the fame of Julius and Pompey. And by him stood all these clerks that wrote of the mighty deeds of Rome; so that if I should tell their names, I must tarry all too long. And on a pillar of sulphur next to him stood Sir Claudian, as if he were in a gloomy frenzy, sooth to say; he bore up all the renown of hell, of Pluto and Proserpine, queen of the dark torments.

Why should I tell more? The hall was as full of them that wrote old histories as trees be of rooks' nests. But it were confusion to hear all the exploits that they wrote of, and what their books were named. But whilst I beheld this sight, I heard a noise swiftly approaching, as it were of bees in an hive towards the time of their swarming; for all the world, even such murmuring it seemed to me. Then I looked about and saw that there came entering the hall a right great company, and that from sundry lands, of all sorts and conditions, poor and rich, that dwell on earth under the moon. And straightway when they were come into the hall, they fell on their knees before this noble queen, and said, 'Of thy grace, bright lady, grant each of us a boon!' And to some of them she granted it forthwith, and some she refused flatly, and to some she granted the very contrary of their request. But truly I tell you I knew not what her reason was, for I knew full well that this folk had each deserved good fame, although they were diversely treated; even as her sister, dame Fortune, is ever wont to serve men.

Now hearken how she requited those who prayed her grace; and yet, lo, all this company said sooth and nothing false. 'Madame,' they said, 'we are folk that here beseech thee to grant us now fair renown and let our achievements have that name; in full recompense for good works, give us good repute.'

'I deny it you,' she said forthwith. 'Ye get no good fame of me, by heaven, and therefore go your ways.'

'Alas and alack!' they cried. 'Tell us, what may be thy reason?'

'Because I list not,' quoth she. 'No man shall speak good or ill of you, in verity, neither this nor that.' And at that she summoned her messenger who was in the hall, and bade him, on pain of blinding, to go speedily and summon Æolus, the god of winds: 'Ye shall find him in Thrace, and bid him bring his clarions, that be full diverse in their tone. That is called Clear Laud with which he is wont to herald them that I please to have praised; and also bid him bring his other clarion, which everywhere is called Slander, with which he is wont to dishonour them that I will, and to shame them.'

The messenger went speedily and found where, in a rocky cave in a country called Thrace, this Æolus held the winds in harsh constraint, and oppressed them under him till they roared like bears, so sore did he bind and press them. This messenger cried on high, 'Rise up,' quoth he, 'and haste thee till thou come to my lady; and also take thy clarions with thee, and speed thee forth.'

And anon he delivered his clarions to a man called Triton to carry, and let go a certain wind, that blew so high and hideously that it left not a cloud in all the long and broad sky. This Æolus nowhere tarried till he was to come to Fame's feet, and with him the man named Triton; and there he stood, still as a stone.

And on this there straightway came another huge company of good folk, and cried, 'Lady, pray grant us fair fame, and let our deeds be known so, in honour of nobility, and so may God bless thy soul! For since we have deserved well, it is right that we be requited.'

'On my life,' quoth she, 'it shall not be; good works shall not avail you, to get good fame of me. But know ye what? I grant you that ye shall have an ill fame and evil praise and worse repute, though ye have deserved fair praise. Now go your ways, ye are sped. And thou, Lord Æodus,' quoth she, 'let see now! Take forth thy trump anon that is called Ready Slander, and blow their renown so that every creature shall say evil and cursedness of them, instead of what is good and worthy. For thou shalt trump thus the contrary of what they have done fairly or well.'

'Alas!' I thought, 'what ill chance have these sorry creatures! For amongst all the crowd shall they thus be shamed guiltless. But what! it must needs be.'

What did this Æolus do but take his black trumpet of brass, fouler than the Devil; and he blew this trumpet as if he would overthrow all the world, so that this foul trumpet's noise went throughout every land as swift as ball from gun when fire is touched to the powder. And such a smoke came out of the end of his foul trumpet, black, blue, swarthy red, greenish, as comes all on high from the chimney, where men melt lead. And one thing more I saw well, that the

461

farther it went the greater it waxed, as a river from its source; and it stank as the pit of hell. Alas, thus guiltless was their shame sounded on every tongue!

Then came the third company and hasted to the dais, and forthwith fell on their knees and said, 'We all be folk that have full rightfully deserved fame, and we pray thee that it be proclaimed even as it is, and blown forth.'

Quoth she, 'I grant it, because it pleases me now that your good works be known; and, in spite of all your foes, ye shall have yet better praise than ye merit, and that anon. Thou Æolus,' she cried, 'let be thy trumpet that is so black, and take out thine other trumpet that is called Laud, and blow it so that their fame spread nimbly throughout the world, but not too speedily, only so that it be known at last.'

'Full gladly, my lady,' he said, and anon drew out his trumpet of gold and set it to his lips, and blew it east, west, north, south, loud as any thunder, so that every creature marvelled at it, so widely ran the sound ere it ceased. And certes all the breath that issued from his trumpet's mouth smelled as if men placed a potful of balm amid a basket full of roses. This favour he did their renown.

And upon that I espied that the fourth band was coming — but certainly they were wondrous few, — and they stood in a row and said, 'Of a truth, bright lady, we have done well with all our power, but we care not for glory. For God's love, hide our works and our name; for certes we have done them out of goodness and for no manner of thing else.'

'I grant your boon,' said she; 'let your works die!'

With that I turned my head and forthwith saw the fifth band, who louted to this lady and fell on their knees anon, and then all besought her to hide their good works also, and said they gave not a leek for fame or such renown; for they had laboured out of piety and love of God, and would naught of fame.

'What!' quote she. 'Be ye mad? And think ye to do good and have no glory for it? Scorn ye to have my name? Nay, ye shall every one of you live! Thou Æolus,' quoth she, 'blow thy trumpet, I command, and that anon, and ring out in music, the deeds of this folk so that all the world may hear of them.' And he blew their praise so clear in his golden clarion that the sound went throughout the world, never so keen and soft; but at last it mounted to the sky.

Then came the sixth band and began to cry earnestly to Fame in this manner: 'Thy favour, dear lady! To tell the very truth, we have done neither this nor that, but been idle all our life. But nevertheless we pray to have as fair a fame and great renown and glory as they that have done noble deeds and achieved all their will, in love as in other other matters; albeit never was brooch or ring or aught else sent us of women, nor once did they think in their hearts to make us even friendly cheer, but were ready to bring us to our graves, — yet let us seem so to the people that all may judge of us that women loved us madly. It shall do us as much good, and avail our hearts to weight ease over against travail, as if we had won it with labour. For that had been dear-bought honour at the cost of all our ease. And thou must do for us yet more; let us be held also as worthy, wise and good, and rich, and lucky in love, for His sake who sits in heaven. Though we may not have the bodies of women, yet, so God save thee, let men fasten on us the credit! That shall suffice us!'

Quoth she, 'By my troth, I grant it! Now Æolus, let see, tarry not, take out thy trumpet of gold, and blow as they have asked, so that every man think them at ease, though they walk in full poor pastures.' This Æolus blew it so loud that it was known through the world.

Then anon came the seventh crowd, and all fell on their knees and said, 'Lady, grant us forthwith the same thing, the same boon, that thou hast done for this last folk.'

'Fie on every one of you!' quoth she. 'Ye gluttonous swine, idle wretches full of the rotten vice of sloth! What, false thieves, would ye be famed as good, and nothing deserve it and never recked thereof? Men ought rather to hang you! Ye be like the tired cat that would fain have fish; but what think ye? He would not wet his paws! Ill luck on your pates and also on mine, if I grant it, or do you favour, to extol you! Thou Æolus, king of Thrace,' quoth she, 'go, blow this folk straightway a sorry favour. And knowest thou what? Even as I shall tell thee forthwith. Say, "These be they that would have honour and do no sort of toil; and do no good, and yet have praise; and desire men should think that *la belle Isolt* herself could not refuse them love, and yet she that grinds at an hand-mill is all too good to ease their hearts." '

This Æolus anon started up, and with his black clarion blew out a sound as loud as winds bellow in hell, and also in truth the sound was so full of mocks as ever apes were of grimaces. And that went around all the world, so that every man began to shout at them and to laugh as a madman, such sorry visages men found in their hoods!

Then came another band, that had done treachery, harm, the greatest wickedness any heart could imagine; and prayed her to grant fair fame, and not to disgrace them, but blow them glory and good name by the clarion. 'Nay, certainly,' quoth she; 'that were a fault. Though there by no justice in me, I list not do it now; I will not grant you this.'

Then a crowd came leaping in, rapping every man about on the pate till all the hall resounded; and they said, 'Lady sweet and dear, we be such folk as we shall tell thee. In good sooth we be rogues, every one of us, and delight in wickedness as good folk in goodness; and rejoice to be known as rogues and full of vice and sins. Wherefore here in a row we pray that our fame be known in all things even as it really is.'

'Verily, I grant it you,' quoth she. 'But who art thou who sayst this, and wearest a stripe on thy hose and such a bell on thy tippet?'

'Madame,' quoth he, 'sooth to say, I am that very rogue that burned the temple of Isis in the city of Athens, lo!'

'Wherefore,' quoth she, 'didst thou that?'

'By my thrift, Madame,' quoth he, 'I would fain have had glory even as other folk in the town had, though they were famous for their excellence and their moral virtue. Thought I, rogues have as great fame, though it be but for roguery, as good folk for goodness. And since I cannot have the one, I will not forgo the other. And to get meed of Fame I set the temple afire. Now let our renown be blown quickly, as ever thou hopest for joy!'

'Gladly,' quoth she. 'Thou Æolus, hearest thou not their prayer?'

'Yes, Madame,' quoth he, 'I hear well. And I will trumpet it, perdy!' And he quickly took his black trumpet and puffed and blew till the sound was at the world's end.

With that I turned around; for one who stood right at my back spoke to me kindly, methought, and said, 'Friend, what is your name? Are you come hither to ask for renown?'

'Nay, in sooth, friend!' I said. 'Gramercy! I came not hither for any such cause, by my life! It suffices me that no man have my name on his lips, even as if I were dead. I myself best know how I stand; for whatsoever I think or suffer I myself will swallow it all, — or certainly the greater part, so far as I have skill.'

'But what do you here then?' said he.

Quoth I, 'That I will tell, the reason why I stand here: to learn some new tidings, some new things, I know not what; tidings of this or that, of love, or such glad things. For certainly he who caused me to come hither told me that I should both see and hear wondrous things in this place. But these be no such tidings as I mean.'

'No?' quoth he.

And I answered, 'No, of a truth! For since I first had wit, I knew ever that folk have desired fame and glory and renown diversely. But truly till now I knew not how or where Fame dwelt; nor yet what manner of person she is, in look or quality, nor the manner of her judgments, till the time I came hither.'

'Lo, what is this which you have heard, which you but now spoke of?' he asked me. 'But now no matter; for I see well what you would hear. Come forth, stand here no longer, and without doubt I will lead you into such another place where you shall hear many a thing.'

Then I went forth with him out of the castle, and saw in a valley below the castle close by such an house that the *Domus Dœdali*, which is called the Labyrinth, was not half so wondrously and curiously fashioned. And evermore swift as thought this wondrous house whirled around, so that it nevermore stood still. And there came out from it such a roar that had the house stood upon the Oise, I believe verily that men might easily have heard it as far as Rome. And the noise which I heard there went on for all the world like the rush of the stone which is shot from the machine. This whole house was made of twigs, yellow, green, red, and some white, such as men whittle for these cages, or make into these panniers or other baskets; so that with the gusts and the whirring of the twigs, this house was full of squeaks and creakings and much commotion. And also this house had as many entries as there are leaves on trees in the summer when they are green; and still in the roof men could see a thousand holes, and more yet, to let out the sound easily.

And by day all the time, and by night, the doors are open wide. There is no porter there to hinder any kind of tidings from passing in; and there is never quiet in that place, that it is not full of tidings, either loud or whispered. And all the corners of the house are full of whisperings and pratings of war, of peace, marriages, rest, labour, journeyings, abidings, of death, life, love, hate, accord, enmity, of praise, learning, of gains, of health, sickness, of buildings, of fair winds, tempests, pestilence of man and beast; of divers changes of estate for men and nations; of trust, fear, jealousy, wit, profit, folly, of plenty, and of great famine, of ruin, of cheap times and dear; of good or ill government, of fire, of divers events. And lo, be ye sure it was not small, this house of which I write; for it was sixty mile in length. Though the timber were not strong, yet the house was founded to last whilst it should please Chance, which is the mother of tidings, as the sea of springs and founts. And it was shaped like a cage.

'Certes,' quoth I, 'in all the years of my life I never saw such a house.' And as I marvelled thereat, I was ware that mine eagle was perched high upon a rock hard by; and I went to him straight and said thus: 'I pray you, for God's love, wait for me a while, and let me see what wonders are in this place. For peradventure I may yet learn some good from it, or hear somewhat that were pleasant to me, ere I go.'

'Peter! that is mine intention,' quoth he to me. 'Therefore I tarry. But certainly I tell you one thing: unless I bring you therein, without doubt you shall never know how even to begin to enter it, so rapidly it whirls around. But since Jove of his grace, as I have said, will do you pleasure with such matters, strange sights and tidings, wherewith to drive away your heaviness, such pity he has on your troubles, which you endure meekly — , and know yourself quite hopeless of all joy, since Fortune has unjustly made the sum of all your heart's repose to languish and be in point to burst, since he of his great kindness will do you pleasure, though it be but little, and gave express command, to which I am obedient, to further you all I can, and guide and direct you aright whither you may hear most tidings, — therefore you shall straightway learn many an one here.'

With this word forthwith he caught me up betwixt his toes and brought me in at a window of this house, methought; and at that the house seemed to stop, and revolved not at all; and he set me down on the floor. But never was seen, and never again shall be, such a congregation of folk as I saw roaming around, some within, some without; certes there are not left in the world so many formed by Nature, now so many creatures dead, so that scarce had I one foot's breadth of room in that place. And every creature whom I saw was whispering privily in another's ear a fresh piece of news, or else all openly spake right thus and said, 'Know you not what has happened lately or now?'

'No,' quoth the other, 'tell me!'

And then he told this and that, and swore it was true; — 'Thus has he said' — , 'Thus he does — ,' 'Thus it shall be — ,' 'thus I heard tell — ,' 'That shall be found — ,' 'That I dare wager — '; so that all the folk alive have not the cunning to relate the things I heard, some aloud, some in the ear. But the most wondrous was this; when one had heard a thing, he came forth to another and straightway told him the same thing that he had heard ere it was a moment older, but in the telling he made the tidings somewhat greater than ever they had been. And not so soon was he parted from him as the second met a third; and ere he was done, he told him everything; were the tidings true or false, he would tell them nevertheless, and evermore with greater increase than the first. Thus every word went from mouth to mouth in all directions, evermore increasing, as fire is wont to kindle and spread from a spark thrown amiss, till a whole city is burned up.

And when that story was fully spread, and had grown greater on every tongue that it ever had been, anon it went up to a window to go out; but ere it could pass out there, it crept out at some crevice and straightway flew forth quickly. And sometimes then I saw a lie and a sober truth at the same time, that by chance drew near to pass out of a window. And when they met there, they were both checked and neither could go out, each so crowded by the other, till each cried shrilly, 'Let me go first!,' 'Nay, but let me! And so thou wilt do so, I here assure thee that I shall never part from thee, but be thine own sworn brother. We will both so mingle together that no man, be he never so angry, can get only one of us, but both at once, all without his leave, come we by morn or night, be we cried aloud or quietly whispered.' Thus I saw falsehood and truth compounded fly abroad as one piece of news.

Thus all the tidings squeezed out of holes straight to the goddess, and she named each after its nature, and allotted to each its duration, some to wax and wane quickly, as does the fair white moon, and let them go. There I could see winged wonders fly fast, twenty thousand in a company, as Æolus blew them about.

And Lord! at all times this house was full of shipmen and pilgrims, with scrips brimful of lies, mingled with sooth tidings or alone by themselves. And also I saw, ah, many a thousand score of these pardoners, couriers and also messengers, with boxes crammed as full of lies as ever vessel was with dregs. And I went about as fast as I could go, and gave all my mind to divert me and to learn, and also to hear news which I had heard of some country (which for my part shall not now be told, for truly it needs not; other folk can sing it better than I can, for all must out, sooner or later, all the sheaves in the barn), — then I heard a great noise in a corner of the hall where men were telling tidings of love, and I began to look thitherward; for I saw every person running as fast as he could, and each cried, 'What is it?' And some said I know not what. And when they were all in a mass, those behind began to leap up, and crowded and climbed up on the others, and lifted up their noses and eyes, and trod hard on others' feet, and stamped, as men do after eels.

At last I saw a man whose name I know not, but he seemed to be a man of great authority . . .

[*Unfinished.*]

The Legend of Good Women

Prologue

A thousand times I have heard say that in heaven is joy and in hell pain; and I grant well that it be so. Nevertheless, well I wot this, that there is none dwelling in this land who has been in either hell or heaven, or who can know of them in any other wise than as he has heard tell or found it written, for none can put his knowledge to the assay. But God forbid but men should believe far more than they have seen with their eyes! A man shall not deem all things false because he has not beheld them of long time. God wot, a thing is none the less true though every person cannot see it. Even Bernard the monk saw not all things, perdy!

Then in all reason must we give credence to these books, through which olden things be kept in mind, and to the instruction of these sages of old time, and believe on these old, approved histories of holiness, of kingdoms, of victories, of love, hate, and other sundry things which I cannot now rehearse. And were old books all gone, then were the key of remembrance lost. Well ought we then to believe old books, where there is none other test by experience.

As for me, though my wit be little, I delight to read in books and in mine heart revere them. In them I have such joy and faith, that there is scarce any sport to draw me from my books, unless it be some festival or else the lovely time of May; but when I hear the little birds singing, and when the flowers begin to put forth, then farewell my studies for that season!

Now I have also this liking, that of all the flowers in the meadow I most love those white and red flowers which men in our town call daisies. To them I have such affection, as I have said, that when May is come, no day dawns upon me in my bed, but I am up and waking in the mead to see these flowers opening to the sun when it rises, in the bright morn, and through the long day thus I walk in the green. And when the sun draws towards the west, then they close and betake them to slumber till the morrow when the day comes — so sore they fear the night. This daisy, flower of all flowers, filled with all excellence and honour, ever and alike fair and lusty of hue, fresh in winter as well as in summer, fain would I praise it if aright I could. But woe is me, for it lies not in my power! For well I wot that folk have reaped the field of poesy before me and have garnered the corn. I come after, gleaning here and there, and am right glad if perchance I find an ear of any goodly words which they have left behind. And if I chance to rehearse again what they have said in their lusty songs, I hope that they will not be ill-pleased, since all is said in furthering and worship of them who are followers of either the leaf or flower. For trust well, I have not undertaken to sing in honour of the leaf against the flower, or of the flower against the leaf, any more than of the corn against the shock. For as to me, neither is dearer; as yet I am retained by neither. I know not who serves the leaf, who the flower; that is no wise the object of my labour. For this work is all drawn out of another tun, of ancient story, ere any such strife was.

But why I spake of giving credence to old books and revering them, is that men should believe authorities in all things wherein there lies none other means of proof. For mine intent is, ere I go from you, to make known in English the naked text of many a history or many a tale, even as authors tell them. Believe them if you list!

When the month of May was almost past, and I had roamed all the summer's day over the green meadow of which I have told you to gaze upon the fresh daisy, and when the sun out of the south drew towards the west, and the flower was closed and gone to sleep, for darkness of the night which she feared, I sped me full swiftly home to mine house; and in a little shady bower that I have, newly embarked with fresh-cut turves, I bade folk lay my couch, and flowers to be strewn thereon, for joy of the new summer. When I had laid me down and closed my eyes, I fell asleep within an hour.

Then I dreamed that I was in the meadow, and was roaming about to see that flower, even as you have heard me tell. Fair was this meadow, methought, all variegated with sweet flowers. No herbs or trees or spicy gums could compare with it; for it utterly surpassed all odours, and also all flowers for rich beauty. The earth had forgot his poor estate of winter, which had made him naked and deject and with the sword of cold had smitten him so sore. Now the mild sun had relieved all that, and clothed him in green afresh. Rejoicing in the season, the little birds that had escaped the snare and the net mocked the fowler who had affrighted them in winter and destroyed their brood, and eased their hearts to sing of him in scorn, and to flout the foul churl who for his covetousness had betrayed them with his sophistries. This was their song, 'We defy the fowler!' On the branches some sang clear lays of love and spring, that it was a joy to listen, in honour and praise of their mates, and for the new, joyous summer; they sang, 'Blessed be Saint Valentine! For upon this day I chose you, my dear heart, and never have I repented.' And then they joined their beaks, and they paid honour and tenderness to each other, and then did other ceremonies right pleasing to love and nature.

I gave myself to hearing their song (for I dreamed I understood their meaning); till at last a lark sang on high. Quoth she, 'I see the mighty god of love! Lo yonder he comes! I see his wings spread!' Then I looked along the meadow and saw him come, leading by the hand a lady clothed in a royal habit of green. She had a net of gold around her hair, and over that a white crown with many flowers; for all the world even as the flower of the daisy is crowned with little white leaves, such were the flowers of her white crown, for it was made all of one fine orient pearl; wherefore the white crown above the green, with the golden ornament in her hair, made her appear like a daisy.

This mighty god of love was clothed in silk embroidered full of green sprigs; on his head was a garland of rose-leaves, all set with fresh lilies. But the hue of his face I cannot tell, for truly his face shone so bright that the eye was astonied with the gleam. For a season I could not look on him, but at last I saw that he held in his hands two fiery darts, red as glowing coals. And he spread his wings like an angel. Albeit men say he is blind, yet methought he could see well enough; for he looked sternly upon me, so that his look even yet makes my heart cold.

He held by the hand this noble lady, crowned with white and clothed all in green, who was so womanly, benign and gentle that though men should seek throughout this world they should not find half her beauty in any being formed by nature. Her name was Alceste the gentle, fair fortune ever befall her, I pray God! For had it not been for the comfort of her presence, I had been dead without help, for fear of Love's words and look; as ye shall learn hereafter, when the time is.

On the grass, behind this god of love, I saw a company of nineteen ladies in royal garb coming at a right gentle pace, and after them came such a train of women that I could not have thought that by any possibility the third part of them or the fourth had ever lived in this world, since God made Adam of earth. And every one of these women was faithful in love. Now was this a wondrous thing or no? For as soon as they espied this flower which I call the daisy, right quickly they stopped all together and kneeled down by that very flower; and after that they went in a circle slowly dancing about it, and sang, as it were in carol-wise, this ballade which I shall tell you.

> Hide, Absalom, thy golden tresses clear;
> Esther, lay thou thy meekness all adown;

And Jonathan, hide all thy friendly cheer;
Martia, the Roman Cato's paragon,
Before our lady's truth vaunt not thine own;
Hide ye your beauties, Isolt and Elaine,
Alceste is here, your glories all are vain.

Thy beauteous body, let it not appear,
Lavinia; and Lucrece of Latian town,
Polyxena, that paid for love so dear,
Warm Cleopatra, with thy regal crown,
Hide ye your truth in love and your renown,
And Thisbe, thou for love that hadst such pain;
Alcest is here, your glories all are vain.

Hero, Laodamia dead of fear,
And Phyllis, hanging for thy Demophon,
And Canacè, spied by thy heavy cheer,
Hypsipyle, that Jason falsely won,
Penelope, thy web is all undone,
Ariadne, Hypermnestra, now refrain;
Alceste is here, your glories all are vain.

When this ballade was all sung, they sat full gently down upon the sweet and soft green grass, in order all in a circle about. First sat the god of Love, and then this lady clad in green with the white crown; and then nigh them all the rest right courteously, according to their station. And then, whilst a man might walk a furlong, in all the place not a word was spoken.

Close by, reclining beneath a grassy slope, I waited, still as any stone, to learn what this folk purposed; till at last the god of love turned his eyes on me and said, 'Who is it rests there?' And I answered his question and said, 'Sir, it is I.' And I came nearer, and saluted him.

Quoth he, 'What do you here in my presence, and that so boldly? For truly a worm were more worthy to come into my sight than you.'

'And why, sir,' quoth I, 'an it please you?'

'Because,' quoth he, 'you are no wise fit. My servants be all wise and honourable; you are my mortal foe, and war against me, and speak evil of mine old servants, and with your works of translation plague them, and hinder men's devotion in my service, and hold it folly to trust on me. You cannot deny it; for in text so plain that it needs no commentary you have translated the Romance of the Rose, which is heresy against my religion; and you cause wise folk to withdraw from me, and think your cool wit that he is but a proper fool who loves with passion, too hard and hot. Well I know hereby that you begin to drivel, as these old fools when their spirit fails; for then they abuse other folk, and know not what is amiss with themselves. Have you not also made in English the poem which tells how Criseyde forsook Troilus, to show how women have gone astray? But nevertheless answer me this now, why would you not also speak well of women, as you have said evil? Was there no good matter in your memory, and in all your books could you not find some story of women good and faithful? Yes, God wot! Sixty books, old and new, you have yourself, all full of long stories, in which both Romans and Greeks treat of sundry women, what kind of life they led, and ever an hundred good to one bad. This God knows, and also all clerks who use to seek out such matters. What says Alerius or Livy or Claudian? What says Jerome, in his treatise against Jovinian? Of pure maidens and faithful wives, of widows steadfast unto death tells Jerome; and that not a few, but I dare say an hundred in succession, till it is piteous and ruthful to read of the woe they endured for their faithfulness. For they were so true to their love that, rather than take a new mate, they chose death in sundry manners, and died even as the story will relate. Some were burned, some had their throats cut, and some were drowned, because they would not be false. For they all kept their maidenhood, or else widowhood or wedlock. And this was not done for devoutness, but for very virtue and purity, and that men should put no blame on them. And yet they were heathen, all the pack, who so sorely dreaded all disgrace. These women of old so guarded their good name that I believe men shall not find in this world a man who could be so true and kind as was the least women in those days. Likewise what say the epistles of Ovid concerning true wives and their travail? What says Vincent, in his Historical Mirror? Also you may hear the whole world of authors, Christian and heathen, treat of such matters. It needs not to write all day about them; but again I say, what ails you to write the chaff of stories and overlook the corn? By Saint Venus, my mother who bare me, though you have abjured my faith, as other old fools have done many a day gone by, you shall repent it in sight of all men.'

Then spake Alceste the worthy queen: 'God, of very courtesy thou must hearken and see whether he can make reply to these charges that thou hast made against him. A god should not thus be moved to anger, but being a deity he should be stable, and also righteous and merciful. He cannot rightfully vent his ire ere he has heard the other party speak. All that is carried to thee in complaint is not gospel-true; the god of love hears many a feigned tale. For in thy court there is many a flatterer, and many an artful, tattling accuser, who din many a thing in thine ears out of hatred or jealous imaginings, or to have familiar talk with thee. Envy — I pray God give her ill luck! — ever washes the foul linen in a great court; out of the house of Cæsar she departs neither by night nor day (thus says Dante). Whosoever departs, never will she be lacking. This man may be accused wrongly, and by rights should be absolved. Or else, sir, because this man is unwise, he might translate a thing not out of malice but because he uses to write books and heeds not of what matter; therefore he wrote the *Rose* and *Criseyde* all innocently, and wist not what he was saying. Or else he was bidden by some person to write these poems, and also durst not refuse it, for ere this he has writ many a book. In translating what old clerks have written, he has not sinned so grievously as if he should in malice endite scornfully of love, out of his own wit.

'A righteous lord should have this in mind, and not be like Lombard tyrants who practise wilful tyranny; for a king or lord by natural right ought to be tyrannical or cruel like a farmer of taxes, doing all the harm he can. He must bear in mind that they are his liege-men, and that his very duty is to show all benignity toward his people, to hear their defences readily and their complaints and petitions in due time when they present them. This is the philosopher's saying, that a king shall maintain his lieges in justice; that is his duty, of a truth, and thereto is a king sworn full deeply, and has been for many an hundred years of old; and to maintain his lords in their station, as it is right and reasonable that they be exalted and honoured and held most dear, for they be demi-gods here in this world. Thus shall he do to both rich and poor, albeit their conditions be not alike, and have compassion on poor folk. For behold the noble nature of the lion! When a fly annoys or bites him, he full gently drives the fly away with his tail; for in his noble nature he deigns not to avenge him upon a fly, as a cur does and other beasts. A noble nature should show restraint, and weigh all things by equity, and ever regard his own high station. For, sir, it is no noble act for a lord to condemn a man without speech or answer; in a lord that is a full foul practice. And if so be the man cannot excuse himself, yet with sorrowful heart asks mercy, and humbly in his bare shirt yields him up wholly to thy judgment, then a god with brief consideration ought to weigh his own honour and the other's trespass. For since there is no cause of death here, thou oughtest the more easily to be merciful. Lay aside thy wrath, and be a little yielding!

'This man has served thee with his art, and has furthered thy religion with his poesy. Whilst he was young he followed thee; I know not whether he be now a renegade. But well I know that by what he has been able to write in praise of thy name he has caused unlearned folk to rejoice in serving thee. He wrote the book called the House of Fame, and also the Death of Blanche the Duchess, and the Parliament of Birds, I believe, and all the love of Palamon and Arcite of Thebes, though the tale is little known; and for thy holy days many hymns, which are called Ballades, Roundels, and Virelays; and to speak of other laborious works, he has translated Boethius in prose, and Of the Wretched Engendering of Mankind, which may be found in Pope Innocent; and he also wrote the life of Saint Cecilia; and also, a long while ago, Origen upon the Magdalene. He ought now to have the less penalty; he has written many a lay and many a work.

'Now as thou art a god and a king, I, thine Alceste, once queen of Thrace, ask thee of thy mercy never to harm this man so long as he lives. And he shall swear to thee, and that straightway, that he will sin no more thus; but even as thou shalt enjoin he shall write of women ever faithful in love, maidens or wives, whatsoever thou wilt; and shall further thee as much as he spake amiss in the *Rose* or in *Crisedye*.'

Forthwith the god of love answered her thus: 'Madame,' quoth he, 'it is long that I have known you to be so charitable and faithful that never, since the world was new, have I found any better toward me. Therefore, if I will safe-guard mine honour, I neither may nor will refuse your petition. All lies with you; do with him as pleases you, and forgive all, without more tarrying. For whosoever gives a gift or does a kindness, let him do it betimes, and his thanks will be the greater. Judge you therefore what he shall do. Go now, thank my lady here,' quoth he.

I rose, and then got me down on my knee and said: 'Madame, may God on high reward you because you have made the god of love to give over his wrath against me; and may He grant me the grace to live so long until I may truly know who you are that have helped me and put me in such hopeful case. But truly in this matter I thought not to have sinned or to have trespassed against love. For an honest man, in verity, has no part nor lot in the deeds of a thief; and a true lover ought not to blame me, though I speak reproach of a false. He ought rather to hold on my side, because I wrote of Criseyde or of the Rose; whatsoever mine author meant, it was in my mind at least, God wot, to exalt faithfulness in love and to cherish it; and to warn folk from falseness and evil by such ensamples. This was mine intent.'

And she answered, 'Let be your arguing, for Love will hear no pleas against himself, just or unjust; learn this from me. You have your pardon; hold by that. Now will I say what penance you shall do for your trespass; understand it now. As long as you live, year by year you shall spend the most part of your life in writing a glorious legend of good women, maidens, and wives, who were ever faithful in love, and you shall tell of the false men who betrayed them, men who all their life do naught but try how many women they can shame, — for in your world that is now held as a sport. And though you list not be a lover, speak well of love. This penance I give you. And I will so pray the god of love that he shall charge his servants in any wise to aid you and shall requite your labour. Now go your way; your penance is but small.'

The god of love smiled, and then he said, 'Know you whether this be maid or wife, queen or countess, or of what degree, who has given you so little penance that have deserved to suffer more sorely? But pity runs soon into a noble heart; that you can see. She manifests what she is.'

And I answered, 'Nay, sir, as I hope for happiness, I wot no more but that I see well she is kind.'

'By mine hood,' quoth Love, 'that is a true saying; and that you well know, perdy, if you well consider. In a book which lies in your chest have you not the story of the great goodness of Queen Alcestis, who was turned into a daisy, — she who chose to die for her husband and also to go to hell in his stead; and Hercules rescued her, perdy, and brought her out of of hell back to happiness?'

And I replied, 'Yes, now I know her! And is this the good Alceste, the daisy, mine own heart's repose? Now I feel well this woman's goodness, that both in her life and after her death her great goodness makes her renown double. Well has she requited me for mine affection which I bear toward her flowers, the daisy. No wonder though Jove should turn her into a star, as Agathon tells, for her goodness. Her white crown bears witness of it; for she had as many excellences as there be small flowers in her crown. In remembrance and honour of her Cybele created the daisy, the flower all crowned with white, as men can see; and Mars gave its redness to her crown, set amidst the white instead of rubies.'

At this the queen waxed somewhat red from modesty, when she was so praised in her presence. Then said Love, 'It was a full great negligence to write about the unsteadfastness of women, since you know their goodness by experience and also by olden stories. Let be the chaff, write well of the corn. Why would you not write of Alceste, and leave Criseyde sleeping in peace? For your writing should be of Alceste, since you know that she is a calendar of goodness; for she taught noble love, and especially how a wife ought to live, and all the bounds that she should keep. Your little wit was nodding that time. But now I charge you on your life that in your Legend you write of this woman, after you have written of other lesser ones. And now farewell, I charge you no more. I will that you begin with Cleopatra; and so continue. And so you shall gain my love.'

And at these words I awoke from my sleep, and I began to write on my Legend even thus.

I *The Legend of Cleopatra*

After the death of the king Ptolemy, who had all Egypt under his rule, Cleopatra his queen reigned; until on a time it befell that out of Rome there was sent a senator to win kingdoms and honours for the town of Rome, as was their wont, that she might have the world under her obedience; and in sooth his name was Antony. As Fortune owed him a disgrace after he had met with prosperity, it so befell that he became a rebel to the town of Rome; and moreover he falsely deserted the sister of Caesar, ere she was aware, and at any cost would have another wife. Wherefore he fell at odds with Caesar and with Rome.

Nevertheless this same senator was a full worthy, noble warrior, in sooth, and his death was full great pity. But Love had brought this man into such a madness and so tightly bound him in his snare, all for love of Cleopatra, that he set all the world at no value. Naught seemed to him so needful as to love and serve Cleopatra. He recked not to die in arms in defence of her and of her right. Also this noble queen in like fashion loved this knight, for his merit and his knighthood; and certainly, unless the books lie, he was of his person and nobility and discretion and hardiness worthy of any creature alive. And she was as fair as the rose in May. And (for it is best to write briefly) she became his wife and had him as she desired.

To describe the wedding and the festival were too long for me, who have undertaken such an emprise as to put in verses so many stories, lest I should neglect things of greater weight and import. For men may overload a ship or a barge. Therefore I will skip lightly to the conclusion, and let slide all the remnant.

Octavian, maddened by this deed, raised an host of stout Romans, cruel as lions, to lead against Antony for his utter destruction. They went to ship, and I leave them sailing thus. Antony was wary and would not omit to encounter these Romans if he could; he laid his plans, and on a day both he and his wife and all his host went forth anon to ship; they tarried no longer. Out at sea it befell the foes to meet; the trumpet sounds on high, they shout and shoot and at sunrise make fierce onset. With grisly sound out flies the huge shot, and furiously they hurtle together, and from the fore-tops down come the great stones. In amongst the ropes go shearing-hooks and grapnels full of claws. This man and that press on with poleaxes; one flees behind the mast, and out again, and drives the other overboard. One pierces another upon his spear-point; one cuts the sail with hooks like scythes; another brings the wine-cup and bids them be glad; one pours peas upon the hatches to make them slippery; they rush together with pots full of quicklime. And thus they pass the long day in battle, till at last (as everything has an end) Antony is defeated and put to flight, and all his folk scatter as best they can.

The queen with all her purple sails fled likewise from the blows that went thick as hail-stones; no wonder she could not endure it. And when Antony saw that chance he said, 'Alas the day that I was born! So on this day I have lost all mine honour!'; and in despair he started out of his wits, and rove himself to the heart forthwith, ere he went further from the place.

His wife, who could get no mercy from Cæsar, fled to Egypt in dread and anguish. But hearken, ye that speak of devotion, ye men who falsely swear by many an oath that ye will die if your beloved be but angered, behold what womanly faithfulness ye may here see. This woful Cleopatra made such lament that no tongue can tell it; but in the morning she would tarry no longer and caused her skilful workmen make a shrine out of all the rubies and fine gems that she could spy out in all Egypt and she filled the shrine with spices and had the body embalmed, and fetched forth this dead corpse and enclosed it in the shrine. And next the shrine she had a pit dug, and put therein all the serpents she could find, and thus she spake: 'Now, beloved, whom my sorrow-ful heart so far obeyed that, from that blissful hour when I swore to be all freely thine, — I mean thee, Antony, my knight — , thou wert never out of mine heart's remembrance so long as I was awake, day or night, were it in weal or woe, in the carol or the dance. And then I made this covenant with myself, that, whatever it were thou feltest, weal or woe, the same would I feel, life or death, if it lay in my power, for the honour of my wifehood. And that covenant, whilst breath remains in me, I will fulfil; and this shall men see well, never was queen truer to her love.'

And at that word with right good heart she leapt naked into the pit amongst the serpents, and there she chose to be buried. Anon the serpents began to sting her, and she received her death cheerfully, for the love of Antony who was so dear to her. And this is truth of history, it is no fable.

Now, until I find a man thus faithful and steadfast, who will so willingly die for love, I pray God may our heads never ache!

II The Legend of Thisbe of Babylon

At Babylon, the town which Queen Semiramis had ditched all around and walled full high with hard tiles well baked, it befell thus. In this noble town there dwelt two lords of high repute; and they dwelt upon a green so nigh each other that there was but a stone wall betwixt them, as often is in great towns. One of these men had a son, one of the lustier in all that land; and the other had a daughter, the fairest that then dwelt in the eastern world. The name of each was brought to the other by women, neighbours round about. For in that country, even now in truth, maidens be full closely and jealously guarded, lest they do some folly. This young man was called Pyramus, and the maid hight Thisbe; Ovid says thus. And so their praise was brought to each other by report, so that as they grew in years their love grew. And certainly, as for their age, there might have been marriage betwixt them, but that their fathers would not assent to it. And both alike burned so sore in love that none of all their friends could hinder them from meeting privily sometimes by craft, and speaking somewhat of their longings. Cover the coals and the fire is the hotter; forbid love, and it is ten times as raging.

This wall which stood betwixt them was cleft in twain, from the top right down, since the old time when it was built; yet this cleft was so narrow and small that it was not visible a farthing's worth. But what is it love cannot espy? Ye two lovers, to say the sooth, ye first found this narrow little crack! And they let their words, with voice as soft as any shrift, pass through the crack, and as they stood there, told all their love-complaints and all their woe every time when they durst. He stood upon the one side of the wall, Thisbe upon the other, to her the sweet sound of each other's voice; and thus they would deceive their warders. Every day they would threaten this wall and wish to God it were beaten down. Thus they would say: 'Alas, thou evil wall! Through thy envy thou hinderest us wholly. Why wilt thou not cleave, or fall in two? Or at least, if thou wilt not so, yet wouldst thou but let us meet once, or once permit us to kiss sweetly, then were we recovered of our cold cares. But nevertheless we be beholden to thee, inasmuch as thou sufferest us to send our words through thy mortar and stone. We still ought to be well pleased with thee.'

When these vain words were uttered, they would kiss the cold stone wall and take their leave and depart. And they were fain to do this in the eventide or wondrous early, lest folk saw them. And long time they did thus, till on a day, when Phœbus was clear and Aurora with her hot beams had dried up the dew on the wet herbs, came Pyramus unto this cleft, as he was wont, and then came Thisbe, and by their faith they pledged their troth to steal away that same night, and to beguile all their warders and flee from the city; and, because the fields were so broad and large, that they might meet at one place at one time, they appointed their meeting to be under a tree where King Ninus was buried. (For old paynims who worshipped idols used then to be buried in fields.) And close by this grave was a spring. And, shortly to tell this tale, this covenant was confirmed wondrous strongly. Long did it seem to them that the sun tarried, ere it went down under the sea.

This Thisbe had so great a feeling and desire to see Pyramus, that when she saw her time she stole away full privily at night with her face craftily wimpled. To keep her pledge she forsook all her friends; alas! it is pity that ever woman should be so faithful to trust man, unless she knew him better! She went to the tree at a right good pace, for her love made her so hardy; and down beside the spring she settled herself. Alas! without more ado a wild lioness, with mouth bloody from strangling some beast, came out of the wood to drink at the spring where Thisbe was sitting. And when Thisbe espied that, she started up, with heart all terrified, and with fearful foot fled into a cave which she saw well by the moon; and as she ran she let fall her wimple and took no heed thereof, so sore was she dismayed, and also glad of her escape. And thus she sat in hiding wondrous quietly. When the lioness had drunk her fill, she roamed about the spring, and anon found the wimple, and rent it all to pieces with her bloody mouth. When this was done, she tarried no longer but took her way to the wood.

At last this Pyramus came, but alack! all too long had he stayed at home. The moon shone, a man could see full well, and in his way, as he came speedily, he cast his eyes down to the ground, and as he looked down he saw the wide tracks of a lion in the sand, and he suddenly shuddered in his heart and waxed pale and his hair stood on end; and he came nearer, and found the torn wimple. 'Alas!' quoth he. 'Alas, the day that I was born! This one night will slay both us lovers! How should I ask mercy of Thisbe, when I am he who have slain her, alas! My prayer to thee to come has slain thee! Alas, to bid a woman go by night to a place where peril might befall, and I so slow! Alas! that I had not been here in this place a furlong before thee! Now what lion there be in this forest, may he rend my body; or what wild beast there be, now may he gnaw mine heart!' And with these words he sprang to the wimple, and kissed it often, and wept over it full sore and said, 'Alas, wimple! there is naught else but that thou shalt feel my blood as well as thou hast felt the bleeding of Thisbe!' And with these words he smote himself to the heart. The blood gushed out of the wound as broad as water when the conduit is broken.

Now Thisbe, who wist not of it, thought thus as she sat in fear, 'If it so hap that my Pyramus be come hither and cannot fine me; he may hold me false and also cruel.' And she came out and spied about after him both with her heart and with her eyes, and thought, 'I will tell him concerning my dread both for the lioness and for all my act.' And at last she came upon her lover, all bloody, beating on the ground with his heels; and therewithal she started back, and her heart began to toss like the waves, and she waxed pale as a box-tree, and for a little season considered him, and then well knew him, that he was Pyramus, her dear heart. Who could write what a deadly mien had Thisbe now, and how she tore her hair, and how she tormented herself, and how she lay on the ground and swooned, and how she wept his gash full of tears; how she mingled his blood with her lamentation, and did paint herself with his blood; how she embraced the dead corpse, alas! How did this woful Thisbe then, how kissed she his frothy mouth so cold! 'Who has done this! Who has been so ruthless, to slay my beloved! O, speak, my Pyramus! I am thy Thisbe who thus calls thee!' And thereat she lifted up his head. This woful man, in whom still remained some life, when he heard the name of Thisbe cried, cast his heavy, death-like eyes upon her and down gain, and yielded up the ghost.

Thisbe arose without noise or outcry, and saw her wimple, and his scabbard empty, and also his sword, which had put him to death. Then she spake thus: 'My sorrowful hand,' quoth she, 'is strong enough for such a task in my behalf, for love shall give me strength and boldness, I believe, to make my wound large enough. Dead I will follow thee, and I will be cause and also partner of thy death,' quoth she. 'And though nothing save death alone could truly separate thee from me, thou shalt now no more part from me than from death, for I will go with thee. And now, ye wretched, jealous fathers of ours, we who were once your children, we pray you that without more ill-will we may lie together in one grave, since love has brought us this piteous end. And may the righteous God grant every lover, that truly loves, more prosperity than ever Pyramus and Thisbe had! And let no woman of gentle blood make bold to place herself in such hazard. Yet God forbid but a woman may be as true and loving as any man! And for my part I shall forthwith make this plain.' And with these words she seized his sword straightway, which was warm and hot with her lover's blood, and smote herself to the heart.

And thus are Pyramus and Thisbe gone. Of faithful men I find in all my books but few more besides this Pyramus, and therefore I have spoken thus of him. For it is rare delight to us men to find a man who can be tender and true in love. Here ye may see that, whatsoever lover there be, a woman has wit and daring to do as well.

III The Legend of Dido, Queen of Carthage

Glory and honour, Mantuan Virgil, be to thy name! I shall follow thy lantern as well as I can, whilst thou leadest, in telling how Æneas forswore himself to Dido. I will follow the tenor of thine Æneid and of Ovid, and will put the substance into verse.

When Troy was brought to destruction by the wiles of the Greeks, and especially by Sinon, feigning that horse, through which many a Trojan was to die, to be an offering to Minerva; and when Hector had appeared after his death, and fire so wild it could not be controlled raged through all the noble tower of Ilium, which was the chief donjon of the city; and when all the land was brought low, and Priam the king slain and done away; and when Æneas was charged by Venus to flee, he took Ascanius his son by his right hand and fled. And on his back he bore with him his old father, y-clept Anchises, and on the way he lost his wife Creusa. And much sorrow had he in heart ere he could find his fellows. But at last, when he had found them, he made ready in a certain hour, and right quickly hied him to the sea, and sailed forth with all his folk toward Italy, as destiny would. But of his adventures on the sea it is not in point to speak here, for it relates not to my matter; but, as I have said, my tale shall be of him and Dido, till I have done.

So long he sailed the salt sea, until with difficulty he arrived in Libya with seven ships, and no larger fleet; and glad was he to hie to land, so shaken was he with the tempest. And when he had gained the haven, of all his fellowship he chose a knight called Achates to go with him to spy out the land; he took with him no greater company. Forth they went, his comrade and he, without any to point the way, and left his ships riding at anchor. So long he walked in the wilderness till at the last he met an huntress; she had a bow in hand, and arrows; her garments were cut short to the knee; but she was the fairest creature that ever nature had formed. And she greeted Æneas and Achates, and thus spake to them, when she met them: 'Saw you,' quoth she, 'whilst you walked wide and far, any of my sisters in this forest, with garments tucked up and arrows in their quivers, walk hard by you, with any wild boar or other beast which they have roused in the hunt?'

'Nay truly, lady,' quoth this Æneas; 'but methinks by thy beauty thou canst never be woman of this world, as it seems to me, but art Phœbus' sister, I believe. And, if so be thou art a goddess, have pity on our labour and woe.'

'Truly, I am no goddess,' she said; 'for here in this land maidens walk with arrows and bow in this manner. This is the realm of Libya where you are, of which Dido is lady and queen;' — and briefly she told him all the occasion of Dido's coming into those parts, of which I list not now to write; it needs not, it were but loss of time. For this is the sum and substance, it was Venus, his own mother, who thus spake with Æneas; and she bade him turn toward Carthage, and forthwith vanished out of his sight. I could follow Virgil word for word, but it would take all too long a time.

This noble queen named Dido, whilom wife to Sychæus, and fairer than the shining sun, had founded this noble town of Carthage, in which she reigned in so great glory that she was held the flower of all queens in nobility, liberality and beauty; so that well was he that once might see her, who was so desired by kings and lords that her beauty had inflamed all the world; so well stood she in grace with every person.

When Æneas was come thither, full privily he took his way unto the chief temple of all the town, where Dido was at her devotions. When he was come into the broad temple, I cannot say if it be possible, but Venus made him invisible — thus says the book, I promise you. And when Æneas and Achates had been over all this temple, they found painted on a wall how Troy and all the land had been destroyed.

'Alas that I was born!' quoth Æneas, 'our shame is known so far over all the world that now it is depicted on every side. We who were in prosperity are now defamed, and that so grievously that I care to live no longer.' And with these words he burst out weeping so feelingly that it was pitiful to behold.

This blooming lady, queen of the city, stood in the temple in royal state, so splendid and also so fair, so young, so joyous, with her glad eyes, that, if the god who made heaven and earth had desired a love, for beauty and goodness and womanhood and seemliness and fidelity whom should he have loved but this sweet lady? There was no woman half so meet.

Fortune, that governs the world, speedily brought in so strange a chance that never yet was so rare a case. For all the company of Æneas, which he deemed had been lost in the sea, came to shore not far from that city; wherefore some of the greatest of his lords by chance came to the city unto that same temple, to seek the queen and beseech her for succour; such renown of her goodness had spread. And when they had told all their distress, and their tempest and their hard case, Æneas showed himself to the queen and freely told who he was. Then who were more joyful than his men, who had found their lord, their ruler? The queen saw how they did him such honour, and ere then she had often heard of Æneas, and in her heart she had pity and woe that ever so noble a man had so lost his heritage. And she beheld the man, that he was like a knight, and well endowed in person and strength, and like to be a full courteous man, and was full fair of his speech, and had a noble visage, and was well formed in brawn and bone. For, next after Venus, he had such fairness that no man could be half so fair, I believe. And he well seemed to be a lord. And because he was a stranger she liked him somewhat the better; as — God save us! — to some folk a new thing is often sweet. Anon her heart pitied his woe, and with that pity love also came in; and thus out of pity and courtesy he must needs be solaced in his distress.

She said, certes she was sorry that he had had such peril and such mishap; and in her friendly speech she spake to him thus and said as ye may hear: 'Be you not the son of Venus and Anchises? In good faith, all the worship and assistance that I can rightly give you, that you shall have. Your ships and your followers I will protect.' Many a courteous word she spake, and commanded her messengers to go that same day without fail to seek his ships and victual them; she sent many a beast to the ships, and presented them also with wine. And she sped her to her royal palace, and ever had Æneas about her. What need to describe the feast to you? He was never better at ease in his life. The festival was well provided with dainties and with splendour, with instruments of music, song and gladness; and many were the amorous glances and devices. This Æneas is come into Paradise out of the gulf of hell; and thus in bliss he recalled his state in Troy. After the meat, this Æneas was led to dancing-halls, full of fine hangings and rich couches and ornaments. And when he had sat down with the queen, and spices had been served and wine passed around, he was led anon unto his chambers, to take his ease and have his repose, and all his folk likewise, to do even as they would.

There was no charger well bridled, nor steed good to go to joustings, nor large palfrey, easy to ride, nor jewel adorned all over with rich gems, nor sacks full of gold, of huge weight, nor any ruby that shone by night, nor noble high-flying falcon for the heron, nor hound for hart or wild boar or deer, nor cup of gold, nor florins newly coined, which could be procured in the land of Libya, which Dido sent not to Æneas. And all that he would have spent she paid. Thus could this noble queen bid her guests as one who knew how to surpass all in generosity.

Æneas, truly, sent also unto his ship by Achates for his son, and for rich gear, both sceptre, raiment, brooches and rings, also some to wear, and some to present to her who had given him all these noble things. And he bade his son to make the presenting and give the gift to the queen. This Achates returned and Æneas was full fain and glad to see his young son Ascanius. But nevertheless our author tells that Cupid, who is the god of love, at the prayer of his mother on high had taken the likeness of the child, to enamour this noble queen of Æneas; but as to that text, be it as it may, I heed it not. But true it is that the queen made such to-do about this child that it is wondrous to hear of; and with good will she thanked him full oft for the gift that his father sent.

Thus was the queen in pleasance and delight with all this new, lusty folk of Troy. And she further inquired about the deeds of Æneas, and learned all the story of Troy. And they twain gave themselves up to converse and diversion all the long day; whence was bred such a flame that luckless Dido had strong desire to be united with Æneas her new guest, and lost her colour and also her health.

Now for the conclusion, the fruit of it all, wherefor I have told this story, and shall continue it. Thus I begin; it befell on a night, when the moon had lifted up her beams, that this noble queen went to her rest, and sighed sore, and tormented herself; she waked and tossed, started up many a time as lovers are wont to do, I have heard tell. And at last she made moan unto her sister Anna, and spake right thus: 'Now, my dear sister, what can it be that makes me so aghast in my dream? This Trojan is so in my thoughts, because methinks he is so well formed and also so like to be a manly man, and also is so courteous and discreet, that all my love and life lie in his keeping. Have you not heard him tell his adventures? Now certes, Anna, if you counsel me so, I would fain be wedded to him. This is all; what more should I say? On him it all hangs, to make me live or die.'

Her sister Anna, as a discreet damsel, spake as she thought and somewhat withstood her; but hereof was so much discourse that it were too long to rehearse. To sum all up, the thing could not be withstood; love will love, it will hold back for no man. The dawn arose out of the sea; this amorous queen charged her attendants to prepare the nets and the spears broad and sharp. A-hunting would she go, this lusty, blooming queen, so this new sweet pain pricked her. To horse went all her lusty folk, the hounds were led to the courtyard, and upon chargers swift as thought her young knights hovered all around, and also a huge company of her women. Upon a stout palfrey white as paper, with red saddle adorned delightsomely, high embossed with bars of gold, sat Dido all covered with gold and gems, and she as fair as the bright morn, that heals sick folk of the night's sorrow. Upon a charger that leapt like flame (yet men could turn him with a little bridle-bit) sat Æneas, like Phœbus in his looks, so lustily was he arrayed after his fashion; and governed his charger as he would, by the foamy bridle with golden bit. And thus I let this noble queen ride forth a-hunting, with this Trojan by her. The herd of harts was found straightway, with 'Hey! Faster! Spur on! Loose the dogs! Loose them! Why will not the bear or lion come, that I might meet him once with this spear?' Thus cried these young folk, and on they went killing all these wild harts, and had them as they would.

Amid all this the heavens began to rumble, the thunder roared with grisly voice; down came the rain thick with hail and sleet and heaven's fire, so sore it affrighted this noble queen and also her attendants that each was glad to flee away. And, in brief, to save her from the tempest she fled into a little cave, and with her went Æneas also; I wot not if any more went with them, the author makes no mention thereof. And here began the deep devotion betwixt the two of them; this was the first morn of their gladness, and the beginning of their sorrow. For there Æneas so kneeled, and told her all his heart and his pain, and swore so deeply to be true to her in weal or in woe, and to change for none other, — as a false lover so well knows how to make his plaint — , that hapless Dido pitied his woe, and took him for a husband, to be his wife for evermore so long as they should live. And after this, when the tempest ceased, they came out in joy and went home.

Evil Rumour rose, and that anon, how Æneas had gone with the queen into the cave. And men deemed as they list. And when the king hight Iarbas knew of it, since he had loved her ever and wooed her, to win her as his wife, he made such lament and heavy cheer that it was piteous and heart-rending to see. But in love it haps ever so, that one shall laugh at another's sorrow; now laughs Æneas, and is in more bliss and wealth than ever he was in Troy. O hapless woman, innocent, full of pity, faith, and tenderness, why didst thou so trust to men? Hadst thou such pity upon their feigned woe, yet hadst before thee so many old ensamples? See ye not all how they be forsworn? Where see ye one who has not forsaken his beloved or been unkind or done her some mischief or robbed her or boasted of his acts to her? Ye can see this as well as ye can read it. Take heed now of this great gentleman, this Trojan, who so well knew how to please her, who feigned him so true and yielding, so courteous and so discreet in his deeds; who so well knew how to perform all due observances, and attend her pleasure at dances and feasts and when she went to the temple and back again home; and fasted till he had seen his lady, and wore in his heraldic devices I know not what for her sake; and he would compose songs, and joust and do many deeds at arms, and send her letters, tokens, brooches, rings, — now hearken, how he shall serve his lady! When he had been in peril of death from hunger and mischiefs on the sea, and desolate, fugitive from his country, and all his folk scattered with tempest, she gave her body and also her realm into his hand, when she might have been a queen of another land besides Carthage and lived in sufficiency of joy; what would ye more?

This Æneas, who had vowed so deeply, was weary of the business within a season, and the hot earnest was all blown by. Privily he had his ships prepared, and planned to steal away by night. This Dido suspected it, and well thought that all was not right; for in the night he lay in his bed and sighed. Forthwith she asked him what displeased him — 'my dear heart, whom I love best?'

'Certes,' quoth he, 'this night my father's spirit has so sore vexed me in my sleep, and also Mercury has delivered a message, that my needful fate is soon to sail to conquer Italy; for this methinks my heart is broken!' Therewith his false tears burst forth, and he took her in his two arms.

'Is that in earnest?' quoth she. 'Will you do so? Have you not sworn to take me to wife? Alas, what manner of woman will you make of me! I am a gentlewoman and a queen; you will not thus foully flee from your wife? Alas that I was born! What shall I do?'

To tell it briefly, this noble Queen Dido visited shrines of saints and did sacrifice, she knelt and cried so that it is piteous to relate. She conjured him and offered to be his thrall, his servant of the meanest rank; she fell at his feet and swooned, her shining golden hair dishevelled, and cried, 'Have mercy! Let me go with you! These lords who are my neighbours will destroy me, only because of you. And, so you will take me now to wife, as you have sworn, then I will give you leave to slay me with your sword right now at eventide, for then I shall die wedded to you. I am with child, — grant my child life! Mercy, lord! Have pity in your heart!'

But all this availed her right naught; for one night he let her lie sleeping and stole away to his followers, and as a traitor forth he sailed toward the great land of Italy. Thus he left Dido in woe and pain; and there he wedded a lady hight Lavinia.

He left a garment and also his sword standing even at the head of her bed, when he stole away from Dido in her sleep, so he hasted to reach his ships. Which garment, when hapless Dido awoke, she kissed full often for his sake, and said, 'O thou garment, so sweet whilst it pleased Jupiter, take my soul now, unbind me from this unrest! I have run out the whole course of fortune.' And then she swooned twenty times, without any succour from Æneas. And when she had made her lament to her sister Anna — of which I cannot write, such pity I have to tell of it — she bade her nurse and her sister go fetch fire and other things forthwith, and said she would do sacrifice. And when she saw her time, she leaped on the sacrificial fire, and with his sword she rove herself to the heart.

But ere she was wounded, before she died, she said even thus, as mine author tells; she wrote a letter anon, which began thus: 'Even as the white swan,' quoth she, 'begins to sing against the time of his death, so to thee make I my lament. Not that I hope to get thee back, for well I wot that is all in vain, because the gods are contrary to me; but since my good name is lost through thee, I may well lose a word or a message upon thee, albeit I shall be never the better thereof; for the same wind that blew away thy ship has blown away thy good faith.' But whoso would know all this letter, let him read Ovid; there he shall find it.

IV The Legend of Hypsipyle and Medea

Duke Jason, thou root of false lovers, thou sly devourer and ruin of high-born women, tender creatures! Thou didst set thy lures and thine enticement for ladies with thy stately appearance and thy words stuffed with pleasantness, and thy feigned troth, and thy manner, and thine obsequiousness and thy humble bearing, and thy counterfeited woe and pain. Where others are false to one, thou art false to two! Ah, often didst thou swear thou wouldst perish for love, when thou feltest no malady save foul delight, which thou callest love! If I live, thy name shall be far spread in English, that thy guile shall be known! Have at thee, Jason! Now is blown the horn for hunt of thee! But certes it is both ruth and woe that love so works with false lovers; for they shall find better love and better cheer than he who has paid for his love full dearly, or has had full many a bloody blow in fight. For ever as tender a capon shall the fox eat, though he be false and have deceived the fowl, as the good-man shall, who has paid therefor; although he have claim to the capon in reason and right, the false fox will get his share in the dark. This ensample well fits Jason, as he dealt with Hypsipyle and Medea the queen.

In Thessaly, as Guido tells us, was a king hight Pelias, who had a brother hight Æson; and when he could scarce walk for age, he gave Pelias the rule of all his realm, and made him lord and king. Of which Æson was begotten Jason, in whose time was not in all that land a knight so renowned for noble bearing, liberality, and strength and lustiness. After his father's death he so bore him that there was none cared to be his foe, but gave him all honour and sought after him. Whereat this Pelias had great envy, imagining that Jason might be so exalted and put in such position by the love of the lords of his realm that he might put him down from his throne. And in his wit by night he compassed how Jason might best be destroyed without scandal concerning his plot. And at last he determined to send him into some far country, where this

Jason might perish. This was his subtle plan, though he showed Jason all affection and loving cheer, lest his lords should espy it.

Not it so befell, since fame spreads widely, that there were great tidings everywhere and many reports that in an isle called Colchis, eastward in the sea beyond Troy, men might see a ram, which had a fleece of gold so shining that nowhere was another such sight. But it was ever guarded by a dragon and many other prodigies all around, and by two bulls all of brass, which spat fire; and many another thing there was. But nevertheless this was the tale, that whosoever would win that fleece, ere he could win it, must fight both the bulls and the dragon. And king Æetes was lord of that isle.

This Pelias bethought him of this fetch, to exhort his nephew Jason to sail to that land to divert himself; and he said, 'Nephew, if such an honour might befall you as to win this famous treasure and bring it into my land, it were great pleasance and honour to me; then were I bound to requite your labour. And I myself will stand all the cost. Choose what folk you will take with you. Let see now, dare you take this voyage?'

Jason was young and lusty of heart, and undertook this emprise. Anon Argus contrived his ships. With Jason went the strong Hercules, and many another whom he chose with him. But whosoever will ask who went with Jason, let him go read *Argonauticon*, for that will tell a tale long enough. Anon Philoctetes hoisted the sail, when the wind was favourable, and they hasted them out of their country of Thessaly. Long they sailed the salt sea, till they arrived at the isle of Lemnos (albeit this is not related by Guido, yet Ovid in his Epistles says this), and of this isle the lady and queen was the fair young Hypsipyle, the shining-bright, who was daughter to Thoas, once the king.

Hypsipyle was walking to divert her and, roaming upon the cliffs by the sea, anon she espied where under an height the ship of Jason was come to shore. In her goodness she sent down speedily to know if any stranger were blown thither by storm during the night, that she might bring him succour, as she used to assist every person and do kindnesses of her very bounty and courtesy. This messenger hied him down and came upon Jason and also Hercules, who were come to land in a cock-boat to refresh them and take the air. The morning was mild and fine. And on his way the messenger met these two lords and right discreetly greeted them and gave his message, asking them anon if they were damaged or in aught distressed, or had need of steersman or victual; for they should in no wise fail of succour, since it was wholly the queen's will.

Jason answered mildly and gently; quoth he, 'I heartily thank my lady for her goodness; truly, we need nothing now, save that we are weary and are come off the sea to divert us, till the wind blow nearer our course.'

This lady was roaming with her attendants along the shore by the cliff to divert her, and found this Jason and the other standing speaking of their matter, as I have said. This Hercules and Jason beheld how this lady was the queen, and greeted her fairly as soon as they had met her. And she took heed, and knew by the fashion of them, by their array and words and cheer, that they were men of noble birth and high degree. And to the castle she led these strangers with her, and did them great honour, and asked them of their labour and travail on the salt sea; so that within one day or two she knew from the folk who were in the ships that they were Jason, full of renown, and Hercules, of great praise, that sought the adventures of Colchis. And she did them more honour than before, and the more time passed, the more she had to do with them, for in very truth they were worthy folk. And she spake most with Hercules; to him her heart inclined, for he seemed to be steadfast, wise, true, discreet of speech, without any other attachment in love, or evil fancies.

This Hercules so praised Jason that he exalted him to the sun, saying that there was not under the high cope of heaven a man half so true in love; and he was wise, hardy, trusty, and rich; and in three more points there was none like him, — in liberality and lustiness he passed all men, living or dead, and also he was right nobly born and like to be king of Thessaly. There was no fault, save that he was afraid of love, and shamefast of speech; he would rather murder himself and die, than have men find him out to be a lover. 'Would to almighty God I could give my flesh and blood (so I died not!), that he might find a wife somewhere, fit for his degree; such a lusty life as she should lead with this lusty knight!' And all this had been shapen the day before by Jason and Hercules; by these two here was contrived a wicked fraud to quarter themselves upon an innocent; for their agreement was to cozen this queen. And Jason was as coy as a maid; he looked piteously but said naught, and freely gave great gifts to her counsellors and officers.

Would God I had leisure to rhyme a full story of all his wooing! But if any false lover be in this house, even as he now does, so did Jason, with feigning and every act of craft. Ye get no more from me, unless ye will read mine author, who tells all the matter. The sum of it is this, that Jason was wedded to this queen, and took of her substance whatsoever he would for his purveyance; and upon her he begat two children. And he hoisted his sail, and never saw her more.

In truth she sent him a letter, which were too long to write and tell, and reproached him for his great infidelity, and prayed him to have some pity on her. And of his two children she told him this, that in truth they were like him in all things, save they knew not how to beguile. And she prayed God that ere long time she who had bereft her of his heart might find him untrue to her also; and that she should be fated to slay both her children, and so might all those that suffered him to have his will of them. And all her days Hypsipyle remained true to Jason, and ever kept her chaste, as his wife; nor ever had she joy in heart, but died for his love in bitter sorrows.

This duke Jason, a dragon and devourer of love, was come to Colchis. Even as the appetite of matter is ever to take form, and may pass from form to form, or like a well that is bottomless, so false Jason could have no peace; for the craving of his appetite to work his will with women of gentle blood, this was all his delight and felicity.

Jason roamed forth to the town which once was called Jaconites, which was the chief city of all Colchis; and he told the cause for his coming to Æetes, king of that land, praying him that he might have his trial to win the golden fleece if he could. To which petition the king assented, and did him honour, as was fit; and so much that he caused his daughter and heir Medea, who was so wise and beautiful that never man saw with his eyes a fairer, to bear Jason company at meat, and sit by him in the hall. Now Jason was a seemly man and full lordly, and had great renown, and of his mien regal as a lion, and goodly of speech and affable, and knew without book all the trade and plenary art of love, and every ceremony thereof. And as Fortune owed Medea a foul mischance, she waxed enamoured of this man. 'Jason,' quoth she, 'for aught I see you have put you into great peril in this thing which you are about. For whoso would achieve this adventure, he cannot well escape death, I believe, unless I be his helper. But nevertheless,' quoth she, 'it is my will to further you, so that you shall not perish but return home safe and sound to your Thessaly.'

'My true lady,' then said this Jason, 'that you have any regard for my death or woe and do me this honour, I wot well that my might and my travail cannot earn it all the days of my life. May God thank you, for I never can. I am your man, and humbly pray you, without more speech, to be my help; but certes I shall not spare for fear of death.'

Then this Medea made known to him from point to point the peril of the adventure and of his battle, and in what unequal combat he must stand, in which no creature save she alone could assure him of his life. And, to go shortly to the point, they were accorded betwixt them two that Jason should wed her as a true knight; and the time was set for him to come at even to her chamber, and there take oath by the gods that never for weal or woe, night or day, would he falsely fail her, to be husband as long as he lived to her who here had saved him from death. And hereupon they met by night, and he took his oath and went to bed. And on the morrow he made haste to arise, for she had taught him how he could not fail to win the fleece and achieve the conflict; and thus she saved his life and his honour and got him a great name as a conqueror, even through the wiles of her enchantment.

Now Jason had the fleece, and returned home with Medea and full great store of treasure. But it was unknown to her father that she went to Thessaly with duke Jason her dear, who afterwards brought mischief upon her. For like a traitor he went from her, and left with her his two young children, and falsely betrayed her, alas! Ever was he a chief of traitors in love; and anon he wedded yet a third wife, the daughter of king Creon.

This is the meed and reward that Medea received from Jason, even for her fidelity and kindness, who loved him better than herself, I believe, and left her father and her heritage for him. And this is the prowess of Jason, that in his days no lover so false was found walking on earth. And therefore in her letter she began thus, when she upbraided him for his falseness: 'Why pleased it me more to look on thy yellow hair than on the boundaries of mine honour? Why pleased me thy youth and comeliness, and the infinite graciousness of thy tongue? Ah, hadst thou died in thine adventure, how much faithlessness had died with thee!' Well can Ovid endite her letter in verse, which were too long for me to set here now.

V The Legend of Lucretia

Now I must speak of the exile of kings of Rome by reason of their horrible deeds, and of the last king, Tarquin, as Ovid and Titus Livy relate. But it is not for that cause I tell this tale, but to praise and memorize that true wife, the faithful Lucrece; for whose true wifehood and steadfastness not only do these pagans extol her but he who is called in our book of Saints' Legends the great Augustine has great pity for this Lucrece, who died in Rome-town. And of the manner of her death I will treat but briefly, and touch but the chief of this thing.

When Ardea was compassed around with Romans full stern and stout, right long lay the siege and wrought but little, so that they lay there half idle, as they deemed. And in his sport the young Tarquin began to jest, for he was light of speech, and said that 'it was an idle existence, no man there did more than his wife. And let us speak of wives, that is best. Let every man praise his own as pleases him, and let us ease our hearts with converse.'

A knight named Collatine arose and spake thus: 'Nay, there is no need to rely on words, but on deeds. I have a wife,' quoth he, 'who is held to be good by all who know her. Go we to Rome to-night and see.'

Tarquinius answered, 'That is good.'

To Rome they came and quickly repaired to the house of Collatine, and alighted, Tarquin and also this Collatine. The husband well knew all the shape of the house, and privily they entered in, for there was no porter at the gate, and at the chamber-door they stopped. This noble wife sat beside her bed with hair unbound, for she suspected no harm. And she was working soft wool, our book says, to keep her from sloth and idleness, and she bade her servants perform their duties, and asked them, 'What tidings hear you? What say men of the siege, how it shall end? Would God the walls were fallen! My husband is so long from this town, wherefore the dread so sore pains me, it stings to mine heart even as a sword, when I think of the siege or of that place. God save my lord, I pray, in His mercy.' And at that she wept full tenderly and took no more heed of her work, but meekly let her eyes fall. And this mien well became her; and also her tears, full of virtue, adorned her wifely chastity. Her look was worthy of her heart, for they accorded in sign and in truth. And at her words Collatine her husband came bursting in, ere she was ware of him, and cried, 'Fear not, for I am here!' And straightway she rose up with blissful countenance, and kissed him, as wives use to do.

Tarquin, this proud king's son, considered her beauty and her demeanour, her yellow hair, her form, her manner, her hue, her words of lament, and saw that her beauty was not feigned by any artfulness. And he conceived such desire for this lady that it burned in his heart like any flame, so furiously that his wits were all forgot. For he well imagined that she could never be won. And ever the more he despaired, the more he coveted her and thought her lovely. His blind pleasure was all he coveted.

On the morrow, when birds began to sing, he returned full privily to the camp and walked sadly by himself, ever freshly recalling her image. 'Thus lay her hair, and so fresh was her hue. Thus she sat, thus spake, thus spun. This was her look, thus fair was she, and this was her demeanour.' His heart has now received all this conceit. And as the sea, all tossed with tempest, will yet heave for a day or two after the storm has all departed, even so, though her form were absent, yet the pleasance thereof was present, — but not pleasance, but rather evil delight or an unrighteous desire with evil intent. 'For in spite of herself she shall be my mistress,' quoth he; 'ever hap helps the hardy. However it ends, it shall be done.'

And he girded on his sword and departed, and rode forth till he arrived at Rome, and all by himself took his way straight to the house of Collatine. The sun was down, and the day had lost its light. And in he came to a privy corner, and in the night stole out like a thief, when everyone had gone to his rest and none had a thought of such treachery. Were it by window or other sly means, he quickly entered in and with sword drawn came speedily where she lay, this noble wife Lucrece. And as she awoke she felt her bed pressed down. 'What beast is that,' quoth she, 'weighs down my bed thus?'

'I am the king's son Tarquin,' said he; 'but if you cry out or make a noise, or awake any creature, by that God who formed man alive, I shall thrust this sword through your heart.' And thereat he leaped at her throat and set the sharp point on her heart.

She spake no word, she had no strength; what should she say? — her wit was all fled. Even as when a wolf finds a solitary lamb, to whom should she lament or make moan? What! shall she fight with an hardy knight? Men well know a woman has no strength. What! shall she cry, or how shall she escape him who has her by the throat, with his sword at her heart? She begged for mercy, and said all she could.

'If you yield not,' quoth he, this cruel man, 'so surely may Jupiter save my soul, as I will slay your groom in the stable and lay him in your bed, and raise the alarm that I found you in such adultery. And thus you shall die, and also lose your good name, for you have none other choice.'

Now at this time these Roman matrons so loved their fair repute, and so dreaded shame, that, what for fear of scandalous talk and fear of dying, she lost wit and breath at once, and lay in a swoon so deathlike that a man might have smitten her arm or head off; she felt naught, fair or foul.

Tarquin, heir to a king, who by lineage and justice shouldst bear thee as a lord and a true knight, why hast thou done dishonour to chivalry? Why hast thou basely wronged this lady? Alack! this was a villainous deed of thee!

But now to the point: I read in the history that after he departed, the mischance which befell was this. The lady sent for all her friends, father, mother, husband together; and with her shining hair all dishevelled, in habit such as women then used to go in to the burial of their friends, she sat in the hall with a sorrowful look. Her friends asked what could ail her, and who was dead? And she sat ever weeping; for shame she could not fetch forth a word, nor durst she look upon them. But at last she told them of Tarquin, this rueful case, all this horrible thing. It were impossible to tell the lament that she and all her friends made together. Had folks' hearts been of stones, it would have made them pity her, so wifely and so true was her heart. She said that for her guilt or infamy her husband should not have a foul name, that she would not permit, in any wise. And they all answered, upon their troth they forgave her, as was just; it was no guilt of hers, it lay not under her control. And they told her many ensamples.

But all for naught, thus she straightway replied. 'Be as be may,' quoth she, 'as to forgiving, I will by no means have forgiveness.' And privily she snatched forth a knife, and with it slew herself. And as she fell, she looked and still took heed of her clothes; for as she fell down she still took thought lest her feet or the like were bare, so well loved she purity and fidelity.

All the town of Rome felt pity for her, and Brutus swore by her chaste blood that for that deed Tarquin should be banished, and all his kinsfolk; and he had the people summoned, and openly told the tale to them all, and openly had her carried on a bier through all the town, that men might see and learn the horrible deed of her violation. And never since that day was there a king in Rome-town; and she was held there to be a saint, and her day was ever dear and hallowed in the calendar of their creed.

And thus ended Lucrece the noble wife, as Titus Livy bears witness. I tell the tale because she was so faithful in love, and never by her will changed to any new lover, and for the sake of the constant heart, steadfast and kind, which men may ever feel in these women; where they set their heart, there it remains. For well I wot Christ himself tells that in all Israel, broad though the land be, he found not so great faith as in a woman; and this is no lie. And as for men, look what tyrannical deeds they do every day. Assay them who will, the truest is full brittle to trust.

VI The Legend of Ariadne

Thou Judge in Hell, Minos, lord of Crete, now thy turn comes, now thou comest into the ring! Not for thy sake only write I this history, but to call to mind once more the great untruth in love of thee, Theseus, for which the gods of high heaven be wroth, and have taken vengeance for thy guilt; redden with shame! Now I begin thy life.

Minos, great king of Crete, who had an hundred great and strong cities, sent his son Androgeus to school at Athens; whence it befell that whilst he was learning philosophy he was slain in that very city, only out of malice. The great Minos, of whom I speak, came to avenge his son's death. Long and hotly he laid siege to Alcathoe. Nevertheless the walls were so strong, and Nisus, king of that city, was so knightly, that he feared little; he took no heed of Minos or his host until on a day the chance befell that the daughter of Nisus stood on the wall and saw all the manner of the siege. It so happed that, watching a skirmish, she set her heart so sore upon Minos the king for his beauty and his chivalry that she thought she must die. And, to hasten over this long story, she caused Minos to win that place and to have the city all at his will, to save or destroy whom he would. But ill he repaid her kindness, and had left her drowning in sorrow and woe, had not the gods had pity upon her. But that story were too long for me now.

Athens also this King Minos won, and Alcathoe and other towns. And this was the outcome, that Minos so hard pressed them of Athens that from year to year they must give him their own beloved children to be slain, as ye shall hear. This Minos had a monster, an evil beast, so cruel that, when a man was brought to him, without pause he would devour him; no defence availed. And verily every third year they cast lots, and as the lot fell, on rich man or poor, he must give up his son and present him unto Minos to save or destroy, or let his beast devour him at his will. And this did Minos out of hatred; all his pleasure was set to avenge his son, and from year to year to make them of Athens his thralls as long as he should live. And when this town was won he sailed home.

This evil custom continued long, until Æeus, king of Athens, must send his own son Theseus, since the lot fell upon him, to be devoured, — for grace there was none. And this woful young knight was led forth straight to the court of King Minos, and was cast fettered into a prison, till such time as he should be devoured.

Well mayst thou weep, woful Theseus, a king's son, thus condemned! Methinks thou wert deeply beholden to any who should save thee from cold cares. And now if any woman help thee, well oughtest thou to be her slave and true lover year by year. But now to return to my tale.

The tower where this Theseus was cast, down in the dark bottom, wondrous deep, adjoined the wall of an outer chamber belonging to the two daughters of King Minos, who in much mirth and joy and comfort dwelt in their great chambers above, toward the chief street. By chance, I wot not how, it there befell that as Theseus was making moan by night, the king's daughter, named Ariadne, and also her sister Phædra, heard all his complaint, as they stood upon the wall and looked upon the bright moon; they list not to go early to bed. And they had compassion of his woe; for a king's son to be in such a prison and be devoured seemed to them great pity.

Then Ariadne spake to her noble sister and said, 'Phædra, dear sweet sister, can you not hear this woful lord's son, how piteously he laments his kindred, and also the wretched plight he is in, and all guiltless? Now certes, it is pity. And if you will assent, by my faith he shall be holpen, whatever we do!'

Phædra answered, 'Certainly I am as sorry for him as ever I was for any man; and for his assistance the best counsel I know is that we cause the gaoler to come privily and speak with us straightway, and bring this woful man with him. For if he could overcome this monster, then he were quit; there is none other help. Let us test him well to his heart's root, whether, if so be he have a weapon, he dare fight this fiend and defend himself, to keep and save his life. For you well know, that in the prison where he must descend, the beast is in a place that is not dark, and has room to wield an axe or a sword or staff or knife; so methinks he ought to save himself. If he be a man he will do it. And we shall also make him balls of wax and tow, that when the beast fiercely gapes, he shall cast them into his throat, to encumber his teeth and slake his hunger. And anon when Theseus shall see the beast choke, he shall leap on him to slay him ere they come more together. This weapon the gaoler shall hide, ere that time, full privily within the prison. And because that dwelling-place winds much in and out, and has such intricate paths — for it is shaped like a maze, — for this I have in mind a remedy, — that by means of a clew of twine he may straightway return the way he went, following ever the thread. And when he has overcome the beast, then he may flee away from this horror and can take the gaoler with him, and advance him at home in his country, since he is son of so great a lord. This is my counsel, if he dare take it.'

Why should I make a longer story? The gaoler came, and Theseus with him; and when all was thus agreed, down fell Theseus upon his knee before Ariadne: — 'Rightful lady of my life, I a sorrowful man,' quoth he, 'condemned to die, after this stroke of fortune will not part from you so long as I have life or breath, but I will thus remain in your service, so that as an unknown outcast I will serve you forevermore, till my heart die. I will forsake mine own heritage, and, as I said, be a page of your court, if you vouchsafe me so great a grace to have but my meat and drink here; and for my sustenance I will still labour even as you will have it, so that not Minos, who never saw me with the sight of his eyes, nor no man else, shall be able to know me, so cunningly and well shall I bear me and so skilfully and meanly disguise me, so that I shall be espied by no man in this world. This I will do to preserve my life and to remain in your presence, who do me this excellent kindness. And I will send this worthy man here, now the gaoler, to my father, and for reward he shall be one of the greatest men of my country. And if I yet durst say it, my fair lady, I am a king's son, and a knight. Would God, if it could be, that you were in my land, all three of you, and I with you to bear you company; then should you see if I lie herein. And if I proffer you humbly to be your page and serve you here, if I should not serve you as humbly there I pray Mars to grant me such favour that a shameful death may there fall on me, and death and poverty upon all my friends; and that after my death my spirit may roam by night and walk to and fro; that I may have the shameful name of traitor, by reason of which may my spirit walk! And if I ever claim higher station, unless you vouchsafe to give it me, may I die a shameful death, as I have said! Have mercy, lady! I can say naught else!'

Theseus was a comely knight to behold, and young, of but three-and-twenty years. Whoso had seen his countenance would have wept for pity of his woe. Wherefore this Ariadne in this wise made answer to his proffer and his appealing look: 'For a king's son,' quoth she, 'and a knight also to serve me in so low degree, God forbid it, for the shame of all women, and grant me such a thing never befall, but send you grace and cunning of heart to defend you and slay your foe in knightly fashion; and grant hereafter I may find you so kind to me and to my sister here that I repent not to have saved you from death! Yet it were better I were your wife, since you are as gently born as I and have a kingdom not far hence, than that I should suffer you to die guiltless or let you serve as a page. It is not meet for one of your kindred, but what is it that a man will not do for fear? As for my sister, since it is so that she must go with me if I depart, or else suffer death, and I too, do you as faithfully cause her to be wedded to your son at your home-coming. This is the final end of this thing. Do you swear to it here, by all that may be sworn on.'

'Yea, lady mine,' quoth he, 'or else may I be all rent by the Minotaur to-morrow! And here have of my heart's blood in pledge, if you will; if I had knife or spear, I would let it out and vow thereon, for I wot only then you will believe me. By Mars, who is chief in my creed, so I may live and not fail tomorrow to achieve my battle, I would never flee from this place until you should see the very proof of my words. For now if I am to say sooth to you, in mine own country I have loved you full many a day, though you wist it not, and most desired to see you of any earthly creature living; by my faith I swear and certify you that for these seven years I have been your devoted lover. Now I have you, and you also have me, my dear heart, duchess of Athens!'

This lady smiled at his steadfastness, and at his earnest words and his look, and spake all softly to her sister in this wise: 'Now sister mine,' quoth she, 'now we be duchesses, both you and I, and assured of royal rank in Athens, and both like to be queens hereafter; and have saved from his death a king's son, as it is ever the wont of well-born women to save a man of gentle blood if they can, in an honest cause, and most of all if he be in the right. Methinks none ought to blame us for this, nor give us an evil name.'

And to endite this matter briefly, Theseus took leave of her, and every point in this covenant was carried out as ye have heard me relate. His weapon, his clew, all the things that I have named, were laid by the gaoler right in the house where this Minotaur had his dwelling, hard by the door where Theseus should enter. And Theseus was led to his death, and he came forth to this Minotaur, and after the instruction of Ariadne he overcame the beast and slew him; and by the clew he came out again full privily when he had slain the beast. Through the gaoler he got a barge, and loaded it with his wife's treasure, and took his wife and her fair sister, and the gaoler also and with them all three stole away from the land by night, and turned toward the land of Œnopia, where he had a familiar friend. There they feasted and danced and sang. And he had in his arms this Ariadne who had preserved him from the beast. Anon he got him another ship there, and also a right great number of his countrymen, and took his leave, and sailed homeward.

And on an isle amid the wild sea, where there dwelt no creature save wild beasts, and of them full many, he brought his ship ashore. And he tarried on that isle half a day, and said he must rest him on land, and his mariners did as he desired. And, to tell the matter briefly, whilst Ariadne his wife lay sleeping, because her sister was fairer than she, he took her by the hand and forth he went to ship, and like a traitor stole off, whilst this Ariadne still slept; and toward his country he swiftly sailed — the wind drive him twenty devils' ways!, — and found his father drowned in the sea.

I list speak no more of him, in faith. These false lovers, may poison be their destruction! But I will return to Ariadne, who for weariness was overtaken with sleep, — full sorrowful her heart may awaken! Alas! now my heart has pity for thee! Right in the dawning she awoke, and groped in the bed and found naught. 'Alas!' quoth she, 'that ever I was created! I am betrayed!' And she rent her hair, and hastened barefoot to the strand, and cried, 'Theseus! my sweet heart! Where are you, — that I cannot find you and may be slain thus by beasts?'

The hollow rocks answered her; she saw no man. And the moon yet shone, and high upon a rock she climbed speedily, and saw his barge sailing in the sea. Cold waxed her heart and thus she said, 'Milder than you I find the wild beasts!' — Had he not sin who thus betrayed her? — 'O, return,' she cried, 'for the pity and sin of it! Your ship has not all its crew!' She stuck her kerchief up on a pole, in case he should indeed see it and remember that she was left and return and find her on the strand. But all for naught, he was gone his way. And down she fell swooning on a stone; and she arose, and in all her sorrow she kissed the prints of his feet where he had passed. And then she spake thus to her bed: 'Thou bed,' quoth she, 'which hast received two, thou shalt answer for two, and not for one only! Where is thy greater part gone? Alas, what will become of me, wretched creature! For though so be a ship or a boat come here, I dare not for dread go home to my country. I cannot counsel myself in this strait!'

Why should I tell more of her lament? It was so long, it were an heavy thing to tell; Ovid records all in her epistle. But I shall tell quickly to the end. The gods helped her, out of pity, and in the sign of Taurus men may see the gems of her crown shining brightly. I will speak no more of this tale; but so this false lover could beguile his true love. The Devil repay him for his trouble!

VII The Legend of Philomela

Thou Giver of its forms to matter, Who has created the fair world, and eternally borest it in Thy mind ere Thou didst begin Thy work, why madest Thou to the shame of man, — or though it were not Thy doing to create such a thing for that end — why didst Thou suffer Tereus to be born, who was so false and perjured in love that when folk mention his name, all things from this world up to the highest heaven are corrupted? As for me, so grisly was his act that, when I read his foul story, mine eyes also wax foul and sore. Even yet lasts the venom of so long ago, and infects him who will behold the story of Tereus of whom I tell.

He was lord of Thrace, and kin to the cruel god Mars, who stands with bloody dart. And with blissful cheer he had wedded King Pandion's fair sweet daughter, who was named Progne, flower of her country (though Juno list not to be at the festival, nor Hymen, who is god of marriage; but ready at the feast, in sooth, were the three furies with their deadly torch; the owl, prophet of woe and misfortune, all night fluttered amongst the roof-beams). The revels, with much singing and dancing, lasted a fortnight or little less. But to pass soon over this history, for I am weary to tell of him, five years he and his wife abode together, till on a day she began to yearn so sore to see her sister, whom for long she had not seen, that she knew not what to say for desire. But she begged her husband for God's love that she might once go to see her sister and return straightway; or else, if she might not go to her, she prayed him to send after her. And this was ever her petition day by day, with all wifely meekness in word and cheer.

This Tereus had his ships made ready, and himself fared forth to Greece to his father-in-law, and prayed him to vouchsafe that Philomela, his wife's sister, might but once have a sight of Progne, his wife, for a month or two, — 'and she shall straightway return to you; myself will both come and go with her, and I will guard her as mine heart's life.'

This aged Pandion, this king, began to weep for tenderness of feeling when he thought to give his daughter leave to go; in all this world he loved naught so much. But at last she got leave, for with salt tears she besought of her father the boon to see her sister, whom she longed after so; and she embraced him with her two arms. And she was so young and fair withal that when Tereus beheld her beauty, and that there was not her peer in attire, and that she was yet twice as rich in goodness, he so set his fiery heart upon her that he would have her, howsoever it went; and with his wiles he kneeled and prayed till at last Pandion spake thus: 'Now, son,' he said, 'so dear to me, I commit to you my young daughter here, who hears the key of all my heart. Greet well my daughter and your spouse, and give her leave to follow her pleasure sometime, that she may see me once ere I die.'

And in sooth he made splendid entertainment for him and for his folk, great and small, who had come with him; and gave him costly gifts, and conveyed him through the chief street of Athens, and escorted him to the sea, and returned home; he thought no evil.

The oars speedily pulled the vessel on, and at last it arrived in Thrace. And up into a forest he led her and privily hasted into a dark cave, and there, willy-nilly, he bade her remain. Whereat her heart shuddered, and she said, 'Where is my sister, brother Tereus?'

And at that she wept tenderly, and trembled with fear, pale and piteous even as the lamb that is bitten by the wolf; or as the dove stricken by the eagle, that escapes from his claws, yet is dazed and afeared lest it be seized again, even so she sat. But it could not be otherwise, this was all: by force this betrayer did his deed, all in spite of her. Lo! here was a manly deed, and a righteous! She cried, 'Sister!', with a loud voice, and, 'Father dear!', and, 'God in heaven help me!' All availed not. And this false thief did this lady yet more harm, out of fear lest she should cry out his shame and openly disgrace him, and he cut off her tongue with his sword; and in a castle he put her privily in prison for evermore and kept her in possession, so that she could nevermore escape him. Ah hapless Philomela, woful is thine heart! God avenge thee and grant thee thy prayer! Now it is time I made a brief end.

This Tereus came to his wife and took her in his arms and wept right piteously and shook his head, and swore to her he found her sister was no more. Whereat this luckless Progne was so woful that her sorrowful heart night broke in twain. And thus I leave Progne in her tears, and will tell on of her sister.

This woful lady had learned in her youth to make embroidery, and in her frame weave tapestry, as women have long been wont to do. And, to tell it briefly, she had her fill of meat and drink, and clothing at her desire, and also could read and compose a thing well enough, but verily she could not write with a pen; but she knew how to weave letters to and fro, so that by the time the year was all gone, she had woven on a large woollen cloth how she had been brought in a ship from Athens, and taken into a cave; and all that Tereus had wrought, she wove it well, and endited the story on the top, how she had been served because she loved her sister. And anon she gave a ring to a page, and by signs prayed him to go to the queen and bear her that tapestry, and by signs she swore many an oath to him that she would give him what she could obtain.

This page straightway repaired to the queen, and gave it her, and told her all the manner of it. And when Progne beheld this thing, for sorrow and frenzy also she spake no work, but feigned to go on pilgrimage to the temple of Bacchus. And in a little while she found her dumb sister sitting weeping all by herself in the castle. Alas for the woe, lament and moan that Progne voiced over her dumb sister! Each took the other in her arms; and thus I leave them in their sorrow.

The rest of the story it boots not to tell, for this is the sum thereof, that thus she was served who never merited ill of this cruel man, nor wrought him harm that she knew of. Well may ye beware of man (if ye list). For albeit he may not for shame do as Tereus did, lest he lose his fair repute, or demean him as a villain or murderer, yet but little while shall ye find him true; this I say, were he now mine own brother (unless so be he can find no new love).

VIII The Legend of Phyllis

By experience as well as authority ye may find, if ye are willing, that evil fruit comes from an evil tree. But I speak this now for this end, to tell you of false Demophon; never heard I of a falser in love, unless it were his father Theseus. — God in His mercy keep us from such an one! — thus may those women pray who hear of him. Now I turn to the substance of my tale.

The city of Troy was destroyed. This Demophon came sailing over the sea to Athens, to his broad palace; with him came many a ship and barge full of his folk, of whom full many were sore wounded and sick and woe-begone. And they had lain long at the siege. Behind him came a rain and a wind, and drove him so fiercely that his sails could not withstand it; rather than all the world he would he were ashore, so the tempest hunted him to and fro. It was so dark he could go nowhere, and his steering-gear had been broken by a wave. His ship was rent so far below, and in such wise, that no carpenter could mend it. By night the sea glowed wildly, as it were any torch, and rolled him now up now down, till Neptune had compassion on him, and also Thetis, Chorus, Triton and all the deities of the sea, and let him come upon a shore whereof Phyllis was lady and queen, the daughter of Lycurgus, fairer to see than the flower in the bright sunshine. Scarce could Demophon win to shore, weak and weary, and his folk wasted by weariness and famine; wellnigh he was driven to the death. His wise folk counselled him to seek help and succour of the queen, and to look what grace he might obtain, and to make a borrowing in that land to keep him from woe and mischance; for he was sick and nigh dead, scarce could he speak or draw breath, and he lay near Rhodope to rest him. When he could walk, he thought it was best to seek for succour at the court.

Men knew him well, and did him honour; for at Athens he was duke and lord, as Theseus his father had been, who in his day was of great renown, no man so great in all that region. And he was like his father in face and form, and false in love; it came to him by nature. As does Reynard the fox, so the fox's son; by nature he knows his old father's ways without teaching, as a drake can swim when it is caught and carried to the water's edge. This honourable Phyllis made him good cheer, well pleased with his bearing and demeanour. But because I am already surfeited with writing of men forsworn in love, and also that I may haste me in my legend, which God grant me grace to finish, therefore I pass on quickly thus. Ye have fully heard the device of Theseus in betraying fair Ariadne, who in pity had preserved him from death. In few words, even so in the same way Demophon trod the same path of his false father Theseus. For he swore to Phyllis to wed her, and plighted her his troth, and picked from her all the goods he could, when he was whole and sound and had rested him; and he did with Phyllis as he would. And well could I, if I list, describe all his doings back and forth.

He said he must sail unto his own land, for there he desired to prepare for her wedding, as fitted her honour and his also. And openly then he took his leave, and swore to her that he would not tarry, but in a month would return. And in that land he ordered matters like a very lord, and received men's obedience well and familiarly, and caused his ships to be made ready, and went home the nearest way he could. And he came not again to Phyllis. So cruelly and sore suffered she for that, alas!, as the stories remind us, that she was her own death even with a cord, when she saw that Demophon had betrayed her.

But first she wrote to him and earnestly begged him to come and deliver her from her pains, as I shall rehearse in a word or two. I will not vouchsafe to toil over him, or spend a penful of ink on him, for he was false in love, even as his sire, — the Devil burn up both their souls! But I will write a word or two from the letter of Phyllis, though it be but a small part.

'O Demophon,' quoth she, 'thine hostess of Rhodopeia, thy Phyllis, so encompassed with woe, must complain upon thee, that thou keepest not the covenant which thou madest, but tarriest over the term set betwixt us. Thine anchor which thou didst drop in our haven gave promise that thou wouldst truly come again ere the moon once completed her circuit; but four times the moon has hid her face since that day thou wentest from this land, and four times she has lighted the world again. But for all that, in very sooth, the Thracian waves have not yet brought the ship from Athens; and still it comes not. And if thou wouldst but reckon up the time appointed, as I or other true lovers should, thou wouldst see I complain not, God wot, before the day.'

But I cannot write all her letter from point to point, for it were a burden to me; her letter was right long and broad. But here and there I have set it in rhyme, where methought she has spoken well.

She said, 'Thy sails return not, nor verily is there any good faith in thy words. But I wot why thou comest not; it is because I was so liberal of my love to thee. And if the vengeance of the gods to whom thou art forsworn should fall on thee for that, thou art not sufficient to bear the penalty. Too much I trusted, well may I complain against thy lineage and thy fair tongue, and thy tears falsely pressed out. How couldst thou weep thus by art?' quoth she. 'Can such tears be feigned? Now certes, if thou wouldst but remember it, this ought to be but small glory to thee, to have betrayed thus a simple maiden! I pray to God, and oft have prayed, that this be the greatest glory of all and the highest honour that ever shall come to thee! And when thine ancestors of old shall be limned, that men may see their worthiness, then I pray God that thou also mayst be limned, that folk may read as they pass by, "Lo, this is he who betrayed with his flattery and basely wronged her who was his true love in thought and deed." And truly, one point more may they see, that in this thou art like thy father; for he beguiled Ariadne, in sooth, with such subtlety and art as thine in beguiling me. And in that point, and not a worthy one, thou followest him and art his heir in very sooth. But since thou hast beguiled me thus sinfully, though thou be harder than any stone, within a season, thou mayest see my body floating even in the harbour of Athens without sepulture and burial.'

And when this letter was sent forth, and she knew how fickle and false he was, anon in despair she destroyed herself; such sorrow had she, alas!, because she had bestowed her love so amiss. Beware of your subtle foe, ye women, since even this day ensamples may be seen; and in love trust no man but me!

IX The Legend of Hypermnestra

In Greece once were two brethren, of whom one was named Danaus, and got many a son of his body, as such false lovers often know how to do. Amongst all his sons there was one he loved best of all; and when this child was born, this Danaus devised him a name and called him Lynceus. The second brother was named Ægyptus, and in love he was false as ever he pleased, and in his days he begat many a daughter, amongst whom he begot of his own wife a dear daughter, the youngest of them all, and let her be named Hypermnestra, which child by her horoscope was born to all good virtues, as it pleased the gods before her birth that she should be the corn of the sheaf. The Weird Sisters, that we call Destiny, ordained for her that she must needs be compassionate, steadfast, wise, and true as steel; and it well accorded with this woman. For though Venus gave her great beauty, she was so compounded by the influence of Jupiter that tenderness, and fidelity, and to dread disgrace, and preserve the good name of her wifehood, — these seemed to her to yield felicity on earth. And at that time of year red Mars was so feeble that he was bereft of his power for ill; Venus repressed his cruel activity. What with her power and other depression by celestial houses, Mars' venom was kept down, so that Hypermnestra durst not handle a knife with evil intent, though it were to save herself. But as the heavens then revolved, she came under evil aspects of Saturn, which made her to die in prison, as I shall afterwards tell.

To Danaus and also to Ægyptus, though they were two brethren, it seemed good to make a marriage betwixt Hypermnestra and Lynceus (for at that time consanguinity hindered not), and appointed it should be on such a day, and the full accord was duly made. The preparation was done, the time was near at hand. And thus Lynceus wedded the daughter of his uncle, and each possessed the other. The torches and the bright lamps burned, the sacrifices were all ready prepared, the incense reeked sweetly out of the fire; flower and leaf were torn up by the roots to make garlands and high crowns. The place was full of the sound of minstrelsy, of the amorous songs of marriage, as was all the custom at that time. And this was in the palace of Ægyptus, who ruled in his house as he would. And thus they wore the day to an end, and friends took leave and went home. The night came, the bride must to bed. Ægyptus hasted to his chamber and privily summoned his daughter. When the house was voided of all folk, he looked on his daughter with joyful mien, and spake to her as ye shall hear. 'Mine own true daughter, mine heart's treasure, since the day when my first shirt was made, or I had my lot at the hands of the fatal sisters, never a thing came so nigh my heart as you, mine Hypermnestra, beloved daughter! Take heed what I your father here say to you, and evermore follow the will of one who is wiser than you. For, first of all, daughter, I love you so that all the world is not half so dear to me! And I would not advise you to your harm for all the wealth under the cold moon. And what is in my mind shall be said straightway, with this attestation, that unless you do as I shall tell, you shall die, by Him who created all! In few words, you escape not from my palace before you die, unless you consent and work after my counsel. Take this to you as my full resolution.'

This Hypermnestra cast down her eyes and trembled as the leaf of the green aspen; deathly waxed her hue and like ashes, and she said, 'Lord and father, God wot I will do all your will, according to my power, so it be no dishonour to me.'

Quoth he, 'I will have no conditions.' And he caught out a knife, sharp as a razor. 'Hide this,' quoth he, 'that it be not seen. And when your husband is gone to bed, cut his throat in two whilst he sleeps. For in my dreams I am warned that my nephew shall be my slayer, but which nephew I know not; therefore I will be secure. If you say nay, by Him that I have sworn by, we two shall fall out, as I have said.'

This Hypermnestra nigh lost her wits, and, to pass thence unharmed, she consented to him; there was none other grace. And with that he took up a flask, and said, 'Give him a draught of this, or two or three, to drink when he goes to rest, and he shall sleep as long as ever you would have him, the narcotics and opiates be so strong. And go your ways, lest he grow impatient.'

Out came the bride; and with full grave countenance, as is oft the manner with maidens, was brought to the chamber with revel and song. And in brief, lest this tale stretch out, this Lynceus and she were soon brought to bed, and every person hasted out at the door.

The night wore on and he fell into slumber. She began to weep full tenderly, and arose, and quaked with fear, as the branch which Zephyrus buffets; and all in that city of Argos was hushed. Now she waxed cold as any frost; for pity so constrained her heart and dread of death so pained her that thrice she fell down in the strife. She arose and staggered here and there, and looked hard at her hands. 'Alas, and shall my hands be bloody? I am a maiden, and, by my nature and my semblance and my raiment, my hands are not shapen for a knife, to reave his blood from any man. What (a Devil!) have I to do with the knife? — And shall I have my throat cut in twain? Then I shall bleed, alas! and perish; and this thing must needs have an end, either he or I must needs die. — Now certes,' quoth she, 'since I am his wife, and he has my troth, it is better for me to die with wifely honour than to be a traitor living in shame. Be as be may, for earnest or mirth, he shall awake and arise, and go his way out by this gutter, ere it be light.'

And she wept full tenderly on his face, and clasped him in her arms, and shook him, and gently awoke him. And when she had warned him and provided his escape, he leaped out at the window from the upper room. This Lynceus was swift and light of foot, and ran full swiftly before his wife. This hapless woman, alas, was so weak and helpless that ere she had gone far, her cruel father had her seized. Alas, Lynceus, why so unkind? Why didst thou not remember to take her and lead her forth with thee? For when she saw that he was gone, and that she could not go so fast or follow him, she sat her down right then, till she was caught and fettered in prison.

This tale is told for this end. . . .

[Unfinished.]

Chaucer's Life and Works

GEOFFREY CHAUCER was born in London about 1340, the son of a wine-merchant more or less known at court. The poet did not receive a university education, and his extensive reading and wide interests were due to his own native mental activity. His connection with members of the court, high and low, was always close, and determined his life. In 1357 he was page in the household of a daughter-in-law of Edward III, and later was squire to the king. In 1359 he had a short and luckless experience in the army. He was married to an attendant and namesake of Queen Philippa about 1366; his wife probably died in 1387; we know of two sons. Between 1370 and 1380 he was sent on some seven Continental embassies, of which the most important to him were in 1372–1373 and 1378, to northern Italy; where in his person English literature came first under the influence of Italian. Between 1374 and 1386 his chief other offices seem to have been two comptrollerships in the London custom-house. In the latter year he sat in Parliament for the county of Kent. During the last twelve years or so of his life he held various minor public appointments, but seems often to have been in straitened circumstances, perhaps owing to his political connections. He died in 1400, and was the first literary man buried in the south transept of Westminster Abbey, how known as Poets' Corner.

The Book of the Duchess, Chaucer's earliest datable poem, was written in or soon after 1369, to lament the death of Blanche, first wife of John of Gaunt, transparently alluded to toward the end of the poem as 'gode faire Whyte'.

The Complaint of Mars (date uncertain) is an allegory, crammed with astrological technicalites of a conjunction of the planets Venus and Mars in the sign Taurus, treated as a meeting of two lovers. It may allude to a particular scandalous *amoura* at court, but this is uncertain.

The Parliament of Birds (1381) celebrates the betrothal of Richard II to Anne of Bohemia; the noble tercel eagle represents the former, and the formel the latter. The two rival eagles represent two other suitors of the princess.

The fragmentary *Anelida and Arcite* (perhaps 1383–1384) is partly based on Boccaccio's *Teseide*. Chaucer's intention in it is not very clear.

The Former Age (the date of this beautiful poem is uncertain) is based as to its first half on a passage in Boethius' *De Consolatione Philosophiæ*.

L'Envoy de Chaucer à Bukton (near the end of 1396) was addressed to the poet's friend Robert Buckton, constable of the castle of Eye, Suffolk; but quite in vain for he was married by January, 1397.

The Complaint of Venus (a late poem) is based on three *ballades* by Sir Oton de Granson, a contemporary poet of Savoy.

The Complaint to His Purse (1399–1400), perhaps Chaucer's last poem, was addressed to King Henry IV.

The *Troilus and Criseyde* (dated by various students between 1377 and 1385) is a very much altered and expanded version of Boccaccio's *Filostrato*. The love-story cannot be traced further back than the twelfth-century *Roman de Troie*, by Benoit de S. Maur, the rest of which was based, not on Homer, but on certain late Latin accounts of the siege of Troy.

The House of Fame (perhaps 1379, doubtless never finished) is Chaucer's free and highly original working up of numerous motives found elsewhere in folk-lore and literature, especially in Virgil and Dante.

The Legend of Good Women (about 1386–1387) the poet intended to be twice as extensive as it is; he may have been diverted from it by the more attractive plan of the *Canterbury Tales*. The lives of Love's martyrs (*legend* being a church-term for an account of a saint's life) are based on various classical sources, especially Ovid's *Heroides*. The prologue is a vivifying of several well-recognized types of contemporary French court-poetry, of which it contains many reminiscences: it exists in two versions, the second of which (about 1394–1395) is here given. In the earlier, Queen Anne has generally been believed to be celebrated under the double guise of the daisy and of Queen Alcestis.

The Canterbury Tales were Chaucer's principal literary work between 1387 and 1400, but contain a few portions written earlier; of his enormous original design for them he completed only about one-fifth. They belong to a type of work ('tales within tales') oriental in origin and very widespread; there is no evidence that they were modelled on Boccaccio's *Decameron*. The unfinished state of the work accounts for certain inconsistencies, and for the want of links between certain of the tales, which have come down to us in about eight separate groups; the order of the groups, however, may be determined by internal evidence. The pilgrims spend three days (probably) on the sixty-mile journey to the most frequented of mediæval English shrines, St. Thomas à Becket's in Canterbury Cathedral.

The Knight's Tale, mentioned under a different name in the prologue to the

Legend of Good Women, was perhaps written about 1384–1386. It is a greatly condensed, and otherwise altered, version of Boccaccio's *Teseide*.

The Man of Law's Tale is Chaucer's splendid poetizing of a passage in English mythical-history as given in the French prose of Nicholas Trivet, a fourteenth-century Dominican friar. The story belongs to a type widespread in folk-lore and mediæval literature. The events are represented as having occurred late in the sixth century; the King Ælla of the tale is he on whose name Gregory the Great made his famous pun when he saw the Saxon slaves in the market-place at Rome.

The Shipman's Tale was originally meant to be delivered by the Wife of Bath, as is shown by a passage early in it where the speaker classes himself among married women. Here, as often, Chaucer neglected to revise.

The Prioress' Tale belongs to a group of stories, slanderous against the Jews, current in the Middle Ages. Another similar story is told of the little St. Hugh of Lincoln, referred to at the end of the poem.

The Tale of Sir Thopas seems to be meant as a burlesque of various inferior romances of chivalry.

The Tale of Melibeus is an expanded translation of a French prose version of the *Liber Consolationis et Consilii*, by the thirteenth-century Lombard, Albertano da Brescia.

The Clerk's Tale is based on Petrarch's Latin prose version of the last tale in Boccaccio's *Decameron*.

The Squire's Tale, which was probably never finished, is doubtless oriental in ultimate origin, but its exact source (if it had one) is unknown. It is to this tale that Milton refers in *Il Penseroso:*

> "Or call up him that left half-told
> The story of Cambuscan bold."

The Second Nun's Tale is based on the *Legenda Aurea* of the thirteenth-century Jacobus à Voragine, Archbishop of Genoa. The fact that it was written long before the rest of the *Canterbury Tales* (it is mentioned in the prologue to the *Legend of Good Women*) accounts for certain inappropriate expressions in the invocation.

The Parson's Tale, too, was not written for its present purpose. Its unknown source was based upon two treatises by two thirteenth-century Dominicans, one on the sacrament of penance, by Raymund of Pennaforte, the other on the seven deadly sins, by Guilielmus Peraldus. The singular recantation at the end was doubtless written at the close of Chaucer's life; just how seriously it is to be taken is uncertain.

Glossary and Notes

The abbreviations following the explanations indicate one or two of the works in which the words explained occur.

Æsculapius, Dioscorides, etc. These were recognized authorities (Greek, Arabic and mediæval European) on medicine. Æsculapius had been transformed from a god into a writer. (*Prol.*)

Agathon. Probably a Greek poet of the fifth century B.C. (*L.G.W.*)

Alan. Alain de l'Isle, the twelfth-century French author of *The Complaint of Nature*. (*P.F.*)

Alcathoe. The citadel of Megara, near Athens. (*L.G.W.*)

Aldiran. A star in or near the constellation Leo. (*Sq. T.*)

Alexander the Great, according to the mediæval romances, flew almost to the heavens in a car drawn by griffins. (*H.F.*)

Almagest. The great astronomical treatise of the Egyptian Greek Ptolemy. (*Mill. T.*)

Alma Redemptoris Mater. A hymn in the breviary ('Gentle Mother of the Redeemer'). (*Pri. T.*)

Alnath. A star in the constellation Aries, by the distance of which from the true equinoctial point could be calculated the amount of the precession of the equinoxes. (*Frankl. T.*)

Amphiaraus. A seer (hence Chaucer calls him a bishop) swallowed up by the earth at the siege of Thebes. (*W.B.P., T. and C.*)

Angle. One of the four most favourable of the twelve 'houses' (which see) or divisions of the sky. (*M.L.T.*)

Anni collecti, anni expansi. Tables of the positions of the planets for large and for small numbers of years, respectively. (*Frankl. T.*)

Annualer. A priest who lives by singing annual masses for the souls in purgatory. (*C.Y.T.*)

Anticlaudianus. A Latin poem by Alain de l'Isle (twelfth century). (*H.F.*)

Ape-wine. Mediæval folk-lore distinguished four manners of being drunk, — ape-, lion-, sheep-, and pig-drunk. (*Manc. Prol.*)

519

Argonauticon. A Latin epic by Valerius Flaccus. (*L.G.W.*)

Argument. A mathematical quantity on which others depend. (*Frankl. T.*)

Argus (or **Algus**). The supposed name of the inventor of the Arabic numerals. (*B.D.*)

Arnold de Villa Nova. A thirteenth-century Frenchman, who wrote a *Philosopher's Rosary*, on alchemy. (*C.Y.T.*)

Ascendent. The part of the heavens just rising, a planet in which (according to astrology) was especially potent; observed particularly at birth. (*Prol.*, *M.L.T.*, *W.B.P.*)

Aspect. A planet's aspect is its position with reference to the others; on this (according to astrology) depends its influence. (*K.T.*, *T. and C.*)

Astrolabe. An instrument used (as the sextant now) for taking the altitudes of the heavenly bodies. (*Mill. T.*)

Astromy. A blunder of the Miller's for *astronomy*. *(Mill. T.)*

Atiteris. Unknown. (*H.F.*)

Atropos. One of the three Fates, who cuts off the thread of life. (*T. and C.*)

Attalia. On the south coast of Asia Minor. (*Prol.*)

Attrition. A lesser degree of contrition, the minimum requirement for a good confession. (*T. and C.*)

Auctor. Often inserted in the manuscripts to indicate that the author is exclaiming in his own person. (*March. T.*)

Aurora. Parts of the Bible in Latin verse, by Petrus de Riga, a twelfth-century Frenchman. (*B.D.*)

Beasts. 'Aërial beasts' refers to the signs of the zodiac (mostly named after animals). (*H.F.*)

Bellona seems to be identified with Pallas (both being war-goddesses). (*A. and A.*)

Belmaria. A Moorish kingdom in Africa. (*Prol.*)

Benedicite. 'O bless ye [the Lord]': a sort of greeting used by monks, then becoming a mild ejaculation. (*K.T.*, *T. and C.*, etc.)

Bigamy. A second marriage, even after the death of the first mate, formerly deprecated by the church (cf. *octogamy*). *(W.B.P.)*

Blood. Each of the four humours (which see) was supposed to be dominant at certain times of the day. (*Sq. T.*)

Book of the Lion. This work of Chaucer's seems to be lost. (*Pars. T.*)

Book of the Nineteen Ladies. An inexact reference to the *Legend of Good*

Women. This curious Retractation at the end of the *Parson's Tale* seems to indicate an attack of contrition at the end of Chaucer's life.

Brooch of Thebes. A magic brooch or bracelet which brought ill-luck (in the *Thebaid* of Statius). (*A. and A.*)

Brunel the Ass. A satirical Latin poem by the twelfth-century Englishman Nigellus Wireker. (*N.P.T.*)

Brutus. According to myth, the great grandson of Æneas who became the first king of Britain. (*Purse*)

Brutus Cassius. Chaucer curiously identifies the two chief conspirators against Cæsar. (*Monk's T.*)

Candace. Probably an Indian queen, who tricked Alexander the Great (according to the romances). (*P.F.*)

Cecilia. The five curious etymologies for the name (as if from *cœli lilia, cœci via*, etc.) are all false. (*S.N.T.*)

Cellarer. A monastic officer who had charge of the wine-vaults. (*Monk's Prol.*)

Centre. A part of an astrolabe (which see). (*Frankl. T.*)

Ceruse. A cosmetic made of white lard. (*Prol.*)

Chance. A term in dicing. (*Pard. T.*)

Chautepleure. The name of a thirteenth-century French song, which became proverbial. (*A. and A.*)

Chichevache. A cow in a folk-lore story, subsisting only on patient wives (and therefore always lean). (*Cl. T.*)

Choler. The red bile, one of the four humours (which see). (*N.P.T.*)

Choleric hot sign. Aries was so-called because it was deemed to be of the nature of the hot humour (which see), red bile. (*Sq. T.*)

Chorus. Perhaps for Caurus, the northeast wind. (*L.G.W.*)

Chough. The allusion is to a story (like that of the *Manciple's Tale*) in which a licentious woman and her maid fool her husband by means of a bird. (*W.B.P.*)

Christopher. An image of St. Christopher worn for good-luck. (*Prol.*)

Church-door. Marriages were sometimes performed at the church-porch. (*Prol., W. B. P.*)

Churl. The man in the moon, — a peasant carrying a bundle of thorns. (*T. and C.*)

Claudian. Claudius Claudianus, the fourth-century writer of a poem *On the Rape of Proserpina* by Pluto; therefore to be regarded as an authority on the other world.

Clerk. An ecclesiastical, acolyte, learned man, or student. (*Prol.*, *Mill. T.*, *T. and C.*)

Coal-fox. Apparently a (partly) black fox. (*N.P.T.*)

Cock's bones. *Cock* is a corruption of *God*. *(Reeve's Prol.)*

Colle. Unknown. (*H.F.*)

Combust. Deprived of power by being too near the sun (said of a planet). (*T. and C.*)

Conqueror of Albion. Henry IV, who had dethroned Richard II. (*Purse.*)

Corinna. Unknown; Chaucer here really uses Boccaccio. (*A. and A.*)

Corpus Dominus, Corpus Madrian. Bits of the Host's hog-Latin; he intends oaths by the Eucharist and (perhaps) St. Mathurin. (*Pri. Prol.*, *Monk's Prol.*)

Cyprian dame. Venus, the goddess. (*T. and C.*)

Cytherea. Chaucer invokes Venus, goddess and planet. North-north-west may be an error for west-north-west. (*P.F.*)

Dane. An Italian form for *Daphne*. (*K.T.*)

Dares and Dictys. The supposed authors of two Latin accounts of the Trojan War, dating from the early Christian centuries; the chief authorities on it in the Middle Ages. (*T. and C.*)

Depardieux. In God's name. (*Fri. T.*)

Depressed. The depression of a planet is the sign where it is astrologically weakest. (*W.B.P.*)

Dictys. See *Dares*.

Dry Sea and Carrenare. Probably two regions in central Asia, of which Chaucer had heard through some book of travels. (*B.D.*)

'Dun is in the mire.' 'The horse is stuck; we are at a standstill' (proverbial). (*Manc. Prol.*)

Dunmow. At Dunmow, Essex, a flitch of bacon is said to have been given to any married couple who had lived a year without quarrelling. (*W.B.P.*)

Eclympasteyre. A supposed son of the god of sleep. (*B.D.*)

Elcanor. Unknown. (*H.F.*)

Envoy. The last stanza of a ballade, supposed to contain an address or application; sometimes used of an entire poem. (*Cl. T.*, *Truth*, etc.)

Exaltation. The sign in which a planet is astrologically most powerful. (*W.B.P.*)

Explicit. 'The end.' (*S.N.T.*, etc.)

Face. A third part of a sign of the zodiac; the face of Mars was the first ten degrees of Aries. (*Sq. T.*)

Fallows. Ploughed land. (*W.B.P.*)

First-moved. *Primum mobile*; according to the Ptolemaic system, the ninth sphere, the daily revolution of which carried all the heavenly bodies around with it, and caused day and night. (*M.L.T.*)

Florin. A third of a pound (6*s.* 8*d.*); worth in Chaucer's day ten or fifteen times as much as now. (*Pard. T.*)

Formel. The female of the hawk or eagle. (*P.F.*)

Franklin. A middling land-holder; (nearly) a country-squire. (*Prol.*)

Ganelon. According to the romances of Charlemagne, the traitor through whom Roland and his army were destroyed by the Saracens. (*Sh. T.*)

Gawain. In the earlier romances of Arthur, a model of courtesy and valour. (*Sq. T.*)

Geoffrey. Geoffrey of Monmouth, whose Latin *History of the Kings of Britain* (about 1136) was one of the most influential of mediæval books. (*H.F.*)

Geoffrey de Vinsauf. A twelfth-century Latin poet, who wrote a lament on the death of Richard I (*N.P.T.*)

Glasgerion. A celebrated Welsh minstrel or bard. (*H.F.*)

Gloss. An explanation or comment on a text; hence sometimes sophistry or flattery. (*Sumn. T., B.D.*)

Golden thumb. A miller's golden thumb was a proverbial expression. (*Prol.*)

Gower. John Gower (about 1332–1408), a friend of Chaucer's and a well-known poet. (*T. and C.*)

Granson. Sir Oton de Granson (d. 1397), a Savoyard poet.

Groat. A coin worth 4*d.* (*N.P.T., Sumn. T.*)

Guido de Columnis (or delle Colonne) wrote a *Trojan History* (about 1287), a chief authority on the Trojan War. (*H.F.*)

Half-course. The sun's half-course in the Ram in April is naturally the second, the first being in March. (*Prol.*)

Hallows. Saints, or saints' shrines. (*W.B.P.*)

'Hazel-woods shake.' *i.e.*, 'that is no news.' (*T. and C.*)

Hermes Ballenus. An incorrect name for a Greek esoteric philosopher. (*H.F.*)

Herod. King Herod appears in the miracle-plays; his noisy habits were the reason for Hamlet's 'it out-Herods Herod.' (*Mill. T.*)

Herse. Daughter to Cecrops, mythical founder of Athens; beloved by Mercury. (*T. and C.*)

Hot, cold, etc. See *Humours*.

House. In astrology the word meant both the sign in which a planet was especially potent, and also a twelfth part of the sky reckoning always from the eastern horizon (see *Angle*). (*Merch. T.*, etc.)

Hugh of Lincoln. A boy said to have been murdered by the Lincoln Jews in 1255; he was canonized. (*Pri. T.*)

Humour. One of four fluids in the body (blood, phlegm, black bile, red bile), the relative proportions of which determined temperament and disease. The qualities heat, cold, moisture and dryness were attributed to them in certain ways. (*Prol., N.P.T..*, etc.)

Ilium. Priam's palace, or the citadel of Troy, according to mediæval accounts. (*B.D.*)

Innocent. Pope Innocent III (1161–1216); Chaucer's translation of his treatise *On Contempt of the World* seems to be lost. (*L.G.W.*)

In Principio. The first words of St. John's Gospel, often used and regarded with peculiar reverence. (*Prol.*)

Iulus and Ascanius. Two names of Æneas' son; Chaucer oddly makes two persons. (*H.F.*)

Janus. The Roman deity Janus, presiding over January, had two faces (and therefore beards). (*Frankl. T.*)

Jape. *To jape* is to talk or behave in a roughly joking way. (*W.B.P.*)

Jovinian. A monk who was furiously attacked by St. Jerome for his alleged worldliness. (*W.B.P., Sumn. T.*)

Jubilee. After a friar's jubilee (at the end of fifty years), he had certain privileges, such as that of going about alone. (*Sumn. T.*)

Julian. St. Julian is the patron-saint of hospitality. (*Prol. H.F.*)

King's Note. Apparently some tune or song. (*Mill. T.*)

Lachesis. The second of the three Fates; her office was to draw out the thread of life. (*T. and C.*)

Lapidary. A book on precious-stones and their virtues. (*H.F.*)

Latten. A composite metal, somewhat like brass. (*Prol.*, etc.)

Layas. A city in Armenia. (*Prol.*)

Legend. The account of a saint's life to be read (*legenda*) on his festival; or a collection of such accounts. In *The Legend of Good Women* the unfortunate ladies are regarded as martyrs to Cupid, and ecclesiastical terms are constantly used.

Limiter. A friar who had the exclusive right to beg within a certain district or certain limits. (*W.B.T.*)

Litharge. Protoxide of lead. (*C.Y.T.*)

Lollius. No such writer is known; some think Chaucer deliberately substituted this name for Boccaccio's, as an authority on the Trojan War. (*T. and C., H.F.*)

Long castle, etc. These words form a sort of cipher for the two persons meant in *The Book of the Duchess* (Blanche of Lancaster and John, Earl of Richmond, commonly called John of Gaunt).

Longinus. According to the legend, the name of the centurion who pierced Christ's side on the cross. (*A.B.C.*)

Lord of the ascendent. A planet in the ascendent (which see), and therefore especially potent. (*M.L.T.*)

Love-days. Days when the clergy were supposed to reconcile enemies and heal differences. (*Prol., H.F.*)

Lymote. Possibly Elymas the sorcerer (*Acts* xiii. 8). (*H.F.*)

Macrobius (about 400 A.D.) wrote a much-read commentary on Cicero's *Dream of Scipio*, which tells of heaven and the future life. (*N.P.T., P.F.*)

Manciple. The steward of a college or inn-of-court. (*Prol., R.T.*)

Manes. According to Roman mythology, the spirits of the dead; regarded by Chaucer as infernal goddesses. (*T. and C.*)

Mansions. The word has two meanings, — the house (which see) of a planet, and the twenty-eight daily positions of the moon. (*Frankl. T.*)

Mare. The mare's words to the wolf are from a fable in which she fools him. (*R.T.*)

Mark. Two-thirds of a pound (13*s.* 4*d*), worth then ten or fifteen times as much as now. (*C.Y.T.*)

Martian. Martianus Capella, a fifth-century satirist who wrote *The Nuptials of Mercury and Philology. (Merch. T., H.F.*)

Martyr. St. Thomas à Becket (killed in 1170), whose shrine at Canterbury was the most popular in England, and whose intercession was especially sought by the sick. (*Prol.*)

Melancholy humour. The black bile, one of the four humours (which see). (*K.T., N.P.T.*)

Mercury. The children of Mercury are scholars, over whom that planet presided. (*W.B.P.*)

Mortify. To change the outward form or shape (a term in alchemy). (*C.Y.T.*)

Multiply. To practice alchemy (*lit.*, to make a small into a large amount of precious metal). (*C.Y.T.*)

'My lief is faren in londe.' A popular song, — 'My wife's gone to the country.' (*N.P.T.*)

Myrrha. A Cyprian princess who (according to Ovid) was changed to a myrrh-tree and wept tears of myrrh. (*T. and C.*)

Nicholas. St. Nicholas (according to his legend) even as a baby refused to eat at fasting-times. (*Pri. T.*)

Noble. A coin worth 6*s.* 8*d.* (*Pard. T., H.F.*)

Nones. One of the breviary services, originally said, about 3 P.M., then at noon (whence our word). (*T. and C.*)

North. The abode of evil spirits was sometimes thought to be in the north. (*Fri. T.*)

Nowell's flood. A blunder for Noe's (Noah's); the Miller was more familiar with the convivial Christmas cry 'Nowell!' than with Holy Writ. (*Mill. T.*)

Octogamy. The marrying of eight wives (cf. *bigamy*). (*W.B.P.*)

Office. 'To say one's office' is to recite the breviary services, which ecclesiastical persons read to themselves when absent from church. (*Sh. T.*)

Oliver. One of the twelve chivalrous paladins of Charlemagne. (*Monk's T.*)

Origen *On the Magdalen*. A lost translation by Chaucer of a work formerly attributed to the church father Origen. (*L.G.W.*)

Orpiment. Trisulphide of arsenic. (*C.Y.T.*)

Pardoner. A seller of indulgences, which are not forgivenesses of sins, but remissions of part or all of the penalties. (*Prol.*)

Paul's porch. The entrance of the cathedral was a gathering place for lawyers. (*Prol.*)

Pax. A sort of disc which was kissed at the 'kiss of peace' in the mass (at the words 'Pax Domini sit semper vobiscum'). (*Pars. T.*)

Perdy. A mild oath, corrupted from 'par Dieu' (cf. *Hamlet*, III, ii, 305). (*Pard. T., C.Y.T.*, etc.)

Phidon's daughters, etc. All these anecdotes of ancient chaste heroines are from St. Jerome's book *Against Jovinian* (whom see). (*Frankl. T.*)

Philosopher. There is a play on the word; a philosopher (= alchemist) might be expected to have plenty of gold. (*Prol*).

Philosophy. The term was especially claimed for their art by the alchemists. (*C.Y.T.*)

Physiologus. A book (of very early date) on the natures of animals. (*N.P.T.*)

Pilate's voice. Pilate (like Herod) was one of the boisterous characters in the miracle-plays. (*Mill. Prol.*)

Pisces is the exaltation (which see) of Venus. (*Sq. T.*)

Placebo. 'I will please', — the first word of an antiphon in the vespers for the dead; also used ironically for a flattering speech. (*Sumn. T.*)

Pluto. Since Pluto was sovereign of the underworld, where the fairies were supposed by the mediævals to live, he is represented as king of the fairies. (*Merch. T.*)

Pons asinorum. 'The bridge of asses,' — the nickname of a proposition in the first book of Euclid; by a rough translation of Chaucer's words, it represents Criseyde's state of perplexity. (*T. and C.*)

Powder-merchant. A tart flavouring-powder. (*Prol.*)

Priapus. The Roman god of gardens; the story alluded to is told by Ovid. (*P.F.*)

Prime. One of the breviary services, said about 9 A.M. (originally at the first hour). Before clocks were common, people often told time from the ringing of the church-bells. (*K.T., T. and C.* etc.)

Princess. Perhaps Isabel, Duchess of York and Princess of Spain. (*Venus.*)

Proportional parts. A table of these is used to make more exact such calculations as based on somewhat rough tables. (*Frankl. T.*)

Pseustis. Unknown. (*H.F.*)

Puella and Rubeus. Two figures used in geomancy, also associated with astrology. (*K.T.*)

Quern. A hand-mill. (*Former Age*).

Qui bien aime, etc. 'Who loves well scarce forgets'; probably the name of a French air. (*P.F.*)

Qui cum Patre. A formula at the end of prayers and sermons, — 'Who with the Father and the Holy Ghost liveth and reigneth', etc. (*Sumn. T.*)

Quintain. A long bar on a pivot; the sport was to hit one end and get out of the way before the other end swung around and hit the player (a feat for which clearly the Cook was in no condition.) (*Manc. Prol.*)

Romance of the Rose. A much-admired thirteenth-century French allegorical poem. The scene is laid in a garden. The first part (by Guillaume de Lorris) is ornate and sentimental; the last part (by Jean de Meun) critical and cynical. (*Merch. T., B.D., L.G.W.*)

Roncesvalles. In Navarre; its connection with the Pardoner is not very clear. (*Prol.*)

Roots. Astrological data. (*Frankl. T.*)

Rum, ram, ruf. Nonsense words in parody of the alliterative verse popular in the northerly parts of England. (*Pars. Prol.*)

Sallows. Willow-twigs, osiers. (*W.B.P.*)

Saturn. Classical deities are constantly identified with the planets. Saturn's astrological influence was sinister; he was the farthest planet known to the mediævals. (*K.T.*)

Scylla. Daughter of Nisus of Megara; she loved Minos and (according to Ovid) was turned into a bird. (*P.F.*)

Senior. The reference is to a book on alchemy (but Chaucer errs as to both the author and the name of the book). (*C.Y.T.*)

Significavit. The first word of a writ inflicting temporal penalties on an excommunicated person. (*Prol.*)

Sir. Formerly the title of a priest. (*Monk's Prol.*)

Sol and luna. Gold and silver (according to the lingo of the alchemists). (*C.Y.T.*)

Spheres. The concentric crystalline spheres in which (according to the Ptolemaic system) the planets and stars were fixed; their revolution within each other produced the 'music of the spheres'. (*Frankl. T., P.F.*)

Stratford-le-Bow. Near London, the seat of an important Benedictine nunnery; the French taught here was presumably Anglo-French. (*Prol.*)

Strode. Probably an Oxford philosopher, later the tutor of Chaucer's son Lewis. (*T. and C.*)

Sumner. An apparitor, whose office was to summon culprits before a church-court (presided over by the archdeacon); which took cognizance of certain classes of offences (cf. the *Friar's Tale*). (*Prol.*)

Tercel, tercelet. The male of the eagle or hawk. (*Sq. T., P.F.*)

Term. An irregular division of a sign of the zodiac, assigned to one or another planet. (*Frankl. T.*)

Theophrastus. The author of a book on marriage. (*W.B.P., Merch. T.*)

Thieves. The 'seven thieves' which pursue the poet are the seven deadly sins. (*A.B.C.*)

Thiodamas. One of the besiegers of Thebes (according to Statius). (*Merch. T., H.F.*)

Thomas. St. Thomas of Kent is Thomas à Becket (see *Martyr*). (*H.F.*)

Toledo tables. Astrological tables, adapted to the latitude and longitude of Toledo. (*Frankl. T.*)

Tortuous ascendent. The ascendent (which see) was tortuous when the zodiac rose obliquely to the horizon. (*M.L.T.*)

Tower of Mercury. A poetic word for the house or mansion (which see) of Mercury. (*Mars.*)

Tregentil. Probably the name of a scribe. (*Rosamund*).

Tremessen. A Moorish kingdom in Africa. (*Prol.*)

Trental. A series of thirty masses for the dead. (*Sumn. T.*)

Trophee. Unknown. (*Monk's T.*)

Tully *On the Dream of Scipio*. (See *Macrobius*.)

Undern. The time of tierce (one of the breviary services), said about II A.M. (*N.P.T.*)

Valerius. The supposed author of a dissuasion against marriage (*W.B.P.*); also Valerius Maximus, a Roman writer. (*Monk's T., W.B.T.*)

Venus' hour. Each of the twenty-four hours of the day (as well as each day of the week) was presided over by one of the planets. (*K.T.*)

Vernage. A sweet, red Italian wine. (*Sh. T.*)

Vernicle. A copy of the napkin of St. Veronica, on which the image of Christ's face was believed to have been miraculously imprinted; copies were brought away as mementos by pilgrims to Rome, where the relic was supposed to be preserved. (*Prol.*)

Vigil. Originally a devout watching, afterwards merrymaking, before a church-festival or a burial. In the latter case it was regarded as similar to the funeral-games of the ancients. (*Prol., W.B.P., T. and C.*)

Vincent of Beauvais. The thirteenth-century author of an encyclopædic work. (*L.G.W.*)

Wade. A hero of Teutonic antiquity, whose story is lost. (*Merch. T., T. and C.*)

White. Obviously a translation of *Blanche*, the name of John of Gaunt's first wife, whose death is lamented in *The Book of the Duchess*.

'Who painted the lion?' The allusion is to a fable of Æsop. The Man pointed out to the Lion in how many pictures men are shown conquering lions; the Lion replied that if lions painted it, it would be otherwise. (*W.B.P.*)

Wicked Nest. A translation of *mau ni* (mod. Fr. *mal. nid*); Sir Oliver Mauny, a Breton knight, was one of the plotters against King Pedro of Castile. (*Monk's T.*)

Zeuxis. Apparently the Athenian painter, whom Chaucer once wrongly took to be a writer. (*Phys. T., T. and C.*)